THE PAPERS OF
BENJAMIN FRANKLIN

SPONSORED BY

The American Philosophical Society

and Yale University

STUPETE GENTES! REPERIT VIVUM DIOGENES

BENJAMIN FRANKLIN

Ministre plenipotentiaire a la Cour de France pour la Republique
des Provinces unies de l'Amerique Septentrionale.

Benjamin Franklin

THE PAPERS OF

Benjamin Franklin

VOLUME 33 *July 1 through November 15, 1780*

BARBARA B. OBERG, *Editor*

ELLEN R. COHN AND JONATHAN R. DULL, *Senior Associate Editors*

KAREN DUVAL, *Associate Editor*

LESLIE J. LINDENAUER, *Assistant Editor*

CLAUDE A. LOPEZ, *Consulting Editor*

KATE M. OHNO, *Editorial Assistant*

New Haven and London YALE UNIVERSITY PRESS, 1997

As indicated in the first volume, this edition was made possible through the vision and generosity of Yale University and the American Philosophical Society and by a substantial donation from Henry R. Luce in the name of Life Magazine. Additional funds were provided by a grant from the Ford Foundation to the National Archives Trust Fund Board. Subsequent support has come from the Andrew W. Mellon Foundation and the Pew Charitable Trusts through Founding Fathers Papers, Inc. Major underwriting of the present volume has been provided by the Florence Gould Foundation and the Kemper Educational and Charitable Fund. We are grateful for the generous support of Ralph Gregory Elliot, Candace and Stuart Karu, and Richard N. Rosenfeld, and for contributions from Mark H. Biddle, Jean Griffin Elliott, Dr. and Mrs. William W. L. Glenn, John and Deane Sherman, Mr. and Mrs. Malcolm N. Smith, and George F. Waters. Gifts from many other individuals as well as donations from the American Philosophical Society, the Friends of Franklin, the Friends of the Franklin Papers, and the Saturday Evening Post Society also help to sustain the enterprise. The Papers of Benjamin Franklin is a beneficiary of the generous and long-standing support of the National Historical Publications and Records Commission under the chairmanship of the Archivist of the United States. The National Endowment for the Humanities, an independent federal agency, has provided significant support for this volume. For the assistance of all these organizations and individuals, as well as for the indispensable aid of archivists, librarians, scholars, and collectors of Franklin manuscripts, the editors are most grateful.

Publication of this volume was assisted by a grant from the National Historical Publications and Records Commission.

Library of Congress catalog card number: 59–12697
International standard book number: 0–300–07040–3

⊗ The paper in this book meets the guidelines for permanence and durability of the Committee on Production Guidelines for Book Longevity of the Council on Library Resources.

Printed in the U.S.A.

Administrative Board

Edmund S. Morgan, Yale University, *Chairman*
Edward C. Carter II, American Philosophical Society
Robert Darnton, American Philosophical Society
David B. Davis, American Philosophical Society
Mary M. Dunn, Schlesinger Library, Radcliffe College
Paul LeClerc, New York Public Library
Robert Middlekauff, University of California, Berkeley
Barbara B. Oberg, Yale University
John G. Ryden, Yale University Press
Gordon S. Wood, American Philosophical Society

Advisory Committee

Thomas Boylston Adams
Thomas R. Adams
I. Bernard Cohen
John C. Dann
Andrew Heiskell

To
DAVID W. PACKARD
in appreciation of his vision, understanding, and encouragement

Contents

Foreign-language surnames and titles of nobility often run to great length. Our practice with an untitled person is to provide all the Christian names at the first appearance, and then drop them; a chevalier or noble is given the title used at the time, and the full name is provided in the index.

*Denotes a document referred to in annotation.

CONTENTS

List of Illustrations

Benjamin Franklin   *Frontispiece*

Line engraving, credited to "N. L. G. D. L. C. A. D. L," and published by
Honoré-Thomas Bligny (from whom Franklin purchased prints and
frames; see our Editorial Note on Accounts). Diogenes, seated before his
tub and holding his lantern, displays a framed portrait of Franklin after
the Cathelin engraving of the Rosalie Filleul portrait that we used as the
frontispiece to vol. 29. The print is entitled "BENJAMIN FRANKLIN
Ministre plenipotentiaire a la Cour de France pour la Republique des
Provinces unies de l'Amerique Septentrionale," and was announced for
sale in the *Journal de Paris* on January 21, 1781. In the lower right corner
is engraved the following dedication, in ungrammatical French: "Presenté
à son Excellence quelle à acceptée le 14 Juillet 1780. Par son très humble
et très Obeissant Serviteur BLIGNY."

This print was produced by rubbing out and reengraving sections of
the copper plate of an earlier engraving by Thomassin after Rigaud and
Autreau. The original engraving showed the same Diogenes holding a
portrait of Cardinal Fleury (1653–1743). Bligny, it has been said, made a
practice of reusing old plates. In this case, four sections were reengraved:
the portrait inside the frame, the motto on the stone platform, the symbols
in the lower right corner, and the area above Diogenes' head. The stone
is inscribed: "Stupete gentes! Reperit vivum Diogenes" (People, be
amazed! Diogenes has found one living). The symbols associated with
Franklin are a broken yoke, a map of North America, and a phoenix (look-
ing very much like the American eagle) sitting on flames from which are
emanating two bolts of lightning. Behind the figure of Diogenes, the artist
added a liberty cap on a pole, and, in the sky, a dove of peace. See Carl Zi-
grosser, "Franklin Portraits in the Rockefeller Collection," *Philadelphia
Museum of Art Bulletin,* XLIV (1948–49), 22–7; Sellers, *Franklin in Portraiture,* pp. 283–4.

The identity of the engraver is unknown. The working drawing, however—a counterproof of the engraving, on which an artist has drawn the
new elements in pen and ink—is in the Rockefeller Collection at the
Philadelphia Museum of Art. This counterproof is signed "Gaucher." We
believe him to be Charles-Etienne Gaucher, a renowned Parisian portrait
engraver whose most celebrated portrait to date—Mme Du Barry
(1770)—was one of several published by Bligny: Roger Portalis and
Henri Draibel, *Charles-Etienne Gaucher, graveur, Notice et catalogue* (Paris,
1879), pp. 6–7, 80–1. Gaucher was inducted into the Lodge of the Nine
Sisters in 1781, and in his capacity as secretary will send Franklin invitations to masonic meetings in future volumes.

Reproduced by courtesy of the Yale University Library.

The only surviving matrices from the Passy foundry. Belonging originally to Claude Mozet, they were acquired first by Hémery and then by Franklin, who brought them to Philadelphia and gave them to Benjamin Franklin Bache. After Bache's death in 1798, his successor William Duane (who married Bache's widow) held onto the foundry equipment until 1806, when he sold it to Philadelphia typefounders Binny & Ronaldson, who may have melted it down. William Duane evidently overlooked these particular matrices in the transfer, and presented them to the Massachusetts Historical Society in 1838. See Rollo G. Silver, *Typefounding in America, 1787–1825* (Charlottesville, Va., 1965), pp. 36–8. Photograph courtesy of the Massachusetts Historical Society.

Two copying presses engraved from the drawing that accompanied James Watt's patent of February 4, 1780. Figures 1 and 2 are views of the rolling press Watt invented, clamped to a table top. Figure 3 shows a screw press, which Watt said might be used instead of a rolling press. From "Specification of the Patent granted to Mr. James Watt of Birmingham, for his new Method of copying Letters and other Writings," *The Repertory of Arts and Manufactures*, 1 (London, 1794), facing p. 20. Reproduced by courtesy of the American Philosophical Society.

Stipple engraving taken from the oil portrait of his family that West painted in 1772. Elizabeth West is seated, with her youngest son and Franklin's godson Benjamin West, Jr., on her lap and her son Raphael standing beside her. West's father John and half-brother Thomas are seated to her right, and the painter stands behind his father. The engraving was made by Georg Sigmund and Johann Gottlieb Facius, who worked for the prominent English engraver John Boydell, and dedicated to "Her Imperial Majesty of all the Russia's." It was published on July 26, 1779, and West sent Franklin a copy on August 16, below. See Helmut von Erffa and Allen Staley, *The Paintings of Benjamin West* (New Haven and London, 1986), pp. 461–2; *Bryan's Dictionary of Painters and Engravers* (London, 1903), I, 186–7; II, 141. See also Jules D. Prown, "Benjamin West's Family Picture: a Nativity in Hammersmith," *Essays in Honor of Paul Mellon, Collector and Benefactor*, John Wilmerding, ed. (Washington, D.C., and Hanover, N.H., 1986), pp. 269–75. Reproduced by courtesy of the British Museum.

Bisque porcelain medallion by Richard Champion, after the Sèvres circular profile medallion. The floral wreath frame is said to have been modeled by Thomas Briand, and is characteristic of Bristol pottery. Although we have no evidence that Franklin ever received his copy, Champion did present two examples to George Washington. One medallion, still in the Franklin family, is reputed to have been presented to Sarah Bache by Louis XVI. See Sellers, *Franklin in Portraiture*, pp. 365, 369–70 and The Metropolitan Museum of Art, *Benjamin Franklin and his Circle* (New York, 1936), p. 46. See also Digges to Franklin, August 18, below. Reproduced by courtesy of the British Library.

The Le Rouge Chart of the Gulf Stream   *facing page* 298

A copy by George-Louis Le Rouge of the northwest quadrant of the Franklin-Folger chart printed *c.* 1769 by Mount and Page in London. The "Remarks for Sailing from Newfoundland to New York" are translated into French, and Le Rouge added an advertisement for his maps, sold from his home on the rue des Grands Augustins, in the bottom right corner.

The circumstances of this chart's publication are still a mystery. A copy at the Bibliothèque nationale was docketed by an unknown clerk as "communiqué par Mr. de franquelin en 1778." Whatever was communicated could not have been Le Rouge's engraving, however, as Franklin seems to have known nothing about the cartographer when he introduced himself at Passy in September, 1780 (see BF to JW, Sept. 18, below). Another copy, given by Franklin to Minister of the Marine Castries in 1783, displays in its margins extensive manuscript remarks on navigation written by Franklin and L'Air de Lamotte (Archives nationales). At the bottom of the sheet, Lamotte wrote: "Copied and printed in Paris at the Expence of M. de Chaumont."

Given that Franklin seems to have met Le Rouge for the first time around September 18, 1780, and that by December, Chaumont was on the verge of bankruptcy (a situation that would remain precarious for years), we believe that a likely time for the chart's publication is early fall, 1780. We are tentatively dating it after September 18.

Reproduced by courtesy of the Yale University Library.

Mr. Kelsy's Grist Mill   405

Henry Laurens   *facing page* 506

Portrait in oil of Henry Laurens, attributed to John Singleton Copley, 1781. Reproduced by courtesy of the United States Senate Art Collection through the Architect of the Capitol.

Contributors to Volume 33

The ownership of each manuscript, or the location of the particular copy used by the editors of each rare contemporary pamphlet or similar printed work, is indicated where the document appears in the text. The sponsors and editors are deeply grateful to the following institutions and individuals for permission to print or otherwise use in the present volume manuscripts and other materials which they own.

INSTITUTIONS

Académie de médecine, Paris
American Philosophical Society
Archives de la Marine, Paris
Archives du Ministère des affaires
  étrangères, Paris
Archives Nationales, Paris
Assay Office, Birmingham,
  England
Bibliothèque Nationale
Columbia University Library
Harvard University Library

Historical Society of Pennsylvania
Library of Congress
Maryland State Archives
Massachusetts Historical Society
McGill University Library
National Archives
New Jersey Historical Society
Public Record Office, London
Richmond Academy of Medicine
University of Pennsylvania Library
Yale University Library

INDIVIDUALS

Mrs. Carl H. Ernlund,
  Cambridge, Massachusetts
The Gallery of History,
  Las Vegas, Nevada

Frederic R. Kirkland,
  Philadelphia, Pennsylvania
Miss Lillian S. Wilson,
  Scarsdale, New York

Statement of Methodology

Arrangement of Materials

The documents are printed in chronological sequence according to their dates when these are given, or according to the date of publication in cases of contemporary printed materials. Records such as diaries, journals, and account books that cover substantial periods of time appear according to the dates of their earliest entries. When no date appears on the document itself, one is editorially supplied and an explanation provided. When no day within a month is given, the document is placed at the end of all specifically dated documents of that month; those dated only by year are placed at the end of that year. If no date is given, we use internal and external evidence to assign one whenever possible, providing our explanation in annotation. Documents which cannot be assigned a date more definite than the entire length of Franklin's stay in France (1777–85) will be published at the end of this period. Those for which we are unable to provide even a tentative date will be published at the conclusion of the series.

When two or more documents have the same date, they are arranged in the following order:

1. Those by a group of which Franklin was a member (*e.g.*, the American Commissioners in Paris)
2. Those by Franklin individually
3. Those to a group of which Franklin was a member
4. Those to Franklin individually
5. "Third-party" and unaddressed miscellaneous writings by others than Franklin.

In the first two categories letters are arranged alphabetically by the name of the addressee; in the last three, by the name of the signatory. An exception to this practice occurs when a letter to Franklin and his answer were written on the same day: in such cases the first letter precedes the reply. The same rules apply to documents lacking precise dates printed together at the end of any month or year.

Form of Presentation

The document and its accompanying editorial apparatus are presented in the following order:

1. *Title.* Essays and formal papers are headed by their titles, except in the case of pamphlets with very long titles, when a short form is substituted. Where previous editors supplied a title to a piece that had none, and this title has become familiar, we use it; otherwise we devise a suitable one.

Letters written by Franklin individually are entitled "To" the person or body addressed, as: To John Adams; To John Adams and Arthur Lee; To the Royal Society.

Letters to Franklin individually are entitled "From" the person or body who wrote them, as: From John Adams; From John Adams and Arthur Lee; From the Committee of Secret Correspondence.

Letters of which Franklin was a joint author or joint recipient are titled with the names of all concerned, as: Franklin and Silas Deane to Arthur Lee; Arthur Lee to Franklin and Silas Deane. "Third-party" letters or those by or to a body of which Franklin was a member are titled with the names of both writers and addressees, as: Arthur Lee to John Adams; The American Commissioners to John Paul Jones.

Documents not fitting into any of these categories are given brief descriptive headings, as: Extract from Franklin's Journal.

If the name in the title has been supplied from external evidence it appears in brackets, with a question mark when we are uncertain. If a letter is unsigned, or signed with initials or an alias, but is from a correspondent whose handwriting we know, the name appears without brackets.

2. *Source Identification.* This gives the nature of the printed or manuscript version of the document, and, in the case of a manuscript or a rare printed work, the ownership and location of the original.

Printed sources of three different classes are distinguished. First, a contemporary pamphlet, which is given its full title, place and date of publication, and the location of the copy the editors have used. Second, an essay or letter appearing originally in a *contemporary* publication, which is introduced by the words "Printed in," followed by the title, date, and inclusive page numbers, if necessary, of the publication. Third, a document, the manuscript or contemporary printed version of which is now lost, but which was printed at a later date, is identified by the words "Reprinted from," followed by the name of the work from which the editors have reproduced it. The following examples illustrate the distinction:

Printed in *The Pennsylvania Gazette,* October 2, 1729.
Reprinted from William Temple Franklin, ed., *Memoirs of the Life and Writings of Benjamin Franklin* . . . (3 vols., 4to, London, 1817–18), II, 244.

The Source Identification of a manuscript consists of a term or symbol (all of which are listed in the Short Title List) indicating the character of the manuscript version, followed by the name of the holder of the manuscript, as: ALS: American Philosophical Society. Since manuscripts belonging to individuals have a tendency to migrate, we indicate the year in which each private owner gave permission to publish, as: Morris Duane, Philadelphia, 1957. When two or more manuscript versions survive, the one listed first in the Source Identification is the one from which we print.

3. An editorial *Headnote* precedes some documents in this edition; it appears between the Source Identification and the actual text. Such a headnote is designed to supply the background of the composition of the document, its relation to events or other writings, and any other information which may be useful to the reader and is not obtainable from the document itself.

4. The *Text* of the document follows the Source Identification, or Headnote, if any. When multiple copies of a document are extant, the editors observe the following order of priority in determining which of the available versions to use in printing a text: ALS or ADS, LS or DS, AL or AD, L or D, and copy. An AL (draft) normally takes precedence over a contemporary copy based on the recipient's copy. If we deviate from the order set forth here, we explain our decision in the annotation. In those instances where multiple texts are available, the texts are collated, and sig-

nificant variations reported in the annotation. In selecting the publication text from among several copies of official French correspondence (*e.g.,* from Vergennes or Sartine) we use the version which is written in the best French, on the presumption that the French ministers used standard eighteenth-century spelling, grammar, and punctuation.

The form of presentation of the texts of letters is as follows:

The place and date of composition are set at the top, regardless of their location in the original manuscript.

The signature, set in capitals and small capitals, is placed at the right of the last line of the text if there is room; if not, then on the line below.

Addresses, endorsements, and notations are so labelled and printed at the end of the letter. An endorsement is, to the best of our belief, by the recipient, and a notation by someone else. When the writer of the notation has misread the date or the signature of the correspondent, we let the error stand without comment. Line breaks in addresses are marked by slashes. Different notations are separated by slashes; when they are by different individuals, we so indicate.

5. *Footnotes* to the Heading, Source Identification, Headnote, and Text appear on the pages to which they pertain. References to documents not printed or to be printed in later volumes are by date and repository, as: Jan. 17, 1785, APS.

Method of Textual Reproduction

1. *Spelling* of all words, including proper names, is retained. If it is abnormal enough to obscure the meaning we follow the word immediately with the current spelling in brackets.

2. *Capitalization and Punctuation* are retained. There is such variety in the size of initial letters, often in the same manuscript, that it is sometimes unclear whether the writer intended an upper or lower case letter. In such cases we make a decision on the basis of the correspondent's customary usage. We supply a capital letter when an immediately preceding period, colon, question mark, exclamation point, or dash indicates that a new sentence is intended. If a capital letter clearly indicates the beginning of a new thought, but no mark of punctuation precedes it, we insert

a period. If neither punctuation nor capital letter indicates a sentence break, we do not supply them unless their absence renders comprehension of the document nearly impossible. In that case we provide them and so indicate in a footnote.

Dashes were used for a variety of purposes in eighteenth-century personal and public letters. A dash within a sentence, used to indicate a break in thought, is represented as an em dash. A dash that follows a period or serves as a closing mark of punctuation for a sentence is represented as an em dash followed by a space. Occasionally correspondents used long dashes that continue to the end of a line and indicate a significant break in thought. We do not reproduce the dash, but treat it as indicating the start of a new paragraph.

When there is an initial quotation mark or parenthesis, but no closing one, we silently complete the pair.

3. *Contractions and abbreviations* are retained. Abbreviations such as "wd", "honble", "servt", "exclly", are used so frequently in Franklin's correspondence that they are readily comprehensible to the users of these volumes. Abbreviations, particularly of French words, that may be unclear are followed by an expanded version in brackets, as: nre [navire]. Superscript letters are brought down to the line. Where a period or colon is a part of the abbreviation, or indicates that letters were written above the line, we print it at the end of the word, as: 4th. for 4.th. In those few cases where superscript letters brought down to the line result in a confusing abbreviation ("Made" for "Mad^e"), we follow the abbreviation by an expanded version in brackets, as: Made [Madame].

The ampersand by itself and the "&c." are retained. Letters represented by the "y" are printed, as: "the" and "that". The tailed "p" is spelled out, as: "per", "pre", or "pro". Symbols of weights, measures, and money are converted to modern forms, as: *l.t.* instead of ₶ for *livres tournois*.

4. *Omissions, mutilations, and illegible words* are treated as follows:

If we are certain of the reading of letters missing in a word because of a torn or taped manuscript or tightly bound copybook, we supply the letters silently.

If we cannot be sure of the word, or of how the author spelled it, but we can make a reasonable guess, we supply the missing letters in brackets.

When the writer has omitted a word absolutely required for clarity, we insert it in italics within brackets.

5. *Interlineations* by the author are silently incorporated into the text. If they are significant enough to require comment a footnote is provided.

Textual Conventions

/	denotes line break in addresses and different hands in notations.
⟨roman⟩	denotes a résumé of a letter or document.
[*italic*]	editorial insertion explaining something about the manuscript, as: [*one line illegible*]; or supplying a word to make the meaning clear, as: [*to*].
[roman]	editorial insertion clarifying the immediately preceding word or abbreviation; supplies letters missing because of a mutilated manuscript.
(?)	indicates a questionable reading.

Abbreviations and Short Titles

AAE	Archives du Ministère des affaires étrangères.
AD	Autograph document.
Adams Correspondence	Lyman H. Butterfield, Richard A. Ryerson, *et al.*, eds., *Adams Family Correspondence* (6 vols. to date, Cambridge, Mass., 1963–).
Adams Papers	Robert J. Taylor, Gregg L. Lint, *et al.*, eds., *Papers of John Adams* (10 vols. to date, Cambridge, Mass., 1977–).
ADB	*Allgemeine Deutsche Biographie* (56 vols., Berlin, 1967–71).
Adm.	Admiral.
ADS	Autograph document signed.
AL	Autograph letter.
Allen, *Mass. Privateers*	Gardner Weld Allen, ed., *Massachusetts Privateers of the Revolution* ([Cambridge, Mass.], 1927) (Massachusetts Historical Society *Collections*, LXXVII).
Almanach des marchands	*Almanach général des marchands, négocians, armateurs, et fabricans de France et de l'Europe et autres parties du monde . . .* (Paris, 1779).
Almanach royal	*Almanach royal* (91 vols., Paris, 1700–92). Cited by year.
Almanach de Versailles	*Almanach de Versailles* (Versailles, various years). Cited by year.
Alphabetical List of Escaped Prisoners	Alphabetical List of the Americans who having escap'd from the Prisons of England, were furnish'd with Money by the Commissrs. of the U.S. at the

	Court of France, to return to America. A manuscript in the APS, dated 1784, and covering the period January, 1777, to November, 1784.
ALS	Autograph letter signed.
APS	American Philosophical Society.
Archaeol.	Archaeological.
Assn.	Association.
Auphan, "Communications"	P. Auphan, "Les communications entre la France et ses colonies d'Amérique pendant la guerre de l'indépendance Américaine," *Revue Maritime,* new series, no. LXIII and LXIV (1925), 331–48, 497–517.
Autobiog.	Leonard W. Labaree, Ralph L. Ketcham, Helen C. Boatfield, and Helene H. Fineman, eds., *The Autobiography of Benjamin Franklin* (New Haven, 1964).
Bachaumont, *Mémoires secrets*	[Louis Petit de Bachaumont *et al.*], *Mémoires secrets pour servir à l'histoire de la république des lettres en France, depuis MDCCLXII jusqu'à nos jours; ou, Journal d'un observateur . . .* (36 vols. in 12, London, 1784–89). Bachaumont died in 1771. The first six vols. (1762–71) are his; Mathieu-François Pidansat de Mairobert edited them and wrote the next nine (1771–79); the remainder (1779–87) are by Barthélemy-François Mouffle d'Angerville.
Balch, *French in America*	Thomas Balch, *The French in America during the War of Independence of the United States, 1777–1783* (trans. by Thomas Willing Balch *et al.;* 2 vols., Philadelphia, 1891–95).

BF	Benjamin Franklin.
BF's accounts as commissioner	Those described above, XXIII, 20.
BFB	Benjamin Franklin Bache.
Bigelow, *Works*	John Bigelow, ed., *The Works of Benjamin Franklin* (12 vols., New York and London, 1887–88).
Biographie universelle	*Biographie universelle, ancienne et moderne, ou histoire, par ordre alphabétique, de la vie publique et privée de tous les hommes qui se sont fait remarquer* . . . (85 vols., Paris, 1811–62).
Bodinier	From information kindly furnished us by Cdt. Gilbert Bodinier, Section études, Service historique de l'Armée de Terre, Vincennes.
Bodinier, *Dictionnaire*	Gilbert Bodinier, *Dictionnaire des officiers de l'armée royale qui ont combattu aux Etats-Unis pendant la guerre d'Indépendance* (Château de Vincennes, 1982).
Bowler, *Logistics*	R. Arthur Bowler, *Logistics and the Failure of the British Army in America, 1775–1783* (Princeton, 1975).
Bradford, *Jones Papers*	James C. Bradford, ed., *The Microfilm Edition of the Papers of John Paul Jones, 1747–1792* (10 reels of microfilm, Alexandria, Va., 1986).
Burke's Peerage	Sir Bernard Burke, *Burke's Genealogical and Heraldic History of the Peerage Baronetage and Knightage with War Gazette and Corrigenda* (98th ed., London, 1940). References in exceptional cases to other editions are so indicated.
Burnett, *Letters*	Edmund C. Burnett, ed., *Letters of Members of the Continental Congress* (8 vols., Washington, 1921–36).

Butterfield, *John Adams Diary*	Lyman H. Butterfield *et al.*, eds., *Diary and Autobiography of John Adams* (4 vols., Cambridge, Mass., 1961).
Cash Book	BF's accounts described above, XXVI, 3.
Chron.	*Chronicle.*
Claghorn, *Naval Officers*	Charles E. Claghorn, *Naval Officers of the American Revolution: a Concise Biographical Dictionary* (Metuchen, N.J. and London, 1988).
Clark, *Ben Franklin's Privateers*	William Bell Clark, *Ben Franklin's Privateers: a Naval Epic of the American Revolution* (Baton Rouge, 1956).
Clark, *Wickes*	William Bell Clark, *Lambert Wickes, Sea Raider and Diplomat: the Story of a Naval Captain of the Revolution* (New Haven and London, 1932).
Clowes, *Royal Navy*	William Laird Clowes, *The Royal Navy: a History from the Earliest Times to the Present* (7 vols., Boston and London, 1897–1903).
Cobbett, *Parliamentary History*	William Cobbett and Thomas C. Hansard, eds., *The Parliamentary History of England from the Earliest Period to 1803* (36 vols., London, 1806–20).
Col.	Column.
Coll.	*Collections.*
comp.	compiler.
Croÿ, *Journal*	Emmanuel, prince de Moeurs et de Solre et duc de Croÿ, *Journal inédit du duc de Croÿ, 1718–1784* (4 vols., Paris, 06–07).
d.	*denier.*
D	Document unsigned.
DAB	*Dictionary of American Biography.*
DBF	*Dictionnaire de biographie française* (19 vols. to date, Paris, 1933–).

xl

Dictionary of Scientific Biography	Charles C. Gillispie, ed., *Dictionary of Scientific Biography* (18 vols., New York, 1970–90).
Deane Papers	*The Deane Papers, 1774–90* (5 vols.; New-York Historical Society *Collections,* XIX–XXIII, New York, 1887–91).
DF	Deborah Franklin.
Dictionnaire de la noblesse	François-Alexandre Aubert de La Chesnaye-Dubois and M. Badier, *Dictionnaire de la noblesse contenant les généalogies, l'histoire & la chronologie des familles nobles de la France . . .* (3rd ed.; 19 vols., Paris, 1863–76).
Dictionnaire historique	*Dictionnaire historique, critique et bibliographique, contenant les vies des hommes illustres, célèbres ou fameux de tous les pays et de tous les siècles . . .* (30 vols., Paris, 1821–23).
Dictionnaire historique de la Suisse	*Dictionnaire historique & biographique de la Suisse* (7 vols. and supplement, Neuchâtel, 1921–34).
DNB	*Dictionary of National Biography.*
Doniol, *Histoire*	Henri Doniol, *Histoire de la participation de la France à l'établissement des Etats-Unis d'Amérique. Correspondance diplomatique et documents* (5 vols., Paris, 1886–99).
DS	Document signed.
Duane, *Works*	William Duane, ed., *The Works of Dr. Benjamin Franklin . . .* (6 vols., Philadelphia, 1808–18). Title varies in the several volumes.
Dubourg, *Œuvres*	Jacques Barbeu-Dubourg, ed., *Œuvres de M. Franklin . . .* (2 vols., Paris, 1773).
Dull, *French Navy*	Jonathan R. Dull, *The French Navy and*

Fortescue, *Correspondence of George Third* — Sir John William Fortescue, ed., *The Correspondence of King George the Third from 1760 to December 1783 . . .* (6 vols., London, 1927–28).

France ecclésiastique — *La France ecclésiastique pour l'année . . .* (15 vols., Paris, 1774–90). Cited by year.

Freeman, *Washington* — Douglas S. Freeman (completed by John A. Carroll and Mary W. Ashworth), *George Washington: a Biography* (7 vols., New York, 1948–57).

Gaz. — *Gazette.*

Gaz. de Leyde — *Nouvelles extraordinaires de divers endroits,* commonly known as *Gazette de Leyde.* Each issue is in two parts; we indicate the second as "sup."

Gen. — General.

Geneal. — *Genealogical.*

Gent. Mag. — *The Gentleman's Magazine, and Historical Chronicle.*

Hays, *Calendar* — I. Minis Hays, *Calendar of the Papers of Benjamin Franklin in the Library of the American Philosophical Society* (5 vols., Philadelphia, 1908).

Heitman, *Register of Officers* — Francis B. Heitman, *Historical Register of Officers in the War of the Revolution . . .* (Washington, D.C., 1893).

Hillairet, *Rues de Paris* — Jacques Hillairet, pseud. of Auguste A. Coussillan, *Dictionnaire historique des rues de Paris* (2nd ed.; 2 vols., [Paris, 1964]).

Hist. — Historic or Historical.

Idzerda, *Lafayette Papers* — Stanley J. Idzerda *et al.,* eds., *Lafayette in the Age of the American Revolution: Selected Letters and Papers, 1776–1790* (5 vols. to date, Ithaca, N.Y., and London, 1977–).

JA	John Adams.
JCC	Worthington Chauncey Ford *et al.*, eds., *Journals of the Continental Congress, 1744–1789* (34 vols., Washington, 1904–37).
Jefferson Papers	Julian P. Boyd, Charles T. Cullen, John Catanzariti, *et al.*, eds., *The Papers of Thomas Jefferson* (26 vols. to date, Princeton, 1950–).
Jour.	*Journal.*
JW	Jonathan Williams, Jr.
Kaminkow, *Mariners*	Marion and Jack Kaminkow, *Mariners of the American Revolution* (Baltimore, 1967).
L	Letter unsigned.
Landais, *Memorial*	Pierre Landais, *Memorial, to Justify Peter Landai's Conduct during the Late War* (Boston, 1784).
Larousse	Pierre Larousse, *Grand dictionnaire universel du XIXe siècle* . . . (17 vols., Paris, [n.d.]).
Lasseray, *Les Français*	André Lasseray, *Les Français sous les treize étoiles, 1775–1783* (2 vols., Paris, 1935).
Laurens Papers	Philip M. Hamer, George C. Rogers, Jr., David R. Chestnutt, *et al.*, eds., *The Papers of Henry Laurens* (13 vols. to date, Columbia, S.C. 1968–).
Le Bihan, *Francs-maçons parisiens*	Alain Le Bihan, *Francs-maçons parisiens du Grand Orient de France* . . . (Commission d'histoire économique et sociale de la révolution française, *Mémoires et documents*, XIX, Paris, 1966).
Lee Family Papers	Paul P. Hoffman, ed., *The Lee Family Papers, 1742–1795* (University of Virginia *Microfilm Publication* No. 1; 8 reels, Charlottesville, Va., 1966).

Lewis, *Walpole Correspondence* — Wilmarth S. Lewis *et al.*, eds., *The Yale Edition of Horace Walpole's Correspondence* (48 vols., New Haven, 1939–83).

Lopez, *Lafayette* — Claude A. Lopez, "Benjamin Franklin, Lafayette, and the *Lafayette*," Proceedings of the American Philosophical Society CVIII (1964), 181–223.

Lopez, *Mon Cher Papa* — Claude-Anne Lopez, *Mon Cher Papa: Franklin and the Ladies of Paris* (rev. ed., New Haven and London, 1990).

Lopez and Herbert, *The Private Franklin* — Claude-Anne Lopez and Eugenia W. Herbert, *The Private Franklin: the Man and His Family* (New York, 1975).

LS — Letter or letters signed.

l.t. — *livres tournois.*

Lüthy, *Banque protestante* — Herbert Lüthy, *La Banque protestante en France de la Révocation de l'Edit de Nantes à la Révolution* (2 vols., Paris, 1959–61).

Mackesy, *War for America* — Piers Mackesy, *The War for America, 1775–1783* (Cambridge, Mass., 1965).

Madariaga, *Harris's Mission* — Isabel de Madariaga, *Britain, Russia, and the Armed Neutrality of 1780: Sir James Harris's Mission to St. Petersburg during the American Revolution* (New Haven, 1962).

Mag. — *Magazine.*

Mass. Arch. — Massachusetts Archives, State House, Boston.

Mazas, *Ordre de Saint-Louis* — Alexandre Mazas and Théodore Anne, *Histoire de l'ordre royal et militaire de Saint-Louis depuis son institution en 1693 jusqu'en 1830* (2nd ed.; 3 vols., Paris, 1860–61).

Métra, *Correspondance secrète* — [François Métra *et al.*], *Correspondance secrète, politique & littéraire, ou Mé-*

	moires pour servir à l'histoire des cours, des sociétés & de la littérature en France, depuis la mort de Louis XV (18 vols., London, 1787–90).
Meyer, *Armement nantais*	Jean Meyer, *L'Armement nantais dans la deuxième moitié du XVIIIe siècle* (Paris, 1969).
Meyer, *Noblesse bretonne*	Jean Meyer, *La Noblesse bretonne au XVIIIe siècle* (2 vols., Paris, 1966).
Morison, *Jones*	Samuel E. Morison, *John Paul Jones: a Sailor's Biography* (Boston and Toronto, 1959).
Morris, *Jay: Peace*	Richard B. Morris *et al.*, eds., *John Jay, the Winning of the Peace: Unpublished Papers, 1780–1784* (New York, Cambridge, London, 1980).
Morris, *Jay: Revolutionary*	Richard B. Morris *et al.*, eds., *John Jay, the Making of a Revolutionary: Unpublished Papers, 1743–1780* (New York, Evanston, San Francisco, 1975).
Morris Papers	E. James Ferguson, John Catanzariti, Elizabeth M. Nuxoll, *et al.*, eds., *The Papers of Robert Morris, 1781–1784* (8 vols. to date, Pittsburgh, Pa., 1973–).
Morton, *Beaumarchais Correspondance*	Brian N. Morton and Donald C. Spinelli, eds., *Beaumarchais Correspondance* (4 vols. to date, Paris, 1969–).
MS, MSS	Manuscript, manuscripts.
Namier and Brooke, *House of Commons*	Sir Lewis Namier and John Brooke, *The History of Parliament. The House of Commons 1754–1790* (3 vols., London and New York, 1964).
Neeser, *Conyngham*	Robert Walden Neeser, ed., *Letters and Papers Relating to the Cruises of Gustavus Conyngham, Captain of the Continental Navy 1777–1779* (New York, 1915).

NNBW	*Nieuw Nederlandsch Biografisch Woorden-boek* (10 vols. and index, Amsterdam, 1974).
Nouvelle biographie	*Nouvelle biographie générale depuis les temps les plus reculés jusqu'à nos jours* . . . (46 vols., Paris, 1855–66).
Pa. Arch.	Samuel Hazard et al., eds., *Pennsylvania Archives* (9 series, Philadelphia and Harrisburg, 1852–1935).
Palmer, *Loyalists*	Gregory Palmer, ed., *Biographical Sketches of Loyalists of the American Revolution* (Westport, Ct., 1984).
Phil. Trans.	The Royal Society, *Philosophical Transactions.*
PMHB	*Pennsylvania Magazine of History and Biography.*
Price, *France and the Chesapeake*	Jacob M. Price, *France and the Chesapeake: a History of the French Tobacco Monopoly, 1674–1791, and of Its Relationship to the British and American Tobacco Trade* (2 vols., Ann Arbor, Mich., 1973).
Proc.	*Proceedings.*
Pub.	*Publications.*
Quérard, *France littéraire*	Joseph Marie Quérard, *La France littéraire ou Dictionnaire bibliographique des savants, historiens, et gens de lettres de la France, ainsi que des littérateurs étrangers qui ont écrit en français, plus particulièrement pendant les XVIIIe et XIXe siècles* . . . (10 vols., Paris, 1827–64).
Rakove, *Beginnings of National Politics*	Jack N. Rakove, *The Beginnings of National Politics: an Interpretive History of the Continental Congress* (New York, 1979).

RB   Richard Bache.

Repertorium der diplo-   Ludwig Bittner *et al.*, eds., *Repertorium*
matischen Vertreter   *der diplomatischen Vertreter aller*
    Länder seit dem Westfälischen Frieden
    (1648) (3 vols., Oldenburg, etc.,
    1936–65).

Rev.   *Review.*

Rice and Brown, eds.,   Howard C. Rice, Jr., and Anne S.K.
    Rochambeau's Army   Brown, eds., *The American Campaigns*
    of Rochambeau's Army, 1780, 1781,
    1782, 1783 (2 vols., Princeton and
    Providence, 1972).

s.   *sou.*

Sabine, *Loyalists*   Lorenzo Sabine, *Biographical Sketches of*
    Loyalists of the American Revolution
    . . . (2 vols., Boston, 1864).

SB   Sarah Bache.

Schelle, *Œuvres de Turgot*   Gustave Schelle, ed., *Œuvres de Turgot et*
    documents le concernant (5 vols., Paris,
    1913–23).

Schulte Nordholt, *Dutch*   J. W. Schulte Nordholt, *The Dutch*
    Republic   *Republic and American Independence*
    (trans. Herbert M. Rowen; Chapel
    Hill, N.C., 1982).

Sellers, *Franklin in Por-*   Charles C. Sellers, *Benjamin Franklin in*
    traiture   *Portraiture* (New Haven and London,
    1962).

Sibley's Harvard Graduates   John L. Sibley, *Biographical Sketches of*
    Graduates of Harvard University (17
    vols. to date, Cambridge, Mass.,
    1873–). Continued from Volume IV by
    Clifford K. Shipton.

Six, *Dictionnaire*   Georges Six, *Dictionnaire biographique des*
    biographique   *généraux et amiraux français de la Révo-*
    lution et de l'Empire (1792–1814) (2
    vols., Paris, 1934).

Smith, *Letters* — Paul H. Smith *et al.*, eds., *Letters of Delegates to Congress* (24 vols. to date, Washington, D.C., 1976–).

Smyth, *Writings* — Albert H. Smyth, ed., *The Writings of Benjamin Franklin* . . . (10 vols., New York, 1905–07).

Soc. — Society.

Sparks, *Works* — Jared Sparks, ed., *The Works of Benjamin Franklin* . . . (10 vols., Boston, 1836–40).

Stevens, *Facsimiles* — Benjamin F. Stevens, ed., *Facsimiles of Manuscripts in European Archives Relating to America, 1773–1783* (25 vols., London, 1889–98).

Taylor, *J. Q. Adams Diary* — Robert J. Taylor *et al.*, eds., *Diary of John Quincy Adams* (2 vols. to date, Cambridge, Mass., and London, 1981–).

Trans. — Translator or translated.

Trans. — *Transactions.*

Van Doren, *Franklin* — Carl Van Doren, *Benjamin Franklin* (New York, 1938).

Van Doren, *Franklin-Mecom* — Carl Van Doren, ed., *The Letters of Benjamin Franklin & Jane Mecom* (American Philosophical Society *Memoirs*, XXVII, Princeton, 1950).

Villiers, *Commerce colonial* — Patrick Villiers, *Le Commerce colonial atlantique et la guerre d'indépendance des Etats-Unis d'Amérique, 1778–1783* (New York, 1977).

W&MQ — *William and Mary Quarterly*, first or third series as indicated.

Ward, *War of the Revolution* — Christopher Ward, *The War of the Revolution* (John R. Alden, ed.; 2 vols., New York, 1952).

Waste Book — BF's accounts described above, XXIII, 19.

WF — William Franklin.

Wharton, *Diplomatic Correspondence*	Francis Wharton, ed., *The Revolutionary Diplomatic Correspondence of the United States* (6 vols., Washington, D.C., 1889).
Willcox, *Portrait of a General*	William B. Willcox, *Portrait of a General: Sir Henry Clinton in the War of Independence* (New York, 1964).
WTF	William Temple Franklin.
WTF, *Memoirs*	William Temple Franklin, ed., *Memoirs of the Life and Writings of Benjamin Franklin, L.L.D., F.R.S., &c . . .* (3 vols., 4to, London, 1817–18).
WTF's accounts	Those described above, XXIII, 19.
Yela Utrilla, *España*	Juan F. Yela Utrilla, *España ante la Independencia de los Estados Unidos* (2nd ed.; 2 vols., Lérida, 1925).

l

Note by the Editors and the Administrative Board

As we noted in volume 23 (pp. xlvi–xlviii), the period of Franklin's mission to France brings with it roughly two and a half times as many documents as those for the remaining seventy years of his life. In the present volume once again we summarize a portion of his incoming correspondence in collective descriptions; they appear in the index under the following headings: commission seekers; favor seekers; intelligence reports; offerers of goods and services.

As we noted in volume 30 (p. lx), Franklin's new French secretary Jean L'Air de Lamotte was responsible for keeping the official letterbook. Many of the copies produced by L'Air de Lamotte are severely flawed. They contain errors of spelling, punctuation, and syntax that could not have been present in Franklin's originals. Regrettably, however, these copies are the only extant versions of much of Franklin's official correspondence dating from this period, and we publish them as they stand.

A revised statement of textual methodology appeared in volume 28 and is repeated here. The original statement of method is found in the Introduction to the first volume, pp. xxiv–xlvii. The various developments in policy are explained in xv, xxiv; XXI, xxxiv; XXIII, xlvi–xlviii.

Introduction

America required one of two things in the fall of 1780: "A Peace—or the most vigorous aid of our allies particularly in the article of money," as George Washington bluntly presented it.[1] Franklin's ministerial responsibilities in the months covered by this volume were determined by this need. His skills in diplomacy and finance were put to new tests as American efforts to obtain support intensified in Spain and the Netherlands and were renewed in France. In age and experience Franklin was the senior minister in Europe, and his colleagues John Jay in Madrid and John Adams in Amsterdam turned to him for information and guidance. He was also responsible for paying their salaries, as Congress had made drafts payable on him at Paris. The mission that united the three men was where to find money for the war against Britain and how to get more of it.

Jay had been in Spain since January, 1780, but he had made scant progress toward his objectives of securing diplomatic recognition, a treaty of alliance and commerce, and financial aid. In July he was optimistic, persuaded that the court and Chief Minister Floridablanca were well disposed toward the United States. By late September, when the two men met at San Ildefonso, it was clear that neither a treaty of alliance nor financial assistance would be forthcoming unless Jay was prepared to relinquish American rights to navigate the Mississippi River. He was not, and Congress, in fact, reaffirmed his instructions on that point on October 4.[2] By the end of the month Jay advised Franklin that there would be no loan from Spain and that his situation there was most "unpleasant."[3]

Adams, whom Congress had appointed to treat for peace when Britain was ready to negotiate, proceeded from Paris to Amsterdam in late July. He would spend the next two years there. Before he departed he enraged Foreign Minister Ver-

1. From George Washington, Oct. 9.
2. From Jay, July 17; Morris, *Jay: Revolutionary*, pp. 824–35; from James Lovell, Oct. 28.
3. From Jay, Oct. 30.

lii

gennes by strongly criticizing the extent and direction of France's aid to the American cause; Adams also resented Vergennes' unwillingness to inform the British about his commission in Europe. The foreign minister promptly declared that he would have no further correspondence with the American and requested Franklin to inform Congress about Adams' behavior.[4] Franklin was caught in the middle, as he had been in June when Adams and Vergennes vehemently disagreed over Congress' devaluation of the currency. He apprised Adams of Vergennes' displeasure, adding that he himself was sorry to see the offending passages in Adams' letters to Vergennes and suggesting that Adams write something to Vergennes to erase the impression the letters had made. Franklin eventually did as Vergennes had asked, however, and forwarded the correspondence to Congress.[5] His accompanying letter to President of Congress Samuel Huntington included an explicit and moving statement of what he believed a proper American policy toward France should be: it is "not only our Duty but our Interest" to be grateful to Louis XVI, and Franklin intended to procure whatever advantages he could for America "by endeavouring to please this Court."[6]

When Adams reached Amsterdam he encountered a serious situation that threatened American credit. Henry Laurens, who had been appointed in November, 1779, to obtain a loan and negotiate a treaty of amity and commerce with the Netherlands, was expected to arrive at any time. Immediately after his appointment, Congress began to draw drafts on him, and the bills were coming into Amsterdam even before Laurens had left the United States. The Amsterdam merchant firm Jean de Neufville & fils dispatched alarmed appeals to Franklin when the bills were presented to them for payment.[7] Laurens, however, had been

4. See the editorial note in *Adams Papers*, IX, 516–20, and Vergennes to BF, July 31.

5. To JA, Oct. 8; to Samuel Huntington, Aug. 9.

6. To Huntington, Aug. 9. For JA's opinion see his letter to BF of Oct. 14.

7. In July they hoped Jay could find the money for the incoming bills drawn on Laurens (Neufville & fils to BF, July 13). In mid-August JA thought that if Laurens had decided not to come or had met with an accident the situation would be critical enough for Congress to appoint someone else with full powers: *Adams Papers*, x, 69.

captured at sea in September and imprisoned in the Tower of London in October.[8] The task of searching for a loan to cover the bills drawn on him fell to Adams, but ultimately, when no loan could be found, the responsibility for covering them devolved on Franklin.

Franklin was confronted by bills of exchange from several directions. He confided to Jay that the quantity of them left him so "terrified" and "vexed" that he was deprived of sleep, and "render'd almost incapable of Writing."[9] With hopes of Spanish assistance dashed and efforts to raise money in Holland unsuccessful, Franklin had no choice but to ask the French for a new loan. His request to Vergennes revealed just how serious the situation was; unexpected drafts had already absorbed much of the money he had, and if he were to protest the bills now presented, the credit of Congress would be destroyed. As the states would easily be able to repay the loan after a few years of peace, and as the work of establishing a free commerce with France was almost complete, Franklin argued, it would be a pity to see it miscarry "for want of 4, or 5 millions of Livres."[1] He had modest success: on October 5 the French government paid the final installment on the loan it had granted late in 1779, and on November 27 it provided an additional one million *livres*.

Fulfilling Congress' 1779 order for supplies for the American army continued to occupy an important part of Franklin's day-to-day responsibilities, and much of his correspondence in the summer and autumn of 1780 pertains to this task. By late September, clothing for the troops was at Lorient, Le Ray de Chaumont had obtained cloth for the officers' uniforms, and John Bondfield had promised to supply cannon.[2] Desegray, Beaugeard fils et Cie. at St. Malo had been requested to dispatch saltpeter, which was subject to special provisions when exported

8. BF tried to intervene for more humane treatment for Laurens by writing to his former friend Sir Grey Cooper. BF also observed that he might do the same for a friend of Cooper's some day: BF to Cooper, Nov. 7.

9. To Jay, Oct. 2.

1. To Vergennes, Sept. 20.

2. From Bondfield, Sept 19; from JW, Sept. 26. For an overview of the progress of the supply order during the period of the present volume see Lopez, *Lafayette*, pp. 197–208.

by anyone but the King. Franklin appealed to his old friend and fellow scientist, Antoine-Laurent Lavoisier, *régisseur des poudres et salpêtres* and son-in-law of Jacques Paulze, a prominent member of the farmers general, to cut through the red tape and secure the necessary passport.[3]

No amount of worrying or soliciting on Franklin's part, however, could move the supplies. The *Alliance*, under the command of Captain Pierre Landais, had sailed with half-filled holds in July. Captain John Paul Jones and the *Ariel* left in early October but were forced back into port by a violent storm. The *Marquis de Lafayette*, a former East Indiaman and now the intended transport for most of the goods, was still in Bordeaux at the end of October. Pleas for supplies continued to arrive from America: the marquis de Lafayette begged for arms, powder, and "fifteen or twenty thousand Compleat Suits" for the "Nack'd, Schokingly Nack'd" troops.[4]

To assist the war effort the women of Philadelphia, mobilized by the Ladies Association that Esther DeBerdt Reed had founded, collected funds to purchase supplies and also sewed shirts for the soldiers. "The women of America have at last become principals" in the Revolution, observed Benjamin Rush. Sarah Bache "had no small hand" in the effort, her husband reported.[5] Franklin (perhaps recalling the stinging rebuke he had given Sally a year earlier for wanting feathers) remarked that the Association refuted the charge that women have no "amor patrie."[6]

The primary theater of the war was in the southern states. Congress had appointed Horatio Gates, who had "burgoyned" the British in 1778, to the command of the army there. Lacking fresh troops and accurate information about the strength and location of British forces, he was defeated at Camden, South Car-

3. See BF to JW, Sept. 27 and Oct. 7; JW to BF Sept 30; BF to Lavoisier, Oct. 22 and Nov. 3.

4. From Lafayette, Oct. 9. The request of the comte de Rochambeau for "troops, ships, and money," was another indication of the enormous needs in America: Mackesy, *War with America*, p. 350.

5. From RB, July 22. See also SB's letter of Sept. 9. For Rush's remark see *Adams Papers*, IX, 530–1.

6. BF to RB and SB, Oct. 4. For his 1779 criticism of SB see XXIX, 613–15.

olina, on August 16. American troops fled, and the Baron de Kalb was mortally wounded.[7] Not until after the period of this volume would Franklin learn of the first check to British hopes of regaining the whole region: the October 7 American victory at Kings Mountain.

Lord North, grown confident by the news of military successes in North America and the suppression of the Gordon Riots in London in June, decided that the time was right to dissolve Parliament. Although he hoped to increase his majority in the House of Commons, the September elections (in which an unusually large number of seats was contested) actually slightly increased the strength of the opposition. In those constituencies where a popular voice existed, it spoke against the government. Although Britain had the military initiative and resources adequate for the moment to win the war, the election reflected, if ever so slightly, a war-weariness among some English country gentlemen and metropolitan radicals.[8]

Several developments that came to fruition in late 1780 and early 1781 were embryonic in the summer and fall. In Europe, additional steps were taken toward the formation of the League of Armed Neutrality, with Denmark and Sweden signing conventions to join it. In America, the Continental Congress began to consider a series of administrative reforms and advances were made toward the ratification of the Articles of Confederation.[9] In Franklin's own life, Arthur Lee and Ralph Izard's criticisms and a threat by John Mathews of South Carolina to move for the American Minister's recall foreshadowed a coming congressional reconsideration of the French mission that would weaken Franklin's authority.[1]

7. From RB, Sept. 10, and from Lafayette, Oct. 9. News of the battle was published in the *Courier de l'Europe* on Oct. 13; see our annotation of the comtesse de La Rouërie to BF, [after Oct. 13].

8. Ian R. Christie, *The End of North's Ministry, 1780–82* (London and New York, 1958), pp. 157–63; Namier and Brooke, *House of Commons*, I, 80–7. See also Mackesy, *War for America*, pp. 363–9.

9. See Lafayette to BF, Oct. 9. See also Jack N. Rakove, *The Beginnings of National Politics: an Interpretive History of the Continental Congress* (New York, 1979), pp. 286–7, and H. James Henderson, *Party Politics in the Continental Congress* (New York, London, and other places, 1974), pp. 263–4.

1. From RB, Sept. 10 and Oct. 30.

A number of Franklin's regular correspondents will become less prominent in future volumes. The chevalier de Kéralio sent his final series of intelligence reports. Sartine, blamed by public opinion for the massive expenditures of money and France's failure to win a decisive victory, was dismissed as naval minister.[2] David Hartley, defeated by his constituents at Hull, ceased writing to Franklin for almost a year. And, finally, the annoying Pierre Landais sailed for America in July, firing off his final epistle to Franklin.

In late July, Franklin ceased his sponsorship of privateers sailing under American commissions. For more than a year he had encouraged John Torris, Luke Ryan, and others to harass British shipping and capture British sailors. On July 24, however, Vergennes advised Franklin that it would be wise to recall the commissions for the remaining privateers. Franklin acquiesced the following day. In August the French foreign minister informed Franklin that henceforth the proper jurisdiction for ruling on prizes taken by American privateers would be the *Conseil des Prises*.[3] As Franklin had never sought the duties in the first place, he must have felt relief. The collapse of the privateering venture meant, however, the dashing of his hopes for capturing significant numbers of seamen to exchange for Americans in Mill and Forton prisons.

In the summer of 1780 Franklin and his grandson Temple apparently helped in the recovery of a runaway slave, "Mr. Montague." Few letters to or from Franklin survive to illuminate the story, but the extant documents indicate that he wrote to the head of the Paris police asking him to help Captain Robeson of the South Carolina navy in recapturing the man; three days later Montague himself, signing his letter "Jean," sent Franklin an eloquent plea to be released from the Petit Châtelet. The tale is fragmentary but intriguing and will unfold in future volumes.[4]

2. Dull, *French Navy,* pp. 199–201. Turgot commented that "Ce pauvre M de Sartine dit à tout le monde qu'il est ruiné, il va quitter sa maison comme trop grande pour sa fortune." *Lettres de Turgot à la duchesse d'Enville, 1764–74 et 1777–80,* ed. Joseph Ruwet *et al.* (Louvain and Leiden, 1976), p. 154.

3. Vergennes to BF, July 24 and Aug. 13, and BF's replies of July 25 and Aug. 15. See also Clark, *Ben Franklin's Privateers,* pp. 164–70.

4. See BF to Lenoir, July 22; from Jean [Montague], July 25.

Franklin seems to have led a fairly modest social life during these months. He apparently had a quiet celebration of the fourth anniversary of the 4th of July. He and Temple ate several times with Madame Helvétius; he dined with Turgot and also with Lavoisier. On August 20 he hosted a dinner for his former colleague Silas Deane, who had arrived in Paris the preceding day. In September he entertained the newly arrived Americans John Thaxter, Jr., and Jeremiah Allen.[5] Several invitations to attend meetings came to him—from the Royal Society of Medicine and from the Loge des Neuf Soeurs, for example—but we have no evidence that he went.[6]

Franklin's typefoundry at Passy, which he had engaged J.-Fr. Hémery to set up, had been in operation for more than a year. In late July the first inventory was drawn up. The foundry had produced more than 5,000 pounds of type, ranging in size from *double canon* to *petit texte*. The numerous entries for the foundry's expenses in Franklin's Cash Book indicate that it was in active operation throughout this period, except for a month-long summer break. In August, Franklin paid a visit to the typefoundry of Simon-Pierre Fournier le jeune.[7]

Franklin's interest in printing also took him into a related field—copying. The London stationer James Woodmason sent him a prospectus for a copying machine patented by James Watt. Franklin himself bought three of Watt's machines, along with the special paper and ink powder required, noting that he approved of the firm's unwillingness to offer credit, "for I think Credit is upon the whole, of more Mischief than Benefit to Mankind."[8] Recalling that years earlier he had devised a copying method himself, Franklin began to discuss various techniques with the abbé Rochon, who came up with his own invention, a machine that could mechanically engrave type. In August the abbé presented it to the Académie royale des sciences, open-

5. See our headnote on BF's accounts and Thaxter to BF, Sept. 22.

6. From Vicq d'Azyr, Aug. 23; from d'Ussieux, [before July 3].

7. See the Inventory of Fonts Cast, [July 22], our headnote on accounts, and Fournier to BF, Aug. 15.

8. BF to Woodmason, July 25 and Sept. 26; Woodmason to BF, Sept. 12 and Nov. 1.

ing his presentation by describing his conversations with Franklin about the new machine.

Franklin suffered a severe and incapacitating attack of the gout that lingered from approximately mid-October until the middle of December. He reported himself continually "harassed" by it.[9] Some of his correspondence lay unanswered, and Temple replied to some letters on his behalf. Madame Brillon, in her witty fable "Le Sage et La Goutte," admonished him that prudence was not his strongest point and listed a few of his faults: overeating, lack of exercise, too much time with women and at chess, and drinking "un peu."[1] He had a respite from his pain in mid-November, however, during which he purchased a pair of crutches. We take this as evidence that he was recovering and expected to resume a more active life.[2]

9. To Samuel Wharton, Nov. 1, and to Lavoisier, Nov. 3.
1. See her letters of [before Nov. 14] and Nov. 14.
2. See the abbés Chalut and Arnoux to BF, Nov. 14 and the headnote on accounts.

Chronology

July 1 through November 15, 1780

July 7–August 16: *Alliance* sails to America.

July 8–August 15: Cruise of privateer *Fearnot*.

July 9: Denmark joins the League of Armed Neutrality.

July 11: Rochambeau and Ternay reach Newport.

July 18: Privateer *Black Princess* returns to Morlaix from her second cruise.

July 25: BF agrees to withdraw American commissions from French privateers.

July 27: JA leaves Paris for the Netherlands.

August 1: Sweden joins the League of Armed Neutrality.

August 1–11: Third cruise of *Black Princess*.

August 8–9: Combined French and Spanish fleet captures valuable Jamaica convoy off the Azores.

August 13: Henry Laurens sails for Europe aboard the *Mercury*.

August 16: Gen. Horatio Gates defeated at Battle of Camden.

August 19: Silas Deane arrives at Passy; abbé Rochon presents his copying machine to the académie royale des sciences.

September 1: Parliament dissolved and new election called.

September 3: Laurens captured aboard *Mercury* and his papers taken.

September 4–October 7: *Ariel* is at the Ile de Groix.

September 10: James Searle arrives in Paris with dispatches from Congress.

September 11: David Hartley defeated at Hull.

September 14: Admiral Rodney's fleet arrives at New York.

September 20: BF asks French government for new loan.

September 20–22: Washington meets with Rochambeau at Hartford.

September 23: Capture of Maj. John André; conference of Jay and Floridablanca at San Ildefonso.

September 25: Gen. Benedict Arnold defects to British.

October 2: Maj. André executed as spy.

October 5: French government pays final 750,000 *l.t.* installment of December, 1779, loan.

October 6: Laurens imprisoned in the Tower of London.

October 7: American victory at Battle of Kings Mountain.

October 7–12: *Ariel* sails for America, is forced by storm to return to port.

October 13: Sartine relieved of post as naval minister.

October 14: Marquis de Castries appointed naval minister; Washington appoints Greene as commander of southern army.

middle of October–middle of December: BF afflicted with severe case of gout.

October 22: Guichen's fleet from the West Indies reaches Cadiz.

October 31: Convening of new Parliament.

November 7–January 3, 1781: D'Estaing brings fleet from Cadiz to Brest.

THE PAPERS OF
BENJAMIN FRANKLIN

VOLUME 33

July 1 through November 15, 1780

Editorial Note on Franklin's Accounts

One new account begins during the period covered by this volume.[1]

XXIX. Franklin's Account with Congress, October 4, 1780, to April 4, 1781: Historical Society of Pennsylvania, 3 pages. An account in William Temple Franklin's hand recording Franklin's official expenditures, including his salary payments and sums given from his "Private Purse" for which he drew reimbursement. These entries are duplicates of items recorded in other accounts, but the personal expenditures will be a particularly valuable record for the period after the Cash Book ends.

We also offer a summary of entries from Franklin's accounts that have not found a place elsewhere in our annotation but that provide insights into his private and public life between July 1 and November 15, 1780.

Account XVI (Cash Book, XXVI, 3.)

This is the last volume that will be covered by the Cash Book, whose final page contains entries through mid-October. If Franklin continued this account in another ledger, it has not survived.

The expenses of the typefoundry continue to be the most consistent entries.[2] Weekly salary payments to the staff (Hémery, Bieuville, Rocque, Madelon, and Garre) stopped from mid-July to mid-August, at which point Madelon was replaced, first by Baudegon, then on September 23, by Sophie. Draonet supplied wood in early July, and Hémery was paid twice for metal, on August 26 and again in mid-October.

Franklin noted some of the sums he loaned on behalf of Congress or gave outright to prisoners. Apart from the loan he extended to Duplessÿ,[3] the only other entry was for "Three poor Frenchmen, who had been in the American Service, made Prisoners & just returned from England." He gave them 72 *l.t.* on October 4.

Jean L'Air de Lamotte received 600 *l.t.* on August 7, wages for his first six months' work as "Clerk." Franklin paid for visits to the baths, bought fruit and flowers from a "Gardner" and an "Old Woman" on

---

1. The following other accounts still apply: VI, VII, XII, XVI, XVII, XIX, XXII, XXIII, XXIV, XXV, XXVI, XXVII, and XXVIII (for which see XXIII, 21; XXV, 3; XXVI, 3; XXVIII, 3–4; XXIX, 3; XXXI, 3; XXXII, 3–4).

2. Hémery's first inventory of type cast at Passy is published below, [July 22].

3. For which see our Editorial Note on the letter from the Marquis de Valory and other Favor Seekers, July 5, below.

September 2, and subscribed to *L'Esprit des journaux français et étrangers* on September 17.

Account XXIII (William Temple Franklin's Account of Family Expences, XXIX, 3).[4]

In this account, the household staff and local tradesmen take center stage. Arbelot and François, as usual, are compensated for their own food when they serve their masters at dinners away from home.[5] Coimet, the cook, and François receive payments for "wages and wine," and Mme Le Mare collects half-a-year's payments for "washing & mending." Franklin settles accounts with Brunel, the carpenter,

---

4. The entries for the second half of 1780 are not in Temple Franklin's hand, as is the rest of this account. They were written by sixteen-year-old Gurdon Saltonstall Mumford (1764–1831), son of the prominent Connecticut merchant David Mumford and Rebecca Saltonstall, and a nephew of Silas Deane, who had sailed to France with Capt. Conkling and arrived in Paris in mid-August. Mumford's father wanted him placed in a mercantile house, but Deane was skeptical of the plan since the youth had arrived with no funds, could not speak French, and had no familiarity with accounting. Franklin put the young man to work temporarily as a clerk. Deane's efforts over the next two years to find him a position elsewhere were unsuccessful, and Mumford ended up living in Passy and working for Franklin for the duration of the war. He later became a successful New York banker and member of Congress. For Mumford's arrival and Deane's reaction see *Deane Papers*, IV, 199; for a biographical account see James Gregory Mumford, *Mumford Memoirs* . . . (Boston, 1900), pp. 211–17.

5. For the first time, we have monthly bills submitted by both Arbelot (who served BF) and François (who served WTF) for their expenses: APS. Arbelot's are for dinners and errands during August, September, October, and December (settled on Dec. 31); François', for meals only, cover every month from August through December (settled on Jan. 7, 1781). BF's social engagements can be traced through these scraps of paper. He and WTF dined with Mme Helvétius once a week during August, three times in September, and twice in October. (BF's last dinner away from home, before being confined with gout, was Oct. 17 at Mme Helvétius' home.) They had several dinners at the home of her neighbor, Mr. Hébert (XXVII, 546n), and in other unspecified locations in "au teule" (Auteuil). When BF went to Versailles, he went without WTF. He dined with Turgot in Paris on Aug. 31 and Oct. 7, with Mme Bertin on Oct. 5, and at Mme Lavoisier's on Oct. 15. Some dinners were listed by the name of the hotel: "de Tours," "de Provence," and the "hotel de Danemarc, rue Jacob," probably so called because Christian VII (XV, 225n) had visited in 1772: Hillairet, *Rues de Paris*, I, 666. Arbelot also accompanied BF to the baths, posted letters, and ran errands which incurred the added cost of passage on the ferry.

Bernard the glazier, La Pierre the tinsmith, and Chabert, who has made him a pair of shoes. Cabaret continues to supply the household with stationery.[6]

On July 4,[7] Franklin purchases six volumes of *Mémoires . . . des Chinois* from the Parisian bookseller Nyon aîné, and on July 30 acquires "a Piece of new invented Black Silk" from M. Perron. On July 15 he pays duty on two cases that had arrived from Ostend, and on September 24 he settles the account of Honoré-Thomas Bligny, who furnished frames and prints. (Bligny published the engraving that is the frontispiece of this volume and showed a proof to Franklin on July 14; see the List of Illustrations.) In October Franklin buys a pair of plated candlesticks, purchases wax tapers, sends six yards of fine flannel to be dyed, and has his watch cleaned. He also pays 240 *l.t.* on October 8 to assist Thiery de la Veau, "on his Notes," to return to his family in Boston.

In August, Franklin receives a number of deliveries of spirituous beverages. A gift of wine from Jonathan Williams, Jr., arrives on August 10,[8] Boutard the *limonadier* furnishes 150 bottles of beer on the 12th, and Franklin orders 50 bottles of champagne on the 19th.[9] All of this can be chilled thanks to the "Person who furnished the Ice during the Summer," who receives 24 *l.t.* On November 13, the purchase of a pair of crutches signals that he is recovering from his attack of gout.

Account XXV (Account of Postage and Errands, XXXII, 3).

Coimet, the cook, once again kept the records for the months covered by this volume. Letters are posted almost daily, and errands in Paris are run nearly that often. Coimet arranged for a carriage for the

6. Also among BF's papers at the APS is a bill submitted by the plumber Delbos on July 9, 1781, for services beginning on Oct. 27, 1780, when he refitted and cleaned a stove.

7. In contrast to 1779, when BF's papers contained various references to the lavish banquet in celebration of Independence Day (see XXX, 44–6), there are no traces of such an event from 1780. JA reported having spent the Fourth of July "very happily with a Number of our Countrymen in Commemoration of our glorious Anniversary" (*Adams Papers*, IX, 498). It is possible that the company dined at Passy on the Queen's Ware china that BF had purchased in June: XXXII, 468–73.

8. See JW to BF, July 29.

9. The day Silas Deane arrived in Paris: *Deane Papers*, IV, 195. BF hosted a dinner for him the following day, a Sunday: *ibid.*, 193.

wine sent by Jonathan Williams, Jr. (see above). The only other expense is 15 *s.* on August 15 for sawing a load of wood.

Account XXVII (Accounts of Public Agents in Europe, XXXII, 4).
Only a few entries, for sums paid by Ferdinand Grand on Franklin's order, are unrecorded elsewhere. On July 10, Mr. Roger received 440 *l.t.* 18 *s.* 6 *d.* for "Gold, Silver & Copper Medals struck by Order of Congress."[1] On September 2, Franklin paid his overdue subscription fee to the *Courier de l'Europe*,[2] and on September 18, the wine merchant Bousie's account was finally settled: 294 *l.t.* for what he had supplied to Silas Deane in 1778.[3] Miss Chaumont received what was due her for the hire of horses and carriages.

From ——— De Frey

ALS: American Philosophical Society

Excellence,   [before July 1, 1780][4]
Je viens encor une fois d'incomoder votre Excellence et de la prier de faire donner cette lettre incluse à mon frere, capitaine de la legion du Comte de Pulasky, qui arrivera ces jours à Paris.[5] Esperant que votre Excellence ne me prendra pas à mauvaise parte cette liberté, je Suis avec la plus profonde Soumission et respect, votre Excellence le tres humble et tres obeissant Serviteur

DE FREŸ
Capitaine de Belgiojoso
au Service de Sa Majeste Imperiale

Notation: De Frey.

1. These must be the medals that Duvivier had engraved (XXXI, 489–91; XXXII, 273, 349, 435–6). We can only guess that Roger was the artisan who actually struck them.

2. A printed notice reminding him to resubscribe as of July, 1780, is at the APS.

3. See XXIX, 175n.

4. Based on a second letter from the captain (XXX, 78), dated Oct. 1, 1780, in which he says that it has been more than three months since he wrote to BF with a letter for his brother. Since he has had no answer from his brother, he fears an accident and asks BF to send him news. APS.

5. After being granted leave by Congress, baron de Frey landed in Bordeaux sometime in early April when he agreed to carry packets to BF: XXXII, 228–9, 230. He writes on Aug. 8, below.

From the Marquis d'Amezaga

ALS: American Philosophical Society

paris Le 1er jlle [1780][6]

Jay toujour Monsieur, étté a chantilly[7] ce qui ma empeché, d'aller vous rendre mes çivilité, monsieur amelot ma baucoup demondé de vos nouvelles ainsy que sa femme,[8] sil dine Lundy prochain, ches eux, vous devries y venir, en me faisant avertir davançe.

Sy vous dines ches vous dimanche Jaurois bien envie daller vous en demonder; faite moÿ faire, un petit mot de reponçe par Le garçon ministre; qui est Monsieur, votre petit fils; a qui Je vous prie de faire mes compliments.

Je Loge rue du bacq vis avis Les convalesçent:[9]

Receves Les assurançe de La veneration, et de L'attachement, avec Le quel Jay Lhonneur dettre Monsieur votre tres humble et tres obeissant serviteur   U[RTADO] M[ARQUIS] D'AMEZAGA

Notation: Damedraga Paris [1st. jy]

From Joshua Johnson

ALS: American Philosophical Society

Sir   Nantes 1 July 1780

I am honord with your Letter of the 22d. Ultimo by which I find you expect my acceptance of the appointment Congress

6. On July 22 and Sept. 2 the marquis wrote to ask BF if he would be dining at home the following day, "demain dimanche." APS. Both of those dates fell on a Saturday in 1780. We presume the present letter also dates from 1780, when July 1 was a Saturday.

7. Historically the seat of the princes de Condé. For Amezaga's friendship with Louis-Joseph de Bourbon, the current prince, see F.-A. Gruyer, *Chantilly: les Portraits de Carmontelle* (Paris, 1902), pp. 37–8.

8. Marie-Françoise-Jeanne Le Gendre (b. 1738), daughter of Paul-Gaspard-François Le Gendre, a *conseiller* in the Paris *parlement* and a *président* of the *chambre des comptes:* Michel Antoine, *Le Gouvernement et l'administration sous Louis XVI: Dictionnaire biographique* (Paris, 1978), p. 8; François Bluche, *Les magistrats du Parlement de Paris au XVIIIe siècle* (2nd ed., Paris, 1986), pp. 245, 314n.

9. The Hôpital des Convalescents was founded in 1652 to afford a rest of two weeks to people coming out of the hospital. It offered no medical care and was closed to priests, soldiers, and domestics, since they could find shelter elsewhere: Hillairet, *Rues de Paris,* I, 133.

confered on me will make my presence, for the execution of that trust necessary in Paris,[1] at the time I accepted of this appointment[2] I did not understand from the Resolution of Congress or your Letter that it was requested I should leave my Family[3] & Business to do that of the Publics without even so much as my Expences being born, nor do I understand those resolutions of Congress in any other light still than that the Accounts are to be laid before me here order this & I am ready to go into an examination of them, but I am reduced to the necessity of informing you that I cannot attend you in Paris. I shall write Congress on the subject and tell them at the time of my Acceptance of their Commission, that I had no Idea of their desiring me to leave Home & that I request a discharge from this trust.—[4] I thank you for your information about the Business of the State of Maryland.[5] I suppose the Act explains itself & that you are acting in conformity to it. I will take the liberty to recommend to you to be certain, that those Gent. will apply the Money to the Payment of the Bills drawn by the Trustees and not set it off against the Demands they have against America. I have the honor to be with much respect.

Your Excellencys most Obedt & most Hble. Servt

JOSHUA JOHNSON

His Excellency Benjamin Franklin Esqr.

1. BF's letter is in XXXII, 570. Johnson had been appointed by Congress to audit the accounts of BF and his former fellow commissioners: XXX, 544n.

2. XXXI, 564–5.

3. Johnson and his wife Catherine by now had four children: Andrew Oliver, ed., *Portraits of John Quincy Adams and His Wife* (Cambridge, Mass., 1970), p. 23.

4. He wrote President of Congress Samuel Huntington on July 20: National Archives.

5. At the request of Gov. Thomas Sim Lee of Maryland, BF had asked the state's trustees in London, James Russell, Silvanus Grove, and Osgood Hanbury, to sell Maryland's stock in the Bank of England so it could liquidate bills of credit. BF was empowered to name a replacement for them if they refused: XXXI, 336–8; XXXII, 401, 523.

From Colonel M. de Sonnemaens

ALS: American Philosophical Society

Sir   Venlo July 1(?). 1780

I had the honour upon the 28th of June 1780 to recive your
Honored answer to my letter,[6] out of the mentioned date apears
that it is impossible within the preschribed 14 days that this our
answere the requered nor desired effect can satisfay. Nevertheless we are surprised our Brother Johan Henry Baron de Wolff
etz. etz. dos, or did not derect follow your Counsell, being you
are the only person capable to give him good Councell not allon,
but lykeways to provide him according to his Rang, Quality, and
Merit compiting and necessair for all Brave, Dapper Gentlemen
Millitair officers generaliter Usewall. Thus done we advise him,
and are very desirous he Should come over and stay here, till all
his wounds be wholy heeled, Then he having Eleven of them it
may be suposed that till such time his wounds are heeled he is not
able to serve. This being all we can say there about at this time,
only take the liberty to recomend him to your High protection
and at the same time heartely to thank you for the honour you
have don us, offering reciproque service in case any occasion
ther too happen.[7] Where with we have the honour with all imaginable respect to name our selves.

Sir.

Your Most Humble and most Obliged Servant.

M: DE SONNEMAENS Collonel

Intelligence from Paris and Other Places

D: National Archives

During the period of the present volume Franklin received through
the courtesy of his friend the chevalier de Kéralio eight intelligence

---

6. BF's June 16 letter (XXXII, 538) actually was to the colonel's wife, a sister of the baron de Wolff or Wulffen, an officer wounded in America who
had sent several requests to BF: XXXII, 111–12n, 457, and following. BF told
her that he had tried unsuccessfully to persuade the baron to visit her while
he recuperated from his wounds, but that he would forward a letter to Wulffen if it arrived within a fortnight.

7. Sonnemaens enclosed his and his wife's invitation to the baron. This
letter, now at the APS, is in Dutch and is dated July 1. BF never delivered it

9

reports; Franklin forwarded them, when the opportunity permitted, to the United States, as he had done with some 260 earlier reports.[8] These were the last that Franklin bothered to send.[9] Their cessation was not a great loss to Congress. Often little more than gossip, their information was outdated by the time it reached Philadelphia. As in past volumes we publish the first intelligence report and summarize the remainder.

(I) Bayonne, July 25: On the 19th an English prize made by the *Comte d'Artois* entered this port; it was the *Charming Nancy* of Portsmouth, carrying salt beef, rice, flour, and some woolen cloth to Gibraltar.[1]

(II) Brest, July 26: Two recently arrived Swedish ships were visited off Ushant by a fleet of twenty-two British ships of the line. A frigate and a lugger have been sent out to reconnoiter and it is possible that the seven ships of the line here will wait to sail until their return.[2] Commandant Hector has received a letter from Naval Minister Sartine, telling him of the impending arrival of a convoy from the Baltic

---

because Wulffen was already en route to his sister's house. Dumas reported him in Brussels on June 29 (Dumas to BF, July 4, below) and he wrote from Venlo, a Dutch city on the Meuse, on July 7, below.

8. A list of them, arranged by place of origin, was eventually compiled at the instigation of then-Secretary of State John Jay and filed with the reports at the National Archives. The lack of communications between August and October undoubtedly was related to Kéralio's absence from Paris.

9. Although Kéralio does not seem to have written BF directly during the period of this volume, he continued to take an interest in American affairs; on Oct. 24 and on Nov. 2 he wrote WTF for information about the Battle of Camden, which he could circulate among German newspapers (APS). For the most recent prior intelligence reports see XXXII, 70–3. None of the present reports is in Kéralio's hand. All were written in French and are now at the National Archives.

1. The *Comte d'Artois* was a privateer, whose capture of the *Charming Nancy* was reported in the Aug. 18 issue of the *Courier de l'Europe:* VIII (1780), 112.

2. The French ships of the line presently at Brest were the *Bretagne*, 110, *Royal Louis*, 110, *Ville de Paris*, 100, *Auguste*, 80, *St. Esprit*, 80, *Languedoc*, 80, and *Northumberland*, 74. The fleet was in the process of being stripped of its ships in order to reinforce the Spanish fleet at Cadiz, whose vulnerability had frightened the French. The British Navy hence enjoyed superiority in French coastal waters : XXXII, 70n; Dull, *French Navy*, p. 366; Jonathan R. Dull, "The French Navy and American Independence: Naval Factors in French Diplomacy and War Strategy, 1774–1780" (Ph.D. diss., University of California at Berkeley, 1972), pp. 335–6n.

escorted by several warships of the northern powers.[3] The King desires us to receive and assist any ships that wish to enter port. Letters from Lisbon report the capture of the frigate *Artésienne*.[4]

(III) Brest, July 31: The ships of the line *Hector* and *Vaillant* have arrived from Lorient.

(IV) Paris, July 31: We have learned from London that the French frigate *Capricieuse* sank after being captured by the British frigates *Prudente* and *Licorne*.[5] A courier from Madrid reports that Admiral Córdoba's Cadiz fleet of twenty-two Spanish and nine French ships of the line has sailed, reportedly for a cruise of ten or eleven days.[6] A squadron from Toulon has arrived in the bay of Cadiz with a convoy.[7]

(V) Paris, August 6: The arrival of the Toulon squadron and convoy has been confirmed. There are various indications that the French fleet will winter in Cadiz. It is said that the formal siege of Gibraltar will begin this autumn. The combined Spanish-French fleet is cruising between Cape Spartel and Cape Ste. Marie. The frigate *Etats d'Artois* has been captured by a 50–gun British ship. A courier from Bordeaux reports the arrival of the *Fier Roderigue* and a convoy of eighteen ships.[8] When it left Chesapeake Bay on June 26 there was not

---

3. Jean-Charles, comte d'Hector (1722–*c.* 1808), was commandant of the arsenal at Brest and became port commandant on Feb. 1, 1781: Didier Neuville, ed., *Etat sommaire des archives de la marine antérieures à la Révolution* (Paris, 1898), p. 136n. The French government hoped that Denmark, Sweden, and Russia, using the mechanism of Empress Catherine II's League of Armed Neutrality, would escort Baltic naval stores to French ports. The Russian Baltic Fleet did sail on June 21, but it extended protection only to Russian ships: Madariaga, *Harris's Mission*, p. 212. It arrived off the English coast in mid-August: *Courier de l'Europe*, VIII (1780), 118 (issue of Aug. 22).

4. The *Artois* (or *Artésienne* or *Etats d'Artois*) was a 40–gun privateer captured off Cape Finisterre by H.M.S. *Romney*, 50: William Laird Clowes, *The Royal Navy: a History from the Earliest Times to the Present* (7 vols., London and Boston, 1897–1903), IV, 52. Possibly this is the same ship as the *Comte d'Artois*.

5. The crew of the *Capricieuse* "displayed the greatest intrepidity in offering so stubborn a resistance to so superior a force": Clowes, *Royal Navy*, IV, 53; *Courier de l'Europe*, VIII (1780), 55–6, 100–1 (issues of July 25 and Aug. 15).

6. On August 8–9 Córdoba's fleet captured a huge outbound convoy for the British East and West Indies; the sixty-one prizes were worth £1,500,000: Mackesy, *War for America*, p. 357; Dull, *French Navy*, pp. 193–4.

7. This convoy of twenty-five supply ships was escorted by four ships of the line: Dull, "French Navy," p. 335n. The Aug. 6 intelligence report indicates that it also included seven ships for the Western Hemisphere.

8. As was reported in the Aug. 15 issue of the *Courier de l'Europe* (VIII [1780], 100). The *Fier Roderigue*, 50, was the largest ship in Beaumarchais'

yet any news of Admiral Ternay. The marquis de Lafayette received a most flattering welcome in Boston. The frigate *Hermione* on which he had traveled subsequently captured three prizes and fought off two British ships; her captain was wounded.[9]

(VI) Bayonne, October 5: A letter from Madrid informs us that Admiral Antonio de Ulloa's[1] squadron of four ships of the line and two frigates has brought into La Coruña as prizes two British ships of the line and a frigate.

(VII) Bordeaux, October 9: On Tuesday the 5th [*i.e.*, 3rd] a privateer frigate from this city arrived with three British prizes. It is reported that the Spaniards have captured two British ships of the line and several frigates.

Paris Le 1er. Juillet [1780]

M. le Cte. d'Estaing part dimanche pour aller, disent bien des gens, prendre le Commandement de la flotte combinée de Cadiz.[2] Ils se fondent Sur ce que ce Général a eu depuis peu plusieurs conférences avec M. de sartine. D'autres prétendent qu'il va tout simplement aux eaux de Baréges, pour consolider la guérison de la blessure qu'il a reçüe l'année passée, et que les conférences qu'il a eües avec M. de sartine, n'ont eu d'autre objet que d'obtenir des graces pour les officiers de son escadre.

Un paquebot arrivé à la Corogne, et depeché de la floride occidentale à apporté la nouvelle de la prise du fort de la mobile par les Troupes d'Espagne; que le général Campbel s'etoit retiré; que le General Galvez marchoit vers Pensacola qu'on ne

---

fleet. She had sailed from Yorktown on June 14 with a convoy of thirty-four merchant ships: Roger Lafon, *Beaumarchais, le brillant armateur* (Paris, 1928), p. 144.

9. Admiral Ternay's fleet, bringing General Rochambeau's expeditionary force to America, reached Newport, R.I., on July 11: XXXII, 72–3n; Rice and Brown, eds., *Rochambeau's Army*, I, 17n. Lafayette, who had gone ahead to announce its arrival, was welcomed in Boston on April 28: XXXII, 333, 414n. In June the *Hermione*, 32, fought an engagement with H.M.S. *Iris*, 32: Clowes, *Royal Navy*, IV, 52.

1. Lt. Gen. of the Navy Antonio de Ulloa (1716–1795) was a distinguished naval officer and scientist: Larousse. His accomplishments, however, did not include the one ascribed to him here.

2. D'Estaing had been appointed to bring the French contingent of the combined fleet to Brest, which he did at the end of 1780: Jacques Michel, *La vie aventureuse et mouvementée de Charles-Henri, comte d'Estaing* (n.p., 1976), pp. 250–60.

prévoïoit pas devoir tenir longtems, et que les prisonniers faits au fort de la Mobile etaient au nombre de 300. hommes de troupes réglées et d'une centaine de milice.[3]

On parle d'une Lettre de M. Joubert commandant en second à la martinique, dans laquelle il est dit que l'escadre de M. de Guichen etoit venüe au Nord de la Martinique, qu'elle y avoit embarqué un renfort considérable de Troupes de débarquement, et que de là elle avoit fait voile vers la Barbade.

Une Lettre de st. Eustache du 15. mai arrivée à Amsterdam, annonce la prise de la Barbade par M. de Guichen. Une lettre précédente du 3. mai annonçait Son débarquement dans cette Isle./.[4]

Notation: Intelligence recd. from Doctr. F March 12 1781

From the Former Crewmen of the *Bonhomme Richard* Aboard the *Alliance*[5]

Copy: American Philosophical Society

Sir,   July 2d. 1780. On board the Alliance.

We take this oppertunity of accuainting your honour of our Cituations at present, we have ben in Irons since Wednesday last[6] and likewise on half Allowance, set side Grog & that we have none. Not withstanding it our determine to remain prison-

---

3. Bernardo de Gálvez, the Spanish governor of Louisiana, captured Mobile in March, 1780. Among his prisoners were about 100 soldiers. His attack on Pensacola had to be postponed, however, largely for logistical reasons: John Walton Caughey, *Bernardo de Gálvez in Louisiana 1776–1783* (Berkeley, 1934), pp. 171–82, 191.

4. After failing to capture Barbados (or any other British island) Lt. Gen. of the Navy Guichen brought his fleet to Cadiz and placed himself under d'Estaing's command: Dull, *French Navy,* pp. 188–90. Joubert was commandant at St. Pierre, the chief commercial port of Martinique: Rice and Brown, eds., *Rochambeau's Army,* I, 228.

5. Jones fowarded this letter to BF on July 5, below.

6. When Landais retook command of the *Alliance* in June he had expelled the former officers of the *Bonhomme Richard* serving aboard the ship. Jones had tried to obtain their release as well: XXXII, 520n, 566n. Landais later said that he had placed the eighty former crewmen in irons because they had mutinied and refused to do their duty: Landais, *Memorial,* p. 102. The preceding Wednesday was June 28.

ers untill we go to America— Excepting your Honour will git us out of this unhappy situation but we depend upon your honour to do the best of your indeaver to relese us as soon as lyes in your power which we expect will be soon, & further if it be no Ditterment to your honour please to send us an answer when you Expect you can obtain us.— And in so doing you will much Oblige your Sirt,(?)   CREW, BON HOME RICHARDS IN CHIEF

(Copy)

Notation: Crew, Bonne Homme Richard, July. 2. 1780

From Mary Hewson   ALS: American Philosophical Society

My dear Sir   Cheam July 2. 1780

Time will not permit to give you more than a hasty line. Accept the resemblance I send you of one whom you esteemed, and do me the favour to give one to Mlle. Beeheron, and another to M. Dubourg.[7] I feel so much the honour of the reception he gave to the books that it makes me presume upon this being no unacceptable present.

Your affectionate   MARY HEWSON

When you have an opportunity be so kind as to send the fourth copy to Mr Williams.

Addressed: Dr Franklin

7. She was sending a print of her late husband, Dr. William Hewson, who had died in 1774: XXI, 209n; BF to Mary Hewson, Dec. 7, 1780, APS. Marie-Catherine Biheron was an old friend of Polly and her mother; Jacques Barbeu-Dubourg (who had died in December, 1779) had offered high praise for Polly's translation of his *Petit Code de la raison humaine:* XXVI, 91n, 361; XXXI, 237n, 361n.

From Pierre Landais

LS: American Philosophical Society

Ship Alliance under Groa 2d July 1780

May it please your Excellency

I write you in Answer to yours of June 24th. as in the former,[8] thinking it was nothing but right in Demanding my people Should be righted. And indeed if there is any time Lost it is by the delay of there payment, my two first prizes, Sweedish Ships,[9] were bro't in on account of the Masters' not furnishing Sufficient proofs of their Neutrality having sent you Copys of them that was received by me from the Masters And Couted [Counted] those that were wanting, therefore I think If the Ships have tarry'd so Long in port before they were judged, & if any damage have been Granted it is the fault of those that were to see the Ships tried— Another Brigantine from Bourdeaux bound to Ireland under protection of the Kings passport, but not yours, was bro't in[1] And I inform'd you in Consequence of the Capture, but never received an Answer, the three prizes sent into Norway[2] I told my officers & Crew on my arrival that you had sent a memorial to the Court of Denmark Demanding payment for them.[3] I must put you in Mind that there were two other prizes sent into the Port of L'Orient, Namely Brigantine May Flower Laden with provisions And the Brigantine, fortune, Laden with Oil & blubber, which were sold and the money remitted to Passy by Mr. Montplesir[4] upon which my officers and Crew have Some Right— I know not whether you have the produce of them in

---

8. BF's letter denied withholding any prize money from the *Alliance*'s crew: XXXII, 585–6. Landais' former letters, those of June 14 and 16 (XXXII, 523–4, 539–40) ask that the prize money be paid to the officers and crew of the *Alliance*.

9. The *Victoria* and *Anna Louisa:* XXVIII, 563. WTF prepared a French translation of this portion of the letter (from "my two first prizes" to the sentence beginning "The delay of the Sailing of the Alliance".) The extract (which also includes a translation of the final sentence, beginning "As soon as") is at the APS.

1. The *Three Friends:* XXX, 12n.

2. The *Union, Betsy,* and *Charming Polly:* XXX, 339–40, 593n.

3. He did: XXXI, 261–5.

4. The *Fortune* and *May Flower* were sold in October, 1779: XXX, 360n. Montigny de Monplaisir was Chaumont's agent in Lorient: XXIV, 278n; XXXII, 560.

your hands or Mr Chaumont which may be the same thing. You order'd the prizes Captur'd in Company to be put into the hands of Mr. Chaumont or his agent.[5] The delay of the Sailing of the Alliance was owing to their not having sold the prizes & paying the Money, which it was Certainly in your power to have Compel'd them to do— Every man has been hard at Work Since I have been on board. As to the Mutinous declerations of My people I have never heard of, But their Claiming their Right And if any Mutiny or Irruption has been made on board my Ship, it was at the Texel & from that time to the 13th Of Last Month, which was the time I took the Command[6] and since that I have Regulated every thing for the best— But is reported to me that Captn. Jones, has held some Conversation with my People in order to raise Discontent and Mutiny on board And at the same time desireing one of them to go immediately on board & acquaint the people of what he had said—[7] I hope If he is in the American Service you will Repremand him for misconduct in this Instance which is unpardonable in a Captain to hold any such Conversation to the Prejudice of the Navy of the United States— If your Excellency should hear of any more such Conduct please inform me. As soon as my people are paid I shall sail and if there is any detention of the Ship hereafter, Congress will judge whose fault it may be, If my people are not paid or Contrary winds detain me, you'l please send your Orders Directly for America which is all the Orders I will Receive, and if I have been faulty in any thing I am going before those that gave me the Command of this Ship, to Answer for my Conduct.

And am with the Greatest Respect your Excellencys most obedient & very humble Servant   P: LANDAIS C.A.

His Excellency B. Franklin Esqr Minister Plenipo, to the United States at Passy near Paris

Notation: P Landais Groa July 2. 1780

5. In orders to Jones: XXIX, 780.
6. For the coup by which Landais seized control of the *Alliance* from Jones see XXXII, 519–21.
7. Landais later claimed that Jones's agent Lt. Richard Dale tried to bribe Thomas Blick (?), one of the *Alliance*'s boatswain's mates: Landais, *Memorial*, p. 111.

From Louis d'Ussieux[8]

Printed invitation with MS insertions: American Philosophical Society

[before July 3, 1780]

VERITE∴ UNION∴ FORCE∴

T∴ C∴ F∴

L∴ R∴ L∴ des Neuf Sœurs, Est convoquée pour le *Lundy 3* du *5*e. mois de D∴ L∴ D∴ L∴ V∴ 5780.[9] à *6* heures *très* précises. *du Soir.*

Vous êtes priés d'y venir augmenter les douceurs de l'union fraternelle. *On y traitera d'affaires essentielles, Le f. Trésorier rendra Ses Comptes, On prendra des Mesures pour Suppléer à la Negligence des ff. musiciens membres de la R∴ L∴,*[1] et lon S'occupera des preparatifs d'une fête Academique.[2]

Je suis, par les N∴ C∴ D∴ F∴ M∴ V∴ T∴ H∴[3] & affectionné Frere,   D'USSIEUX

        *2*e Secrétaire D∴ L∴ R∴ L∴

        Des Neuf Soeurs.

8. D'Ussieux's term as second secretary of the Neuf Soeurs masonic lodge began in the second year of BF's *vénéralat:* XXXII, 331n.

9. La Respectable Loge des Neuf Soeurs . . . De l'année de la Vérité 5780. The masonic year began on March 1.

1. In 1780 there appears to have been a general defection of musicians from the Neuf Soeurs: of nineteen musician members in 1778–1779 only three maintained their membership. Whatever measures were taken at the July 3 meeting, it was not until March 19, 1781, that another musician was affiliated with the lodge; see d'Ussieux's invitation for March 19, 1781 (APS). For the list of musician members in 1779 see Louis Amiable, *Une Loge maçonnique d'avant 1789* (Paris, 1897), p. 339; for the length of their memberships see Le Bihan, *Francs-maçons parisiens,* under the names given in Amiable.

2. BF's invitation for the *fête,* July 31, announces a reception for the candidate Choffar, readings, a concert, and a banquet. APS. Pierre-Philippe Choffard (1730–1809) was a draughtsman and engraver: *DBF;* Le Bihan, *Francs-maçons parisiens.*

During the period covered by this volume BF received two more printed invitations. The first was for a meeting on Aug. 28, at which emblems and legends were to be chosen for lodge tokens. The second one, for "Lundy 18 du présent mois" of 1780, either September or December, announced a concert and banquet to which BF was "Spécialement invité à vous y trouver." The new meeting place was at "lhotel de Bullion par la ruë Coqueron [Coq-héron]."

3. Par les noms connus des frères maçons votre très humble.

L'adresse ordinaire de la Loge est à M. FAIN, Entrepreneur des Bâtimens du Roi,[4] rue Sainte Croix de la Bretonnerie, vis-à-vis celle des Billettes.

Addressed: A Monsieur / Monsieur Le Docteur / franklin / N.·. S.·. ./. A Passy

To Jacques-Donatien Le Ray de Chaumont

ALS: The Gallery of History, Inc. (Las Vegas, Nevada, 1993)

Cher Ami, [on or after July 3, 1780][5]

Notre Intention en donnant l'Ordre de ne pas payer leurs Portions a ceux qui avoient signé le Mutinerie,[6] n'etant qu'un Expedient temporaire pour les reclamer; il me semble qu'actuellement il sera mieux de rapeller cette Ordre; parceque il y a en Amerique des Loix pour les punir; & je crois qu'il sera bon de payer les portions de ces gens en France plutôt qu'en Amerique, parceque ils ont nombre des Creanciers à l'Orient qui perdront beaucoup de leur Droits si l'Argent est envoyé en Amerique, & cela causera grand Clameur. Je suis donc d'Avis de payer à Messrs. Puchelberg tout ce qui est dû aux Matelots & aux Officiers du produit des Prises. On evitera par ce moyen nombre de Soupçons & de Censures— BF.

Addressed: A Monsieur / Monsieur de Chaumont

To Puchelberg & Cie.

Copies: National Archives, Library of Congress

Gentlemen Passy July 3. 1780

I have just received the Letter you did me the honor of writing to me the 28 past, acquainting me that you are appointed by

4. Jean-François Fain (XXXI, 373n).

5. The day on which BF first learned that Puchelberg & Cie. was representing the crewmen of the *Alliance:* BF to Puchelberg & Cie., immediately below. This letter probably does not date from much later, however, as the *Alliance* sailed for America on July 7; see Landais' letter of the date.

6. See XXXII, 245n, 506–7.

the Officers & Crew of the Alliance Frigate to be their attorneys & Agents to receive for them what may be due to them of Prize Money.[7] I am glad to hear of this appointment, & wish it had been made sooner. But the Demand of their Shares is not rightly made upon me who never received any of the money for which their prizes have been sold, & do not intend to meddle with any such money. M. de Chaumont who was intrusted with the equipment of that Squadron, & was impower'd by the Captains, by a Joint instrument in writing to receive the prizes,[8] has I suppose received, or will receive & pay the whole that can be obtain'd; for as to the prizes sent into Norway, Satisfaction for them has been refused,[9] not a farthing has been received on their account, nor likely to be at present. I will communicate to Mr. Chaumont your Letter, but I think it will be proper for you to write to him yourselves; I do not apprehend you can meet with any difficulty in the affair, otherwise I would offer you my best Services—

I have the honor to be Gentlemen Your most obedient & most humble Servant   Signed B FRANKLIN

To Messrs. Puchelberg & Co

Boston June 20th. 1781 The above is a true copy attested,
SAM BRADSTREET

From Cornelis Van der Oudermeulen

ALS: Library of Congress

Monsieur   Amsterd: ce 3 Juillet 1780
Avant mon depart pour la Nord Hollande, où je dois me rendre ce Soir pour vaquer pendant 10 a 12 jours aux affaires de la Compagnie,[1] j'ai cru qu'il convenoit de repondre aussi la-

---

7. XXXII, 618–19.

8. For this agreement see XXX, 223, 459.

9. BF had been so informed by the Danish government, which had turned over Landais' three prizes to the British: XXX, 591–4; XXXI, 261–3; XXXII, 75–6.

1. He was director of the Amsterdam chamber of the Dutch East India Company: XXXII, 418.

coniquement qu'il m'est possible a la lettre dont votre Excellence m'à honoré le 22. du mois passé.[2] Elle ne m'est parvenue que hier.

En consequence j'ai lhonneur de vous presenter quelques idées Sur la feuille cÿ jointe.[3] J'espere que par cette explication vous sentirez plus dans son entier la baze sur laquelle le plan proposé repose. J'avoue qu'il auroit demandé un plus ample detail, mais considerez je vous prie que la matiere est 1°. de la derniere delicatesse, & 2°. qu'un Plan de cette nature demande qu'on expose Ses Idées le plus succintement qu'il Soit possible, afin de prevenir les inconveniens que les Memoires trop long (Selon l'experience que j'en ai) produisent assez Souvent, & a ce qui me paroit ce n'est pas un mal que sur un objet de cet importance, on pense, et on reflechisse, quelques tems. Je sens au reste que c'est en Amerique que la proposition doit en premier lieu etre goutée, avant qu'on puisse rien entreprendre ladessus en Europe. C'etoit à cause de cela pour aplanir bien des difficultés, que j'ai offert de faire le Voÿage. Mais maintenant que vos Idées me paroissent encore trop eloignées des miennes il convient de temporiser: peut être qu'un jour Votre Excellence observera que mes idées ont été plus ou moins analogue aux circonstances actuelles des affaires politiques. Du moins il me semble qu'elles sont propres pour

2. XXXII, 572–3. It had criticized van der Oudermeulen's proposal for establishing privileged commercial companies in America (XXXII, 536n).

3. A three-page memoir defending his proposal. He knows the Americans are self-sufficient except for luxury goods, but they gradually will become the leading traders of the universe and will render themselves masters of most commerce. Generally private commerce is more profitable but in war commercial companies can spread losses around and can band merchants together for mutual protection of their ships. It is to America's advantage to extend its commerce at the expense of the English. The companies he proposes will be more advantageous to Americans than to Europeans. Britain and Holland being the two chief commercial nations will attempt to hinder the Americans. The Dutch executive [William of Orange, the stadholder] is acting in the interests of the British court. In spite of the efforts of Amsterdam, it is unlikely The Hague will agree to the proposed alliance [with the United States]. The Americans should enter into relations with European merchants, who will encourage their sovereigns to protect this commerce, which will gradually spread throughout Europe. Freedom of commerce is contrary to the interests of the colonial powers; it is only by their jealousy of each other that the goal can be reached.

parvenir le plutot au but qu'on Se propose. Une fois que Votre État Seroit parvenu à ce qu'il desire, alors les choses S'etabliront de soi même, & selon que les circonstances d'*alors* le demanderont. Mais en attendant pour atteindre cet Epoque, il me semble qu'insensiblement on doit tacher de déranger la position actuelle du Commerce même, car Selon mes petites lumieres il paroit que par les choses qui se passent, que tot ou tard le Commerce Se transferera dans le N. d Ame. Tel est la Vicissitude auxquelles les affaires humaines sont Sujettes, vouloir Sÿ opposer, c'est vouloir se mettre contre un torrent impetueux—plus on cherche à retarder l'evenement qui aura certainement lieu dans les Siecles à venir, plus grand Sera le degat qui naturellement en pourra resulter un jour. Pour le moment la grande question Se borne à ceci. Les Finances sur le continent en E. Suffisent elles pour soutenir les enormes depances qu'il ÿ à encore à faire? Enfin pour ne pas entretenir pour le môment trop longtems Votre Excellence. Je prie d'observer que le Plan en question à pour but: Savoir:

1°. D'étendre le Commerce & la Navigation du Nord Am: & des Européens du *continent*.

2°. De nuire 1, 2, 3, et porter par la 8, a la 4, d'ou 5, 6, 7 &c.[4]

3°. De rependre de plus en plus 13, Sur 14.[5] &

4°. De 9 & 10 de plus en plus par la 11, 12.[6]

Mais sur toute chose Je prie de considerer que ma proposition pour former la Compe. previligiés en Ame. n'est fondée que sur la necessité actuelle des Choses, car qu'on ait S.V.P. toujours en vue qu'une Puissance qui à eu une augmentation dans son commerce Sur les Import. & Export. pendant le cours de ce Siecle pour environ *16 millions de Livr. St. annuellement* ne se persuade pas si facilement. Il faut pour cela non seulement prendre Son re-

---

4. Dumas must have provided the key to van der Oudermeulen's code, as is promised in the postscript, because BF interlined his decoded version of the following three paragraphs (as he also did for the coded portion of the attached memoir). The present one reads (using BF's spelling), "De nuire da Commerce d'Angleterre et porter par a Coup, a la Source, d'où derive la Force maritime, &c."

5. "De repende de plus en plus le Commerce, sur [le] Continent de l'Europe."

6. "De soutenir & nourir de plus en plus, par l Esprit Antianglicain."

cours à la force ouverte, mais encore à beaucoup de moÿens imperceptibles. (Il est bon de dire que mes idées par ce mot *d'imper.* n'est entendu que relative. au commerce).

Je prie Votre Excellence de m'accuser la reception de la presente, d'annuler ces feuilles et de Secretter a jamais mon nom. N'aiant dans tout ceci d'autres vues que de randre autant qu'il me soit possible de Services à ma Patrie, et à mon Prochain.

J'ai lhonneur d'etre avec un profond respect,

Monsieur De Votre Excellence Le tres humble & tres Obeissant serviteur   C: V: D: OUDERMEULEN

Pour l'intelligence des Chiffres cÿdessus, Votre Exce. recevra quatre mots par Mr. D.——

To Joseph Gardoqui & fils

Copy:[7] Library of Congress

Gentlemen,   Passy, July 4. 1780.

Your respected Letter of the 25th. past[8] came duly to hand. Captain Haraden (whose Bravery in taking and retaking the Privateer give me great Pleasure) is very good in offering the Spare Room in his Ship for the Service of the States. Having lately received the enclosed List of Articles wanted in America[9] which came under a Cover directed to me without a Letter and not having funds in my hands at present to purchase the same, I imagine it may possibly be that Order which the Captain mentions as intended for you, and therefore send it, that so, you may if it should suit you, execute the whole or any Part, after consulting with Mr. Jay the American Minister at your Court, as to the Payment. We cannot otherwise profit of Capt. Haraden's Offer. For tho' we have here as much Goods of another kind, as make a Bulk of 500 Tons ready to ship, I imagine it will not suit the General Pickering to come to france for the Part she could take; and I am

7. In the hand of BF's secretary, Jean L'Air de Lamotte, as are most of the Library of Congress copies of BF's letters in the present volume.

8. Actually June 21: XXXII, 563–4. The date on the recipient's copy can easily be read as a "25."

9. Of which we have found no other record.

about agreeing this Morning for the freight of the whole here.[1] I thank you for the obliging Offers of your friendly Service at Bilbao, which I shall make use of on Occasion. The Communication of any fresh News you may receive from America I shall take as a great favour. If in any thing I can be of use to your House, it will give me Pleasure, being, With great Esteem, Gentlemen, &c.

Messrs. Joseph Guardoqui and fils Negociants à Bilbao.

From Charles-Guillaume-Frédéric Dumas

ALS: American Philosophical Society; copy: Algemeen Rijksarchief

Monsieur   La Haie 4e. Juillet 1780
En conséquence de l'honorée vôtre du 22 Juin, j'ai envoyé votre Lettre à Mr. C. van O——, qui m'en a accusé la réception. J'ai envoyé pareillement copie à Messieurs Van de Perre & Meyners de celle que vous m'avez écrite à leur sujet.[2]

Les Etats d'Hollde. se sont séparés, pour ne se rassembler que le 26 de ce mois. Il ne S'est rien passé d'interessant. L'armement ici va très lentement, & les résolutions à cet égard, et à l'égard de la négociation avec la Russie, se traînent de même.[3] 5 & 958

1. BF is referring to a meeting with Chaumont and JW, who had arrived in Passy on or before July 1 (JW to Gourlade & Moylan, July 1, Yale University Library). JW had written BF on June 9 (XXXII, 497–8) that if he were unsuccessful in obtaining a ship at Lorient he would come to Paris. BF's meetings with JW and Chaumont led to the latter's purchase of a large merchant ship named the *Breton*. He chartered the vessel to JW to carry the supplies they had assembled for the American army (for which see XXXI, 267–8): Lopez, *Lafayette*, pp. 198–9.

2. On June 22 BF wrote two letters to Dumas (XXXII, 568–9) as well as one to van der Oudermeulen (for which see our annotation of the latter's July 3 letter). One of the ones to Dumas promised Congress would do justice in the case of the *Berkenbosch*, a Dutch ship captured by John Paul Jones. Van de Perre and Meÿners were the ship's owners: XXXII, 429, 494–5. Her arrival in Boston was reported in the June 30 issue of the *Courier de l'Europe*, VII (1780), 428.

3. A major problem facing both the States of the Province of Holland and the States General of the Netherlands was the seizure of Dutch ships by the British Navy on suspicion of carrying naval supplies to France. (See, for example, XXXI, 369n.) Two ways of countering such seizures were outfitting warships to provide convoy protection and joining the League of Armed Neutrality to protect neutral shipping. Dumas' prior correspondence frequently had discussed these approaches.

brouillent continuellement tout, & 30 suit machinalement leurs impulsions.[4] Les Anglois intriguent plus encore ici qu'à Petersbourg-même: Les brouilleries qu'ils excitent & fomentent en Allemagne au sujet de l'élection d'un Coadjuteur de Cologne,[5] sont calculées en grande partie pour embarrasser cette rep., & empêcher qu'elle ne s'occupe avec succès du rétablissement de sa Marine. Voilà, Monsieur, l'état des affaires. C'est une Comédie monotone, dont toutes les scenes se ressemblent. Les uns ont toujours en tête l'augmentation des forces de terre; les autres, avec raison, le rétablissement de celles de mer.

Je viens de recevoir une Lettre du Baron de Wufflin de Bruxelles 29 Juin, où il me marque, Monsieur, que vous lui avez remis des Lettres de grande importance pour moi; qu'il Seroit déjà en chemin pour me les remettre; mais que ses plaies, rouvertes, l'obligent d'aller passer quelques jours à Venlo chez sa Soeur, dont il m'a donné l'adresse, pour lui écrire là. Il y a 36 lieues d'ici à Venlo. J'ignore quel peut être le contenu & le volume de ces Lettres, & si elles pressent, ou non: ainsi je n'ose ni ne puis lui marquer de me les envoyer; & j'en suis pourtant en peine. Si vous vouliez, Monsieur, m'apprendre en attendant ce que c'est, je serois plus tranquille, & pourrois peut-être prendre des mesures pour les avoir, si Mr. De Wufflin tardoit de me les apporter.

Ma santé est fort dérangée par les chagrins & les émotions journalières. ———— ne finit pas. Quelquefois il se montre bon. Ensuite, à l'instigation, apparemment, de mon ennemi, il n'est plus content de ce qu'il a exigé de moi, & que j'ai voulu faire: il

4. According to the code devised by Jones and revised by Dumas (XXXI, 345–7, 460n), these numbers stand respectively for the pro-British Duke of Brunswick, British Ambassador Sir Joseph Yorke, and Stadholder William V of Orange, all of whom opposed the augmentation of the Dutch navy. BF has added above the line the names for which the numbers stand.

5. Although Cologne was generally regarded as being under French influence the Austrians were exerting pressure to elect Archduke Maximilian Franz (1756–1801), the youngest of Empress Maria Theresa's children, as coadjutor to the archbishop-elector. He did become coadjutor in 1780 and archbishop-elector in 1784: *Gaz. de Leyde*, supplements to the issues of June 9, July 4, and July 28, 1780; Constant von Wurzbach, ed., *Biographisches Lexikon des Kaiserthums Oesterreich* . . . (60 vols., Vienna, 1856–90), VII, 109–10.

exige ce que je ne puis faire Sans me déshonorer & perdre.[6] Ajoutez à cela, Monsieur, que tout ce qui tient ici à certain parti, c'est-à-dire, toute la Haie, m'évite & me décrie, & me suscite des désagrements jusque chez moi; enfin, que ma femme languit depuis longtemps d'une facheuse maladie: Et vous n'aurez encore qu'une idée foible de mon état actuel; car je ne dis pas tout. Mon unique espoir est que de bonnes nouvelles de l'Amérique, & 484,[7] changeront ma Situation ici en mieux. Dieu veuille nous amener bientôt l'un & l'autre.

Il court ici un bruit fort extraordinaire à l'égard du C. Jones. Landais, dit-on, S'est emparé de son Vaisseau en vertu de Sa Commission Américaine. Cela me met en peine pour vous, Monsieur, parce que votre autorité seroit commise là-dedans, & aussi pour les paquets de Dépeches au Congrès, que je vous avois adressé pour Mr. Jones, & une autre Lettre pour le Congrès, que j'avois adressée à Mr. Williams à Nantes, pour la lui faire tenir.

Dans ce moment je reçois l'incluse de Mr. C—— van O——[8] avec priere "de vous la faire parvenir, parce qu'elle est nécessaire pour servir d'intelligence à une autre qui partit hier par une autre voie.— Il se flatte, ajoute-t-il, qu'en réponse vous goûterez mieux ses idées."

Je suis & serai tout le reste de ma vie avec le respectueux & inviolable attachement qui vous est voué, Monsieur, Votre très-humble & très-obéissant serviteur,   DUMAS

Passy à S.E.M. Franklin

Addressed: à Son Excellence / Monsieur B. Franklin, Esqr. / Min. Plenipe. des Etats-Unis / &c. *Passy./.*

Notation: Dumas la haie July 9. 80

6. Dumas here seems to be lamenting the deterioration of his relationship with French Ambassador La Vauguyon and blaming the banker Georges Grand; see XXXI, 347; XXXII, 165–6 and following.

7. Laurens. Henry Laurens, who had been selected by Congress to negotiate a loan in the Netherlands, finally sailed from Philadelphia in mid-August: XXXII, 192n.

8. Van der Oudermeulen's July 3 letter, above.

From Timothy Kelly

ALS: American Philosophical Society

Excellent sr   St Malo. July 4th. 1780

Repeatedly I have wrote to your Excellency, when in the
Black Prince Privateer of Boston under the Commands in both
Cruizes of Capt Marshant & Dowlin wherein we took Prizes and
Ransoms to a Considerable Amount.[9] The Names of sd. Prizes
as Clark of our former Privateer I always sent your Excellency
an Account thereof in Journal Manner. When our Misfortune
happened of being run on shore by the Tartar Frigate thro their
Mistake[1] we made the best of our way to Dunkerque, where not
meeting with the Generous Usuage we Expected was Constrained thro Necessity to Embark in the Cutter The American
union, under a french Commission, and is now detained here by
as I can Understand by an Order from Ministry.[2] Excellent Sr.
such usuage as Americans Subjects Sustains in France Viz. being
wronged by Torris of Dunkerque and afterwards Stopped will
be a means if not prevented to hinder (as is has done some already) our Countrymen Irish, from leaving Ireland to Join in our
Just Cause, There remains 22 of us here our Capt is gone to yr.
Excellency to Demand. Justice and Liberty for us to set out to
Sea on our Intended Cruize. Yr. Excellency will please to Dirrect
to Timothy Kelly at Monsr. de Segrey[3] in St Malo. Rems. [re-
mains] with Respects yr. Excellency's Most humble Sert.

TIMOTHY KELLY

Addressed: To / His Excellency Benjamin / Franklin Minister for
the united / States at the Court of France / at Passy near Paris

Notation: T. Kelley. July 4. 1780

9. Kelly had been acting as a clerk for more than a year (see XXIX, 718n),
but this is his first extant personal letter. The *Black Prince* was from Dunkirk,
although her first captain, Stephen Marchant, may have been from Boston:
XXVIII, 471n.

1. BF had learned of the loss of the *Black Prince* from one of her principal
owners, John Torris: XXXII, 259–60. The vessel responsible, however, was
the French privateer *Calonne*.

2. See the complaint of Joseph Myrick, captain of the *American Union:*
XXXII, 616–17.

3. Presumably of the firm Desegray, Beaugeard fils & Cie.

To Gourlade & Moylan

Copy: Library of Congress

Gentlemen   Passy, July 5. 1780.

I wrote to M Williams on the 27th. Ult. inclosing an oder to
the Commanding officer of the Alliance to take on board that
frigate as many of the arms &c as he could conveniently Stow,
and to give a Receipt for the same.[4] I at the same time signified
my Desire to have the Arriel fitted and dispatched with the utmost Expedition.[5] M Williams is now here and consequently has
not received my Letter, I therefore gave him a Duplicate of the
Order to forward to you, and I have now to request that the remainder of the Powder and Arms may be shipped on board the
Ariel, and that frigate dispatced under the Command of Commodore Jones as soon as possible.[6] If there should remain any
Room after loading the Arms and Powder let M Williams's
Cloathing have a preference to all other Goods— If the Bonhomme Richard's men are released from the Alliance there will
be enough for the Ariel, if not you must get together as many as
you can, and in Addition I will order some others to join who
have lately arrived at St. Malo.

You will please to inform me in answer to this when You think
the Ariel will sail and I will take care to have my Dispatches
ready for her, I am Gentlemen Your most humble Servant

Messrs. Gourlade and Moylan.

4. XXXII, 615–16 and, for the enclosure, XXXII, 613.

5. XXXII, 612–13. The *Ariel* was a French sloop of war on loan to Capt.
John Paul Jones to carry supplies to America: XXXII, 442–3, 467–8.

6. JW, when he was in Lorient at the end of June, had instructed Gourlade
& Moylan to take charge of receiving and organizing the bales of clothing
that were arriving from Nantes and Brest, and to check them against the invoices. Clothing for the officers, marked "FO," was to be kept separate. They
would receive further directions at a later date, and should charge all expenses for this operation to BF, who would reimburse them: JW to Gourlade
& Moylan, June 25, 1780. JW wrote them again on July 1, from Passy, enclosing the duplicate of BF's letter mentioned in the present one, and asking
them to execute BF's orders. Both of JW's letters to the firm are at the Yale
University Library. The first of the Lorient firm's bills was submitted to BF
on July 19; WTF kept a list of them as they were presented in what he called
the Bill Book, part of which is at the APS. The Gourlade & Moylan entries
begin on July 19, 1780, and run through Feb. 28, 1781.

To John Paul Jones

Copy: Library of Congress

Dear Sir   Passy, July 5. 1780.

I received yours of June 21. with the Papers it inclosed from M. Genet, who had kept them a Day or Two to translate them for the Minister.[7] I approve much of your humanity and Prudence. But am sorry in the Letter to Dr. Bancroft, you Complain of your friends who are in no fault.[8] They spare you, and have not even hinted that if you had staid on board where your Duty lay in stead of coming to Paris, you would not have lost your Ship. Now you blame them as having deserted you in recovering her. Tho' relinquishing to prevent Mischief was a Voluntary act of your own for which you have Credit.— Hereafter, if you should observe on occasion to give your officers and friends a little more praise than is their Due, and confess more fault than you can justly be charged with, you will only become the sooner for it a Great Captain. Criticising and censuring almost every one you have to do with, will diminish friends, encrease Enemies, and thereby hurt your affairs.— I continue as ever, Dear Sir. &c.

Honble. Comme. Jones.

To James Moylan

Copy: Library of Congress

Sir,   Passy, July 5. 1780.

I received your favour of the 25th. past,[9] and am much obliged by the Pains you took to get my Letters delivered on board the

---

7. Jones had described how his intervention kept the French from firing on the *Alliance* when she left Lorient for the anchorage at the Ile de Groix: XXXII, 565–7. The minister is Sartine.

8. Among his other complaints Jones told Bancroft in a June 27 letter that the French officers at Lorient had acted "rather like Women than Men": Bradford, *Jones Papers*, reel 5, no. 1123. He also said that "If 299 Sits Still in this matter I shall pronounce him and 868 Philosophers indeed!" We suspect that 299 stands for "Franklin" in a private code to which BF was not privy; 868 represents "you." For a list of documents using the code see James C. Bradford, *Guide to the Microfilm Edition of the Papers of John Paul Jones* (Alexandria, Va. and Cambridge, Eng., 1986), p. 121.

9. XXXII, 594–6.

Alliance. Please to return me that which Capt. Landais refused to receive, putting your Note of that Refusal on the back of it.

In yours (Gourlade & Moilan) of March 14.[1] You mentioned the receiving 4571 *l.t.* 5. 4. tournois as a Ransom for the ship friendship and Cargo taken by Comm. Jones, which Sum you had passed to the Credit of my Account. Capt. Jones at the same time informed me by Letter that he had intended to burn that Ship; but the Capt. Driburgh having been excedingly useful to him as a Pilot, he had taken his Ransom merely to have the means of rewarding him by giving him the Money, & which he desired my approbation.[2] As it did not belong to me to receive or Dispose of such Monies, I Spoke to Comm. Jones about it, and desired him to request your taking that Sum from my Account which I hope is done. But Capt. Driburgh being in want of Money here, I advanced him Ten Louis on a Draft he gave me on a Merchant in Dunkerque, which Draft is not paid, and therefore I request that out of the Money Capt. Jones may think fit to order for him, you would retain for me those ten Louis. As to the rest, I make no doubt that upon a proper Representation of Circumstances the Consideration intended by Comm. Jones for that poor Man's Services will be approved of, by those, to whom the Allowance of his Accounts shall appertain.

With great Esteem I have the honour to be Sir,—&c.

Mr. James Moylan.

From John Paul Jones

ALS: American Philosophical Society

Sir,   L'orient July 5th. 1780.

Since the 23d. ult. I have been doing my best to bring our Affairs here back again to Order; or at least to be able to proceed for Philadelphia with the Ariel. The enclosed papers will best explain the circumstances of Landais' beheaviour and of my endeavours to counteract him and his Advisers in thier schemes to defeat the Plan that you had Adopted in consent with this Gov-

1. Missing.
2. XXII, 101.

ernment for conducting the Public Stores to America.— You will see, by the within letter of the 2d. from the Sailors of the late Bon homme Richard,[3] that moderation was not likely to effect their enlargement.— Yesterday I was in the Afternoon, on the Parade in the Port with Mr. Blodget the Purser of the Alliance, and directed him to accompany me on Board the Ariel with two or three of my Officers in Order to examin the State of Accounts of the People of the Alliance previous to the division of Prize Money.— Blodget refused to attend me.— I repeated my Order, and took hold of his Coat, as he appeared to intend running away.— He then called for the Guard, and demanded to be put in Prison.— The Guard came and, without any Order or request on my part, took Blodget into Custody.— I gave an immediate Account of the Affair to the Commandant and Officers of the Port; and afterwards sent M. de Thevenard the letter whereof the within is a Copy. M. de Thevenard sent for me again this morning, and begged me to commit the matter entirely to his management:— he said he would take the whole upon himself, and believed he should be able thro' the means of Blodget to Obtain the Seamen within mentioned from the Alliance.[4]

I have not yet heard the effect of my letter to the Crew of the Alliance; but it is my Opinion they will not weigh Anchor before they are hopeless of receiving Money.

I am and will be Always, with the heighest and most Affectionate respect Dear Sir, Your most Obliged and faithful Friend

JNO P JONES

N.B. I am honored with yours of the 27th.—[5] and by a letter of the 28th. from M. de Genet I find that you must that day have

3. Above.

4. Jones enclosed copies of a June 20 set of orders by Port Commandant Thévenard to arrest any officer or crewman of the *Alliance* designated by Jones, a July 3 letter from Jones to the ship's company of the *Alliance* offering them their prize money if they would reconsider their situation (*i.e.*, if they returned the ship to him), and a July 4 letter to Thévenard asking him to deliver Blodget to the *Ariel*. The latter two documents are reproduced in Bradford, *Jones Papers*, reel 6, nos. 1141, 1144. Blodget was aboard the *Alliance* when she sailed for America, as during her voyage he signed two Aug. 10 petitions (National Archives).

5. XXXII, 612–13.

recd. my former letter with explainatory Papers that was missing.[6]

His Excellency B. Franklin Esqr. &c. &c.

Notations in different hands: J. P. Jones, L'Orient July 5. 1780 / Comme. Jones.

From the Marquise de Lafayette

ALS: American Philosophical Society

ce mercredy [on or before July 5, 1780][7]

Je ne puis, monsieur refuser a un homme de mes parens qui veut partir pour Lamerique, est muni d'un passeport de monsieur de montbarey, et qui a déja obtenu de mr De Sartine a La reccommandation de mr Le Mal. De Noailles[8] une Lettre pour Pauljones, de vous Supplier de vouloir bien lui donner des Lettres pour Le Congrès, je vous demande bien pardon de mon importunite je vous supplie d'agréer mes excuses, ainsi que Lassurance de ma recconnoissance que minspireront vos bontés pour mr Le Baron D'arross.

Rendes justice monsieur a La sincerite des sentimens avec Lesquels j'ai lhonneur detre votre très humble et très obeissante servante.   NOAILLES DE LAFAYETTE

From the Marquis de Valory and Other Favor Seekers[9]

ALS: American Philosophical Society

On July 5, 1780, in the document printed below, the marquis de Valory solicits Franklin's help in cashing a payment made to him in

6. Undoubtedly XXXII, 565–7.
7. The first Wednesday before July 10, the day the baron d'Arros, who carried this letter, writes to remind BF of his promise to answer the marquise (below).
8. Her grandfather, the duc de Noailles: XXX, 258.
9. Unless otherwise indicated, all the letters discussed here are in French and at the APS.

American currency.[1] Eleven other people in the course of the following four months were to seek assistance from the American minister in solving a wide range of problems having to do with money.

A former infantry major who signs himself Dalgres,[2] writing from Paris on September 19, encloses three bills of exchange amounting to 1710 *l.t.* sent to him from Nantes. He has already presented them to banker Grand who said the affair must be conducted through Franklin. A note in Chaumont's hand specifies that the papers seem to be in order but that payment should be made only on the originals because the notaries in Les Cayes (a town in St. Domingue) would not be able to detect a forgery. A notation indicates that this letter was answered on September 20th, but we have no further record of the response.

From Rabastens in the Albigeois comes a letter written on September 29 by a chevalier de Poteins. He alludes to a previous message (presumably lost) in which he had asked Franklin to help him cash in French currency the sum of 134 continental dollars which he owns. Please answer him soon. His needs are pressing.

Sir John Lambert, the Parisian banker who had already communicated with Franklin on June 20 (XXXII, 45), writes in English on September 26. He pleads the cause of "a poor American captain," Benjamin Bucktrout, whose three bills of the U.S.A., amounting to a total of 120 dollars, were refused by Franklin because they had not been duly endorsed. The writer, having already returned them to the Amsterdam bank from which they emanated, now offers that bank's guarantee and his own as to their validity. Could Franklin please reconsider? He did, as attested by an endorsement in Temple's hand, crediting his grandfather's change of mind to "consideration of this Letter."

These are the straightforward cases. The others are somewhat more complex.

Four correspondents relate a tale of woe. Louis Gourlet Duplessÿ, a former sergeant in Col. Livingston's regiment, pensioned as an invalid by the United States of America, is currently living in Noyon,

1. Charles-Jean-Marie de Valory (b. 1750), whose family was of Florentine origin, was colonel by rank but still occupying the position of *capitaine commandant*, Regiment Royal-Lorraine, cavalry. He became *colonel en second* in the Bourbonnais regiment, infantry, in September, 1781: from information provided by Bodinier. See also Mazas, *Ordre de Saint-Louis*, II, 352n; *Etat militaire* for 1780, p. 362.

2. Pierre-Philippe Duval Dalgrés (b. 1728), originally a dragoon, was sent to St. Domingue in 1762, where he became lieutenant, then captain in the Boulonnais regiment (1773): Bodinier. See also *Etat militaire* for 1777, p. 266.

Picardy. He had been residing for twenty-six years in Quebec when the Anglo-American war broke out and rather than take up arms against France and the United States, as the new Governor wanted him to do after the fall of Quebec, he threw his fate with that of the United States, raised a corps of fifty Canadians, took part in several battles—the last of them in Rhode Island—and was captured. It was impossible for him to go back to Canada after his exchange, so he decided to rejoin his family in Paris. While in the capital in July, 1780, he paid a visit to Franklin and obtained the promise of his protection, along with some financial help.[3] Finally back with his own people in Noyon, he discovered that his own little capital had been spent in his absence. On August 11 he sends Franklin a letter (not in his own hand) explaining that his only hope for survival lies in the payment in France of his American pension. Along with his American certificates, the petitioner encloses one from the lieutenant general of police in Noyon.[4] A follow-up, in his own hand this time, is sent on September 13. One year later, on September 10, 1781, Lieutenant Montfort, *maître de camp de cavalerie* in Noyon, urges Franklin to come to the aid of Duplessÿ and to send back his certificates.[5]

Also returning empty-handed from America, a man named Baudin writes on September 12 from St. Martin on the Ile de Ré. He had left for Pennsylvania, he says, two and a half years previously with a fairly large capital but was captured before disembarking and thrown in a

3. On July 22 BF loaned 48 *l.t.* to Duplessÿ, "a poor wounded Canadian who had been in our Service since 1776 in Col. Livingston's Regiment & was made Prisoner at Rhode Island—to help him down to his Relations in Picardy." Cash Book. Duplessÿ signed one of BF's printed promissory notes for the amount. Only one other promissory note dates from the period of this volume: BF loaned Robert Cains, of Taunton, 24 *l.t.* on Sept. 15. Both Duplessÿ and Cains appear on the Alphabetical List of Escaped Prisoners. Also listed are John Adain and John Doughty, who received 12 *l.t.* apiece on Nov. 3.

4. The first of those certificates, dated Albany, Jan. 10, 1777, is signed by Regnier, lieutenant-colonel of a regiment of Canadians and attests that Duplessÿ served to the best of his abilities as lieutenant in Capt. Duncan Campbell's company of Canadians from Jan. 23 to Dec. 20, 1776. The second one, dated June 19, 1779, and signed by Lt. Maynard, certifies that Duplessÿ, now incapable of joining Col. Livingston's regiment, is recommended for duty in the corps of invalids. Both are in English. James Livingston commanded the 1st Canadian Regiment of the American Army: Fred Anderson Berg, comp., *Encyclopedia of Continental Army Units: Battalions, Regiments and Independent Corps* (Harrisburg, Pa., 1972), p. 16.

5. This letter is at the University of Pa. Library.

New York jail. As soon as he got out, he enlisted on a privateer. He was soon taken again and sent back to the same jail for another six months, after which he sailed directly for France having lost his entire fortune but for 156 Virginia dollars. He now needs Franklin's help, desperately. His follow-up message, of October 18, covers the same ground. The sole difference is that the 156 dollars have become 165.[6]

Salvator Le Séque, a sailor, living in Lorient, sends to "Monseigneur franqueline en Bassadeur des ámériquins" an undated letter sometime around August 12. His son Louis Salvator Le Séque was working as a cabin boy. The ship on which he served perished, and the father now seeks his son's share of the prize money. Franklin endorsed the letter, "Gave this poor Man 6 Livres."[7]

Captain Richelot, writing from Rennes on October 1, suffered tribulations that exceed all others. Sent back to France after the fall of Charleston, he was captured five times, four times at sea and the fifth in Charleston. He is presently so debilitated by the lack of food that he keeps falling ill, which has prevented him from taking Franklin's orders in Paris. Worse yet, the enemy has confiscated all the money he has earned in commerce while employed by Congress and he is left with only some continental paper currency that is non-negotiable in France. What he desires from Franklin is a letter that will insure that his military advancement is not hampered by his lengthy stay in Europe. He also wants guidance as to the necessary steps to preserve the value of the currency he holds, now that a congressional resolution has altered the size of bills, as he heard on the day of his departure.

Some correspondents are not too happy with the way Franklin is reacting to their requests. On September 15, the Nantes firm of Wilt & Delmestre, Junr. complains that he is too slow in accepting the bills of exchange drawn upon him in America: some of them have been almost one month in his hands, not causing them any anxiety but much

6. This was Augustin Baudin, the son of François, a merchant who had written as early as March 21, 1777, to extol the potential commerce between America and the Ile de Ré (XXIII, 512). Baudin *fils*, who had gone to Paris the following August (*Deane Papers* II, 112), sailed early in 1778 on the *Deane* (XXV, 494n; Baudin *père* to Col. Thomas Conway, Feb. 13, 1778, APS). On March 28, 1780, he deposited at the French consulate in Baltimore two certificates of $1,000 each that had been issued on Dec. 13, 1779, in Philadelphia (National Archives).

7. BF noted the gift of the 6 *l.t.* in his Cash Book on a page headed Aug. 12, 1780: "To Salvator, a poor Man who had lost his son in Capt. Wicks." "Wicks" was Lambert Wickes. The muster book for his *Reprisal*, lost in 1777, is incomplete so we find no other record of the son: Clark, *Wickes*, pp. 375–6.

inconvenience. Convinced that this is simply a matter of negligence on the part of Franklin's secretaries, they urge him to remedy the situation. Franklin noted "Repondue" on the top of their letter.

The Italian poet Bassi[8] reminds Franklin in no uncertain terms, on September 18, that some two months previously Franklin had tacitly agreed to subscribe for six copies of Bassi's forthcoming *Recueil de poésies Italiennes, i.e.,* Franklin let the poet know by an intermediary that his answer would be coming via the *petite poste*. Now that the printer is about to insert the names of the subscribers, it is time to pay the fifty-four *l.t.* that are due. He repeats his reminder the following day and sends a messenger to collect the money. Both letters come from Paris.

The last two letters in this category have to do with money in a more oblique way. Madame Dubois' message of September 2 is quite mysterious. Franklin, it seems, promised to give her some advice and she rejoices in the thought that he is not confusing her with those indelicate souls whose only idol is money. Sensing that he trusts her, she will explain her case in a totally open way when she has the honor of meeting him the following Monday around 9 a.m. if that day and time are convenient to him.[9]

As to Joseph Blanchard, who writes on September 28 in the third person, he has a complicated story to tell. While serving two masters, Teyleur and Trambell (Tyler and Trumbull)[1] as interpreter, he has been accused of stealing two bags of money that had been furnished by the Grand bank and left for a night in John Adams's residence at the Hôtel de Valois. He in turn intimates that the theft was committed by his colleague Provin. Foucault (Chaumont's son-in-law?), Ostinn (Austin?) and someone named Jackson at the Hôtel de York (probably Edward Jackson Jones who wrote from there on July 13, below)

8. Anton-Benedetto Bassi is best known for introducing Italian literature to the French: Antonio Pace, *Benjamin Franklin and Italy* (Philadelphia, 1958), pp. 239–40. Some time between Feb. 18 and April 10, 1780, he sent out a printed announcement of two courses he was planning to give, one on the Italian language, the other on English. He identifies himself as belonging to the Academies of Sienna, Rome, Padua, Bologna, etc. and as having taught at Oxford. A scrap of paper, possibly taken from BF's guest book, mentions that Bassi had sent the Doctor a brochure called *Observations sur les poètes italiens*. On July 10, 1780, the *Journal de Paris* announced the publication of that work.

9. BF gave her 48 *l.t.* as "Charity": Cash Book.

1. For Col. John Steele Tyler and John Trumbull's arrival in France see XXXII, 244–5, 308. In July they arrived in London. We have found no other trace of this episode.

also figure in his hopelessly garbled account. Conclusion: he requests Franklin's protection and help.

Three people pine for news. The marquise de Castries[2]—whose husband was to become minister of the navy the following month—wonders on September 14 whether Franklin can tell her anything about her son who is part of the squadron led by Ternay and Rochambeau. She hears that it has reached Rhode Island.

A man named Bertrand, who identifies himself as *ancien commissaire des guerres aux colonies,* writes on September 29 from Paris to enquire whether Franklin knows anything about Joseph Redmond, an Irishman who has been for forty years a resident of Philadelphia and who was a sheriff there about eight years ago. Is he still alive? If not, when did he die? This is of the utmost importance for the writer, who was in conversation with Vergennes when Franklin arrived the previous day in the company, as he later learned from Gérard de Rayneval, of a visitor from Philadelphia.[3] Franklin apparently failed to answer this query, for Bertrand wrote again, on January 10, 1781, inclosing a duplicate of his first letter, at the suggestion of Rayneval.

From Ludwigsburg in the duchy of Württemberg comes, on October 31, a request from Gottlob Friedrich Ruthardt, a merchant. His brother Christian Wilhelm emigrated to Philadelphia six years ago to make his fortune in commerce. No news was received from him after the first two years and now a letter from Baltimore talks about his death. The writer begs Franklin to inquire about the matter and, if need be, to have a death certificate sent to him. A notation on a French abridged version of this long letter (written originally in German) indicates that it was answered. Indeed, in his follow-up note of December 9, in German, Ruthardt acknowledges Franklin's letter of November 14. Our assumption is that Franklin said that he did not know the fate of Ruthardt's brother, as the writer now encloses three identical letters to Evangelical Lutheran clergymen at Philadelphia, as well as two letters from relatives of his, with a request that Franklin forward them.

2. Gabrielle-Isabeau-Thérèse de Rosset de Fleury was married in 1743 to Charles-Eugène-Gabriel, marquis de Castries: *Dictionnaire de la noblesse*, VI, 539. Their son, Armand-Charles-Augustin de La Croix, comte de Charlus and later duc de Castries (1756–1842) wrote an account of the American campaign: *DBF;* Bodinier, *Dictionnaire;* Sydney W. Jackman, ed., *A Middle Passage: the Journal of Armand-Charles Augustin de la Croix de Castries . . .* (Boston, 1970).

3. This may have been James Searle, for whom see Huntington to BF, July 12.

Other people need Franklin's help in forwarding their mail to America.

From the Academy at Liege, W. Brent asks on July 17 for two letters to be sent off. He presumes Franklin has heard of the battles in the West Indies and the defeat of the Americans. He writes again on July 25, enclosing another letter and giving war news. Both his messages are in English.

On August 1, Tudesq, the mayor of Cète (Sète in Languedoc), begs Franklin to forward a package to his brother-in-law, Jean Thouron, a sea captain who has built several ships in Maryland (or maybe in Virginia) in unsuccessful attempts to send merchandise to France. The writer plans to ship a second packet, just to be safe. Franklin's love of humanity, and of the French in particular, is so well known that he feels no qualms in doing so.

A lieutenant-colonel of a regiment of dragoons named Forestier encloses two letters that are to be remitted to M. de Villefranche. He is writing from Angers on September 5.[4]

Using English on September 18, Alexander Gordon, principal of the "Scotch College" (Collège des Ecossais) in Paris, avails himself of the privilege of being a friend of Mrs. Strange[5] to enclose some letters for Mr. Griffin. "One of them is from his Lady's Aunts and, I suppose, contains nothing of any importance."

The wife of Mr. de Flad,[6] captain of the Royal Deux-Ponts regiment currently in the Rochambeau corps in America, has asked her friend de Puchelbel to help her send a letter safely to her husband either through Franklin or any other way he indicates. Writing from Paris on October 3, Puchelbel asks BF to add her letter to his packets to America.

In German and in a very shaky hand Baron Wilhelm Augustine von Steuben entreats Franklin, on October 18, to forward letters to his son. His letter comes from Cüstrin.[7]

Finally, no survey of favor-seekers would be complete without people who recommend themselves or others.

J. Lepine, who lives in Paris, thanks Franklin on November 13 in excellent English for having recommended his translating abilities to a

4. Forestier (XXIV, 74; XXVI, 692–3) was presently lieutenant-colonel of the Dragons du Roi: *Etat Militaire* for 1780, p. 389.

5. Perhaps Isabella Strange, the wife of the engraver Robert Strange.

6. Charles-Louis Flad (b. 1738), whose career eventually took him to Cayenne as French commandant: Bodinier, *Dictionnaire*.

7. He previously had written from the same place to ask BF about his son or to forward letters to him: XXX, 617; XXXI, 474; XXXII, 49–50.

Mr. Bromfield[8] who in turn recommended him to Mr. Andrews. They have both been satisfied enough to give him written certificates. He now humbly solicits the continuance of such august patronage.

On July 26, Fallavel, who repeatedly refers to Franklin as his friend, renews a plea: to grant a letter of introduction to America in favor of young Dezoteux, whose own message to him is enclosed.[9]

On July 14, a *receveur des impositions* named Jacqué, who writes from Châtillon-sur-Sèvre, pleads with Franklin to communicate his remedy against dropsy. He has long wanted to ask this but has refrained for fear of committing an indiscretion. Now, thinking of the good this would do in his province of lower Poitou and mindful of Franklin's benevolence, he feels emboldened.[1]

Joseph Mazurié[2] makes an impassioned plea on September 18 for the use of Landerneau as a Breton port and for the freedom of maritime commerce in general. He is indignant because two American ships have been forbidden to unload their cargo anywhere but in Brest and urges Franklin to discuss the matter with the controller general of finance. He encloses the text of the memorandum he would like Franklin to send.

Monsieur.   Bordeaux Ce 5 julliet 1780.

Estant un militaire qui connaist très peu Le cours des especes en papiers des colonies uniées un particulier qui en estait pourvú, et qui me devait m'en ayant donné en payement une assez forte Somme, je vous serais bien obligé de me faire donner Les Moyens d'en avoir le payement, Ou au moins de me faire indiquer ou il faut faire enregistrer ma Creance Sur Les colonies uniées, et Si elle porte interest. Malgré que j'eusse grand besoin de Ces fonds, je suis trop bon Cytoyen pour ne pas prendre pa-

8. Probably Henry Bromfield, Jr.

9. Pierre-Marie-Félicité Dezoteux, later baron de Cormatin (1751–1812), a captain of dragoons. He does sound quite impatient when writing Fallavel from Lorient, on July 22: he has been waiting for Franklin's letters for six weeks now, but he still has fifteen days before Capt. Jones sets sail. Please hurry. Dezoteux fought in America as aide de camp of baron de Vioménil, emigrated to England during the French Revolution and became one of the leaders of the Chouans or counter-revolutionaries: Bodinier, *Dictionnaire.*

1. BF had been receiving similar requests about dropsy remedies since 1777: XXV, 178; XXVI, 144; XXIX, 155.

2. In earlier days he had announced his intention of leaving Landerneau and setting up business in Brest: XXVI, 210.

tience, ainsy que tous les arrangemens que voudrat faire Le congrés, La seule chose que je desire de Sçavoir c'est comment il faut S'y prendre pour assurer en france la créance, et a quelles epoques a peu pres on serat payé.

Je vous demande mille pardons de troubler un instant des moments qui Sont tous Si pretieux pour L'humanité et pour ma patrie, je vous prie de Croire que l'estime et La Veneration que jay L'honneur de vous porter egalent Le Respect avec Lequel je suis Monsieur Vostre très humble Serviteur

LE MQIS DE VALORY colonel d[*torn.*:'infanterie] Chez mr. Le grix president des tresoriers de france a Bordeaux

From Dumas

ALS: American Philosophical Society

Monsieur,   Lahaie 6e. Juillet 1780

J'ai eu l'honneur de vous écrire le 4e. Aujourd'hui j'ai celui de vous dire qu'il est arrivé à Amsterdam un petit Bâtiment Américain *the Fame Capt. Nic. Lamprell,*[3] parti de Salem le 4e. de May. J'en ai vu 2 passagers Mr. Isaac White de Salem,[4] & Mr. Ed. Jones de Boston,[5] qui Sont venus ici chez moi.

Mr. White avoit reçu le 1er. May des Depeches de Mr. le Marquis de la Fayette pour Mr. l'Ambassadeur de fce. [France] ici. Un Exprès les lui avoit apporté de nuit, après que Mr. De la Fayette, arrivé le 30e. Avril avoit passé une partie de la même nuit à les préparer & expédier.[6] Cela faisoit un paquet de 4 bons doigts d'Épaisseur. Leur voyage fut heureux jusque sur le *Dog-*

3. Nicholas Lamprell's vessel was a 10-gun brig: Claghorn, *Naval Officers,* p. 178; Allen, *Mass. Privateers,* p. 126.

4. Isaac White (1753–1780) was a Salem merchant: Lawrence Park, "An Account of Joseph Badger, and a Descriptive List of His Work," Mass. Hist. Soc. *Proceedings* LI (1917–18), 181; Allen, *Mass. Privateers,* pp. 157–8.

5. Possibly the Edward Jones (1751–1835), who lived on Milk Street: Mass. Hist. Soc. *Proceedings,* 2nd ser., XX (1906–7), 409.

6. Lafayette spent April 28 to May 2 in Boston: Louis Gottschalk, *Lafayette and the Close of the American Revolution* (Chicago, 1942), pp. 77–80. We have found no record of his contacts with the French ambassador in the Netherlands, the duc de La Vauguyon.

ger bank, banc entre l'Angleterre & le Jutland; là, environ les 56.° 36', ils furent chassés tout un jour par un Corsaire portant pavillon Anglois. Ils jeterent leurs dix canons pour S'alléger, & même quelques marchandises. Enfin ils furent pris. Le Corsaire envoya du monde, qui visita leurs papiers, qui, conforme à leur déclaration, comme quoi ils étoient Américains, eussent dû engager le Corsaire à les laisser aller, puisque c'étoit *la Princesse de Robec, Cape. Cornu de Dunkerque*.[7] Mais lui, continuant contre toute raison, de feindre, leur dit que, cela étant, ils étoient bonne prise, & qu'il alloit les conduire à Douvres, & les passagers eurent ordre de passer à son bord. White, à qui le Dr Cooper[8] avoit expressément ordonné de jeter les Dépêches, si le salut de sa patrie lui étoit cher, en cas de prise, avoit pris la précaution de les mettre dans un sac avec un boulet, de les suspendre hors du Navire à une ficelle, & d'ordonner à un homme affidé de couper la ficelle S'il lui donnoit un certain signe, se voyant enlever, donna le signe & les Dépeches allerent à fonds, ainsi que les autres Lettres, & Lettres de change à [*lui*] qu'il y avoit jointes. Enfin le Cape. Cornu ne pouvant plus les méconnoître, leur dit qu'il alloit les conduire en france; & ce fut avec peine qu'ils obtinrent de pouvoir aller à leur destination. Tout ce procédé est contraire, ce me semble, à l'art. 29 du Traité de Commerce entre la France & l'Amérique.[9] Le plus facheux c'est la perte des Dépêches. J'ai conduit le Sr. White chez M. l'Ambassadeur, qui a demandé une Déclaration signée de lui de tout cela. Dès que je l'aurai, j'en tirerai une copie & s'il y a quelque différence avec ce que j'en dis ici, je vous la marquerai, Monsieur. En attendant, j'ai cru devoir vous donner connoissance de cela, Monsieur, afin que vous puissiez en porter plainte, si vous le croyez à propos.

Du reste, le Sr. White a déclaré, que tout étoit bien à son départ. Les Recrues se levoient, & la Taxe se collectoit, avec facilité. Mr De la Fayette Se préparoit à partir pour l'Armée & vers

7. The *Princesse de Robecq* recently had ransomed five ships: *Courier de l'Europe* VII (1780), 364, issue of June 2, 1780.

8. Dr. Samuel Cooper, an ardent supporter of the Franco-American alliance.

9. Which governed meetings between privateers and merchantmen: XXV, 622–3.

le Congrès. Il assure que la prise de Charlestown n'aura nullement découragé les Américains.

Je suis avec un très-grand respect, Monsieur De V. Exce. le
très-humble & très-obéissant serviteur   DUMAS

Passy à S.E. Mr. Franklin

Addressed: à Son Excellence / Monsieur B. Franklin, Esqr. /
Min. Plenipe. des Et. Unis / &c. / Passy./.

Notation: Dumas la haie July. 6. 80

From John Diot & Co.   ALS: American Philosophical Society

Honoured Sir   Morlaix the 7th. July 1780
   This Serves to Acquaint Your Excellency that the Black
Princess American privateer,[1] which after too long a detention,
Sailed from Isle Bas [Isle de Batz] Road on Thursday Evening,
took 8 prizes, which the Weakness of her Crew, forced Captn.
Macatter to Ransom, but on sonday 2d. Instant, Being about 3
leagues off Milford, he Saw 3 sails of Merchantmen Which he
gave chace to, and Came up with the brig Padmore Captn.
Solomon Williams, from Chester bound to London, with 28 four
pounders Iron Guns, and after takeing out of her, the Captain, 4
hands and Two Women passengers he Sent her to harbour, under Command of Wm. Ripner and three men, With a man and a
boy prisoners he left on board.
   Said prize Came in this Road, Yesterday morning after a Very
narrow Escape, haveing been chaced by an English privateer,
Close to the harbour mouth and most under the fort.
   We have deliver'd to the Admiralty office all the papers Relative to Said prize and Every thing Seeming to be Regular, We are
in hopes that your Judgement in Condemnation will be issued
Soon; The Two prisoners were put in Gaol.

1. Diot managed the privateers outfitted by John Torris, including the
Black Princess, while they were using Morlaix, as well as handling their
prizes: XXIX, 783; XXXII, 460–3. During her present cruise (June 29–July 18)
the *Black Princess* took twenty-six prizes, including the brig *Padmore:* Clark,
Ben Franklin's Privateers, pp. 146–54.

Mr. Torris has forwarded us The Judgements of the Peter and friendship prizes,[2] which we deliver'd to the Admiralty office, and We gratefully Thank your Excellency for same.

We have the honnour to be with due Respect Honoured Sir Your most Obedient and Most Humble Servants

JN DIOT & CO

To His Excellency B. Franklin Minister for the Congress at the Court of France Passy

Notation: Mr. Diot & Co. July 7. 1780

From Dumas

ALS: American Philosophical Society

Monsieur, Lahaie 7e. Juille [1780]

La protestation, en Allemand, de la minorité du Chapitre de Munster, m'ayant été communiquée ce matin, je me suis tout de suite mis à la traduire, pour pouvoir vous l'envoyer ce soir.[3] Cette piece me paroît très-bien faite. D'ailleurs la matiere est de la plus grande importance, puisqu'il s'agit du futur Electeur de Cologne & Evêque de Munster. Je la crois de la façon de Mr. De Furstemberg[4] Administrateur de l'Evêché de Munster, grand Génie; mais ce n'est qu'une conjecture de ma part. Je pense que cela vous fera plaisir. Un vilain mal aux reins m'empêche presque d'écrire. Je suis avec un grand respect, Monsieur Votre très-humble & très obeissant serviteur DUMAS

Passy à S.E. Mr. B. Franklin

Notation: Mr. Dumas la Haie July. 7. 80

2. Prizes of the *Black Prince*. BF, who counted on the privateers to bring in prisoners to exchange for Americans in British jails, had sent the condemnations to Torris on June 26: XXXII, 602–3.

3. The protestation was against the impending election of Archduke Maximilian Franz as coadjutor to the archbishop-elector of Cologne. Dumas' French translation is at the APS. See also Dumas' letter of July 4, above.

4. Franz Friedrich Wilhelm, freiherr von Fürstenberg (1729–1810) was vicar general of the bishopric of Münster and a rival candidate to the archduke: *ADB;* Alfred Baudrillart *et al.,* eds., *Dictionnaire d'Histoire et de Géographie Ecclésiastiques* (25 vols. to date, Paris, 1912–), XIX, 300–4.

From Landais

LS: American Philosophical Society

Alliance at Groix 7th July 1780.

May it please your Excellency

I have waited 'till now for your Order for Sailing as you announced me another letter in yours of the 24th. June,[5] to Come by the next Post—but since you have wrote me nothing and that you charged me in that letter with the prejudicial delay of the Sailing of the Alliance, and given no hopes of having my People righted, I have prevailed upon them to go to our own Country to seek Justice.

I have for my own part been treated very ill, and my Purser[6] has been Put into Prison, but I hope We will have Satisfaction for the injury and I now acquaint you that I am getting under Sail to go to America.[7]

I have the Honor to be Your most Obedient humble Servt.

P: LANDAIS Captain of the Alliance

Doctor Franklin

Notation: P. Landais Groix July 7. 80

From the Baron de Wulffen

L:[8] American Philosophical Society

Sir   Venlo the 7th. jullett 1780

I have the Honour to late your Exelance know that am in tollerable good health arrived here at Venlo, where, where I am oblidged to rest Some days,[9] meen time them depeches your Ex-

---

5. XXXII, 586. See also XXXII, 539–40.

6. Nathan Blodget.

7. He sailed two hours later: Landais' court martial testimony, Jan. 2, 1781 (National Archives). The *Alliance* arrived in Boston on Aug. 16: XXXII, 9n. This is Landais' last extant letter to BF.

8. The signature is in the hand, unknown to us, of the person who wrote the letter for him.

9. He spent only a few weeks with his sister and brother-in-law. By Aug. 1 he was in Amsterdam, where he reported himself partly recovered from a recent indisposition and worried only that "le bon Dieu" would preserve BF for his important work. He concluded, "Nos amis Vous donnerai de Lettres, donc Votre Excellence n'est pas encore informé de nouvelles extraordinaires

elance Sent along are Delivered in good hands in the Hague,[1] His Exelance Knowing I' am wishing nothing more than to Return again to my post to which End have the Honour to hould my Self Recomended to your Exelance thanking your Exelance for the alrady Received protection and Honours Subschryet myself with diepst Respect, Sir your Most Humble and most obedient Servant   JOHAN HENRICK DE WULFFEN

P.S. Exelance favour me with a letter of answer to this an I Shall have the Honour to wait your Exelances further orders in here

To Antoine-Raymond-Gualbert-Gabriel de Sartine

Copy: Library of Congress

Monseigneur,   Passy le 8. Jullet 1780.

Un Corsaire nommé l'union de l'Amerique, qui a été expedié de Dunkerque avec une Commission du Roi, mais équipé avec des Americains et des Irlandois étant chassé dans le Port de St. Malo a été arrêté par ordre de la Cour, et on dit que l'équipage doit être envoyé à l'Orient pour être mis àbord les vaisseaux du Roy qui sont dans ce port. Voilà, Monseigneur, le rapport qui m'en a été fait.[2]

Comme la perte de son équipage sera ruineuse pour le Capitaine Meyric qui est un Americain et un des proprietaires de son Bâtiment, et qui aura l'honneur de vous presenter celle cy. Je prie, votre Excellence de vouloir bien, (Si la chose est faisable) favoriser son humble requête et lui permettre de continuer Sa Croisiere.

---

et je me recommande à lavenir de votre protection." On Oct. 9 he wrote in German from Rotterdam a final letter complaining of being ill-treated in spite of BF's protection. Both of these letters are at the APS.

1. Presumably to Dumas; see Dumas' letter of July 4.

2. BF had been asked to intervene with Sartine by both Joseph Myrick (XXXII, 616–17), and Timothy Kelly (on July 4, above). For the prizes the *Union Américaine* made while cruising from Dunkirk in the summer of 1780 see Anatole-Louis-Théodore-Marie, Marquis de Granges de Surgères, ed., *Prises des Corsaires français pendant la Guerre de l'Indépendance (1778–1783)* (Paris and Nantes, 1900), pp. 26–9.

Ce Capitaine a deja fait cinq Prises et comme lui et son Equipage sont au fait de la navigation sur la côte d'Angleterre, Je ne doute point que ce Corsaire ne soit capable de faire beaucoup de tort au Commerce de Gabotage [Cabotage] de l'ennemi commun. Capitaine Meynik m'a dit que parmi tout son Equipage il n'a qu'un françois qui est établi depuis plusieurs années en Amerique où il a laissé une femme et des Enfans, Je suis avec respect, Monseigneur, Votre tres humble et tres obeissant serviteur

M. De Sartine

From Sartine

Copy: Library of Congress

A Versailles le 9. Juin [*i.e.*, July] 1780.[3]
Je reçois, Monsieur, votre Lettre du 8. de ce mois au sujet de l'Equipage du Corsaire l'Union Americaine, detenu à St. Malo; je donne les Ordres que vous me demandès pour que cet Equipage soit laissé à la Disposition du Capitaine et pour que celuicy ait la liberté de renprendre la Mer avec son Bâtiment.

J'ai l'honneur d'etre avec une parfaite Considération, Monsieur, votre très humble et très obeissant Serviteur.

(signé) DE SARTINE.

M. Franklin.

To Anne-Louise Boivin d'Hardancourt Brillon de Jouy

AL: American Philosophical Society

ce 10 Juillet 80
Dites moi, ma chere Amie, de vos nouvelles. Vôtre Saignée,[4] l'a-t-il reussi de vous soulager? Croyez vous que nous pouvons esperer d'avoir la Felicité de vous voir ici, avec les cheres en-

3. The month was probably miscopied by L'Air de Lamotte. Sartine is acknowledging BF's letter of July 8, immediately above.
4. The first indication of an illness that would afflict Mme Brillon for many months.

fants, Mercredi prochaine, aprés midi, pour prendre le Thé chez nous? Nous aurons les Mesdemoiselles Alexander,[5] qui seront charmées de vous rencontrer. Je prierai aussi vos Voisines.[6]

Il me semble, que quand vous étés en Santé, vous ne prenez pas assez d'Exercice pour la tenir. Je vous conseille de promener tous les jours une heure, dans votre belle Jardin s'il fait beau tems, autrement dans votre Maison. Ou si vous n'avez pas autant de loisir, prenez une Exercice plus fort en moins de temps, qui sera la même chose. Vous pouvez faire cela, en descendant & remontant l'escalier dans vôtre Jardin, ou dans le Maison, pour un quart d'heure, en chaque jour avant diner.

Addressed: A Madame / Madame Brillon / Passy[7]

From the Baron d'Arros[8] and Other Commission Seekers
ALS: American Philosophical Society

Of the fifteen people who either applied for a commission in the American army between July 1 and November 15, 1780, or recommended someone for a commission, as far as we know only the first, the baron d'Arros, had the connections to elicit Franklin's support. His letter of July 10 is printed below.[9]

Also writing on July 10 was Louis-Germain Dupin d'Assarts, from the Nivernais, who begs a chance to shed his blood for America and to find a haven for his family. Seven years ago he took advantage of

5. Since Mariamne had married JW, the remaining Alexander *demoiselles* were Bethia (23), Christine (17), Jane (15), Isabella (11), and Joanna (9): XXIX, 534n; Charles Rogers, *Memorials of the Earl of Stirling and of the House of Alexander* (2 vols., Edinburgh, 1877), II, 34–5.

6. Mme Geneviève-Elisabeth Le Veillard and her daughter Geneviève (XXXI, 125n). See also Louis Batave, "Les eaux de Passy au XVIIIe siècle," *Revue du dix-huitième siècle*, II (1914), 121.

7. The address is in imitation of Mme Brillon's writing.

8. Quite possibly Jean-François, baron d'Arros d'Argelos (b. 1730), the future commandant of the *Languedoc* when it sailed with de Grasse's fleet from Brest in March, 1781. He was named *garde-marine* in 1744, *lieutenant de vaisseau* in 1756, captain in 1772, and *chef d'escadre* in 1784: *DBF*.

9. Unless otherwise specified, the following documents are in French and located at the APS.

the gullibility of a young woman and, prompted by his religion and his honor, married her. His mother disapproved of the marriage and deprived him of all his resources. Having no money he has been unable to find employment. He speaks German, Italian, and Latin. He is robust of temperament and fit for any work. Five years ago he wrote the King of Prussia seeking a position and he encloses a translation of Frederick's answer as well as copies of documents testifying to his gentle birth, his honorable conduct, and the military experience of his family, including that of his grandfather Philippe Dupin de Coeurs, a *chevalier de St. Louis.*[1]

Three days later Charles de Dyke writes from Stralsund in Swedish Pomerania. Bored with garrison life this young infantry first lieutenant seeks at least that rank in the American army where he can learn his profession and find honor under the flags of liberty. He asks that his travel expenses to America be paid.

On July 14 Jacques-Dominique de Roberdeau[2] of Haguenau, Alsace, introduces his son. He has ascertained that his father and General Daniel Roberdeau's were brothers, separated after the revocation of the Edict of Nantes.[3] Now he wishes to cement his friendship with the general by sending one of his two sons to support the American cause. The son, for eight years an officer in the infantry and the *troupes à cheval,* is an excellent subject, calm and discreet.[4] He speaks French, Latin, German, and will soon master English. The father has written to Montbarey, Vergennes, and Sartine to obtain recommendations and passage to America. He asks Franklin for a letter of introduction to their relative and his friend the general.

Roberdeau carried another letter of support, written on July 30, by M de Barth, the general syndic of Alsace, who recommends Roberdeau as a young man of much promise. On September 3 at Paris Roberdeau himself asks whether he may call the next day and take Franklin's orders.

1. Dupin writes again on Sept. 17, asking for a reply to his letter. A notation by WTF says that the letter was answered. On Jan. 15, 1784, Dupin writes once more, enclosing that answer to show that he is no mere adventurer. He and his wife are completely destitute. They have pawned all their belongings to satisfy masters who taught them both a trade, and can no longer provide for themselves and their four children. He asks for an advance.

2. For whom see XXV, 672.

3. BF had forwarded correspondence between the brigadier general of militia and his Alsatian cousin several times: XXVI, 258; XXVIII, 354; XXIX, 72, 78; XXX, 604.

4. He was a lieutenant in the Bercheny regiment of hussars: *Etat militaire* for 1780, p. 383.

Herman Esser, a former officer in the Dutch army, on pension since 1752, writes from Venlo on July 22 concerning propositions made by M de Wolffen (*i.e.*, the baron de Wulffen). Wulffen, who claims to be head of a corps of dragoons in the service of America, has offered him a company in the same corps and on July 7, in Esser's presence, wrote to Franklin for his approval and the authority to confer on Esser the rank of captain with three months advance wages.[5] Wulffen left on the thirteenth for The Hague, where Esser was to join him once he heard from His Excellency. Esser and his youngest son, age fourteen, await only a word from Franklin before departing. His second son, a cadet in the Dutch army, will want to follow them to be with his older brother, already in America serving as a lieutenant.

On August 2 Major de Pfortzheim announces his arrival in his country, at Arlon, Luxembourg. In very uncertain French the major suggests that in writing he is following Franklin's instructions, and he hopes that Franklin will accord him "sa bien viellane et haute protection prés des ettatts unis" to pursue his vocation.

From Arpajon in the Ile-de-France a M Garnier writes in English on August 19: "Though neither a rich nor a nobleman born, yet do I chearfully desire in this time of war, to get useful." He has served in a regiment of dragoons for six years and speaks the English tongue without any foreign accent. He will be in town the following Wednesday to wait upon Franklin "according to your answer."[6]

The vicomte de la Motte, a retired infantry lieutenant colonel, writing on August 23 from La Tremblade in Saintonge, recalls an earlier offer to volunteer his services in the American army in exchange for his rations. While Franklin had discouraged him in a friendly way, the vicomte still yearns to contribute "au grand ouvrage de La Liberté americaine," and proposes now to lead a corps of three hundred seasoned soldiers to be stationed with a naval squadron for defense of its ships and to aid in expeditions and raids.

Another former commission seeker, officer O'Sullivan de Bearhaven of the infantry regiment of Dillon, renews a now-missing request on September 1.[7] Writing in English he states that Colonel Conway and Dr. McMahon had recommended him earlier but that Franklin had not then "an ocation of Rendering me that multiplisity of Service." He is, however, a "Nevew to Genl. o Sullivan" whom

---

5. For Wulffen's missing letter of July 7 see BF to Esser, July 29, below.

6. BF wrote on Aug. 21, below, to discourage Garnier.

7. For the O'Sullivans of Beare see *DNB*. For a summary of his regiment's role during the Revolution see Balch, *French in America*, II, 22–5.

he is anxious to join.[8] He says that Franklin's writing in his favor to John Paul Jones now at Lorient would "the more induce him to afford my Passage on the Hariel."[9] He has also written to Count Dillon to sollicit Franklin on his behalf.[1]

On October 7 Douillemond, a baillif from Vendenois near Bar-sur-Aube in Champagne, writes on behalf of an unnamed officer who has served nine years in the *gendarmerie* headquartered at Lunéville in Lorraine. The lieutenant of cavalry is twenty-five, tall, and well-formed. If he could find service in America and the proper rank he would go over on the first ship. All this must be kept quiet for the marquis de Castries[2] would greatly regret losing him.

Mutel de Boucheville, a *conseiller* at the *Cour des Comptes* of Normandy,[3] recommends his sixteen-year-old son on October 10. Charles-Pierre, chevalier de Mutel, inspired by the praise of Lafayette and Rochambeau, seeks a place in one of the regiments that have gone over to the islands. Then in forty-three verses, mainly classical alexandrines, the father praises Franklin as "Le Nestor de Boston respecté par le Temps" and depicts the visions of military glory that have inspired his son to want to fight for "Waginston secouant l'affreux joug de la vaine Albion." In a postscript he adds that his son has completed his studies, can draw, has studied geography, and learned the books of Mr. Bezou.[4]

8. The writer must have been a *neveu* of Gen. John Sullivan only in the broadest sense of being a relative. The general had resigned on Nov. 30, 1779: *DAB.*

9. The *Ariel* departed Lorient on Sept. 5 but remained in Groix Roads for over a month: Morison, *Jones*, p. 304. A Jeremie O. Sulivan was a cadet volunteer aboard the *Ariel* according to the list of volunteers described in our annotation of Jones to BF, Sept. 23, below.

1. Comte Arthur Dillon had transferred command of his regiment to comte Theobald de Dillon in April, 1780: John Cornelius O'Callaghan, *History of the Irish Brigades in the Service of France* ... (Glasgow, 1870), pp. 50, 52.

2. At present Castries was *commandant général* and *inspecteur* of the gendarmerie: *Etat militaire* for 1780, pp. 73, 142.

3. Jacques-François Mutel de Boucheville (1730–1814) was also a writer and poet: Larousse.

4. Etienne Bézout (1730–1783), of the Académie royale des sciences, was a celebrated mathematician and the examiner for the royal corps of artillery. His *Cours de mathématiques* ... (4 vols., Paris, 1770–72) was the textbook for candidates to and students of the artillery corps: *DBF;* François-André Isambert *et al., Recueil général des anciennes lois françaises* ... (29 vols., Paris, 1821–33), XXVII, 66–7.

A former major in the Walloon regiment of Smissaert[5] and a chevalier de St. Louis, M de Bernard de Chasteauvieux writes on October 20 from Namur, Austrian Netherlands. His twenty-five-year-old son, who began his career as a cadet and ensign in the same Walloon regiment, has just sold his post of lieutenant in the naval regiment of Binting in the Dutch service which he had held for three years, serving in Surinam to put down an uprising of blacks. Not content with the pace of his advancement the son now wishes to enter, with Franklin's protection, the service of the "Treize Cantons unis" and to raise a volunteer corps of one hundred men from around Liège. All he asks is the means and a place to assemble, clothe, arm, and embark the men.

Two Englishmen write in English from Leghorn on October 27. Walter Williams and Helenus Scott[6] had left England to go by land to India with Colonel Mathews, second in command on the Malabar Coast and a relative of Williams. Mathews, however, was detained in London and they have since resolved to offer their services to General Washington. They ask for passports and the name of a port in France from which they should embark for America. One of them leaves an estate in Wales of five hundred pounds a year and the other gives up his appointment in the Army. They enclose letters of introduction to the governor and chief people at Bombay.

Monsieur   versailles le 10 juillet 1780

Javois eù l'honuer de porter â votre exelence, únne letre de madame la marquise delafaÿete au suget de mon voÿage pour Boston;[7] vous me fites l'honuer de me dire que vous repondriés a madame la marquise il faut que votre exelence l'et oublié puisque on na rien resú de vous â lhotel de noailles; vous sçavès combien madame de lafaÿete (a qui je l'honuer d'epartenir) a des Bontés pour moÿ, et a quel point elle sinteresse a mon sort; votre exelence ne se repentira pas de mavoir rendù service, dailleur lexperience de 34 áns de servisse, et trois gúeres que je faite mont mis en meme de conetre mon metier, que je serés heureux de pouvoir le metre en activité chès les etats réunis de lamerique nos

---

5. The regiment was named for Jan Carel Smissaert (1684–1747): *NNBW*, II, 1329.

6. Scott (1760–1821), a physician, had studied medicine at Edinburgh from 1777 to 1779. He entered the medical service of the East India Company, and for thirty years served chiefly in the Bombay presidency: *DNB*.

7. See her letter above, on or before July 5. BF wrote to Samuel Huntington on the baron's behalf, immediately below the present document.

alliés vous pouvés avoir grande confiance en moÿ, je suis militaire et je ne desire autre chose que detre rendù a Boston, je me chargeré avec plaisir des comisions que vous voudré bien me donner, aÿé la Bonté dadresser vos letres a madame la marquise delafaÿete a lhotel de noailles ruë st honoré a paris./.

Je l'honuer detre avec ún tres profond respect, de votre exelence Monsieur Votre tres humble et tres obeissant serviteur

LE BARON D'ARROS

Notation: d'Arros, Versailles 10. Juillet 1780.

To Samuel Huntington

LS:[8] American Philosophical Society; copy: Library of Congress

Sir   Passy July 10th. 1780.

I am requested by Madame la Marquise de la Fayette, whom no body can refuse, to give the Bearer, M. le Baron d'Arros, a Letter to your Excellency. I have acquainted him that our Armies are fully officer'd, that there was no Probability of his being employed, that it was contrary to my Orders to recommend any foreign Officer for Employment, that such a Recommendation, if I were to give it, would therefore do him no Service, & that I could not give him the least Expectation or Encouragement to go over to America, but would rather advise him to remain in France. All this has had no Effect to change his Resolution. He thinks his long Experience and Skill in his Military Profession, will recommend him: and I have only to request of your Excellency, that you would shew him that Countenance and those Civilities, that his Zeal for our Cause & his Connections with a Family we all so much esteem & love, may entitle him to.

I have the honour to be with the greatest Respect, Sir, Your Excellency's, most obedient and most humble Servant.

B FRANKLIN

His Exy. S. Huntington Esqr. President of Congress.

8. In WTF's hand.

To Sartine[9]

Copy: Library of Congress

Sir Passy, July 10. 1780.

I beg your Excellency to accept my thankfull Acknowledgment for your favour to the Captain of the American Union, in permitting him to continue his Cruize. You have made him & his People very happy, and have very much obliged Your Excellency's obedient and most humble Servant.

Mr. De Sartine.

To the Comte de Vergennes

LS:[1] Archives du Ministère des affaires étrangères; copy: Library of Congress

Sir Passy July 10th 1780

I received the Letter your Excellency did me the honour of writing to me, dated the 1st Instant, together with the Papers accompanying it, containing the Correspondence with Mr Adams.[2] I have taken some Pains since to understand the Subject, and obtain Information of the Facts, from Persons lately arrived, having received no Letters myself that explain it. I cannot

---

9. In response to his of the previous day, above.

1. In WTF's hand.

2. Foreign Minister Vergennes' letter actually was dated June 30: XXXII, 625–7. For several weeks he and JA had been conducting an acrimonious correspondence about the March, 1780, devaluation of American currency to a fortieth of its nominal value: XXXII, 527n, 573n. Recently JA had escalated the conflict by criticizing French naval efforts and by again raising the question of informing the British of his appointment as peace commissioner. In late July, JA chose to leave France for the Netherlands: Butterfield, *John Adams Diary*, II, 442–3n; IV, 243–5, 250–2; *Adams Papers*, IX, 516–29, 536; X, 1–4, 16–18, 32–51, 56–8; James H. Hutson, *John Adams and the Diplomacy of the American Revolution* (Lexington, Ky., 1980), pp. 66–73. BF also wrote Vergennes' *premier commis* Joseph-Mathias Gérard de Rayneval on this date enclosing "the Original Letter of Mr. Adams, of which Mr Franklin has taken the copy" (AAE); that enclosure was a memorandum JA had sent Vergennes: XXXII, 625n.

say that I yet perfectly understand it; but in this I am clear, that if the Operation directed by Congress in their Resolution of the 18th of March, occasions from the Necessity of the Case, some Inequality of Justice, that Inconvenience ought to fall wholly on the Inhabitants of the States, who reap with it the Advantages obtained by the Measure. And that the greatest Care should be taken, that Foreign Merchants, particularly the French who are our Creditors, do not suffer by it. This I am so confident the Congress will do, that I do not think any Representations of mine necessary to persuade them to it.[3] I shall not fail, however, to lay the whole before them. And I beg that the King may be assured, their Sentiments and those of the Americans in general, with regard to the Alliance, as far as I have been able to learn them, not only from private Letters, but from authentic public Acts, differ widely from those that seem to be express'd by M. Adams, in his Letter to your Excellency,[4] and are filled with the strongest Impressions of the Friendship of France, of the generous manner in which his Majesty was pleased to enter into an equal Treaty with us, and of the great Obligations our Country is under for the important Aids he has since afforded us.

With the sincerest Respect, I have the honour to be, Sir. Your Excellency's, most obedt. & most humble Servant.

B FRANKLIN

His Exy. the Count De Vergennes.

Endorsed: M. de R[5]

3. Had BF made such representations he would have undercut JA as well as risking his own reputation. On Aug. 9, below, he did send Samuel Huntington copies of JA's letters to Vergennes, but he did not directly discuss the currency devaluation.

4. JA had argued that the alliance was beneficial to France as well as to the United States, had minimized the damage done by the devaluation to the French holders of American currency, and had criticized French demands for an exemption: *Adams Papers,* IX, 460–70.

5. This assigns to Gérard de Rayneval responsibility for preparing a response.

From Gourlade & Moylan[6]

Extract:[7] Archives du Ministère des affaires étrangères

[July 10, 1780]

You will find from the Perusal of these Papers (Copies of the Correspondence between Capt. Landais & M. Moylan) that *we do not refuse* furnishing the Fregate Alliance with the Provisions necessary for the daily Support of her Crew.[8]

Extract of a Letter from Messrs. Gourlade & Moylan, dated July 10. 1780, to B. Franklin.

From Francis Hopkinson   ALS: Historical Society of Pennsylvania

My dear Friend.   Philada. July 10th. 1780

I did myself the Pleasure of writing to you pr. Mr. Carmichael;[9] since which, I have not heard from you in Return, but flatter myself there may be a Letter on the Way. Come when it may, it will be truly acceptable.— Since your Departure my chief Pleasure is in conversing with Mr. Rittenhouse on Philosophical Subjects. This Gratification, however, I but seldom enjoy. Both he & myself are so closely engaged in public Business as to leave little Time for those agreeable Enquiries.— He is certainly a very able, friendly & communicative Philosopher— He is an Honour to his Country as a Man & as a Man of Science—

---

6. In answer to BF's of June 24 (XXXII, 584–5).

7. This extract and two others (Schweighauser's letters of July 15 and Sept. 7, both below) were made by L'Air de Lamotte in 1783 for Thomas Barclay to use in his review of BF's accounts: Barclay to BF, Dec. 16, 1783, AAE. French translations of the extracts are also at the AAE.

8. The copies of the Landais-Moylan correspondence are missing, but Landais had complained to Puchelberg, the American commercial agent in Lorient, that Moylan was refusing to cooperate and asked that action be taken against him: Landais to Puchelberg, June 16, 1780 (National Archives).

9. William Carmichael, who sailed from Philadelphia on the *Confederacy* on Oct. 26, 1779, probably carried Hopkinson's Sept. 5 letter (XXX, 298–300). Eleven days before the ship sailed, however, Hopkinson did give Carmichael funds to purchase any new "Phylosophical Machines" for him: XXX, 299n.

I am sure you will join me in this Opinion.— As to Politics & News I trouble you not with them—you have enough on those Subjects from all Quarters.— I only say we [*torn:* go?] on—ever keeping in View the main & ultimate [*torn:* object?] vizt. Liberty & Independence to the rising Generation— But I will not enter into so large a Field. I only wish the Continuance of your Friendship & Esteem, which I shall always endeavour to deserve.

Being my dear Sir with all affection & Regard.— Your Friend & humble servt   FRAS HOPKINSON

Honble Dr. Franklin

Addressed: Honourable / Dr. Franklin / favourd by Hon[le.] Mr. Searle

Endorsed: F. Hopkinson Letter of Friendship

From Puchelberg & Cie.   LS: American Philosophical Society

May it please Your Excellence,   LOrient 10th. July 1780

We see by the Letter Your Excellence did us the honnour to write to us on the 3 Cort. [Current], that the demand for prize Money due to the Frigatte Alliance, must be solely made upon M. de Chaumont for his having Receiv'd, or being likely to Receive in short all the money which might Result thereof.

We write to day in Consequence to the said Gentleman, and humbly beg Your Excellence's assistance and protection for the cause of your Countrymen, if any difficulty might fall out on this head.[1]

Your Excellence be pleased to accept of our humble thanks for the advice you give to us about the prizes sent into Norway, and that not a farthing is like to be gathered thereof for what we are truly sorry.

We have the honnour to be with great Respect May it please Your Excellence Your Most obedient humb Serv:

PUCHELBERG & CO

---

1. On July 31 Chaumont wrote the firm, promising to pay the officers and crew of the *Alliance* or their agents as soon as he received the funds: National Archives.

The frigatte Alliance being under sail since yesterday[2] M. Schweighauser will send to your Excellence in short the account of the furnitures we have been obliged to make to her, for account of the Congress.

To his Excellence Doctor Franklin Passy.

Notation: Puchelberg, L'Orient 10. July. 1780.

From Madame Brillon   AL: American Philosophical Society

Mon bon papa   [after July 10, 1780][3]
J'ai été dans un état violent, et je suis excéssivement foible; quand vous voudrés me venir voir un moment, je vous recevrés avéc grand plaisir, mais de longtems je ne pourrai vous allér chérchér:/: Mon ami ma machine est foible, le sort m'a déstiné a souffrir, je souscris a cét arrést, n'y pouvant rien changér; je n'ai rien a me reprochér je fais de l'éxercisse, je vis sagement; j'aime mes amis, et surtout mon papa je désire qu'il me le rende, c'est le bonheur le plus cértain sur lequel je puisse comptér:/:

Addressed:[4] A Monsieur / Monsieur franklin / A Passy

To Landais   Copy: Library of Congress

Sir,   [July 11, 1780]
    There are on board the Alliance five Cases of Types shipped by Mr. Jona: Williams of Nantes in consequence of My Orders, two of which were shipped when the alliance was at L'Orient last year, the other three were put on board at L'Orient in May last, and for which no Receipt was given.[5]

2. According to Landais' later testimony he sailed on the 7th; see our annotation of his letter of that date.
3. In answer to his of July 10, above.
4. In another hand.
5. For the cases of type see XXVI, 547; XXVII, 392–3; XXVIII, 505; XXIX, 347. As the *Alliance* had already sailed we do not know what happened to them when they reached America.

All these Cases are addressed to Mr. Watson in Connecticut, but as I Since hear that the said Mr. Watson is dead & the purchase of these types being recommended by Governor Trumbull of Connecticut as being much wanted for the public Benefit; I hereby direct you to take proper Care of the said five Cases of Types, and on your Arrival in america to deliver the Same to the Order of his Excellency Governor Trumbull who will apply for the same and for so doing this Shall be your Warrant.

Given at Passy this 11. day July 1780.

To the Commanding Officer on board the Continental frigate Alliance.

Committee for Foreign Affairs to Franklin and John Jay

Copy and transcript: National Archives; copy: Massachusetts Historical Society

Sirs   Philadelphia 11 July 1780

Congress have appointed the Honorable Henry Laurens Esqr to solicit a loan of Money in the United provinces of the low Countries, in order to facilitate his Success the enclosed resolution, has been passed.[6] We need say nothing to explain or urge it, except that it is thought a Mark of attention and confidence due to those powers named in it; that their interest, if the State of politics inclines them to exert it, will have a good effect, and that the want of Money makes this loan a very Capitol object to the United States. You will, we are sure, give Mr Laurens every assistance in your power, and solicit the countenance of the court where you reside to forward his Negociations. Till Mr Laurens shall arrive, Mr Adams is commissioned and empowered to undertake that business, and in case of his Disability, Mr Dana is in

6. As James Lovell explained in a letter of this date to Jay (Smith, *Letters*, xv, 432–3), this resolution was one directing the two American ministers to inform the French and Spanish courts of Laurens' mission and solicit their support: *JCC*, xv, 1250.

like Manner Commissioned and empowered.[7] We are Sir, your
mo. Hum. Servt   Signed JAMES LOVELL
                                                  WM. C. HOUSTON[8]

To the honorable Benja Franklin Esqr. & the honorable John Jay
Esqr

From the Committee for Foreign Affairs: Two Letters

(I) ALS:[9] American Philosophical Society; LS: Historical Society of
Pennsylvania; copies: Archives du Ministère des affaires étrangères,
National Archives, Library of Congress (two); transcript: National
Archives; (II) ALS: American Philosophical Society; press copy: Library
of Congress; copy and transcript: National Archives

I.

Sir   Philada. 11 July 1780

After the repeated Remonstrances you have made to Congress on the Subject of Bills of Exchange the inclosed Resolution[1] we are well aware, will need an Apology. We regret
that you should have so much Trouble and be put upon so many
Expedients in matters of this Kind, well knowing how delicate
a Point it is to solicit further Advances after so many have already been made. Congress attending to your Letters & Representations has taken this Step with Reluctance But the present
Crisis when not only the Preparations for a vigorous Campaign
call for large Expenditures but the Expectation of a cooperating

---

7. For these June 20 resolutions see *JCC*, XVII, 534–7. Congress also sent
commissions to JA and Dana; JA, already in the Netherlands, received his on
Sept. 17: *Adams Papers*, IX, 453n.

8. Two of the three current members of the committee for foreign affairs.
The other was Robert R. Livingston of New York: *JCC*, XV, 1302.

9. The ALS of both (I) and (II) are in the hand of James Lovell, who enclosed them with his letter of Oct. 28, below.

1. A resolution of May 19 directing that $25,000 in additional bills of ex-
change be drawn on BF and a similar sum on John Jay: *JCC*, XVII, 438. Twelve
days later, a second resolution ordered the committee for foreign affairs to
notify the two ministers: *ibid*, p. 475. Copies of these resolutions are with BF's
papers at the APS and at the University of Pa. Library.

Force make great Additions necessary, has induced Them to risque the Sum mentioned. The Bills will not be drawn faster than indispensible Exigencies may require, and it is to be hoped that this mode of commanding Cash will not be again resorted to.

We are Sir Your obedt. Servants

JAMES LOVELL
WM CHURCHILL HOUSTON

3d Copy

Honble. Benja. Franklin

Addressed: Honorable / Doctor Franklin / Minister plenipory./ &c. / France

II.

Sir   Philada. 11 July 1780

We are to communicate to you that Congress entertain a favorable Sense of the Attention & Services of Monsr. Chasseaulx his Most Christian Majesty's Consul at the Port of Bergen in Norway in the late Affair of the Prizes sent in there by the Squadron commanded by Capt. Jones,[2] and we beg you will present through the proper Chanel the Acknowledgements to be made for the polite Respect shewn to the Interests of the Citizens of these States.

We are Sir Your very humble Servants

JAMES LOVELL
WM CHURCHILL HOUSTON

3d Copy

Hon. Benja. Franklin

Addressed: Honorable / Doctor Franklin / Minister plenipory. &c. / France

---

2. Congress so resolved on May 31: *JCC*, XVII, 476. Chezaulx had assisted the prize crews: XXX, 336–7, 340, 342–3, 591–4.

From Sartine

Copy: Library of Congress

Versailles le 11. Juillet 1780.

Mr De Sartine a l'honneur d'envoyer à Mr. Franklin une Lettre pour M. de la Granville[3] Commissaire de la Marine à l'Orient pour qu'il soit delivré un Passeport à la Dame Angloise recommandée de Mr le Ministre Plenipotentiaire des États Unis de l'Amerique et Mr. De Sartine a l'honneur de l'assurer de son très sincere Attachement./.

From Thomas Digges

ALS: Historical Society of Pennsylvania

Dr. Sir   July 12 1780

I got Your obliging favor of the 25th June[4] by Mr. Burn & am very thankful for your attention & civility to Him. He is a very excellent young Man & may be useful to You or Yours hereafter, in case You should have anything to do at Lisbon, for which place He will set out in a month or two & where He is the head of a Merchantile House inferior to no other English one in that Country.

I mentioned to Mr S. H——y Your thanks for a second offer of some Jama Rum, & your readiness to make him some acceptable return. I put in as from you, a hint for the release of Captain C——m, who has been again taken & about this period is expected to arrive at Dartmo in a privateer which Mr H——y partly owns.[5] I told Him one good turn deserves another, & that you had by my recommendation got releasd from a french goal one of His own Captains about a year ago & for which He was very thankful.[6] If Mr. H——ys letter gets to Dartmo in time for the Captain of the Privateer before Captn. C——m is committed, I hope he will be releasd in consequence, but I fear if it gets to hand after Committment, there will be no hopes of liberating Him his name being so offensive.

3. Jean-Charles-Bernardin Charlot de La Grandville: XXXII, 299n. The enclosure was probably Sartine's letter agreeing to a passport for Mrs. Shrowdy; see BF's letter to her of July 13.

4. XXXII, 590–1. Digges had expected William Burnes's return from Paris: XXXII, 109–10, 620.

5. For the capture of Conyngham by the Dartmouth privateer, of which Samuel Hartley was a part owner, see XXXII, 361.

6. Possibly either Capt. Currie of the *Henry* or Capt. Colley of the *David:* XXX, 529n; XXXI, 376–7.

I observe what you say about the medal & have hinted to Dr. P—ce, Mr Paradise & Mr Jones that no further applications are to be made.[7] I rather wonder that the Portrait of the Bishop had not reachd You before the 25th. ulo. I think it was many weeks before that, that Mr Bowens of ostend acknowlegd the safe receipt of it & that it should be forwarded on. I have got our friend Mr W———t to promise the undertaking another portrait I solicited you for, I think by what we have got, & the picture in Miss Georgianas possession we may make something out of it.[8]

Mr. Hodgson has informd You about the ansr. of the Board, on seeing M Sartines Letter they desird Mr H to draw up a memorial stating the circumstances of the case & we are not without hopes, tho faint ones, that the Cartel may again go.[9]

Our friend David is quite desponding, & feels much for the want of wisdom in our Rulers here for not adopting any one measure that will lead to accomodation with America; He has been incessantly upon this, & I believe Am———n Indepe. would be the summit of His Wish.[1] So far from our wise heads thinking about, nothing but the extreem reverse is now talkd of. Since

7. The Royal Society medal that John Paradise and William Jones had urged be given to BF for his efforts on behalf of Capt. James Cook: XXXI, 448–9 and following. They were friends of Dr. Richard Price: XXX, 532.

8. The portrait of Jonathan Shipley, Bishop of St. Asaph, was made by his daughter Georgiana. It did not reach BF until early 1781: XXXII, 422, 432–3, 437. François (Frans)-Jacques-Arnould Bowens (or Bauwens) was born in Ostend in 1741. He was descended from a family that had emigrated from County Cork, Ireland. Baron Isidore de Stein d'Altenstein, *Annuaire de la Noblesse de Belgique* (Brussels, 1860), pp. 264–5. Mr. W———t must have been Joseph Wright, who in 1782 would paint a likeness of BF: XIV, 149n. He had recently exhibited a portrait of his mother, Patience Wright: Sellers, *Franklin in Portraiture*, p. 143.

9. William Hodgson had not as yet written BF about the reaction of the Board of Sick and Wounded to Sartine's failure to deliver French-held prisoners in exchange for Americans in British prisons: XXXII, 236–8. As there was an insufficient number of American-made prisoners in France, the British-American prisoner exchange had come to a halt. On July 3 Hodgson transmitted to the Board Sartine's explanation of why the last British cartel ship had to return empty (XXXII, 305–6, 556). In his covering letter, dated July 4 (APS), Hodgson suggested that the British send American prisoners to France on credit or send them to New York for exchange in America.

1. Wishful thinking on Digges's part as David Hartley was not yet prepared to accept American independence. For his latest effort to arrange a compromise peace see his letter of July 17, below.

the affair of Chas. Town nothing but unconditional submission is talkd of. I do assure you Sir the great folks here look as much now upon America being in their power as they did the first day General Gage was sent to Boston. Nothing can exceed the infatuation. They look upon No Caroa. and Virga. as already theirs, that Maryland must follow, & they give out with confidence they have a considerable body of the people in Connecticut now in Arms for England. Since the quelling of the late Riots & Insurrections,[2] & restord a little peace and order to a Capital that was for five whole days in possession of a Mob, they Think they can subdue the whole world. They Brag still of being masters of the Sea in the West Indies, (I dare say they will next claim a dominion over the air) That Rodney will infallably intercept & ruin the Spanish fleet, that Tearney's Squadrn. is a sure & easy prey to Adml Graves, & that the Channel fleet is to shut up the port of Brest & keep the Spanish fleet from again joining &ca &ca.[3]. This is not only the language, but seemingly the firm beleif of the Court, the Ministry, & their out Runners; The flame has spread in the City, & many thinking people are led to a beleif of it & are actually purchasing pell-mell in the Stocks, which have risen upwards of five pr. Cent lately. There is no standing against the present torrent of folly & I lean towards it in order to make my exultation the greater when some future day of gloom & sorrow may turn up. We may expect great & important news both from Ama & the Wt Indies in a few days; If it does not turn up different from what is generally, nay almost universally, expected here I shall be very much deceivd. There is no arrivals or news from any part of Ama. since the Despatches fm. Chas Town, to keep us the more in the dark as to the state of things in that Country, not one private Letter was recd. by the last packets.

It seems as if the New York fleet,[4] wch was ready abot 2

2. The Gordon Riots of June 2–9: XXXII, 501–2.

3. The British failed to follow up their recent victories. They proved unable to intercept either Admiral Solano's Spanish fleet en route to the West Indies or Admiral Ternay's squadron bringing Rochambeau to America or to prevent the ships of the Brest fleet from sailing individually to Cadiz: Dull, *French Navy*, pp. 187–94.

4. A vital provisions convoy which did not leave Cork until August 14: Bowler, *Logistics*, p. 135n. Digges had predicted that it would sail in mid-June: XXXII, 423.

months ago, will not be permitted to sail till we hear the actual destination of Monsr Teirnay; abot. 60 Ships compose it, & twenty or 30 others are intended for the West Indies by a Convoy very soon.

I am Sir Your obt. Servt JOHN THOMPSON

12 July 1780

From Samuel Huntington LS: American Philosophical Society

Sir Philadelphia July 12. 1780

I take the Liberty of introducing to your favourable Notice the Honble James Searle Esquire the Bearer.[5]

This Gentleman hath been for some Time past, and now is a Member of Congress for the Commonwealth of Pennsylvania, and comes to Europe charged with Business of Consequence from that State.

The Honour that State hath conferred upon him, and the Confidence they have placed in him, render it needless for me to add any Thing in Support of his Character.[6]

Mr Searle will present you with Bills to the Amount of one thousand Pounds Sterling drawn by Order of Congress, in Favour of the President & Supreme Executive Council of Pennsylvania, upon their Minister at the Court of Versailes.[7]

---

5. James Searle (1733–1797), a Philadelphia merchant and member of the Pa. militia, was elected a delegate to the Continental Congress in November, 1778. He was generally allied with the radical Lee-Adams faction and served on several committees, including the committee of commerce (XXXI, 520n). Sent to Europe to obtain a loan for Pennsylvania, he left Chester on July 14 and arrived in Brest on Sept. 1: Arthur Ervin Brown, "A Philadelphia Merchant in 1768–1791," *PMHB*, XIX (1895), 399; Mildred E. Lombard, "James Searle: Radical Businessman of the Revolution," *PMHB*, LIX, (1935), 286–7; *DAB*. For Searle's mission see Smith, *Letters*, XV, 412, 421, 438–9; William B. Reed, *Life and Correspondence of Joseph Reed* (2 vols., Philadelphia, 1847), II, 450–65.

6. Above the following two paragraphs BF has written in red ink the notation "N° 3 / Extract of a Letter &c" and marked them in the margin.

7. Congress on July 6 directed the Board of Treasury to supply the bills: *JCC*, XVII, 590.

I lament the Necessity which hath occasioned so many Draughts upon you and hope the Affairs of these United States may soon be regulated in such Manner as to prevent the like Necessity in future.

I presume the Committee of foreign Affairs (to whose Department it belongs) have transmitted you from Time to Time the needful Information, and material Intelligence relating to American Affairs.[8]

The Particulars of the Seige and Capitulation of Charlestown you will doubtless receive before this comes to hand.

Your Letters of the 30th of September, 4th of October & 17th of October 1779 and 4th of March 1780 have been received and laid before Congress.[9]

I have the Honour to be with every Sentiment of Respect and Esteem Sir your most obedt hbble Servt   SAM. HUNTINGTON

The Honble Benjamin Franklin Esqr

Endorsed: President Huntington's Recommendation of Mr Searle, &c July 12. 1780

From John Paul Jones

LS: American Philosophical Society; AL (draft): Library of Congress

Honored and dear Sir,   L'Orient July 12th 1780

Your Letter of the 5th Currt. gives me more pleasure than any other I have had the Honor to receive from you; because it affords me the Strongest proof of your affection. I observe however with regret that my Letter to Doctor Bancroft has given you offence: It was a private Letter, and as far as I can remember, is the only one I have ever written mentioning your Name, that I would not have freely Submitted to your perusal.

I need not remind you that I never sought after the Command of the Alliance;— But when I had taken it upon me, not only in

8. The committee had written BF two letters on the previous day. The most recent extant letters prior to these were from committee members William Churchill Houston (February 9) and James Lovell (February 24 and May 4): XXXI, 466–8, 520–2; XXXII, 354–5.

9. See XXX, 420–1, 463–74, 547–50; XXXII, 36–42.

Obedience to yours, but to the Orders of the King as here in enclosed;[1] it was natural for me to expect to have my authority Supported; and you know that Captain Landais Letter to you in the latter end of May[2] for orders to re-take the Command of the Alliance, and which, when you shewed it to me, gave me the first intimation of his Ideas on that Head, was sufficiently alarming to have required the immediate Interposition of Government.— Before I took the Step of coming up to Paris, in April, I had the Alliance compleatly refitted and, with near four hundred Men on Board, was ready for the Sea. The Men and Officers absolutely refused to weigh Anchor, before they received Satisfaction respecting their Wages and Prize Money.— The strongest Letters from the Parties concerned, and from indifferent Persons, had been frequently written to Paris on the Subject and had produced no effect.— M. de Chaumont had turned a Deaf Ear, made a thousand insignificant difficulties, and given as many Unmeaning Promises.—[3] In this Situation my Journey to Paris was on my part Undertaken with great reluctance and in complyance with the pressing Advice of every American Gentleman here except Mr. Lee and Mr. Cummings[4] whom I did not Consult.— You did not appear to disapprove of my Journey; and if I had not been sent back empty handed at last, no Revolt would have happened in the Alliance; But soon after my return when the people saw that they had no certainty to receive their Just dues before their departure; Mr. Lee found means to persuade them that I had Joined with you and Chaumont &c. to amuse and defraud them; and that as they had been decoyed into *privateers* Under the Title of Continental Ships, they could hope for no Justice from our hands, but must go to America and make their Complaint to Congress; For if they did not revolt from my

---

1. BF had recommended, but not specifically ordered Jones to take command of the *Alliance:* XXX, 537–8. French Ambassador La Vauguyon, however, had ordered Jones to take over the *Alliance*, so a French officer could take command of the *Serapis:* XXXI, 120n, 150n. The enclosure may have been a copy of those orders: Bradford, *Jones Papers,* reel 4, no. 876.

2. XXXII, 439–40.

3. XXXII, 213–14n. In 1779 Chaumont had been in charge of outfitting Jones's squadron for sea: XXIX, 240n.

4. The merchant James Cuming.

Command I would certainly carry them on another expedition and perhaps they would not See America during the War.— Under such circumstances I am convinced that Tourville[5] himself could not have prevented their Plot from succeeding; And I believe you will find I have not been to Blame in that Respect.— The Armament of the Ariel is far advanced.— I shall embark as much as possible of the powder Arms and Clothing, and I could be ready for Sea within ten Days if I had a sufficient number of Seamen.— Four Men only have arrived here from St. Malo.— One of these an Officer, I have sent back this morning (Mr. Jones Wheeler)[6] with the necessary Letters to engage Thirty or Forty American Seamen that He says he left behind Him. Should these Men Arrive I shall be ready to Sail a few days afterwards. They will I believe require some advance Wages; and Writing or obtaining from Court a strong Letter to the Commissary at St. Malo might have a good effect. It is my duty to inform you that the Officers and Men of the Bon homme Richard who are now doing their duty on board the Ariel appear to expect payment of their Wages and Prize Money some days at least before they Sail. M. de Montplaisir this moment assures me that M. de Chaumont has not yet given Him any possible means of Paying on that Account a single Sol.— I mention this, that I may not be reflected Upon for the obvious Consequences. I beg leave to Assure you that I will pay the greatest Attention to your kind Advice; and that it shall ever be my highest Ambition to merit Your Affectionate Friendship— being with the highest Esteem and Respect, Honored and dear Sir your most Obliged and most Obedient Servant

JNO P JONES

[*In Jones's hand:*] His Excellency B. Franklin Esqr. American Minister Plenipotentiary in France at Court.

Notation: John P Jones L'Orient July 12. 1780

5. Anne-Hilarion de Cotentin, comte de Tourville (1642–1701) was the most celebrated French admiral of the 17th century: Larousse.

6. Jonathan Wheeler was a gunner aboard the *Ariel* who later deserted: John S. Barnes, ed., *The Logs of the Serapis-Alliance-Ariel under the Command of John Paul Jones, 1779–1780* (New York, 1911), p. 20; Bradford, *Jones Papers*, reel 6, no. 1259. Jones's orders to him are reproduced in Bradford, *Jones Papers*, reel 6, no. 1153.

From Achille-Guillaume Lebègue de Presle

ALS: American Philosophical Society

ce 12 juillet 80

Jai Lhonneur de prevenir votre Excellence que je crois avoir trouvé une maison tres convenable au jeune Medecin Americain.[7] Mr Desault chirurgien[8] qui fait des cours de chirurgie avec succès consent a le prendre en pension et a lui faciliter Létude de la langue francoise, ainsi que de la chirurgie theorique et pratique, comme il a deja fait pour mr lunn de Philadelphie qu'il a eu chez lui. On m'a rendu le meilleur temoignage de la societé de mr Desault. Il est doux, honnete, et a une parente qui est avec lui. Il demande douze cent livres de Pension. Comme il n'a point de chambre libre, il faudra en prendre une dans le voisinage; et j'en ai vu plusieures a louer dans la maison voisine, a 12 et 15 livre par mois, toute meublée.

Sa demeure est, comme le desire ce jeune medecin, tres près de l'hotel dieu et des Ecoles de chirurgie ou il y a un petit hopital.[9] C'est dans la rue des Lavandieres a peu de distance du College

7. Almost certainly Dr. John Foulke (XXXII, 283n). In an undated letter he thanks WTF for "the civil part he has taken in procuring the appartments at Paris." APS.

8. Pierre-Joseph Desault (1744–1796), the great French surgeon, was important in the development of clinical instruction of medicine and surgery. A member of the Collège et Académie royale de chirurgie and a *démonstrateur* of anatomy and surgery at the Ecole pratique de dissection, Desault also taught privately in an amphitheater at his residence. On Oct. 8 the *Jour. de Paris* announced that Desault's course would begin. See *DBF;* Charles Coury, *L'enseignement de la Médecine en France des origines à nos jours* (Paris, 1968), pp. 106–7, 150; Pierre Huard, "L'Enseignement médico-chirurgical," in René Taton et al., eds., *Enseignement et diffusion des sciences en France au XVIIIe siècle* (Paris, 1964), pp. 224, 225.

9. The Hôtel-Dieu, where Desault conducted the surgical clinic, was the main general hospital. Until 1878 it was located on the south side of the *parvis* of Notre-Dame. In 1775 the Ecoles de chirurgie were moved to new quarters just off rue de la Harpe, buildings now occupied by the Ecole de Médecine: Hillairet, *Rues de Paris,* I, 461; II, 235–6; Coury, *L'enseignement de la Médecine,* p. 94; Charles C. Gillispie, *Science and Polity in France at the End of the Old Regime* (Princeton, 1980), pp. 249–50; Huard, "Enseignement médico-chirugical," p. 197n.

de beauvais,[1] et de la rue st jacques. Comme c'est mon quartier je Souhaite que cette pension convienne dans L'esperance de pouvoir temoigner au jeune Americain par mes services, combien je desire de faire des choses qui Soient agreables a votre excellence.

Je suis avec respect votre tres humble serviteur
LEBEGUE DE PRESLE
Rue st jacques la seconde porte cochere
au dessus de la rue des mathurins

Endorsed: Ansd

Notation: Le Begue de Presle. 12 juillet 1780.

To Mrs. ———— Shrowdy

Copy: Library of Congress

Madam,   Passy, July 13th. 1780

Messrs. Foulke and Fox[2] having signified to me your Desire of going to England in some of the Cartel Ships from L'Orient and requested me to obtain for you, Monsr. De Sartine's Permission.— Herewith I have the honour of Sending you a Letter from that Minister to Monsr. de La Granville,[3] by which you will find he has been pleased to grant your Request, and has given Orders accordingly.

With great Respect, I have the honour to be Madam Your most obedient and most humble Sert.

Mrs. Shrowdy.

1. In the rue Jean-de-Beauvais, where the Faculté de médecine was housed in the former quarters of the Ecole de droit: Gillispie, *Science and Polity,* p. 216; Hillairet, *Rues de Paris,* I, 672.
2. The two young Philadelphians John Foulke and George Fox had come to France in the spring. They met JW in Lorient and it may have been there that they learned of Mrs. Shrowdy's request: XXXII, 283n, 313–14, 562.
3. See Sartine's letter of July 11.

From E. Jackson [Edward Jackson Jones][4]

ALS: American Philosophical Society

Paris 13th. July 1780.

A very near Relation of Dr. Cadwalladers[5] of Philadelphia presents his respectfull compliments to His Excellency Benjamin Franklyn Esqr. and wishes to have the honor of an Audience— He has taken the Liberty of sending by the bearer, the London papers from the 20th. Ulto. to the 4th. Inst.

E. JACKSON
à L'Hotel de Yorck Rüe Jacob Fauxbourg st. Germain

Addressed: A Son Excellence Benjamin Franklyn / Ministre Plenipotiniare / des Etats Unies de L'Amerique / Septentrionale / a Passy

Notation: Jackson Paris. no date

From Jean de Neufville & fils

ALS:[6] American Philosophical Society

Honour'd Sir!   Amsterdam the 13th July 1780.

Though with some reluctance we take the Liberty to trouble your Excellency again, she will excuse us we hope as saving the reputation and the Credit of the United States is our only motive.[7]

4. In a memoir enclosed with his next letter, that of Aug. 11, below, he calls himself Edwd. Jones. Later he signs himself E.J. Jones; see his letter published under Aug. 18.

5. The late Dr. Thomas Cadwalader (1, 209n), whom BF knew for some fifty years. Cadwalader's maternal grandfather Edward Jones (1645?–1737) had five sons, one of whom may have been the writer's relative: *DAB* (under Cadwalader); *PMHB*, XVII (1893), 235.

6. In the hand of Jean de Neufville, as are the other ALS from the firm in this volume.

7. The Dutch firm had accepted a dozen bills of exchange on behalf of Henry Laurens, who was reportedly en route to the Netherlands to negotiate a loan. When he did not arrive, the firm wrote several concerned letters to BF, who in response assured them Laurens would resolve their problems on his arrival: XXXII, 441, 459–60, 473–4, 480–1, 534–5, 571, 589–90.

Our Laws do not admitt any bills to be only enregistrated when not Accepted they are generally protested, and So they must. We thought however upon previous consultation and the extraordinary situation of the Cause of Mr Laurens absence that most of the bearers would be satisfied that we should give an attestation when each bill had been presented, on the hint Your Excy were pleased to give us about it, and we tried it severall times since agreable to the inclosed modell;[8] butt farr from being satisfied therewith they send all a Notary to have the bills protested in due form today again a house doing bussiness even for the Convenience pretended to do the Same and Send the protest to Londn. so no choice being left, we have again Accepted.

About Mr Laurens being retired early from Charlestown Congress we were informed received proper intelligence, butt none as farr as we know about her departure. So methodes absolutely must be found in Europe, if we intend to show regard for the honour of the United States. It is miraculous mostly that by so many Vessells as already arrived there hath been no greater quantity remitted, as which we could resolve to stop a vessell which gott a quantity on board Distroy'd her papers and the other which brings the duplicates was not yett heard of. Every day however we tremble now to see this or any other Vessells from the Continent or our own Colonies Arrive with a larger quantity; and we think your Excellency can find no fault nor shall we to be blamed before Congress, if we do not go any further now by want of any Certainty of rembursements. We thought however, we should again propose to your Excellency wether for a remitted summ of one or two hundred thousand Gilders we might not draw in the manner formerly proposed. This might perhaps go a great Lenght and we have some hopes that the Hone. john jay at Madrid if it laid in his power would also lend us assistance if such a way could be agreed upon.[9] If this should still apear not practicable to your Excellency then we fell on the idea of trying a Loan. We have gott the honour to represent verbally and by letters that something might be expected in that

8. We have not located Neufville's enclosed model.
9. They wrote Jay for assistance: Morris, *Jay: Revolutionary*, pp. 763–4.

way. We should not have mentiond this if the Cause had not been so urgent, and perhaps your Excellency will have other measures to prescribe which would answer the Same purpose which we confess not to know, for Your Excellency had already mentiond that she had given up all idea of making loans in Holland,[1] and by what hath happend before this prudence was not butt ruled by experience.

We may say however that the American spirit here hath been encouraged severall times since by some favourable events and that with some private Persons we should from time to time have made up Some money which now could have been of Service. Since the capture of Charlestown there should be certainly not many in favour of this entreprise, butt those expectations are momentaneall, and every opportunity may be adopted. We never could yett engage positively for any Summ at once we can do it best again in this moment, nor can we try any thing butt upon a proper power. All other ways for Securing the money for the payment of those bills should they be closed. We flatter our selfs however that we could herewith prevent the worse. It should at least not faile by want of endeavour nor should we en-trusted there with expose the Credit of Congress to new risqs. To assure your Excellency that we rather should leave every-thing undone then to make that suffer again we can not express equally to our feelings; and here of persuaded by our selfs we have made a generall plan fr. Such a power. We take the liberty to inclose it.[2] We will only mention that though it extends to two million we think we must make the first triale for much less. This must be foreseen with prudence and we engage to give the most exact Account of our proceedings; the terms your Excy formerly

1. xxx, 540. The firm had earlier attempted with little success to raise a 1,500,000 florin loan for Congress in the Netherlands: xxviii, 629–31; xxix, 101–2n, 151, 586–7, 655, 661–2, 692–5, 759; xxx, 28, 465–6, 589–90.

2. At the National Archives is a five-page memoir in Neufville's hand la-beled "Copy of those papers, which we have send to His Excellency B Franklin, &ca. &ca., concerning a Loan of Two Million Holld. Currcy. to be made in Holland." It includes a "Formule d'Autorisation du Congress" and a "Formule d'obligation de Son Excellence B Franklin . . . "; copies of the two "formules" are at the APS. This memoir, however, may instead relate to Neufville's February, 1779, negotiations with BF as it also discusses a title that he had wished for his firm: xxviii, 629–31.

fixed us were 10 p Ct. viz 1 p Ct. Annum.[3] We found those rather low then, and so they Should be still may they be exceeded we wish to know to facilitate the dispatch of any Summ of consequence, if not we will try what may be done, for farr from viewing to gain by it only, this our proposall only tends to cover the bills which provisionally might suffer.

Hath all our endeavours since we enter'd into so large a Scale of bussiness as to view at the Independence of America and a conection between both countries been extended to promote this. We should be sorry to fall short in it at any instance, may your Excellency be assured thearoff[?] as of the most perfect and extended Regard, with which we have the honour to be always Honourd Sir Your Excellencys most devoted and most Obedient humble Servants   JOHN DE NEUFVILLE & SON

From Jean-Baptiste Le Roy ALS: American Philosophical Society

Vendredy 14 Juillet [1780][4]

J'ai vu, mon Illustre Docteur, M. De Maillebois[5] et comme vous lui avez donné le choix du Jour il a pris Jeudy prochain 20 de ce mois. Ainsi ce jour là nous aurons l'honneur de vous voir et de causer avec vous. Je m'ennuye d'étre privé depuis Si Long tems de ce plaisir et de cet Avantage. Recevez les Sinceres assurrances de tous les Sentimens d'attachement que Je vous ai voués pour La Vie   LE ROY

P.S. Si par hazard mon Illustre docteur il arrivoit quelqu'obstacle dans cet Arrangement Vous voudrez bien m'en prevenir, afin que J'en avertisse M. De Maillebois. Mille complimens Je vous prie a Monsieur Votre petit fils.

---

3. BF had earlier agreed to pay a 1 percent commission to either Neufville or the rival firm of Horneca, Fizeaux & Cie.: XXVII, 322; XXVIII, 631n; XXX, 465–6.

4. The only time during BF's stay when July 14 fell on a Friday.

5. The comte de Maillebois had served with BF, Le Roy, and others on a commission appointed by the Académie des sciences to investigate Jean-Paul Marat's experiments on the nature of fire: XXIX, 105–7, 213, 311.

Addressed: a Monsieur / Monsieur Franklin / Ministre Plénipotentiaire des / treize Etats unis de LAmérique / en Son hôtel / a Passy

Notation: Le Roy 14 Juillet 1780.

From Robert Mease

ALS: American Philosophical Society

Sir   L'Orient July 14. 1780

I am this day favoured with a letter from Mr. Jonathn Williams, desiring me to give you what information I am able, respecting the comparative value of hard money, bills of Exchange and the circulating currency of America, at the time I left Philadelphia.[6]

In compliance with his request, permit me Sir, to inform you That interest bills on the Commissioners and those drawn by Mr. Holker the French Consul at 30 days sight sold at 45 paper dollars for one dollar of 5 livers Tournois[7] and were considered to be scarse specie being more negociable both at Home and in the West Indias, and the credit of bills not well established bore an advance generally of 15 to one more than the bills above mentioned, to which may be added that it had chiefly got into such hands as necessity or a great advance only could call it from, and had been in some instances up to 70 for one and higher about two or three weeks before my departure at which time it had fallen to 55 a 60, and it was generally believed that paper money must still appreciate through the late measures taken for that purpose,[8] (though much complained of) and that the quantity in circulation was verry inadeqte. to the necessaries of Life and the prices of Goods. Bills upon London were to be had sometimes and

6. Mease left Philadelphia in May. By June 27 he was in Lorient and had forwarded to BF letters and newspapers that he carried from America: XXXII, 336, 609.

7. This is the same exchange rate for bills on Europe that Pelatiah Webster gave in May: XXXII, 339.

8. Congress' March 18 devaluation of the currency. The ratio of paper currency to specie was indeed about 60 to 1: XXXII, 339; Ferguson, *Power of the Purse*, p. 32.

were sold much about the old rate which was reduced into the present circulation at its depreciated state. That is £160 the rate of Exchange for £100 Sterling[9] and that sum multiplied by 60 the present state of depreciation gives £9600 for £100 Steg. Some time before I came away I was asked more, but it had got lower afterwards and it was the prevalent opinion that it must of necessity still grow better. The necessaries of life rose(?) from 80 to 120 of the former prices and imported goods from 150 to 300.— I intend shortly to pay a visit to Paris when I propose having the pleasure of paying my respects to you in person.—

I have the honour to be Sir verry respectfully Your most obedient Humble Servant   ROBERT MEASE

Addressed: A Monsieur / Monsieur Franklin / Ministre plenipotentiare des Etats Unis / De l'amérique a la Cour de france / A Passy près paris

From Jonathan Williams, Sr.

ALS: American Philosophical Society

Hond sr   Boston July 14th. 1780

I take this opportunity to Send you a small Box of Crown Soap that I Recd from your Sister Who has been here On a Visit,[1] is now return'd in good helth & Spirits, & I belive more happy now then I ever new her. I repeated to her that I Stood ready to advance her any money she stood in need of agreeable to your Orders her greatfull hart was effected. She told me that she hoped the Income of the house would be soficient.

Notwithstanding all discouragement our Political State grows Better. The Loss of Charlestown was indeed a disagreeable Circumstance but the arival of our Fleet at Rhode Island makes up

9. Roughly the same rate of exchange for Pennsylvania pounds sterling on London that prevailed at the beginning of the war: John J. McCusker, *Money and Exchange in Europe and America, 1600–1775: a Handbook* (Chapel Hill, N.C., 1978), p. 186.

1. Jane Mecom went to Boston to visit her granddaughter Jenny: Van Doren, *Franklin-Mecom*, pp. 201, 203; I, lxi.

for it, now we are all, more then ever, through the Continent in high Spirits, & do & Shall exert ourselves to give our Enemies a decive blow & I hope Soon finish the Blooddy Contest, two days ago One of the Transports ariv'd in to our harbour yesterday Landed the Troopes as they march'd up State Street they Passd through the Acclamations of the people they had three Cheeres by a great multitude as they Passd.[2] I think they look'd full as well & behav'd much better then I ever saw Britians that is the Officers did not Look so much Like Tyrants nor the Soldiers so much like Slaves. We are all well my Wife & Children Joine in Duty & Love to you & yours Belive me Ever Your Dutyfull Nephew and most Hble servant JONA. WILLIAMS

N.B. My Only Brothers onley Son is dead[3]

Addressed: His Excellency Benjamin Franklin Esqr / In / Passy / France / per Capt Sampson[4]

To John Ross

Copy: Library of Congress

Dear Sir   Passy July 15. 1780

I have received your favour of the 9. July.[5] I should be very glad to have it in my Power to satisfy every body, and send all the Supplies immediately to America, which the late Disturbance on board the Alliance has in a great measure prevented. I understand that the Alliance would carry a considerable Part of the Stores, and the Ariel the Remainder, but this first Ship is gone with little or nothing, and I now hear that the other is too small to take what is left.

The Court of France who have assisted us with the Ariel, will certainly expect her to be employed to carry out the Supplies

2. The day after their landing in Boston the troops began marching to Providence: *Boston Gazette, and the Country Journal,* July 24, 1780.

3. John Williams' son Jonathan (I, lviin; XXIX, 307n).

4. Simeon Samson of the *Mars;* see our annotation of Samuel Cooper's July 25 letter to BF, below.

5. Missing. For Ross's attempts to have his goods placed on ships bound to America see XXXI, 499, 501, 524; XXXII, 18, 284–6, 364–5.

they have also assisted us with, in Preference to any other Goods; The most essential of these Supplies are the Arms and Powder, and M. Moylan informs me these are as much as the Ariel will carry, there will therefore remain no Question whether to prefer your Goods or the Cloathing made in this kingdom, tho' if their should be any Room left, I confess it appears to me that the latter should be shipped first.— Methinks you may be able to persuade the Customs-House Officers to permit you to land the Goods under an obligation to reship them as soon as you can find occasion, and when I can get the other Supplies away, I will endeavour to make Room for yours; at present the Ariel must be dispatched with what She can carry, and I can only recommend to you to deposit the Goods till a Ship is procured on freight, unless you can find some Vessel at L'Orient which can take them in, and go under the Ariels Convoy.

M. John Ross.

From Alexis Judlin[6]   ALS: American Philosophical Society

Monsieur   Ce Samdi, 15 juillet 1780
    Comme je n'ai pas eu lhonneur de vous trouver chez vous jai laissé une lettre de la part d'un Mr: de Votre Connoissance,[7] au quel vous avés permi, de vous faire peindre, comme cela vous serés trop incomode de vous transporter chez moi et que je ne pourés point non plus vous donner des seances chez vous, Si vous pouviés me Confier pour quelque jour un portrait de vous qui fut resemblant jaurès le plaisir de Contenter celui qui desir votre portrait vous pouvés être assuré Monsieur que j'aurés tout

6. A miniaturist who had exhibited at the Royal Academy of London from 1773 to 1776, and who would have several pieces in the Parisian Salons of 1791 and 1793: Sellers, *Franklin in Portraiture*, pp. 135–6, 317–19. Judlin had been commissioned in the spring to paint a portrait of BF for Simon-Pierre Fournier le jeune. BF had agreed to sit for the artist as a special favor to Fournier, but explained that he would have preferred Judlin to copy the Duplessis portrait: XXXII, 349–50, 362–3. As it happened, BF was never at home when Judlin had called and, as this letter makes clear, the artist was now giving up hope of obtaining a sketch from nature.
    7. Fournier; the letter has not been found.

76

les soins possible pour le portrait que vous me pretterés,[8] j'ai lhonneur d'etre Monsieur Votre tres humble serviteur

JUDLIN
peintre De la Reine

Addressed: a Monsieur / Monsieur Franklin / à Passy

Notation: Judlin 15 Juillet; Paris 1780.

From Schweighauser

Extract:[9] Archives du Ministère des affaires étrangères

[July 15, 1780]

Having just received Advice from Messrs. Puchelberg & Company[1] that the Alliance Sailed the 8th. Instant, I seize this Post to acquaint you therewith. *Notwithstanding the positive orders I gave to the above House not to furnish any longer to that Frigate,* they write me that they have been obliged to continue, no other House there having presented itself to do it.

Extract of a Letter from J.D. Schweighauser of Nantes, dated, July 15. 1780 to B. Franklin.

From Samuel Cooper   ALS: American Philosophical Society

My dear Sir,   Boston July 17th. 1780.

I wrote you not long since by the Rambler from Salem, and the Pallas from Newbury Port[2] and have now too much Reason

8. We do not know which of the Duplessis portraits was lent, as Judlin's miniature has not been located (see Sellers, *Franklin in Portraiture*, p. 319). He completed it by Aug. 15; see Fournier's letter of that date.

9. The extract was made in 1783; see our annotation of Gourlade and Moylan, July 10, above.

1. It was Schweighauser, acting as American commercial agent in Nantes, who had appointed Puchelberg in 1778 to oversee American affairs at nearby Lorient: XXVII, 59, 62n.

2. One of these vessels may have carried Cooper's only extant recent letter, that of May 23 (XXXII, 414–16). There were a number of vessels named *Rambler;* the *Pallas* was a 14–gun brigantine commanded by Hector McNeill: Allen, *Mass. Privateers,* pp. 232, 247–9.

to fear that the Vessel in which Mr Austin sailed from hence the latter End of Jany, or the Beginning of Feby, is lost, as we have hitherto received no Account of it: By that Gentleman I wrote you largely.[3]

This will be delivered to you by Mr Bromfield,[4] Son of Henry Bromfield Esqr, whose respectable Family and Connections, and whose Reputation not only as a Merchant, but from the public offices he has so worthily sustained, you are not unacquainted with: His Brother Mr Bromfield late Merchant in London,[5] and the Frowns he received from the Ministry upon Account of his distinguished Attachment to [*torn:* the?] American Cause, which obliged him to leave England, must also [*torn:* be?] known to you. The young Gentleman by whom I write, and who is much esteemed here, goes to England to look after his Father's Property combined there with his Uncle's; from whence he wishes to transfer it in the most advantageous Manner to France, where also, he has some important Accounts of his Father to settle. From your Philanthropy, and Inclination to secure the Property of every good Subject of the United States, I doubt not of your Readiness kindly to afford him your Countenance and aid in every Measure proper to be taken on these Occasions. This will be a particular Favor to a very deserving Gentleman and Family, for whom a Number of your Friends here are much interested.

I am Sir, with every Sentiment of Respect and Friendship, Your most obedient and very humble Servant

SAMUEL COOPER

Addressed: His Excellency Benjamin Franklin Esqr. / Minister Plenipotentiary from the United / States of America. / At the Court of Versailles.

Notation: Dr. Cooper 17 July 1781

3. Jonathan Loring Austin had recently arrived in France: XXXII, 528. We do not know of any letter from Cooper that he carried.

4. Henry Bromfield, Jr. (XXVII, 503n), the son of a Boston merchant. In 1768 his father had taken him to England and placed him under the supervision of his uncle Thomas: Daniel D. Slade, "The Bromfield Family," *New England Hist. and Geneal. Register,* XXVI (1872), 141–3.

5. For Thomas Bromfield see XXI, 157n, 216; XXII, 161n.

From Thomas Digges

ALS: Historical Society of Pennsylvania

Dr. Sir   Monday July 17. 1780

Since my letter to you of the 12th. I have seen Jas Garnet[6] who is loungeing & going so idly about the Streets, & whom I have detected in so many lies, that I think it necessary to apprise you of Him in order that Monsieur Chamont may be warnd not to pay too implicit faith to what Garnet may write. He told me had drawn two Bills on Him before He gave me the one for 12 Guins abot. the 8th of last month: as he told me he was taken in a Ship of Mr Chamonts & carryd into Ireld. & that He was sure of getting the command of another vessel of Mr Chamonts now fitting out, I readily lent him the money to get away, without wch He seemingly could not have movd. At Ostend He took up eight Guis [guilders] more in my name of Mr Bowens, went as He tells me from thence to Dunkirke, then post to Nantes, & so back via Ostend to London, which He had not possibly time to do. When I taxd him hence he prevaricatd & lyed most abominably, but persisted He returnd on accot of yr. sending Him an order to embark on board P. Jones, whom He said He did not like well enough to go to Sea with. I wrote to you & Mr A. by Him under date the 8th June or 7th, I do not recollect which.[7] I am much afraid He sacrificd my letters, & when you have an oppery [opportunity] should be glad to know whether yrs. got to hand or not. I fear I shall be 20 Guins out of pocket by Him, but prudence obliges me to keep up an outward civility, as yet I have not heard whether His bill on Monr Chamont was paid or not. It will be no new matter to me to get it protested, for accept the one you paid me drawn by a Dr. Jas Brehon[8] I have never had a bill paid, nor any remittance from any one of my Countrymen passing hence.

In my letter of the 12th. I mentiond the mode I had used towards helping Capt. C——m; We have no answers yet, but not

6. James Barnett, Jr., whom Digges had sent in June to deliver letters to Passy: xxxii, 501n.

7. He had written JA on the 8th, BF on the 10th: xxxii, 500–3; *Adams Papers*, IX: 392–400.

8. XXIX, 530, 577, 666, 701; XXXI, 356.

destitute of hopes but we may succeed. Capt. M——y[9] has also had fresh hints given Him.

I have good reason to think this will be put into the Post Office at Ostend tomorrow morning (Tuesday) and by that means will most likely inform you sooner than advices by the Regular post from London that a mail in 37 days from Jama. gives an accot. that The Expedition from that Island to the Spanish main Commanded by Kemble, but generally calld Dallings Expedn had succeeded so far to take Fort St. Juan on a River of that name not far from Carthagena or rather in the quarter of Nicarauga Lake.[1] No particulars are yet transpird, but the clamour which is usual on every slight success is gone forth to a greater degree than for the fort Omoa.[2] It appears the Expedition got an easy footing near Cape Gracios a Dios towards the 20th April, & from thence proceeded up the River St. Juan to the Fort, before which they were near three weeks. Report says the Garrison offerd the sum of 4, million of Piasters as a ransom to the Place; (at 3 / 4 *d* ea [3*s*. 4*d*. each] is 660,000£ Ster). I dont believe the fee simple of the whole settlement was worth so much. However, nothing less than millions are talkd of or will be beleivd— perhaps a few hours may paint the Expedition but as of trifling consequence. The same packet brings accots that the Spaniards & Indians have broke up the Settlement of English in the Black River in the Bay of Campeachy, & driven all the English to the Island of Rattan. This Jamaica Packet appears to have saild the begining of June,

9. Like Gustavus Conyngham, Capt. John Manley was confined at Old Mill Prison, Plymouth: XXXI, 418–19; XXXII, 320.

1. The July 18 issue of the *London Courant, and Westminster Chronicle* gave a detailed account of the news from Jamaica, from whence Gov. John Dalling sent some 1,000 regulars and volunteers to attack Nicaragua. Conspicuous for his gallantry during the expedition was young Horatio Nelson. The expedition eventually failed because of disease: Mackesy, *War for America,* pp. 335–6.

2. Omoa was captured during a 1779 expedition to Honduras, whose success was equally ephemeral: *ibid.,* pp. 275, 316–17, 335. The Black River settlement mentioned below was also in Honduras and the island of Rattan (Roatán) lies off it. The Bay of Campeachy (Bahía de Campeche), however, is well to the northwest, on the opposite side of the Yucatan peninsula: *ibid.,* p. 226.

had only 37 days passage, came thro the Windward passage with the whole Jamaica fleet, *upwards of two hundred Sail,* & left them in safety from the Cruisers in those Seas. This fleet is expected to arrive in a week or ten days. And in a little time after, one from the Leward Island of abot 120 Sail.

There is also a Packet from Chas. Town with a multitude of Letters, none of wch are yet out, but this packet cannot bring any material news, having saild but three days after the last publishd accots. from Genl Clinton; But the cry is that No Carolina has submitted to Engd. & that Virga will certainly do the like. I am yrs &ca &ca   W S. C[3]

Notation: July 17. 1780

From Henry Grand   ALS: American Philosophical Society

Monsieur   Paris ce 17 Juillet 1780.

J'ai eu lhonneur de remettre hier à Monsr. J. Williams la Notte des payemens qui me paroissoient regarder vôtre dépense particuliere depuis l'Epoque du 11 fevrier 1779. Les comptes que jai eu(?) Celui de vous remettre depuis des Etats Unis vous mettront à même de collationer cette Notte.[4]

Vous trouverez ci joint, Monsieur, le mandat que vous tirates Sur moi, conjointement avec Mr. Dean, le 2 Mars 1778, pour la somme de £3600.[5] & qui vous étoit échappée de la Mémoire vous voudrez bien avoir la bonté de me la renvoyer après vous en être Servi.

Je Suis avec Respect Monsieur Votre tres humble & très obeiss. Servitr   Hy. GRAND

Addressed: A Son Excellence / Monsieur Bn. Franklin / Passy

Notation: Grand Paris. 17e. Juillet 1780

3. William Singleton Church, one of Digges's aliases.
4. Henry Grand had been reviewing BF's accounts; see XXXII, 98–9.
5. Recorded in *Deane Papers,* III, 28. "Sur moi" refers to his father Ferdinand Grand, on whose behalf he was writing.

From David Hartley

Reprinted from William Temple Franklin, ed., *Memoirs of the Life and Writings of Benjamin Franklin, LL.D., F.R.S., &c ...* (3 vols., 4to, London, 1817–18), II, 266–8.

My dear friend,   London, July 17, 1780.

Inclosed I send you a copy of a conciliatory bill which was proposed in the house of commons on the 27th of last month. It was rejected.[6] You and I have had so much intercourse upon the subject of restoring peace between Great Britain and America, that I think there is nothing farther left to be said upon the subject. You will perceive by the general tenor of the bill that it proposes a general power to treat. It chalks out a line of negociation in very general terms. I remain in the sentiments which I ever have, and which I believe I ever shall entertain, viz. those of seeking peace upon honourable terms. I shall always be ready and most desirous to conspire in any measures which may facilitate peace. I am ever, your most affectionate,   D. HARTLEY.

From John Jay

Copy:[7] Library of Congress; AL (draft):[8] Columbia University Library

Dear Sir,   madrid 17 July 1780.

I have had the Pleasure of receiving your favours of the 13th. & 25th. of June last.[9]

After having recd. Part of the money lodged with marquis d'

---

6. Thomas Digges had already informed BF about the debate in Parliament on the proposed bill: XXXII, 622–3. The bill is printed along with Hartley's letter in William Temple Franklin, ed., *Memoirs*, II, 266–8. JA forwarded to the President of Congress an English translation of a French text of it that had appeared in the *Courier de l'Europe: Adams Papers*, IX, 500–1.

7. In L'Air de Lamotte's hand and we presume made from the recipient's copy. With it are copies of the enclosures.

8. With a number of deletions and interlineations, which are detailed in Morris, *Jay: Revolutionary*, pp. 793–6. We have used Jay's draft to correct Lamotte's errors in copying.

9. XXXII, 515–18, 592.

Yranda,[1] I sent for another Part, not chusing to receive the whole at once, and intending to leave in his hands the Balance due to you. I recd. for Answer that I might receive the whole, but not a Part. There was no Choice, and I recd. it accordingly. No Remittances from Congress have arrived. I have written to them on the subject,[2] and am now feeding on your Ballance choosing rather to do this, than humiliate my Constituents, by running them in Debt for my Bread here.

The Papers enclosed with this will make known to you the Exact State of affairs at this Court.[3] I have been permitted to accept Bills to amount of between ten and twelve thousand Dollars; and as the Court and particularly the Count de florida Blanca seem well disposed towards us, I hope this unpleasant Measure will terminate Well, these Papers should have been sent you before, but I have been long waiting for Count Montmorin's Courier, by whom I would rather transmit them than by the Post, for Reasons which you will be at no Loss to conjecture. From these Papers you will naturally conclude, that it is very far from being in my Power to afford M. Ross the aid mentioned in your Letters. On the Contrary, I find myself constrained to request the favor of you to lodge here, for M. Carmichael and myself, a further Credit, to enable us to receive what may be due on account of our Salaries— We shall otherwise be very soon in a very disagreable Situation.— To take up money from Individuals would not be eligible or reputable and it would not be prudent to trou-

1. For Jay's benefit BF in February had placed a credit of almost 20,000 *l.t.* with the marquis d'Yranda, a Madrid banker: XXXI, 513. Congress had made BF responsible for paying the salaries of Jay, Carmichael, JA, and Francis Dana: XXX, 543.

2. Jay to President of Congress Huntington, July 10 in Wharton, *Diplomatic Correspondence*, III, 843–4. See also his May 23 letter to Robert R. Livingston in Morris, *Jay: Revolutionary*, pp. 757–9.

3. Jay sent several enclosures: Floridablanca to Jay, Feb. 24, March 9, June 7, and June 20; Jay to Floridablanca, March 6, April 25, April 31 [*i.e.*, April 29], June [9], June 19, and June 22; Vergennes to Jay, March 13; Jay to Vergennes, May 9; and part of "Anecdote Historique" of Sir John Dalrymple. For the last of these see our annotation of Carmichael to BF, July 18; for Jay's correspondence since his arrival in Spain see Morris, *Jay: Revolutionary*, pp. 698–793, and Henry P. Johnston, ed., *The Correspondence and Public Papers of John Jay . . .* (4 vols., New York and London, 1890–93), I, 254–380.

ble Government, already a little sore about the Bills, with further Requisitions at present. I am also obliged to make this Request without being able to give you other assurances respecting the Time of Repayment, than that the proceeds of the first Remittances I may receive, shall be Applied to that In preference to any other Purpose, I cannot However think the time will be very distant, as Remittances may now be made in Bills of Exchange. But if I should be deceived and if the Servants of Congress here, must live a while on Credit they may seek and find with others, I think it most decent to recur to their ally. France I know has already done great things for us and is still making glorious Exertions—I am also sensible of your Difficulties and regret them, tho' I am happy in reflecting, that since they must exist, they have fallen into the Hands of one whose abilities and Influence will enable him to sustain and surmount them at a Court, which does not appear inclined to do things by Halves.

I should be surprised at the Treatment your Letters I sent to Nantes have met with, had I not experienced too many Strange things to be much surprised at any.

It is necessary you should be informed that the papers inclosed with this are known to Count Montmorin, and therefore are probably no secret to his Court. I am on good terms with the Count, whom I esteem as a man of abilities, and am pleased with as a friend to our Country. As France had interested herself deeply in our Cause, had done us essential Benefits, and had been requested to interpose her friendly offices for us here, I could not think of withholding from him all the Confidence which these Considerations dictate—especially as no personal Objections forbid it. To have conducted the Negociations with Finesse, unnecessary Secrecy, and equivocating Cunning was irreconciliable with my Principles of action, and with every Idea I have of Wisdom and Policy— In a Word, France and America are and I hope always will be allies; and it is the Duty of each Party to cultivate mutual Confidance and Cordiality. For my own Part while their Conduct continues fair, firm, and friendly, I shall not only remain strongly attached to their Interest and gratefull for their Benefits, but Shall endeavour to transmit the same Impressions to my Posterity.

Mrs. Jay is much Pleased with and Thanks you for the Print you was so kind as to send her. It is a striking Likeness. I find that

In France great men like their Predecessors of old, have their Bards— Yours seem to have mounted high mettled Pegasus, and to have been inspired (if Brydenes [Dryden's?] Doctrine be right) by electrised muses. Your Strictures are just, tho' a little Severe while there are young Telemachus, and fascinating Calypsos in the World, Fancies & Penns and Hearts will sometimes run Riot in Spite of the mentors now and then to be meet with.

Your Danish Correspondent was very civil as well as very much embarrassed, I am pleased with both Circumstances they indicate more Caution in future, but I fear the present Case will continue without Remedy.

I receive no Letters but what have passed thro' the fire once and often twice, and that is not the worst of it. For I am sure that some have been suppressed. I wish therefore that such as you may favor me with be sent either by Courier, or in some other Way that you may have Reason to confide in.

I am, Dear Sir, with very sincere Regard Your most obedient Servant   (signed) JOHN JAY

p.s. Mrs. Jay had a Daughter born the 9 Inst.[4] They are both well. Benevolent minds enjoy Events grateful to others, I cannot forbear telling you this little piece of news.

His Excellency B. Franklin Esqe.

From Benjamin Franklin Bache

ALS: American Philosophical Society

Mon cher grand Papa   Geneve Le 18 Juillet 1780
    J'ai reçu vôtre lettre[5] avec beaucoup de plaisir parcequ'il y avoit long temps que je n'avois eu de vos nouvelles et De celles de mon Papa et de ma maman. J'ai donné le gouter que vous m'avés acordé[6] et je vous en remercie beaucoup j'en fus très con-

---

4. Susan Jay, their second child, was born on July 9 and died on Aug. 4: Morris, *Jay: Revolutionary*, pp. 703, 710, 851.
    5. Missing.
    6. In June BFB had won the prize for the best translation from Latin into French. With his grandfather's permission he celebrated according to Genevan custom with a *goûter* for his classmates: XXXII, 559, 561.

tent ainsi que tous mes amis je ne vous envoie pas une pièce de dessin parce qu'elle n'est pas tout à fait finie mon maître étant malade.[7] Je languis beaucoup d'avoir fini mes classes pour pouvoir aller voir mon papa et ma maman je ferai tout mon possible pour les faire aussi bien que je les ai commencées. Je vous souhaite une aussi bonne santé que la mienne ainsi qu'à mon cher papa et à ma chere maman faites bien mes amitiés à mon ami Cockran[8] et encoragès le à venir à Genève. Mr et Md Marignac vous présentent bien leurs respects. J'ai l'honneur d'être Mon cher grand papa Votre très humble et très obeissant petit fils

B FRANKLIN B

BF

Addressed: A Monsieur / Monsieur Franklin / Ministre Plenipotentiaire des Etats / unis de l'amérique recomandée à / Monsieur Grand Banquier ruë / Montmartre / A Paris

From William Carmichael: Extract

Reprinted from William Temple Franklin, *The Private Correspondence of Benjamin Franklin, LL.D., F.R.S., &c...* (2nd ed.; 2 vols., London, 1817), II, 461.

Madrid, July 18, 1780.

I thought, until the receipt of your letter (of the 17th June)[9] that Mr. Jay had sent you Sir John Dalrymple's Memorial, and other papers while I was at Aranjuez. He sends them, however, by this courier, and I think you will be amused in reading Sir John's *Reveries.*[1]

   Mr. Cumberland,[2] a former Secretary of Lord Germaine, suc-

---

7. BFB first mentioned sending the drawing on May 30: XXXII, 444.

8. Charles Cochran.

9. XXXII, 540–3.

1. Jay's letter of the preceding day is above. For Sir John Dalrymple's abortive peace mission see XXXII, 290–1n, 409n. His "reveries" refers to the memoir titled "Anecdote Historique," which included his peace proposals: Wharton, *Diplomatic Correspondence,* III, 727–31.

2. Richard Cumberland (1732–1811), secretary of the Board of Trade, had been sent by the British government to forward any Spanish peace proposals. He arrived at the royal palace of Aranjuez on June 18: *DNB;* Samuel Flagg Bemis, *The Hussey-Cumberland Mission and American Independence: an Essay in the Diplomacy of the American Revolution* (Princeton, 1931), pp. 44–60.

ceeds Sir John. His residence gives no uneasiness to the Count de Montmorin,[3] which with the assurances that we receive from the Count de Florida Blanca, ought to remove *our* apprehensions.

To —— Rinquin
Copy: Library of Congress

Sir   Passy, July 19. 1780.
   I received the honour of yours dated the 14th. Instant.[4] containing the Pieces relative to the Padmore a Prize taken by the Black Princess; and I Send you here with the Judgment thereupon.[5] I have the Honour to be, Sir, &c.

M Rinquin.

To Schweighauser

AL (draft):[6] American Philosophical Society; copy: Library of Congress

Passy, July 19. 1780.
In order to have the old arms,[7] conveyed to America in the cheapest manner, I request you to have the Gun Barrells Locks

---

3. On July 18 Ambassador Montmorin reported to Vergennes that Spanish Chief Minister Floridablanca was not displeased by the idea of giving the French a little disquietude so they would be more amenable to the joint campaign plans he favored. AAE.

4. Missing.

5. We have not located BF's prize judgment. Rinquin, the clerk of the Admiralty of Morlaix, had been communicating with BF for the past half year about prizes of the *Black Prince* and *Black Princess;* see, for example, XXXI, 400–1.

6. In JW's hand. JW had been in Passy since the beginning of July (see our annotation of BF to Gardoqui & fils, July 4) and left on the evening of the 19th, arriving in Nantes late on July 21. (JW to French & Cie., July 22, Yale University Library; to BF, July 25, below.) BF probably used him as a secretary for drafting both this letter and the following one, which was written on the verso of this sheet.

7. Muskets that the commissioners had bought in 1777; see XXIV, 100–1, XXVIII, 497–9, and for Schweighauser's involvement, XXIX, 263. See also Rasquin's letter of Sept. 12, below.

Bayonnetts & Iron or brass furniture of them closely packed in small Cases so as to take up the least Room possible. The Cases may be the exact length of a Gun Barrell & being about a foot broad & deep they will contain as many as a man can easily manage, & thereby make convenient & handy ballast, which will be an inducement for Ships to take them on a reasonable freight. I do not think the Woodwork of the arms worth sending, as I understand the principal Part must be new Stocked which had better be done in America. Care must be taken to have the Barrells & Locks cleaned & oiled, at least so well as at their arrival they may not be in a worse condition than they now are, as this Operation does not require much Skill common Labourers will answer the purpose in case you cannot obtain armourers. In the Course of a month I may perhaps have an Opportunity of sending what you may then have ready and at about that time I shall be glad to know the quantity.

The arms already repaired if any remain unshipped, must go as they are.

Mr. Schweighauser.

To Jonathan Williams, Jr.

L (draft):[8] American Philosophical Society; copy: Library of Congress

Passy July 19. 1780.

I have already given you Powers to freight a Ship to carry out the public Stores & I now confirm them. If you agree with Mr. de Chaumont for the Breton or other large Ship to pay the Freight in France, you may draw on me for the amount of it. I approve of Mr de Chaumont's proposition for the Cloathing he has at Nantes & authorize you to accept it.[9] As soon as you have made out the Invoices let me know the amount that I may draw my

8. In JW's hand. See our annotation of the previous letter.

9. No written version of Chaumont's proposal survives, and we suspect that these negotiations may have been oral. He seems to have offered to sell the cloth at cost. Details of the agreement are revealed in later documents, but for a summary see Lopez, *Lafayette*, pp. 202–3.

Bills on Congress for the same.— If Mr Schweighauser should have anything for the public ready to ship when you load the Ship you may freight, and there should be sufficient Room without excluding any part of the other Stores you will on his Application permit him to embark what he may have to send.

For any other Matter relative the Business I have intrusted you with I refer to your own judgment & rely on your best Exertions for the public Good.

Mr Williams.

Notation in Franklin's hand: BF to J. Williams July 19. 1780 Approbation of M. Chaumont's Proposition to sell Cloth, & authorizing [?] to accept of it.

From John Ross   ALS: American Philosophical Society

L'Orient 19th. July 1780.

I have the honour of your Excellencey's much Respected favour 15th. Inst:— The disturbance on board the Alliance must be attended with delay's & difficultys in geting forward the Stores. Therefore, it being evident Your Excellencey's plan have been deranged by the measure's of that faction, much to the dishonour & prejudice of the United States & foreseeing the impossibility of the Ariel carrying even half the arm's ordered on board.— My last of the 10th. Inst:[1] woud inform you of my determination; agreeable to which, the 123 Bales are now on board the Brigg St. Luke Capt: Clark[2] which I hope will be approved of.— So soon as the bills of Lading are Signed, one shall be Sent accompanying the order for the Freight.

It will be proper to recommend this Brigg to the protection of Captain Jones Commander of the Ariel dureing the Voyage, if it can be done consistent with your Excellys Views & the Service of the States— As well as Such other American Vessels that are ready to proceed with him for America.— All kinds of stores

1. He must mean the 9th, the date of a letter (now missing) that BF acknowledged in his reply of July 15.
2. Joseph Clark: Claghorn, *Naval Officers,* p. 60.

whether on public or private Accots. being essentially necessary to get safe home.

The Duke of Linster, Captain Souder,[3] will proceed with the Ariel, in which Vessel, I propose to Embark. If your Excellencey shoud have any further Commands to commit to my cares— I shall pay attention to the delivery of them on my Arrival, if I have but the good fortune to get home Safe.

With particular Respect and Regard, I have the honour to be Your Excellenceys Most obedient very humble JNO. ROSS

Passy

His Excellencey Benjamin Franklin. Minister Plenipoty. from the United States at the Court of Versailles

From the Vicomtesse de Clermont-Tonnerre[4]

AL: American Philosophical Society

le 19 juilliet 1780

MDe. La Vtse De tonnerre a lhoneur De faire mille Complimets a monsieur le Docteur franklin et Celuy de luy envoyer deux Lettre pour les etats unis affin qu'elle parviennent plus Surment a Leurs destination elles Sont de mr le chr De failly qui a eté longtems aux Service des etats unis[5] mde. De tonnerre Sest

3. John Souder of Philadelphia: *ibid.*, p. 291. Ross intended to sail to America on the *Duke of Leinster*, which he expected to be ready in ten to twenty days: Ross to WTF, July 19 (APS).

4. Anne-Marie-Louise Bernard de Boulainvilliers, the former Mlle de Passy, who was married to the vicomte Gaspard-Paulin de Clermont-Tonnerre (XXXI, 280n).

5. Philippe-Louis de Failly (1735–1804), a *chevalier de la croix de St. Louis* since 1772, was a captain in the Anjou regiment: Bodinier, *Dictionnaire*. He enlisted as a volunteer in the American army on Dec. 1, 1776, and received a commission of lieutenant colonel by Congress on Aug. 13, 1777, effective Dec. 1, 1776: *JCC*, VIII, 638. Failly served under Gates at Saratoga, under Washington at Valley Forge, and under Lafayette at the battles of Monmouth and Newport: Failly to BF, Feb. 5, 1784 (APS). He was breveted a colonel on Oct. 27, 1778, and retired at the end of that year: *JCC*, XII, 1068; Lasseray, *Les Français*, I, 211–12. His name appears on a list of sums advanced for various purposes in 1779, showing that Congress paid him $125 on March 13. National Archives.

chargé de Suplier monsieur le docteur de franklin denvoyer Ses lettres avec un de Ses paquets elle espere ne pas Luy etre importune en Luy demandant Cette grace ayant Saisit cette ocasion avec empressement pour le faire Souvenir des habitents du chateau de passy mde. Sa mere[6] et elle Se plaignent du tems quil y a quelles n'ont eu lhoneur de le voir et de luy offrir Lhomage de Leurs attachement.

Notation: Mde. Tonnerre.

From Dumas

ALS: American Philosophical Society; AL (draft):[7] Algemeen Rijksarchief

Monsieur,   La Haie 20e Juillet 1780.

Comme tout est en vacance & absent d'ici, & que les Etats Provinciaux d'Hollande ne se rassembleront que le 26, je n'ai rien à marquer quant aux affaires publiques, si ce n'est que 10 à 12000 prussiens cantonnés en Westphalie ont ordre de se tenir prêts à S'approcher de Munster au premier signal qui leur en sera donné, à ce qu'on dit.

Le Baron de Wulffin, dont j'ai parlé dans une de mes précédentes,[8] m'a envoyé de Venlo, où il est, un gros paquet par la poste, qui m'a couté un port exorbitant. Je m'en serois consolé, Si, comme il me l'annonçoit, il y avoit eu des affaires de grande importance. Mais ce sont les Journeaux du Congrès du 1er. Mars 1779 jusqu'au 30 Mars 1780, à la réserve de diverses pieces qui manquent entre deux; & puis un paquet de gazettes de Pensylvanie depuis le commencement de cette année jusqu'au 3e. May. Pas un mot de Lettre avec. Ainsi j'ignore de qui cela vient. Je m'apperçois seulement que les Gazettes, &c. ont appartenu à des Membres du Congrès. Ce que j'y vois de plus interessant pour

---

6. Marie-Madeleine-Adrienne d'Hallencourt Bernard, marquise de Boulainvilliers.

7. Dated July 18 and chiefly consisting of a copy of the congressional resolution which Dumas subsequently encoded.

8. Above, July 4.

nous, & que je crois devoir vous transcrire du Journal du Congrès de Mars, c'est l'article suivant.

"Thursday March 23d. 1780
Resolved, That the thirty-two and ¼ MLBPUCYQTXOTRY
& twinty-nine 610. 765. Specified in the invoice & bill of Lading, from 873. S.S. 484. 812'd. 136. STW. 618. MYLBO. 840.
MBTRLXDTXPLOBTLXLTYCTLSSTVWLCDPB.   322.
533. & 300. be 618. 41. & BTCAEP. of these 7. & that the said S.
484. be 226ed. 322 873. 846. 610. 232426½ Dollars, being the Cost
& charges."[9]

Si vous savez quelque chose, Monsieur, du sort de cela, je me recommande. De mon côté, j'y serai attentif.

948. 842. a 888. 484. would do great things 95. 68. & be 431.
610. its 89ers. by 296ing. 357. 222ence. 948. 642. & 519.[1] Dans
mon opinion il y a longtemps qu'on eût dû le faire. Cela auroit donné un très grand relief au crédit de l'Amérique: & cela peut le relever encore très à propos ici. Dieu veuille que le tout arrive.

Je suis toujours avec mon respectueux attachement, Monsieur
Votre très-humble et très-obéissant serviteur   DUMAS

J'espere d'apprendre que les Dépêches pour le Congrès que Mr. Guilon vous a portés de ma part, Sont en bonnes mains & qu'elles ne sont point sur l'Alliance. Il faut que Mr. J—[2] [torn: ait fait de?] grandes fautes dans sa conduite; car ce qui vient de lui arriver seroit incompréhensible pour moi sans cela.

Cette Lettre a été retardée deux ordinaires, parce que je n'étois pas bien. Il n'y a pas grand mal: car, excepté ce qui est chiffré, il n'y a rien d'essentiel. Je l'ai rouverte. Vous Savez sans doute, Monsieur, que la Cour de Danemarc vient de faire aux autres

9. BF interlined his decoding of this resolution: "Resolved, That the thirty-two and ¼ barrels of Indigo and twenty-nine of Rice specified in the invoice & bill of Lading from the [Honorable H.] Laurens ship'd [by] him on board the brigantine *Adriana* Josiah Hill master, for Martinico [and] Europe, be on the risque of these States & that the said H Laurens be credited the sum of 232426 ½ Dollars, being the cost & charges." At the bottom of the letter he calculated 232,426 divided by 40, presumably to obtain the amount in specie dollars. The actual resolution differs slightly: *JCC*, XVI, 281.

1. "With such a value Laurens would do great things at Amsterdm. & be independent of its Bankers by establishing good correspondence with Paris & Madrid."

2. Jones.

Cours la même déclaration que la Russie, quant à la Neutralité armée.[3] Ici l'on est plus lent. Nos deux Plénipotentiaires, qui doivent régler cela à Petersbourg, sont seulement sur leur départ.[4] Le Baron de Wulffin a passé ici. J'espere qu'il pourra partir incessamment sur un vaisseaux de Virginie, qui est prêt à mettre à la voile d'Amsterdam. Il m'a emprunté deux Ducats.

Addressed: A Son Excellence / Monsieur B. Franklin, Escr. / Min. Plenipe. des Etats-Unis / &c. / *Passy.*/.

Notation: Dumas la haie July 20. 80

To Jean de Neufville & fils[5] LS and copy: Library of Congress[6]

Gentlemen   Passy, July 21. 1780.
   I declined having any Concern with the Bills drawn on M. Laurens, because I had no Orders nor Advice concerning them, and knew nothing of their Amount, and because he himself was daily expected to arrive in Holland. But being lately informed that the Congress Stopt the Proceeding in those Drafts soon after it commenc'd,[7] having adopted the better Plan of borrowing at home by issuing new Paper Money bearing Interest; and calling in all the old by Taxes; and that the Sum drawn for on that Gentleman is not considerable, & the Destination of M. Laurens may be changed or delayed; I have concluded to pay those you

3. The Danish declaration was accompanied by a convention with Russia, signed on July 9: Sir Francis Piggott and G.W.T. Omond, eds., *Documentary History of the Armed Neutralities 1780 and 1800* . . . (London, 1919), pp. 219–21, 233–8; Madariaga, *Harris's Mission*, pp. 188–9.
   4. Ministers Plenipotentiary Baron van Wassenaer Starrenburg and Baron van Heeckeren tot Brantsenburg had been selected by the stadholder to negotiate a convention with Russia as a prerequisite to the Netherlands' joining the League of Armed Neutrality. On July 5 the States General approved their instructions: *Repertorium der diplomatischen Vertreter*, III, 268; Fauchille, *Diplomatie française*, pp. 511–12.
   5. In answer to theirs of July 13.
   6. Both the LS and the copy are in L'Air de Lamotte's hand. The LS is actually a photostat of the document and is in the Woodrow Wilson Papers at the Library of Congress.
   7. See BF's July 26 letter to Dumas, below.

have already accepted; and if the others are presented to me here, I will continue to accept them till his Arrival, unless Some good Reason should appear or arise to the Contrary, in which Case I will return them immediately, that the Possessors may protest them.

As to the Loan you formerly proposed to commence, and of which you now repeat the Proposition, it being now more than a Year since you undertook to procure and produce to me Subscriptions of Sums for that Purpose, which might induce me to engage in it, and you having not hitherto from the low State of our Credit in Holland, found any such Subscribers, I am fully of Opinion that the Project is not at this time praticable. And if it were yet as long as there is a possible Expectation of the Arrival of M. Laurence, I should not think it right for me to anticipate him in a Business that would more properly appertain to his Employment. I thank you nevertheless for the zeal & Readiness you show to serve the Interests of the United States; and have the Honour to be with great Regard, Gentlemen, your most obedient & most humble Servant   B FRANKLIN

Messrs. John Neufville & Son.

recd(?)

From Alexander Small   ALS: American Philosophical Society

Dear Sir   Hotel de York Paris [before July 22, 1780][8]

Being thus far in my way to England,[9] and being informed that you live out of Town, I take this Opportunity of enquiring of your Welfare, and beg to know whether Capt Nairn, Brother to Mr Nairn in Cornhill, gave you a paper on Ventilation, and the History of it.[1] I hope to receive a favourable Answer to these

8. Dated on the basis of BF's letter of July 22, below.

9. The Scots army surgeon, F.R.S., and long-time friend of BF (IX, 110–11n and XIX, 105n) was on his way back to London from Minorca, where he had been since 1775 (according to his "Observations on the Gout," for which see BF's letter to him of July 22).

1. Small's paper on ventilation included a number of BF's views on the subject. In early 1777 he proposed to send BF a draft; see XXIII, 486–91, 497–8.

particulars, and ever remain Dear Sir Your Faithful humble Servant   ALEXR SMALL

Addressed: A Monsieure / Monsieure le Docteure / franquelain a pacie

Notation: Alex Smal Paris.

To John Paul Jones   Copy:[2] Library of Congress

Dear Sir,   Passy July 22. 1780.
     I received yours of the 12th. and one preceding. I am glad you took mine of the 5th as it was intended in friendship— It had appeared to me, that you hurt your own Views, and weaken'd your own hands by a censorious [quarellous?] Disposition that obstructed your Acquisition of . . .
     . . . at your Request and to prevent Mischief, the orders were not caried into Execution,[3] I could see no foundation you had to complain that the Government had deserted you. It seemed to me that taking to your self the Credit you merited for the Prudence and Humanity of that Request, and then blaming the Government for not having acted contrary to it, was an Inconsistence, and that being right in the first, you must be wrong in the last, which could only be placed to the Account of the Disposition above mentioned. However that is all over.
     I have spoken to M. De Chaumont again this morning relative to the Prize money. That arising from the Sales of the Serapis and Countess, is not I think in his Hands; but he will do all he can to forward the Payment.
     I am glad to hear you are so near being ready for sailing. I shall send down my Dispatches about the End of next Week.
     With best Wishes for your Health, Honour and Hapiness, I am ever Your faithful friend and humble Servant.

Honble. Commodore Jones.

2. In BF's letterbook, where a portion of the letter is torn out. We indicate with an ellipsis the missing section.
3. Apparently the French orders to prevent by force the *Alliance* from leaving Lorient: XXXII, 565.

To Jean-Charles-Pierre Lenoir[4]   Copy: Library of Congress

This letter was written in response to a plea[5] from Capt. William Robeson of the South Carolina navy, now in Paris, regarding a runaway slave. Robeson had purchased this "little Negro Boy" from Lieut. Peter Amiel. The young man had disappeared on May 31, the eve of Robeson's intended departure for Lorient. Robeson was forced to delay his journey by several days, during which time he wrote twice to Temple asking him to keep a look-out for "Mountacue," whom he expected would flee to the neighborhood of his former master in Passy. The captain had notified the police, was prepared to reward the captor, and had left instructions with John Adams on how to proceed once the slave was apprehended.[6]

The present letter suggests that "Mr. Montague," as Robeson would later call him,[7] had only recently been discovered. Franklin gave the captain this letter of introduction to Lenoir, but his involvement in the affair was far from over. Three days later the slave, signing himself "Jean," directed to Franklin an eloquent plea for his release from prison, where Robeson had evidently ordered him placed (below, July 25). Whatever the minister plenipotentiary may have done to effect his release has not surfaced, but as our annotation to that document shows, the slave was reunited with his master. The following year, after both Robeson and Montague had been captured by the British and made their way back to France, Montague again eluded the captain. This time, Temple persuaded him to lodge with the Franklin household while waiting for Robeson to accept his demands for new terms of employment as a free man.[8] Finally, in 1782, only days before their ship was due to set sail from Nantes, Montague once again "[gave Robeson] the slip," and was the subject of more anxious letters to Passy.[9]

The latter parts of this story will be told more fully in future volumes. For his part, Robeson maintained that his treatment of Montague was "to a fault both Bountiful and kind."[1] Montague's story,

4. Head of the Paris police.
5. If it was a written petition, it has since disappeared.
6. Robeson to WTF, June 1 and June 3, 1780. The captain's instructions to JA have not survived, but he did carry dispatches for JA to Lorient: *Adams Papers*, IX, 369.
7. Our earliest example is in his letter to WTF, Sept. 11, 1781. APS.
8. WTF to Robeson, Sept. 3 and 8, 1781. APS.
9. Mumford to WTF, May 18, 1782, and JW to WTF, June 4, 1782. APS.
1. Robeson to WTF, Sept. 11, 1781. APS.

told only by his behavior and by the one letter he wrote to Franklin, suggests that he thought otherwise.

Monsieur,   Passy, July 22. 1780.

Le Capt. Robinson au Service des Etats Unis que J'ai l'honneur de vous presenter a besoin de l'autorité de votre Excellence pour recouvrer un Négre qui s'est évadé de son service et qui lui appartient. Je ressentirois particulierement l'assistance que vous voudrez bien lui accorder et que les Loix et L'Equité reclament en sa faveur.

J'ai l'honneur d'être &c. &c.

M. Le Noir.

To Alexander Small

Reprinted from William Temple Franklin, *The Private Correspondence of Benjamin Franklin, LL.D., F.R.S., &c . . .* (2nd ed.; 2 vols., London, 1817), I, 65–6.

Passy, July 22, 1780.

You see, my Dear Sir, that I was not afraid my masters would take it amiss if I ran to see an old friend though in the service of their enemy. They are reasonable enough to allow that differing politics should not prevent the intercommunication of philosophers who study and converse for the benefit of mankind. But you have doubts about coming to dine with me. I suppose you will not venture it; your refusal will not indeed do so much honour to the generosity and good nature of your government, as to your sagacity. You know your people, and I do not expect you. I think too that in friendship I ought not to make you more visits as I intended: but I send my grandson to pay his duty to his physician.[2]

You enquired about my gout, and I forgot to acquaint you, that I had treated it a little cavalierly in its two last accesses. Finding one night that my foot gave me more pain after it was covered warm in bed, I put it out of bed naked; and perceiving it easier, I let it remain longer than I at first designed, and at length fell asleep leaving it there till morning. The pain did not return, and

2. Small inoculated WTF shortly after BF assumed responsibility for him: XIII, 323n, 443n.

I grew well. Next winter having a second attack, I repeated the experiment; not with such immediate success in dismissing the gout, but constantly with the effect of rendering it less painful, so that it permitted me to sleep every night. I should mention, that it was my son who gave me the first intimation of this practice. He being in the old opinion that the gout was to be drawn out by transpiration. And having heard me say that perspiration was carried on more copiously when the body was naked than when clothed, he put his foot out of bed to increase that discharge, and found ease by it, which he thought a confirmation of the doctrine. But this method requires to be confirmed by more experiments, before one can conscientiously recommend it. I give it you, however, in exchange for your receipt of tartar emetic,[3] because the commerce of philosophy as well as other commerce, is best promoted by taking care to make returns.

I am ever, Yours most affectionately, B. FRANKLIN.

From Richard Bache

ALS: American Philosophical Society

Dear & Hond. sir Philadelphia July 22d. 1780.

The last time we had the pleasure of hearing from you was on the arrival of the Marquis de la Fayette.[4] Having just recd: an ac-

3. BF may be referring to Small's "Observations on the Gout," a paper that reported the author's own experiences with gout since 1770 and his experiments with various treatments. A combination of bark and an emetic seemed to be the most effective, but the attendant vomiting was unpleasant. Therefore, in mild cases, Small recommended taking a grain of emetic tartar (gradually increasing the dose to two grains) with a dram of bark (cinchona) mixed in water gruel, and followed by more than a half pint of gruel.

BF had L'Air de Lamotte copy Small's paper; he corrected that copy, noted at the top, "Written by Mr Small, at Minorca 1780," and sent it to Vicq d'Azyr (presumably under cover of his letter of Sept. 11, below). The MS is presently in the archives of the Académie de médecine, Paris, and bears the notation, "Remis par M franklin." The marquis de Turgot had the piece translated and printed (BF to Small, Dec. 7, Library of Congress). It appeared in the September issue of the *Jour. de médecine, chirurgie, pharmacie, &c.,* LIV (1780), pp. 224–36.

4. Lafayette arrived in Boston in April; see our annotation of the Intelligence Reports, July 1.

count of the arrival of the French Fleet at Rhode Island, we please ourselves with the expectation of hearing of you, if not from you.

Sally with her two youngest Children are in the Country, at our Friend Mr. Duffield's, returning a visit that the Miss Duffields made us in the Winter;[5] she and the Children are well— Will stays in Town on account of going to School, he shews a good deal of Genius, but much inattention; as he advances in years, I trust the latter will wear off— I long to hear how Ben comes on, in his Learning, and whether he makes such improvement, as our fond wishes suggested he would do, at the Geneva Accademy— It would give us pleasure to hear, that you had found leisure enough to visit him at Geneva, but I suspect your time has been more importantly employed; the Journey might conduce to your health, & be a means of prolonging a Life, that is not only of so much consequence to us, but to the World in general— Formerly you used to find a Journey absolutely necessary for you, every now and then; surely you must think it equally so now, unless the Climate of France should agree with you better, than any other Climate you have heretofore lived in.

I herewith send you the Newspapers; some I shall also send you by another Conveyance sailing at this time— The loss of Charles Town seems to have roused us out of the Lethargy we have been in, for two years past— I trust we shall make such exertions this Campaign, as to render the United Force of our Good Ally, of real and substantial use.

The Females of our City have been interresting themselves in behalf of the soldiers of our Army, by collecting donations, to be applyed to their use & comfort; this plan was first set on foot here, and I have the pleasure to tell you, that Sally has had no small hand in it;[6] it is likely to obtain thro' the different States;

5. For Edward Duffield and his family see xxx, 334–5, 352.

6. The Ladies Association, led by Esther DeBerdt Reed, wife of Governor of Pennsylvania Joseph Reed, was organized to persuade American women to forego "vain ornaments" and donate the money saved to the American troops. The movement, which its founders intended to be the first large-scale women's association in American history, was announced in the *Pa. Gazette* on June 21. SB solicited contributions in her district (Market to

99

New Jersey & Maryland have already adopted it—[7] It has put our Soldiery in the highest good humour, & for this end, believe me, something of this sort was necessary—

Many of the Merchants & Landed Men of this City have subscribed liberally towards establishing a Bank for very laudable & generous purposes, you will see in the papers an account of it, I will therefore refer you to them.[8] Remember me with Will to Temple & Ben— Accept our Love & Duty & believe me to be Dear sir Your ever affectionate son   RICH: BACHE

I herewith send you a Letter for Capt. Droüart, from his Son, who impatiently wishes to hear from his friends.[9]

Dr. Franklin

From Tristram Dalton   ALS: American Philosophical Society

Sir   Boston July 22nd. 1780.

I am honor'd with your Favors of the 17 October last respecting the Compensation order'd by the good King of France, for Reperation of the loss of the Brigantine Fair Play,[1] & did

---

Chestnut Streets), corresponded with near-by communities, and took over the leadership of the group when Esther Reed died in September. For the Association and sb's role in it see Mary Beth Norton, *Liberty's Daughters: the Revolutionary Experience of American Women, 1750–1800* (Boston and Toronto, 1980), pp. 177–88; Lopez and Herbert, *The Private Franklin*, pp. 225–6.

7. New Jersey had done so by July 4 and Maryland by the 14th: Norton, *Liberty's Daughters*, p. 183.

8. The Bank of Pennsylvania: Ferguson, *Power of the Purse*, pp. 56, 136n; Smith, *Letters*, XV, 481. The Bank and its subscribers are discussed in the June 21, 28, and July 5 issues of the *Pa. Gazette*.

9. Henry-Dieudonné Droüart de Givricourt was the son of [Charles-François-Robert?] Droüart, chevalier, seigneur de Lezey: *DBF*, XI, 802. RB forwarded to BF correspondence between the father and son: RB to WTF, Sept. 13, 1779, and Nov. 5, 1783; the chevalier to BF, June 13, 1781, and Droüart de Givricourt to BF, June 14, 1785. All these documents are at the APS.

1. XXX, 544–5. Dalton, one of the owners of the *Fair Play*, had sent BF documents relating to its accidental sinking by a Guadeloupe shore battery: XXIX, 486–8. He sent the present letter (along with several depositions now with BF's papers at the APS) via the *Mars*, Capt. Simeon Samson: *Adams Correspondence*, III, 419–21.

flatter myself, that there would have been no further Occasion of troubling or interrupting your more important Business, on this account, but that of asking Acceptance of the Owners unfeigned Thanks for the Attention bestowd thereon, & my gratefull Acknowledgements for personal Expressions— Which indulgent Favor of believing them true, both with Respect to the Owners & myself, be pleased to grant— The Order on the Government of Guadaloupe for said Indemnification, has been acknowleged & Application made by Mr. Bingham,[2] for Observation of it, who after repeated Addresses on the Subject, has received for answer, that further Representation must be made to the Court of France, & payment be orderd there, as their Chests were empty—[3] This Evasion puts the concern'd to the disagreable Task of renewing their Application to the Fountain Head of Justice, which they see with the greatest Pleasure is untainted & pure— They therefore, by me their Agent, presume to entreat your further Attention to the Affair that it may be finished, if possible by having the Payments order'd in France, as the Governor of Guadaloupe[4] is said to be not friendly to the Subjects of the United States, and in this instance has evaded the Execution of his royall master's Orders— That this should give the least possible Interruption to your other & infinitely greater Concerns, I have enclosed every Paper, and mentiond every particular to my esteemed Friend, the Honble. Mr. Dana, asking the Favor of his Attention, & Correspondence on the Subject— To him therefore permit me to refer if any Enquiry more is necessary—

The greatest Confidence is placed in the Justice which sways

2. Bingham, congressional agent in Martinique from 1776 to 1779, had been acting as an intermediary in the case: XXVIII, 350; XXIX, 393.

3. The French government was reluctant to incur the expense of sending specie across the Atlantic. The French expeditionary force in America was also bothered by a shortage of specie: Lee Kennett, *The French Forces in America, 1780–1783* (Westport, Conn. and London, 1977), p. 67.

4. Bache-Alexandre, comte d'Arbaud de Jouques, served as governor of Guadeloupe from 1775 to 1782: *DBF; Almanach Royal* for 1782, p. 168 and for 1783, p. 170. He had supported an appeal by the *Fair Play*'s captain: XXIX, 486n.

the Heart of his most Christian Majesty, and in the mode by which Application will be made in this Affair—

I have the honour to be with the most profound Respect & Esteem Your Honor's Most Obedient & most humble Servant

TRISTRAM DALTON

Honble. Benjamin Franklin Esqr.

Addressed: His Excellency / Benjamin Franklin Esqr: / Minister Plenipotentairy of the / United States of America at the Court / of Versailles, / Passy near Paris

Notation: Tristram Dalton. Boston July 22 1780

Endorsed:[5] Tristram Dalton Esq. Papers relating to the Loss of the Fairplay Brigantine—

Hémery's Account of the Fonts Cast at Passy

MS: American Philosophical Society

Franklin had engaged J.-Fr. Hémery in the spring of 1779 to set up a typefoundry at Passy; the regular payments for workers' salaries and supplies have been noted in previous volumes.[6] Here is the master founder's first inventory, drawn up, perhaps, because the shop was preparing to close for four weeks.[7] The manuscript is in a scrawled hand that often rendered terms phonetically and did not maintain a strict order of items. What emerges from the jumble of information is that the foundry had produced more than 5,000 pounds of type in an assortment of eleven sizes and, in some cases, multiple faces.[8]

Providing English translations or even modern equivalents for Hémery's terminology is problematic. Before type sizes were standardized the names by which fonts were identified denoted dimensions that were only approximate, and varied from founder to founder.

5. The endorsement appears on a sheet that served as a cover for the enclosed papers and is addressed to BF.

6. See XXVIII, 586n; XXIX, 463n; XXX, 3; XXXI, 3.

7. Salary payments ceased between July 22 and Aug. 19; see our Editorial Headnote on Accounts, under Account XVI.

8. Hémery was casting letters from matrices he had acquired from Claude Mozet when he took over the Mozet foundry in 1760; see Marius Audin, *Les Livrets typographiques des fonderies françaises créées avant 1800* (Paris, 1933), pp. 99–102.

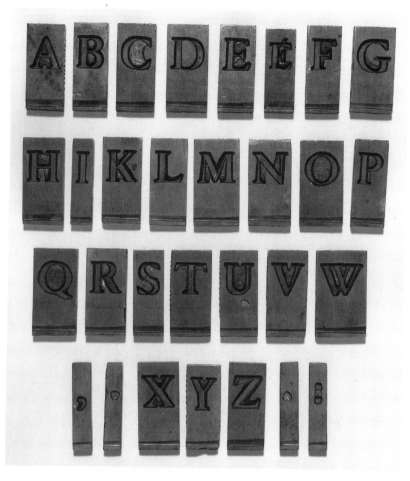

Matrices of Deux-Point Petit Canon

Moreover, eighteenth-century English terms were not exact translations of the French; English type corresponded only roughly to the sizes made across the Channel, and the two were not interchangeable. In 1737 Pierre-Simon Fournier le jeune had proposed a system of standardization, measuring by units called points, which was similar in concept to the scheme created by Sébastien Truchet in the 1690's for the Imprimerie royale. Didot l'aîné would recalibrate the point around 1781; his system of measurement and numeric designation eventually became standard.[9]

We list here Hémery's body sizes from largest to smallest, translating them into the English terms that Franklin himself used,[1] and supplying modern point-size equivalents: *double canon* (French canon, 56 point), *gros canon* (two-line great primer, 44 point), *trimégiste* or *deux gros romain* (double great primer, 36 point), *petit canon* (two-line English, 28 point), *gros parangon* (great paragon, 22 point), *petit parangon* (double pica, 20 point), *gros romain* (great primer, 18 point), *St. Augustin* (English, 14 point), *cicéro* (pica, 12 point), *petit romain* (long primer, 10 point), *petit texte* (brevier, 8 point).

[July 22, 1780]

Etat des fonte fait à passie premierment

Le double Canon romain & italique cadras
espas[2] pes 146 lb. à 1 livre la livre fait . . . . 146 *l.t.*
Le gros canon ordinaire romain & italique
laitre de deux point[3] 133 lb. à 1 *l.t.* la livre fait . . . . . 133 *l.t.*

9. James Mosley, ed., *The Manuel Typographique of Pierre-Simon Fournier le jeune, together with* Fournier on Typefounding, *an English Translation of the Text by Harry Carter* (3 vols., Darmstadt, 1995), III, xvi and xxxv–xxxvii of Carter's translation, 351–2, 354, 400–8.

1. These are based on three documents: BF's translation of a second inventory made on Jan. 27, 1781, which he called "Account of the Contents of the 34 Boxes of Printing Letters, &c., cast at Passy," and two undated lists which we conjecture he made around the time the printing office was being packed for shipment back to America, c. February, 1785. APS.

2. A font of *double canon*, including both roman and italic, with quadrats and spaces. Both quadrats and spaces were used to add blank space to a line of type; the latter, being smaller, were customarily used between words to justify a line.

3. "Lettres de deux point." Two-point or two-line letters were capitals twice as large as the font, and were used in conjunction with it, often as initial letters. BF began the text of each of his bagatelles with a two-point letter.

plus des vignete et crochait[4] pour La fonte
3 lb. à quarante sol la livre fait .... 6 *l.t.*
une fonte de deux Gros rom ou trismegisse
68 lb. à vien [vingt] sol fait .... 68 *l.t.*
une fonte de petit Canon romain et italique
Cadras Espas Laitre de deux point à 1 *l.t.*
fait 88 lb .... cy 88 *l.t.*
un gros parangon romain & italique Cadras
Espas Laitre de deux point 103 lb. à 22 sol
fait .... 113 *l.t.* 6 *s.*
plus des philet[5] Corp de petit romain triple
double fient [fine?] et gras à quarante sol fait ...... 90 *l.t.*
plus des interligne 32 lb. à trente sol fait .... 48 *l.t.*
un petit parangon romain & italique Cadras
et spasse Laitre de deux point 173 lb. à
22 sols fait .... 190 *l.t.* 6 *s.*
plus des vignete de parangon 8 lb. à
quarante sol .... 16 *l.t.*
des Cadras dadition[6] de 2 point de Gros
Canon et Creux 37 lb. à vient sien
[vingt cinq] sol fait .... 46 *l.t.* 5 *s.*
plus une fonte de Cicero marqué 264 lb.
à 2 *l.t.* 10 *s.* fait .... 660 *l.t.*
Le petit romain aublique[7] pes 160 lb. à 3 *l.t.*
La livre .... 480 *l.t.*
Le petit romain Gros oeille[8] pes 909 lb.
Conpré Les Cadras Les Especes, Laitre de
deux point à 1 *l.t.* 16 *s.* fait La somme de .... 1636 *l.t.* 4 *s.*
un cicero romain et font italique Cadras,

---

4. "Vignettes et crochets": flowers and square brackets.
5. "Filet": brass rule, cast on the same body as the font. They came as single, double, or triple, thin (generally called *maigre*, in French) or thick (*gras*).
6. "Quadrats d'addition": quotations.
7. Both this and the *cicero marqué* refer, we believe, to a rare sloped roman typeface probably commissioned by BF. The *cicero* was used in the French Loan Certificate: xxx, facing p. 346. Our thanks to James Mosley, St. Bride Printing Library, London.
8. Large-faced.

Espas, Laitre de deux point pes 767 lb.
à 1 *l.t.* 10 *s.* fait . . . . 1150 *l.t.* 10 *s.*
plus Le Cicero italique de fantaisie⁹ qui
paise 123 lb. a 1 *l.t.* 15 fait . . . . 215 *l.t.* 5 *s.*
une fonte de Cicero Gros oeille porta sont
blanc Cadrais Espas à vec sont italique pes
452 lb. à 1 *l.t.* 9 *s.* fait . . . . 645 *l.t.* 8 *s.*
une fonte de Gros romain et sont italique
Cadras Espas Laitre de deux point pes
650 lb. à 1 *l.t.* 4 *s.* fait . . . . 780 *l.t.*
plus des vignette à quarante sol 65 lb. fait . . . . 130 *l.t.*
Cadras, Espas de petit romain 2 lb.
à 1 *l.t.* 16 *s.* fait . . . . 3 *l.t.* 12 *s.*
une fonte de st augustin romain et Litalique
Cadras Espas Laitre de deux point à 1 *l.t.* 5 *s.*
et pes 392 lb. fait . . . . 490 *l.t.*
une fonte de petitxte romain & italique
Cadras Espas, Laitre de deux point pes
655 lb. à quarante sien sol fait . . . . 1473 *l.t.* 15 *s.*

fait à passi Le 22 julliet 1780

[*The following additions in Franklin's hand:*]
Omitted Signes d'Almanach
5 ¼ lb. à 45 *s.* la livre . . . . 26 *l.t.* 5 *s.*

$$\overline{8634: \quad 6}$$

Half the Petit Text sold & sent to Connecticut —— to be deducted viz 327 lb. ½ weight.¹

Notations by Franklin: Hemery's Acct of the Founts cast, their weight and Value, to July 22. 1780 / Acct of the Founts

9. We believe that these letters, which BF called "fancy italic," were the ornamental capitals that Luther S. Livingston cited as being so distinctive: *Franklin and His Press at Passy* (New York, 1914), pp. 105–6. BF used them in a number of official forms and in the bagatelles.

1. This type was finished in early March; see XXXII, 69n. According to the Cash Book entry of March 6, the font of brevier weighed 327 ½ lbs., but BF also sent 15 lbs. of rules, 10 lbs. of interlines, and 2 ½ lbs. of signs and planets.

From Alexander Small

ALS: American Philosophical Society

Dear Sir   Wednesday Noon [after July 22, 1780]

When I had the pleasure of seeing You I did not know that we were to quit our present Habitation before five O'Clock. I therefore trouble with this, to desire that you will by him send Your Commands for England, and the paper I left with you.[2]

Let your Evening and Morning Contemplation be the Inscription on the Peace of Munster.[3] As much depends on *You*, in Proportion to *your neglect* of the Means, in that proportion will the *Deaths* the *delay* occasions be laid to *your* Charge. Blessed are the Peace Makers,[4] said the preacher of Peace and Good will to Men. Let your Speedy appearance in London give Joy to thousands; and to none, more than to Dear Sir Your Faithful and Affectionate Servant   ALEXR SMALL

Addressed: To Dr Franklin / Passey

Notation: Small.

From ———— Champion and Other People with Goods and Services to Offer

ALS: American Philosophical Society

During the months covered by this volume Franklin received only four offers to supply goods or to establish factories in America.[5] The earliest, published below, comes from a supplier to the French army at the Hôtel royal des Invalides. That same day, July 24, the Parisian firm of Magniel Montauban & Cie., on the rue de Bourgogne, "Maison de M. Joly,"[6] offers to furnish all military clothing according to the prices

2. Possibly his "Observations on the Gout," which BF had copied; see BF's letter to Small of July 22, above. The two men had also discussed Small's work on ventilation.

3. The French treaty with the Holy Roman Empire as part of the Peace of Westphalia (Oct. 24, 1648).

4. "Blessed are the peacemakers: for they shall be called the children of God.": Matthew 5:9.

5. All the letters discussed are written in French and deposited at the APS.

6. The *hôtel* at number 50 was built in 1772 for Jean Joly, *secrétaire des commandements du prince de Condé:* Hillairet, *Rues de Paris,* 1, 233.

and yardages listed in an attached inventory, the suits being constructed *à la française*. In addition and with the same economy, they can supply collars, shirts, cockades, gaiters, and haversacks.

Writing from Liège on October 23, Jannesson offers his services to set up one or several paper and cardboard factories. He has just built one in Liège[7] and would like to branch out. He also offers to provide the workers and machinery necessary to the operation of an iron foundry, an enterprise more in line with the native expertise in iron work and arms manufacturing.[8]

On October 30 Jean Delmot of Leiden offers his services as agent to furnish cannons, cannonballs, mortars, bombs, rifles, pistols, in short, "tout ce qui concerne l'artillerie." He promises quality and low prices, and will take orders from Franklin or Dumas, "chargé Dit on des affaires De L'amerique unie."

Paris Le 24 Juillet 1780./.

Fourniture de Trouppes

Le Sr. Champion Negotiant a Paris Et Chargé de fourniture des trouppes a L'Honneur d'offrir a Monsieur Francklin Ministre Et Ambassadeur des Etats et Provinces de L'Amerique de Fournir tous Les Etoffes, Chapeaux Et generalement tous Les fournitures aux mêmes Prix que Les marchez qui Lui ont Eté Passés Par Le Ministre tenant Le Departement de la Guerre Et Suivant Les mêmes Echantillons Cachetés et adoptés Par Messieurs Les Commissaires des Guerres.[9] Les Fournitures des trouppes Etant La seule Branche de Commerce Qu'il adopte, il se flatte que Peu de Personne sont aportés de Les faire avec autant de Connoissance Et à un Prix aussi modique Que Lui. En outre Elévé dans Les fabriques, il Peut faire Jouir des avantages que Son travail Lui a Acquit. La Celeritée avec la quelle il Peut

7. His return address identifies him as "Directeur et sociétaire de la manufacture de papier de la Boverie Lez-Liège." Boverie lies east across the Meuse River from the center of Liège and is no longer a separate town.

8. Liège was at this time a principal city in the manufacture of arms and BF had received offers from *liégeois* gunmakers before: XXV, 465–6; XXVIII, 12; XXIX, 35.

9. As *secrétaire d'Etat au Département de la Guerre*, Montbarey was also director and general administrator of the Hôtel Royal des Invalides for whose troops Champion is the supplier. For the eight *commissaires ordonnateurs des guerres* see the *Almanach Royal* for 1780, pp. 234–7, and pp. 179–80, for the administration of the Invalides.

Executer des ordres Lui Peut faire meriter une Preference qu'on
Lui a deja accordé dans Beaucoup d'occasion.

CHAMPION
Entrepreneur des Fournitures de trouppe
a L'Hotel Royal des Invalides Et Rue
des Marais faubourg St Germain a Paris

Notation: Champion, Paris 24 Juillet 1780.

From John Diot & Co.
ALS: American Philosophical Society

Honored Sir   Morlaix July the 24th. 1780

We did our Selves the honnour to write to you the 7th. Instant,
to acquaint you with the arrivall in this harbour, of the prize Padmore Capn. Salomon William, Loaded with 28 Twenty four
pounds Cannons.[1]

This Serves to forward to Your Excellency an abstract of the
Journal of the Black Princess privateer,[2] Captn. Edwd. Macatter
commander, that came in to this harbour on the 18th. Instant at
night. She Landed next day 26. Ransomers for £10500. Stg, and
16 prisonners, whereof Subjoined a List of their names, proceeding from the brig Padmore, and from Two Vessells they destroyed at Sea.

Captn. Macatter Expects that Your Excellency will cause them
16 prisonners and two Sent in the prize Exchanged for a like
Number of Americans now lying in Gaol in England.

We understood by the Commissary here,[3] that those prisoners were to be Sent off this week by the Britannia Carteel Ship

1. About July 23 BF seems to have written to Diot & Co. in response to
their letter of the 7th. All that remains of BF's letter, however, is the following fragment in his letterbook: "present Difficulty.
I sent the 19th Instant, to Morlaix, the Condemnation of the Padmore
Prize, which I hope will prove valuable to you. I have the Honour to be, &c."
Our estimate of the date of this fragment is based on its position in the letterbook immediately following BF's letter to Jones of July 22. BF to Rinquin,
July 19, above, was the covering letter for the condemnation he had sent.
2. The enclosures are missing.
3. His name was Boucault: Diot & Co. to BF, Aug. 16, below.

now lying in this road; Your Excellency will undoubtedly take care that they Shou'd be exchanged for French prisonners, for, endeed, not one Single man wou'd go out in the Cutter again, were they not persuaded that the above prisonners Wou'd Serve to their own exchange, had they the misfortune of being taken.

Being all what occurrs at present We have the honnour to be Very Respectfully of Your Excellency The most obedient and Most Humble Servants   JN DIOT & Co.

His Excellency B. Franklin

Notation: Diot & Co. July 24. 1780

Francis Hopkinson to the American Commissioner or Commissioners

Three ALS:[4] American Philosophical Society

Gentlemen./   Philada. July 24th. 1780

Since my last of the 27th. of June[5] the following Sets of Exchange have issued from my office vizt.

To the State of Maryland

	dlr		Dolr
7 Sets	100 each	No. 1–7	700
5	200	1–5	1000
1	300	1	300
1	500	1	500
			2500

To the State of Pennsylvania

	dlr		dol
4 Sets	100 each	No. 8–11	400
19	200	6–24	3800
12	300	2–13	3600
8	400	1–8	3200
8	500	2–9	4000
			15,000

4. The ones we do not print are marked "Triplicate" and "Quadruplicate."
5. For which see XXXII, 63n.

To the State of Rhode Island

	dol		dllr
5 Sets	100 each	No. 12–16	500
5	200	25–29	1000
			1500

To the State of Connecticut

	dolr.		Dollr
4 Sets	100 each	No. 17–20	400
6	200	30–35	1200
5	300	14–18	1500
1	400	9	400
1	500	10	500
			4000

To the State of Virginia

	dor		dolr
5 Sets	200 each	No. 36–40	1000
2	300	19–20	600
1	400	10	400
			2000

Also

	dlr		dollr
150 Sets	12 each	No. 2126–2275	1800
100	18	1958–2057	1800
25	24	2173–2197	600
25	30	2691–2715	750
			4950

I have the Honour to be Gentn. Your very humble Servt.

FRAS HOPKINSON
Treasr. of Loans[6]

6. During the months covered by the present volume Hopkinson dispatched several other lists of loan office bills, compiled to help American commissioners in Europe distinguish valid certificates from counterfeit ones. On Oct. 23, as directed by the Board of the Treasury, he sent the numbers and denominations of interest bills issued to New York, Pennsylvania, New Hampshire, South Carolina, Georgia, Connecticut, Delaware, New Jersey, Rhode Island, and Massachusetts. He also reported that as he had received no orders to provide similar information for the new emissions of larger bills, which were likely to become very complex, he would omit sending their

(No. 18)

(Duplicate)

Addressed: To The Honourable / The Commissioner or Commissioners / of the United States of America / at Paris / (No. 18) / (On public service) / (Duplicate) / To be sunk if in Danger of falling into the Hands of the Enemy

From Vergennes: Two Letters

(I) and (II) copy: Library of Congress; draft:[7] Archives du Ministère des affaires étrangères

I.

a Versailles le 24 Juillet 1780.

M. L'Ambassadeur de Hollande continue, Monsieur, à se plaindre de la Prise du Navire la Flora, faite par le Corsaire le Prince Noir,[8] Vous êtes trop éclairé pour ne pas sentir que l'armateur de Ce Corsaire, Sujet du Roi et domicilié à Dunkerque,[9] ne peut reconnoitre d'autre Autorité que celles de Ses Juges naturels; que par conséquent la Legitimité de Sa prise ne peut être jugée qu'en France et selon les loix Francoises: s'il en étoit autrement, il en resulteroit que les François seroient les maitres de se rendre In-

---

numbers unless requested otherwise. On three occasions Hopkinson gave notice of duplicate sets of bills he had signed to replace original ones that had been lost: on Sept. 18, Nov. 3, and Nov. 6, he wrote that he had signed the fifth, sixth, seventh, and eighth sets of various bills, amounting to $396, $72, and $156 respectively. All the documents mentioned are at the APS.

7. The draft of the first letter is in the hand of Gérard de Rayneval, except for the postscript, which is in Vergennes'. A notation indicates a copy of this letter was sent to Sartine. We have corrected from the draft L'Air de Lamotte's minor omissions and misspellings. Rayneval also drafted the second one. The day of the month, given as "31," and the year may have been added later. We assume L'Air de Lamotte, working from the recipient's copy, was correct in dating it the 24th.

8. A Dutch brig that the *Black Prince* captured on April 7, a few days before the privateer was shipwrecked: XXXII, 259. For La Vauguyon's complaints see particularly XXXII, 550n.

9. John Torris.

dépendants de l'Autorité du Roi selon leur bon Plaisir dans le Royaume même, en arborant un Pavillon Etranger; or une Pareille Jurisprudence seroit le renversement de tout Ordre, et il seroit impossible à Sa Majesté de la tolerer sans compromettre les droits Inherents à sa Souveraineté.

Le Roi m'a chargé, Monsieur, de vous faire connoitre ces Principes, et de vous prevenir en même tems que son Intention est que la Contestation relative à la prise de la Flora soit portée pardevant les Tribunaux du Royaume, et qu'elle y soit jugée selon les loix et reglemens etablis pour les Corsaires François. Cette Marche est d'autant plus conforme à vos propres Principes, que selon ce que vous m'avez fait l'honneur de me mander le 18. Juin dernier,[1] les Corsaires Américains doivent reconnoitre les Loix des Pays où ils Ameneront des Prises. Ainsi le Prince Noir est dans le cas d'être jugé en France, soit qu'on le regarde comme François ainsi qu'il l'est, soit qu'il ait le droit de se dire Americain en vertu des Lettres de Marque dont il est pourvû.

J'ai l'honneur d'être très sincerement, Monsieur, Votre tres humble et très obeissant Serviteur.　　　(signé) De Vergennes

J'estime, Monsieur, que le meilleur moyen d'éviter tout Embarras, est de retirer les Lettres de marque que vous avez pu accorder à des Sujets du Roi et de ne plus leur en expedier aucune. Ils ne s'en serviroient que pour inquietter la Navigation des Puissances Neutres, et rien ne seroit plus formellement contraire aux Intentions de sa Majesté et à ses engagemens.

(signé) D.V.

M. Franklin

II.

à Versailles le 24 Juillet 1780.

Je me fais un veritable plaisir, Monsieur, de vous donner une nouvelle marque de ma Confiance, en vous Communiquant les Resolutions ci-jointes du Congrès. Vous y verrez avec la même satisfaction que nous, la Sensation agréable qu'a fait la nouvelle de la Destination de M. de Ternay et de Rochambeau, ainsi que

1. XXXII, 553–4.

les Efforts que le Congrès se propose de faire pour concourir au Succès des Operations de ces deux officiers.[2]

J'ai l'honneur d'être très sincerement, Monsieur, Votre très humble et très obeissant Serviteur (signé) DE VERGENNES.

M. Franklin.

To Franco and Adrianus Dubbeldemuts[3]

Copy: Library of Congress

Gentlemen, Passy, 25. July 1780.

I received the Honours of yours, without Date,[4] relating to the Ship called Gouderoos, which you mention as taken first by the English, and afterwards retaken by an American Privateer, and sent into New-York. I do not well understand this Account, New-york being itself in the Hands of the English. I shall chearfully do any Service in my Power for the owners; and request they would send me Extracts of Letters they have received from their Captain, by which the Fact may be better explained to me. Your Letter has been accidentally mislaid, or I should have answered it sooner. I have the Honour to be.

Messrs. F. & A Dubbeldemuts.

To Van der Oudermeulen

Copy: Library of Congress

Sir, Passy, July 25. 1780.

I received duly the Honour of yours of the 3d. Instant. Supposing you are by this time returned from N Holland, I write this

2. Vergennes enclosed French translations of a May 19 circular letter to certain states by President of Congress Huntington, May 20 and May 22 congressional resolutions, and a May 24 letter from Huntington to French Minister La Luzerne: Smith, *Letters*, xv, 154–6, 185; *JCC*, xvii, 442–3, 447. These documents concerned American cooperation with Ternay's squadron and Rochambeau's army. Library of Congress.

3. The last extant letter in a three-year correspondence with the Rotterdam merchants, for whose beginnings see xxv, 122–4.

4. XXXII, 321.

Line just to acquaint you that my Sentiments continue the same as in my former Letter;[5] and that in my Opinion, the Merchants of America are not likely to form any Such Company's as proposed. The Congress cannot authorize it having no Power to make Laws for Such Purposes; and any one or two States doing it without the rest would answer little purpose. But I wish you to communicate upon it with his Excellency M Adams, who knows the present State of that Country better than I do, & who will deliver this into your hands. You may explain more fully to him than can well be done by Letter, and with more Safety.— I have the Honour to be.

M. C V. d' Oudermeules.

To Vergennes

LS:[6] Archives du Ministère des affaires étrangères; copy: Library of Congress

Sir,   Passy July 25. 1780.

The Intention of his Majesty, (which you have done me the honour to signify to me in your Letter of the 24th Instant) to have the Contestation relative to the Taking of the Ship Flora, brought before the Tribunals of the Realm, there to be judged according to the Laws and Rules established for French Privateers, appears to me so perfectly right, that I acquiesce in it with Pleasure. I had the Honour of acquainting your Excellency in mine of the 18th. past,[7] with the Motives urged to me for granting an American Commission to the Black Prince. I was afterwards (without seeking or desiring it) drawn into the Exercise of a kind of judicial Power respecting her Prizes, by being assured that your Tribunals refused to judge of Prizes made by American Cruisers, and by being shown the 11th. Article of the King's Regulation of Sept 27. 1778. directing the Officers of the Admiralty to send me Copies of all their Proceedings, and the Papers relating to any Prize brought into your Ports by such Cruisers,

5. XXXII, 572–3.
6. In WTF's hand.
7. *I.e.,* June 18: XXXII, 552–5.

which it was alledg'd was intended to enable me to judge of the Legality of those Prizes, which Judgement was therefore demanded of me.—[8] A Letter too, which I had the Honour of receiving from M. De Sartine, seem'd to confirm this, viz:

"Versailles le 27. 7 bre 1779

J'ai l'honneur, Monsieur, de vous envoyer les Procédures instruites par les Officiers de l' Amirauté de Brest concernant la Prise le jeune Dominique, et huit Rançoms faites par le Corsaire Americain le Prince Noir. Vous savez, Monsr, que le Conseil de Prises n'a pas jugé convenable de prendre connaissance de ces sortes de Procédures; et je vous prie de m'accuser la Reception de ces différentes Pieces.

J'ai l' honneur d'etre &ca. (signé) DE SARTINE[9]"

These, if I have acted improperly, are my Excuses. I shall as you advise, withdraw the only two Commissions[1] I have issued to Privateers fitted out by the King's Subjects; being with the greatest Consideration & Respect, Your Excellency's most obedient and most humble Servant.   B FRANKLIN

His Exy. Count De Vergennes.

Endorsed: M. de R[2]

To James Woodmason

ALS and press copy: Assay Office, Birmingham, England

When James Watt, working in Birmingham in the summer of 1778, succeeded in developing a method of copying letters by mechanical

8. BF had been urged by Francis Coffyn to judge the *Black Prince*'s prizes: XXX, 271–3, 311–12, 360–1. The French regulations of Sept. 27, 1778 (XXVII, 648n) are printed in Sir Francis Piggott and G.W.T. Omond, eds., *Documentary History of the Armed Neutralities 1780 and 1800* . . . (London, 1919), pp. 100–2.

9. XXX, 409.

1. BF actually had issued four commissions—to Stephen Marchant and Patrick Dowlin for the *Black Prince*, to Edward Macatter for the *Black Princess*, and to Luke Ryan for the *Fearnot*—but only the latter two were still active: XXIX, 495–6; XXX, 536; XXXI, 446; Clark, *Ben Franklin's Privateers*, pp. 165–6. For BF's disillusionment with the privateers see XXXII, 602–3.

2. Rayneval, who drafted Vergennes' response: below, Aug. 13.

means, he did so in order to spare himself work. But he was soon convinced to patent the process and market the materials. James Watt & Co. received a patent in May, 1780, for a copy press that would soon change the lives of Franklin and many of his contemporaries.[3]

Watt & Co. advertised for subscriptions through various London stationers, the chief one being James Woodmason of Leadenhall Street. To their one-page "Proposals for Receiving Subscriptions, for an Apparatus, by which Letters or other Writings may be copied at once . . . ," they attached a sample (or "specimen") which consisted of a single, copied sentence written in an elegant hand: "Time, Labour & Money are saved, Dispatch & Accuracy are attained, and Secrecy is preserved by this newly-invented Art of copying Letters and other Writings."[4]

Woodmason, who had visited Franklin in June, 1779, and sold him an order of paper,[5] must have sent him multiple copies of this proposal, to judge by the present letter. His cover letter, now missing, must also have described the copying process well enough for Franklin

3. BF did not receive the copy presses ordered in the present letter until February, 1781. The method involved taking a letter written with special ink, letting it dry, laying over it a dampened tissue-thin piece of unsized paper, and applying pressure with either a rolling press or screw press. The result was a mirror-image whose ink penetrated the tissue completely, creating a positive image on the verso. The ink feathered somewhat in the tissue, however, creating a slightly blurred appearance. For Watt and his invention see Samuel Smiles, *Lives of Boulton and Watt* (Philadelphia, 1865), pp. 265–8; Silvio A. Bedini, *Thomas Jefferson and His Copying Machines* (Charlottesville, 1984), pp. 10–15; James H. Andrew, "The Copying of Engineering Drawings and Documents," in *Transactions*, Newcomen Society for the Study of the History of Engineering and Technology, LIII (1981–82), pp. 1–15.

4. A photograph of the "Proposals . . . " with its attached "specimen" is in the Birmingham Museum of Science & Industry. This circular was soon followed by a second one, three pages in length, which countered the fears of many London bankers and business leaders that this method might be used by counterfeiters. Watt pointed out that his copying paper was so distinctive—tissue-thin and unsized—that it could never be confused with the original, and the ink of the copy was never as sharp. Moreover, copper-plate blanks (such as those that were used for bills and notes) could not be copied by this method. He repeated that the machine would be demonstrated several days a week at Woodmason's shop, where parties could also obtain copies of the "Proposals . . . ". BF's copy of the "Proposals" has been lost; the second circular is at the APS.

5. See XXXII, 441–2, and for the background of the paper order, XXX, 609–12.

to have tried it himself (as he says here). The attempt apparently stimulated Franklin to recall a copying method he had devised years earlier in America. He demonstrated his method to the abbé Rochon, and their discussions inspired the abbé not only to improve upon it, but also, by mid-August, to invent an entirely new kind of engraving machine.

Franklin's technique for "printing almost as quickly as one could write" is known to us only through the abbé's reports, described below. It involved writing on paper with a gummy ink over which he sprinkled a powder of fine sand or iron filings. He ran this sheet through a rolling press, made a negative impression on a copper plate, and used that plate to produce duplicates. The method, although fast, produced copies "bien désagréables à la vue," according to the abbé, who decided that Franklin's method could be improved by writing directly on a specially varnished copper plate with a steel point, etching the writing into the plate with a nitric acid solution, and printing a negative copy. From this reverse imprint, one could make a positive copy by applying wetted paper and running it through a rolling press. (This last step was doubtless inspired by Watt's method.) If multiple copies were desired, one could print any number of reverse sheets from the copper plate, and press a fresh sheet of copying paper onto each one.

Rochon soon wondered about the feasibility of mechanically engraving type. He invented a small machine that pressed individual letter-punches into a plate of copper, allowing for letter-spacing and line-spaces, which was capable of creating an entire page of text that would look like print. The process was quick, the machine was portable, and it could be operated by virtually anyone. Rochon anticipated that it would be particularly useful in the battlefield and on shipboard.

The abbé presented his engraving machine to the Academy of Sciences on August 19, opening his report by describing his conversations with Franklin about copying methods and admitting that he would never have become interested in the art of engraving had it not been for these discussions.[6] The Academy enthusiastically endorsed it, and Rochon published a detailed description, along with several plates, in his *Recueil de mémoires sur la mécanique et la physique* (Paris, 1783).[7] As for his method of copying handwriting, based on Franklin's

6. His report, read into the minutes on Aug. 19, is in the *pochette* of the same date at the Académie des sciences, Paris.

7. His chapter on the engraving machine is on pp. 323–47; it ends with a copy of the Academy's report, dated Dec. 22, 1781. Another person who was enthusiastic about the invention was the abbé Morellet, who believed it was

method, he explained it years later to Thomas Jefferson, who took careful notes.[8]

Sir   Passy, July 25. 1780

I sometime since ordered the Payment of your Account for the Paper, which I hear is arrived at Rouen.[9]

I thank you for the Proposals relating to the new-invented Art of Copying. I have distributed the Specimens among such as I thought likely to use or recommend the Invention. And I have myself made a faint Attempt to practise it, as you will see by the Sample enclos'd. But as I love to encourage Ingenuity, you may put me down as a Subscriber, and send me three of the Machines, wch. are for some Friends.[1] With great Regard, I am, Sir, Your most obedient and most humble Servant   B FRANKLIN

P.S. It is probable I may send another Order for Paper, it being much admired here.

Mr Woodmason

Notation: B: Franklin July 25 1780

---

far more important than Watt's copy press. Morellet tried to interest Shelburne in financing the manufacture of the engraving machines in England, using Rochon himelf to train the workmen. Dorothy Medlin, Jean-Claude David, and Paul LeClerc, eds., *Lettres d'André Morellet* (2 vols. to date, Oxford, 1991–), I, 426, 428n.

8. See *Jefferson Papers*, X, 323–4, 325–6.

9. We had assumed in vol. 30 (p. 612) that since BF ordered payment for this paper on May 30 (XXXII, 441–2), it meant that he had received it. This was evidently not the case. To add to the confusion, WTF's household accounts (Account XXIII, XXIX, 3) record a payment of 7 *l.t.* 3 *s.* on July 9 for "Expences of Paper from Rouen." BF may have sold a portion of the shipment to the abbé de la Roche, who paid him 70 *l.t.* 4 *s.* for paper on Sept. 17: Cash Book.

1. Although BF may have intended to give away all three machines, when they finally arrived in February, 1781, he kept one for himself. The other two went to JW and the marquis de Turgot: JW to WTF, Feb. 12, 1781, Yale University Library; BF to the marquis de Turgot, April 25, 1781, Library of Congress.

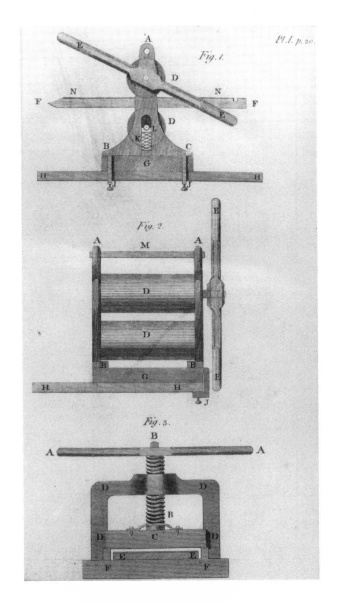

Pl. I. p. 20.

Fig. 1.

Fig. 2.

Fig. 3.

James Watt's Copying Machine

From Samuel Cooper

ALS: American Philosophical Society

My dear Sir,   Boston July 25th. 1780.

I have but a Moment to write by the Mars a Vessel belonging to this State, the Voyage having been kept secret upon political Accounts.[2]

I congratulate you on the Arrival of the Fleet from Brest, under the Orders of the Chevalier de Ternay, at Newport, after a Passage of about ten Weeks; not a single Vessel of the whole Fleet missing.

You will hear before this reaches you of the Loss of Charlestown, in which Genl. Lincoln and his whole Army were made Prisoners of War, and four Continental Frigates taken. The Place, it is said, was well defended; but the Enemy having Command of the Sea Coasts, having received repeated Reinforcements from N. York, and the Difficulty we found in sending Aid and supplying it with Provisions, occasioned it's Surrender on the 12th of May. This Loss, and the Arrival of the Marquis de la Fayette who apprized us of the Armament coming from Brest, awaken'd the States; great Exertions, considering our Circumstances, have been made, and are still making, to reinforce the Army of Genl. Washington. This State has voted 5000 Men for 6 Months: and 5000 Militia for three Months: Great part of this Force has already joined, or is near the Army. Tho the Term is so short in which they are to serve, it is at a vast Expence the Men are raised, the Produce of Land, and Labor of all Kinds being at a greatly advanced Price. The People, however, discover a noble Attachment to their honorable Cause in the Manner of bearing these Burdens.[3] I should have mentioned before that one Thing that contributed to rouze us to the present Exertions was, the Irruption of almost the whole Force at New york, into the Jerseys, where the Britons and their Mercenaries renewed a

2. The mission of the *Mars*, 22 (Simeon Samson commanding), was to bring back goods for the state of Massachusetts. The vessel left Boston on Aug. 1 and reached the entrance to the Loire on Sept. 10. On her return voyage she carried musket barrels provided by JW: John A. McManemin, *Captains of the State Navies during the Revolutionary War* (Ho-Ho-Kus, N.J., 1984), pp. 163–7; Lopez, *Lafayette*, pp. 206–7.

3. Three weeks previously Abigail Adams had made a similar comment: *Adams Correspondence*, III, 371.

Scene of Barbarities equal perhaps to any Thing of the Kind they had ever before exhibited. This is saying not a little. They were however, nobly opposed by General Green with an handful of Troops and the Jersey Militia. They retired precipitately having lost, by the best Accounts we can obtain 900 kill'd and wounded. Our own Loss was but small. Springfield was burnt, many Women abused, and Mrs Calder the Wife of a Clergyman who had distinguished himself in the Cause of his Country, cruelly murdered.[4]

In the Midst of our Joy at the Arrival of the Fleet from France, and of our Exertions for the Campaign, we have two days ago received an Account that a British Fleet is off Newport, supposed to be Graves joined with Arbuthnot. Our Accounts mention about 16 Sail, 8 of which are of the Line— Ternay has but 7 of the Line, and but few Frigates. We hope soon to see his Second Division from Brest; for if we have not a Naval Superiority on these Coasts, I expect little from this Campaign, and that Britain will hold New york Charlestown and other important Posts, in Spite of all the Efforts we can make.[5] We wish the approaching Season of Hurricanes may lead part of the French Ships there to these Seas. This Continent is the Core of the War, which ceases with the Repulse of the Enemy from their Stations here.

This will be delivered to you by my Kinsman Richard Cooper, Son of my eldest Brother, who tho young has been some time in the Naval Service of his Country, and from his good

4. On June 7 Baron Knyphausen, commanding at New York in Clinton's absence (XXXII, 340n), led 5,000 troops on a raid into New Jersey; Gen. Nathanael Greene was in charge of the American defense. After a skirmish at Springfield on the 23rd, Knyphausen retreated to Staten Island: Mark Mayo Boatner III, *Encyclopedia of the American Revolution* (New York, 1966), pp. 1045–7; Richard K. Showman *et al.*, eds., *The Papers of General Nathanael Greene* (8 vols. to date, Chapel Hill, 1976–), VI, 9–11, 14, 24, 29–42. On the first day of the incursion a British soldier shot and killed Hannah Ogden Caldwell, wife of the Rev. James Caldwell, at Connecticut Farms, N.J.: Larry R. Gerlach, ed., *New Jersey in the American Revolution 1763–1783: a Documentary History* (Trenton, 1975), pp. 312–13.

5. By July 22 seven ships of the line under the command of Rear Admirals Marriot Arbuthnot and Thomas Graves were off Newport: John A. Tilley, *The British Navy and the American Revolution* (Columbia, S.C., 1987), p. 194. The "second division" of Rochambeau's expeditionary force never left France: XXXII, 71n.

Conduct is like to be advanced in this Service as fast as his Age will allow.[6] He will esteem it an Honor to wait on our Minister at the Court of France. I cannot forbear again to commend to your kind Notice my dear Boy at Passy,[7] and am with every Sentiment of Respect and Friendship, my dear Sir, Your's for ever,

SAML: COOPER.

I have wrote you not long since by the Pallas from Newbury Port, and the Rambler from Salem.

Notation: Dr. Cooper 25 July 1781

From Jean [Montague][8]

ALS: American Philosophical Society

Monseigneur,   du petit Chatelet Ce 25: Juillet 1780.

Jai l'honneur de vous assurer de mon tres humble respect. Jai celui de vous Faire Sçavoir que Japartient á Monsieur le Capitaine Robson, il ma Fait des ménaces de me Fraper pour lors jai trouvé Monsieur Tessier Gentilhomme qui desire faire mon bonheur; Monsieur Robson la Scü et ma Fait arreté et fait constituée prisonnier au petit chatélet parceque le Commisaire lui á dit qu'il ny ávoit pas d'esclave en France;[9] Je ne demande pas mieux de rentrer chez Monsieur Robson; parceque Sy je n'avois

6. Richard Wibird Cooper (1761–1810) was the son of Samuel's brother William (1721–1809): Frederick Tuckerman, "Thomas Cooper, of Boston, and His Descendants," *New England Hist. and Geneal. Register,* XLIV (1890), 56–8.

7. His grandson Samuel Cooper Johonnot: XXXII, 117, 415, 561n.

8. For background to this letter and an explanation of the surname that we have supplied see the headnote to BF's letter to Lenoir, July 22.

9. Criminal prisoners were held in the Petit Châtelet, one of three dungeons making up the central prison system of Paris and located on the left bank at the entrance to the Petit Pont. A month later the King ordered its demolition as part of Necker's prison reform: François-André Isambert *et al., Recueil général des anciennes lois françaises* (29 vols., Paris, 1821–33), XXVII, 376–9. See also Hillairet, *Rues de Paris,* II, 260–1; Charles C. Gillispie, *Science and Polity in France* (Princeton, 1980), pp. 248–9.

While there was a tradition of granting freedom to slaves who set foot on French soil, the edict of Aug. 9, 1777, forbade entry into France to all people of color. JW described the edict as forbidding "any Negroes from the French Islands to be brought into the Kingdom"; those that were brought in were kept in custody until they could be sent to the West Indies and sold as

pas été detourné par Mr. tessier Je n'aurois Jamais sorty. Je vous Suplie, Monseigneur, de vouloir bien faire mes excuses à Monsieur Robson; et que je Ferez tous ce qu'il dependera de moy pour le contenter s'etois qu'il voulois me Faire Baptiser, Jespere de vos bontés que vous voudrez bien me Faire rendre justice, il y á de ma Faute du peu dexperience que jai, n'etant pas avancé en áge, je reitere de vous Suplier de vouloir bien parler pour moy á Monsieur Robson.[1] Je vous en serez toute ma vie reconnoissant et vous Suplie de me Croire avec tout le respect qui vous est düe en áttendant une petite réponse, Monseigneur

> Votre tres humble et tres obeissant serviteur soumis
> JEAN
> neigre de Mr. Robson

Addressed: A Monsieur / Monsieur Frankley / Ministre des Boxtonniens / en Son hotel á passy pres / paris / á Passy

Notation: Jean Negre de M. Robson du petit Chatlet 25 Juin 1780.

From Rudolph Erich Raspe ALS: American Philosophical Society

Honoured Sir,   London. July. 25. 1780.

The kindness, wherewith Your Excellency was pleased last year to receive Baron Waiz[2] and would have received me at Passy, engages me to the warmest acknowledgments and obliges me in consequence of my duty to Your Excellency and to the bearer of this to direct and to recommend to Your care Baron

---

slaves: JW to BF, Feb. 9, 1781, University of Pa. Library. For the edict of 1777 and subsequent amendments see Isambert, *Recueil général des anciennes lois,* XXVI, 81–4, 131, 189, 213, 257–8. See also Lucien Peytraud, *L'Esclavage aux Antilles Françaises avant 1789, d'après des documents inédits des Archives coloniales* (Paris, 1897; reprint ed., Pointe-à-Pitre, 1973), pp. 391–401.

1. According to the *arrêt* of Sept. 7, 1777, the slave's expressed willingness to return to his master's service was essential to his release: Isambert, *Recueil,* XXVI, 131. This letter seems to have served the purpose. Robeson conveyed Montague back to Nantes, evidently "in the bottom of his Post Chaise," and arrived some time before Aug. 8: George Fox to WTF, Oct. 12 (APS); JW to WTF, Aug. 8 (APS).

2. The baron Waitz von Eschen (XXX, 150).

Podmanniczky, a Nobleman from Hungaria,[3] whose learning, zeal, ingenuity and interest must operate a happy revolution in the learning and useful Arts of his country, as soon Protestants will be looked upon at Vienna with the same eye as they are in France under Mr. Neckers administration.

He has met here with great distinction amongst the Nobility as well as amongst the Learned. Being received a Member of several learned Societies and in particular of the Royal Society, it will be in his power to give Your Excellency some accounts of Your friends amongst them, and though he should not tell You, I must, that according to the new principle of taxing free People, which of late has crept even into the Royal Society,[4] he has been taxed 30. Guineas for his admission.[5]

Dr. Graham, the Prince of Quacks, has set up in the Adelphi a Temple of Health and pretends to do and does wonders with his electrical, magnetical, aerial, aetherial and musical influences—in open defiance to the Faculty. His house is crowded, he gets money and the Faculty begin to follow his example in setting up electrical mills for the sake of health and money.[6]

3. Baron Joseph Podmaniczky (1756–1823) was a Protestant peer of Hungary who held various political appointments under Emperor Joseph II. He served as a counselor to the Fiume government, a member of a commission to study the Austrian customs system, and an Austrian representative to Paris in 1815. It was in his palace that the seven-year-old Franz Liszt first performed: *Magyar Eletrajzi Lexicon* (3 vols., Budapest, 1967–81), II, 423. See his letter below, after July 25.

4. The baron, described in his certificate of membership as "a gentleman well versed in various branches of Litterature & especially Natural History," was elected to the Royal Society on June 8, 1780. One of his sponsors was BF's friend Jean-Hyacinthe de Magellan: Royal Society, *Journal Books*, XXX, 27; Royal Society, *Certificate of Membership Book*, IV, 44.

5. By the original statutes of the Society fellows were required to pay an admission fee of 40 s. They were also expected to make weekly contributions of 1 s. toward its expenses. In lieu of these weekly charges, however, fellows could choose to pay a fixed sum at the time of admission. In 1776 this fee had been set at 26 guineas: *The Record of the Royal Society of London for the Promotion of Natural Knowledge* (4th ed., London, 1940), pp. 83, 94–5, 288.

6. For Dr. James Graham (1745–1794) see the *DNB*. He describes his house (located at the Royal Terrace, Adelphi, overlooking the Thames River) and his "most powerful Medico-electrical Apparatus" in *A Sketch: or, Short Description of Dr. Graham's Medical Apparatus, &c.* (London, 1780), pp. 3, 89.

Though there is a deal of madness in that, it will be productive however of some good experiments, and at the end turn out an improvement of Science; for good comes from evil, which I hope and wish may be the case of this and of Your Excellency's country.

Mr. Williams's Lectures on the principle of universal toleration and benevolence have not yet operated these desirable virtues in the minds of the Publick;[7] nevertheless he continues warm in their interest and sympathizes with me in the warmth of that dutiful respect, wherewith I have the honour to be Your Excellency's most obedient humble Servant   R. E. RASPE.

Orders and commands to be directed to Mr. Digges.

Addressed: To His Excellency / Dr. Benjamin Francklin / Minister of the United States / of America / at / Paris.

Notation: Raspe July 25. 1780

From Vergennes

Copy: Library of Congress; draft:[8] Archives du Ministère des affaires étrangères

a Versailles le 25 Juillet 1780.

Je viens de recevoir, Monsieur, une Lettre de M. Jon: *Loring Austin* se disant agent pour l'Etat de Massachusset,[9] comme je ne connois point ce Particulier, je ne puis que vous renvoyer Sa Lettre, parce que je ne saurois recevoir que par votre Canal les demandes qui interessent soit les Etats unis en general, soit chaque Etat en particulier.[1] Je crois devoir vous observer d'ailleurs que

7. David Williams' *Lectures on the Universal Principles and Duties of Religion and Morality . . .* (2 vols., London, 1779) was based upon a course of lectures on moral philosophy that he delivered at the Margaret Street Chapel. In the fall of 1778 he had sent BF proposals for their publication: XXVII, 354–5; XXXII, 378–9; J. Dybikowski, *On Burning Ground: an Examination of the Ideas, Projects and Life of David Williams* (Oxford, 1993), pp. 62–3, 306.

8. In the hand of Gérard de Rayneval.

9. Austin, who had brought to France the news of Saratoga (XXV, 102–3), had returned to obtain a loan for the state of Massachusetts: XXXII, 250–1n, 528; *Adams Papers*, VIII, 309n. Unsuccessful in France, he proceeded to Amsterdam, where he found lodgings with Francis Dana: *Sibley's Harvard Graduates*, XVI, 306. We have not located a copy of his letter.

1. BF had served as an intermediary for state requests to France: *e.g.*, XXX, 205.

les Circonstances actuelles ne nous permettent pas de prendre en Consideration l'Objet de la Lettre du Sr. Austin.

J'ai l'honneur d'être tres sincerement, Monsieur, Votre très humble et très obeissant Serviteur   (signé) DE VERGENNES.

M. Franklin.

From Jonathan Williams, Jr.

ALS: American Philosophical Society; copy: Yale University Library

Dear & honoured Sir.   Nantes July 25. 1780.

I arrived here in 50 Hours after I left you & found all my Family well.— I received by last Post from Morlaix, where I hear a Cartel is arrived, a Letter from Capt Manly of which the inclosed is Copy, poor Cunningham is yet alive as you will see.—[2] I wish it were possible to get all these poor Fellows exchanged, you see by the Letter that the English endeavour to persuade them that the Fault lays on our side which is no doubt an Artifice to induce them to enter the English Service & they have in some measure succeeded. I am making all ready for the Breton as fast as possible and hope soon to hear from Mr de Chaumont about her coming round.

I am ever with the greatest Respect Your dutifull & Affectionate Kinsman   JONA WILLIAMS J

It is said here that the Spanish Fleet has joined M de Guichen.

From Baron Joseph Podmaniczky

AL: American Philosophical Society

This Sunday morning. [after July 25, 1780][3]
Baron Podmaniczki presents his respectfull compliments to Dr:

2. Writing to JW from Mill Prison, on July 16, Manley described the despair among prisoners at the failure of an exchange, which seemed to be the fault of the French. He tried to escape, but was caught and confined to the black hole. Eight Americans have defected, and entered English service. In a postscript, he added that Gustavus Conyngham had arrived a few days since, and was recovering. The copy of Manley's letter, certified by JW, is at the APS.
3. The date of Raspe's letter introducing him, above.

Franklin, and takes the liberty of asking the permission to wait upon him to day at dinner; the day of his leaving this town being fixed on next Wednesday; But as one of his Friends, the Brother of Mr: de Walkiers St: Amand[4] has entreated the Baron to procure him the honour of the Doctors acquaintance, he would take it as the most particular favour if the Doctor would excuse him if he brings him along with him. Mr. and Mrs. le Roy and Mr: Magellan from London have as the Baron heared, a mind of calling likewise upon the Doctor.

Addressed: à Monsieur / Monsieur le Docteur / Franklin, Ministre Plèni: / potenciere de l'amerique / Septentrionale / à Passy.[5]

Notation: Baron Podmaniczki

To Dumas

LS:[6] American Philosophical Society; copy: Library of Congress; transcript: National Archives

Dear Sir,   Passy, July 26. 1780.

I wrote to Mrs: De Neuville by the last Post[7] in answer to theirs of the 14th. I hope they received my Letter. It signified that I would accept the Bills drawn on M. Laurens. I find by a Vote of Congress on the 4th of March, that they then stopt drawing,[8] and

4. Charles-Louis Walckiers de St. Amand, a young Brussels "electrician" whom Jan Ingenhousz had recommended to BF (XXXII, 345). The brother mentioned here is probably Edouard-Dominique-Sébastien-Joseph (1758–1837), a wealthy banker, prominent freemason, and Belgian patriot; he became a vicomte in 1786. Information courtesy of Georges Walckiers. For further details see *Biographie Nationale Publiée par l'Académie Royale des Sciences, des Lettres et des Beaux-Arts de Belgique* (44 vols., Brussels, 1866–1986), XXVII, 37–42.

5. In a corner of the address sheet, BF wrote the following series of homophones in French and English, evidently unfinished: "é ai ais ois / a, ai, ay, ei, eigh,".

6. In the hand of L'Air de Lamotte. As it is badly worn, we have supplied from the copy some missing words.

7. Above, July 21; it was written in answer to theirs of July 13.

8. On that date Congress resolved "That the Board of Treasury be directed to suspend the sale of any more bills of exchange, till the further order of Congress": *JCC*, XVI, 228.

I am informed no more Bills have been issued since. I could not relish those Gentlemen's Proposal of Mortaging *all our Estates* for the little Money Holland is likely to lend us. But I am obliged to them for their Zeal in our Cause.

I received and thank you for the Protest relating to the Election of the Coadjutor.[9]

You seem to be too much affected with the taking of Charlestown. It is so far a Damage to us as it will enable the Enemy to exchange a great Part of the Prisoners we had in our hands, otherwise their Affairs will not be much advanced by it. They have successively been in Possession of the Capitals of 5 Provinces, viz. Massachusetts Bay, Rhode island, Pennsylvania, New York and Georgia; but were not therefore in Possession of the Provinces themselves. New-York and Georgia still continue their Operations as free States; and so I Suppose will S. Carolina. The Cannon will be recover'd with the Place; if not, our furnaces are constantly at work in making more. The Destroying of our Ships by the English is only like shaving our Beards, which will grow again. Their Loss of Provinces is like the Loss of Limbs which can never again be united to their Body.

I was sorry to hear of your Indisposition. Take care of yourself. Honey is a good thing for Obstructions in the veins. I hope your Health is by this Time re-established.

I am less committed than you imagine in the affair between Jones & Landais. The latter was not dispossessed by me of his Command, but quitted it. He afterwards took into his head to resume it, which the former's too long stay at Paris gave him an Opportunity of effecting. Capt. Jones is going in the Ariel frigate to America, where they may Settle their Affairs as they can.

The Capt. Cornu of Dunkerque, who occasioned the Loss of our Dispatches, is himself taken by the English.— I have no doubt of the Truth of what Mr. White told you about the facility with which the Tax was collected.—[1]

9. An enclosure to Dumas' July 7 letter, above.
1. This paragraph was written in response to Dumas' July 6 letter, above. The *Princesse de Robecq* was captured by the warships H.M.S. *Ariadne* and *Fly: London Courant, and Westminster Chronicle*, July 5, 1780 (which gives the privateer captain's name as Robert Corun).

That same Baron de Wulffen has not pleased me, having left little Debts behind him unpaid, tho' I furnished him with 20 Guineas. As he had been with his Brother at Venlo before he saw you where he might get Money. I wonder at his borrowing of you.

I thank you for the Vote of Congress you send me dated the 23d March.— I imagine 484 went in that Vessel to 533, and may have been detained there for Convoy.[2]

Your Dispatches by M. Gillon are in the Alliance, which sailed the 7th. or 9th. Instant.

This will be delivered to you by his Excellency John Adams Esqr. whom I earnestly recommend to your best Civilities. He has never been in Holland and your Counsels will be of use to him.

My best Wishes attend you, being ever Dear Sir, Your most obedient and most humble Servt.   B FRANKLIN

Endorsed: [July?] 26 [*illegible*] Mr. Franklin

William Temple Franklin to John Adams

AL: Massachusetts Historical Society

Passy 26. July 1780

Mr Franklin junr. has the honour of sending herewith to his Exy Mr Adams, his Grandfathers Dispatches for Holland; & has that of wishing him his Health, & an agreable Journey./.[3]

2. The Congressional resolution is the one Dumas had sent on July 20, above. "484" is the code number for Laurens; "533" represents Martinico (Martinique).

3. On the afternoon of the 26th JA went to BF's residence at the Hôtel de Valentinois for a passport. At one o'clock the following afternoon he and his sons John Quincy and Charles set out for the Netherlands: Taylor, *J.Q. Adams Diary*, 1, 35–6; Butterfield, *John Adams Diary*, II, 442.

From Antoine-Laurent Lavoisier

ALS: Harvard University Library

Monsieur   Paris 26. juillet 1780./

Le S. fouquet qui aura lhonneur de vous remettre la présente
lettre, est un sujet intelligent, attaché très anciennement au Service des poudres de france, qui a passé il y a quelques années en
amérique, pour y construire des fabriques de poudre.[4] L'objet de
son voyage se trouvant rempli à la Satisfaction du congrès des
etats unis, il vient de repasser en france. Le congrés avoit pris
l'engagement de faire les frais de son retour, et il avoit été embarqué à cet effet Sur la frégate la considération, armée par le
Congrès pour ramener M. Gérard en france.[5] Le gros tems ayant
obligé ce batiment de relacher à la martinique, le S. fouquet y est
resté cinq mois à Ses frais, et pendant cet intervalle de tems, il a
dépensé beaucoup d'argent, de sorte que l'objet du congrès, qui
étoit de le renvoyer en france sans qu'il lui en Coutat rien, ne Se
trouve point rempli. Dans ces circonstances le S. fouquet a recours
à votre justice pour obtenir le remboursement des frais qu'il a fait
pendant Son séjour à la martinique. Le S. fouquet est un homme
zelé et intelligent, qui paroit avoir fait en amerique des établisse-
mens utiles. Il est digne de vos bontés et de votre protection.

Je Suis avec respect Monsieur Votre très humble et très obeissant serviteur   LAVOISIER

From the Abbés Chalut and Arnoux to Franklin
and John Adams

AL:[6] American Philosophical Society

dimanche. [before July 27, 1780][7]

Les abbés Chalut et arnoux ont l'honneur de souhaiter le bon-
jour aux deux respectables deputés du Congres general. Ils sont

4. Nicolas Fouquet and his son Marc (XXVII, 207–8n) served in the American army from November, 1777, until October, 1779. The elder Fouquet's
letter, Aug. 2, is below.
5. The frigate carrying Gérard was the *Confederacy:* XXX, 357–8n.
6. In the hand of Arnoux.
7. The day JA, who had been in Paris since Feb. 9, left for the Netherlands:
WTF to JA, July 26, above; XXXI, 473n. Also possible is sometime in July, 1781,

bien fachés de ne pouvoir pas se rendre à l'honneur de leur invitation, pour vendredi prochain ils sont empechés Ce jour là, ce qui excite leurs regrets.[8]

Addressed: A Monsieur / Monsieur franklin / Ministre plenipotentiare / des états unis d'Amerique / à *Passy.*

From Edward Macatter

LS: American Philosophical Society

Hond. sir   Morlaix the 28th. July 1780.

My friends and Agents in Morlaix, Messrs. Jno. Diot & Co, have forwarded to Your Excellency an abstract of my Journal and have acquainted you that I brought 18 prisonners, which were lodged in the Gaol of this Town.[9]

This day the Commissary of this town[1] has acquainted me that he intended to send over to England, by the Britannia Carteel ship Captn. John Floyd Master, the above prisonners; the Uncertainty of their being to be Exchanged hereafter for Americans, has induced me to Request from the Commissary that they Shou'd not be Sent off, untill fresh Orders be issued from Your Excellency for their fate, and I woud like Rather to maintain 'em in Gaol at my Own Expences, than to have 'em lost for the Congress.

Altho' the remaining time of my Cruize is but Short, I hope to make it Good, and that 'ere 'tis over, I Shall fetch great many more Prisoners in So much as to be Worthwhile Sending a Carteel Ship Over to England to have a like Number of my poor distressed Countrymen Exchanged, God may Send it!

I Expect Your Excellency will take Care that these 18. prisonners of myne Shall not be Exchanged, but for a like number of

---

when JA was back in Paris for a few weeks, summoned by Vergennes to consult on proposals for mediating between the warring powers: *Adams Correspondence,* IV, 170n.

8. The abbés also wrote (in Chalut's hand) on Tuesday, Sept. 26, [1780], accepting BF's invitation for the following Friday. APS.

9. Diot & Co. had reported on July 24, above, that the *Black Princess* had brought in sixteen prisoners.

1. Boucault.

Americans, for, Endeed, not one single man wou'd go any more to Sea with me, Were they not Sure Your Excellency wou'd do so.

I Still must Crave your Protection and good Offices, and I Shall Spare no Opportunity to prove to Your Excellency that I am not undeserving of Same, Nay at the risk of my Life and bottom.

The favor of your answer I beg your Excellency will direct for me to Messrs. Jno. Diot & Co.

I Expect to sail to morrow, if the wind answers.

I Remain Most Respectfully Honored sir Your most obedient and most Humble Servant   EDWARD MACATTER

To His Excellency B. Franklin

Notation: Capt. Maccatter. July 28. 80

To Herman Esser[2]   Copy: Library of Congress

Sir,   Passy, July 29. 1780.

I cannot give you the last Encouragement to go to America in Expectation of Service in the armies of the United States. There are already more officers in the Country than they can find Employment for, and many are returned to Europe, because they could not be placed. I have not authority to promise Commissions, nor has M. de Wolffen.[3] I never received any letter from him mentioning you or any Propositions he had made to any officer. I have had only one Letter from him since he went to Holland, which was dated the 7th. Instant, and which only acquainted me that he was well at Venlo, and had forwarded my Pacquets to the Hague.[4] I would advise you not to undertake a hazardous and expensive Voyage to America upon any Promises

2. In answer to his of July 22, discussed in our annotation of the commission seekers, July 10, above. L'Air de Lamotte has here miscopied his name.

3. Although Wulffen was offering Esser a commission he was not even still considered to be in American service: Fitzpatrick, *Writings of Washington,* xv, 206n.

4. For the packets see Dumas' letter of July 20.

made to you by a Person not authorized to make them. I have the Honour to be.

M. Le Capt. H. Elser à Venlo.

To Schweighauser Copy: Library of Congress

Sir, Passy, July 29. 1780.

I daily received yours of the 15. Instant.[5] By a Letter from Mrs. Gourlade and Moylan dated the 10th. I am assured that they never refused to continue supplying the Alliance with the necessary Provisions: Therefore a Charge from your Correspondent at L'Orient on that Account, will not be rightly brought against me.

In my last I mentioned that I might possibly in the Course of the Month have an Opportunity of shipping the old Arms. M. Williams will inform you when it offers. By that Vessel if not already gone, you may send young Slade and Miss Clarke. The Promisory Notes you formerly took from Officers payable to the President of Congress, I suppose you have already sent, if not, they may go by the same Opportunity. If the Notes sign'd were single, and not Triplicates, it will be well to keep the Originals, & send attested Copies. The Accounts against the American Captains who staid so long at Nantes by improperly [*word or words skipped?*] should also be sent over.

I never settled the affair of the Swedish Prizes,[6] being in Expectation that the Claimants would have prosecuted Capt. Landais for their Damages if they had a right to any. I should have been containted to have seen the disputed brought before the Courts in France, to whose Jurisdiction all our Cruisers are directed to submit their Prizes brought into this kingdom. I depend on your being able to defend the Captain on the Proof that the Swede did not produce his Papers to show the Prizes was

5. Brief extracts of this letter, and the next one mentioned, are printed above.
6. Two ships taken by Landais in early 1779: XXVIII, 488, 563. Swedish Ambassador Creutz repeatedly protested the incident: XXX, 295n; XXXI, 362–3.

neutral property till after they was brought in; and in this View I returned you all the Papers. When I afterwards wrote to have them again in Order to discourse on the Subject with the Swedish Ambassador you answered that to save Postage, they being bulky, you would send them by some good private Hand. I never received them; and the Swedish Ambassador saying nothing more to me on the subject, I forgot it. Capt. Landais was in France from October 1779 till July 1780. And as the Claimants neglected to Sue him here, they must now follow him to America, where is no doubt they will meet with the Justice that may be found due to them.— If they resolve to do this, it will be well to transmit authenticated Copies of those Papers to the Congress; and Will pay the Charges you may be at in getting them transcribed.— For I suppose they are still in your Hands.

With great Regard I have the Honour to be Sir, &c.

P.S. July 29. Since writing the above, I have received your Respected Letter of the 25th.[7] It seems to me that you have made some mistake in your Calculation both of the Expence of the Boxes and of the Number of Gun Barrels they will contain for 334 Boxes at 60 in a Box, will contain 20040 instead of 3000 lb. as you mention. But having measured a Musket Barrel, I find that Box which is a foot broad and foot deep in the Inside, will, if the Barrels are placed Muzzels and Breeches together, hold ten Rows of ten in a Row which is 100 in Each Box; and therefore 200 such Boxes will be sufficient, and at 5 *l.t.* a Box will cost only 1000 *l.t.* tho I should imagine that in agreeing for such a Number you might have them much cheaper.— If the Barrels are already no better than old Iron, it will not be worth while to send them at all. If they are yet in a State to be servieable as Gun Barrels, and would be reduced by the Rust to old Iron by being sent loose and open, the Sum of 1000 *l.t.* to preserve them in Boxes will not be ill laid out. Therefore on the whole supposing my Calculation nearly Right I am still of Opinion that Boxes should be made for those that are good & Servieable. Perhaps the Barrels may be something thicker than that I have measured, in Which case the Boxes must be a little larger, but will not therefore cost much

7. Missing. BF forwarded it to JW; see the following document.

more. I approve of your disposing of the Beef, and of such other Lumber as is not worth sending.

M. Schweighauser,

To Jonathan Williams, Jr.

AL (draft): American Philosophical Society; copy: Library of Congress

Dear Jonathan,   Passy, July 29. 1780

By a Letter from M. Schweighauser I find you were arrived: I hope you found all well. He writes me a Letter relating to the 20,000 Musket Barrels which I send for your Perusal & Opinion, with a Copy of my Answer. You will return it to me.[8] I find in his Account of the Arsenal, that the rest are gone or pack'd, & I should think it hardly worthwhile to unpack them. Indeed I do not find any Muskets pack'd with Stocks, except 30 Cases from Holland which I suppose are good and new. I wish to know where the Ship is, and when you begin to load. I also want much to know what Bills you have drawn on M de Chaumont, and when payable, and whether you have now drawn for the whole, and what the Amount. I am

Mr Jonath. Williams

BF. to J Williams July 29. 1780 Desire to know what Bills have been drawn on Mr de Chaumont & the Amount

From Francis Coffyn   ALS: American Philosophical Society

Hond Sir.   Dunkerque 29. July 1780.

Agreable to The unfortunate Captain Conynghams request, I have The honour to enclose a Copy of a letter I received from him dated Mill prison the 10th. inst,[9] The general protection

8. JW did so on Aug. 3, below, but the enclosed letter is now missing.

9. In the enclosed letter Conyngham reported that his treatment in prison was "most cruel," his captors taking even the "necessaries of life" from him. He asked Coffyn to notify BF of his situation so that he might procure some relief, as his health was unfit to endure the hardships of prison.

your Excellency chearfully grants to those who suffer by the calamities of The warr, and the particular attachment, you have allways profess'd, for The man who now claims your Excellency's assistance, render all recommendation in his behalf needless; Therefor I shall only add, That if I can be instrumental in the execution of The acts of benevolence, your Excellency will readely bestow on him, nothing shall be wanting on my part to alleviate his distress,[1] and to convince your Excellency of the profound respect with which I have the honour to remain Your Excellencys most obedt. & most devoted humble Servant

FRANS. COFFYN

From Silas Deane   ALS: American Philosophical Society

My Dear sir   Rochelle 29th July 1780
I arrived at Rochfort Two Days since after Forty Three Days passage from York in Virginia,[2] and came here last Evening to Visit a Friend. The length of Our passage, has prevented my being the Bearer of any News from America, later than what you are already acquainted with, for which Reason I shall take Nantes in my way and pass a few Days there with Mr. Williams, and shall have the happiness in a Week or Ten Days of embracing You at Passy.[3] I had Letters from Philadelphia a few Days before I left Virginia, Mr Bache & Your Daughter must have been well then, or I should have been informed of the Contrary, as my Letter was from Our Mutual Friend Mr Morriss, You will conceive easier, than I can express, my impatience, after so long & unexpected an Absence, to see You, & to converse on many Subjects proper only for a private interview. I pray You present my Compliments to Mr Franklin & to Mr. Chaumont, & Family &

1. Coffyn was not the only one concerned for Conyngham. On July 26 the merchant Jonathan Nesbitt sent Conyngham a credit of £50 and told him he had written BF about his situation by the last post: Neeser, *Conyngham*, pp. 198–9. We have not found such a letter from Nesbitt.

2. Deane sailed on the *Fier Roderigue: Deane Papers*, IV, 149, 153, 175–6.

3. Deane reported his arrival as Saturday, Aug. 19; he took his "old lodgings" with his former colleague BF in the Hôtel de Valentinois: *Deane Papers*, IV, 195–6. BF loaned him 1200 *l.t.* on Sept. 2: Cash Book.

be assured that I am with the sincerest Attachment & Respect My Dear sir Your Most Obedt. & Very Hume. servt.   S DEANE

I pray You to forward the inclosed. I have Two or Three Letters for You, but they are of a very old Date, having received them in December last at Virginia, where I pass'd the Winter. I should however have sent them on but they are at Rochfort with my Baggage.

His Excellency B Franklin Esqr.

Notation: Silas Deane Esqr. Rochelle 29 July. 1780

From Jonathan Williams, Jr.

ALS: American Philosophical Society; copy: Yale University Library

Dear & hond Sir.   Nantes July 29. 1780.

I wrote you per last Post since which your Case of wine has been sent to the Messagerie.[4] M de Francis arrived in Town from Rochelle last Evening he came passenger in the Fier Rodrigue which arrived at Isle de Rhe after first seeing her Convoy of 18 Sail safe in the Bordeaux River. M Dean is a passenger in the Fier Rodrigue. M de Francis[5] tells me he left maryland the 14 June & at that Time they had no news of the Chevalier Ternay.— Our People are not in that State of despondence on accot of the Loss of Charlestown as has been represented, they are no doubt sorry for it but they are as firm as ever and will always support the Cause. I suppose you will have Letters by the Post from Rochelle & Bordeaux and consequently know all the Details: My Letters will not come to hand 'till Tuesday next. I have it not therefore

4. While at Passy, JW had so praised the Bordeaux wine supplied him by V. & P. French & nephew that he made his friends' "mouths water for a taste of it." On July 22, the day after he returned to Nantes, he requested the firm to ship one hogshead of the finest Bordeaux to each of three addressees: BF, Bancroft, and JA. Yale University Library. (He also ordered, the same day, a large English cheddar cheese taken from a prize ship at Lorient to be sent to Mme Helvétius: JW to James Cuming, July 22, Yale University Library.)

5. Théveneau de Francy, Beaumarchais' secretary, who was returning from his mission to America where he signed a contract with Congress. See XXVII, 137, 382–3; XXVIII, 528n.

in my Power to give you any particulars, As soon as I know anything further I will give you all that is interesting, and in turn I shall be obliged to you for such Information as you can with propriety give me.

The Jane a large Ship of 320 hhds of Tobacco sunk at about 60 Leagues from the Capes & the Fier Rodrigue saved the Crew.

I am ever with the greatest Respect Yours most dutifully & Affectionately JONA WILLIAMS J

Doctor Franklin

To Thomas Digges

Copy: Library of Congress

Dear Sir,   Passy, July 30. 1780.

I received yours of the 29th. past, and of ⁶ Inst. but that you mention as sent by Barnet never came to Hand,⁷ and he has already play'd so many cheating Tricks in France that I do not expect to see him here again. It is an Irishman who having been once employed in one of our Privaters, and taken, has ever since he escaped from England rambled about Europe pretending to be an American and sometimes a Relation of mine, borrowing Money or running in debt everywhere.⁸ I am heartily sorry that you have been so robbed by him, and by his Scotch Acquaintance.

I am much obliged to your friend for his kind Intentions of sending me Spectacles of the Cherokee Chrystal.⁹ Enclosed is the Glass you require.

By this time you will probably have heard from Capt. Cunningham. He has been very unfortunate, and very ill treated. I have unaccountably mislaid your last Letter. But I think there was some mention in it of applying to M. Samuel Hartley relat-

6. From the description, below, of the last letter BF had received from Digges, he must mean that of July 12; apparently he had not yet received Digges's of the 17th. Both are above. Digges's letter of June 29 is in XXXII, 620–4.

7. Barnett had carried a now-missing letter of June 8; see XXXII, 620, and Digges to BF, July 17.

8. For Barnett's prior financial dealings with BF see XXVIII, 69–70, 322.

9. XXXII, 620.

ing to the Exchange of Cunningham.[1] Perhaps it may not be wise to show him the Enclosed Letters. Till we can procure the Captain's Liberty, I recommend him to your kind assistance in supplying him with what may be necessary.

Don't be discouraged by the present Triumph of a People who are so easily elated. God governs, and the Second' Hour of their Insolence may be as short as the first.

Enclos'd is a Letter for M. Peters,[2] I am obliged to send it to you to be forwarded, because I do not know his address. I am.

Mr. Digges.

To John Jay

LS:[3] American Philosophical Society; two copies: Library of Congress

Dear Sir,   Passy, July 31. 1780.

I write this Line just to acknowledge the Receipt of your Favour of the 17th. & Mr. Carmichaels of the 18th. (with the Pacquet of Papers in good Order,) which I shall soon answer fully. At present I can only say that I have given Orders for a Credit to you of another 1000 £ Sterg., to be proportionally divided between you: I hope the Remittances will arrive before this Sum is expended. I find myself obliged to advance likewise to Messrs. Adams & Dana.

I congratulate you & Mrs. Jay sincerely on the Birth of your Daughter; being with sincere Esteem, Dear Sir, Your most obedt & most humble Servant   B FRANKLIN

His Excy. J: Jay Esqr

Addressed: A son Excellence / Monsieur Jay, &ca &a / A Madrid.

Endorsed: Dor. Franklin 31 July 1780 Recd. 18 Augt. 1780 / mentions his havg ordered a Credit of 1000 £ Ster

1. See Digges to BF, July 12.
2. The recipient surely was William Peters, whom Digges had located for BF: XXIX, 492, 530, 581, 666, 736. The letter may have been from his son Richard.
3. In WTF's hand.

From William Strahan[4]

ALS: American Philosophical Society

Dear Sir   London July 31. 1780.

The young Gentleman who will have the Honour to put this into your Hands, Mr. Richard Henderson, is a Son of a worthy Scotsman long since settled in Maryland. He has resided here above seven Years past, and comes to France, by the Advice of his Father, purely with a View to his farther Improvement in the Study of the Law. Presuming on our ancient Friendship, I take the Liberty to recommend him to your good Counsel and good Offices. Whether he should remain in Paris, or retire to Dijon, Rheims, or any other Parliamentary Town, you will best be able to determine.— Your Countenance and best Advice is all he wants, and these I hope you will readily give him; and you may be assured he will duly estimate, and acknowledge with Gratitude the Honour and Advantage he must derive from your friendly Notice of him. You will, at the same time, confer a great Obligation on Dear Sir Your most obedient Sert

WILL: STRAHAN

My best Respects to Mr. Alexander,[5] I pray you, when you next see him

Addressed: Benjamin Franklin Esqr. / Paris

Notation: Strahan 31 Juillet 1783

From John Torris

ALS: American Philosophical Society

Honnd. Sir   Dunkerque 31st. July 1780.

On receit of the Letter you did me the Honnor to write me,[6] I have Immediatly Handed to My lord De Calonne our Inten-

4. Written in response to a July 25 request from Thomas Moore of Clarges St., London, for a letter of introduction to BF for Richard Henderson. He explained that the young man, who had been educated in Scotland, proposed to study in Rheims or perhaps Dijon for two years. APS.

5. Probably William Alexander.

6. Missing. Undoubtedly it was written on or after July 25, when BF informed Vergennes, above, that he would withdraw American commissions from French-owned privateers.

dant,[7] a Memorial Showing the Dangerous Consequences attending to the Armatteur, & nay to the State, the Withdrawing the American Commission to our Black Princess, & that, at any rate, there is an Impossibility of recalling it untill her three months Cruise are out.[8] 'Twill be forwarded to Mylord De Sartine; & I can assure, Your Excellency, That you will be entreated to Continue me your favours, which I Shall ever most gratefully acknowledge. My orders to Macatter are very positive never to Touch or Mollest in the Least, any Neutral Vessell whatsoever, Till now He has most Carefully obey'd them, & I am so positive that He will never meddle with any one, that I have offer'd whatever Security which may be requiered for the Same.

The Princess is now at Sea to Compleat her Cruise,[9] & I expect She will Come here round by the North, & indeed, 'Twou'd be must unjust & ungenerous to all, & nay it is utterly Impossible, to recall her Commission before her Three months Cruise are finisht.

The Black Prince is lost a great while past,[1] & his Commission is given up.

The Sales of the flora's Small Cargoe have Produced but 14,000 *l.t.*, & I wait for your Excellencys determination relative to the disposall of the Same, favor of the Captor, to which I See no further difficulties, as the Dutch Shippers give it freely up, by acknowledging it is the Property of the Ennemy, except the 31. Bales of Clover Seeds. I say I am but waiting for this Produce, to settle diffinitevely with my Concerns & the Crew, who drive me to distraction, altho' I have over paid the most.

I Beseech your Excellency will also forwd. as soon as Possible your Condamnation for the Black Princess's Ransoms.

---

7. Charles-Alexandre de Calonne (1734–1802) was intendant of Flanders. He became controller general of finance in 1783: *DBF*.

8. The three months presumably dated from May, when the new *Black Princess* assumed the commission of an earlier privateer of the same name and undertook her first cruise: Clark, *Ben Franklin's Privateers*, pp. 131–3.

9. She did not sail from the roadstead of Morlaix until Aug. 1: Diot & Co. to BF, Aug. 7, below.

1. In April: XXXII, 259–60.

I have the Honnor to be with greatest respect Honnd. Sir Your Excellency's Most obedient & most Hble Servant   J. TORRIS

His Excellency Dr. Franklin./.

Endorsed: 31 July 1780

Notation: Torris

From Vergennes

LS: National Archives; draft:[2] Archives du Ministère des affaires étrangères; copies: University of Pennsylvania Library, Library of Congress, Massachusetts Historical Society; transcript: National Archives

à Versailles le 31. Juillet 1780.

Le caractere dont vous etes revétu, Monsieur, votre sagesse et la confiance que je mêts dans vos principes et dans vos sentiments, m'engagent à vous communiquer la correspondance que je viens d'avoir avec Mr. Adams;[3] Vous trouverés, je pense, dans les lettres de ce plénipotentiaire, des opinions et une tournure qui ne répondent ni à la maniere avec laquelle je me suis expliqué avec lui, ni avec la liaison intime qui subsiste entre le Roi et les Etats unis. Vous ferés de toutes ces piéces l'usage que votre prudence vous suggérera. Quant à moi je desire que vous les fassiés passer au congrès afin qu'il sache la conduite que Mr. Adams tient à notre égard, et qu'il puisse juger s'il est doué autant que le congrès le desire sans doute, de l'esprit de conciliation qui convient à une besogne aussi importante et aussi délicate que celle qui lui est confiée.[4]

J'ai l'honneur d'être très Sincérement, Monsieur votre très humble et très obéissant Serviteur./.   DE VERGENNES

Mr. francklin

2. In Gérard de Rayneval's hand.

3. With the transcript is a list of the letters Vergennes now forwards to BF, as well as a list of those he had sent BF at the end of June (for which see XXXII, 626n). The July letters, which are numbered 6 through 14, are JA to Vergennes, July 13, 17, 21, 26, and 27, and Vergennes' responses of July 20, 25 (with enclosure), and 29: *Adams Papers,* IX, 516–29; X, 1–4, 16–18, 32–51, 56–8.

4. For an analysis of JA's motives in conducting such a provocative correspondence see *Adams Papers,* IX, 516–20.

Notations in different hands:[5] Original Letter of Count de Vergennes to Dr Franklin, on sending him Mr Adams's Correspondence. / Letter from Ct de Vergennes to Doctr. Franklin July 31. 1780 with 9 Numbers from 6 to 14 inclusive

To Dumas

Transcript: National Archives

Sir   Passy 1st. Agt. 1780.

The Bearer of this, Mr. appleton, is lately arrived from Boston. He is recommended to me as a young Gentleman of excellent character, & as such, I beg leave to introduce him to your acquaintance and Civilities.[6]

With great Esteem, I am Dear Sir your most obedient & most humble Servant.   B. FRANKLIN.

M. Dumas.

From Sartine

Copy: Library of Congress

Versailles le 1er. Aout. 1780.

Je crois devoir vous prevenir, Monsieur, que M. Boucault Commissaire à Morlaix me marque que le Corsaire la Princesse Noire lui a remis 26. otages et 16. prisonniers Anglois. Je vous prie de ne pas differer de me faire connoitre si ce Commissaire peut remettre ces Prisonniers, a titre d'Echange pour le Compte des Americains, au Capitaine du Parlementaire Anglois la Britannia qui se trouve dans ce moment à Morlaix,[7] ou s'ils doivent rester

---

5. The first notation is by WTF. The second was made after the document reached the United States, most probably in February, 1781 (*JCC*, XIX, 174).

6. John Appleton had been recommended to BF by Samuel Cooper: XXXII, 109. While he was in Paris Appleton sent BF an undated note accepting his invitation to have dinner on Sunday. APS. After leaving Paris he met JA in Leiden and accompanied him to Amsterdam: *Adams Correspondence*, III, 390n; Taylor, *J.Q. Adams Diary*, I, 52.

7. In accordance with the cartel arrangements formalized in March, 1780. During the war the British returned more than 31,000 French sailors in exchange for some 16,000 of their own: Olive Anderson, "The Establishment of British Supremacy at Sea and the Exchange of Naval Prisoners of War, 1689–1783," *English Hist. Rev.*, LXXV (1960), 82n.

dans ce Port à votre Disposition. Dans le cas où M. Boucault ne les auroit pas encore remis au Capitaine Anglois; ce qu'il auroit pu faire, croyant devoir profiter de cette Occasion, pour les renvoyer en Angleterre, et pour lors J'aurai l'honneur de vous envoyer le Reçu qu'il aura exigé du Capitaine de ce Parlementaire.

J'ai l'honneur d'être avec la Consideration la plus distinguée, Monsieur, votre très humble et très obeissant Serviteur

(signé) DE SARTINE.

M. Franklin.

To Edward Macatter[8]

Copy: Library of Congress

Sir,   Passy Augt. 2. 1780.

I congratulate you on the Success of your late Cruize. I see by the English News Papers that you have much alarmed the Enemy's Coasts, and done great Damage to their Commerce,[9] your Bringing in so many Prisoners is another considerable Service, and you may depend on having your generous Intentions fulfilled in the Exchange and Deliverance of so many Americains. Therefore if the British Cartel ship is not gone I wish they may be put on board her, a Receipt being taken for them by the Commissary, that they are sent on account of America; which Receipit will be remitted to me. I have the Honor to be, with much Esteem for your Activity, and Bravery, Sir,

Capt. Macatter.

To Sartine

Copy: Library of Congress

Monseigneur,   Passy, le 2. Aout 1780.

J'ai l'honneur de vous remercier de l'information contenue Dans la lettre que vous avez eu la bonté de m'ecrire hier au sujet

8. In answer to Macatter's of July 28, above.
9. The exploits of the *Black Princess* were reported, for example, in the July 17, 18, 19, 22, and 24 issues of the *London Courant, and Westminster Chronicle*.

des 16. Prisoniers amenés a Morlaix par le Corsaire la Princesse noire, ainsi que de l'offre que votre Excellence a bien volue me faire, de les envoyer en Angleterre par le parlementaire anglois qui est actuellement dans le port— J'accepte volontiers cette proposition et je prie votre Excellence de donner ses ordres en Consequence, et qu'on me remette le reçu du Capitaine Parlementaire, comme quoi il les reçoit pour le Compte des Americains—

Je suis avec Respect, Monseigneur, de votre Excellence le tres humble et tres obeissant serviteur.

M. De Sartine

From Nicolas Fouquet[1]

AL: National Archives

2 aout 1780.

Le Sieur fouquet a lhonneur de remettre à Son Excellence Monsieur francklin un memoire quil le Suplie dadresser aux Etats unis de l'amerique. Il a pour objet de demander une gratiffication de 1500 *l.t.* pour indemnité les depenses que le S. fouquet a été obligé de faire pour repasser En france ayant été forcé de quitter la fregate la Consideration lors de relache à la martinique et n'ayant pû obtenir Son passage Sur la fregate l'aurore Suivant les certifficats qu'ils joint a son memoire.[2]

Le S. fouquet Espere que Monsieur francklin qui a pris Connoissance des temoignages authentiques de satisfaction qui lui ont été donnés par les Etats voudra bien appuyer Son mémoire aupres d'Eux de sa recommandation et faire part à mm. les Regisseurs généraux des poudres de france de la reponse quil recevera.[3]

Endorsed: M. Fouquet's Memoire

1. For the gunpowder-maker see Lavoisier's letter of July 26.
2. Fouquet's memorial to Congress, dated Aug. 2, explains that the unexpected death of his wife required him to return to France to tend to his affairs and to care for his children. In support of his claim for expenses at Martinique he attached certificates from Gérard and from Parsons, Alston, & Co., American agents at St. Pierre. National Archives.
3. BF forwarded Fouquet's letter, memorial, and certificates with his letter to Huntington, Aug. 9, below. It was read in Congress on Feb. 22, 1781, and referred to the Board of War: *JCC*, XIX, 185. For a summary of testimonials

To Vergennes

LS:[4] Archives du Ministère des affaires étrangères; copy: Library of Congress

Sir   Passy Augt 3d. 1780.

It was indeed with very great Pleasure that I received and read the Letter your Exy. did me the honour of writing to me, communicating that of the President of Congress and the Resolutions of that Body relative to the Succours then expected:[5] For the Sentiments therein express'd are so different from the Language held by Mr Adams, in his late Letters to your Excellency[6] as to make it clear that it was from his particular Indiscretion alone, and not from any Instructions received by him, that he has given such just Cause of Displeasure, and that it is impossible his Conduct therein should be approved by his Constituents. I am glad he has not admitted me to any Participation in those Writings, and that he has taken the Resolution he expresses of not communicating with me or making use of my Intervention in his future Correspondence;[7] a Resolution that I believe he will keep, as he has never yet communicated to me more of his Business in Europe than I have seen in the News Papers. I live upon Terms of Civility with him, not of Intimacy. I shall as you desire lay before Congress the whole Correspondence which you have sent me for that purpose.

With the greatest & most sincere Respect, I am, Sir, Your Excellency's most obedient and most humble Servant

                                          B FRANKLIN

His Exy. the Count de Vergennes

Endorsed: M. De R.[8]

---

given by the various states for which the Fouquets had worked see the report submitted by the Board of War on Oct. 12, 1779, recommending a payment beyond the sum mentioned in their contract: *JCC*, xv, 1164–5.

4. In WTF's hand.

5. Above, July 24.

6. Discussed in Vergennes to BF, July 31, above.

7. In his July 27 letter to Vergennes: *Adams Papers*, x, 49.

8. This generally would indicate that Rayneval was expected to draft a reply, but, as far as we know, none was sent.

From Dumas   ALS: American Philosophical Society

Monsieur,   La Haie 3e. Août 1780.

L'Assemblée d'Hollande vient de se séparer pour jusqu'au commencement de Sept. Il ne S'y est rien passé d'interessant. Les deux Plénipotentiaires de la Rep. sont partis pour Petersbourg,[9] avec les Instructions, selon lesquelles ils doivent demander, qu'on garantisse les possessions de la rep., tant en Europe qu'aux deux Indes; Amsterdam persiste dans sa protestation contre ces Instructions,[1] & notamment contre cette demande inutile, qui ne tend qu'à traîner l'affaire en longueur: elle vouloit que l'on envoyât tout simplement à Mr. Swart le Résident de la rep. à Petersbourg, la résolution de L.H.P.[2] où l'accession de la rep. à la neutralité armée est résolue, sans condition, & qu'immédiatement après la signature faite en conséquence entre le dit Résident & le Ministere Russe, la Rep. fît une Déclaration aux Puissances belligérantes, analogue à celle de la Russie. *D'autres*, au contraire, ont espéré de faire échouer toute cette combinaison. Sur ces entrefaites, la déclaration inopinée du Danemarc a étrangement déconcerté ces derniers; & leur embarras vient de redoubler par une Déclaration à peu près semblable de la part de la Suede. Notre Ami pense qu'ils ne pourront plus reculer, sans encourir généralement le blâme d'avoir désobligé la Cour de Russie, & sacrifié le Commerce de cette rep. à celle de la Gr. Br., & en conséquence il soupçonne que, les Plénipotentiaires ont été munis d'un ordre secret, pour ne pas insister plus que de raison sur la condition susdite de la garantie.[3]

388. 259es. 601. 262. 610. YEB OEUPYQMBEXCGTNU

9. Wassenaer Starrenburg and Heeckeren tot Brantsenburg reached Danzig on Aug. 13 and St. Petersburg on Aug. 30: Fauchille, *Diplomatie française,* p. 526.

1. An English translation of a June 29 Amsterdam protest on the subject appears in Wharton, *Diplomatic Correspondence,* III, 829–32; Dumas enclosed a French translation with his Aug. 22 letter to BF, below.

2. "Leurs Hautes Puissances," the States General of the Netherlands.

3. The suspicions of Pensionary of Amsterdam Engelbert-François van Berckel, "Notre Ami," were incorrect, as the plenipotentiaries did not have authority to retreat from the demand: Fauchille, *Diplomatie française,* pp. 512–13. For Dumas' system of code names see XXIX, 6n.

385ing. 731d a 373. 720. 610. 382s. 322. 394 endeavours to NBYCC 873n. 701.[4]

Le Baron de Wulffen vient de jouer un sot rôle ici. Sans se souvenir qu'il a été ci-devant dans ce service, &, comme on l'assure, d'en avoir déserté, il a voulu dans un second voyage à Lahaie aborder le Stadhouder à la parade en Uniforme Américain, on lui a fait ordonner de se retirer incessamment de lahaie, ou qu'on le feroit arrêter. Ce qui me mortifie le plus, c'est que cela a fait redoubler l'espionnage à mon sujet: car on sait qu'il a été chez moi.

Dieu veuille, Monsieur, que vous puissiez recevoir bientôt quelque bonne & grande nouvelle de l'Amérique.

Je suis avec un grand respect, Monsieur Votre très-humble & très-obéissant serviteur   D

Passy à S. E. M. B. Franklin

Addressed: à Son Excellence / Monsieur B. Franklin, Esqr. / Min. Plenipe. des Etats-Unis / &c. / Passy./.

Notation: Mr Dumas La Haie Aout. 3. 80.

From Penet, D'Acosta frères & Cie.

ALS: American Philosophical Society

Nantes August 3d. 1780

We beg leave to recommend to your care the annex'd packet for Mr. Philip Mazzei from the State of Virginia.[5]

4. Decoded by BF as, "He does not doubt of our duke of Brunswick having receivd a great quantity of Guineas for his endeavours to cross the Project." The stadholder's adviser Duke Louis of Brunswick-Wolfenbüttel was generally regarded as pro-British.

5. Possibly a packet Gov. of Virginia Thomas Jefferson had sent by the *Fier Roderigue.* Mazzei was waiting for his credentials, letter of instructions, and remittances from the state to reach the Nantes merchant firm, which was refusing to honor his letter of credit on them: XXXI, 247–9, 414–15; *Jefferson Papers,* III, 341, 376. Almost a year later Mazzei still had not received the packet, although BF said he had forwarded it: Penet, D'Acosta frères & Cie. to BF, July 31, 1781 (APS); BF to them, Aug. 8, 1781 (Library of Congress).

We have the honor to be Sir Your most obedient & very humble servants   PENET D'ACOSTA FRERES & Co

The Hble. Doctor Franklin.

Addressed: To / His Excellency / the Hble. Doctor Franklin

Notation: Penet d'Acosta, Nantes August 3. 1780.

From Jonathan Williams, Jr.

ALS: University of Pennsylvania Library; copy: Yale University Library

Dear & honoured Sir.   Nantes Augt 3. 1780

I have received your Favour of the 29 Ulto. with Mr Schweighausers Letter to you & a Copy of your Answer, the former of which I return inclosed. I have given my Opinion as you desire on a Paper annexed.[6]

I have heard nothing from M de Chaumont about the Ship since I left Passy. I suppose he has not yet received a decisive Answer from Bordeaux where the Vessell is. As soon as I receive answers to the Letters I have written to him I hope the matter will go on expeditiously, in the mean Time I am preparing so as to prevent any Delay on my part.

I inclose a List of the Bills as you desire,[7] the amount you will see at the Foot. I have not yet drawn for all because I delay drawing as much as I can in order to avoid payment before you receive the Funds, and on the whole it will be found none has been advanced.

I am with the greatest Respect Dear & hond Sir Your dutifull & affectionate   JONA WILLIAMS J

---

6. That sheet, in a clerk's hand, is also at the University of Pa. If the 20,000 gun barrels are "not worth the boxes," as BF has written, then JW agrees that they are not worth sending to America. He recommends having a disinterested party determine which should be sold for old iron. If the guns already packed are newly stocked and repaired, they should remain as they are. Barrels only should remain as they are. But old arms with old stocks should have the stocks removed before shipping, since the [old] wood is useless and cannot serve again. The locks and barrels should be oiled before packing.

7. Missing.

P.S. Inclosed is an order on Mr. Puech & Co for 12 of Capt. Hutchins Maps & Pamphlets.[8]

Notation: J. Williams Augt. 3. 1780

From Joseph-Mathias Gérard de Rayneval

Copy: Library of Congress

A Versailles le 4 Aout 1780.

L'avt. [avant] derniere lettre que M. Le Cte. de Vergennes vous a addressée,[9] Monsieur, étoit accompagnée de plusieurs Lettres originales de M. Adams, comme nous en avons besoin, vous m'obligerez beaucoup Si vous voulez bien avoir la Complaisance de Me les renvoyer le plus promptement qu'il sera possible.

J'ai l'honneur d'être avec autant de Considération que d'attachement, Monsieur, votre très humble et très obeissant Serviteur. (signé) GERARD DE RAYNEVAL

M. Franklin.

From William Hodgson

ALS: American Philosophical Society

Dear sir London 4 Augt. 1780

I recd your favor of the 19th June[1] with the sundry inclosures & immediately upon recept thereof I waited upon the Commissioners of Sick & Hurt & laid before them the Substance of yours to me. I found no Impression was to be made upon them as to the mode of exchanging for French in lieu of those in Holland but they seemed to come into an Idea I suggested of making a short Memorial on the Subject which they promised to lay before the Lords of the Admiralty. I therefore drew one, Copy

8. On March 15, Hutchins had written JW from Passy, requesting these items which were under JW's care (see XXXII, 121n). Evidently, JW had transferred them to Puech fils & Cie.; on the bottom of Hutchins' letter to him, he drafted an undated note to the Paris firm requesting them to remit to BF twelve each of Hutchins' maps and brochures of the interior of North America. APS.

9. On July 31, above.

1. XXXII, 556–7.

of which you have inclosed.[2] I hope it will meet your Approbation. I called upon the Board again this day to know if any Answer, but as yet they have not recd any, from above, as soon as they do I was promised to be made acquainted. We have here a report that Congress had (upon receipt of the News concerning the Boston Cartels) stopped all further exchange with New York.[3] I coud wish as soon as you recive authentic Information thereof that you woud furnish me with a Copy, There are other Impressions which weigh, with Politicians besides the just & fit— I shoud likewise take it as a favor if you coud oblige me now & then with such American News papers as may come to your hand & you can Spare great Events, seem to be in Expectation. I hope the Cause of Liberty & Justice will triumph finally. I am with great respect Dr sir your Most Obed sert

WILLIAM HODGSON

Addressed: Dr. Franklin / à Passy

Notation: William Hodgson London Augt. 4. 80

To Gérard de Rayneval

Copy: Library of Congress

Sir,   Passy, Aug. 5. 1780.

Herewith you will receive the Letters you write for.[4] But as I purpose to send them, or Copies of them, to the Congress, agreable to the Request of the Count de Vergennes, and have not yet had time to copy them; I suppose you will return them to me.[5] I have the Honour to be &c

M. Gerard de Raynevall

2. The July 4 letter described in our annotation of Digges to BF, July 12.

3. The exchanges with New York were local cartels for naval prisoners with which Congress did not concern itself: William M. Fowler, Jr., *Rebels under Sail: the American Navy during the Revolution* (New York, 1976), pp. 260–1. Congress currently was discussing the far different question of the exchange of army prisoners. It followed Washington's advice in deciding to exchange only officers: Fitzpatrick, *Writings of Washington,* XIX, 148–9; *JCC,* XVII, 705–6. The Boston cartels were the *Bob* and *Polly,* which the British refused to recognize: XXXI, 365–7, 418, 469.

4. Above, Aug. 4.

5. On Aug. 7 Gérard de Rayneval wrote BF, enclosing three letters and promising to send two others momentarily (Library of Congress). Among

To Sartine LS:[6] Archives de la Marine; copy: Library of Congress

Sir,   Passy, Aug. 5. 1780.

Having just received these Letters under Cover to me from New- England, I Send them immediately to your Excellency. Being with great Esteem, and Respect, Sir, Your Excellency's most obedient and most humble Sert.   B FRANKLIN

His Excellency Mr. de Sartine

Endorsed: M d F[7] expédies la réponse a toutes les lettres que j'ai recuës de M de la Touche[8] pour la faire partir par l'ariel

Notation: accuser à M Franklin la reception des paquets Et le remercier Rep(?) le. 7. dudt.

From Pierre Bon de Corcelles[9] ALS: American Philosophical Society

⟨August 5, 1780, at Moudon in the canton of Bern, in French: The enclosed plan for a subscription in favor of your country has long been on my mind but I could not bring myself to publish it, convinced as I was that the United Provinces would achieve independence on their own. But the fall of Charleston prompts me to bring it out, imperfect as it is, because of my haste and lack of current news. It has been distributed in Switzerland and nearby

---

BF's papers at the APS are copies of JA's letters to Vergennes of July 13, 17, 21, 26, and 27 (for which see Vergennes to BF, July 31). Among his papers at the University of Pa. Library are copies of the July 27 letter and Vergennes' July 29 response.

6. In L'Air de Lamotte's hand through "Sir" in the complimentary close. The remainder is in WTF's hand.

7. Possibly standing for M. de Fresnaye. Pierre de La Fresnaye was *premier commis* of the naval ministry's bureau of ports and arsenals: *Almanach de Versailles* for 1780, p. 241.

8. Louis-René-Madeleine Le Vassor de La Touche (XXVII, 78n) was captain of the *Hermione*, which had taken Lafayette to Boston: XXXII, 142n; Idzerda, *Lafayette Papers*, II, 372. Presumably he sent letters via BF, who here relays them to Sartine.

9. The enthusiast for the American cause had written seventeen months earlier seeking land in Pennsylvania: XXIX, 52, 54–6. We have not located his enclosed plan.

places but slowly and without enthusiasm. I wish to send you one thousand copies of my pamphlet for your constituents. Please do not refuse this humble gift, and tell me where I should direct it.⟩

From Sartine
Copy: Library of Congress

Versailles le 5. Aout 1780.

Le Capitaine John, Monsieur, ci-devant Commandant du Navire le Hope Weel pris par le Corsaire le Prince Noir et conduit à Dunkerque,[1] me représente qu'il est detenu à st. Omer avec son Epouse, un Pilote et un Mousse[2] depuis le mois de 7bre. et demande son Echange avec Instance, je vous prie de me faire connoitre, si vous desirez que ces trois Prisonniers soient renvoyés a titre d'Echange pour le Compte des Americains, et dans ce cas J'aurai l'honneur de vous faire passer le reçu du Capitaine du Batiment de Cartel Anglois auquel ils seront reunis.

J'ai l'honneur d'être avec la Consideration la plus distinguée, Monsieur, votre tres humble et tres obeissant Serviteur.

(signé) DE SARTINE

M. Franklin.

To ——— de Illens
Copy: Library of Congress

Sir, Passy, Augt. 6. 1780.

I have received the Letter you did me the honor of Writing to me the 28th. past with the Copy of one of the 24. June.[3] By the Description you give of the Declaration or certificate of the Treasurer, and their names, with the Interest to be paid for your money 7. per Cent it appears to me that it is in the Treasury of

1. The captain of the *Hopewell* was John Bell; he and the other prisoners were brought to Dunkirk on Sept. 24, 1779: Clark, *Ben Franklin's Privateers*, pp. 84, 87.
2. According to the lists we describe in XXX, 440n, the pilot was Henry Davis, or Davies, while the ship's boy was William Hope, age 12.
3. The letter of June 24 is printed in XXXII, 588–9. The one of July 28 (XXXII, 588n) enclosed a copy of the earlier one and asked again how to obtain his money.

the State of South Carolina and not in that of the general Congress, who have never agreed to pay more than 6. per Cent. and whose declarations or Certificates do not mention Pounds but Dollars, and are assigned by Fras. Hopkinson Treasurer of Loans. The Particular Circumstances of that State, (South Carolina) at present, (their Capital and Ports being in the Hands of the English) must make it difficult for you at this Time to withdraw your funds; But as the State Subsists, there is no doubt but it will in time justly perform its Engagements, and that you will receive your Money with Interest. There has been a general Depreciation of the Value of Paper Money in America, not made by Order of Congress, as it seems you have been told, But growing naturally and gradually from its too great quantity. The Congress have advised the Several States to call in their proportions of it by Taxes; and tho' the Depreciation was so great as that 60. or 70. Paper Dollars were at length actually valued only as one of Silver, they advised that Silver Dollars Should not be received in the Payment of those Taxes as worth more than forty of Paper. This was probably to enforce the Payment of the Taxes in paper only, the End being to call it in and destroy it. But tho' the People in general have suffered the Loss occasioned by the depreciation it has only operated as Tax upon them, from which Tax those who lent their Money to the Congress are secured by a Resolution of Congress of the 18th. of April last in the following Words.

"Resolved,

"That Congress will, as soon as may be, make such Provision for discharging the Loans that have been made to these United States on Loan office Certificates, as that the Holders of them Shall Sustain no Loss hereon by any Depreciation of the Bills Loaned, Subsequent to the respective Dates of said Certificates."[4]

This Example Sent by Congress with Regard to the general Loans, will doubtless be followed by the Several States with regard to their particular Loans, so that you will not suffer by Depreciation.

4. *JCC*, XVI, 374–5. Holders of loan office certificates received treatment far more favorable than that of currency holders, who lost $^{39}/_{40}$ of their investment by the March 18, 1780, devaluation: Ferguson, *Power of the Purse*, pp. 51–2, 68–9.

If Charlestown should be retaken, which is not improbable; or if the Enemy Should abandon it, as they have done Successively the Capitals of massachusetts Bay of Pensylvania, and of Rhode island, when they found that the Reduction of the Capital did not reduce the Province, and that their being posted in those Towns where they have always been confined, served only to divide their forces, and hurt them by Idleness; The Port of Charlestown will then be open, the Produce of the Country may then be exported, and by that means your Money be remitted to you. Your Correspondent may then if you Order it, sell your Stock in the Funds, and vest the Money in Indigo or Such other Commodities as you may direct.

I have the honour to be, Sir,

P.S. If you should want any farther Explanation that I can give you, please to mention it,[5] and I will answer immediately.

M. d'Illen Negociant a Marseille.

To John Torris

Copy: Library of Congress

Sir,   Passy, Aug. 7. 1780.

I received yours of the 31st. Past. I hope you will obtain a favourable Answer to your Memorial, which I Shall endeavour to promote. All the Proceedings relating to the Flora will be received by the Council of Prizes, who will decide upon the whole, therefore I can give no farther Orders relating to her Cargo. I enclose the Judgment on the Black Princess's Ransoms in her Cruise of may last.[6] The subsequent ones are not yet come to

---

5. He waited until Jan. 31, 1783, to answer the present letter. APS.

6. BF enclosed a copy of the certificate, which resembles other handwritten certificates used for multiple prizes (*e.g.*, xxx, 361–3). It condemned five prizes, the *Live Oak* (£100 ransom, John Reed ransomer), the *George* (£100 ransom, Peter Thomas ransomer), the *Saville* (£400 ransom, John Yeates and Jhon [John] Graham ransomers), the *Fortunes Favor* (£105 ransom, Williams Phlips [Philips?] ransomer), and the *Triton* (£3000 ransom, Robert West ransomer). These prizes were taken by the *Black Princess* on May 29: Clark, *Ben Franklin's Privateers*, pp. 133–4.

hand. I congratulate you on her late Successes, and have the honor to be, Ser.

P.S. Please to inform me whether a Captain Jhon formerly of the Hopewell, taken By the Black Prince & now at St. Orient with his Wife a Pilot and Boy; remains there as a Hotage for Ransom Money not yet paid, or whether he is merely a Prisoner, together with the Pilot and Boy. I desire your Answer to this by return of Post; M. De Sartine having wrote to me[7] to know if I chose to send them in the Cartel to England to be exchanged.

M. Torris.

From John Diot & Co. ALS: American Philosophical Society

Honored sir   Morlaix the 7th. August 1780.

Captn. Macatter haveing desired us to open and answer the Letters that might come for him after his departure, We Shall hereafter answer the purport of Your Excellency's Letter to him, dated Augt. 2d., by Causeing the prisoners of the Black Princess to be sent off by an other Carteel Ship, lately arrived in this road.[8]

This Serves meerly now to acquaint, Your Excellency, With the Safe arrivall at Pontusval,[9] Small harbour about 10 Leagues hence, of the Prize brig Entreprize, James Martimor former Master, from Liverpool to Plymouth, loaded with Coals, Rum, Earthen Ware and Cheese, taken the 4th. Instt. by the Black Princess, and brought in by William Rippner that brought before the prize Padmore. He was Chaced Close in by Two Guernzey Privateers.

There is three prisoners in the prize, which we'll Cause to be sent here along with the others.

All the papers and Clearances belonging to her, we have With us, and Shall have 'em Carefully forwarded to Your Excellency by the admiralty officers of Brest. The Princess went off from

7. Above, Aug. 5.
8. Apparently the *Britannia* had sailed without the *Black Princess*' prisoners: Sartine to BF, Aug. 7, below.
9. Near Brignogan Plage, some 20 miles west of Morlaix.

Isle Bas road the first Instt. in the Evening, and the 4th. She had 6 Ransoms besides the above prize.[1]

We Most Respectfully Remain of Your Excellency The Most obedient and Most Humble Servants   JN DIOT & CO

To His Excellency B. Franklin

Notation: Diot & Co: Augt. 7. 1780

From John Paul Jones

LS: American Philosophical Society; AL (draft) and transcript: National Archives

Honored & dear Sir,   L'Orient August 7th 1780

I am honored in due Course with your esteemed favor of the 22d. Ult.— I send this by an Express that has given me no warning, but sets out immediately; so that I have not time to be very particular—[2] The Ariel is in the Road, nearly ready for the Sea— I have taken on Board 146 Chests of Arms and 400 Barrels of Powder; I believe I shall be able to carry very little besides: But this is more than was carried on Board the Alliance by one half the Cannon excepted which took up no Room, being in the place of Ballast. Enclosed I send you a Correspondence I have had here respecting Wages and Prize Money.—[3] I have obtained no answer nor satisfaction whatever from Gourlade & Moylan respecting the Prize Money. Mr. De Montplaisir has at last explained what he means and what I suppose M. de Chaumont has meant by a Roll *en Regle*. This is what I should never have guessed at— A Ledger stating in French the Account Current of every Man.— His demand has been complied with.— He has at last given up the Idea of commencing the Mens Wages in June who were Enlisted and had served several Months be-

1. The Aug. 1–11 cruise of the *Black Princess* is described in Clark, *Ben Franklin's Privateers*, pp. 155–6.

2. At this point the draft contains a lengthy passage which has been lined through.

3. Bradford, *Jones Papers*, reproduces a number of Jones's July letters to Gourlade & Moylan and to Montigny de Monplaisir: reel 6, nos. 1164, 1166, 1170, 1175–77, 1180.

fore. But he insists on deducting so much pr. Livre for the Hospital of Invalides.— This I cannot take upon myself to Allow; because these Men the Americans who served with me in the Bonhomme Richard never had any pretentions to that Hospital or received from it any benefit Whatever. And in America I should find myself in utter discredit with the Seamen in General— for I promised these Men when I enlisted them their wages without any deduction at the rate of Five Livres per Dollar— And as Mr. Garneir[4] can tell you I was authorised by the Minister to make with them that Bargain.— But there remains another difficulty.— M. de Montplaisir will only give the means of paying the wages of the few officers and Men of the Bon homme Richard (45 in number) who are now with me in the Ariel.—[5] I can obtain no satisfaction from him respecting the payment of the Wages of Men who have been carried away in Irons and are suffering for my sake in the Alliance after having Fought so bravely by my side in the Bonhomme Richard.— I leave you to judge how these things must distress me, and in what light I must appear to the Worthy Class of Men I am destined to Command in america.— I desire only to be certainly informed in what Bankers Hands of Paris the Wages and Prize Money in question will be Lodged (for I cannot expose myself to the Risque and damages of having my Bills protested should I draw either on any person here or on M. de Chaumont) and that I may be authorised to Draw Bills on that Banker on my arrival in America for the Ballance that may remain due when the Ariel Sails; and that in the meantime I may be furnished with an account of Sales of the Prizes.— As I have no Clerk all the within papers are originals except No. 1. and No. 2. Your Excellency will therefore please to return them to me by the Bearer.— Mr. Gillon of South Carolina has taken much pains to promulgate that you wrote him a Letter with an assurance *that the Bon homme Richard was a Privateer.* This has already done me much harm; and as it is not true, I beg your Excellency to contradict it.— I am and will be ever with the most profound Esteem and Respect

4. The former diplomat Charles-Jean Garnier.
5. Crew lists of the two ships are provided by John S. Barnes, ed., *The Logs of the Serapis-Alliance-Ariel under the Command of John Paul Jones 1779–1780* (New York, 1911), pp. 3–16, 20–21.

Honored and dear Sir Your most affectionate Friend and obliged Servant   JNO P JONES

Private I beg leave to mention a circumstance for your Observation.— The Court sent no orders whatever here either by Express or otherwise to Stop the Alliance by Force.—⁶ Landais was a mere Cat's Paw in the Affair: And as a Friend who really Loves you, I must tell you I am persuaded your malicious Rivals levelled the Blow against You rather than me.

N.B. The Bearer is a Friend of mine the Count de Vauban whose pressing affairs call him back to Paris; but who will arrive here again the 15th. in order to Embark with me.⁷

His Excellency Benjamin Franklin Esqr. &c. &c.

Notation: J. P. Jones L'Orient August 7. 1780

From Sartine: Two Letters

(I) and (II) copies: Library of Congress

I.

Versailles le 7. Aout 1780.

J'ai reçu, Monsieur, la Lettre que vous m'avez fait l'honneur de m'écrire le deux de ce mois relativement aux 16. prisonniers qui ont été remis par le Capitaine du Corsaire la Princesse Noire de Mr. Boucauld Commissaire à Morlaix vous verrez, Monsieur, par la Lettre que je viens de recevoir⁸ les raisons qui l'ont determiné à ne pas remettre ces Prisonniers au Capitaine du Parlementaire Anglois la Britania, ainsi que vous desirerez.

Je vous prie de me renvoyer la Lettre du Sr. Boucauld auquel je mande qu'il doit profiter du premier Batiment de Cartel pour

---

6. Jones had claimed the same thing at the time: XXXII, 565.

7. In order to join Rochambeau as an aide-de-camp. Jacques-Anne-Joseph Le Prestre, comte de Vauban (1754–1816) was the grandson of a cousin of Louis XIV's great master of fortification: Larousse; Bradford, *Jones Papers,* reel 5, no. 1103.

8. Not located.

faire repasser en Angleterre tous les Prisonniers faits par les Corsaires Americains qui se trouvent dans son Quartier.

J'ai l'honneur d'être avec la consideration la plus distinguée, Monsieur, votre tres humble et très obeissant Serviteur,

(signé) DE SARTINE

M. Franklin.

II.

A Versailles le 7. Aout 1780.

J'ai reçu, Monsieur, avec la Lettre que vous m'avez [*fait*] l'honneur de m'écrire le 5. de ce mois les dépeches à mon Adresse qui vous sont parvenues. Je vous suis très obligé de me les avoir envoyées promptement.

J'ai l'honneur d'être avec la plus parfaite Considération, Monsieur, Votre très humble et très obeissant Serviteur.

(signé) DE SARTINE./.

M. Franklin.

From the Baron de Frey ⟶ ALS: American Philosophical Society

Excellence ⟶ Paris le 8. d'aoust 1780./.

Etant obligé d'aller aprés diner a Versailles, ou je résterois deux jours pour finir mes affaires, je viens prier Votre Excellence d'avoir la bonté de m'envoier (:par le porteur:) encore quatre L'ouis d'or pour pouvoir faire cet Voiage.[9] Votre Excellence peut etre assuré, que pour vendredi matin je viendrois à Passy pour vous remettre le 20. guinée que V: E. aura eû la bonté de m'avancer, car je Suis Sur en mon retour de Versailles de récevoir mon argent de chéz moi, aiant récu avec le dernier Courier l'avis— La noble facon de penser, qui caractérise Votre Excel-

9. The baron repeated his request the next day since BF had not been at home on Aug. 8. A note, in WTF's hand, at the bottom of Frey's Aug. 9 letter indicates that BF advanced him the money: "Reçu quartre Louis d'ors pour remettre a M. Frey ce 9 Aoust 1780. Pierre Jacquinot. sa Marque." APS. Jacquinot, whose mark follows WTF's note, was probably the *porteur* referred to in the Aug. 8 letter.

lence me fait ésperer qu'elle voudra bien encore m'accorder ma demande, cet la seul grace que j'ose demander à V: E: et celle de me croire pénetrée de reconoissance. En attendant j'ai l'honneur d'etre avec un profond Respect di Votre Excellence très humble et très obeissant Serviteur

DE FREŸ

Capitaine au Service des Etas Unies de l'amérique

Notation: De Frey, Paris le 8. d'Aout 1780.

To Samuel Huntington

LS:[1] National Archives; ALS (draft) and copy: Library of Congress; transcript: National Archives

Sir,   Passy, Augt. 9. 1780.

With this your Excellency will receive a Copy of my last dated May 31.[2] the Original of which, with Copies of preceding Letters, went by the Alliance, Capt. Landais who sailed the Beginning of last Month; & who I wish may arrive safe in America; being apprehensive that by her long Delay in Port from the Mutiny of the People, who after she was ready to sail refused to weigh Anchor 'till paid Wages &ca. she may fall in the Way of the English Fleet now out, or that her Crew, who have ever been infected with Disorder and Mutiny, may carry her into England. She had on her first coming out, a Conspiracy for that purpose;[3] besides which her Officers and Captain quarrel'd with each other, the Captain with Commodore Jones, and there have been so many Embroils among them that it was impossible to get the Business forward while she staid, and she is at length gone without taking the Quantity of Stores she was capable of taking, and was order'd to take. I suppose the Conduct of that Captain will be enquired into by a Court Martial. Capt. Jones goes home in the Ariel, a Ship we have borrowed of Government here, and carries 146 Chests of Arms and 400 Barrels of Powder: To take

1. In WTF's hand except for the complimentary close and the postscript, which are in BF's.
2. XXXII, 448–53.
3. See XXVIII, 486–9.

the Rest of the Stores and Cloathing I have been obliged to freight a Ship, which being well armed and well manned will I hope get safe. The Cloaths for 10,000 Men are I think all made up; there are also Arms for 15,000, new & good, with 2000 Barrels of Powder; besides this, there is a great Quantity of Cloth I have bought, of which you will have the Invoices sent by Mr Williams; and another large Quantity purchased by Mr Ross; all going in the same Ship.

The little Authority we have here to govern our armed Ships, and the Inconvenience of Distance from the Ports, occasion abundance of Irregularities in the Conduct of both Men and Officers: I hope therefore that no more of those Vessels will be sent hither, 'till our Code of Laws is perfected respecting Ships abroad, and proper Persons appointed to manage such Affairs in the Sea Ports. They give me infinite Trouble; and tho' I endeavour to act for the best, it is without Satisfaction to myself, being unacquainted with that kind of Business. I have often mentioned the Appointment of a Consul or Consuls.[4] The Congress have perhaps not yet had time to consider that Matter.

Having already sent you by different Conveyances, Copies of my Proceedings with the Court of Denmark, relative to the three Prizes deliver'd up to the English, and requested the Instructions of Congress, I hope soon to receive them. I mentioned a Letter from the Congress to that Court, as what I thought might have a good Effect.[5] I have since had more Reasons to be of that Opinion.

The unexpected Delay of Mr Deane's Arrival has retarded the Settlement of the joint Accounts of the Commission, he having had the chief Management of the Commercial Part, and being therefore best able to explain Difficulties. I have just now the Pleasure to hear that the Fier Rodrigue with her Convoy from Virginia is arrived at Bordeaux, all safe, except one Tobacco Ship that founder'd at Sea, the Men saved. And I have a Letter from

4. *E.g.*, XXIX, 556; XXXII, 39. Congress finally acted on BF's request in November, when it named the paymaster general of the army, Col. William Palfrey, as consul: *JCC*, XVIII, 1018; Smith, *Letters*, XVI, 314–15; Richard K. Showman *et al.*, eds., *The Papers of General Nathanael Greene* (8 vols. to date, Chapel Hill, 1976–), III, 167n.
5. See XXXII, 451.

Mr Deane that he is at Rochelle, proposes to stop a few Days at Nantes, and then proceed to Paris, when I shall endeavour to see that Business compleated with all possible Expedition.

Mr Adams has given Offence to the Court here by some Sentiments and Expressions contained in several of his Letters written to the Count de Vergennes. I mention this with Reluctance, tho' perhaps it would have been my Duty to acquaint you with such a Circumstance, even were it not required of me by the Minister himself. He has sent me Copies of the Correspondence, desiring I would communicate them to Congress; and I send them herewith. Mr Adams did not shew me his Letters before he sent them. I have in a former Letter to Mr Lovell, mentioned some of the Inconveniences that attend the having more than one Minister at the same Court;[6] one of which Inconveniencies is, that they do not always hold the same Language, and that the Impressions made by one and intended for the Service of his Constituents, may be effaced by the Discourse of the other. It is true that Mr Adams's proper Business is elsewhere, but the Time not being come for that Business, and having nothing else here wherewith to employ himself, he seems to have endeavour'd supplying what he may suppose my Negociations defective in. He thinks as he tells me himself, that America has been too free in Expressions of Gratitude to France; for that she is more obliged to us than we to her; and that we should shew Spirit in our Applications. I apprehend that he mistakes his Ground, and that this Court is to be treated with Decency & Delicacy. The King, a young and virtuous Prince, has, I am persuaded, a Pleasure in reflecting on the generous Benevolence of the Action, in assisting an oppress'd People, and proposes it as a Part of the Glory of his Reign: I think it right to encrease this Pleasure by our thankful Acknowledgements; and that such an Expression of Gratitude is not only our Duty but our Interest. A different Conduct seems to me what is not only improper and unbecoming, but what may be hurtful to us. Mr Adams, on the other Hand, who at the same time means our Welfare and Interest as much as I, or any Man can do, seems to think a little apparent Stoutness and greater Air of Independence & Boldness in our Demands,

6. XXVII, 139–40. JA also felt that it would be best to have a single minister for each foreign court: *Adams Papers*, VIII, 161–2.

will procure us more ample Assistance. It is for the Congress to judge and regulate their Affairs accordingly. M. De Vergennes, who appears much offended, told me yesterday, that he would enter into no further Discussions with Mr Adams, nor answer any more of his Letters. He is gone to Holland to try, as he told me, whether something might not be done to render us a little less dependent on France. He says the Ideas of this Court & those of the People in America are so totally different, as that it is impossible for any Minister to please both. He ought to know America better than I do, having been there lately; and he may chuse to do what he thinks will best please the People of America: But when I consider the Expressions of Congress in many of their Publick Acts, and particularly in their Letter to the Chevr de la Luzerne of the 24th of May last,[7] I cannot but imagine that he mistakes the Sentiments of a few for a general Opinion. It is my Intention while I stay here, to procure what Advantages I can for our Country, by endeavouring to please this Court;[8] and I wish I could prevent anything being said by any of our Countrymen here that may have a contrary Effect, and increase an Opinion lately showing itself in Paris that we seek a Difference, and with a View of reconciling ourselves to England: Some of them have of late been very indiscreet in their Conversations.

I received 8 Months after their Date the Instructions of Congress relating to a new Article for guaranteeing the Fisheries. The expected Negociations for a Peace appearing of late more remote; and being too much occupied with other Affairs, I have not hitherto proposed that Article. But I purpose doing it next Week. It appears so reasonable and equitable that I do not foresee any Difficulty. In my next I shall give you an Account of what passes on the Occasion.[9]

7. Congress expressed its gratitude for the King's "unremitted Attention to the Interest of these United States" and his "great and generous Efforts in their Behalf": Smith, *Letters*, xv, 185.

8. As Thomas Pickering remembered it, Lovell called BF "an old Rascal" for these words: Charles R. King, ed., *The Life and Correspondence of Rufus King* . . . (6 vols., New York, 1894–1900), v, 108. In 1811, JA criticized this letter: Gerald Stourzh, *Benjamin Franklin and American Foreign Policy* (2nd ed., Chicago and London, 1969), p. 159.

9. For the instructions on fisheries see xxx, 226–30. BF's meeting with Vergennes, if it occurred, produced no results.

The Silver Medal order'd for the Chevr De Fleury, has been deliver'd to his Order here, he being gone to America. The others for Brigadier General Wayne, and Colonel Stuart, I shall send by the next good Opportunity.[1]

The two thousand Pounds I furnish'd to Messrs. Adams and Jay, agreable to an Order of Congress, for themselves and Secretaries,[2] being nearly expended & no Supplies to them arriving, I have thought it my Duty to furnish them with farther Sums, hoping the Supplies promised will soon arrive to reimburse me, and to enable me to pay the Bills drawn on Mr Laurens in Holland, which I have engaged for, to save the publick Credit, the Holders of those Bills threatening otherwise to protest them. Messrs De Neuville of Amsterdam had accepted some of them. I have promised those Gentlemen to provide for the Payment before they become due; and to accept such others as shall be presented to me. I hear and hope it is true, that the Drawing of such Bills is stopt and that their Number and Value is not very great.

The Bills drawn in favour of M. De Beaumarchais for the Interest of his Debt are paid.[3]

The German Prince who gave me a Proposal some Month's since for furnishing Troops to the Congress, has lately desired an Answer. I gave no Expectation that it was likely you would agree to such a Proposal, but being press'd to send it you, it went with some of my former Letters.[4]

M. Fouquet, who was employed by Congress to instruct People in making Gunpowder, is arrived here after a long Passage. He has requested me to transmit a Memorial to Congress which I do inclosed.[5]

The great publick Event in Europe of this Year is the Proposal by Russia of an armed Neutrality, for protecting the Liberty of Commerce. The Proposition is accepted now by most of the

1. XXX, 416–17; XXXI, 422–3, 489–91; XXXII, 39, 200–1, 273, 349, 435–6, 450.

2. See XXXII, 37.

3. On June 12 BF had received congressional orders to do so: XXIX, 707–8; XXX, 463–4. On Sept. 20, below, he sent Vergennes a list of his financial obligations, including that to Beaumarchais.

4. Probably the proposal presented by Stadel in October, 1779: XXX, 567–8.

5. Fouquet's request is above, Aug. 2.

Maritime Powers. As it is likely to become the Law of Nations that free Ships should make free Goods, I wish the Congress to consider whether it may not be proper to give Orders to their Cruizers not to molest Foreign Ships, but conform to the Spirit of that Treaty of Neutrality.

The English have been much elated with their Success at Charlestown. The late News of the Junction of the French and Spanish Fleets, has a little abated their Spirits; and I hope that Junction, and the Arrival of the French Troops and Ships in N. America will soon produce News that may afford us also in our Turn some[6] Satisfaction.

Application has been made to me here requesting that I would solicit Congress to permit the Exchange of William John Mawhood, a Lieut. in the 17th Regiment, taken Prisoner at Stony Point July 15th. 1779, and confined near Philadelphia:[7] or if the Exchange cannot conveniently be made, that he may be permitted to return to England on his Parole. By doing this at my Request the Congress will enable me to oblige several Friends of ours, who are Persons of Merit & Distinction in this Country.

Be pleased, Sir, to present my Duty to Congress, & believe me to be, with great Respect, Your Excellency's most obedient and most humble Servant   B FRANKLIN

P.S. A similar Application has been made to me in favour of Richard Croft, Lieut in the 20th Regiment, a Prisoner at Charlotteville.[8] I shall be much oblig'd by any Kindness shown to that young Gentleman, and so will some Friends of ours in England who respect his Father. BF.

To his Excellency Saml. Huntington Esq. President of Congress.

Notations in different hands: Aug. 9. 1780 from Doctr. Franklin read Feb. 19. 1781[9] / Alliance sailed without Stores. Jones to come in the Ariel with Arms and powder. Another Ship to bring

6. In the draft, lined through, "room for Exaltation."

7. He is listed in Worthington Chauncey Ford, comp., *British Officers Serving in the American Revolution, 1774–1783* (Brooklyn, 1897), p. 126.

8. *Ibid.*, p. 54 (where his name is spelled "Crofts"); xxx, 572–3. As far as we can determine Congress took no action on behalf of either prisoner.

9. *JCC*, XIX, 174.

Cloaths. Requests that no Vessels of War may be sent to France till a Code is perfected respecting Ships abroad. Affair with Denmark. Mr. Adams has given—has recd. the Instructions relative to guarantying the Fisheries—embarrassed by Bills drawn on him.

To Samuel Huntington   AL (draft) and copy: Library of Congress

Sir,   Passy, Augt. 10. 1780

Having but just been acquainted with this Opportunity which goes directly,[1] I have only time to write a few Lines; and only leave to send a Letter without any Pacquets of News Papers.

Count d'Estaing is gone to Spain to take the Command of the United Fleet.[2]

The important Alliance of the Neutral Powers for the Protection of Trade, is nearly compleated It has met with some Delays & Obstructions in Holland thro' English Influence, tho' the Plan is more particularly to the Advantage of that State wch. subsists by Commerce & Carriage.

The Emperor is gone to Russia on a Visit to that Empress.[3]

The Disposition of this Court towards us continues as favourable as ever; tho' some Displeasure had lately been unluckily given to it; which perhaps will be explain'd to you by M. le Chevr de la Luzerne.

The Departure of the Supplies obtained here last Spring has met with Delays from various unforeseen Causes: Some are however gone in the Alliance: more will go in the Ariel Comme. Jones; and the rest, being the greatest part in a large Ship we have chartered. There is in all Clothing made up for 10,000 Men, 15000 Stand of Arms, 2000 Barrels of Gunpowder, some Can-

1. The recipient's copy of this letter is no longer extant. The bearer of it may have been the comte de Vauban, whom we know carried BF's dispatches to the *Ariel:* Jones to BF, Sept. 23, below.

2. He did not reach Cadiz until Sept. 26: Jacques Michel, *La vie aventureuse et mouvementée de Charles-Henri, comte d'Estaing* (n.p., 1976), p. 255.

3. Joseph and Catherine met as planned in June, the first cautious step in the *rapprochement* of Austria and Russia: XXXII, 164n; Madariaga, *Harris's Mission*, pp. 216–19.

non; and a good deal of Cloth &c unmade-up. I hope all will safely arrive before Winter.

The Ariel will sail next Week with my fuller Dispatches.[4]

I have furnished Messrs Jay & Adams with the Moneys you ordered; and more since, those Sums being expended, and no Supplies arrived to them.

I have paid the Interest Bills to M. Beaumarchais.

I continue to pay punctually your Loan Interest Bills[5] and I have to prevent their being protested, promis'd Payment of those Bills arrived in Holland drawn on Mr Laurens, who has not yet appear'd. I am anxious to support the Credit of Congress. They will not suffer me to lose my own. But if these *extra* Demands are multiplied upon me, & no Supplies sent, I must become a Bankrupt: For I cannot continually worry the Court for more Money.

The Privateers Black Prince & Black Princess, with Congress Commissions issued here by me, and mann'd partly with Americans, have greatly harrass'd the English Coasting Trade, having taken in 18 Months near 120 Sail.[6] The Prince was wreck'd on this Coast, the Men saved. The Princess still reigns, and in a late Cruize of 20 Days between June 20 & July 10, took 28 Prizes, some very valuable.

I must repeat my Motion that the Congress would appoint Consuls in the principal Ports, to take care of their maritime and commercial Affairs; and beg earnestly that no more Fregates may be sent here to my Care.

Much Clamour has been made here about the Depreciation of our Money, but it is a good deal abated. I wish however to be furnish'd with authentic Informations of the Intentions of Congress[7] relative to that Matter.

Mr Adams is gone to Holland for a few Weeks. Mr Dana remains here.

4. BF had written more fully to Huntington on Aug. 9, above.

5. Here BF deletes the following passage: "Mr Jay has found Means to pay all that were arrived drawn upon him".

6. Clark, *Ben Franklin's Privateers*, p. 177, computes the total, including the prizes of the *Fearnot*, as 114.

7. BF originally concluded this sentence, "to do Justice to Strangers, which I am satisfied they will take care to do."

I am told Complaints are likely to be made against me by Messrs Lee & Izard & Capt Landais. If such should be laid before Congress,[8] I wish to receive Copies of them; and knowing the Uprightness and Clearness of my own Conduct, I have no doubt of answering them to Satisfaction. I hear you have already had some Sheets of the kind from Mr Lee.

Be pleased to present my dutiful Respects to Congress, and assure them of my most faithful Services.

I have the Honour to be, with great Respect Sir Your Exy's &ca

p.s.[9] The Fier Rodrigue with her convoy from Virginia are all safe arrived except one Vessel that founded at Sea the Men saved.

To his Excelly. S. Huntington Esqe. President of Congress.

To Francis Lewis
Copy: Library of Congress

Sir,   Passy, Aug. 10. 1780.

I received the Honour of your's written by Order of the Board march 28th.[1] We were at the time preparing to send back the alliance laden with Several kinds of the military stores.

An unfortunate Quarrel between Capt. Jones & Landais and a mutinous Spirit among the men, encouraged by the latter as appears by his Correcting with his own hand & transmitting to me the Declaration of 125 of them, not to weigh anchor till they were paid wages and Prize money &c. threw every thing into confusion and occasioned a long and expensive Delay of her Sailing.[2] The Particulars you will hear from Capt. Jones. She departed at last, without taking near the quantity She ought to have

8. BF here deletes the phrase, "and are thought worth". Lee and Izard were "not very reserved" in their comments about BF, at least according to James Madison (Smith, *Letters*, XVI, 304), but they were cautious enough not to launch a direct public attack.

9. In WTF's hand.

1. On behalf of the American Board of Admiralty, Lewis had asked BF to order the *Alliance* back to America and had requested drafts (plans) of French warships: XXXII, 162–3.

2. See XXXII, 244–5n, 506–7, 586.

done.— I formerly sent Drafts to the best frigates, which I believe were received.[3] But I shall endeavour to get more as you desire. You have not mentioned the Rates, but I suppose you do not mean Ships of the line. I shall do what I can to obtain Satisfaction for the Daphne.[4] Be Pleased to present my Respects to the Board and be assured that I am, with great Esteem. Sir.

Honble. Francis Lewis Esqe. of the Board of Admiralty at Philadelphia.

To James Lovell

LS[5] and transcript: National Archives; AL (draft) and copy: Library of Congress

Sir   Passy Augt. 10. 1780.

I received on the 12th of June 1780 Copies of your several Favours of April 29. 1779. June 13. 1779. July 9th. & 16th. Augt 6. & Sept. 16th. 1779.—[6] You will see by this what Delays our Correspondence sometimes meets with. I have lately receiv'd two of fresher Date, viz. Feb. 24. & May 4.[7] I thank you much for the News-Papers & Journals you have from time to time sent me. I endeavour to make full Returns in the same Way. I could furnish a Multitude of Dispatches with confidential Informations taken out of the Papers I send you, if I chose to deal in that kind of Manufacture: I know the whole Art of it; for I have had several volunteer Correspondents in England, who have in their Letters for Years together communicated to me Secrets of State extracted from the News Papers, which sometimes came to hand in those Papers by the same Post, and sometimes by the Post before.[8] You and I send the Papers themselves. Our Letters may appear the leaner, but what Fat they have is their own.

---

3. Perhaps BF refers to the drafts of Capt. Jacques Boux's frigate (the *Indien*, later *South Carolina*), which the commissioners had sent: XXIII, 421.

4. About which Lewis had written in May: XXXII, 358–9.

5. In WTF's hand.

6. XXIX, 397–400, 683; XXX, 87–8, 109–11, 194–6, 348–9.

7. XXXI, 520–2; XXXII, 354–5.

8. Thomas Digges fits the description.

I wrote to you the 17th. Octr. and the 16th. of March,[9] and have sent Duplicates, some of which I hope got to hand. You mention receiving one of Sept. 30. & one of Decr 30.[1] but not that of Oct. 17.— The Cypher you have communicated, either from some Defect in your Explanation or in my Comprehension, is not yet of use to me;[2] for I cannot understand by it the little Specimen you have wrote in it. If you have that of Mr Dumas, which I left with Mr Morris,[3] we may correspond by it when a few Sentences only are required to be writ in Cypher, but it is too tedious for a whole Letter.

I send herewith Copies of the Instruments annulling the 11th & 12th Articles of the Treaty.[4] The Treaty printed here by the Court omitted them, and number'd the subsequent Articles accordingly.

I write fully to the President.[5] The frequent Hindrances the Committee of Correspondence[6] meet with in writing as a Committee, which appear from the Excuses in your particular Letters; and the many Parts of my Letters that have long been unanswer'd, incline me to think, that your foreign Correspondence would be best managed by one Secretary; who could write when he had an Opportunity without waiting for the Concurrence or Opinions of his Brethren, who cannot always be conveniently got together. My chief Letters will therefore for the future be address'd to the President 'till further Orders.

I send you enclosed some more of Mr. Hartley's Letters. He continues passionately to desire Peace with America, but wishes we could be separated from France.

9. XXX, 547–50; XXXII, 122–4. The former was received on March 4.
1. The two are actually the same letter, that of Sept. 30: XXX, 420–1. The duplicate of Lovell's Feb. 24 letter (XXXI, 520–2) mistranscribed the date of BF's as Dec. 30: Smith, *Letters*, XIV, 441n.
2. XXXI, 521–2n.
3. XXII, 404–7.
4. XXVII, 330–2. Lovell had inquired about them on May 4: XXXII, 354.
5. To Huntington of Aug. 9, above.
6. *I.e.*, the committee for foreign affairs, of which Lovell was the most active member. It had been called the committee of secret correspondence when BF was a member in 1775–76; see XXIV, 12.

With great Esteem, I have the honour to be Sir Your most obedient & most humble Servant. B FRANKLIN

Honble. James Lovell Esqr.

Notation: Aug. 10. 1780 Doctr. Franklin to JL recd. Feb. 18. 1781

To Schweighauser   Copy: Library of Congress

Sir,   Passy, Augt. 10. 1780.

On Tuesday the 8th. Instant, sundry Bills drawn by you upon me, amounting to upwards of 30,000 *l.t.* were presented at my House,[7] and an immediately [immediate reply?] urged. Being that Day at Versailles,[8] and not returning till late in the Evening, I gave my answer the next Day that having no Advice of the said Bills and not knowing on what account they could be drawn, I did not accept them.

I think I had formerly objected to the Drawing of Bills for the Amount of an account before the same had been delivered in, & a sufficient time allowed for examining and considering it; which appeared to me a part of a fair Dealing. I know however that I objected to your drawing at a few *days* date which might be expired before the Bills could be presented instead of so many Sight[9] and that you promised to conform to the latter method for the future and did so accordingly in your subsequent Bills, these however were drawn a 8 Days Date; and your Letter of advice With the account (if your correspondent had authority to make it which I think he had not with any Right to expect my paying it) unaccompanied with Vouchers, tho' the Payment was so hastily and prematurely demanded.

On receiving your & my Letters I find the Case between us stands thus. June 20 you wrote to me, that Capt. Landais had summoned your Correspondents to furnish his Wants in *conse-*

7. A fragmentary account in WTF's hand, listing the amounts of these bills, is at the APS.

8. Probably for the regular Tuesday audience for foreign diplomats (XXIX, 627n).

9. BF's extant correspondence with Schweighauser does not include such an unambiguous objection, but see XXX, 139, 353.

quence of the Orders he brought to you from navy board, and that you knowing there had been Disputes, had requested M. Thevenard the Commandant to give your Correspondent Orders how to act, till my Orders should arrive. I answered you June 24. that "I should have no Objection to your supplying the Alliance with such *Provisions* as might be *necessary* for the *present subsistance* of the *People* that are on board her, many of whom are exchanged Prisoners, honest and good Men who ought not to suffer *Famine* for the Folly of Capt. Landais. But the king having given orders for paying all the *necessary Charges* of that ship during her present Relache at l'Orient, I did not see why the Application had been made to you, unless the provisions furnished ever since her arrival there had been lately Stopt, which I had heard Because this was unecessarily bringing a Present Expence upon me, besides commencing a new Account of Disbursements in another House, that will rather tend to confuse the affair, & answer no good purpose. Adding I shall therefore write by this Post to L'Orient requesting, that if the Provisions have been stopt on Acct. of Capt. Landais Misconduct they may nevertheless be continued for the Sake of the poor People."[1] You will observe, that this Permission to supply, was conditional in case the *Provisions* furnished otherwise had been stopt on Account on the Capt. Landais Misconduct. That it mentions only *provisions* & those necessary for the *present Subsistence,* not Sea Stores for the Voyage; Subsistence too for the *People,* not superfluities for the officers; and it was to prevent their suffering famine, not to regale them with Luxuries. By the Return of the Post from l'Orient,[2] I was informed that the Provisions had not been Stopt, and it appeared to be merely the Will of Capt. Landais to take them, with every thing else he had a fancy for, from your Correspondents who it seems were very willing to furnish him liberally. You now in yours of the 3d. Instant[3] speak of my having approved his [this] *measure.* I do not find among the Copies of my Letters any other Approbation than what is contained in the

1. XXXII, 586–7. Schweighauser's June 20 letter is missing.
2. Probably Gourlade & Moylan to BF, under July 10, above, of which only an extract survives.
3. Missing.

above. If you have any Such, please to send me a Copy of it. As to the above, you were at the time so far from considering it as an Approbation, that you acquaint me in your answer of fully [July] 15. that you had given *positive Orders*, to that House not to *furnish any longer to that Frigate*, and that they nevertheless had continued to do it; excusing themselves with this Slender Reason, that no other House had *presented itself* for that purpose.[4] It was not to be expected that another house would present itself to M Messrs. Puchelberg & Co. with such an offer; but it might have been decent for them to have informed themselves, before they undertook a Business that was in execution by another House, whether that House had refused or was willing to continue it.— You cannot but see upon reflection, that were the Disbursements necessary, your Observation that it is very immaterial to me, whether they were made by you or Messrs. Gourlade & Moylan is ill founded; Since in one Case they would have been paid by the king who would not probably have demanded payment till the Peace, if ever, and in the other case they are demanded of my with a promptitude and urgency that it in usual it not unfair and cannot but bed disagreable[5] especially when I consider that the Ship was well fitted for the Sea and on the point of sailing when Capt. Landais took possession of her, and yet an Account of near 32000 Livres is run up against her in a few Weeks, great part of it for Luxuries and Superfluities in extravagant Quantities, and, (if my judge of those I do not know by those I do) at very extravagant Prices. Upon the whole, since you consider it as a necessary Compliance with the orders, you received from the Navy Board,[6] I must refer you to them for the Consideration and allowance of your Account. They have neither given me Orders nor furnished me with money to pay Such Account; and I am persuaded, whatever respect they may with me have for yourself, they will not this Expence be much pleased

4. All that remains of Schweighauser's July 15 letter is an extract, above.

5. Probably what BF wrote was, " . . . of me with a promptitude and urgency that it is unusual if not unfair and cannot but be disagreeable."

6. The Eastern Navy Board had directed Landais to apply to the American agent (*i.e.*, Schweighauser) for supplies and necessaries; see XXVIII, 255–6.

with the Conduct of Capt. Landais or your agents. I have the Honour to be

M Schweighauser

To Robert Troup[7]

LS:[8] National Archives; copy: Library of Congress

Sir,   Passy, Aug. 10. 1780.

I received the Letter you wrote me by Order of the Board of Treasury, dated Sept. 29. 1779. requesting me to procure Medals to be struck here agreable to the Several resolutions of Congress you inclosed to me. I have got one of them finished, that in Silver for Colonel Fleury; & two others, with the same Devices relating to Stony Point, one for Major General Wayne in Gold and one for major Steuart in Silver. They are well done, by the king's medallist; But the Price is high, each Die costing 1000 Livres. Col. Fleurys is delivered to his Order here, he being returned to america. The other two will go by the first good Opportunity.[9] I shall also forward the Engraving of the others as fast as possible.— Be pleased to present my Respects to the Board, who I wish had furnished me with the Devices proper for the Other medals, the Difficulty of pleasing myself with regard to them occasioning some Delay. I have the honour to be Sir, Your most obedient and most humble Servant   B FRANKLIN

Robert Troup Esqr. Secretary to the Board of Treasury.

Notation: Letter from doct Franklin Passy Aug 10. 1780 to R Troup Secy bd. of treasy Read March 23. 1781

---

7. Secretary of the Board of Treasury. His letter of Sept. 29, 1779, to which this is the answer, is published in XXX, 416–17. For the medals which are the subject of this letter see the references cited in our annotation of BF to Huntington, Aug. 9, above.

8. In L'Air de Lamotte's hand. The complimentary close is in BF's.

9. On Aug. 21, BF purchased from Duvivier six cases for the medals: Account XXIII (XXIX, 3).

To Tristram Dalton

Sir,   Passy, Augt. [11] 1780.[1]

I wrote to you the 17th. of October last, on the Subject of your unfortunate Brig.[2] I suppose you received that Letter, as the Vessel I sent it by arrived.[3] I now enclose a Copy of the Answer I some time since received to my Application on your Behalf, together with a Copy of a Letter I wrote immediately on receiving that Answer.[4] I have since heard nothing more of the affair. The minister of the Marine has in this time of War an infinity of Business. I suppose it has slipt his Memory; But I will remind him of it, tho' I cannot say I have much hopes of Obtaining a Reconsideration. I have the Honour to be Sir, &c.

Tristram Dalton Esqe. Newbury Port, New England.

To Thomas Sim Lee

Sir,   Passy, Augt. 11. 1780.

I received your Excellency's Letter of the 4th January, enclosing an Act of your General Assembly, appointing me to nominate a Trustee for carrying the same Act into Execution, in Case the Trustees heretofore appointed should neglect or refuse it.[6] I transmitted the Original Act, (retaining a Copy) to Mr. Rus-

1. The letter comes between two others of that date in BF's letterbook. It is not a response to Dalton's letter of July 22, above, which BF would not have had time to receive. BF and JA had discussed the *Fair Play* incident, and Francis Dana also was familiar with Dalton's concerns: *Adams Papers*, VIII, 356; Dalton to BF, July 22.

2. XXX, 544–5.

3. Probably the *Mercury*, which had reached Martha's Vineyard in February: XXX, 473n, 618–19n.

4. In June Sartine had announced the payment of 15,000 *l.t.* as compensation for the sinking of the *Fair Play*, a sum which BF argued was insufficient: XXXII, 596, 614–15.

5. In the hand of L'Air de Lamotte.

6. XXXI, 336–8.

sel, and desired an immediate Answer from the Trustees.[7] He answered after some Time separately, that he had written on the Subject to Mr. Hanbury, who was then at Bath for his health; that Mr. Hanbury had reply'd he should return to London in about a Month; that they would then consider the Affair and send me a decisive Answer.[8] It is now near two Months since, and I have not heard from them. I will write again by the next Post. I am inclined to think it probable, from some Circumstances, that they will neither execute the act themselves, nor transfer the money to another Trustee of my Appointment. And the Bank, I believe, will not pay the money, but to the Order of those who deposited it, and not in compliance with any Act of an American assembly. I gave my Reasons for this Opinion to Mr. Carmichael,[9] who proposed to communicate them to your Excellency.[1] As soon as I can get an Answer from the old Trustees, I shall forward it, with what I can farther learn concerning the affair. I am very sensible of the Honour done me by your Excellency and the general assembly in the Appointment. Be pleased to accept, & present, my Thanks; and be assured that any Service in my Power to render you or your Province, will afford me great Pleasure. With great Respect, I have the Honour to be, Sir, Your Excellency's most obedient & most humble Servant.

B FRANKLIN

His Excellency Thos. Tim Lee Governor of Maryland.

From Dumas

ALS: American Philosophical Society; AL (draft) or copy: Algemeen Rijksarchief

Monsieur,   La Haie 11e. Août 1780.

J'ai reçu la très-agréable vôtre des mains de Son Exc. Mr.

7. XXXII, 401.

8. XXXII, 523.

9. XXXII, 542–3.

1. Perhaps this promise was in his letter to BF of July 18, of which only an extract, above, is still extant. Carmichael had refused a more direct involvement in the business: XXXII, 290.

Adams.[2] J'ai taché de lui rendre le séjour de la Haie agréable, & de satisfaire sa curiosité; & j'ai lieu de penser qu'il est content de moi. J'ai eu l'honneur, entre autres de le présenter à M. l'Ambassadeur de France. Enfin je l'ai accompagné jusqu'à Leide; & j'espere de le revoir quand il repassera, pour continuer de lui être utile.

La maniere gaie dont vous parlez, Monsieur, du désastre de Charlestown, pour m'en consoler, produit l'effet que vous vous êtes proposé. Je fais de mon mieux pour que le même effet ait lieu dans les têtes de nos amis en ce pays; & je souhaite que nous recevions bientôt des nouvelles propres à rabattre les fumées qui sont montées dans celles des Anglomanes, au milieu desquels je fais ici en attendant une figure bien mortifiante, celle d'un hibou placé en plein jour au milieu d'un bois rempli d'oiseaux, qui tous l'insultent par leurs cris. Si l'extrême oeconomie que je dois observer, me laissoit une douzaine de Louis de reste, j'aurois volontiers passé ce mois de vacances, où rien ne se fait à Lahaie, à Amsterdam & dans ses environs, tant pour le bien des affaires, que pour ma santé, qui souffre de cette position désagreable.— Je suis bien sensible, Monsieur, à l'obligeant intérêt que vous prenez à ma santé. Je n'ai plus ces obstructions dans les reins; & j'espere que les chaleurs de l'Eté passeront, pour me rétablir entierement d'un espece d'accablement ou d'épuisement qui me reste.

Je suis bien aise de voir que l'affaire de Mr. Jones ne vous compromet en rien, Monsieur.

Voici la copie de la Déclaration notariale du Sr. Is. White, &c. que j'ai remise à S. E. M. l'Ambr. de Fce.[3]

Le Baron de Wulfen, & sa famille de Venlo ne me plaisent ni les uns ni les autres. Ils ont voulu m'excroquer encore de l'argent par une assignation tirée sur moi de 8 Ducats, que j'ai refusé de payer.

---

2. Dumas met with JA at The Hague on Aug. 7 and 8. On the 9th they met Ambassador La Vauguyon and then visited Leiden: Taylor, *J.Q. Adams Diary*, 1, 46–8. JA brought to Dumas BF's letter of July 26, above.

3. Dumas enclosed a three-page English translation (in his own hand) of a July 25 notarized statement by Isaac White, John Samuel, and Alexander Oarkney, or Orkney, of the brig *Fame*. They asked compensation for the goods they had thrown overboard when the *Princesse de Robecq* chased them; see Dumas to BF, July 6, above.

J'apprends que Mr. Silas Deane est arrivé dans le fier Rodrigue. Peut-être est-il actuellement à Passy. Permettez, en ce cas, Monsieur, que je place ici les assurances de mon respect pour lui, & l'espérance qu'il m'aime toujours.

J'étois à Leide quand Mr. Appleton a passé ici avec votre Lettre de recommandation.[4] Je l'ai vu un moment à Leide, & lui ai témoigné mes regrets de n'avoir pas été chez moi. Il est allé avec Mr. Adams à Amsterdam.

J'espere que Mr. Wm. Franklin votre cher fils est constamment bien portant, & m'honore toujours de son amitié.

Je suis avec le plus respectueux attachement, Monsieur Votre très-humble & très-obéissant serviteur   DUMAS

Permettez, Monsieur, que je vous rappelle l'espérance & promesse que vous m'avez faites dans une de vos Lettres du commencement de l'année passée, d'écrire à mon sujet au Congrès, pour qu'il ratifie mon état d'Agent des Etats-Unis par une Résolution & Commission en forme,[5] qui m'assure enfin *une existence à l'abri des évenemens, des chicanes & des Intrigues.* Il ne m'étoit jamais venu dans l'esprit, depuis le commencement où je fus honoré des ordres et commissions de l'hon. Committé des Affaires étrangeres,[6] *au nom du Congrès,* que j'eusse autre chose à craindre pour mon sort, que le mauvais succès de la Révolution Américaine. Mais depuis le commencement de l'année passée, il m'est revenu des Discours qu'ont tenu divers Américains, & ils m'ont lâché à moi-même (entre autres Mr. TULBO,[7] qui paroît fort prévenu contre moi) certaines insinuations, comme si les Commissions & engagemens du dit Committé n'avoient nullement l'importance & la solidité que je croyois; sans me convaincre, ces discours & ces insinuations n'ont pas laissé de me causer à moi, & surtout à ma famille, des inquiétudes qui ont répandu beaucoup d'amertume journaliere sur ma vie. Exposé à toute la haine ici d'un Puissant Parti, ne pouvant compter sur l'amitié &

4. BF to Dumas, Aug. 1, above.
5. Dumas had asked to be commissioned American *chargé d'affaires* in the Netherlands and BF had promised to propose it to Congress: XXVIII, 427, 507; XXIX, 421–2.
6. In December, 1775, BF had written Dumas on behalf of the committee of secret correspondence to ask his services: XXII, 288–9.
7. Probably Dumas meant "TKLBO," the cipher for "Izard."

sur la considération des amis de l'Amérique, qu'autant qu'ils verront que le Congrès se soucie de moi, il est naturel que je sollicite qu'il veuille enfin m'honorer d'un moment d'attention; & l'espérance que vous voudrez bien me donner à cet égard, Monsieur, m'est très-nécessaire pour rassurer ma femme & ma fille, à qui l'on ne cesse de remplir la tête de terreurs de toute espece sur mon sort, & par conséquent sur le leur.

Passy à Son Ex. M. B. Franklin

Addressed: à Son Excellence / Monsieur B. Franklin, Esqr. / Min. Plenipe. des Etats-Unis / &c. / Passy./.

Notation: Dumas la haie Augt 11 1780

From Gourlade & Moylan   ALS:[8] American Philosophical Society

Honord Sir   L'Orient 11th. August 1780

We are persuaded that Commodore Jones Kept you regularly advised of the State of the Frigate Ariel wch. was the reason we did not trouble you on the same subject since our letter to you of the 19 ulto.—[9] That vessel has been in the Rode since the 29th. of said month and nothing now delays her departure but the settlement of the Bon homme Richard's prize money & wages. We wish you & Mr. Le Ray De Chaumont woud fall on some plan to bring these matters to some conclusion, otherwise the delay of the Ariel will be attended with aditional & heavy expence, for all vessels in port are continually in want.

We have the honor to be respectfully Honord Sir Your most obedient & most humble Sts   GOURLADE & MOYLAN

The Honorable B. Franklin Esqr. Minister plenepotentiary from the United States of America at passÿ

Addressed: The Honorable / Benj: Franklin Esqr. / Minester plenepotentiary from / the United States of America / at / Passÿ

8. In the hand of James Moylan. A French translation, made by WTF, is at the APS.

9. Missing. We do know that on that date they ordered Pothonnier & Cie. to draw a bill on BF for 5,494 *l.t.*, 1 *s.*, 11 *d.* According to WTF's list of bills, it was accepted on July 29. For that list, see our annotation of BF to Gourlade & Moylan, July 5.

Notations: Gourlade & Moylan L'Orient August 11. 1780 / Repondue le 19. augt

From William Hodgson
ALS: American Philosophical Society

Dear sir   London 11th Augt. 1780

I wrote you on the 4th Instant in which I stated the actual Situation of the Negotiation for the further exchange of your people & referred you to the Copy of a Memorial I had drawn & sent to the Comrs. of Sick & Hurt on the Subject.

Since then I had a Message from the Board of Sick & Hurt desiring to see me, I waited upon them accordingly & they shewed me a Letter from the Lords of the Admerality on the Subject of the Memorial I had presented. It consisted of the recital of my propositions & concluded by this Declaration that having taken the same into Consideration they coud not depart from their former Resolution. viz to exchange Man for Man of the American prisoners against Man for Man of his Majestys Subjects taken by American Vessells in Europe.[1] I am exceedingly sorry my endeavours have been attended with so little success, but I flatter myself you will do me the Justice to believe no Zeal of Mine was wanting on the Occasion— I shall be happy if on any future Occasion I can be of the least use in forwarding the Cause of Humanity, Liberty, Peace or Reconcilement but as Milton says— "How can true Reconcilement, grow where Wounds of deadly hate, have pierced so deep."[2]

I am Dr sir very Respectfully Your most Obed & Hble Sert
WILLIAM HODGSON

Dr Franklin

Addressed: Dr Franklin / Passy

Endorsed: Answer'd Aug. 25.

1. Philip Stephens, secretary of the Board of Admiralty, communicated to the Commissioners of Sick and Wounded Seamen on Aug. 5 the Admiralty's decision not to depart from their policies on prisoner exchange: Stephens to Commissioners, Aug. 5, 1780, National Maritime Museum.

2. *Paradise Lost,* Bk. IV, lines 98–9.

From Edward Jackson Jones

ALS: American Philosophical Society

Sir. August 11th. 1780.

In consequence of the case I have submitted to your consideration, I have to inform you that I waited on the Spanish Ambassador and received yesterday for answer that as he had no orders to advance money to Spanish subjects passing through France, he must beg to decline it and concluded with recommending it to me to apply to you as the most proper Person.—³ My applying to you however has not been the effect of his Advice, nor any Merit as an American—on the contrary I apply to you in your private capacity, being perfectly sensible, that my Family would be very happy in a similar situation to render any of yours the same service.— I want to leave Paris as soon as possible to go to Bourdeaux where I have a Correspondent and from Whence I mean to embark.— To pay therefore any sum that might be advanced to me here, I would wish to draw on myself payable at Thirty days sight—and to secure the Lender, deposit in his hands, an Accepted draft of mine on John Goddard Esqr. of the Plantation Office in London,⁴ payable the first of December next for One hundred pounds—as I do not want so much as that sum, it must be returned to my Correspondent at Bourdeaux the moment my draft is paid.

If this mode of accomodating myself fails the consequences must be truly serious, as I have already been insulted by my Landlord and tomorrow morning is the last moment he has allowed me.— It would give me much pain to solicit you in a matter that might in its consequences tend to injure your Fortune—

3. Presumably Jones had applied to Ambassador Aranda because, as he claimed in a three-page memoir titled "Case," he had resided as a merchant and planter in Spanish Louisiana from 1776 to 1778. En route to Bordeaux he and his goods were captured by a Bristol privateer and taken to Ireland. Following an unsuccessful lawsuit he proceeded to London, Ostend, and then Paris, where he was awaiting £100 from his friend William Irving, Esqr. According to the memoir, Jones was originally a New Yorker who with two brothers had owned a mercantile house in West Florida from 1768 to 1775 and who had briefly commanded a company of New York volunteers. APS.

4. John Goddard was one of the two clerks of the reports at the Board of Trade: *The Royal Kalendar . . . for the Year 1780* (London, n.d.), p. 111.

but I hope that the smallness of the sum added to the security I offer will effectually remove every apprehension of that Kind.[5]

I have the Honor to be Sir Your most Obedt. & most humble Servt.   E. JONES

His Excellency Benjamin Franklin Esqr.

Addressed: His Excellency Benjamin Franklin Esqr / at Passy

Notation: E. Jones. Paris August 11. 1780

From Sartine

Copy: Library of Congress

Versailles le 11. Aout 1780.

J'ai l'honneur de vous envoyer, Monsieur, les procedures des Prises et Rançons faites par le Corsaire Americain le Prince Noir. et qui ont été instruites par l'Amiraute de Morlaix.[6] Comme le Conseil des Prises ne prend pas connoissance des prises faites par des Corsaires munis de commission des Etats unis, je crois devoir vous envoyer ces Pieces./.

J'ai l'honneur d'être avec la consideration la plus distinguée, Monsieur, votre très humble et très obeissant Serviteur

(signé) DE SARTINE

Je vous prie Monsieur, de vouloir bien m'accuser la Reception de ces procedures.

M. Franklin.

From John Torris

ALS: American Philosophical Society

Honnd. Sir   Dunkerque 11th. Augt. 1780.

The Judgement your Excellency sends me for the five first Ransoms of the Black Princess I have Recd. & am thankfull for the Same.[7]

5. Jones's appeal was successful. On Aug. 11 BF loaned him 720 *l.t.* (30 *louis*): Account XXVII (XXXII, 4).

6. Not found.

7. BF sent it on Aug. 7, above.

I had already been Told the Intentions of our Councill for Prises, relative to the Flora; the Same I cannot conceive, & I think the Judgment Issued by your Excellency, Conformable to the King's Réglement 28th. June 1778, must have it's exécution or be appeald to Congress.

I have no Answer yet relative to the Commission of the Princess who is Sailed the 2d. Instt., But am not uneasy on the Subject, & your Excellency will wait till the Cruise is out. The Poor Capt. John Bell with his Boy,[8] are Still at St. Omers I think— They are meer Prisonners, His Brig Hopewell havg. been Taken by the Black Prince & afterwd. retaken by the Ennemy. 'Tis really a great misfortune for John Bell to have Sufferd so long a Time, & I have often wished for his Exchange, & in doing the Same, 'Tis granting an act of Humanity.

I respectfully am Honnd. Sir Your Excellency's Most Humble & most obedient Servant   J. TORRIS

His Excellency Dr. Franklin./.

Notation: Mr. Torris. Augt. 11. 1780

To John Paul Jones: Two Letters

(I) ALS: National Archives; (II) LS:[9] National Archives; copy: Library of Congress

I.

Sir,   Passy, Augt. 12. 1780
You are hereby directed to proceed as soon as possible with the Ship under your Command, to the Port you can best make in North America, and deliver the Arms, Powder & other Stores, to such Officers of Congress as are appointed to take Care of such Matters, for which this shall be your Order.

I am, Sir, Your most obedient humble Servant   B FRANKLIN

8. For whom see our annotation of Sartine to BF, Aug. 5. BF inquired about them in his letter to Torris of the 7th.

9. In the hand of L'Air de Lamotte. The final sentence of the postscript is in WTF's hand; the one just above it is in BF's.

To the honourable Commodore John P. Jones, Esqr. at present commanding the Ship Ariel in the Service of the United States,

Notation: No. 38. Augt. 12 1780 Orders from Dr. Franklin to Capt. Jones, to sail with the Ariel to America

II.

Dear Sir,   Passy, Aug. 12. 1780.

I received yours by the Count de Vauban,[1] and I send by him my Public Dispatches, requesting you to sink them if necessary. I am glad you are so near ready for sailing. I return all the Papers that were enclosed in yours, and send Copies of some others which perhaps may be of use to you in your future affair with Landais. Depend upon it I never wrote to Mr. Gillon that the Bonhomme Richard was a Privateer. I could not write so, because I never had Such a Thought. I will next Post send you a Copy of my Letter to him;[2] by which you will see, that he has only forced that Construction from a vague Expression I used merely to conceal from him, (in answering his idle demand that I would order your Squadron, then on the Point of Sailing, to go with him to Carolina) that the Expedition was at the Expence and under the Direction of the King, which it was not proper or necessary for him to know. The Expression I used was that the *Concerned* had destined the Squadron for another Service. These Words, the *Concerned,* he & the Counsellor,[3] have interpreted to mean the Owners of a Privateer. I shall send per Post some private Letters for my american Friends, for which I had not time by your Express. If you Should be Still at L'Orient when they come, it is well; but do not wait a Moment for them if you are ready to sail & the Wind Serves. Adieu. I wish you a prosperous Voyage, a happy Sight of your Friends and Country, and that you may be receiv'd with all the Honour you have so justly merited.

1. Jones to BF, Aug. 7, above.
2. Of July 5, 1779: XXX, 36–7.
3. Probably a reference to Arthur Lee, who had completed his legal studies in 1775: Louis W. Potts, *Arthur Lee, a Virtuous Revolutionary* (Baton Rouge and London, 1981), p. 138. Lee and Gillon had supported Landais' claims to the command of the *Alliance:* XXXII, 509–11, 519, 560.

I am ever, Dear Sir, Your most obedient & most humble Servant   B FRANKLIN

P.S. I Say nothing about the Prize money having never had any thing to do with it. But I will endeavour to forward the Payment to those honest Fellows who are gone to America.

Pray let me know if the Dispatches I formerly sent down to go with you in the alliance are gone in her. There were Letters containing the proceedings about Capt. Landais.

My Respects to Mr Wharton, Mr Ross, &c.

Mr Wm T. Franklin wishes Health, Honour & Happiness to his Friend the Commodore.

Honble: Comme. Jones.

Notation: From his Excellency Dr. Franklin Passy, August 12th 1780 No. 7.

From Pierre-François de Boy[4]

ALS: American Philosophical Society

from Paris the 12th: August 1780

May it please your Honour
Sir

I have Given Myself, My Petition, the 10th: of this Month, to the Minister of the Marine, I take the Liberty to Sent, to your Honour, the Copy of it,[5] et I humbly Beg you to present it to him, And to favour it, With a Word too your protection.

I have lost all my things, When the British troops have taken Brunswick, I have, Also, Suffer'd Great deal in your Country, by

4. De Boy (1737–1793) was a militia captain in St. Domingue before receiving his brevet as a major in the American army. He served with Gen. Hugh Mercer in New Jersey (where he lost his effects) and Gen. John Sullivan. When he was unable to obtain a regimental posting he resigned his commission. During the last ten years of his life he went to the Dutch East Indies, became a member of the Society of the Cincinnati, and, just before his death, served as a captain in a French infantry regiment: Bodinier, *Dictionnaire; JCC,* V, 852; De Boy (or de Bois) to Congress, March 10 and April 17, 1778, and Jan. 1 and Feb. 7, 1779 (National Archives).

5. A one-page listing of his previous military postings (APS).

Making the War During three years. My Commission is Bearing date the 7th. october 1776. till 9th. April 1779. in Which time the Hble: Congress Grant'd me thouzand Dollars, as Gratification, and to Defray My Expence to go to France,[6] but the Ennemys have taken me prisonner (on the Brick the Eagle Captne: Ashmed) and Stol'd me &ca; having bring me to St: Kits.[7]

Very Much oblig'd, to your honour, to See Mr. De Sartine about this Matter, and to pray him to Employ me accordingly to My Wishes; and I Will be very Gratefull to all your kindnesses,[8] I am With Great Respect Sir of your Honour the Most Obedient and Most Humble Servant

> DE BOY
> Major D'Infanterie au Service des Etats unis
> de L'Amerique a L'hotel De Berlin
> rue De Grenelle St. honoré

N.B. the Hble: Congress in their Journals have Written My Name, De Bois but t'is De Boy

Notation: Du Bois. Paris Augt. 12. 1780

From William Carmichael

Copy: Library of Congress

Dear Sir,   St. Ildephonso Aug. 12th. 1780.

I did myself the Honor of answering yours of the 17th. of June by a Courier from the French ambassador, but not having the Copy of my Letter to you, with me here, I cannot recollect the Date. M. Jay Sent by the same conveyance Sir John Dalrymples memorial and others papers.[9] M. Cumberland Still remain at Madrid, but as the Count de Montmorin doth not appear uneasy in this Account, altho' his Court is as much interested as we are, the Residence of this Gentleman doth not give us so much

6. *JCC*, XIII, 432–3, but see also *JCC*, XIV, 570.

7. The *Eagle* was taken to Nevis, adjacent to St. Kitts; see Dumas to BF, Oct. 20.

8. He wrote again on Aug. 24 to renew his request and volunteer to return to America (APS).

9. Carmichael's letter is dated July 18, and Jay's July 17; both are above (Carmichael's in extract).

Apprehension, as we should otherwise feel from this Circumstance and the Misterious Conduct of this Court.

Our affairs are in much the same Situation as when I last wrote, but I hope a little time will remove our doubts and show more clearly the Intentions of his Catholic Majesty. We are without remittances or Information from Congress,[1] altho' the Count de Montmorin hath received Letters from the Chevalier de La Luzerne as late as the 12th. of May.

The uneasiness which you have so often experienced in a similar Situation will lead you to compassionate ours at present, and as M. Deane is probably now with you, I hope you will prevail upon him to give us an ample detail of the actual State of america & of our Friends there, which it will be proper to convey by a Courier from the Court. I cannot too often repeat my Sense of the Friendly Conduct of the Ct. de Montmorin's Conduct.

I have been assured by the Gentlemen I mentioned to you in my last that no such manuscripts exists on the Library of the Escurial, as those mentioned by Sir J. D.

The Courier that brings this informs us of the arrival of a Convoy from St. Domingo at Cadiz.[2] The Ct. D'Estaing hath been received with much Distinction here, & various Conjectures are formed of his Destination. He hath frequent and long conferences with the Ministers, & appears to be in very good Spirits.[3] It is hoped, that the Cadiz Grand Fleet which sailed the 29th. Ulto. consisting of 36. Sails of the Line hath Joined that of Ferrol, which will make it amount to 40.[4] Mr. . . . .[5] had much

1. On this date Carmichael compiled a list of bills of exchange in his possession. They included three payable on BF at Paris, each for 1,500 *l.t.* Two were dated Aug. 3, 1780, and the third Aug. 12: Public Record Office.

2. Nineteen merchant ships escorted by the frigate *Boudeuse* left Cap-Français on June 20 and arrived at Cadiz on Aug. 6: *Courier de l'Europe*, VIII (1780), 160, issue of Sept. 8.

3. D'Estaing had arrived at the palace of San Ildefonso on Aug. 2 for war strategy discussions with the Spaniards: Jacques Michel, *La Vie aventureuse et mouvementée de Charles-Henri, comte d'Estaing* (n.p., 1976), p. 254; Dull, *French Navy*, pp. 195–6.

4. Although the fleet's primary mission was the defense of incoming convoys it had the good fortune on Aug. 8–9 to capture almost all of a large British convoy worth £1,500,000; see our headnote on intelligence reports, above, July 1.

5. At this point there is a gap in the letterbook.

to gain. M. Jay informs me that he has written to you on the subject of Money. I am much afraid to touch on that thing, but necessity must plead my Excuse. I therefore beg leave to tel you, that I have touched only 4800. Livres of my Salary since my appointment (now near nine months) & that the money you remitted M. Jay, is almost expended, without the least hopes of my receiving any more. My Expences since I left America amt. to upwards of 700 pounds sterlg. I mention this to you without knowing how far it will be in your Power to assist us.

I have not received from my name sake the Copies of Letters which you mention to have passed between Messrs. Grand & Lee.[6] Depend upon it, that the Latter will do you all the Injury that malice can contrive and put in Execution. The Print you sent to Mrs. Jay hath served to excite Curiosity.

I know no present that I can make to the Princess de Masserano[7] & Several others that will be so agreable; when we are in love with the Talents & reputation of any one, we wish to know something of his Physiognomy, and to have frequent occasions of contemplating it, If therefore my name sake will send me a few Copies of the same print, He may command my Services to procure him any thing in a similar way in this Country.

The Ct. de Montmorin honors me with such particular marks of Friendship & Esteem, that any of the Couriers to him will charge themselves willingly with the Care of them. I intreat you to mention me in the proper manner to those I had the Honor of seeing with you at Paris, particularly to Mr. Chaumont & family Mr. Grand & the family of the marquis de la fayette, whom no doubt you often see.

I have the Honor to be with the highest Respect Your Excellency's most oblid. & most obedient Servant

(signed) William Carmichael

P.S. I have received a very civil & polite Letter from the Baron de Schulenburgh[8] in answer to one I wrote him.

6. BF had said WTF would send them: XXXII, 541.

7. Princess Charlotte Louise Masserano, the French-born wife of Felípe Ferrero de Fiesco, Prince de Masserano, a Piedmontese living in Madrid: Morris, *Jay: Revolutionary,* pp. 774–5n, 856.

8. Friedrich Wilhelm von der Schulenberg, a Prussian minister with whom the commissioners had communicated: XXIII, 327n.

Have you any correspondence with that Court?

The Baron de Ramel[9] late Minister of Sweden at this Court is probably at Paris, I beg you to mention to him the sense I have of his Civilities, if you should chance to see him.[1] . . . and Friendship manner, which I attribute entirely to his desire of showing on all occasions the Union that subsist between his Court and the United States.— The Cte. D'Estaing observes the same Conduct. I have given you the trouble of reading Letter written with bad ink, and the moment before the Departure of the Courier from whose Dispatches you will probably obtain more Information than this Letter gives you. It will however I hope convince you, that I seize every Opportunity of assuring your Excellency how I am Your obliged & humble Servant.

(signed) W. CARMICHAEL.

To B. Franklin Esqe.

From Thomas Mehaney[2]   ALS: American Philosophical Society

Sir   Fortune Prison August the 13 Day 1780

I Take this Opertunetey to Let you know of My unhapey State At Present Sir I Belong to Capt Jones. I Was taken in one of his Small Boats of Ireland I Was Sent in persute after his Boat that they Run Away With & when We Landed they Made prisners[3] [torn: of] Us And Sent us to this Prison.[4] [I . . . h] I Am in Grate Nead of Some Money Sir I Was in Plymouth Prison from the yeare 1776 and then exchange & I Whent Un Board of Capt Jones in the yeare 1779 Sir if your honer please to Let Me have Some Releaf Derect it to the Revent Mr thos Wren of Porth-

9. The Baron von Ramel was Swedish envoy extraordinary to Spain in 1779–80: *Repertorium der diplomatischen Vertreter*, III, 416.

1. There is another gap in the letterbook here.

2. Originally from Kittery, he had been captured aboard either the *Dalton* or the *Charming Polly* and had been exchanged on Dec. 20, 1778. His name was sometimes spelled Mahony: Kaminkow, *Mariners*, p. 125.

3. The left margins of both sheets are torn, obliterating several words. We have supplied them, where possible, in brackets.

4. For the capture of the *Bonhomme Richard*'s boat see XXX, 445–6.

mouth or Let him Supply Me With Clothes and a Small trifel of Money it twill Be the Means of Geting of My Librtey

P.S. Sir I have Ben All Most A 12 Month in this Prison And I hav Not had Any Cloathes and I Am Naked but I Mean to Stand it but tell the Last Minet [*torn: one word missing:*] Men is entren out Dayle Sir I [*torn:* am?] your fathfull Sarvent THOMAS MEHANEY

Addressed: To / the / honred Docter / franklin At / Paris in france

Notations: Mehaney Thomas Augt. 13. 1780. / Prisoners

From Vergennes

Copy: Library of Congress; draft:[5] Archives du Ministère des affaires étrangères

A Versailles le 13 Aout 1780.

J'ai l'honneur de vous envoyer, Monsieur, copie d'une Lettre que le Roi écrit à M. l'Amiral de France;[6] vous y verrez la Jurisprudence qui sera suivie desormais à l'égard des Armements Americains qui se feront dans les Ports du Royaume; elle est conforme aux Principes que j'ai developpés dans la Lettre que je vous addressai le 24 Juillet dernier; et aux quels vous avez adheré. Vous m'obligerez, Monsieur, en me marquant si vous avez retiré les commissions dont étoient pourvus les Corsaire le Prince et la Princesse Noirs.

J'ai l'honneur d'être très sincerement, Monsieur, Votre très humble et très obeissant Serviteur. (signé) DE VERGENNES.

M. Franklin.

5. In Gérard de Rayneval's hand.
6. In the letterbook is a copy of the King's Aug. 10 letter to the duc de Penthièvre, who as admiral of France regulated prize matters. It ordered that henceforth all prizes sent into French ports by American privateers armed in France would be treated in the same manner as prizes made by French privateers. This letter was published as a broadside, "Lettre du Roi à M. l'Amiral, Concernant le Jugement des Prises faites par les Corsaires que les Etats-Unis d'Amérique arment dans les Ports de France" (Paris, 1780).

From Sartine

Copy: Library of Congress

A Versailles le 14. Aout 1780.

J'ai reçu des Représentations, Monsieur, de la part des Armateurs du Corsaire Madame, du port de Granville, au Sujet de 23. Etrangers provenant du Corsaire qu'on fait passer à l'Orient pour l'armement du Sr. Paul Jones; Ils demandent ou que ces Etrangers leur soient rendus, ou de leur rembourser les Avances qu'ils leur avoient payées, les ayant engagés à de hauts Prix, même chèz eux, par des officiers qu'ils avoient envoyés exprès. Vous sentez que le Roi ne peut être dans le cas d'entrer dans l'Examin des dedommagements que les armateurs de ce Corsaire reclament à cet égard; vous connoissez la Nature de l'armement du Sr. Paul Jones; je ne puis que m'en rapporter à vous sur les mesures a prendre pour faire cesser les Representations sur cet objet.

J'ai l'honneur d'être avec une parfaite consideration, Monsieur, Votre très humble et tres obeissant Serviteur.

(signé) DE SARTINE.

M. Franklin.

To Vergennes

LS:[7] Archives du Ministère des affaires étrangères; copy: Library of Congress

Sir, Passy Augt 15. 1780.

I received the Letter your Excellency did me the honour of writing to me the 13th. Instant, enclosing a Copy of the King's Letter to M. the Admiral of France, concerning the future Judgment of Prizes brought in by Privateers fitted out in France, under Commissions of Congress. I accordingly transmit to the *Conseil des Prizes*, for their Judgment, some late *Procés verbaux* taken at Morlaix and sent to me by the Admiralty there.[8] I have written to the Owners of the Black Prince & Princess, recalling their Commissions. The Answer I have received is, that the

7. In WTF's hand.
8. Probably the ones BF had told Torris on Aug. 7, above, that he was awaiting.

Black Prince is wrecked upon the Coast, and her Commission therefore void: That the Princess is out upon a Cruise, and that as soon as her Cruise is finished her Commission shall be returned to me; unless Permission can be obtained from Government to continue acting under it, which the Owners say they have applied for.[9] I have had no other Interest in those Armaments than the Advantage of some Prisoners to exchange for my Countrymen.

With great Respect, I am Sir Your Excellency's most obedient & most humble Servant   B FRANKLIN

His Exy. Count De Vergennes.

Endorsed: M. de R.[1]

Notations in different hands: Août 15. Envoyé copie à M. de Sartine le 18. 7 bre. 1780. / rep le 21 aoust

From Simon-Pierre Fournier le jeune

ALS: American Philosophical Society

Monsieur   Paris Le 15 aoust 1780

Je me Suis fait honneur en entier de votre Portrait a mon beau pere, qui étoit avec moi, et Principalement ma femme, qui a été au Comble. Je vous en Réitere mes très humbles Remercimens votre Portrait fait sur mon ame million de fois Plus de Plaisir que Les accessoires que j'ai cru devoir y faire. Jai été trop sensible a La maniere honnête et délicate avec Laqu'elle vous vous y etes Prété Pour ne Pas Persuader ma femme du cadot en entier. Je me suis flatté que vous me Permettriéz Cette juste Réfexion qui au yeux de ma femme et moi me fera toute La vie honneur, (étant de votre aveu que j'aye votre Portrait):[2] Je desirerois Bien monsieur savoir Le jour de Cette semaine que vous me ferés L'honneur de venir voir ma fonderie. Si je vous Le demande, Monsieur, C'est Pour ne Point méloigner de Chez moi Pour avoir Le bonheur de vous recevoir avec Monsieur votre fils. Honnorez moi d'un mot de réponse.

9. BF's letter to Torris is missing, but Torris' July 31 reply is above.

1. Rayneval.

2. Fournier's precise meaning in this torrent of gratitude is difficult to fathom, but the portrait of BF for which he is so thankful was painted by Judlin; see the artist's letter, above, July 15.

Jay l'honneur d'être avec La Plus haute considération, Monsieur, Votre très humble et très obéissant serviteur

FOURNIER LE JEUNE

Addressed: A Monsieur / Monsieur franklin / à Passy.

Endorsed: make a little Answer to this that we will come on Friday next[3]

Notations: Rep / Fournier Le Jeune le 15. aout 1780.

From James Lovell

ALS and AL:[4] American Philosophical Society; copies: Archives du Ministère des affaires étrangères, National Archives, Library of Congress; transcript: National Archives

Honble. Sir   15[-22] Augst. 1780

Tho I cannot procure the Signatures of the Committee of foreign Affairs at this Moment[5] nor the Resolve of Congress respecting Bills to be drawn on you to the amount of one hundred thousand Dollars passed 2 or 3 days ago, payable at 90 days Sight, yet I should be blameable if I did not thus far notify you. The Breach upon our Taxes at the Southward by the Possession which the Enemy have there made this disagreable Step necessary for the express purpose of supporting Genl. Gates in that Department.[6]

3. BF distributed 12 *l.t.* to Fournier's workmen on that occasion, Aug. 18, which he withdrew from his account the day before: Account XXIII (XXIX, 3).

4. The former was enclosed with Lovell's Oct. 28 letter, the latter (which is missing the second paragraph) with his Sept. 7 letter, both of which are below. The copy at the AAE, also lacking the second paragraph, is in WTF's hand. The National Archives copy (which is published in Smith, *Letters,* XV, 585) and the transcript contain an additional paragraph: "Notwithstanding the mention made in our Journals long ago, of giving you a Secretary, no vote has lately been taken for the purpose."

5. Of the other committee members (*JCC,* XV, 1445), Eliphalet Dyer did not attend Congress during 1780, while Robert R. Livingston and William Churchill Houston were in attendance during only parts of August: Smith, *Letters,* XV, XV, XX.

6. The resolves were adopted on Aug. 9. Six days later supplementary ones specified the mechanics of the financial operation: *JCC,* XVII, 712–14, 733–4. On June 13 Congress had selected Maj. Gen. Horatio Gates to com-

The Honble. Mr. Laurens will be able on any Questions from you in corresponding to give you whatever the Gazettes do not convey. Your most humble Servant   JAMES LOVELL

P.S. Aug. 22d I now add the Resolves

From Jacob Tucker[7]   ALS: American Philosophical Society

Forton Prison. August 15th 1780

May it Please your Honour.

I hope my Necesity at this time will Appologize for the Freedom I have taken In Acquainting you of my Situation, being now a Prisoner almost 27 Months being Destitute of Cloathing & Every Necessary of Life should Be Glad Your honour Would Take it into Consideration & send me some money to Releive My Real Wants. Your Honour Must understand That I Served in Defence of my Country on board The Continental frigate Boston Saml. Tucker Commander (and being a near Relation of Capt Tucker.) On our Cruize from L'Orient 7 Days We Captured The John & Rebecca.[8] I Was put on board of her And on our passage to Boston was taken by the Porcupine frigate And Brought to England Where I have Remained Ever Since[9] & When we shall get Relieved God only knows. Our Allowance here is hardly Enough for nature to subsist on. I hope Your honour Will Consider the Above & send me a little Relief And the favour Done Will be Ever Acknowledged by Your honour's Most Obedient Humble Servant   JACOB TUCKER

Addressed: A Son Excellence / Son Excellence Binjamin Franklin / ambassadeur plenipotentiaire des etats unis / et in-

---

mand the southern military department: *JCC,* XVII, 508. On Aug. 16 his army was crushed at the Battle of Camden.

7. A former quartermaster aboard the frigate *Boston:* John H. Sheppard, *The Life of Samuel Tucker, Commodore in the American Revolution* (Boston, 1868), p. 339.

8. The *John and Rebecca* was a Scotch brig captured on June 19, 1778, by Capt. Samuel Tucker (XXVI, 216–17n), six days after leaving Lorient. Jacob Tucker was mate of the prize: Sheppard, *Life of Tucker,* pp. 292, 294.

9. He was committed to Forton on Aug. 28, 1778, and is listed as having been pardoned for exchange on Dec. 11, 1779: Kaminkow, *Mariners,* p. 192. Either the entry is erroneous or the pardon was rescinded.

depandants de l'amerique a la cour / de france. a Son hotel a Passy prés / Paris

Notation: Tucker Jacob Augt. 15. 1780.

To Sartine: Three Letters

(I), (II), and (III) copy: Library of Congress

I.

Sir,   Passy, Augt. 16. 1780.

I received the Letter your Excellency did me the Honour of writing to me the 14 Instant relating to some foreign Seamen which had been engaged for the Madame of Granville, but are now with Capt. Jones. The Demand of the Owners of that privateer seems to be just; and I shall write by the first Post to Capt. Jones to give them satisfaction either by returning The Seamen, or reimbursing the advances, as those Owners shall Chuse. With great Respect, I am &c.

M. De Sartine.

II.

Sir,   Passy, Augt. 16. 1780.

M. Macreery, An American Merchant now in France,[1] is desirous of prosecuting the following Plan of Commerce in Order to furnish North America with the Manufactures of France. He proposes to load his Ships with Provisions and Lumber proper for your Islands, to take their produce in Exchange and bring the Same to France returning to North America with the Value in manufactures. He requests a Permission for this Circuitous Trade, and that it may be carried on in North American Vessels, as such, paying no other Duties than these usually paid by French Subjects. If consistent with the Laws and Interests of this kingdom, he may be favoured with such a Permission, I wish it may be granted to him, with great Respect, I am, Sir[2]

---

1. MacCreery (or McCreery, XXII, 487n) had been back in France for four months: XXXII, 230–1.

2. The letterbook indicates that this letter was translated into French and sent to Sartine. A copy of the translation follows in the letterbook.

III.

Sir,   Passy, Augt. 16 1780.
I have just received a Letter from Capt. Conklin of the Brig Whim,[3] fitted out at New-London a Port of the United States, and belonging to one of their Subjects, acquainting me that the said Brigantine unfortunately ran on Shore in the Night of the 22d. past near la Tranche on the Coast of Poitou, but is got onto the isle de Rhé where She is repairing her Damages. That the Admiralty there, have taken Possession of her and the Cargo & detain the same, till they shall receive Orders from the Conseil des Prizes, to restore them, as the Cargo of Tobacco is wetted, and will suffer more, if not Speedily taken care of, the said Captain requests I would endeavour to obtain the Dispatch of that Order. I send herewith the Papers that have been transmitted to me, by which the Property & Consignment are manifested; and I beg the favour of your Excellency to expidite the Orders that the Conseil des Prizes shall judge right to be given on this occassion. With great Respect, I am &c

M. De Sartine.

To Elizabeth and Benjamin West

ALS: McGill University Library

Passy, Augt. 16. 1780
I received by the hand of Mr Strange,[4] and contemplated with great Pleasure, the Representations of my dear Friends Mr and Mrs West, & their Children,[5] contain'd in the fine Print they

3. Joseph Conkling (b. 1739), from Connecticut, was captain of the brigantine *Whim*, 12, owned by Joseph Packwood. Returning from France, she arrived in Boston in May, 1781: Claghorn, *Naval Officers*, p. 69; Louis F. Middlebrook, *History of Maritime Connecticut during the American Revolution 1775–1783* (2 vols., Salem, Mass., 1925), II, 243. Conkling's letter is missing.
4. Robert Strange, who frequently carried correspondence between BF and his friends in England: XXXI, 404n.
5. The painter and his wife had been friends of BF's in London. Their children were Raphael Lamar and Benjamin, Jr., BF's godson: XVII, 195n; XIX, 274, 373.

The West Family

have been so kind as to send me.[6] I pray God to bless them all, particularly my Godson, and grant them to live as long as I have done, & with as much Health, who continue as hearty as a Buck, with a Hand still steady, as they may see by this Writing. I hope yet to embrace them once more in Peace: In the mean time I wish them every kind of Felicity, being with sincere Respect & Esteem Theirs affectionately   B FRANKLIN

Mr & Mrs West

Addressed: To / Mr West / History Painter / London

Notation: Dr. Franklin

From Jacques Le Brigant[7]   ALS: American Philosophical Society

à Treguier en Bretagne Le 16e aug: 1780.

Most honourable, an Most honouret doctor,

Ce que Je prens La Liberté de vous addresser[8] seroit très propre à dètruire une des Barrières que Le Genéral Conwai[9] supposoit dernierement devoir faire un obstacle durable à L'indepandance des etats unis, qui vous ont tant D'obligation. Il démontre que Les Langues des Colonies Angloises, n'ètant que des dèbranchemens de Celle des Anciens *gaulois* et des *Bri-*

6. The engraving is described in our List of Illustrations.

7. Le Brigant (1720–1804) was a lawyer as well as a prolific linguist whose publications are now obscure. Known for his imagination, which brought him ridicule as well as respect, he maintained that all the world's languages derived from Breton. He had recently published this theory in his *Eléments de la langue des Celtes-Gomérites ou Bretons; Introduction à cette langue, et par elle à toutes celles de tous les peuples connus* (Strasbourg, 1779). For an extensive biographical sketch see Prosper-Jean Levot, *Biographie bretonne . . .* (2 vols., Vannes and Paris, 1852–57); see also Quérard, *France littéraire.*

8. He enclosed a large chart which compared the Lord's Prayer in English, Scottish, German, Irish, Welsh, and French with the same text translated six different ways into Breton, or "Gomerite." By rearranging the word order of the Breton versions, he hoped to demonstrate the similarities between "Gomerite" and each of the other languages.

9. Thomas Conway, the former American general, who was now serving with the French army in Flanders: *DAB.* We have not been able to trace the comment he supposedly made.

taniens, rien de plus facile que de rapprocher Les filles de La mére, et de resserer de plus en plus encor des Liens, que l'amour de La Liberté, que Leurs ancètres genereux preferoient à La vie, et que Leur assosciation Doit rendre indissolubles pour toujours.

Vous êtes trop judicieux pour ne pas sentir Le mèrite d'une Telle dècouverte et pour refuser Les moiens de L'appliquer au Bien être du nouvel état. C'est un descendant de ces anciens Britaniens qui Les offre, qui avec La franchise, et le caractère de sès pères, différens de Leurs cruels hôtes, Les pirates Saxons, conserve encore Le fil de sa descendance, Le sang de sès pères, Leur Langage, et Leur nom. Je suis avec tous Les sentimens d'estime, et de respect qui vous sont dus, Sir, your most obédient humble servant   Le Brigant, Lawier freres(?)

From John Diot & Co.   ALS: American Philosophical Society

Hond. sir   Morlaix The 16th. August 1780.

We did ourselves the honnour to Write to you the 6th. Instant,[1] to acquaint Your Excellency with the arrivall at Pontusval of the prize Enterprize, taken the 4th. by the Black Princess; this Serves now to forward to your Excellency the *Procés Verbaux* and Examinations taken by the Admiralty board of Brest, Which We hope will deem your approbation.

Since, the Said privateer Came in this Road again, on Friday night,[2] with an other prize Called the St. Joseph, Captn. Ashweek Master, from Waterford bound to Labradore, taken the 9th. Instant, and 6 Ransomers, as par Particulars mentioned in the Abstract of the Journal hereinclosed. She landed allso 18. prisoners, whereof the Names are at foot of the Journal, which we deliver'd to Mr. Boucault, the Commissary, Who is to Send them off to morrow by the Indian Prince Carteel Ship, John Pearce commander.

Said Commissary will undoubtedly forward to Your Excellency Said Pearce's receit for the above prisonners, and

1. Actually Aug. 7, above.
2. Aug. 11.

We don't doubt but you have allready got the Receit for the former prisonners, Which are going by the Same Carteel Ship—[3]

The Black Princess is to Sail again to morrow from hence, bound to an other Short Cruize and then for Dunkirk.

With due Respect We have the honnour to be, of Your Excellency The Most Obedient and Most humble Servants

JN. DIOT & CO

His Excellency B. Franklin Minister Plenipotentiary from the United States of America to the Court of France Passy.

Notation: Diot & Co. Augt. 16. 1780

From John Jay

AL (draft): Columbia University Library

Dr Sir   Madrid 16 Augt 1780

On the 17th. July I wrote a Letter enclosing Copies of several interesting Papers, by Count Montmorins Courier. This Conveyance appeared to me as direct & secure as any I could expect to meet with. I hope you have recd. this Letter. You will percieve from it my Situation, which is really such as to constrain me to repeat my Request for a further Credit—pray let me hear from you by the Return of the Post. I ought now to be at St. Ildefonso—but I cannot go there and to Market too. Whatever Letters you may send me, should be under Cover to some Person here—the house of Druillet[4] are friendly and I believe would take Care of them.

The Fate of the Bills drawn on me is not yet decided— I cannot tell you why in this Letter. I hope for the best, & do my best.[5]

Mr De Neufville writes me that you have saved the Credit of Mr Laurens Bills— I am very happy to hear it, and I am sure our Country are much obliged to you. It appears to me that Mr De

3. None of the documents mentioned above are among BF's papers.
4. Drouilhet and Co., who later became Jay's bankers: Morris, *Jay: Peace*, p. 133.
5. Deleted: "I believe there is but little Corn in Egypt."

Neufville merits the thanks of america on this occasion, and If so he certainly ought to receive them.[6]

Whether my Friends in america have forgot me, or whether their Letters cannot find the way here I know not, but the Fact is that I have recieved scarce any, & but one public one since I left the Delaware— we ought to have some other way of conveying Letters than the Post.

We have lost our little Girl— Adieu.

I am Dear Sir with very sincere Regards Your most obt Servt

His Exy Dr Franklin

Notation in Jay's hand: To Dr Franklin 16 Augt 1780 Dr. [deliver] to Mr Grand covering the former[7]

From Madame Brillon

AL: American Philosophical Society

[after August 16, 1780][8]

Il m'est impossible mon bon papa d'allér ce matin déjeunér avéc vous; je suis toujours foible, souffrante et de plus fort affligée du désastre de la maison Bouffé vous sçavés combien ces dames sont mes amies![9] Faittes moi l'amitié mon chér papa de témoignér a mdes de Boullainvilliér et de Tonnére[1] combien je suis chagrine de pérdre l'occasion de me trouvér avéc élles, elles ont eu mille attentions pour moi pendant ma maladie,[2] et sont venuës me voir

---

6. Neufville & fils wrote Jay on July 28; he responded gratefully on Aug. 16: Wharton, *Diplomatic Correspondence*, IV, 15, 34.

7. On the verso Jay drafted a letter to Ferdinand Grand directing him to forward the enclosed to BF: Morris, *Jay: Revolutionary*, p. 803.

8. The date is established by Mme Brillon's reference below to the collapse of the banking firm of Bouffé & fils, which failed on Aug. 16, 1780: Lüthy, *Banque protestante*, II, 455n; *Journal politique, ou Gazette des gazettes* (Bouillon, Austrian Netherlands), September, 1780, *seconde quinzaine*, p. 50.

9. While the banking firm of Bouffé & fils is listed on the rue d'Orléans-Saint-Honoré (now rue du Louvre) in the *Almanach des marchands*, the Bouffé family resided in Passy and belonged to the Brillon-Le Veillard circle: XXVI, 437n.

1. The marquise de Boulainvilliers and her daughter the vicomtesse de Clermont-Tonnerre (XXVIII, 284n).

2. See BF's letter of July 10, above.

deux fois depuis; la premiére fois j'étois allér prendre l'air au bois, la seconde j'étois dans mon lit un de mes premiérs soins lorsque je pourrai faire quelques visittes sera de les allér remercier; adieu mon ami a ce soir, je compte absolument sur vous mes filles sur monsieur franklinét:/:

Addressed: A Monsieur / Monsieur Franklin / a Passy

From John Adams

ALS: American Philosophical Society

Sir   Amsterdam³ August 17. 1780
    I never was more amuzed with political Speculations, than Since my Arrival in this country.— Every one has his Prophecy, and every Prophecy is a Paradox.— One Says America, will give France the Go By. Another that France and Spain, will abandon America. A Third that Spain will forsake France and America. A Fourth that America, has the Interest of all Europe against her. A Fifth that She will become the greatest manufacturing Country, and thus ruin Europe. A Sixth that She will become a great and an ambitious military and naval Power, and consequently terrible to Europe.
    In short it Seems as if they had Studied for every Impossibility, and agreed to foretell it, as a probable future Event.
    I tell the first, that if the K. of France would release America from her Treaty and England would agree to our Independance, on condition we would make an Alliance offensive and defensive with her, America ought not to accept it and would not, because She will in future have no security for Peace even with England, but in her Treaty with France. I ask the Second, whether they think the Connections of America of So little Consequence to France and Spain, that they would lightly give it up?— I ask the third, whether the Family compact⁴ added to the Connection with America is a trifling Consideration to Spain? To the fifth, that America will not make manufactures enough for her own

3. Where JA had arrived on Aug. 10: Taylor, *J.Q. Adams Diary,* I, 52.
4. *I.e.,* the Franco-Spanish alliance signed in 1761 by Louis XV and his cousin Charles III and still in force.

Consumption, these 1000 years.— To the sixth that We love Peace and hate War So much, that We can Scarcely keep up an army necessary to defend ourselves against the greatest of Evils, and to secure our Independance which is the greatest of Blessings; and therefore while We have Land enough to conquer from the Trees, Rocks and wild Beasts, We shall never go abroad to trouble other nations.

To the fourth, I Say that their Paradox is like several others, viz. that Bachus and Ceres did mischief to mankind when they invented Wine and Bread. That Arts, Sciences and Civilization have been general Calamities &c.

That upon their Supposition all Europe ought to agree, to bring away the Inhabitants of America, and divide them among the nations of Europe to be maintained as Paupers, leaving America to grow up again, with Trees and Bushes, and to become again the Habitations of Bears and Indians, forbidding all navigation to that quarter of the globe in future.— That Mankind in general, however are probably of a different opinion, believing that Columbus as well as Bachus and Ceres did a service to mankind, and that Europe and America will be rich Blessings to each other. the one Supplying a surplus of manufactures, and the other a surplus of raw materials, the Productions of Agriculture.

It is very plain, however, that Speculation and disputation, can do Us little service. No Facts are believed, but decisive military Conquests: no Arguments are seriously attended to in Europe but Force.— It is to be hoped our Countrymen instead of amusing themselves any longer with delusive dreams of Peace, will bend the whole Force of their Minds to augment their Navy, to find out their own Strength and Resources and to depend upon themselves.— I have the Honour to be, with great Respect, your most obedient servant   JOHN ADAMS

His Excellency Dr Franklin

Notation J. Adams. Augt. 17. 1780

From Le Roy

ALS: American Philosophical Society

De Paris rue de Seine ce 17 Aout 1780.

Permettez vous Monsieur, et Illustre ami, que J'aye L'honneur de vous ecrire, pour vous prier avec Instance de vous intèresser auprès de M. De Sartine, pour M De Boy de Marseilles, qui a èté fait prisonnier en combattant pour la bonne cause en Amèrique, et qui a déja Lhonneur d'être connu de vous.[5] Je ne vous engagerois pas à cette démarche, connoissant votre Sagesse, et votre Circonspection prudente, Si Sa demandé ne me paroissoit pas parfaitement juste. En effet qu'y a t il de plus fondé, que de demander à être encore employé, et dans le grade que comporte nos Services, après avoir Servi Le Roi, et l'Amèrique pendant Vingt trois ans,[6] et Setre trouvé dans plusieurs actions Importantes, et notamment en Amèrique à la prise du Genl. Bourgoyne. Il est digne de vous Monsieur et Illustre ami, de vous intèresser au Sort de Ces françois Génereux, qui Se Sont empressés de passer dans le Nouveau Monde, pour Se joindre aux braves Americains, pour Soutenir la bonne cause. Jespere donc que vous voudréz bien m'accorder la grace que Je vous demande pour M De Boy, D'autant plus que Je n'entrevois pas dans la Sollicitation que Je vous prie de faire à M. De Sartine pour lui, rien comme je vous l'ai dit qui puisse blesser vos principes, et La Sage circonspection qui dirige toutes vos demarches.

J'ai Lhonneur dêtre avec les Sentimens les plus distingués d'éstime et d'attachement Monsieur et Illustre ami Votre très humble et très obeïssant Serviteur   LE ROY

M. Franklin

Notation Le Roy Paris Augt. 17. 80

---

5. De Boy had written BF on Aug. 12, above, but there is no indication BF otherwise knew him.

6. The enclosure to de Boy's Aug. 12 letter indicates he had fought at the Nov. 5, 1757, Battle of Rossbach, the most notorious French defeat of the Seven Years' War.

From Vergennes

Copy: Library of Congress; draft:[7] Archives du Ministère des affaires étrangères

A Versailles le 17. Aout 1780.

M. de Sartine, Monsieur, m'a fait remettre un mémoire qui lui a été présenté par le S. Jackson Jones Sujet des Etats Unis de l'Amerique Septentrionale, lequel se trouve actuellement à Paris, ou un enchainement de Malheurs le reduit à la necessité de solliciter un emprunt d'argent pour retourner dans sa Patrie. Je vois par le Memoire que j'ai l'honneur de vous communiquer ci-joint[8] que le S. Jackson Jones S'est deja adressé à vous, Monsieur, et que vous lui avez fait une avance de Trente guinées pour sureté de laquelle il a deposé entre vos mains une Lettre de change acceptée sur Londres.[9] Avant de prendre un parti sur cette Demande, Je souhaiterois savoir votre Opinion, Monsieur, sur la personne de cet Americain, ce qui peut être venu à votre Connoissance des faits qu'il expose, le Degré de Sureté que presente l'Effet qu'il vous a remis tant pour l'avance que vous lui avez faite que sur celle dont il a encore besoin, l'Echeance fixe de cet éffet, enfin l'égard que peut meriter ce Particulier et la mesure d'intérêt que vous y prenez. Je vous serai très obligé de vouloir bien me le mander en me renvoyant la piece ci-Jointe.

J'ai l'honneur d'etre très parfaitement, Monsieur, Votre &c.

(signé) De Vergennes

M. Franklin.

---

7. In the hand of Jean-Baptiste Luton Durival, for whom see Durival to BF, Aug. 21.

8. Missing.

9. Jones had requested the money (which he received) on Aug. 11, above.

To James Russell[1]

Copy: Library of Congress

Sir, Passy, Augt. 18. 1780.

I had the Honour of receiving a Line from you dated the 13th. June,[2] in which you acquainted me, that Mr: Hanbury was at Bath the 10th. drinking the Waters for his Health, but would certainly be in Town in a month or sooner, when I might depend on an answer to a Letter I had written to the Trustees. That Answer has possibly been sent but never came to my hands, of which I thought it right to acquaint you requesting a Copy, which if sent under Cover to any merchant at Paris will be more likely to reach me. With great Respect I have the Honour to be, Sir, &c.

M. James Russel.

To Vergennes

LS:[3] Archives du Ministère des affaires étrangères; copy: Library of Congress

Sir, Passy, Augt. 18. 1780.

I received the Letter your Excellency did me the honour of writing to me yesterday relating to Mr. Jackson Jones. I knew nothing of him 'till his Appearance here. He has shown me a Letter of Governor Johnston's by which it appears that Mr. Jones was establish'd in a Trading House of good Credit in West Florida, while Johnston was Governor there;[4] He show'd me also a Bill of Lading for a considerable Quantity of Merchandize which he Shipt lately from London to Florida. These Papers I believed to be genuine, and knowing some of his Friends in America, I advanc'd to him 30. Louis, on his Bill payable at Bourdeaux at 30 Days sight, where he said he could command Money.

---

1. The letter which BF promised Thomas Sim Lee on Aug. 11, above, that he would send by the next post.

2. XXXII, 523.

3. In the hand of L'Air de Lamotte, except for the last six words of the complimentary close, which are in WTF's.

4. George Johnstone was governor of West Florida from 1763 to 1767: DNB.

This Sum was to pay about 15. Louis, a pressing Debt he had contracted at his Lodgings, and to bear the Expences of his Journey to Bourdeaux which he intended immediately I thought, & he then seem'd to think that Sum sufficient. His Staying here and endeavouring to borrow more Money, is what I don't understand, & do not like. I begin to be a little doubtful of him, and have this Morning written to London[5] to have an immediate Enquiry made whether the Bill he left with me, drawn on a Mr. Goddard of the Plantation Office at Whitehall and accepted by him, is good. It is not payable till the first of December next. I return his Memorial enclosed and am, with the greatest Respect, Sir Your Excellency's most obedient and most humble Servant

B FRANKLIN

His Excellency Mr. Le Comte De Vergennes

Notation: M. [durival?]

From ———— David[6]   AL: American Philosophical Society

à Paris le 18. aoust 1780.

M. David Secretaire de Legation de la Cour Palatine a l'honneur d'envoyer à Monsieur francklin un Paquett qui lui a eté adressé par l'academie de Manheim.[7] Il a celui de lui rendre en meme tems ses hommages./.

Addressed: a Monsieur / Monsieur francklin Ministre / Plenipotentiaire des Etats unis de / de L'amerique près du Roy / a Passy

Notation David Paris le 18. Aout 1780.

5. BF wrote Digges, who acknowledged the now-missing letter in his Aug. 25 response, below.

6. David (XXV, 241) had served the Elector Palatine at the French Court since 1768: *Repertorium der diplomatischen Vertreter,* III, 304.

7. The packet undoubtedly contained the fourth volume of the *Transactions* of the Palatine Academy of Sciences, which the abbé Jacob Hemmer had promised to send BF as soon as it was printed: XXVII, 457. The volume, he said, would include four of his essays on electricity. Hemmer's note to BF, announcing the presentation of the "dernier volume physique de l'academie de Manheim," is dated Manheim, Aug. 8, 1780, and written in French: APS.

Benjamin Franklin

From Thomas Digges

ALS: Historical Society of Pennsylvania

Dear Sir   London Augt. 18. 1780

I recivd your letter of the 30th ulo. [ultimo] & forwarded Mr Peters Letter thro the means of His Bankers Messrs. Fuller, son & Co. The Spectacle glass has also been deliverd by our frd J T—p—e[8] who was the person that applyd for it. He talks of pushing homewards very soon via Holland. A particular friend of mine, left for me about 3 weeks ago, both with Mr Bowens of Ostend & Mr De Neufville of Amsterdam a small parcell wch were to be forwarded to you in my name. They contain porcelane representations of Washington & yourself. I beleive the artist faild in doing yours or it was broke in the carriage so that I cannot say whether that will be forwarded on or not.[9]

That Irish theif Jas. Barnet is still in London, & most likely will be soon taken on some high way robbery. I never was so deceivd & cheatd by a man in my life, cheifly owing to Mrs. W——t & a worthy man from So Caroa. (Mr Ch—n—ng) whom He also took in.[1] As my letters both to yourself & Mr J A, nor those to Josa J——n from Mr. Ch—n—g, never got to hand, I am fearful He has made some improper use of them. What vexes me most is, that the Scoundrel went from hence to Ostend purposely to take Mr Bowens in for 8 Guins. on the strength of a common recommendatory Letter from me to Him, & which I shall be under an obligation to make good.

This will be carryd abroad and put in the Post at Ostend by Mr. Saml H—tl—y whom I wrote you relative to Capt C——m

8. For the spectacle glass see XXXII, 220, 620. The bearer was John Temple.

9. The particular friend was probably the artist himself, Bristol ceramicist Richard Champion (1743–1791), for whom see the *DNB* and Elias and Finch, *Letters of Digges*, p. 40n. A rival of Wedgwood, Champion gave up the china manufactory in 1781 and three years later emigrated to America. The portraits were bisque porcelain medallions; BF's was surrounded by a gilded wreath and framed by a thick border of delicately sculpted flowers. As Digges suspected, the BF portrait was not sent. The Washington medallion, forwarded by Neufville, arrived in October; see below, Neufville & fils to BF, Sept. 18, and BF to Digges, Oct. 9. For more information on the BF medallion see the List of Illustrations.

1. Probably the artist Patience Lovell Wright (XIV, 149n) and John Channing, a South Carolina planter living in London (XXVII, 130n). The references in the following sentence are to John Adams and Joshua Johnson.

& who offerd you the Jama Spirit. He is a considerable mercht. of this place & a uniform friend to the cause of our Country. He goes to Holland & thence to Paris on similar business to that Mr. Barber was some time ago upon. He takes Mrs H——y abroad with Him & they will wait upon you if they visit Paris.[2]

I had laid a scheme conjointly with Mr. H (who owns part of the Ship wch took Capn. C——m) to get Capn C releasd in consequence of Your having got two of Mr H——ys Captains liberated in France.[3] The proper letters were written to the other owners at Dartmo, but it was Capn C——ms fate to be recommitted & put in the Black hole before our letters could get to hand. Since that pereod nothing could be done for Him towards getting his release. My friend at Plymo got early orders to supply all his wants & writes me he has done so & keeps an eye to his future intentions.[4] His health has been very bad, but he is now better. He was I understand 40 days in the black-hole & all the letters sent to Him were stopt & sent up to the Admiralty as was the case with some former ones I wrote to his now companion Capt. M—n—y.[5] This person would have effected his Escape had he been prudent & took advice of not coming out of Goal but singly; instead of this three or four others were taken with Him & carryd back. My frd. has also orders to supply Him with the necessarys He may want. We are not quite so well off in point of assiduity & cleverness in our Plymo friend as we are in that of Portso.[6] but intentions are equally good. I beleive numbers stand now about 180 in one & 68 in the other prison. The board of Sick & Hurt have given a derect refusal to any Exchange but imme-

2. Barber, a business partner of Samuel Hartley, had come to Paris in January on "some secret merchantile Business": XXXI, 353–4. Hartley had previously sent BF some Jamaica rum: XXXII, 590. His cousin David sent a letter of introduction for him to JA on Aug. 14: *Adams Papers*, X, 74.

3. Probably Capt. Currie of the *Henry* and Capt. Colley of the *David:* XXX, 529–30; XXXI, 376–7.

4. Rev. Robert Heath, Digges's agent at Old Mill Prison, Plymouth, had assisted Conyngham during an earlier captivity: XXX, 376, 491, 622.

5. Captain John Manley: XXXI, 418–19n.

6. Rev. Thomas Wren assisted prisoners at Forton Prison, Portsmouth, where by now they outnumbered those at Old Mill: XXV, 416–17n; XXXI, 364–5; XXXII, 80.

diately man for man between this & france. It is a pity the American Cruizers do not hold more Prisoners & pay less attention to Ransoms.

Your Donation of six pence a week to each man[7] was very gratefully & thankfully receivd. It has commencd near four weeks & my friends regularly pay it in. The dispondence among the men from the appearance of never getting exchangd is our greatest evil, & much argument is necessary to deswade them from Entering, which too many have done.

I have read your inclosures about Capt. C——m & the treatment of others carryd into Lisbon. For the present nothing can be done about it, & I lay up these complaints in a little bag to open on a future occasion. One of the most abominable practices of all is the robbing of almost every neutral Ship which is seen in the Channel by English Privateers *under American Colours* and committing acts of insult & theft that would disgrace Pirates. I have publishd many of these cases lately & continue to do so whenever I can get at names. I cannot pass by the mention of Lisbon without informing You that a Mr. ——— Dohrman has on many occasions shewn extraordinary civility & attention to many Amns who were carryd in Prisoners there some of whom I have seen in England.[8] Mr Dohrman is a Nephew to the Dutch Consul Mr Gildermester.[9] I am sorry to say it out of the whole British Factory, near a hundred of whom I know got very handsome Consignments & profits from Ama. not one (Mr Burn excepted) that have shewn the Americans any quarter. Nay they are openly hostile against them at a time too that I am very sure it is the wish of that Court to see the American Ships enter & trade unmolested. I know that Country & People very well, & I wish a proof could be drawn of their acceptance of American ships by some one or other unarmd merchantmen going from America there for a market.

---

7. XXXII, 591.

8. BF already had been told several times about Arnold Henry Dohrman's generosity: XXVI, 211; XXVII, 451; XXVIII, 545–8; XXIX, 682; XXX, 10–11.

9. Perhaps the Lisbon merchant Jan Gildemeester (1743?–1799), although he seems rather young to be Dohrman's uncle: Elias and Finch, *Letters of Digges*, p. 251.

As you must have recd accots. by the fleet lately arrivd in France from Chesapeak[1] to as late dates as the 10 or 15th June I can send you nothing new from that quarter. Clintons arrival from the soward at N York is the latest accots we have had from America.[2] A Ship is arrivd at Whitehaven which left Hallifax the *11th July* & brings no accots whatever from thence, the quarter of N York, or more south, nor any the least tidings of Monsr Ternays or Greaves's Fleet.[3] The folly of all the Southern parts of America "coming in" as it was set forth with such industry, begins to abate considerably. The affair *now* they say must be decided in the West Indies, & most likely it is before this day. Nothing talkd of but the Russian bears and the northern league. Six sail still in the Downs & others they say are gone down Channel with their trade. Many attempts are made to laugh at this armd neutrality & ridicule it as nothing; but serious people look upon it to be wearing a solid & consistant face, by which the Dutch & other maratime powers will get what they have been long aiming at "That free Ships shall make free goods". When this is establishd it will go near to annihilate the claim of Britain for the sole sovereign Dominion of the Sea. What measures will be adopted by our wise Ministry in respect to this northern Confedracy cannot easily be discoverd. They will hardly embroil themselves by stopping and searching these neutral combind fleets; nor does it appear they will totally acquiesce at least without the appearance of resistance to that hostile confederacy: I am informd They are going on in their usual way of littleness, & have given such ambiguous & equivocal orders to the Captns. of men of war that they will not know how to act under them— Thus they hope to preserve Engld from a northern war without tarnishing the British Flag.

The N York fleet has at last saild; abot 40 Ships under Con-

1. The convoy brought by the *Fier Roderigue: London Courant, and Westminster Chronicle*, Aug. 17.

2. Clinton returned to New York from Charleston on June 17: *London Courant, and Westminster Chronicle*, July 31.

3. Graves's squadron had arrived at Sandy Hook on July 13, three days after Adm. Ternay arrived at Newport with Rochambeau's expeditionary force: John A. Tilley, *The British Navy and the American Revolution* (Columbia, S.C., 1987), p. 193. See also our annotation of Cooper to BF, July 25, above.

voy of one Frigate & they go directly for the Hook.[4] There are no troops on board it tho the Papers say there are. I dont find any *civil* officer has saild or is going to their stations in So Carolina; It therefore appears to me that this Country does not expect to hold that very long, & that a military is the best Government for a Conquerd People.[5] I dont find the war is meant to be pushd from thence towards No Caroa. or Virginia. I beleive no plan is fixd on for opperations in that quarter; They seem to trust intirely to the Depradations of detatchd partys of the Troops, & to the exigencies of the day. I am with the highest respect Dr Sir Your mo obligd & ob Sert   W S. C

His Excelly B F

Notation: Augt. 18. 1780.

From Edward Jackson Jones

ALS: American Philosophical Society

Sir!   Friday 1 O'Clock [August 18 or 25, 1780][6]
   The Croud incident to the day, rendering my seeing you very precarious, I have taken the liberty of addressing you to remind you of my passport which if I do not get today may put me to an expense that I am by no means capable of bearing.
   You will pardon me Sir, if in the distracted situation I am in, I tell you that you have involved me in a state that death itself is preferable to.— You assisted me with a *part of* what was really necessary to get me out of Paris—and by informing Mr. De Vergennes that you had furnish'd me with the *whole* you have pre-

4. The long-delayed provisions convoy for New York (more than forty merchant ships escorted by the frigate *Hyena*) sailed for Sandy Hook on Aug. 13 and arrived three months later: *London Courant, and Westminster Chronicle*, Aug. 18; Bowler, *Logistics*, p. 135.
   5. When Clinton left South Carolina no decision had yet been reached on the establishment of civilian government: Willcox, *Portrait of a General*, pp. 312–13.
   6. If Vergennes received by messenger BF's letter of the 18th, above, on the morning of that day, the present letter could have been written that afternoon. More likely it was written the following Friday.

vented his intended good Offices.— The note for £100 was never meant to pay you with—the draft upon myself is a convincing proof of the assertion—and if it had been of no value my Honor would have remained unsullied by paying my debt to you.— My ability and not the means by which I became indebted, was the point to be consider'd— and I can safely declare that with one half the proofs I have in my possession, I ought to have establish'd a confidence necessary to obtain the loan of Fifty pounds— indeed the readiness with which the French Minister consented is a convincing proof— I shall take the liberty of calling on You at Passy to offer you the remaining security I have left—[7] whose real value will amount to much more than your demand—and then I hope you will have no objection to my returning to London where as soon as I have accomodated myself and got such letters of recommendation as my sudden departure prevented me from obtaining I shall take Paris in my way to Bourdeaux.—

I am Sir Yours respectfully   E.J. JONES

His Excellency B. Franklin Esqr

Addressed: A Son Excellence / Benjamin Franklin / Ambassadeur des Etats / de L'Amerique Septentrionale / chez Monsr. de Vergennes

Notation: E.J.Jones. Friday 1 OClock

From Mademoiselle ———— de Poliange

ALS: American Philosophical Society

Monsieur   Paris rue des Sts. peres no. 59. le 18 aout 1780./.

J'eus l'honneur de vous remettre le 18 de juin dernier un petit mémoire Concernant mon parent mr. vigeral qui fut pris par les Anglais Sur un corsaire américain le 5 mars 1778.[8] Il fut Con-

7. Apparently he did not. In a letter dated "Saturday afternoon" he apologizes for not calling the previous night in consequence of BF's request. He has just returned from Versailles and, not wishing to interrupt, requests an appointment between 8:00 and 9:00 this evening. APS.

8. The one-page memoir, undated but in Mlle de Poliange's hand, states that Gabriel Vigeral was born at Vertaison near Clermont-Ferrand. Twenty-

duit a Portsmuth, et de la transféré à Winchester. On n'a point eu de Ses nouvelles depuis la fin du mois de mars 1779; et depuis Cette époque il n'a pas été possible d'apprendre Ce quil est devenu quelques recherches qu'on ait faites a cette occasion. Vous m'aviez fait la grace de me promettre Monsieur que vous donneriez des ordres pour de nouvelles perquisitions soit à londres ou ailleurs, et vous aviez eu la bonté dajouter que vous daigneriez me faire instruire du resultat de vos recherches. Je Crains que vos occupations ne vous aient fait perdre de vüe les interets de mon parent et jespére que vous me permettrez de vous les rapeller et de vous Conjurer Monsieur d'avoir la bonté de me faire écrire Ce que vous aurez appris Sur Son Sort. Je Serai infiniment reconnaissante de Cette grace, et je vous Supplie d'agréer L'assurance du profond respect avec lequel jai Lhonneur Detre, Monsieur Votre trés humble et trés obeissante Servante

DE POLIANGE

Notation Mde. De Poliange Paris 18. Aout.

To ——— de Pavara

Reprinted from Henkels Catalogue No. 1384 (December 18, 1925), p. 39.

Passy, Augt 19, 1780.
Mr Franklin presents his compliments to M. de Pavara, & returns his Book with many Thanks.

From Philip Mazzei
ALS: American Philosophical Society

Sir, Genoa, August 19th. 1780.
The bearer of this will be my noble friend Mr. Celesia,[9] whom you will probably remember, as he was Minister of this Repub-

---

four years old and five feet tall, his upper lip is stitched on the left side. The family contacted John Bell, Commissioner for Sick and Hurt Seamen, who answered only that Vigeral was no longer at Winchester. APS. An English translation is published in Smith, *Letters*, XXI, 246n.

9. Pietro Paolo Celesia (1732–1806), a Genoese diplomat who had served as minister to London. He was a frequent correspondent of Mazzei: *Dizionario Biografico Degli Italiani* (43 vols. to date, Rome, 1960–); *Reper-*

lick in London from the year 55 to 60, & in consequence of his superiour talents must have been well acquainted with several of your worthy friends there. He is esteemed here for what he really is, an ornament to his Country, & his opinion is greedily sought for in the most important affairs of the State. He intends to pass a few weeks, perhaps 2. months in Paris. In giving him this letter to you I have in view not only your mutual satisfaction in conversing with each other, but likewise our publick interest. Such people ought to be candidly informed with the situation of our affairs, especially as the enemies are so industrious in spreading false reports to our prejudice. He will be able to inform you, that I have not been idle in my endeavours to confute them. I shall set out for Florence in a few days, & would be much obliged to you for the favour of a letter, as soon as convenient,[1] to inform me of such things as may be apt to dispose the minds of the People there, & especially of the Sovereign, in our favour. I have the honour to be with respect & esteem, Sir, Your Excellcy's: most Obedt. & most humble Servant   PHILIP MAZZEI

P.S. I wish that my letters may be given to Mr. Favi[2] to be sent under cover for greater security.

From "Comte" Julius de Montfort de Prat: Two Letters

(I) and (II) ALS: American Philosophical Society

I.

⟨Paris, August 19, 1780, in French: I am the innocent victim of a terrible woman, Mme de Villeneuve. She will not forgive me for

---

torium der diplomatischen Vertreter, II, 138; Margherita Marchione, Stanley J. Idzerda, and S. Eugene Scalia, eds., *Philip Mazzei: Selected Writings and Correspondence* (3 vols., Prato, Italy, 1983), I, 6n, and *passim.* On Aug. 19 Mazzei also wrote to JA and Thomas Jefferson to introduce the Genoan: *Adams Papers,* X, 81–2.

1. By mid-October he was in Florence: Marchione, *Mazzei,* I, 246.

2. Francesco Favi, the diplomatic representative of the Republic of Ragusa who on Sept. 9, 1780, also became secretary of legation in Paris for the Grand Duke of Tuscany: Wayne S. Vucinich, ed., *Dubrovnik and the American Revolution: Francesco Favi's Letters* (Palto Alto, Calif., 1977); *Repertorium*

having proposed marriage to her daughter, who is of age and free to dispose of her fate. She has not ceased visiting Inspector Brugnière and Commissary Ninnin; unable to destroy me through civil law they decided to resort to criminal law.[3] They persuaded a simple and credulous wheelwright named Macon to pursue me for not having paid for a carriage I purchased, even though I still have three months to do so, and for signing myself since my return from America as "Montfort d. P." instead of "Prat-Montfort" in order to dupe people. I am even accused of not having held the rank of major in America, but of having been a servant.[4] These calumnies resulted in my arrest. Held incommunicado, I am at this moment finally able to write.

Respectable representative of a nation I served at the price of great suffering, you will not abandon me in my hour of distress when my only failing consists in a few debts which I soon will be able to repay. As to my name, I never hid that I was originally named Prat. No one can be harmed if I call myself Montfort. Everyone in our province knows that my father, Jean-Baptiste-Julien Prat, seigneur du Tour Lavaissiere, *avocat* at the *Parlement* of Toulouse, lived honorably from the income of his estates.

Now that my honor is under attack, I trust you will deliver me an ambassadorial certificate stating that J. Ant. J. Prat, comte de Montfort, served with distinction as a captain and a major in the

---

der diplomatischen Vertreter, III, 451; Antonio Pace, *Benjamin Franklin in Italy* (Philadelphia, 1958), p. 98.

3. The self-proclaimed count (actually Jean-Antoine-Justin Prat) was arrested on Aug. 4 on suspicion of fraud. He had given Jean-Marie Macon, a *maître charron*, three 1,000 *l.t.* notes signed the "comte de Montfort" in partial payment for an English traveling coach. When Macon learned the title of nobility was fictitious, he issued a complaint and Prat was arrested. The police inspector was de Brugnières, boulevard du Temple (*Almanach Royal* for 1780, p. 406). Imprisoned at the Grand Châtelet, Prat was examined by Commissaire-Enquêteur Jean-Baptiste Ninnin (*Almanach Royal* for 1780, p. 374), whose papers at the Archives Nationales (Y 15083 B) provide numerous details about the case. One such detail is Prat's boast that his prospective bride (Mlle. de Villeneuve) was worth 40,000 *l.t.*, but she is not otherwise identified. His career during the French Revolution and later is described in Bodinier, *Dictionnaire*, p. 497.

4. For once Prat seems to have been accused falsely; he had been a major in the American Army and was wounded at Brandywine: XXVIII, 481n.

American army in order that I may use it with the certificate signed by Secretary of Congress Thomson.
I hear that M. Deane has arrived. He certainly will confirm the good reputation I enjoyed in America. So too will the letter from your friend General Roberdeau[5] and so also can testify the doctor from Philadelphia[6] whom your son would have met had he been able to dine at my house the day before I was arrested. You have all the reasons in the world to perform this act of justice.⟩

II.

⟨Undated but written later the same day, in French: Sir, your testimony is absolutely critical to my case. Please ask me in an official manner for the documents I left with you in Passy. Since they have been seized by the police, this is the only way I have to bring them to the judge's attention. Do not abandon me.[7]⟩

5. While serving in Congress Daniel Roberdeau (who was also a brigadier general of militia) had sat on a committee dealing with French officers (XXIV, 11n), but his recommendation of Prat is missing.

6. The Philadelphian probably was Dr. John Foulke. He seems to have been in Paris at this time: George Fox to WTF, Aug. 29, 1780 (APS). Prat's Aug. 2 invitation to WTF is at the APS.

7. On Aug. 23 the increasingly desperate Prat, still imprisoned at the Grand Châtelet, wrote to François and Arbelot, two servants in the Franklin household, asking them to plead his cause with their master (APS). How incredible, he said, that the Doctor should refuse his request for a certificate of service in the American army. As for his debts, they were contracted in good faith, with no intention of deceiving anyone. Two days later he sent another appeal to BF, covering the same points (APS). A notation in WTF's hand indicates that he, WTF, answered the following day, but we have no further record of it or of Prat.

BF seems to have first had a favorable opinion of Prat; see, for instance, XXX, 44, 564–5. But later he may have been influenced by an undated letter from Capt. Paul Bentalou (XXXII, 387n) to Prat protesting the latter's duplicitous use of a title of nobility and demanding letters from his parents in Prat's possession. Bentalou wrote an April 4 covering letter to a Monsieur Bessiere at Versailles, who must have provided BF with both letters, now at the APS. These may be the papers to which BF referred when he wrote on the verso of a printed advertisement from a "Chirurgien Herniare" named Garreau, "Papers concerning Montforts being a Count."

From Sartine Copy: Library of Congress

Versailles le 19. Aout 1780.

J'ai reçu, Monsieur, avec La Lettre que vous m'avez fait l'honneur de m'ecrire le 16 de ce mois, les pieces relatives au Brigantin Américain le Whim, entré à l'Isle de Rhé pour se reparer après avoir fait côte pres de Trance en Poitou. Je me suis empressé de faire passer ces pieces au Conseil des Prises et je ne doute pas que ce Tribunal ne rende son Jugement le plus promptement possible.

J'ai l'honneur d'etre avec la Consideration la plus distinguée, Monsieur, Votre très humble et très obeissant Serviteur

(signé) DE SARTINE

M. Franklin.

William Temple Franklin to Gourlade & Moylan

Copy: Library of Congress

Gentlemen, Passy 19. Augt. 1780.

I am directed by My Grandfather to acknowledge the Receipt of your favour of the 11. Instant. & to inform you that he immediately communicated it to M. Le Ray De Chaumont, who this Day told him that he had sent down Orders to M. De Montplaisir for the immediate Settlement of the Wages & Prize money of the Bonhomme Richard. So that this affair now rests intirely with that Gentleman.[8] My Grandfather who is very Anxious for the sailing of the Ariel, hopes no Time will be lost in finishing this Business, it being the only obstacle to her Departure. With great Respect, I have the Honour to be, Gentleman,

(signed) W T. FRANKLIN.

Messrs. Gourlade et Moylan.

---

8. Chaumont, however, had paid no prize money and only part of the *Bonhomme Richard* crew's wages by mid-December, when the *Ariel* sailed to America: Thomas J. Schaeper, *France and America in the Revolutionary Era: the Life of Jacques-Donatien Leray de Chaumont, 1725–1803* (Providence, R.I., and Oxford, 1995), p. 276.

From Sartine

Copy: Library of Congress

A Versailles le 20. Aout 1780.

J'ai reçu, Monsieur, la Lettre que vous m'avez fait l'honneur de m'écrire le 16. de ce mois relativement au S. Macreery Négociant Americain qui se propose d'importer d'Amerique dans les Colonies Françoises des objets de Commerce utiles à ces Dernieres, et rapporter en france les Denrées coloniales qu'il aura reçues en retour. Les ports de France et ceux des Colonies étant ouverts aux neutres pendant la Guerre Le Sr. Macreery peut sans aucune Difficulté suivre la Branche de Commerce qu'il se propose d'établir tant que la Guerre durera, et sa Majesté accorde avec encore plus de plaisir à Ses alliés une Facilité qu'elle a cru ne pas devoir refuser aux sujets des puissances Neutres.

J'ai l'honneur d'etre avec la Consideration la plus distinguée, Monsieur, Votre très humble et très obeissant Serviteur.

(signé) DE SARTINE.

M. Franklin.

To Joseph Conkling

Copy: Library of Congress

Sir   Passy, Augt 21. 1780.

Immediately upon the Receipt of yours acquainting me with your Misfortune, and the Vessel & Cargo was in Possession of the Admiralty, I apply'd to the Minister of the Marine, & laid before him the Papers you enclos'd to me with your Letter requesting that the said Vessel & Cargo might be delivered to the Consignees.[9] Inclos'd I send you the answer. I have just received from him.[1] I hope the Orders will arrive by the same Post with this Letter. I have the Honour to be, Sir,—

Captain Conklin Commr. of the Brigantine Whim of New London now at la flote in the Isle of Rhé. chez M. de Chezaux.

---

9. See BF to Sartine, Aug. 16.
1. Sartine to BF, Aug. 19, above.

To ——— Garnier

Copy: Library of Congress

Sir, Passy 21. Augt. 1780.

I received this Day the Letter you did me the Honour of writing to me on the 19th. Inst.[2] and I lose no Time in Answering it in Order to save you the Trouble of coming out to me here. I must inform you then, Sir, that your Request of Commission in the Army of the United States, is totally impracticable: That Army being long since more than fully officered: Almost all the foreign officer who have gone to America to seek Employment in their Profession have returned, not being able to obtain any: And the Congress to prevent as much as possible others from undertaking so fruitless a Voyage, have sent me the most positive Instructions not to give the smallest Encouragement to any Persons whom so ever to go to America, with views of obtaining Military Preferment. Your desire of gaining useful Knowledge is praise Worthy & your Goodwill to our Cause requires my most Thankful acknowledgments which please to accept. I have the Honour to be &c.

M. Garnier.

To John Paul Jones

Copy: Library of Congress

Dear Sir, Passy, Augt. 21. 1780.

I received a few Days since a Letter from M. De Sartine which I have mislaid, or would send you a Copy you have however the answer enclosed, by which you will perceive the purport of it.[3] This Day the Captain of the Madame has been with me, and left an account of the Advances, which appeard to me very high, and I proposed to return the Men;[4] but he seem'd not to desire that chusing rather to have the Money. I am eternally perplext with

2. For his letter see our headnote to the letter from the Baron d'Arros and Other Commission Seekers, July 10.

3. Sartine's letter of Aug. 14 and BF's reply of the 16th are both above.

4. From Jones's response of Sept. 23, below, we know that BF enclosed a list of the crewmen of the privateer *Madame* whom Jones supposedly had taken for his own crew.

this sort of Business and overwhelmed with the Expence. I now repent having been persuaded to join in asking for the Ariel, as the Charge of her outfit is likely to be infinitely more than the Value, of the freight of what she can carry, by which she appears to be an improper Vessel and besides I see no likelihood of her ever sailing. I cannot understand why the prize money is not paid. I am always told that Orders have been given to pay it. It is an affair I never had anything to do with, and wish to keep my hands clear of all such money as long as I live, for I have long since observed that the Receivers and payers are subject to much suspicion, and Censure, and have more Trouble than Profit.— If there are Difficulties that cannot be got over but by Time, it does not seem to me just that our Vessel should be detained in Port at an immense charge to the States, on acct. of the Claims of a few men upon their agents Arising from their Service in another Ship.— If they chuse to stay in France till the Claims can be adjusted it seems to me they should be set on Shore to wait the Event at their own Expence; and if the Ship cannot sail without their Help, then let us return her to the Government; and find some other Way to convey our Goods. I am sorry for the poor Men, and wish I could remedy their Case, but I do not see how; the affair not being, & having never been in my Hands. I nevertheless advanc'd to you a Thousand Louis d'ors to be apply'd in relieving and satisfying them for the Present[5] which I suppose you applied accordingly tho' I have not yet received your account of the Application, that advance it seems has had no Effect and I can do no more. M. Chaumont tells me, that the Money would have been paid long since, if you had by a proper Muster Roll made the Sum Due appear. I understand you have now furnished such a Roll to Mr. ————[6] Let me know what is done in Consequence, and whether you can get the Vessel out or not, for we cannot longer go on in this Mad Management. I am ever, with great Regard, Sir,

Comme. Jones.

5. In March, 1780: XXXII, 130n.
6. Undoubtedly Montigny de Monplaisir; see Jones to BF, Aug. 7.

From Jean-Baptiste Luton Durival[7]

AL (draft):[8] Archives du Ministère des affaires étrangères

21. aout 1780.

M. le Cte. de Vergennes, M, ne se déterminera sur la demande de M. Jackson Jones, qu'après avoir reçu l'éclaircisst. [éclaircissement] que vous lui annoncez sur cet effet. En attendant le Ministre auroit desiré savoir non seulement quel dégré de confiance merite la Lettre de change que M. Jackson a déposée entre vos mains, mais encore la valeur de cet effet. Vous ne vous êtes pas expliqué Sur ce der. article. Je vous prie, M, de vouloir bien me le mander, ou à M. le Cte. de Vergennes lorsque vous voudrez bien lui communiquer l'eclaircisst. que vous attendez d'angleterre à ce sujet.

J'ai l'honneur d'être avec un respectueux attacht., M. &a

M. franklin.

From Vergennes

Copy: Library of Congress; draft:[9] Archives du Ministère des affaires étrangères

A Versailles le 21. Aout 1780.

J'ai reçu, Monsieur, La Lettre que vous m'avez fait l'honneur de m'écrire le 15. de ce mois. Nous n'empecherons pas nos Corsaires de prendre le Pavillon Americain pourvu qu'ils ne pretendent pas que ce Pavillion les soustrait à l'autorité des Loix et des Tribunaux du Royaume. C'est une Condition qu'il sera de votre Sagesse de prescrire à tous ceux que vous jugerez à propos d'accorder des Lettres de Marque.

---

7. Durival (1725–1810), originally from Lorraine, was the foreign ministry's *premier commis* responsible for financial affairs: Jean-Pierre Samoyault, *Les Bureaux du secrétariat d'état des affaires étrangères sous Louis XV: Administration, personnel* (Paris, 1971), p. 284; *DBF*. This is the first of several letters he exchanged with BF on various topics.

8. Begun at the bottom of a French translation of BF to Vergennes, Aug. 18, above.

9. In the hand of Gérard de Rayneval.

J'ai l'honneur d'être très sincerement, Monsieur, Votre tres humble et très obeissant Serviteur. (signé) DE VERGENNES.

M. Franklin.

From Dumas

ALS: American Philosophical Society; copy:[1] Algemeen Rijksarchief

Monsieur, La Haie 22e. Août 1780

Je n'ai rien présentement d'interessant à vous faire parvenir, si ce n'est la traduction que j'ai faite du Protest fait il y a près de deux mois par la Ville d'Amsterdam.[2]

Je fis hier une visite au Prince de Gallitzin, Envoyé de Russie, à qui je donnai un petit Mémoire, pour réfuter l'opinion, où l'on est assez généralement, que le Commerce de l'Amérique est en rivalité, quant aux productions, avec celui de la Russie, c'est à dire, que les Américains porteroient en Europe les mêmes articles que l'on trouve chez les Russes, & par conséquent n'avoient rien à prendre chez ceux-ci. Je lui ai fait voir les articles que les Américains prendroient d'eux en si grandes quantités, qu'ils Seroient obligés annuellement de leur payer pour solde une partie de l'or & de l'argent qu'ils tirent des Indes occid. Il m'a dit qu'il Sentoit la vérité de mes observations, & qu'il en feroit usage.

Vous trouverez, Monsieur, ci-joint, Un morceau que j'ai fait insérer dans les Gazettes.[3] J'espere que vous en serez content.

L'Election de l'Archiduc à Munster a été unanime. La Minorité du Chapitre, ne se voyant Soutenue ni par la France, ni par la Prusse, ni par la Hollande, S'est rangée le 15 du côté de la Majorité; & le 16 l'Election a eu lieu.[4]

1. A brief summary, which is dated Aug. 24.
2. For this enclosure (APS) see our annotation of Dumas to BF, Aug. 3.
3. A supposed letter from London minimizing the significance of the British capture of Charleston: *Gaz. de Leyde*, Aug. 22 (sup.). Dumas identifies it in his copy.
4. The election of Archduke Maximilian as coadjutor of the bishopric of Münster was reported in the same supplement of the *Gaz. de Leyde*. A week earlier he had been elected coadjutor of the archbishopric of Cologne: *London Courant, and Westminster Chronicle*, Aug. 26.

Je suis toujours avec un très-grand respect, Monsieur Votre très-humble & très-obéissant serviteur   DUMAS

Passy à S. Exc. Mr. B. Franklin

Addressed: à Son Excellence / Monsieur B. Franklin, Esqr. / Ministre Plenipe. des Etats-Unis / &c. / Passy./.

Notation Dumas la haie. Augt. 22. 1780

From Jonathan Williams, Jr.

ALS: American Philosophical Society; copy: Yale University Library

Dear & honoured Sir.   Nantes Augt. 22. 1780

Since my Return from Passy I have not received a Line from Mr de Chaumont relative to the Breton although I have frequently written to him on the Subject; I have received Letters from him on other matters but not a word of the Breton. I am at a loss to account for this & I wish you would please to put him in mind of the Business, for if we are not expeditious we shall not get the Cloathing out before Winter. If the Breton was at L'orient now I could load her in ten Days.

I am ever with the greatest Respect Your dutifull and affectionate Kinsman   JONA WILLIAMS J

Doctor Franklin

Endorsed: Mr Williams Augt. 22. 1780 Cannot account for his not hearing from M. de Chaum. concerning the Breton could load her in ten Days

To John Torris   Copy: Library of Congress

Sir,   Passy, Augt. 23. 1780.

Inclos'd I send you Copy of an Answer I have received from his Excellency the Comte de Vergennes upon the subject of your Privateers continuing to act under American Commissions.[5] I

5. Vergennes to BF, Aug. 21, above.

believe the Shipping french Seamen as well as the taking of the flora, contributed to raise the alarm against you. I trust you will give Strict Orders to your Captains, that for the future they abstain from every Infringement of the Laws of this Country; and if they observe those Orders, I suppose they may now continue acting with those Commissions. But for the future the Proceedings relating to their Captures must be laid before & Judged by the Conseil des prises, agreable to the Orders of Congress contained in the Commissions, and the King's Order of the 10th. Instant,[6] of which I also send you a Copy. I congratulate you on the Success I hear Capt. Ryan has lately had,[7] and wishing you a Continuance of Good fortune. I have the Honour to be, Sir,

Mr. Torris.

From Félix Vicq d'Azyr

ALS: American Philosophical Society

Monsieur,   ce 23 aout 1780

L'assemblée publique de la Societé royale de medecine aura lieu mardi 29 de ce mois;[8] cette compagnie qui Se fait gloire de vous compter au nombre de Ses membres ma chargé de vous y inviter. Votre presence est un encouragement pour elle qu'elle vous prie de ne pas lui refuser.

6. For which see our annotation of Vergennes to BF, Aug. 13.

7. Luke Ryan was captain of the privateer *Fearnot*, which had recently arrived in Dunkirk after a successful cruise: Clark, *Ben Franklin's Privateers*, pp. 157–63; *Courier de l'Europe*, VIII (1780), 111, issue of Aug. 18, 1780. The present communication ends BF's involvement with Torris' privateers and is his last extant letter to the shipowner.

8. On Aug. 19 the society had sent BF tickets for this meeting and expressed the hope that he would attend (APS). The assembly convened in the *pavillon de l'Infante* of the Louvre. Vicq d'Azyr delivered eulogies of two former members and received high praise for his oratory, which showed him to be "le digne émule des d'Alembert & même des Condorcet": Bachaumont, *Mémoires secrets*, XV, 274. For the social and political significance of his eulogies see Daniel Roche, "Talents, Reason, and Sacrifice: the Physician during the Enlightenment," in Robert Forster and Orest Ranum, eds., *Medicine and Society in France* . . . (Baltimore and London, 1980), pp. 66–88. For details of the assembly see *Jour. de Paris* for Aug. 29, 31, and Sept. 1 and 2.

Je Suis avec Respect, Monsieur Votre tres humble & tres
obeissant Serviteur   VICQ DAZYR
                                                     Secretaire perpetuel

Mr franklin à passy

Notation Vicq d'Azir. 23 aout 1780.

To Schweighauser

Copy: Library of Congress

Sir,   Passy Augt. 24 1780.
      I received yesterday the Honour of your Letter of the 19th.
Instant,[9] where in you mention my having paid your former Accounts of Disbursements on the frigate Alliance and other Vessels, which you suppose was done with the approbation of Congress. The Congress have never yet had the Opportunity of
giving their Opinion of those Accounts, and if they had Approved of them, it does not follow that they will approve of this,
nor if I paid them to serve you and prevent your being long out
of your money, does it follow that I am obliged to pay every subsequent Account that you or your Agents may think fit to present me. I had no order to make these Payments but I ventured
to pay them because I imagined the Accounts to be just. I cannot
venture to pay this, because I think unjust. The Navy Board by
whose Order you say you furnish'd the Supplies are proper and
good Judges of the Account: to them you ought to present it for
payment. And you should not, methinks endeavour to avoid
their Judgment and extort that Payment from me who am very
ignorant of the Value as well as of the Necessity of those Supplies. But if I were ever so expert in such Matters, it would be impossible for me to judge of the Justice of the Charges by the
Manner in which they are stated. For Example.
      To Arnous, Timber Merchant for Sundries 1551. l.t. not men-
tioning what these Sundries were, nor what Price. *To La Riviere,
for Rum, Flour, butter, &c. 1194. l.t. 14. 6.* no mention of Quantity or Price. *To Beauvais, Grocer 1158.16.0* not saying even for
what Goods. *To Blodget, for Shirts 2650 l.t.* not a word of the
Number or Price. *To idem for Linen Jackets and Stockings 1673.*

9. Missing, but undoubtedly in answer to BF's letter of Aug. 10.

l.t. 5 o. No Notice taken of the Quantity or Number or Rates. These articles are Specimens only, not the whole. The greatest Part of the Account is of the same kind. Most of the Articles lump'd, without price or Quantity. Many of these Articles must probably have been unnecessary, Such as the Timber, the Cordage, the Bunting, the ship being fitted for Sailing before Capt. Landais went on Board. The latter Article too seems in Quantity enormous, and Article one in which the Price & Quantity are mentioned appears Clearly extravagant in both as 5 lb. Sealing Wax at 12 Livres a lb. which is nearly double the Value of the Best and 10 times more than he could want during the Voyage, to make the Capt. Accountable for the propriety of these Disbursements his Orders should appears, and his Approbation of the Several Accounts.

But such is the Account you have offerd me, naked of every customary Formality, not a Date to any Article, not an Authority for any Article. The first of them with two Words inserted might as well have served for the whole. The Account would then have stood thus, *to Arnous Timber Merchant for Sundries. 31668. l.t. 12. 3.* This would have been nearly as satisfactory. And yet the Payment of this Account is what was demanded peremptorily by Drafts upon me even before I had a sight of it. And you take offence at my mentioning the Deficiency of Vouchers, as Reflection upon your Character for Probity, which you say is well established through all word, and this too is the Account which you are extreamly surprised at my not paying immediately, and which you threaten me you will pay yourself by selling Goods I have intrusted you with. If I do not comply with your Demand Permit me to say, that if I had paid it I believe my Constituents would have been *extreamly supprised.* And if your Character as a fair Dealer, is universally established, which I do not call in question, it was no established I imagine by rendring such Accounts nor will it be continued and supported by using such methods to extort the payment of them.

On considering the above with my preceeding Letters you will easily perceive that my paying the Account and afterwards demanding it of the King, must be improper & impraticable.

From the Character given of Captain Landais by one of his

friends, I entertained the Opinion of him which you mention. But if he order'd and approv'd of the Articles & Charges in this Accounts, I must change that Opinion.

You mention with some resentments my putting this Vessel in other "Hands than those of your representative at L'Orient"[1] you are misinformed in the fact. As the Expence was intended to be the King's, the Agent of the ministers had a Right to employ whom he pleas'd, and he did not consult me. I have taken no Business out of your Hands; I have in respect to you and your Appointment suffer'd it to take in Course there, tho' I must own I have as mentioned in former Letters, been dissatisfied with the Commission you charge of 5 per Cent.[2] Half the Money it was I suppose in this false Persuasion that I had wrong fully taken the Ship out of his Hands, that your representative reassumed the supplying while executing by her Another House, and persisted in it as you have told me contrary to your positive Orders. Upon him you seem to have some just Claim of Satisfaction. But if you excuse him, and take the affair upon yourself, then, I think as I said before, your proper method is, to send your account to the Navy Board of the eastern Department in consequence of those Orders you alledge the supplies where made. If they approve of it, they will discharge it. If you are longer out of your money then you ought to be, they will allow you Interest. But I forbid absolutely your selling any of the Goods I have deposited with you, to pay Debts, which not being of my contracting, nor contracted by my order, are not justly demandable of me. You are certainly Accountable to me for these Goods, and must restore them entire.

I am glad the Boxes will hold so many of the Gunbarrels, I did not think they would be so heavy. But as the making Smaller Boxes will encrease the Number and augment the Expence, I believe we must adhere to the Dimensions, and put up with the Inconvenience of their Weight. I have the honour to be, Sir,.

M. Schweighauser

1. M. Puchelberg: xxvii, 62n.
2. See, for example, xxix, 497.

From Philip Balliau

ALS: American Philosophical Society

Sir   From Dunkerque Prisone Agust the 24 1780

As I ade the Misfortune to Be Taken By Amerequin Priviteer[3] In Sconneur Belonging to Jersey Caled the May Flower Bound to Newcastle I was Brought to Dunkerque Presone. There I Was Told By the Commesary of Dunkerque to Right to your honneur. I hope you Be So good to Right to the Comesaire of Dunkerque that Wee May Be Exchange In the first oportunite.

I Ramain your Most Humble Servant   PHILIP BALLIAU

Addressed: Dr. Banj: Franklyn, / Plenepotentiaire Des Etâts / Unies de L'Amerique / à / Passy.

Notation: Bailliau. Dunkerque. Augt. 24. 80

From Fournier le jeune

ALS: American Philosophical Society

Monsieur   Ce 24 aoust 1780

Jay l'honneur de vous envoyer L'adresse du nouvel orgue, C'est Chez Mr Maugeaunt horloger Rüe du Pourtour st Gervais.[4] Si vous voulés vous y Rendre demain vendredy moi vous y Sachant Je ne manquerai Point de m'y trouver: Cela sera sur Les midy (tout Sera Pret).[5] Je suis fort aise que Cela me Procure L'honneur de vous Renouveler L'assurance de mon Respectueux attachement avec Lequel Je ne scesserai dêtre toute ma vie, Monsieur, Votre très humble et très Obéissant Serviteur

FOURNIER LE JEUNE

Ma femme me Charge de vous assurer de Ces Complimens

Addressed: A Monsieur / Monsieur francklin / A Passy

Notation: Fournier le Jeune. Paris 24 Augt. 80.

3. Undoubtedly the *Union Américaine.*

4. Neither the clockmaker nor the organ have been identified, but given the combination, it is possible that Fournier was offering BF the chance to hear one of the fantastic mechanical organ clocks that were so popular at the time. A variety of them are pictured in Arthur W.J.G. Ord-Hume, *Barrel Organ: the Story of the Mechanical Organ and Its Repair* (South Brunswick and New York, 1978), following p. 204.

5. BF did not go the following day; see Fournier's letter, below, Sept. 4.

To William Hodgson

Copy: Library of Congress

Dear Sir,   Passy, Augt. 25. 1780.

    I have received your Favour of the 11th. Instant. I have only time by this Oportunity to enclose and send you the Receipts of the Capt. of the Cartel, for some English Prisoners I have lately releas'd.[6] There were a Number sent before, of which I can not find at present the Receipt. I shall continue sending as they may arrive, in order to settle my particular Account honestly. But I still complain about the Boston Cartel People,[7] and other Breakers of Parole. With great Esteem, I am, Dear Sir, &c.

M. Hodgson.

From Thomas Digges

ALS: Historical Society of Pennsylvania

Dr. Sir   London 25 Augt 1780

    I did not receive Your letter of the 18th. handed me by Mr H. time enough for the Office Hours to make enquiry of or about Mr. G——d;[8] But I calld there this Evening & went to Mr G——s Lodgings, where neither His Landlady or the Servant could give me further accots. of Him than that He had been near three weeks in the Country but *where* they could not tell. I shall call at the office again in the morning & get his direction, with which I can make the necessary enquiry as to his accepted Bill; but I fear it will be a post or two before I can inform You further; You may depend however no time shall be lost on my part. As Mr. G—— seems to turn out but an underhand Gentn. I am rather afraid for your Bill.

    I wrote you twice very lately.[9] Since which there is nothing new save the arrival of a small Brig from Boston to Bristol wch arrivd the 23d after a passage of 32 days so that She saild abot the

6. Not located.

7. *I.e.*, those sent from Boston aboard the *Bob* and *Polly*.

8. BF's letter of the 18th is no longer extant. G——d is John Goddard upon whom Edward Jackson Jones had drawn to repay the 30 *louis* BF had loaned him: Jones to BF, Aug. 11, above.

9. We know of only one other letter Digges wrote BF over the past month, that of Aug. 18, above.

21 or 22d July. She appears to be purchasd by Mr J Temples Bror. [Brother] in order to move Himself & Family to settle in Ireland He being ill in a Consumption.[1] We have no regular accots as yet by this vessel nor can I immediately find J. T to inform myself whether He has any. The publick receivd accot by this vessel is, That Monr Ternay arrivd safe at Rhode Island & had landed His men abot. 6,000 which had gone from the Island to the Continent.[2] Three of the transports of His fleet had seperated from Him on the Coast of America & put into Boston. The troops on board them were immediately marchd for Providence. When this vessel saild there were no accots in Boston of Adml Greaves's arrival on the Coast nor any sort of news from N York as to Clintons Expedn. up the North River. In the rough as it was told this day at Change the news is not lookd upon as favorable, but rather the reverse, & will add to the gloom still very conspicuous for the loss of a whole Fleet lately taken by the Combind fleet.[3] I dare say when it comes to be given in detail, it will still cast a deeper gloom.

I find my friend Barnet has been playing similar tricks in Bruxelles to those he playd me. He there went by the name of Billinger.

Dr. S——tt receivd with great thankfulness the pass——t you sent for His Baggage.[4] He went out in the N York fleet which saild the 10th. & much fears are expressd for this fleet. Mr. John Bowman of the State of Georgia (where He has a Considerable propery in Land & blacks) Desires me to supplicate a similar pass for His Baggage. He means to go out in a running Ship to Savanah in a fortnight or 3 weeks. I meet Him frequently at our

1. Robert Temple (1728–1782), an older brother of John Temple's, was a Loyalist from Charlestown, Mass., who had chartered the brig with the permission of the Mass. Council: Elias and Finch, *Letters of Digges*, p. 254n; Sabine, *Loyalists*, II, 349–50; *London Courant, and Westminster Chronicle*, Aug. 26, 1780. The various items of war news reported below appeared in the same issue of the *London Courant*.

2. It was only 1,500 ill soldiers and sailors who were removed from the Newport area to Providence and Bristol on the mainland: Lee Kennett, *The French Forces in America, 1780–1783* (Westport, Conn., and London, 1977), p. 49.

3. *I.e.*, the large convoy captured on Aug. 8–9.

4. Digges had requested a passport for Dr. Upton Scott's baggage: XXXII, 446–7, 503, 620.

freinds in Mincing Lane (Mr. V——s) and have been enough in the habits of intimacy with Him for two Years back to know Him to be perfectly right in politicks & principles with regard to His Country. He was at Paris & known to you abot. two or 3 years ago.[5] If you can oblige Him be pleasd to cover the pass To *Messrs.* Wm. Hodgson & Co. better *Messrs.* than Mr. & the sooner forwarded the better.

Our Reverend friend Mr W——[6] has been some days with me & we have put Your welcome donation to the Prisrs on a good footing. It commencd the 18th. ulo. at F——n to 152 Privates & 43 Officers 6d. pr wk to Ea. The numbers are not exactly known at M P——. M W——n will be in Town again in 6 or 8 days when I will settle the exact advance on this charity & draw a bill on you as heretofore for the amot to that day. I am with the highest Esteem Dr Sir Yr. obligd & obt Ser   W:S:C

Addressed: A Monsr. Monsr. B. F— / Passy

Notation: 25 Augt 80

From ——— Aillaud[7]   ALS: American Philosophical Society

Monsieur,   ce 26 aout [1780]
    Le triste etat dans lequel Melle Basseporte se trouve actuellement ne me permettant plus de me flatter que je puisse joüir en-

5. Bowman had written BF in October, 1777: XXV, 45–6. Benjamin Vaughan lived in Mincing Lane, London: XXXII, 381n.
    6. Wren, who assisted Americans in Forton Prison. "M P——," below, is Mill Prison.
    7. Mme Aillaud must have been the assistant of Madeleine-Françoise Basseporte (xv, 115n), who died on Sept. 5, 1780, at the Jardin du roi where she was *peintre du roi pour la miniature.* Mlle Basseporte was praised for the scientific precision of her paintings of plants and animals, and she attracted to the Jardin members of the Académie des sciences, prominent painters like Van Loo, and distinguished amateurs like the antiquarian Caylus. Rousseau commented that while nature gave life to plants, it was she who preserved it: Mamès-Claude-Catherine Pahin Champlain de la Blancherie, *Essai d'un tableau historique des peintres de l'école françoise, depuis Jean Cousin, en 1500, jusqu'en 1783 inclusivement* (Paris, 1783, reprinted Geneva, 1972), p. 241; *DBF;* Yves Laissus, "Le Jardin du roi," in *Enseignement et diffusion des sciences en France au XVIIIe siècle,* René Taton *et al.,* eds. (Paris, 1964), pp. 311, 334.

core longtemps du plaisir detre aupres d'elle, je crois devoir me donner des mouvemens pour tacher pendant qu'elle existe, de massurer une pension sur sa charge.[8] Cela depend principalement de Monsieur De Buffond[9] que vous connoissez particulierement, et si vous vouliez bien Monsieur avoir la bonté de lui recommander le petit memoire que jay lhonneur de vous envoyer je serois assurée du succès de ma demande. Joze me flatter que vous voudréz bien maccorder cette grace je me fonde sur l'estime dont vous honnorés Melle Basseporte et dont jay eté temoin l'orsquelle a eu lhonneur de vous reunir chez elle avec Monsieur De Buffond.

Je suis avec respect Monsieur Votre tres humble et tres obeissante servante   AILLAUD

Notation: alliaud

From Jonathan Williams, Jr.

ALS: American Philosophical Society; copy: Yale University Library

dear & hond Sir   Nantes Augt 26. 1780

I have this day received a Letter from Mr de Chaumont, in which he tells me, he has purchased the Breton[1] & that she will be ready to take in at L'orient by the last of next Month, so that what I wrote you by the last Post need not be shewn to him, since the Business is now going on, and you may depend it will on my Side go on briskly. I wish the Ariel was gone, for I do not want this operation to be known 'till then; Mr de Chaumont also wishes it may not yet be known.— I think it will be well worth while for Government to grant you a Ship of War to go with the Breton, for it will be a reinforcement, to Mr. de Ternay & the

----

8. Mlle Basseporte succeeded to her office on the death of Claude Aubriet (1665–1742), her teacher (*DBF*). The office, or *charge,* entitled her to a salary, heavily taxed but supplemented by several pensions: Marcel Roux *et al.,* comps., *Inventaire du fonds français: graveurs du dix-huitième siècle* (9 vols. to date, Paris, 1930–62), II, 154–5.

9. Georges-Louis Le Clerc, comte de Buffon, *intendant* of the Jardin du roi: XV, 141–2n.

1. Chaumont purchased the *Breton* from Simon Jauge & fils for approximately 400,000 *l.t.:* Lopez, *Lafayette,* p. 199.

Bretons Cargo which will exceed a million, ought to be well protected. As the Breton will want Sailors I intend by the Desire of
Mr de Chaumont to get as many as I can to go on board her, for
this Purpose it will be necessary for you to give a permission for
Americans to embark, for otherwise it cannot be openly done.
We are forbid to take french Sailors, & the french therefore do
not pass american Ones, tho' the Captains of french Vessells take
them secretly; but any american (if we had a Consul to support
him) could take these Sailors away from a frenchman. If therefore I had a Permission from you to engage american Sailors for
the Breton, & an order from Mr de Sartine that no French Vessell shall engage american Sailors when they are wanted for the
public Service of america, I could engage many & very much facilitate the Expedition, and at the same time prevent our Sailors
from going into other Employ, which very much hurts our Trade
here. I am making out the Invoice of the Goods you take of Mr
de Chaumont & will send it to you as soon as it is done.

I hear with pleasure by the Way of Spain that Mr de Ternay
is arrived at Rhode Island.

I am with the greatest Respect Dear & hond Sir Your dutifull
& affectionate Kinsman   JONA WILLIAMS J

Endorsed: Letter from M Williams Aug 26. 1780 Mr. de Chaumont writes to him that he has purchased the Breton—ready to
take in by the last of September

From John Diot & Co.[2]   ALS: American Philosophical Society

Honored sir   Morlaix the 27th. August 1780.

We did ourselves the honnour to Write to your Excellency the
16th. Instt. to forward you an Abstract of the Journal of the
Black Princess privateer, and to acquaint you with the arrivall in
this harbour of the prize St. Joseph.

We now think it our duty to forward to Your Excellency all
the *Procès Verbaux* and documents relative to Said Prize,
whereof, from the undenial proofs of it's Lawfullness, we have
Reasons to Expect that a Speedy Condemnation will Soon issue.

2. The last extant letter from the firm. We have not located the enclosures
to it.

Your Excellency has undoubtedly been served in Time by the Commissary with the receit of Capn. Pearce of the Indian Carteel Ship for the English Prisoners that the Princess brought and which We deliver'd to him, thro' your orders.

Mr. Jas. Willis Merchant in London and Chief owner of the Cargoe of the prize Phillip,[3] whereof All the documents, Letters and documents Were Sent to Your Excellency, has wrote to us many a Letter to Request we Shou'd Send to him Some Invoyces, without which he can not Claim one Shilling from the Underwritters; these Invoyces are among the papers that you have and We wou'd deem it a great favour, if Your Excellency wou'd be pleased to Send 'em to us, and we'll forward 'em to the owners, whom they are of the Greatest moment to, and Very fruitless to any one Ellse; We do write to Said Mr. Willis that we do Apply to Your Excellency for the Complyance of his Request, which if agreed to, will Oblidge us greatly, as it will be the means of our being paid of some Cash we lent to a Mr. Stevens passenger on board the Phillip and which the former will not pay, unless we furnish him with the Invoyces he Requests.

We Crave the favour of Your Excellency Compliance to the Above, Mean While, With due Respect We have the Honour to be Truely, Your Excellency's Most Obedient and most Humble Servants   Jn Diot & Co

His Excellency B. Franklin Minister Plenipotentiary from the Congress at the Court of France Passy

Notation: Diot & Co. 27. Augt. 1780

To John Ross

Copy: Library of Congress

Sir,   Passy, Augt. 28. 1780.

I received yesterday your favour of the 23d.[4] proposing a Ship to be freighted for our Goods. I some time since put that Busi-

---

3. The *Philip* was captured on Feb. 26 by the *Black Prince* and *Black Princess:* Clark, *Ben Franklin's Privateers,* p. 110. BF had sent Diot & Co. a prize judgement: XXXII, 307.

4. Missing.

ness into the Hands of M. Williams, who has agreed for a Ship accordingly, that is large enough to take all we have to send.[5] He will inform you of the Particulars. I am nevertheless thankful to you for your Obliging Attention to this important Business; and am, with great Esteem, Sir, your &c.

M. Ross

From Jonathan Williams, Jr.

ALS: University of Pennsylvania Library; copy: Yale University Library

Dear & hond Sir.   Nantes Augt 28. 1780.

The Bearer Mr Jeremiah Allen of Boston is a Gentleman for whom I have a great Friendship and Esteem;[6] we were Companions in our Infancy, and from that Time I have had more Reason to increase than diminish my Attachment. I beg leave to recommend him to your notice and am as ever Your dutifull & affectionate Kinsman   JONA WILLIAMS J

The Hon. Doctor Franklin.

Notation: Jona Williams Augt 28. 1780

From Thomas Digges   ALS: Historical Society of Pennsylvania

Dr Sir   29 Augt. 1780

I recd yr. letter of the 18 Int. & answerd it, as far I could do so, by frydays post.[7] Since that period I have been twice to the office where Mr G——d is a Clerk, & the answers to my questions about Him were rather extraordinary. I could find out nothing but that He had been 3 or 4 weeks in the Country (neither his Bror Clerks nor his Landlady at His Lodgings could tell *where* in the Country) but that if I left a line at the office it would be de-

5. The ship Chaumont had just purchased; see JW's letter of Aug. 24.
6. Allen also carried with him from Boston a letter of introduction from JW's father; see XXX, 536.
7. Above, Aug. 25.

liverd to Himself. I have wrote Him a line just to ask if such a bill (*copying* it *exactly from Yrs*) was a good bill & requesting His Ansr. as soon as He conveniently could. I am afraid by what I could discover that you have been flung out of 30 Guineas. The moment I get any information about Him you shall certainly have it.

I mentiond to You on fryday that a Flag of Truce brot. by Mr R Temple had arrivd at Bristol. He is not yet come to Town but is to be here tomorrow— There are no passengers, but a Mr Bromfield whom I have seen, and a master & super Cargoe of a Ship richly laden & lately taken going from Corke to N York & carryd into Boston. I need not recapitulate to you any particular news recd from Mr B—mf—d. It is in substance extreamly pleasing to me & very different to what has been put forth with such assiduity by ministry & their runners ever since the news arrivd of the Capture of Chas. Town. This accot has been rather confirmd to me since the arrival of the last packet from N York, where it appeard on the 11th July the Garrison was aiming rather at securing themselves than making any excursions against the American Army declard now on all hands to be too well posted for Mr Clinton to attempt an assault.[8] Bromfield says they had heard of a fleet of Engs men of War arriving at Hallifax abot the 8th. July wh must be Greaves's fleet. We suppose here from the various accots lately recd. that it is intended by Genl Washington & Monsr. Ternay to make an attack on N York. Accots are this day recd at Loyds that the outward bound Quebec fleet had been met near the Island of N Foundland on the 12th July by the Confederacy Amn Frigate & 2 small privateers who made an easy capture of twelve out of sixteen ships—[9] The other four escapd & told the dismal tale at St. Johns N Foundland from whence the accot comes to Bristol & it is authentic. Well done Yankee say I. This fleet was met by 3 french men of war abot 5 weeks ago soon after they saild from Corke these men of war then took but two of the fleet wch were afterwards retaken.

8. This news, as well as the shipping news below, was reported in the Aug. 29 issue of the *London Courant, and Westminster Chronicle.*

9. The *Confederacy* was not involved in the captures, which were made by the privateers *Brutus, Essex, Jack, America*, and *Stark: Pennsylvania Gazette, and Weekly Advertiser,* Aug. 23 and 30, 1780.

We were much in the dumps here on this & the late Capture near Cape St Vincents, and very much so at the news by the New York Packet wch *only* substantially informd us that Clintons army was far too weak to effect any offensive opperation—we are however today got *up* again. The Leeward Island, the Oporto, & two of the Et. India homeward bound ships are reported to be all safe arrivd at Falmouth, & in consequence of this immence great news, we are *now* mighty enough to war with all the world. The cry is that Ministry ought to be hangd if they do not immediately declare war against Russia, Holland, Denmark & Sweeden for their late perfidy in forming an offensive league agt. the commerce of this Country.

I am with the highest regard Dr Sir Yr Obligd & Ob Ser

W.S.C

Notation: Augt. 29. 1780.

From Jonathan Williams, Jr.

ALS: University of Pennsylvania Library

Dear & hond Sir   Nantes Augt 29. 1780.

I beg leave to introduce to your Notice Mrs Blake her Daughter & two Sons. This Lady is the Wife of William Blake Esqr of South Carolina & one of the most respectable Men in that State.[1] He came hither with his Family about three Years, since & went himself to america where he now is; He was in Carolina but not in Charlestown at the Surrender. Mrs Blake proposes to go to England to put her Children at School, & then return to her Sister at Brussells. For this Purpose she will want your Pasport which I request you to give her & I shall be particularly obliged to you for every mark of Civility shewn her, having the highest

1. Anne Izard Blake (b. 1741) was a cousin of Ralph Izard's. She and William had three children: *S.C. Gen. and Hist. Mag.*, I, 161–2; II, 231–2. JW owed a debt of gratitude to William Blake (XXVI, 40n), who was one of the American merchants at Nantes who had acted fairly toward him during the dispute over his accounts in 1779. Blake returned to America in the spring of that year: XXIX, 196n.

Esteem & Regard for Mrs Blake, and her Husband is my particular Friend.[2]

I am as ever with the greatest Respect Dear & hond Sir Your dutifull & affectionate Kinsman   JONA WILLIAMS J

Notation: Jon. Williams Nantes August 29. 1780

From Dumas   ALS: American Philosophical Society

Monsieur   Lahaie 31e. Août 1780

J'ai eu l'honneur, dans une de mes dernieres,[3] de vous parler d'un Mémoire que j'ai donné au Mine. [Ministre] de Russie ici, pour détruire l'opinion que les Anglomanes ne cessent d'entretenir, comme Si le Commerce des Américains Septentrionaux étoit en rivalité avec celui de la Russie, & pour faire voir qu'au contraire ils feront un trafic direct avec la Russie très avantageux à celle-ci, en y allant chercher de ses productions, comme Chanvre, Lin, Toiles à voiles, Cordages, Cuivre, Cuirs rouges, Drogues, &c. & y portant de leurs productions avec celles des Indes occid. & même de l'or & de l'argent. Je n'ai pas eu le temps de garder copie de ce Memoire qui a paru faire plaisir au Mine. Mais j'ai fait une démarche pareille dans une Lettre que j'avois d'ailleurs à écrire au Chargé d'affaires de Suede près de la rep., présentement à Spa., qui est de ma connoissance. Après lui avoir parlé de l'attente où l'on est ici de voir le Roi son maître,[4] & d'autres choses, j'ajoute ce qui suit:

"Dieu bénisse la neutralité armée. J'espere qu'elle aboutira à rendre la paix aux deux hémispheres. Elle rectifiera bien des opinions, que certaines gens ne cessent d'entretenir, & d'autres

---

2. In a letter to WTF of the same day, JW asked his cousin to take particular care of the Blake party (which included, in addition to the children, a "maid & servant"). JW had directed them to the Hôtel d'York. APS.

3. Aug. 22, above.

4. Peter von Heidenstam had been Swedish *chargé d'affaires* in the Netherlands from April, 1779, to July, 1780; he later was *chargé* in Copenhagen: *Repertorium der diplomatischen Vertreter*, III, 405, 411–12. King Gustavus III of Sweden was at Spa for its famous mineral waters before making a visit to the Netherlands: *Gaz. de Leyde*, Aug. 22, 1780 (sup.).

de croire, sur les suites qu'aura le Commerce illimité des Am.
avec toutes les nations Européennes. A les en croire il Se trou-
veroit en rivalité avec celui des nations circum Baltiques, & notamment de la Suede. Rien de plus faux. Les Am. n'ont cultivé
du Chanvre & du Lin, & fourni d'autres munitions navales qu'à
force de ce qu'on appelle *Bounties*. Ces articles leur étoient pres-
crits parmi ceux que les Angl., dans leur Acte de navigation, appellent *enumerated commodities*.[5] Ils s'adonneront à d'autres articles plus avantageux pour eux à porter en Europe. Les Angl.
devront recourir à la Suede pour du Goudron, &c. comme avant
la Reine Anne. Les Américains-mêmes iront chercher chez vous
du Chanvre, Lin, Toile à voile, Cordages, Cuivre, & de vos
Manufactures de Laine, de Coton, d'Alun, soufre, poudre,
laiton, acier, &c. Ils vous porteront en échange du Tabac, Ris,
Indigo, Rum, & de toutes les productions des Indes occid. Ci-
devant les prétendus Rois de la mer s'approprioient tout cela."

L'Article de Philadelphie, dans la Gazette ci-jointe,[6] a fait une
bonne impression sur les esprits ici. Je n'ai aucune nouvelle de
Mr. Adams. Il m'avoit dit qu'il m'écriroit quelquefois d'Amsterdam; mais il ne le fait pas.

Je suis avec mon respectueux attachement, qui vous est connu,
Monsieur Votre très-humble & très-obéissant serviteur DUMAS

Passy à S. E. M. B. Franklin

Addressed: à Son Excellence / Monsieur B. Franklin, Esqr. /
Min. Plenipe. des Etats-Unis / &c. / Passy./.

Notation: Dumas la haie Augt 31. 80

5. The Navigation Act of 1660 began the process of restricting specified
or "enumerated" colonial exports, initially predominantly agricultural, to
ports in Britain and Ireland; in 1705 and 1729 naval stores were added to the
list: Charles M. Andrews, *The Colonial Period of American History* (4 vols.,
New Haven and London, 1934–38), IV, 85–6, 102. This was designed to
weaken the dominance of the traditional Baltic suppliers, like Sweden, of
naval stores to the British Navy.
6. Probably "Extrait d'une lettre de Philadelphie du 15 Juin," which appeared in the Aug. 29 issue of the *Gaz̧. de Leyde*. It reported the establishment of an Academy of Arts and Sciences in Massachusetts and the selection
(on Jan. 21) of a number of new members by the American Philosophical Society.

From Jean de Neufville & fils

ALS: American Philosophical Society

Honored Sir!   Amsterdam 31 August 1780.

May it please your Excellency! That having not receivd an answer to our Last,[7] proposing to continue to Accept the bills drawn on Henry Laurens Esqr.; we may Suppose that the quantity drawn hath been a trifle, and that your Excellency had no objection to our going on, as we had begun, in which the approbation of Your Excy. Shall always be of no little Consequence for us; We have lately gott no Aman. Vessells here, though now there is one fm. Philadelphia and one from Virginia, they are not come up yett, nor their Letters deliverd.

We have a report that an English Convoy of 54 Sail have fallen into the french and Spanish hands Among their combind fleett[8] may this prove true as we wish!

As Your Excellency hath not prescribed us the manner in which she should [*torn: one or two words missing*] provide for our Rembursement for the bills mentiond we hope she wont take it amiss that we renew our adress in this respect, as there is butt two ways either by Remittances or draufts, and as we have no what is Called in France *Jours de grace*, we shall look upon it as a favour to Receive your Excellencys Directions there About; and at every other opportunity in which we could Convince her of our Readiness to serve the American Cause, and to obey any private Comands; as we have the honour to be with the most perfect esteem and all unfeignd and unreserved Regard.

Honourd Sir! Your Excellencys most devoted and most Obedient humble Servants.   JOHN DE NEUFVILLE & SON

7. Probably that of July 13. Obviously the firm had not yet received BF's July 21 letter. Both are above.

8. News of the capture reached London on the morning of Aug. 22 and Leiden on or by Aug. 31: *London Courant, and Westminster Chronicle*, Aug. 23; *Gaʒ. de Leyde*, Sept. 1 (sup.).

From Jean de Neufville & fils

ALS: American Philosophical Society

Honourd Sir!   [on or after August 31, 1780][9]

May we thank your Excellency for the late favour she honourd us with of the 21st: instant as we are now sure that the bills
drawn on the Hone. Henry Laurens will be further out of danger, and your Excy will answer for the same; We shall now wait
for your Excellencys dispositions for our rimbursement either
that we may draw or have the money remitted; and if we may be
approved, we shall with pleasure continue to accept those bills
under the guarantie of your Excellency for our Remburse in
time; giving exact notice or even copies of those we accept, as
no alteration then shall take place, from what hath been done untill now and the absence of Mr. Laurens will be less thought or
talked off untill we know how this may turn;— Should we on the
countrary offer, as your Excellency proposes to send those bills
for Acceptance, this may be attended with trouble and opposition, the bills being drawn to be accepted and payd in Amsterdam; some bearers to hurt the cause, would not be satisfied, &
present a risk in sending and returning the same, which otherwise would give us not more nor less trouble;— Should some
good reason appear or arise, Which made your Excellency resolve to have them afterwards protested, we will comply therewith at the first notice. We are sensible that this methode will influence here the American Spirit for the best.

Since your Excellency desired us to procure a subscription for
a Million and a half or Two Million,[1] we have never tried it
openly, knowing we should not be able to fulfill it at once, the
proposalls now made for a loan was grounded on the hopes and
expectation to find (if no others could) the funds for those bills

9. This document clearly appears to have been written after the firm's letter of Aug. 31, immediately above. We suspect that soon after writing it the
firm belatedly received BF's letter of July 21. On Sept. 18, below, the firm
refers to the present letter as being written on August 31. Moreover, rumors
of the capture of St. Lucia, discussed in the last paragraph of the present letter, were also discussed in the Sept. 1 issue of the *Gaz. de Leyde* under the
date of Aug. 30.

1. The unsuccessful 1,500,000 florin loan on behalf of Congress that BF
had authorized Neufville to raise (for which see the firm's July 13 letter).

drawn on Mr. Laurens and being at 6 Month we might have engaged what money offerd, without ever hurting the Credit of Congress.— We are sensible to the frendly manner, in which Your Excy took it, and her kind expressions; we shall endeavour to deserve the Same, promoting the American intrest when it lays in our power.

We had the pleasure of seeing the Baron Wulfing Aide de Camp to the great Genall. Washington on generall recomendations given him by your Excelly. We doubt not butt with most part of the Americans, he will be satisfied with our reception.

It is told and generally believed that the French and Spanish fleet have joind may we soon receive some favourable Accounts from America and see that cause favourd all over as much as we wish.

We this moment were presented with a portret of the great Genal. Washington with a desire it should be forwarded to your Excelly who may guess at the hand from which it comes, butt we are forbidden to tell it untill we get leave for it; so we begg leave to be excused on this point butt we shall forward it by the first opportunity.

Great news are reported again fm. America, St Lucia taken, Abt. Barbados and Antigua, butt we dare not trust to any untill we know it to be well confirmd.

We have the honour to be with all Respectfull Regards Honourd Sir! Your Excellencys most obedient & most humble Servants   JOHN DE NEUFVILLE & SON

From Amelia Barry

ALS: American Philosophical Society

Most Dear Sir,   Leghorn 1st Sept. 1780

An English Paper mentions that you are actually preparing to return to America; I hope it is not true: Surely you will not risque your person in America, till the contest be finally determined, and your safety ascertained: Should success attend the British arms, your Virtue your Talents, nor your years, would shelter you if in their power, from vindictive treatment: Know you not my revered Sir, that an Injurer seldom forgives? And erring man is too too apt to view with impatience, to say no worse, the person who gave him counsel that he had not virtue or resolution to follow; and the heavier the consequences of his error and obstinacy may be, resentment often rises in proportion; & to the idea of the wise Friend, is annexed that of the lost Good. If there is any truth in this observation, your Virtue becomes your Crime. Think then, my dear Sir, before you make the dangerous experiment: if your health is not so good as you wish, might not the milder air of Italy be of service to you? Glut not ignoble revenge, with a voluntary sacrifice of such a life as yours. Aristides listened to, & assisted, the meanest voice of his country, tho' to his condemnation; he merited the appellation of Just, but would you Sir, have allowed it to him, had the Ostracism been in use in his Enemies Country, & he had waved the interests of his own, and the regard he owed to his personal safety, by submitting his conduct to their arraignment, & promoted his own condemnation?[2] Let then your Amelia, who claims a kind of right in her revered paternal friend, be heard. In the days of prettling infancy you loved me; the favored, tho' unfortunate child of a Lady most dear to you, & honored by me;— the fd. [friend] too of you Sally, may speak: the event then of this important year, may Heaven inspire you to wait in Europe! For I have a presentiment that if you revisit America, anguish will be the lot of your friends, tho' a noble consciousness of integrity, and true philanthropy may (and assuredly will,) give a lustre to your setting Sun.— Yet after all, I hope that I am misinformed; if so, one line saying "I do not leave Europe my Child" will be truly acceptable; but if you realy go a few parting lines with a precious "God bless you & yours" I implore before you embark, & may all my fears prove vain!

Permit a word or two on the subject of Govr. Pownall.—

2. The Athenian general and statesman Aristeides (d. *c.* 468 B.C.) was known as "the Just"; he was sent into exile when he came into conflict with Themistocles. During the proceedings to ostracize him an "illiterate and illbred peasant," unaware that he was talking to Aristeides himself, requested his assistance in casting a vote for banishment. Asked what harm the great general had ever done him, the peasant replied, "None . . . But I cannot stand hearing everyone call him The Just." Aristeides silently helped him cast his vote: David Sansome, ed. and trans., *Plutarch: The Lives of Aristeides and Cato* (Warminster, England, 1989), pp. 37–9; M.C. Howatson, ed., *The Oxford Companion to Classical Literature* (2nd. ed., Oxford and New York, 1989), pp. 54–5.

When I was honored with your letter I applyed to that Gentn. I waited 2 or 3 months without having heared from him. I then wrote again & had an immediate ansr. which I had the honor to transmit you an extract from in a letter under the 1st May, but as it may have miscarried I subjoin another.[3]

"I was not silent to your application for any other reason but that I did not know what to answer to write: & having left the whole of the publication & account of the sale of the map & topographical description to Mr. Almon the Editor, & desiring him (which he tells me he has done) to write to Doctor Franklin, & to send him an acct. of what Profetts (all charges deducted,) he can afford to remit on your account, for whose benefit I always intended such surplus profits: I was in hopes you would have heared from the Docr. on the subject. I have this day since the receipt of your letter from Legn. of the 27th March spoken again to Mr. Almon & desired him to write again to Docr. Franklin. He has promised me that he will, I will therefore beg of you to address yourself to Doctor Franklin for such answer as he in consequence of Mr. Almon's state of the acct shall be able to give you; & likewise you may address yourself to Mr. Almon Bookseller in Picadilly London. Whether my Letter to Docr. Franklin ever arrived at his hand, I do not know, & cannot guess, never having recd any acknowledgment of its receipt &c &c &c."

I immediately wrote the Mr. Almon & informed him of the authority I had from you Sir, to apply for the profits arising from the sale of the Map, but have never heared from him. I have therefore dear Sir, to entreat the favor of you to let me know wt. he says to you, as I shall suspend further application to him till I have the honor of a line from you.

With the most sincere and ardent wishes for your health happiness & glory I have the honor to be My Dear Sir, your most obliged & devoted Humble Servant   A. BARRY.

Docr. Franklin.

Notation: A Barry 1 Sep. 80

3. Mrs. Barry was seeking royalties for a new edition of a map made by Lewis Evans (her father). She had last written on May 1, where she also refers to a now-missing letter from BF: XXXII, 331–3.

From Henry Coder (Coderc)

LS:[4] American Philosophical Society

Monsieur Le Docteur,   à Pezenas le 1er. septembre 1780

Quinse jours aprés Etre arrivé dans ma chaumiere des blessures Se Sont réouvértes, et aprés Six Mois de Souffrances je Meurs pénétré des bontés dont vous avés d'aigné m'honorér.[5] Je vous Supplie S'y l'occasion S'en presente de les repandre Sur Ma famille, je vous reponds d'avance quils En Sont dignes, et je Meurs content dans l'espérance que vous aurés Egard à Ma derniere demande.

Je Suis avec Veneration Monsieur Le Docteur Votre trés humble et trés obeïssant Serviteur.   CODERC

From the Baron de Frey

ALS: American Philosophical Society

Excellence   Paris le 1: Sepbre. 1780./.

Je prens la liberté de vous envoier par mon domestique le 20. L'ouis d'or, que V: E: à eû la complaisance de m'avancer.[6] Et en même tems je pris V: E: de vouloir rémettre au porteur les trois L'oan office Certificats de 1000 d'ollr ch'aqune, qu'elle à entre ses mains—

Je conte de partir mardi prochaine pour l'Orient ou Bourdaux

---

4. In the hand of his mother, who writes on Sept. 7, below.

5. Coder announced his departure for Pézenas (in Languedoc) in an undated note written around six and a half months before this letter, about mid-February. He intends to sell his *patrimoine* in Pézenas and to purchase merchandise needed in America, where he plans to settle with his brother (XXVII, 406–7n), "qui Est aussi determiné que moi a Sacrifier Sa vie Et Sa fortune pour La Defense de votre Cause Et de vivre Et mourir avec des hommes Vertueux Et Libres." He warns that BF's former suppliers were countering charges of defective supplies by saying they were paid with worthless bills. If BF still needs supplies from France he should turn to the provinces, Languedoc in particular, where he will find high quality but reasonably priced goods. Had Coder received further orders after the initial one for 1,300 uniforms, he would have obtained supplies from towns all over the kingdom reputed to have the best cloth, equipment, and arms. Hist. Soc. of Pa. For Coder's role in the early search for supplies and his order of uniforms see XXIII, 362–5; XXIV, 366–7; XXV, 62n, 71–2.

6. On Sept. 2 BF credited "Col. Frey" for "the 20 Guineas I had lent him." Cash Book.

pour m'en rétourner en amérique, si V: E à quelques Ordres a me donner je passerois dimanche ou l'unedi a Bassy pour les récevoir. En attendant j'ai l'honneur d'etre avec Respect. di Votre Excellence très humble et très obeissant Serviteur

DE FREŸ

Capt: au Service des

Etas Unis de l'amerique

Notation: Frey 1. 7bre. 1780.

From Thomas Digges   ALS: Historical Society of Pennsylvania

Dr. Sir   London 1st Sept 80

I calld again this day at the office where a Bill given you was made payable & I could learn no intelligence of mr. J. G——d more than I had before: He was in the Country but *where* or when He returnd no one could tell. I have no ansr. to the letter wrote to him (& left at the office) wch. containd only an enquiry whether the Bill was good or not. Dr. F——ll being down in Cheshire for some days I could not make the necessary Enquiry whether Mr. Jones the drawer of the Bill on Mr. G——d, was known to Him or not.[7] I will do every thing in this business that can be done & give you the earliest information—at present I have no hopes to give you that the bill is a good one.

We have no news since the last post by wch. I wrote you,[8] save that a *general* opinion prevails that the Parliament was this day dissolvd.[9] There is much bustle in consequence of it, & by every appearance the ministry will get as many if not more Corrupt L——ds into the next as they have had in the late Parliat.

Adml G——y has resignd the Command of the Channel fleet, and Darby has retird, both said to be in disgust at Palissers

7. Jones is Edward Jackson Jones. J. G.——d stands for Goddard and F——ll for Dr. John Fothergill. Mr. G——d is Grand. T——le, whom Digges mentions below, is Robert Temple.

8. On Aug. 29, above.

9. The sudden dissolution of Parliament on Sept. 1, a year early, surprised the opposition but failed to improve the North ministry's majority in the House of Commons: Cobbett, *Parliamentary History,* XXI, 767; Namier and Brooke, *House of Commons,* I, 80–87; Ian R. Christie, *The End of North's Ministry, 1780–1782* (London and New York, 1958), pp. 41–163.

appointt to Greenwich Hospital.[1] Digby wth thirteen Ships saild on tuesday last supposd on a Short Cruise in the Channel.[2] It will be lucky for Him if He does not fall in with the Combind fleet now hourly expected.

I have seen Mr. Robt. T——le who came in the Cartel from Boston to Bristol, and the accots. of the state of things which I receive from Him are in the lump, & I may say totally, very pleasing. No fears of the Yankies "*coming in*" as the term & expectation here. He is in very bad health & brings away three handsome Daughters, comely & full grown, & which must be a loss to any young Country.

He seems to have taken his final leave; but His passport from the State is worded in handsome terms to himself, & expressive that He may return whenever He pleases. He sold his Whole Property to one of the Traceys[3] who supplyd Him with the Ship (in wch. came 7 or 8 passengrs. bound or obligated as those by Mitchell & Dunken were in Decr last to release a like number of Americans here)[4] on condition & penalty of 3,000 £ Str. He should see the ship safe to a port of France or Spain. This cannot possible be done here, for they will not admit her as a Cartel or allow any Excha. of Prisoners. 'Tho the most remarkable civility has been shewn to Mr T—— & the vessel at Bristol, & Mr Stephens of the Admiralty has given orders She Shall not be seizd but permitted to return. This return means to Boston *empty*, but to no other place. Mr. T—— obligation is to put the Vessel in a port of France or Spain so that He must stand the

1. Adm. Geary actually resigned for reasons of health, not because Sandwich had appointed the controversial Vice Adm. Hugh Palliser (xxviii, 251n) as governor of Greenwich Hospital. Vice Adm. George Darby (xxix, 296n) not only did not retire, but eventually was named as Geary's successor: Mackesy, *War for America*, pp. 353–4, 357–9; N.A.M. Rodger, *The Insatiable Earl: a Life of John Montagu, fourth Earl of Sandwich 1718–1792* (New York and London, 1994), pp. 250, 281–2.

2. *London Courant, and Westminster Chronicle*, Aug. 31, 1780. Rear Adm. Robert Digby continued as second-in-command after Geary's resignation: *DNB* under Digby.

3. Nathaniel Tracy (xxix, 332n) and his brother John (1753–1815) were partners in the Newburyport firm of Jackson, Tracy, & Tracy: Elias and Finch, *Letters of Digges*, p. 6n.

4. Mitchell and Dunkin were captains of the *Polly* and *Bob:* xxxi, 365, 418.

risque of running Her to Fr or Spain at any rate. This makes Him uneasy, & I dare say you will hear more of the case as it opens more. I wish this Country would do the handsome thing, & allow this vessel to carry a Cargoe to Morlaix. They may do worse.

I am calld upon by the post & am in a hurry Yrs wth. very Grt. Esteem   W S. C

Addressed: Monr. Monr. B. F / Passy

Notations: Sept 1. 80 / Sept. 1st. 1780.

From Alexander Fleming[5]   ALS: American Philosophical Society

Sir   Kirkliston Near Edine 4 Septr 1780

The great & important transactions You have for some Years been engaged in, will perhaps have totally extripated from your Memory the least Remembrance of me, or my Name— I had the honor to Spend some days with You, & My friends Mesrs Henry Marchant, Edd Church & J Stewart at Glasgow in Nov 1771—[6] I have never had the pleasure to hear from Mr Marchant since He went to America— At that period I & many of My friends had been purposing to go to that Country upon the troubles subsiding, and as that I hope is at no great distance I have wrote, M Marchant, but not knowing any way of Conveying a letter to Him but by way of France, & totally Ignorant of Any Other direction for Him, that what I have put on the Letter, I have taken the Liberty to send it to You begging as the Most singuarly favour You may do me the honour to forward it to Him— That

5. The older brother of John Fleming, a Scottish printer. John was married to the sister of Edward Church (mentioned below): J. Bennett Nolan, *Benjamin Franklin in Scotland and Ireland 1759 and 1771* (Philadelphia, 1938), p. 175.

6. The Rhode Island lawyer Henry Marchant (x, 316n) had accompanied BF on his trip through Scotland in 1771. Marchant and Edward Church (xviii, 257n) traveled together from London, joining BF in Edinburgh. According to Marchant's diary, BF, Fleming, Church, and Mr. Stewart of Maryland dined together on Nov. 12, 1771. Stewart was probably George Stewart, eldest son of Anne Digges Stewart and Dr. George Stewart, Thomas Digges's uncle: xviii, xxvii, 145, 251n, and *passim;* Nolan, *Franklin in Scotland*, p. 187; Elias and Finch, *Letters of Digges*, p. xxiv.

Heaven may preserve & protect Your Valueable life is the earnest prayer of Sir Your most Oebedient & Very humble Servant ALEXR FLEMING

P.S. The inclosed well meant Pamphlet gave much satisfaction here

Notation: Allen Flemming Kirklington Sept. 4. 1780—

From Fournier le jeune ALS: University of Pennsylvania Library

Monsieur Ce 4 Septembre [1780]
   Je vous Prirerai de me donner Votre jour dans cette semaine ainsi que votre heur Le Plus commode Pour Voir et entendre cet orgue fameux qui vous fera un Grand Plaisir, je ne métois Point rappellé que Par votre Lettre vous demandiés Sil étoit Possible de Remettre a vendredy Premier Septembre j'aurais du vous marquer que cétoit très Possible c'est oubli de ma part dont je vous Prie de m'excuser: Le jour que vous Prenderes Sera Le Mien. Bien Sûrement je Crois que L'effet de L'instrument doit flatter Plus Le soir qu'a midy, a cause de La tranquilité qui Regne dans L'air. Vous êtes Monsieur Plus apporté que Personne d'en juger. Honnorez moi dune Réponse et Le jour, et l'heur que vous Prendrez Je Prévienderez celui qui doit Le toucher Pour m'y trouver.[7]
   Je suis avec La Plus Parfaite Considération Monsieur, Votre très humble et très Obéissant Serviteur FOURNIER LE JEUNE

Je Présente Mes Compliments Bien sinceres a Monsieur votre Petit fils.

Chez Mr Maugeaunt horloger

Rue du Pourtour st Gervais

[*In Mme Fournier's hand:*] Permettés, Monsieur, que je joigne à

---

7. Fournier wrote again on the following day, apparently in answer to a response from BF (now missing). The appointment would be set for Friday, at 7 o'clock. APS. We have found no other trace of this rendezvous.

la lettre de Mon Mari l'assurance de Mes très humbles respects, et De Ma Sensibilité a votre Souvenir.

Addressed: A Monsieur / Monsieur francklin / A Passy

Notation: Fournier le jeune

From Esther Smith[8]   ALS: American Philosophical Society

Sir.   London the 4 Septr. 1780
I intreat you to Pardon the liberty I have taken in Addressing you, and Beg your Patience, while I explain the reason of my Temerity. I have a worthy Husband, a Resolve Smith who has the Happiness of being employed in the Service of his Country in the Civil line of Life. His dwelling at Philadelphia, from whom I can get no intelligence although I have wrote by many ways. But I have now an opportunity by a Gentleman on whom I can depend to deliver this, if he should be so happy as to be admitted to the Honor of an Interview. If it is not too great a Favor would be very Thankful you would be pleased to forward the inclosed.

I am with the greatest Respect Sir Your most Obedient Humble Servant   ESTHER SMITH

Notation: Esther Smith. London sept. 4. 80

From Vergennes

Three copies: Library of Congress;[9] draft: Archives du Ministère des affaires étrangères

A Versailles le 4. 7bre. 1780.
Vous vous rappelleréz, Monsieur, par l'Arte. 29. du Traité d'Amitié et de Commerce conclu entre le Roi et les Etats Unis

8. Her identity eludes us. We have made some revisions to her punctuation and capitalization: we have altered periods after "Husband" and "Philadelphia" to commas and introduced capital letters to two words that follow periods, "His" and "But".

9. All three are in the hand of L'Air de Lamotte; we print from the one in the legation letterbook.

de l'Amerique Septentrionale, il a été convenu que les deux Parties contractantes auroient la faculté de tenir dans leurs ports respectifs, des Consuls, Vice Consuls Agents et Commissaires dont les fonctions seroient reglées par une Convention particuliere.[1]

En Consequence de cette Stipulation, et pour d'autant mieux cimenter son Union avec les États Unis, le Roi a nommé des Consuls pour les Principales places de l'amerique Septentrionale.[2] Mais les fonctions de ces officiers n'ayant pas encore été reglées d'une maniere fixe et uniforme il est a craindre qu'il ne s'éleve des contestations à ce sujet. Le seul moyen de les prevenir, est de faire la convention indiquée dans l'art. 29e. que j'ai raporté plus haut. Je ne doute pas, Monsieur, que le Congrès ne soit entierement d'accord avec le Roi à cet égard; mais J'ignore Si ce Corps se croit suffisamment autorisé pour Conclure cette même Convention.[3] Il est possible que chacune des Provinces constituant les Etats Unis croye que cette matierre lui appartient privativement à l'assemblée qui les represente. Il est donc necessaire que cette question preliminaire soit éclaircie avant que nous proposions au Congrès d'agréer notre Projet de convention. Aussitôt, Monsieur, que vous m'aurez fourni sur cette matiere les Eclaircissements dont j'ai besoin, je les mettrai sous les yeux du Roi, afin qu'il puisse determiner la marche qu'ils lui paroitront éxiger de sa Part; et si ce que je desire beaucoup, le Congrès vous autorise à entrer en Négociation avec nous, Je m'empresserai de vous developper notre sistème et nos vues. Ce que je puis vous assurer d'avance, c'est que la plus parfaite reciprocité leur sert de base. Cette Vérité me semble devoir engager le Congrès à vous donner les Pouvoirs les plus amples. Il peut être certain que nous ne proposerons que des arrangements aussi convenables pour les Sujets des Etats Unis que pour ceux de sa Majesté.

1. This was originally article XXXI (xxv, 624), but in the interim two articles (XI and XII) had been dropped at the request of Congress.
2. At present there were two French consuls, Jean Holker in Philadelphia and Joseph, chevalier de Valnais in Boston: Abraham P. Nasatir and Gary Elwyn Monell, eds., *French Consuls in the United States: a Calendar of their Correspondence in the Archives Nationales* (Washington, D.C. 1967), pp. 561–2, 568.
3. A valid concern, as a year later the matter had not yet been resolved: *JCC*, XXI, 895.

J'ai l'honneur d'être très sincerement, Monsieur, Votre tres humble et très obeissant Serviteur.   (signé) DE VERGENNES

M. Franklin.

From Le Roy

ALS: American Philosophical Society

[c. September 5, 1780][4]

J'envoye, Mon cher Docteur Savoir de vos nouvelles et s'il est vrai, comme on me l'a dit que vous avez eu nouvelles de l'arrivée de M. De Rochambeau en amérique. Recevez les Sincères assurrances de tous les Sentimens d'attachement que Je vous ai voués pour la Vie   LE ROY

Addressed: a Monsieur / Monsieur Franklin / Ministre Pleponitentiaire / des Etats unis de l'Amèrique

From Gabriel-Louis Galissard de Marignac: Bill for Benjamin Franklin Bache's Schooling[5]

ADS: American Philosophical Society

[September 5, 1780–February 5, 1781]

Monsieur Franklin doit pour la pension de Monsieur son petit fils depuis le 5e. 7bre. 1780

jusqu'au 5. Fevrier 1781. 5 Mois	£229—	″	″—
Papier, encre & plumes	2—	10 —	″—
4. Rubans de queuë	1—	6 —″	—
pre. [paire] boucles	1—	3 —″	—
Canif	″—	4	—6—
pr. être allé différentes fois à la Comédie	9—	4 —″	—
5. Mois blanchissage	7—	10 —″	—
pr le Maitre à nager	7—	″	—″—

4. The supplement to the Sept. 15 issue of the *Gaz. de Leyde* published an extract of a letter from Versailles, dated Sept. 5, announcing the arrival that morning of dispatches from Ternay and Rochambeau, safely arrived at Rhode Island.

5. For Marignac's previous statement, which covered the period beginning May 5, 1780, see XXXII, 355–6.

pr. racommoder ses bas	4—	4—6—	
pr. des ports de lettres	5—	3 —″—	
pr. des couleurs	″—	9 —′—	
pr. gands	1—10	—′—	
Un porte crayon	″— 6	—″—	
2. Carreaux de vitre	″—13	—″—	
écritoires	″—12	—′—	
pr. avoir blanchi ses habits,			
Vestes & Culottes d'été	3—	″ —′—	
Une armoire	7—12	—′—	
Cahiers	1— 9	—′—	
Pr. le compte du Marchand	43— 7	—″—	
Pr. l'achapt de trois paires			
bas de Galette	7—	″ —″—	
Chapeau	3—15	—′—	
Payé à Mr. Prestreau	14—17	—″—	
Pr. ses étrennes & celles qu'il			
a été obligé de donner	36— 9	—′—	
Pr un reméde	1—	″ —′—	
Pr. des chaussons de peau	1— 9	—′—	
Payé pour le Compte du tailleur	26— 8	—″—	
pr. le maitre du dessin	16—	″ —′—	
Pr. le Maitre d'Anglois	29— 4	—′—	
Pr. le Maitre de danse	4—	″ —″—	
Papier fin	″—10	—′—	
Perruquier avec Poudre & pommade	15—	″ —′—	
Cordonnier	12—	″ —″—	
Pr. ses Dimanches à 10 s. par semaine	22—	″ —′—	

£515—15 —″—

argt. de France 853 *l.t.*—13 s. pr. acquit

MARIGNAC

Endorsed: Mr Grand is requested to pay this Bill on the private Acct of his humble Servant B FRANKLIN[6]

Passy, Feb. 10. 1781

6. The payment is recorded on March 2, 1781, in BF's Private Account with Ferdinand Grand, Account XVII (XXVI, 3).

From Osgood Hanbury, Silvanus Grove, and James Russell[7]

ALS:[8] American Philosophical Society

Sir   London 6t: September 1780

The not having had it in our power to transmit to you sooner a precise answer to your several favours has given us much concern; We trust you will not impute any intentional delay to us when we assure you that for our Guidance in the business we took the earliest opportunity of having a fair and impartial State of our Case, as Trustees, prepared and laid before Mr. Wallace[9] his Majesty's Attorney General, and Mr: Mansfield,[1] Who it is expected will be appointed Solicitor General, whose opinions we have the honour to inclose you;[2] upon the perusal of which we persuade ourselves you will readily see that in the very particular situation in which we stand, as Trustees under the several Acts of Assembly, we are compell'd to the disagreeable necessity of refusing to comply with the Request made to us by your favor of the 20th: of May. We yet beg leave to observe that when the favorable Opportunity occurs that we can discharge our Trust with honor and fidelity we shall have the greatest satisfaction imaginable in so doing; In the interim we hope that from

7. In answer to BF's of May 20 (XXXII, 401) requesting that they as trustees for the state of Maryland see the stock it owned in the Bank of England and pay its bills; for details see XXXI, 336n.

8. In Grove's hand.

9. James Wallace (1729–1783), a friend of Alexander Wedderburn's, was solicitor general from 1778 to 1780 before becoming attorney general (1780–82, 1783): Namier and Brooke, *House of Commons*, III, 593.

1. James Mansfield (1734–1821) replaced Wallace as solicitor general in September. He served until the fall of the North government in March, 1782, and again in 1783: *DNB;* Namier and Brooke, *House of Commons,* III, 109–10.

2. Dated Aug. 28, their joint opinion warned that the trustees could not "with safety" sell the stock or pay the bills: Jacob M. Price, "The Maryland Bank Stock Case: British-American Financial and Political Relations before and after the American Revolution," Aubrey C. Land, Lois Green Carr, and Edward C. Papenfuse, eds., *Law, Society, and Politics in Early Maryland* (Baltimore and London, 1977), p. 8. Maryland threatened to seize the trustees' property in that state if they refused to pay bills of exchange drawn on them: *ibid.*, p. 9; Morris L. Radoff, ed., *Calendar of Maryland State Papers. No. 2: The Bank Stock Papers* (Annapolis, 1947), pp. xv–xvi.

your Candor and that of your Governor and State of Maryland our conduct will receive the most friendly interpretation. We have the honor to be with the highest Esteem and respect Sir, Your Most Obedient humble Servants   OSGOOD HANBURY
SIL: GROVE
JAMES RUSSELL

P.S. We also inclose you the Act you transmitted to us agreeable to your desire.

B Franklin Esqr

Notation: Osgood Hanburg. Silas Grove & James Russell 6 Sept. 1780

To Gourlade & Moylan   Copy: Library of Congress

Gentlemen,   Passy, Sept. 7 1780.

There have been presented to me for Acceptance, within these few Days. The following Drafts of yours on me: viz:

For 1246. *l.t.* 10. in favr. of M. Boy   } Datet 23d
For 1186. *l.t.* 19 in favr. of M. Quartresages } Augt. 1780.
& For 900 *l.t.*— in favor of M. Termier lainé, dated 25. Augt. 80.[3]

They are all drawn at two Usances, and said to be on Acct. of the frigate l'Ariel.— I have accepted them nothwithstanding I have not recd. any Advice concerning them. This is contrary to my general Rule, and I desire you will immediately furnish me with the Account on which they are founded; & that in future you would always do so, previous to your drawing upon me.

3. These three bills are listed on WTF's roster of bills drawn on BF by Gourlade & Moylan (for which see our annotation of BF to the firm, July 5). The signature of Louis Quatrefages must have been difficult to read; WTF also mistook it. He was one of the principal merchants of Lorient, and *chef des magasins:* Lüthy, *Banque protestante,* II, 454; *Almanach des marchands,* pp. 295–6; Gérard Le Bouëdec, *Le Port et L'arsenal de Lorient . . . ,* (5 vols., Paris, 1994), II, 187. The merchant families of Boy and Fermier are both cited in Le Bouëdec, *Le Port de L'arsenal de Lorient,* II, 186.

Pray inform me if Capt. Jones has sailed, & if not what it is that detains him.

Messrs. Gourlade et Moylan.

To Vergennes

LS: Archives du Ministère des affaires étrangères; two copies: Library of Congress

Sir   Passy, Sept. 7. 1780

I received the Letter your Excellency did me the Honour of Writing to me the 4th Instant, on the Appointment of Consuls.— I have not yet received any Orders or Instructions from the Congress relating to that Object. I shall transmit to that Body a Copy of your Excelly.'s Letter;[4] but as the Office of Consul has not been heretofore in Use in America, and they may therefore not be so well accquainted with the usual Functions & Powers of such an Officer in Europe, as to send me Instructions equally compleat & perfect with those your Excelly. could send to M. de la Luzerne, if the Convention were to be treated there, I would submit it to your Judgment whether that Method may not be the best and shortest.—[5] As it is a Matter of the same general Nature with others that are enumerated among the Powers of Congress in the Articles of Confederation tho' not particularly mentioned:[6] And as the Grant in the 29th Article of the Treaty is to the *States United,* and not to each separately and farther, as the having a Consul for each State, or thirteen American Consuls in each port of France, would be of more Expence & Inconvenience than of real Utility, I cannot imagine that the Authority of Congress to make the necessary Convention will be disputed by the particular States.

4. He does not appear to have done so.

5. In July, 1781, La Luzerne proposed a consular convention: *JCC,* XXI, 792–804.

6. This was an issue still to be decided, even after the Articles of Confederation were ratified on March 1, 1781; see our annotation of Vergennes to BF, Sept. 4.

With the greatest Respect, I have the honour to be, Sir, Your Excellency's, most obedient & most humble Servant

B FRANKLIN

His Exy. Ct De Vergennes.

From Vicq d'Azyr

LS: American Philosophical Society

Monsieur.   Ce 7 7bre. 1780.

La société Royale de Médecine Connaissant les talens et Les Lumieres des différens Médecins Résidens dans l'Etendue de Votre Pays, s'est fait un devoir de leur Conférer Le titre de Correspondans;[7] Elle a Crû que Ce témoignage du juste hommage qu'elle Rend à leur Capacité, leur deviendrait plus précieux en passant par Vos mains et elle Vous prie instamment de leur faire parvenir les paquets Cyjoints qui renferment le diplome qui Constate leur nommination.

J'ai L'honneur d'etre avec Respect Monsieur, Votre très humble et très obeissant serviteur   VICQ DAZYR

La société a aussi L'honneur de Vous adresser quelques programes des prix qu'elle a proposes dans sa dre [dernière] seance publique.[8]

[*In Vicq d'Azyr's hand:*] M. Franklin.

Notation: Vicq d'Azir le 7. 7bre. 1780.

7. The royal letters patent of 1778 allowed the Society sixty foreign associates and an unlimited number of correspondents. For the role of the correspondents see Caroline Hannaway, "Medicine, Public Welfare and the State in Eighteenth Century France: The Société Royale de Médecine of Paris (1776–1793)" (Ph.D. diss., Johns Hopkins University, 1974), pp. 115–16, 118–20, 135, 154–7. See also Charles C. Gillispie, *Science and Polity in France at the End of the Old Regime* (Princeton, 1980), pp. 195–6, 200n.

We have found no indication of whom the Society wished to name as correspondents. It may have been the First Medical Society in the Thirteen United States of America, who in May had asked BF for help in establishing a correspondence with the Société royale de médecine: XXXII, 366–7.

8. Two prize subjects were announced. The first, designed to promote the benefits of maternal breastfeeding, asked respondents to determine which women should abstain from nursing their infants and to base their memoirs

From ——— Bonnes Coder[9] ALS: American Philosophical Society

Monsieur   à Pezenas le 7e. Septembre 1780

Jé viens de perdre mon fils, je vous demande pour moy, et ma pauvre famille la continuation des bontés que vous aviés pour luy, car nous n'avons j'amais démérité les bontés du Roy, et de la patrie, ny celles de tous les honnetes Gens.

Jé suis avec respéct Monsieur Votre trés humble et tres obeïssante Servante   BONNES CODER

Notation: Coder. Pezenas le 7. Sept. 1780.

From Dumas   ALS: American Philosophical Society

Monsieur,   La haie 7e. 7bre. 1780

Je vous félicite de tout mon coeur de la bonne nouvelle de la prise des Flottes Angl. pour les Indes-or. & occid.[1] C'est un grand coup, non seulement pour la France & pour l'Espagne, mais aussi pour l'Amérique: car il dérange toutes les opérations de l'ennemi; & voilà l'Aml. Hugue aux Indes or.,[2] Rodney aux Indes occid., D'Ally à la Jamaique,[3] & Cornwallis à Charlestown & Clinton même à N. York, sans secours, & par conséquent réduits à l'inaction pendant le reste de la Campagne: & d'un autre côté, Mrs. De Guichen, Solano,[4] Lamotte

---

on observation and experience. The second question concerned the nature and treatment of dropsy: *Jour. de Paris,* Sept. 2. For the Society's prize competitions see Hannaway, "Medicine, Public Welfare and the State," pp. 122–5, 161–3.

9. Henry Coder's mother and amanuensis for his farewell letter of Sept. 1, above.

1. The prizes taken by Córdoba reportedly included five ships for the East Indies and more than fifty for the West Indies: *Gaȝ. de Leyde,* issue of Sept. 5, 1780. There is a list of fifty-five prizes and their destinations in the Sept. 19 issue of the *London Courant, and Westminster Chronicle.*

2. Rear Adm. Edward Hughes (*DNB*) commanded the British fleet in the Indian Ocean: XXIX, 450.

3. *I.e.,* Gov. John Dalling.

4. José Solano y Bote, Marqués del Socorro (1726–1806) recently had escorted a vital troop and supply convoy to Havana via Guadeloupe: *Enciclopedia Universal Ilustrada Europeo-Americana* (80 vols., Madrid, c. 1907–33); Dull, *French Navy,* pp. 188–9, 368.

Piquet,[5] Ternay, Rochambaut & notre Genl. Washington, en auront les coudées plus franches. Il me tarde beaucoup d'apprendre ce qui s'est passé dans leurs différents départemens.— Les Américain, de leur côté, ont fait la capture, près de Terre-Neuve, d'une 12ne. de Vaisseaux de la flotte de Québec.[6] On m'apprend d'Amsterdam, que 2 vaisseaux y viennent d'arriver, l'un de la Virginie, & l'autre de Philadelphie; & que leurs rapports sont favorables. J'espere qu'ils apprendront bientôt en Amerique, ce qui vient de se passer en Europe. Je voudrois bien avoir été à même de leur porter cette nouvelle en personne. Peut-être cela m'eût rétabli la santé, qui continue de n'être pas des meilleures. Les chaleurs m'ont extrêmement affoibli. On m'a conseillé de changer d'air; & je n'aurois pas été faché de faire quelque séjour à Amsterdam: mais la dépense m'a retenu.

Les Etats d'Hollande sont assemblés ici. J'ai vu notre ami. Mais il ne croit pas qu'il S'y passera grand'chose.

Je suis avec un grand respect, Monsieur, Votre très-humble & très-obéissant serviteur   DUMAS

Passy à Son Exc. Mr. B. Franklin

Addressed: à Son Excellence / Monsieur B. Franklin, Esqr. / Min. Plenipe. des Etats-Unis / &c. / Passy./.

Notation: Dumas la haie, Sept. 7. 80

From James Lovell

Two ALS: American Philosophical Society; copies: Archives du Ministère des affaires étrangères,[7] National Archives, Library of Congress; transcript: National Archives

Hond Sir   Sepr. 7th. 1780

With a Letter of former date,[8] I have to inclose to you some further Proceedings of Congress respecting Bills drawn upon

5. La Motte-Picquet commanded an independent squadron in the West Indies for much of 1780: Auphan, "Communications," p. 498.

6. See Digges to BF, Aug. 29.

7. In WTF's hand.

8. Lovell wrote the present letter at the bottom of a duplicate copy of his Aug. 15 letter, above. He enclosed the other ALS with his letter of Oct. 28, be-

you,[9] and to acknowledge the Receipt of yr. Letter of May 31st.[1] I think I can venture now to assure you that not a single Draught more will be made upon you, let the Occassion be ever so pressing, But you must be entreated to work with all Energy as to the past. You cannot conceive the whole Train of Necessities which led to such Decissions after what you had written.

Congress have called for 3 millions more estimating in Silver to be pd. by the last of December.[2] Nothing but the Weight of Taxes will put an End to the Levity with which our Currency is treated.

New York has empowered her Delegates to cede part of her western Claims; it is recommended to others who have such like to relinquish also a Portion and Maryland is anew invited to close the Ratification of the confederating articles.[3] We must as a Whole show more Vigor than of late. Your most humb Sert.

JAMES LOVELL

Honble. Doctr. Franklin

Addressed: Honorable / Doctor Franklin / Minister Plenipoy. / France

---

low, amending the first sentence to read, "With 3plicates & 2plicates of former dates . . . ".

9. On Aug. 23 and 30 Congress had passed resolutions ordering the board of treasury to draw bills of exchange on BF for $150,000 and $29,105 (specie) respectively: *JCC,* XVII, 763, 794, 796. Upon receiving these resolutions BF sent copies to Vergennes. He also sent copies of the resolutions mentioned in Lovell's Aug. 15 letter, the two Lovell covering letters, and the resolution the committee for foreign affairs had sent on July 11: BF to Vergennes, Nov. 19 (AAE). Other copies of these documents are with BF's papers at the APS.

1. XXXII, 448–53. Its reception was noted in Congress on Sept. 1: *JCC,* XVII, 798.

2. *I.e.,* paid by the states: *JCC,* XVII, 783.

3. Citing what New York had done (on Feb. 17), Congress on Sept. 6 appealed to the other states to surrender their western lands claims in order to make possible the adoption of the long-stalled Articles of Confederation: *Public Papers of George Clinton, First Governor of New York . . .* (10 vols., Albany, 1899–1914), V, 499–502; *JCC,* XVII, 806–7.

From Schweighauser

Extract:[4] Archives du Ministère des affaires étrangères

[September 7, 1780]

Your Excellency wants me to have my Recourse on the above House [Puchelberg & Co. respecting the Disbursements for the Alliance][5] unless I excuse them. I cannot excuse them interely; because they have acted *against* my *positive & repeated Orders;* but it seems that they have been so much intimidated by Capt. Landais's Threats, that they have not dared in a manner refuse him, and I am always obliged to bear this Advance, as they are established in that Port by me as a House *en Comendite.*—[6]

Extract of a Letter from M. Schweighauser to M. Franklin, dated Sept. 7. 1780.—

From John Torris

ALS: American Philosophical Society

Honnd. Sir   Dunkerque 7th. sep. 1780.

I have Communicated to our Brave Capt. Macatter the Letter your Excellency did me the Honnour to write me the 23d. ulto., with the Copies therein Inclosed.— He will Strickly abide to your Commands & directions, & Preserve His American Commission.—[7] He will be again ready for Sea in a Short Time.— We are both gratefull for all your Excellency's favors.— I Shall Conform to your Directions & to those Contained in the Letters abovementd., altho' they are Contrary to the *Reglement* of the 24. Sep. 1778.— As to the Shipping of French Sailors, We only Take those granted to Foreign Bottoms.

4. The extract was made in 1783; see our annotation of Gourlade and Moylan, July 10, above.

5. The brackets are on the MS.

6. A translation of this extract, also at the AAE, renders this as "comme une Maison de commission."

7. Macatter accepted instead a French commission and served Torris until he was captured in October, 1781. He was eventually released: Torris to BF, Feb. 6, 1782 (APS); Clark, *Ben Franklin's Privateers,* p. 174. BF received no letters from Torris during the intervening seventeen months.

I am with utmost respect Honnd. Sir Your Excellency's Most Hble & most obedient Servant   J. TORRIS

His Excellency Dr. Franklin./.

Notation: Mr. Torris. Sept. 7. 1780

From Samuel Cooper   ALS: American Philosophical Society

My dear Sir,   Boston Septr. 8th. 1780.

Having very Short Warning of an Opportunity to France by Bilboa, I can only give you a short and abrupt Account of Things here.

Last Monday all the Towns of this State assembled for the Choice of a Governor, Lt Governor, and Senators, according to the new Constitution. In this Town Mr S. Adams had 1. Vote, for Governor, Mr Bowdoin 64. Mr Hancock 853. This last Gentleman has a great Majority thro the State, and will without doubt be chosen Governor of it. It was urged in his Favor at the Elections that he took an early, open and decided Part in the Opposition to the oppressive Measures of Britain; that in this he generously risqued his Life and Fortune; and that it was expected that we should appear to be the same People we were when the Controversy began by giving our first Honor to those who distinguished themselves at that Time, and that a contrary Conduct would disappoint our Friends in Europe and gratify our Enemies.[8]

The Alliance arrived here some Weeks ago with Dr. Lee, who is still in Town.[9] This Vessel appears to me to have left France in an unjustifiable Manner, tho I cannot yet obtain the particular Circumstances. Landais did not hold his Command thro the Voyage, which was either relinquished by him or wrested from

8. Hancock pulled large majorities in every county and won the election with more than 90 percent of the vote: William M. Fowler, Jr., *The Baron of Beacon Hill: a Biography of John Hancock* (Boston, 1980), p. 244.

9. Arthur Lee was one of the fifteen passengers who arrived on Aug. 16 aboard the *Alliance:* XXXII, 9n.

him.[1] All the Passengers, as well as Officers and Sailors are highly incensed against him; and Dr Lee as much as any one. A Court of Inquiry is now sitting upon this Matter, in which the Dr has given a full Evidence against the Captain which represents him as insane. The Officers and Men complain loudly of being kept out of their Prize Money; this may make a temporary Impression upon some here, but People of Discretion wait for Accounts from France on the other Side: and I pledge myself that your Honor will appear clear thro this whole Matter.

Soon after the Chevalier de Ternay arrived at Rhode Island with his Squadron from Brest, the British Fleet at N. york having received a Reinforcement from England appeared before that Place, and being superior to the French have hitherto prevented our designed military Operations; so that unless the second Division[2] soon arrives from Brest, or an Addition be made to the Strength of Ternay from some other Quarter, our Hopes of striking an important Blow this Campaign will vanish. About the Time the British Fleet made it's appearance before N. port, Genl. Clinton embarqued his Troops at New york so as to occasion an Apprehension that he designed to attack our Allies on R. Island.[3] This afforded an Opportunity for the Militia of this State, at the Call of the French General, to manifest their Alertness in flying to the Aide of our good Friends thus threatned. Many thousands were at or near R. Island at a very short warning, which made an agreeable Impression on the Minds of the Admiral and General of France, and their respective Corps'.[4]

1. During the voyage Landais so alienated the officers, passengers, and crew that the officers unanimously selected Lt. James Degge to assume command. On the *Alliance*'s arrival the Eastern Navy Board removed Landais from the ship. Eventually both Landais and Degge were court martialed: Richard B. Morris, "The Revolution's Caine Mutiny," *American Heritage* XI, no. 3 (April, 1960), 10–13, 88–91.

2. Two additional regiments for Rochambeau which were unable to join him: XXXII, 71n.

3. Clinton did take a sizeable troop detachment to Huntington Bay on the north shore of Long Island, but after various delays cancelled plans to attack Newport: Willcox, *Portrait of a General*, pp. 326–330.

4. Rochambeau had requested 2,000 troops to assist him: Idzerda, *Lafayette Papers*, III, 108n.

The British Troops, however, never approached to attack New port, and by the Aid of the Militia it was soon put into such a Posture of Defence as to defy their whole Force.

We have lately reinforced Genl. Washington's Army at an high Bounty and Wages:[5] This Reinforcement, from too sanguine a Dependence on the present Campaign is only for six Months; Should the War continue another Year as it is very likely, We must have a naval Superiority here to do any Thing important. Could we remove the British Force from this Continent, the Stroke would be decisive; No Exertion should be spared either here or in France for such a Purpose, it seems the only effectual Method of obtaining Peace, and till this is done, all is at Hazard. We have had warm Hopes that the combined Forces in the W. Indies would have carried Jamaica, but our last Accounts from that Quarter have no Expectation of such an Attempt.

I received by the Alliance the Caracaturas you were so kind as to send me. They afford a striking Picture of Barbarity, and I have disposed of them in such a Manner as to do Good.[6]

I am much obliged to you for the Regard shown to my little Grandson in France,[7] who I hope will one day promote in some Measure the Views of the Alliance. I am my dear Sir, with unalterable Friendship, and every Sentiment of Esteem, Your obedient humble Servant　　　　　　　　　　　　SAML. COOPER.

His Excellency Benjn. Franklin Esqr.

Notation: Dr. Cooper Sept 8 1780

---

5. By Aug. 17 Washington had received 1,700 militia from Massachusetts: Fitzpatrick, *Writings of Washington*, XIX, 393.

6. We have not been able to locate any copies of this print or prints, which must have been the first of the illustrations of British cruelty that Congress had asked BF and Lafayette to have engraved in France: XXIX, 590–3; XXXII, 65–6. References to this project are infuriatingly scarce. Chaumont financed the printing of one engraving on an "American subject" in April, for which he later sought reimbursement (XXXII, 66n); in December, BF reported to Lafayette that he had found an excellent engraver (to Lafayette, Dec. 9, Library of Congress).

7. BF had reported to Cooper on the safe arrival in France of Samuel Cooper Johonnot: XXXII, 117.

From James Cuming

ALS: American Philosophical Society

Sir   L'Orient 8th. Septr. 1780

I have the pleasure to inform you that the Ship Jay, Harman Courter ship Independence, Thos. Truxtun and Brigt. Patty Thomas Reads arrived here yesterday.[8] The Public despatches by the Jay I am informed were forwarded from Brest the despatches by Captn. Truxtun were sent under care of a Mr. De Mattey/ I have forwarded you a packet of Newspapers by this post that came by Truxtun. He and Read left the Capes the first ulto. You will have all the news in them.

The Jay and Independence are fine Vessels. The first carries 18 nine pounders and came in with upwards 60 men. I shall augment the Crew if men are to be had— The Independence carries 12 French four pounders and seventy men. If you can oblige me with Freight I shall be able to give the Vessels such despatch as may encourage my friends in America to carry on a more considerable Trade to this Country than they have hither to. The Jay may take from 250 to 300 Tons and the Independence about 100 Tons on Freight more than I at present propose shipping on board them.[9]

I have the Honour to be Sir Your most Obdt. Hble Servt

JAS. CUMING

The Hble. Benjamin Franklin Esqr. Passy

Addressed: A Son Excellence / Monsieur Benj: Francklin / Ministre plenipotentiaire des / Etats unis de l'Amerique / à Passy / prés Paris.

Notation: Jas. Cuming L'orient 8 Sept 80

8. The *Jay* was commanded by Harmon Courter (xxv, 682), the *Independence* by Thomas Truxtun (*DAB*), and the *Patty* by Thomas Read (Claghorn, *Naval Officers*, p. 252). All three ships were fitted out in Pennsylvania and carried letters of marque: Charles Henry Lincoln, comp., *Naval Records of the American Revolution 1775–1788* (Washington, D.C., 1906), pp. 350, 357, 410.

9. The *Independence* sailed again on Sept. 26 and reached Philadelphia five weeks later. While he was in Lorient Truxtun had infuriated Jones by his failure to salute the *Ariel:* John A. McManemin, *Captains of the Privateers during the Revolutionary War* (Ho-Ho-Kus, N.J., 1985), p. 351; Eugene S. Ferguson, *Truxtun of the* Constellation: *the Life of Commodore Thomas Truxtun, U.S. Navy, 1755–1822* (Baltimore, 1956), pp. 39–42.

London 8 Sept 1780

In Consequence of this passport[1] Mr Robt Temple Charterd The Brig Temple 120 Tonns, no Guns, Capt. Jno Fletcher,[2] 11 Seamen From Mr Tracey at Newbury Port, & binds Himself to Tracey that the Vessel shall be put in safety into a French or Spanish Port—which Mr Temple thought could be effected as a Flag of Truce. This has been refusd Him by Lord G. Germain, the Admiralty, & the board of Sick & Hurts. The papers of the vessel has been seiz'd & lodgd wth the Commissioners of the Customs but the Admiralty have given *an order for their restoration & that the Ship shall not be stopd or molested but permitted to depart*. But where She is to depart to no one can tell at present. A few British Seamen was permitted to Navigate the vessel home on Condition a like number of Americans here were releasd— These Seamen have been pressd on board Men of War, There are only three persons left on board, & no *British* Seamen will engage to go in her either to America or a port of France & Spain. As She is *allowd to depart*, I think the best way to clear Her empty for one port & go into another. We want to get Her to Bilboa, & if She is taken by a French or Spanish Cruiser, Going there, I suppose You will be troubled to get Her releasd— Her flag papers & the vessels being known will secure Her from American Privateers & the English Clearance from all British Cruizers—most likely the vessel will go & trust to these risques.

None of the English Parole Prisoners Passengers in Her, can obtain the terms for "releasing here Americans of equal rank or return to Boston in six months" of the People in Office here.

1. At the top of the first page of this letter Digges copied a Mass. Council resolution of July 3, 1780: Elias and Finch, *Letters of Digges*, pp. 263–4. This permitted Robert Temple to charter a ship to transport himself, his wife, their three daughters and two or more servants to Ireland and for them to return to Massachusetts whenever his affairs permitted. Temple was authorized to take with him to Ireland prisoners on parole. If they could not obtain an equal number of American prisoners in exchange they would return as prisoners to the United States. The vessel was to carry a flag of truce. Digges copied the resolution from a copy attested by deputy secretary John Avery.

2. There was a Capt. John Fletcher from Newburyport: Claghorn, *Naval Officers*, p. 111.

They have been assiduous to do it but meet with flat refusals at the Secys. Office, the admiralty, & the board of Sick & hurt. Either the Capn. or one of our frds. who came in Her will be with you soon & state the whole Case.[3]

You have been informd of the State of Mitchells case (the Cartel to Bristol in Decembr last) He obtain a gratuity for his loss of time, & the price of his Ship wch was seizd, 2900£ this was paid Him by acceptances of his own bills of Mr J. Jackson a Secy of Lord Sandwichs[4] at the Bank of Engd 3 mos after date. I was obligd to indorse two of 500£ each to help him away. When these bills became due the 29th Augt. they were noted for non Payment & are still unpaid tho the acceptor is amply able & *must* discharge them— I guess the money being just at this period useful to his Electioneering Schemes at Huntingdon[5] is the cause of delay, but they are fairly promisd for payt the 14th.

You will see by the inclosures what has been done about your matter between Jones & Mr Goddard. Both in his letters to me & to Jones (wch I forward you herewith) He acknowledges *the acceptance* therefore *He is liable & must pay.* If you will indorse the bill to me I think I can get it (at least as much as You have advancd thereon) but your letter covering it must express that *value* has been given therefor. I can pass it as a Credit to Your accot. & this will be as *value* to me. Your name has never been mentiond or hinted at. Goddard can know nothing of me, & I wrote to Him about this bill as at the desire *of a frd* in France who had given money on it. You will therefore act as you think fit in this matter.

3. On Sept. 10 four prisoners on parole—Conolly McCausland, master of the *Jane*, William Stewart, the ship's surgeon, James Campbell and Marcus McCausland, passengers—wrote BF about their inability to obtain American prisoners in exchange. They asked BF for a certificate to protect them in case they were captured. Digges added a covering letter (dated Sept. 12) attesting to their good faith. These letters, which are at the Hist. Soc. of Pa., are printed in Elias and Finch, *Letters of Digges*, pp. 267–9.

4. George Jackson (1725–1822) was second secretary to the Board of Admiralty: *DNB;* Namier and Brooke, *House of Commons*, II, 668–9.

5. Sandwich's estate was in Huntingdonshire. The two seats at Huntingdon were won by his candidates without a contest on Sept. 8: Namier and Brooke, *House of Commons*, I, 311–12, 516; N.A.M. Rodger, *The Insatiable Earl: a Life of John Montagu, fourth Earl of Sandwich 1718–1792* (New York and London, 1994), p. 69.

It is a little extraordinary that Mr Goddard can never be seen, & that they still say at the Office He is in the Country but they know not where. By these appearances, as well as from the tenor of His Letter to me & Mr Jones I am apt to think it has been some jumble between Jones & Him to raise a little ready Cash & that it is not convenient now for Him to pay His acceptances, & wch. He can be obligd to do by Law provided He has effects. I think of giving him a line or two in ansr. to his Letter to me (a Copy of which I annex)[6] saying that I had forwarded Jones's Letter to my frd. at Paris, who having advancd money on the strength of His acceptance which is not denyd by Him, that He certainly would expect payment for such advance when the bill became due, & that it would be regularly presented & prosecuted for in case of failure. Expecting to hear from You further on this head by return of Post, I remain with great esteem Dr Sir Yr obligd & ob Serv   W S C

From John Jay

AL (draft): Columbia University Library; copy: Library of Congress

Dr Sir   St. Ildefonso 8 Septr 1780

My last to you went under Cover to Monsr. Grand from Madrid.[7] I have not been favored with any Letters from you since the one inclosing a Letter of Credit in my Favor from Mr Grand to Marq. DYranda.[8]

Mr. Deane has been long arrived and I have not yet recd. a Line from him.[9] I cannot account for this. Intelligence from Am. might have been very useful. I have recd. but one, and that an unimportant public Letter since I left Philadelphia. You cannot

6. At the bottom of the final page Digges copied a Sept. 5 letter from Goddard stating that he would not pay Jones's bill as it had been obtained by promises not complied with. He asked Digges to forward a letter to Jones via his, Digges's, friend (*i.e.*, BF): Elias and Finch, *Letters of Digges*, p. 266.

7. Above, Aug. 16.

8. Above, July 31, although we have no specific record of the enclosure.

9. Two letters from Deane were en route: *Deane Papers*, IV, 195–7, 218–19.

conceive how little Information and how few Letters reach me from our Country. Whenever [*you*] write to me, send your Letters either to the French Embassador or under Cover of Marq. DYranda. The Post is the most precarious of all Conveyances. No Letters suspected to be for or from me pass safe by it— many are suppressed and the Remr. [Remainder] inspected. Our affairs here go on heavily. The Treaty is impeded by the Affair of the Missippi,[1] and the Fate of my Bills is not yet decided— I have been permitted indeed to accept to the Amt of abt. 14,000 Dollars,[2] and this Circumstance gives me more Hopes for the Rest than any thing else— The Fact is there is little Corn in Egypt— This entre nous.

Cumberland is here still. His Hopes and Fears are secret—he went from hence a few Days ago and is soon expected back again—[3] to what policy are we to ascribe this— I am told we have nothing to fear— it may be so, but my Faith is seldom very extensive—if we have nothing else to fear we have always Danger to apprehend from such a Spy so situated, so surrounded by inquisitive communicative and some say friendly Irishmen—[4] In short I wish you cd. hear me think, but that like most other wishes is vain, and I must leave Time to inform you of many things which at present must not be written. Be so kind as to de-

1. Floridablanca's representative James Gardoqui had recently proposed that Jay offer to surrender America's claims to navigation of the Mississippi in exchange for Spanish financial aid: "Jay's Account of Conferences with Gardoqui and Del Campo," Henry P. Johnston, ed., *The Correspondence and Public Papers of John Jay* . . . (4 vols., New York and London, 1890–93), I, 394–5.

2. But, as Carmichael told the committee for foreign affairs the following day, more than $40,000 of bills had been presented to Jay: Wharton, *Diplomatic Correspondence*, IV, 53.

3. Cumberland in fact had just returned to the Spanish court with an unsatisfactory reply from Secretary of State Hillsborough to Floridablanca's feelers: Samuel Flagg Bemis, *The Hussey-Cumberland Mission and American Independence: an Essay in the Diplomacy of the American Revolution* (Princeton, 1931), pp. 84–90.

4. The Irishman was Father Thomas Hussey (1741–1803), the Spanish secret agent who had arranged the Cumberland mission: *DNB;* Richard B. Morris, *The Peacemakers: the Great Powers and American Independence* (New York, Evanston, London, 1965), pp. 51–65.

liver the enclosed Letters and believe me to be with sincere Regard & Esteem Dr Sr Your most obt Servt

His Exy Dr Franklin.

Note in Jay's hand: To Doctr Franklin 8 Septr 1780

From Thomas Read   ALS: American Philosophical Society

Honoble. Sir   LOrient sept. 8th 1780

Having Arrived here yesterday in a Mercht. Vessell from Philadelphia which Place I left the 25th July Having Leave from Congress to make this Voyage—[5] by the Post I have sent you a Packet Deliver'd me by Mr. Beach[6] and have Inclos'd you a paper from the Press of the morning I left it.

Admiral Ternay was Arrived with his fleet at Rhode Island, and in a few days after Admiral Greaves arrived at N York with Eight Sail of the Line, and sail'd in two days again, his Destination was not known when I Left Philad. On My Passage I fell in with a fleet from 70 to 100 Sail Standing to the Westward in the Latt 48.° 10′ Long 17.° 30′ with the wind at S E the 24th August that wind Continued with us till we Arriv'd in this port.

I Expect to Leave this the Last of this month. If your Excellency has Any Commands Either Publick or Private Shall be happy in Executeing of them.

I am am with Due Respect your Excellency most obedient Humble Servant   THOMAS READ

Addressed: His Excellency / Dr. Benjn. Franklin / Minester Plenepotentiary / from the United States / at the Court of / France

Notation: Read Thomas, L'orient Sept. 8. 1780

5. On July 22, Capt. Read took out a letter of marque for the Pa. brig *Patty:* Charles H. Lincoln, comp., *Naval Records of the American Revolution, 1775–1788* (Washington, D.C., 1906), p. 410. Previously he had carried cargoes and dispatches for the American Commissioners: XXVII, 159, 172, 175. He arrived at Lorient accompanied by the Pa. brig *Polly* and returned to America the following month: John A. McManemin, *Captains of the State Navies during the Revolutionary War* (Ho-Ho-Kus, N.J. 1984), pp. 289–90.

6. Probably RB's letter of July 22, above.

From Sarah Bache

ALS: Yale University Library

Dear and Honoured Sir   Philadelphia Sept. 9 1780

I have been much disapointed so many Vessels have arrived lately and not one single line from you,[7] and if a Mr Esra Johnes[8] had not called to let me know how you all did, we should not have heard wether you were well or not, the account he gives us of your health and spirits is very pleasing to us—tis but a few days since I came from Mr Duffields, were I have been with the two youngest Children all Summer, they are and have been perfectly well, tho it has been the most Sickly Summer ever known in town, & particularly fatal to young Children,[9] Betsy was very unwell when she went out, but the good air and water very soon recovered her, tis remarkable that the Pump water all through the town, is not half as good and sweet as it was before the British came—which makes me wish more than ever for a House in the Country to stay during the hot weather, tho the whole Family at Benfield were so kind and Afectionate, to me and the dear little Babies, that I shall ever feel the strongest atachment to them, Yet while there I am obliged to be seperated from Mr Bache and Willy, Mr B. is well and has wrote several times to you lately, its not in my power to write to either my Nephew or Son by Capt All,[1] I trust they will be pleased to hear we are all well through you, they will excuse my not writing when I tell them I am very busily imploy'd in cutting out and making shirts, and giving them out to make to the good women of my acquaintance, for our Brave Soldiers, You will see by the news Papers that there has been a Collection amongst the good Women as a reward to the Soldiers, and our beloved General chooses the money to be laid out in an aditional shirt to what they are allowed, the Ladies are unwilling to lesen the money by paying People to make them,

7. Although BF wrote on June 27[-August 12], the last extant letter that SB could have received from him is his of March 16: XXXII, 115, 610–11.

8. An Ezra Jones wrote WTF on Feb. 11, 1780, offering to carry letters for BF. He hoped to sail on the *Luzerne* (the *Chevalier de La Luzerne*). APS.

9. For confirmation of SB's assessment see Elaine Forman Crane, *et al.*, eds., *The Diary of Elizabeth Drinker* (3 vols., Boston, 1991), I, 372–3.

1. The ship captain Isaac All, who previously had carried letters to BF: XXVI, 37–8.

and have determined to do them among themselves,[2] I hope you will aprove of what we have done, as much of my time before I went out of town as well as since my return has been taken up in forwarding this Subscription—

Mrs S Wright[3] in a letter I have just received from her says: "I most Sincerely rejoice to hear your Honoured father is Bless'd with health, may it long continue, may his added years be as many and as happy as I wish them to be, and he may then be able to vie with any of the old Patriarchs— But is the account in the papers fact that he has taken, or it about taking a Journey to the Court of Spain; I felt a sensible concern at reading it, sure some less valuable life than Dr Franklins might have been sent to traverse so Inclement a tract of Country, from its great heats & other inconveniencies as I imagine spain to be—" she tells me in a few days she shall compleat her 83d Year: her letter is a very beautifull one if I had time I would send you a Copy—

Willy begins to learn his Book very well and has an extraordinary memory, he has learnt these last Holidays the speach of Anthony, over Ceasors Body, which he can scarcely speak without tears— when Betty looks at your picture here and at Mr Duffields, she wishes her Grand Papa had teeth that he might talk to her, and has frequently tried to tempt you to walk out of the frame to play with her, with a peice of Apple pie, the thing of all others she likes best, Louis is remarkable for his sweet temper and good spirits, he has never been indisposed one moment of his life, he is the very picture of Willy as Betty is of Benjamin, I think I see him when I look at her, she sings a great deal, several tunes very perfect and we think sweetly, the utmost of Lou's performence is to make faces, take Betty off when She cries, call George,[4] and crawl about as Will did when first you came home, but he is but just 11 months old, in time I hope to have it in my

2. For SB's participation in the Ladies Association see RB's letter of July 22. Washington had declared that shirts for the soldiers were the highest priority: Fitzpatrick, *Writings of Washington*, XIX, 71, 167.

3. An acquaintance of BF's for almost thirty years, Susannah Wright also exchanged a few letters with DF and SB. The highly accomplished woman lived in western Pennsylvania and became something of a tourist attraction for visitors to the area: IV, 210–11n.

4. Formerly BF's slave, he now belonged to the Baches: Lopez and Herbert, *The Private Franklin*, p. 293.

power to write you something better about him, all I wish now is to give you a picture of the little Family just as it is. Willy and Betty send their duty with that of your Afectionate Daughter

S BACHE

From the Baron de Frey

ALS: American Philosophical Society

Excellence Paris le 9 septe 1780./.

Je Suis au déséspoir d'etre forcé d'importuner encore Votre Excellence, mais n'aiant pas encore pu terminer mes affaires, attendant jour en jour des lettres de mon Pêre, et me trouvant dans ce moment très embrassé pour pouvoir payer vingt cinque L'ouis d'or pour un lettre de change, que je dois paier aujourdhuy, faute de quoi je serois exposé à de grand désagrement, car celui a qui je dois paier le 25 Louis d'or, m'avéz menacé de me faire arretter Si je ne lui remboursé pas son argent dans la journé. Je viens donc prier V: E: très instament d'avoir la bonté et de m'avancer cet somme, je rémettrois en attendant entre les mains de V: E le bigliets cijoint. Je ne doute pas que Votre Excellence voudra bien accorder cet grace à un officier, qui a l'honneur d'etre Capitaine au service des Etas Unis de l'amerique, et elle peut etre persuadé, que sitot que j'aurois arrangé, mes affaires je partirois pour m'en rétourner en amerique.[5] Si jaurois Scû ou m'addresser allieurs je n'aurois pas été Si hardi d'importuner V: E: En attendant je la prie de vouloir bien m'accorder ma demande, et de la remettre au Porteur. Cet la seul grace que j'ose demander a Votre Excellence et celle de me croire pénetrée de reconoissance. J'ai l'honneur d'etre avec un profond Respect. Di Votre Excellence trés humble et trés obeissant serviteur. DE FREŸ

Capt: au service des
Etas Unis de l'amerique

Notations: De Frey, Paris le 9. 7bre. 1780. / [*in William Temple Franklin's hand:*] Ånsd in the Neg.

5. Returning to America that October, de Frey was captured and held prisoner until July, 1781. He fought as a volunteer under Lafayette at Yorktown. Congress accepted his resignation in November, 1781, and he returned to France with certificates from Washington and Lafayette: Lasseray, *Les Français*, I, 222–5; *JCC*, XXI, 1142–3; Idzerda, *Lafayette Papers*, IV, 513–14.

From Jean-Joseph Dusaulx[6] ALS: American Philosophical Society

Monsieur   paris le 9. 7bre. 1780.

J'ai l'honneur de vous envoyer la Lettre dont je vous ai parlé il y a deux jours, et que M. d'Alembert m'a écrite pour vous demander des nouvelles du Fils de M. Michaëlis.[7] Je Suis avec les Sentimens les plus respectueux Monsieur Votre très-humble et très-obéissant Serviteur   DUSAULX

Addressed: A Monsieur / Monsieur Francklin / Ministre plénipotentiaire / des Etats unis d'Amerique / a passi.

Notation: Dusaulx. Paris 9. Sept. 1780.

From Sir Edward Newenham

ALS: American Philosophical Society

Dear Sir   Belcamp near Dublin 9 Sept. 1780

I beg leave to Introduce, the Bearer, Mr John Collins of the City of Dublin to your favor;[8] I would not presume to take such repeated Liberties, was I not most firmly convinced that Mr: Collins will discharge himself with Integrity.

He will have the Honor to acquaint your Excellency with his Intentions; should they prove favourable, & agreable, to the Interest of the truly Magnanimous, & Virtuous, United States of North America, your protection will greatly add to those favors, I have received from your Excellency; Favors I shall Ever most Gratefully acknowledge, & hope, in March next, personally to thank You for.

6. The popular French man of letters: XXIX, 123n.

7. D'Alembert (XXIV, 220n) asked Dusaulx to tell BF that he had received a letter from Johann David Michaelis (XIX, 446), the distinguished Orientalist and theologian of Göttingen. Expressing "respect infini" for BF, Michaelis wanted news of his son Christian Friedrich who, though a surgeon in the Hessian troops, "ne tue personne, soit françois, soit ameriquain, quoiqu'il soit dans l'armée du General Clinton, et qu'il ne fait metier que de guérir": d'Alembert to Dusaulx, Sept. 4, 1780, Hist. Soc. of Pa. Christian Friedrich became a councillor and Professor of Medicine at Marburg and was elected to the APS in 1785: *ADB*, XXI, 688, under his father; Whitfield J. Bell, Jr., "A Box of Old Bones . . . ," APS *Proceedings*, XCIII (1949), 171–2.

8. He was actually Thomas Collins; see his letter of Sept. 28, below.

Our Parliament began with Spirit, but at the Close of the Late Session, they forfeited Every Title to Virtue & Honor; their latter Acts record their Infamy—upon their own Journals—[9]

The four Americans, that I mentioned to your Excellency in my Letter of the 23 of July last,[1] have been released, without any Expence; & I suppose they have paid their respects to you, in their way to Bourdeaux—

I have the Honor to remain with the most Perfect respect & Esteem Your Excellencys Most obt: & very Humble sert

EDWD NEWENHAM

Notation: Edward Newenham. Belcamp near Dublin Sept. 9. 1780

From Thomas Ruston[2]

Translation:[3] American Philosophical Society

⟨London, September 9, 1780, in French: The world marvels at the wisdom and maturity shown by the American Congress in

---

9. The session of the Irish Parliament concluded on Sept. 2. During August opponents of British policy, the Patriots, were defeated on two major issues, the Mutiny bill and the sugar tariff. The "latter acts" of the parliament may refer to resolutions passed in both the Commons and the Lords condemning the August 17 addresses by the radical Merchants Corps of Volunteers, Independent Dublin Volunteers, and Liberty Volunteers: Maurice R. O'Connell, *Irish Politics and Social Conflict in the Age of the American Revolution* (Philadelphia, 1965), pp. 247–54.

1. Missing. Newenham's most recent extant letter to BF is that of June 25, 1779: XXIX, 739–40.

2. Ruston, a physician practicing in London and Exeter (XXI, 157n), identifies himself as the author in his Sept. 29 letter, below. He had taken a great interest in business since his 1771 or 1772 marriage to a wealthy heiress and was, according to the later testimony of George Washington, "a warm Friend of the American cause": James McLachlan *et al.*, eds., *Princetonians: a Biographical Dictionary* (5 vols., Princeton, 1976–91), I, 404–5.

3. Made from the English original (now missing) by the abbé Morellet: BF to Ruston, Oct. 9, below. A partial copy of this translation is at the Bibliothèque Municipale de Lyon, with a note on it in Morellet's hand that he had translated the piece because it was so similar to BF's way of thinking. Information kindly communicated to us by Dorothy Medlin.

organizing a country that has so recently conquered its freedom. The only weak point of this new administration—a flaw it shares with all European nations excepting England and Holland—has to do with the handling of public credit. That American paper currency should have fallen into discredit in spite of the country's vast resources is proof that Congress is not yet aware of the basic principles governing this subject.

Allow me some background explanation.

Europe has long accepted the idea that public credit can only be maintained when grounded on a certain quantity of gold or silver specie. The French, for instance, carried this view to extremes, but without worrying whether such specie was in the hands of private people or of the government, so that their credit sank and has only begun to be salvaged in the last few years. In England, on the other hand, the paper money in circulation represents vastly more than the coinage in existence. This can be verified in pp. 363–443 of the first volume of the Witworth edition of Dr. Davenant, as well as in Dr. Price's *Observations on the Nature of Civil Liberty,* p. 74.[4]

Furthermore, one would be grossly mistaken in believing that only gold and silver are the proper basis for currency. Their intrinsic value is less than that of iron, a metal of greater use to humanity. Were it not for the myth surrounding gold, a pound of it would be less valuable than a single bushel of wheat. Paper credit is as good as silver or gold, better even, and more convenient as witnessed by the preference that the Dutch, who know as much as any nation about money, show it in depositing their papers of credit in the bank. See Dr. Franklin's remarks on the Board of Trade's report.[5]

To those who object that bills are only as valuable as the belief that they can be exchanged for silver or gold, I shall answer that it is not so, that what counts is the certainty that the other

4. Charles Whitworth, ed., *The Political and Commercial Works of Charles D'Avenant . . .* (5 vols., London, 1771); Richard Price, *Observations on the Nature of Civil Liberty . . .* (London, 1776).

5. Possibly BF's "Scheme for Supplying the Colonies with a Paper Currency," which he wrote in February, 1765: XII, 47–60. The Board of Trade in January and February of that year had been holding hearings on the paper money problem in the American colonies: XI, 176n.

person owns some form of property. Is there one knowledgeable merchant in the world who will sell one whit cheaper if he is paid in cash?

According to Dr. Price, the paper money of the colonies is more stable than that of England because it is not exchangeable for cash upon presentation, because a debtor is legally authorized to have it accepted as payment, and because it does not sustain as monstrous a debt as that of England. Indeed, should such a debt occur in times of exceptional necessity, it can be extinguished within four or five years through taxes on that paper money. Why, then, did the value of paper money fall so low in America? It is because of the public's ignorance of the true nature of credit.

In order to put their finances in good order, the Americans should gather complete knowledge of their debts and of the conditions under which they have been contracted. Having heard that a bank may soon be established in Philadelphia,[6] I make the following suggestions:

1. That all credits be placed in a common fund or in separate funds; that the creditors not be allowed to demand reimbursement but only transfer within the funds, leaving the government free to reimburse all or part of those funds when convenient.

2. That taxes be levied in order to pay scrupulously the interest which has been agreed upon. That a Bank be established for that purpose, and compensated for its services. That a fund large enough to secure the public's trust be created, said fund made up by various kinds of properties (real estate and other), by a subscription and a sale of shares, and by land mortgages, and that the government stand as a guarantor behind the bank.

The Bank should receive all taxes and keep careful accounts. All negotiations of public funds should be done through it, and it should handle silver and gold and operate a mint whenever necessary. It should be allowed to lend money under certain restrictions both to private people and to the government, up to the amount of taxation for that year. Branches should be opened in

6. He may be referring to the Bank of Pennsylvania; see RB's letter of July 22. Robert Morris submitted his proposal for a national bank to Congress on May 17, 1781, three days after promising to accept the position of superintendent of finance: *Morris Papers*, I, 61, 66.

provincial towns, in order to supplant eventually the local banks. 3. When the Bank's credit is solidly established, both within the country and without, it will be able to borrow at more advantageous conditions and to solicit loans at stipulated interests from various European nations.

The rates of exchange should be fixed according to the place with which one is trading but the Bank should not enjoy a monopoly on those operations. It should keep out of small or precarious commercial operations, so as to eliminate any risk of harming the national credit.

The only valid objection to such a plan is that this is wartime and America is invaded by an enemy army, not the most propitious moment for opening a bank, but keep in mind that both England and Holland were in worse shape than the United States when they started their central banks. This is definitely the moment to act.

The proposed bank is somewhat different from most of the ones already established in Europe, to wit:

The Amsterdam Bank is used only for deposits and transactions within the city.

The Scottish banks offer loans only on land mortgages.

The Bank of England, which resembles most the one I am suggesting, assists private commerce through its own credit.

Please believe, Sir, that my only intention is to be of help to a cause endorsed by reasonable people all over the globe and to pay homage to your honesty and your talents. Should you wish to comment, I can be reached at the Carolina Coffeehouse.⟩

From the Baron Stürler[7] ALS: American Philosophical Society

Votre Excellence! Paris le 9. Septemb 1780

Comme c'est moi qui ai prété a Mr. de Frey les vingt Louis pour retirer les billets qu'Il avoit entre Vos mains! afain de le metre en meme de pouvoir les Négotier pour se procurer les moyens de retourner a Votre Armée en Amérique, ou Il Sert comme Capitaine dans la Legion du Comte Poulawski; et qu'Il vient me

7. Possibly Johann Friedrich Stürler vom Altenberg (xxviii, 353–4n).

rendre les dits billets; m'assurrant qu'Il n'a pu trouver a s'en défairre ici. J'esperre que Votre Excellence Voudra bien les reprendre de ma part pour en disposer Comme Elle le jugera bon, et de me renvoyer les Vingt Louis, que j'ai eu l'honneur de Vous fairre remetre par mon Domestique, de la part et avec la letre de Mr. de Frey, le deux du courant;[8] pour rétirer les dits billets, ce que je n'ai fait que pour obliger un officier que je connais daileurs avantageusement, et que je voyais en un tres grand Ambaras. Seul Motif qui m'a engagé a me pretter aux Solicitations de Mr. de Frey a cet Egard, ce dont j'espere Votre Excellence voudra bien ètre persuadé, comme du Respect avec Le quel je Suis De Votre Excellence Le tres humble Servitteur   LE BN: STURLER

Notation: Sturler Paris le 9. Septembre 1780.

To Stürler

Copy: Library of Congress

Sir,   Passy, Sept. 10. 1780.

M. De Frey has, I think, quitted our Service, and is excused by the Congress from the Necessity of returning. I nevertheless lent him 16. Guineas on his Promise of repaying me in a few Days. He broke that Promise and borrowed 4. Guineas more of me on a new Promise, which he likewise broke; for when he paid me it was much after the Time. I do not like to be troubled with such uncertain Borrowers or their affairs, or their Pledges. I therefore return the Billets he has sent me, thro' your Hands and desire to be excused lending him any more Money.[9] I am sorry if this Refusal should happen to be any Inconvenience to you, but

8. BF credited de Frey's payment on Sept. 2; de Frey's letter was dated Sept. 1, above.

9. Three weeks later, however, BF did lend de Frey more money. On Sept. 30, at Paris, de Frey drafted a letter of exchange: "A dix jour de Vue de celle ci ma Seconde lettre de change (la premier netant pas paié) Payé à l'ordre de Monsieur Benjamin Franklin Ecuyer Vingt Louis dor valeur récu, qui vous posseroy au Comte de Votre très humble Serviteur." APS. Endorsed by BF, the letter was addressed to Monsieur Strekfisen, probably Jean-Georges Streikeisen, a merchant banker and consul for Prussia at Bordeaux: Lüthy, *Banque protestante,* II, 216. Frey received 480 *l.t.* (20 louis) on Sept. 30. Account XXVII (XXXII, 4).

as I have had no part in occasioning it, I hope you will likewise excuse me. With great Esteem and Regard I have the honour to be, Sir, &c. &c.

M. le Baron Storler.

From Richard Bache

ALS: American Philosophical Society

Dear & Hond. sir   Philadelphia Sepr. 10th. 1780.

I fully expected to have had the pleasure of a Line from you by some of the late arrivals from France, but am totally disapointed— I wrote you not long since by the Captains Read & Truxton, & sent you the papers,[1]— this, with the Papers up to the date, I shall commit to Captain All's care, who has in charge a Vessel of my Friend Morris, & intends for L'Orient[2]— Dr. Lee, tho' he has been arrived some time in Boston, has not reached this yet,[3] I am told he is preparing a formidable battery, which he intends opening against you, when he shall arrive here; Mr. Izard has been here some time,[4] he was pretty open mouthed against you, when he first came, but finding himself little attended to, is not so vociferous as he was—perhaps he only waits the junction of his Friend Lee, when they intend to try their united force against you, & probably expect the aid of some of the Massachusetts Delegates—A—— and L—,[5] who, if I am well informed, would rather some other friend were Minister at the Court of Versailles,— Your old Friend Gates has been less fortunate to the Southward, than he was to the Northward; he has been under the necessity of making a rapid retreat from the

1. Presumably his letter of July 22, above. Both captains had just arrived at Lorient: Cuming to BF, Sept. 8, above. BF had last written RB on June 27: XXXII, 609–10.

2. Capt. Isaac All made a quick voyage, arriving barely a month later: All to BF, Oct. 16, below. He was captain of the brig *Virginia*, which did not return to Philadelphia until April 23, 1781: *Pa. Gazette*, April 25, 1781.

3. Arthur Lee did not reach Philadelphia until mid-October: Smith, *Letters*, XVI, 211.

4. Izard had arrived in Philadelphia by Aug. 1: Smith, *Letters*, XV, 500n.

5. Samuel Adams and James Lovell: Smith, *Letters*, XVI, xix–xx.

neighbourhood of Camden in South Carolina;[6] depending too much upon raw Militia who would not face the Enemy, he has met with a disgrace; the few Continental Troops we had there behaved nobly, made good their retreat with the loss of General De Calb, who is said to be mortally wounded, & in the hands of the Enemy; besides the General we lost about 350 Men,— I have no other News,— We long to hear from you & Ben,— Sally & the Children join me in Love & Duty— I am ever Dear sir Your affectionate son   RICH. BACHE

Dr. Franklin

Addressed: His Excelly. / Dr. Benjamin Franklin / Minister Plenipotentiary from the United States / of No. America at the Court of [*crossed out:* Versailles] / per Capt. All.

Notation on address sheet: L'Orient October 15th. 1780 Recd: & forwarded, by Yr most hble Servt J. NESBITT

To John Bondfield   Copy: Library of Congress

Sir,   Passy, Sept. 11.[7] 1780.

I do not recollect I have ever had any Account what became of the Cannon you procur'd to be cast by Order of the Commissioners.[8] I wish to be particularly inform'd by the Return of the Post. And if any of them, or any other military Stores belonging to the Congress are Still in your Hands, this is to request that you would immediately Ship them on board the Vessel which was heretofore call'd the Breton, but now the Marquis de la Fayette, and which is at present in your Port. With great Esteem, I have the Honour to be, Sir, &c. &c.

M. Bondfield.

6. Preliminary reports of the defeat at Camden appeared in the Sept. 6 issue of the *Pa. Gazette.* Gates's success in the north was the Battle of Saratoga.

7. Or possibly 15; see Bondfield's reply of Sept. 19. The numeral "11" is quite clear on this copy, but either the copyist or the feverish Bondfield misread the original.

8. The commissioners had ordered him to ship 56 cannon; according to Jones they were now at Lorient: XXIX, 628n; XXXI, 517–18; XXXII, 30.

281

To Vicq d'Azyr

LS:[9] Académie de Médecine, Paris; copy: Library of Congress

Monsieur,   Passy, Sept. 11. 1780.

J'ai reçu les paquêts que la Societé Royale a confié à mes soins[1] et je ne manquerai pas de les faire tenir à leur addresse par la premiere Occasion convenable. Je suis persuadé que ces Messieurs seront fort Sensibles à l'honneur que la Societé leur a fait, et j'espere qu'ils seront de bons et utiles correspondants.

Un de mes Amis un des premiers Chirurgiens à Minorque[2] m'a envoyé differentes pieces que je remêts entre vos mains, étant possible que vous y trouviez quelque chose qui puise concourir au but de votre Excellente Institution.

Celui qui vous remettra cette lettre est M. foulk jeune Americain d'un excellent caractére, qui est venu à Paris avec le dessein de se perfectionner dans la connoissance théorique et pratique de la medecine et de la Chirurgie.[3] Permettez moi de le recommander à vos bons offices et conseils et je vous serai très obligé des bontés que vous voudrez bien avoir pour lui.

Jai l'honneur d'être avec becoup d'Estime, Monsieur, Votre très humble et très obeissant Serviteur,   B Franklin

M. Vic d'Azir

Notation: repondu

9. In L'Air de Lamotte's hand.
1. See Vicq d'Azyr's letter of Sept. 7.
2. Alexander Small. We do not have a complete record of his writings, and can only speculate about these enclosures. One of them was undoubtedly "Observations on the Gout" (for which see BF to Small, July 22, above). The only other papers we know of, only some of which have survived, concerned the ventilation of hospitals; see, for example, what we presume was an early draft of one: XXIII, 486–91. BF submitted a group of them to Vicq d'Azyr with his letter of July 20, 1781 (Bibliothèque de l'Académie nationale de médecine): minutes of the Académie de médecine, July 31, 1781. Whether or not the papers BF submitted in 1781 included a revised version of something he had already presented, is unclear to us.
3. For John Foulke see Lebègue de Presle to BF, July 12. Vicq d'Azyr was at the center of efforts to reform medical training and the profession: Charles C. Gillispie, *Science and Polity in France at the End of the Old Regime* (Princeton, 1980), pp. 196–8. For a thorough treatment of his reforming efforts see Caroline Hannaway, "Medicine, Public Welfare and the State in Eighteenth

From James Searle

AL: American Philosophical Society

Hotel de Lusignan Rue des Vielles Etuves
Che Monsr. Grison
Monday 11th. Septr. 1780

Mr. Searle of Philadelphia presents his respectfull Compliments to Dr. Franklin, & has the pleasure to Send him two packets, & Seven letters with which he had the honor of being Charged by the Drs. Friends in America.

Addressed: Honble. / Benjamin Franklin Esquire / Passy

Notation: [*torn: word missing*] Searle 11. 7bre. 1780.

From Dumas

ALS: American Philosophical Society

Monsieur   La haie 12e. 7bre. 1780

Au pied de la Lettre, il ne se passe rien ici d'interessant. Les Etats d'Hollde. ont mis en commission la requête de quelques Marchands d'Amst., pour obtenir la franchise du transit pour les munitions navales qu'ils font passer en France par le Canal de Gand, l'Escaut, l'Oyse, le Canal de Briare & la Loire à Nantes.[4]

L'inaction des Etats-Generaux est encore plus grande. Ils attendent d'apprendre que leurs Plenipes. [plénipotentiaires] n'ont rien fait en Russie.[5] Le Roi de Suede est attendu en ce Pays revenant de Spa d'où il partira dans la huitaine, à ce que me marque de là son chargé d'Affaire.[6] Je verrai demain le Prince de Gallitzin, pour lui remettre un Livre qu'on m'a envoyé pour lui. Je lui donnerai en même temps une note, que je lui ai promise, de ce que les Anglois appelloient enumerated commodities dans

---

Century France: the Société Royale de Médecine of Paris (1776–1793)" (Ph.D. diss., Johns Hopkins University), 1974.

4. A way of sending much-needed masts to the French Navy without fear of British interception; the first ones reached Nantes in November: Dull, *French Navy,* p. 208n.

5. They had just arrived in St. Petersburg; see our annotation of Dumas to BF, Aug. 3.

6. Former *chargé d'affaires* von Heidenstam.

leur monopole Americain.[7] Les Gazettes ci-jointes vous feront voir, Monsieur, que nous avons soin ici de profiter des papiers que nous ont apporté les derniers vaisseaux arrivés d'Am à Amst.

J'espere que Mr. Wm. Franklin & Mr. Bancroft se portent toujours bien, & me recommande à eux pour des nouvelles dès le moment que vous en aurez de bonne.

Je suis toujours, Monsieur, avec le plus respectueux attachement Votre très-humble & très-obeissant serviteur   DUMAS

Je vois par une Lettre de Mr. J. Adams qu'il se plait beaucoup à Amsterdam.[8] Je suis bien content de la maniere dont Kniphausen l'incendiaire a été reçu dans Jersey. 1500 h. disputer pouce à pouce le terrain à 5000, & les obliger à s'en retourner d'où ils étoient venus, c'est savoir la guerre comme les Européens les mieux aguerris. Beni soit le Genl. Green, & les braves troupes.[9]

Passy à Son Exc. M. B. Franklin

Addressed: à Son Excellence / Monsieur B. Franklin / Min. Plenipe. des Etats-Unis / &c. / Passy./.

Notation: Dumas la haie Sept 12. 80

From Gérard Rasquin[1]

ALS: Historical Society of Pennsylvania

Monsieur   a charleville Le 12. 7bre 1780

Gerard Rasquin Negociant a charleville sur meuse, et ancien Reviseur a La manufacture Rojàle de tulle a lhonneur de vous

7. See Dumas to BF, Aug. 31.

8. JA told Dumas he was "very happy" at Amsterdam and uncertain when he would leave: *Adams Papers*, X, 126.

9. See Cooper to BF, July 25. Greene's report of his victorious campaign appeared in the supplement to the Sept. 8 issue of the *Gaʒ. de Leyde*.

1. This is the first in a series of letters from a man who would not let BF ignore him. Rasquin was the father-in-law of Mercier, the *contrôleur des armes* in the manufactory of Charleville-Mézières with whom JW had negotiated a contract for the repair of arms, on behalf of the American commissioners, in 1777, and who later launched an unsuccessful lawsuit against JW: XXIV, 100–1; XXVIII, 497–9; XXXI, 233. Mercier subcontracted the work to Rasquin, who attempted to "debauch" or hire away workmen from Liège, a

Representer humblement, que d'ans L'année mil Sept Cent Soixante Dix sept ajänt accépte La Commande faite a Monsieur Mercier Controleur Dans Le tems En Cette manufacture dans Le mois de juin même année, et une autre plus Considerable de Monsieur Williams Deputé Des Etats unis [une Commande plus Considerable][2] Consistant En fourniture Des Differente Sortes de pieces D'armes pour Le Radoubbement des fusils; ils S'etoit fait un devoir de Remplir L'intention de Monsieur Williams Ce qui etoit Contenue dans L'Etat des pieces à fournir.

Pour Satisfaire plus promptement je n'ait trouvé pas assé D'ouverier dans charleville, je fus obligé D'aller á Liege au Risque de ma vie; je me suis trouve arretté par Des ordres que L'on avoit obtenus Sur des faux Exposé et pour avoir ma Liberte Cest une perte pour moy de Cinquante Louis.

Cette Commande touchait a Sa fin, Lorsque je fus obligé D'aller a tulle ou Le Roy m'avoit nommé pour Remplir La place de Reviseur dans Sa manufacture, jEcrivis, alors a Monsieur Williams que quoique je ne Seroit plus Resident a charleville, javois un frere qui feroit accélerer L'ouvrages et ma femme feroit Les Envojs á L'ordinaire. Mr Williams Repondit qu'ils n'en falloit plus faire et arretat ainsi Les Restant des Commande et des Marchandises qui etoient prete à partir, et Entre Les mains Des ouverers, avec Lequel javoit fait des marchés, Cest qui mes Causes un prejudice Exorbitant, javois fait des avances a Ces ouveriers pour faire Diligenter Votre Commande jy ait Emplojez toutes ma fortune, et par L'injustice, du premier ouverer de Mr Williams; La Voila Renversé. Les fournitures ne Sont pas Complette, il m'est Reste quantite des pieces qui ne pouvoient Servir qu'a Ce Suget et qui maintenant ne Sont plus De Debit.

Quel Sort plus Deplorable, pour paier Ces ouveriers, il ma fallu faire Des Emprunt, Comment Rembourser Si Ces marchan-

highly illegal practice. Rasquin was imprisoned on July 21, 1777, but released a month later through the intervention of Vergennes: Rasquin's memoir, [July, 1777], Hist. Soc. of Pa.; ———— to French Minister Plenipotentiary Honoré-Auguste Sabatier de Cabre (*Repertorium der diplomatischen Vertreter*, III, 123), Aug. 9, 1777, AAE; Sabatier to Vergennes, Aug. 20, 1777, AAE; Vergennes to Sabatier, Aug. 29, 1777, AAE. As Rasquin says in the present letter, he was subsequently named to a new post and turned over the business to his brother and wife, whereupon JW cancelled the order.

2. The brackets are on the MS.

dises mes Restent, Cest à vous Monsieur à jetter un coup D'oeil de Compassion Sur Le Sort d'un pere des familles, d'un negociant reduit a La misere, Si par votre protections il ne peut obtenir L'Emplojs des Marchandises qu'on Luy avoit Commandé, Cest Votre justice qu'implore un honeste homme qui attends de votre Reponse Le Coup qui decidera Sa fortune et Son Sort.

D'aigné jetter Les yeux Sur Les tablaux des La Commande et Des Envojs qui ont èté faite vous jugeréz parce qui Reste a fournir Du Domage Excessif quil Encoure il prira Les Seigneur pour Votre prosperite et Sera pour La Vie avec Reconnesance Du plus profond Respect Monsieur Votre tres humbles et tres obeissant Serviteur   RASQUIN

Endorsed: Rasquin's Complaint against Williams

Notation in William Temple Franklin's hand: A. M. Franklin. Recd. 14 sep. 1780.[3] / See B Fs Lettr to Ct Vergennes dated 24 Nov. 80 / No. 11

From James Woodmason   ALS: American Philosophical Society

Sir   London 12 Sept: 1780

The 3 Machines for Copying of Writings which you subscribed for, are now ready to be deliverd to your Order.[4] I beg the favour of you to order payment to be made on delivery. as Messrs: Watt & Co: have deliverd none without. Each Machine is £6/6s. & the packing Cases 6s/ more. The Paper which is particularly prepard is only to be had from me at 18s/pr Rm insides. The Copying Ink Powder will be necessary to be had also at 18s pr dozen. The Copy which you sent will not stand any time. Ours will stand as long as the original. I am Sir Your most Obedt. hble Servt   JAMES WOODMASON

Dr: Franklin

Addressed: Dr: Franklin / Passy / a Paris

Notation: James Woodmason. London 12 sept. 80

3. That same day BF had WTF forward this letter to Nantes; see JW's letter of Sept. 26.

4. See BF's letter to Woodmason, July 25.

To James Searle   ALS: Miss Lillian S. Wilson, Scarsdale, N.Y. (1955)

Sir   Passy, Wednesday morning Sept. 13. 1780

I received the Letters and Pacquets you were so good as to send me by Mr Dana on Monday,[5] and I thank you for your Care of them. I sent my Grandson the same Afternoon to congratulate you on your Arrival, and to request the Honour of your Company at Dinner this Day. But he did not meet with you. I was out all Day yesterday at Versailles, and so the Repeating of the Message happen'd to be omitted. If you are not otherwise engaged I shall be glad to see you. My Grandson will conduct you.[6] With great Regard, I have the honour to be, Sir, Your most obedient and most humble Servant   B Franklin

Honble. Mr Searle

From Samuel Potts[7]   AL: American Philosophical Society

Hotel De Tours sept. 13. 1780

Mr. Potts and party present their Compls. to Dr. and Mr. Franklyn, request the favour of their company at dinner next Friday at ½ Past Two, oClock.[8]

Addressed: Benj. Franklyn Esqr / at / Passy

Notation: M. Potts. Sept. 13. 1780.

5. See Searle to BF, Sept. 11. Searle informed Dana that Congress had empowered JA to seek a loan in the Netherlands pending the arrival of Henry Laurens; Dana left immediately for Amsterdam to inform JA: *Adams Correspondence,* III, 416–17. BF provided him with a signed printed passport dated Sept. 11 (Mass. Hist. Soc.); for the passport's format see XXXII, 413n.

6. On Sept. 16 Searle wrote WTF that he would dine with BF the following day (APS). Presumably he received little encouragement from BF about the prospects of obtaining a loan for Pennsylvania in France, as a month later he proceeded to the Netherlands: BF to Dumas, Oct. 2 and Dumas to BF, Oct. 20, both below.

7. Comptroller general of the Inland Office of the British post office. BF had known him in England, and Potts had supplied WF and the New York printer James Parker with London newspapers: X, 149n; XII, 427n; XIV, 92, 186–7n, 220, 238.

8. The next Friday was Sept. 15. On Sept. 14, BF provided a passport to assist Potts, his wife, his relations Mr. Hindley and Mr. J. Potts, and three ser-

From Joseph Conkling

LS: American Philosophical Society

Sir   La Flotte, Isle de Ré September 14th. 1780./.

I was in hopes at the Receipt of the Letter Your Excellency honoured me the 21st. ulto. that it would not be long before I should had the Delivery of my Brigg the Whim & Cargoe, but as yet, I am told, there are not the least orders about it, from the Conseil-des-Prises to the Officers of the Admiralty at Sables D'Olonnes, this delay is of the greatest prejudice to the Tobacco, being Still at La Tranche, where it will be very difficult, when bad weathers comes on on the Coast there, to Ship the same for La Rochelle where it must be carried to be sold, and the time coming on late for my returning to New London, all this so much affected me, that I did fall very sick and was confin'd in bed long time, I make use of my recovery to Humbly beseech Your Excellency to renew your good Offices, to get a Speedy order from Said Conseil-des-Prises, which I am told do not meet often, and which I would beg to be Observed to the Minister of the Marine, and that my case is so very unlucky, that without a Speedy liberty, I fear I shall hardly make of my Cargoe to pay the Charges, all this grieves me to the Heart by the Loss my owner[9] Shall be at, therefore most intreat Your Excellency to be so good, to do all favourable possible for him who beg to remain Very Respectfully Sir Your Most obedient and most Humble Servant

JOSEPH CONKLING

To His Excellency Dr. Franklin at Passy./.

Notation: Conkling Joseph. Isle de Rhe, Sept. 14. 1780.

From Jonathan Williams, Jr.

ALS: American Philosophical Society; copy: Yale University Library

Dear & hond Sir   Nantes Sept. 14. 1780.

Inclosed is a Packet & two Letters which I received by the Mercury Capt Samson. This Ship is fitted out by the Massachu-

---

vants in their safe return to England. A copy (or retained draft), in WTF's hand with interlineations by BF, is at the APS.

9. Joseph Packwood.

288

setts State to carry over the Stores it was expected Mr Austin would have been able to provide;[1] but in consequence of his failure (for I do not understand he has in the smallest Degree succeeded)[2] she is here without money & yet in need of very considerable Supplies for the Payment & subsistance of her People as well as for the outfitts of the Ship which will not be inconsiderable. Capt Samson will wait on you & I suppose will give you an account of his Situation, he will at the same inform you of his having captured & sent into Boston a Portuguese Vessell laden on Irish Account & bound to Cork, the Captain I believe will make a Reclamation of his Vessell & Freight & you may therefore expect some application from the Portuguese Ambassador:[3] Capt Samson carries his Papers with him & will no doubt be able to justify his Conduct.

It appears by all the Letters I have received that great Expectations were formed about the second Division to reinforce Mr De Ternay and Capt Samson had even a Letter for the Commander of the supposed Division in case he should meet him on the Passage. This Letter I have sent to Mr de Sartine & wish it may put the Ministry in mind of sending out a second Division which I am afraid they have forgotten.

I suppose your Letters will inform you of all the news there is so I need not mention any. My Uncle[4] arrived safe at Providence New England.

I have sent almost all the Cloathing to L'orient to be ready for the Breton, I only wait to hear from Bordeaux to judge of the Time of her getting into L'orient & then I shall give Mr Schweighauser Notice to have all he has on hand in readiness.

I am ever with the highest Respect Dear Sir Your dutifull & affectionate Kinsman   Jona Williams J

1. XXXII, 250–1n. The ship actually was the *Mars*. On Sept. 14, JW wrote to Austin that, if he had not already left Paris for Amsterdam, as he had indicated he would in a letter of Sept. 8, he should wait for the arrival of Capt. Samson. Samson would discuss his instructions with Austin directly, but they included orders to return as a ship of war and try to make as many prizes as possible in the event that no goods or freight had been procured. The letter was addressed to either Paris or Amsterdam. Yale University Library.

2. Austin's letter to JW of Sept. 8 had intimated as much.

3. See Branco to BF, Oct. 7.

4. John Williams; see XXXII, 184.

I have lately received a considerable Sum in Bills on Mr Jay. Do you think they will be paid?— I shall be obliged to you for one word on this Subject.

Endorsed: Mr. Williams Sept. 14. 1780 Has sent almost all the Clothing to L'Orient

From Benjamin Franklin Bache

ALS: American Philosophical Society

Mon cher grand papa   [*c.* September 15, 1780][5]

J'avouë qu'il y a très longtems que je ne vous ai écrit c'est pourquoi je vous écris une lettre assez longue pour vous donner de mes nouvelles. Je pense toujours à vous et je vous envoye pas la pièce de dessin, parceque je veux en faire quatre differentes je fais tous mes efforts pour vous contenter et pour avoir un autre prix l'année prochaine.[6] Je crois que mes maitres sont contents de moi ou du moins je fais tous mes efforts pour les contenter. J'espere que vous vous portès bien ainsi que mon cousin et mon ami cockran. J'espere qu'il n'est pas encore parti pour l'amerique. Je souhaterois beaucoup qu'il vint a Genéve en pension chés Mr de Marignac pries le, s'il vous plait, de faire mes amities de ceux de la pension en general et faites bien mes compliments à mon cousin, et quand vous aurès l'occasion d'ècrire à mon cher papa ou à ma Chere maman dites leurs que je fais tous mes efforts pour les contenter. Mr. de Marignac vous présente bien ses respects.

Je suis votre très humble et obeissant petit fils   B F B

Endorsed: recd Sept. 20. 80

Addressed: A Monsieur / Monsieur Franklin / Ministre Plénipotentiaire des provinces/unies de l'Amérique auprés de sa / Majesté trés chrétienne, recommandée / à Monsieur Grand Banquier ruë / Montmartre / A Paris

5. BF's endorsement says that he received the letter on Sept. 20; we estimate five days for delivery.
6. See his letter of July 18.

From Dumas

ALS: American Philosophical Society

Monsieur   Lahaie 15e. 7bre. 1780.

L'Assemblée d'Hollande se Sépare aujourd'hui, & comme j'ai déjà eu l'honneur de vous en prévenir, Sans avoir rien fait.

Ce qui est plus intéressant, c'est que je m'apperçois que plusieurs de nos grands, fort Anglomanes, & fort intéresses dans les fonds Anglois, commencent enfin à prendre l'allarme sur ces fonds, & à témoigner même leurs craintes à cet égard.[7]

Le public revient aussi des fausses idées dont on l'avoit imbu depuis le malheur de Charlestown, quant à la disposition de la masse du Peuple Américain vers une réconciliation avec la marâtre.

Vous verrez, Monsieur, par le feuillet ci-joint,[8] que les amis de l'Amérique, de leur côté, font de leur côté de leur mieux pour désabuser le public à cet égard. De pareilles insertions font beaucoup de bien. J'espere que vous aurez bientôt de bonnes & grandes nouvelles à m'apprendre dont je vous promets de faire bon usage. Je suis toujours avec le plus respectueux attachement, Monsieur Votre très-humble & très obéissant serviteur DUMAS

Passy à S. E. M. Franklin

Addressed: à Son Excellence / Monsieur B. Franklin / Min. Plenipe. des Etats Unis / &c. / Passy./.

Notation: Dumas la haie Sept 15. 80

From Chaumont

AL: American Philosophical Society

[after September 16, 1780]

Extrait d'unne Lettre de Bordeaux ecritte a M de Chaumont par Mrs. S. Jauge et fils[9] en datte du 16. 7bre. 1780.

7. The alarm seems exaggerated. The *Gaz. de Leyde* of Sept. 15 (sup.) reported the funds at 115, whereas seven weeks earlier they were reported at 116½ and twelve weeks earlier at 111: *Gaz. de Leyde,* issues of June 20 and July 28.

8. Quite possibly another item in the supplement to the Sept. 15 *Gaz. de Leyde* describing various manifestations of the continued American enthusiasm for their cause.

9. Simon Jauge et fils, important Bordeaux *armateurs* from whom Chaumont purchased the *Breton:* JW to BF, Aug. 26, above.

291

M. Bromfield [Bondfield] n'a pas de Canons de 12 lb il
n'a que 28 Canons de 18 lb et 28 Canons de 24 lb. de Bale
qu'il est prest a delivrer Sur un ordre de M. franklin.

M. de Chaumont prie M. franklin de luy envoyer L'ordre pour
que Ces Canons Soyent Remis a Mrs. Jauge pere et fils. Les
Canons de 24 lb. de Balle Seront Remis en amerique aux Com-
missionaires du Congrès, et Les Canons De 18 lb. Seront pris en
Remplacement de Ceux que J'ay fait delivrer a L'orient. M.
franklin en devera encore de 12 lb. de Bale mais il n'y en a pas a
Bordeaux.

40 en Tous
28 de 18
12 de 12

Notation: Extrait d'une Lettre de Bordeaux à M De Chaumont.
par Jauge

From Chaumont   AL: American Philosophical Society

[on or after September 17, 1780][1]
M. de Chaumont a L'honneur de Communiquer a Son ami M. le
Docteur franklin unne Lettre quil a Receu de L'orient[2] et qui luy
prouvera que M. Jones est peu propre a faire aimer Les francais
par les americains.

J'ay L'honneur aussi de prevenir mon Bon ami M. Le Docteur
franklin que les derniers pacquets qu'il m'avait Confié pour
L'amerique et que J'avais fait partir Sous pavillon imperial par

1. The enclosed letter from Lorient, dated Sept. 13, would have taken at
least four days to reach Passy.

2. It was from Chaumont's agent Pierre-André Montigny de Monplaisir,
who complained that Jones refused to furnish him a muster roll and that the
crew of the *Ariel* threatened to throw him overboard if he came aboard their
ship. It is filed with the present letter at the APS. Monplaisir paid only 45
crewmen (*viz.*, those who had formerly served aboard the *Bonhomme
Richard*), which angered the others: Thomas J. Schaeper, *France and America in the Revolutionary Era: the Life of Jacques-Donatien Leray de Chaumont,
1725–1803* (Providence and Oxford, 1995), pp. 275–7.

unne Corvette partie d'ostende, ont été Jettés a la mer. La Corvette est rentrée pour en prevenir et en attendre de Nouveaus. J'escris en Consequence a M. de vergennes et Je les Luy demande pour les faire partir demain S'il est possible, parceque J'ay unne occasion Seure pour les envoyer Jusqu'au port de mer.

Notation: M. Chaumont Sept. 13 80

From Dumas

ALS: American Philosophical Society; AL (draft): Algemeen Rijksarchief

Monsieur,   Lahaie 17e. 7bre. 1780.

Je crois devoir profiter de la poste de Rotterdam, qui part demain pour la France, pour vous communiquer ce qui suit plus promptement. Un ami vient de m'écrire, que *quoiqu'il ne puisse pas supposer que je puisse ignorer l'arrivée d'un Mr. Searle* ou *Searce* (car je ne puis pas bien lire le nom tel qu'il est écrit) *il croît cependant devoir m'en parler, & m'apprendre, qu'il est vraisemblablement destiné pour la Hollande.*—[3] Il ajoute, qu'en tout cas, comptant sur mon amitié, il m'impose la condition de ne pas en faire la moindre mention, ni de bouche ni par lettres.— Cette condition, Monsieur, ne Sauroit avoir lieu entre V. E. & moi.— Au contraire, je ferois très-mal de ne pas vous communiquer l'avis. Ayez la bonté, Monsieur, de vouloir bien me répondre là-dessus: 1°. Si l'avis est fondé: 2°. en quoi consiste la mission de cette personne: 3°. comment je dois me conduire à son égard, lorsque nous Saurons quelque chose de plus positif sur ce qui la regarde.— Mes sentimens, Monsieur, vous sont trop connus, & doivent l'être aussi au T. H. [Très Honorable?] Congrès par le Committé des affaires étrangeres, pour qu'il soit nécessaire de les répéter ici en détail.— J'ai été & suis toujours prêt, à respecter & servir tout Plénipotentiaire que les Etats-Unis jugeront à propos d'envoyer pour traiter avec cette Rep.; & l'on doit être convaincu, que personne en ce pays ne remplira ces devoirs avec plus de fidélité & des prétentions plus modestes.— Et d'un autre

---

3. As indeed he was; see BF's reply of Oct. 2.

côté j'ai la juste confiance, qu'après tout ce qui s'est passé depuis ces 5 ans, les Etats-Unis ne m'abandonneront point, en m'oubliant, à être la victime complete de leurs ennemis, qui sont devenus les miens, un objet d'indifference, ou, tout au plus, de pitié pour leurs amis, & de dérision pour tous ceux qui me connoissent. Un tel cas Seroit à la fois, & trop indigne d'eux & trop choquant pour moi, qui ne le mérite pas; pour que je puisse Supposer un instant que ce Seroit jamais le mien.— Il seroit bon, néanmoins, que je fusse en état de répondre à ceux qui pourront me demander ce qui en est du sujet en question; & notamment à *notre Ami*, qui ne manquera pas, quand je le reverrai, de me questionner là-dessus.

Je suis toujours avec le plus respectueux attachement Monsieur Votre très-humble et très-obéissant serviteur   DUMAS

Passy à Son Exc. M. B. Franklin

Addressed: à Son Excellence / Monsieur B. Franklin / Min. Plenipe. des E. U. &c. / Passy./.

Notation: Dumas la haie Sept 17. 80[4]

To Thomas Digges   Copy: Library of Congress

Dear Sir,   Passy, Sept. 18. 1780.

I am sorry you have had so much trouble about Jones's Affair. When he borrow'd of me the 30. Guineas, he gave me the enclosed Bill;[5] acquainting me that he could command Money at Bordeaux where he was going, and would pay it there to my Order. He never went to Bordeaux, but is gone back they Say to London. Thirty Days Sight of Such Bill, is in reality 30 Days date because he must have seen it when he wrote it—By enquiring at Dr. Fothergills perhaps you may find him. & demand it of him. If you recover it, that will be so much in your Hands on my Acct I gave him a Receipt for the Bill of Mr. Goddard's Acceptance acknowledging that it was put into my hands as a Security

4. On the address sheet is also BF's calculation of a bill to be paid; see our annotation of BF to Woodmason, Sept. 26.
5. Missing. Jones is Edward Jackson Jones.

for the 30 Guineas lent. I will deliver up the Bill on payment of the Money and return of the Receipt. He behav'd here very foolishly and fraudulously. I wish all American Fools & Knaves would stay at Home, for the Credit of their Country, I am ever, your affectionately

M. Digges.

To Joshua Johnson

Copy: Library of Congress

Passy, Sept. 18. 1780.

The Trustees of the Maryland Funds in London have at Length sent me their Answer,[6] importing that by the Advice of Counsel learned in the Law, they find they cannot safely do what is required by the Act of the new State, and as at present the Stock cannot be sold or transferr'd but by them, the Execution of the Act seems now impossible. Nevertheless if you think you can do any thing in the Business that may be of Service to the State of Maryland according to the Act, I shall with Pleasure appoint you Trustee for that purpose. Be so good as to forward the Enclosed to the Governor, when you have an Opportunity of Sending to that Province.[7]

Having had some Dispute with M. Schweighauser about the Payment of an Account, of which I send you a Copy, together with Copies of the Letters that have passed between us on the Subject, I have, as you will see advised him to send it over to the navy Board[8] But to have it first examined by you as Inspector of the public Accounts. I imagine it may be within the Intention of your Appointment; but if not, I think your Examination of the

6. Hanbury, Grove, and Russell to BF, Sept. 6, above.

7. On Oct. 10 Johnson wrote Gov. Lee enclosing a copy of the present letter and stating he could see no prospect of his being of use: J. Hall Peasants, ed., *Archives of Maryland*, XLVII, *Journal and Correspondence of the State Council of Maryland (Letters to the Governor and Council) (7), 1781* (Baltimore, 1930), p. 79.

8. In his letter to Schweighauser of Aug. 10, above. The only other intervening letters still extant are BF to Schweighauser, Aug. 24, and an extract of Schweighauser to BF, Sept. 7; both are above.

Accounts, may be of Service, and therefore request you would undertake it, and give your Judgment on it as soon as possible.

With great Regard, I have the honour to be Sir,

P.S. If you have not a Copy of the Maryland Act, I will send you one.

M. Johnson.

To Thomas Sim Lee

Copy: Library of Congress

Sir,   Passy, Sept. 18. 1780.

The foregoing is a Copy of my last:[9] since which I have received a Letter from the Trustees of the Maryland Funds in London, and the Opinions of Counsel they have consulted, Copies of which I send enclos'd.[1] As the Trustees refuse to do any act by which they may be divested of those funds, I do not see that my Appointment, of a Person to do the Business, can have any effect. I have nevertheless offerd the Appointment to M. Joshua Johnson,[2] if he should think any thing can be done in the affair, as possibly may be by persuasion, and offering them private Security. I shall embrace with pleasure every Opportunity that may be afforded me, of being Serviceable to your State; and am, with great Respect. Sir, Your Excellency's most obedient and most humble Servant.

His Excellency Thos. Lee Esqe. Governor of Maryland.

To John Ross

Copy: Library of Congress

Dear Sir,   Passy Sept. 18. 1780.

I received your favour of the 11th. with the Accounts, Bill of Lading &c. of the Goods you have Shipped.[3] If you remember

9. Above, Aug. 11.
1. See Hanbury, Grove, & Russell to BF, Sept. 6.
2. The letter immediately above. As far as we know, that letter and the present one mark the end of BF's involvement.
3. Missing, but see the following document.

right I promis'd only to assist you in the freight, but you have drawn upon for almost an equal Sum over and above, on Account of Charges, Commissions &c. These kind of Encroachements are disagreable, as well as inconvenient. I have however accepted your Bills; But do not try me any more in that Way.

I never could understand the Delay in Payment of the Prize Money, &c. I never had any thing to do with that Money; and as it seem'd to have some Connection with a Quarrel between two of my friends, M. de Chaumont & Capt. Jones, I did not incline to meddle with the Affair, because I would not be drawn into the Dispute. It would have been right, I think, if Capt. Jones had apply'd directly to M. de Sartine.

With great Esteem, I have the Honour to be,

M. Ross.

To Jonathan Williams, Jr.   Copy: Library of Congress

Dear Jonathan,   Passy, Sept. 18. 1780.

M. De Chaumont tells me the Ship will be ready to take in Goods by the End of this Month. You will make the necessary Preparations, that as little time may be lost as possible, it being of the utmost Consequence that the Clothing should arrive before Winter. M. Ross has Shipt 123 Bales of his Goods for the Congress in a Vessel from L'Orient. I do not know if that be all he had. As you will have Room you can take some of the arms which may be shipt by Mr. Schweighauser. I have desired him to confer with you on the Subject. There is also 100 Tons of Salt Peter at St. Maloes: which, if you can take M. Chaumont thinks will be best and cheapest, Risque considered, transported by Land.[4] You will consider this, and give me your Opinion.— M. Le Rouge Geographe rue des grands Augustins, has deliver'd me 15 of Hutchin's Maps & Books, and requests an Order to

4. The American commissioners had purchased the saltpetre in 1778 from Desegray, Beaugeard fils & Cie. of Lorient. There it had remained; they ordered Schweighauser first to ship it to America, then to sell it locally, and finally to hold it for export once again: XXVII, 63, 287; XXVIII, 153, 458, 558–9; XXX, 325.

have the Rest put in to his Hands for Sale. I know not where they are, nor that I have any thing to do with it. Have you? He is, I believe a proper Person.[5] My Love to the good Girls, and believe me ever.

Your affectionate Uncle.

M. Williams.

From Thomas Digges

ALS: Historical Society of Pennsylvania

Dr. sir   London 18 Sept 1780

As the bearer Mr Jones is known to you as well as his companion Mr Paradise I need not ask your usual civility to be extended to them.[6] They are two excellent men & of the right

---

5. Georges-Louis Le Rouge, a military engineer born in Hanover around 1712, was named *géographe du roi* by Louis XV and was an important Parisian map publisher. His most recent folio works had been reprintings and translations of maps of North America: *Atlas Amériquain Septentrional* (1778) and *Le Pilote Amériquain Septentrional* (3 parts, 1778–79). The details of Le Rouge's life are obscure, and it has generally been assumed that these volumes signal the end of his activity: Quérard, *France littéraire*, and R. V. Tooley, *Maps and Map-makers* (7th ed., London, 1987), p. 44. He continued to publish individual maps and volumes of engravings through 1790, however, which he announced in the *Jour. de Paris*.

Le Rouge's extant correspondence with BF begins in November, 1780, and continues through early 1782; in March, 1781, aided by BF, he published a translation of the Hutchins pamphlet BF mentions in the present letter. Curiously absent from their correspondence is the most signicant link between the two men: Le Rouge reengraved the Franklin-Folger chart of the Gulf Stream. We reproduce the Le Rouge chart in this volume, believing that after Sept. 18 is the earliest possible date. Further details are provided in the List of Illustrations.

The original Franklin-Folger chart, as yet undiscovered when we discussed it in XV, 246–8, was located by Philip L. Richardson in 1980. See his articles, "Benjamin Franklin and Timothy Folger's first printed chart of the Gulf Stream," *Science*, CCVII (1980), pp. 643–5, and "The Benjamin Franklin and Timothy Folger Charts of the Gulf Stream," in M. Sears and D. Merriman, eds., *Oceanography: the Past* (New York, Heidelberg, Berlin, 1980), pp. 703–17.

6. The scholars Sir William Jones and John Paradise were considering emigrating to America: Garland Cannon, *Oriental Jones: a Biography of Sir William Jones (1746–1794)* (Bombay, Calcutta, New Delhi, 1964), pp. 78–9.

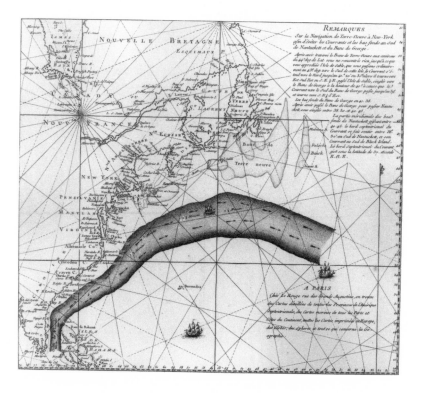

The Le Rouge Chart of the Gulf Stream

sort to fix themselves in our Country where I am not without hopes of seeing them settled in a year or two. They will wait upon you immediately on arrival at Paris & return hither in a fortnight after. I hope to hear from you by their return, & to receive any Amn news papers wch may be laid aside as useless to you.

They frequently contain matter useful to publish in this Country, especially where such matter expresses the strength, fortitude, & determind resolution of Ama. to exert herself towards the exterpation of the British army. The minds of the people here are getting reconcild apace to the Independe of Ama. & these publications help them on. The language now spreading abroad in the western quarter of the Town[7] is that the *new* Parliat. will very early go upon the business of declaring Amn. Independence, & getting the best terms with that Country that Circumstances will permit; but whether this is only an artful language, held out to serve Election purposes, or to raise the Stocks, or is really meant, I cannot determine. It is spoke of in Circles of the great folks perfectly attatchd to the Court. If our wise Rulers have a spark of wisdom left they must soon go to some such work. The Country in general is earnestly wishing for Peace and how can this be got but by getting rid of the American War. People of all descriptions in Politicks are alarmd for the critical situation in which England now stands, even the Toreys and Court Runners have given up the late language of all the Southern Colonies "*coming in*"—that the People of Ama were all ripe to declare for England—that the Capture of Chas Town was the conquest of the States—that the Amns & their allys were quarrelling—that they had nothing left to carry on the war &ca &a. &a.

Some late captures and arrivals from Ama. have opend their eyes to the actual state of things in that Country, & they have learnt that the American mind is not subdued—that they have the means, & are carrying on an active offensive Campaign—that their allies have given them an effectual aid of Ships & Troops, & have been receivd most Cordially—that the People

7. In the vicinity of the court, which was then located in the western part of London.

are not tired with the pleasures of self Government—that they do not despise a free trade, nor begin to think the ministry just, honest, wise or good enough to place themselves at their feet. As America has been long lookd upon by a great majority of this Country to be lost to England, these appearances do not effect the minds of the people half so much as the state of things nearer home. Ireland, tho at present divided by partys brought on by the intrigues of the Court, is lookd on as lost, at least the absolute dominion of it, to this Country & that no further revenue or places can be got from thence but such as the People chuse to give. The northern armd Confederacy is a bitter pill, and is lookd upon as a direct hostile act to this Country— Since the two Russian Ships, (which were loaded with Naval Stores from Petersburgh to France) have been given up,[8] the peoples minds are easier as to a war with those powers, some blame the ministry for their pusilanimity, others rather wish it so than get into a deeper war, but all say it will soon give the House of Bourbon a Superiority at Sea, & this will be a dreadful blow to the Sovereign Lords of the ocean. The affairs in the West Indies are spoke of with dejection & chagrin. Tho not mentiond in the late gazette, it appears Rodney has sent 10 of his Ships down to succour the Jamaica Squadron,[9] which Island is supposd in imminent danger. It is not at all improbable but the spanish flag is this day waveing on some of its Forts.

The Capture of the whole outward bound July fleet will be a dreadful blow to all the Islands & to Rodneys fleet in particular for there were in it 10 or 12 transports loaded wth naval Stores, masts, sparrs &ca for that fleet, besides Provision Ships. Two of the line of his fleet is lately arrivd in a shatterd Condition at Plymo. They were convoy to the 1st Augt. homeward bod [bound] Leeward Island fleet, but seperated from it in a violent

8. The seizure of these ships provoked strong Russian protests: Madariaga, *Harris's Mission*, pp. 233–4, 365–6.

9. The mission of the ten ships of the line was to escort transports and merchant ships to Jamaica and then to take a convoy back to England: W.M. James, *The British Navy in Adversity: a Study of the War of American Independence* (London, New York, Toronto, 1926), p. 218.

Storm wch. happend the 3d Int. & contind for three days.[1] As none of the trade came in with the men of war & only 8 or 10 of eighty vessels are yet arrivd it is feard a great number has been lost. This, with the former extraordinary Capture, the taking of 12 out of the Quebec Ships on the banks N foundland (wch I am told are worth from 30 to 35,000 £ ea) will be a death blow to the gentry at Loyds, & prevent some of their names from appearing to the Government loan of 1781 for the twenty or twenty two millions which the premier will want.[2] I do not pity these chaps a bit, for it has been by the prayers and addresses & the conversation & opinions of these & such like, that the war has been prolongd.

There is yet no accots of Greaves's arrival in America. The first arrivals from N York must determine it—the expectations of the people are much up for accots. from that quarr many people think the Port of N York must be blockd up or accots must have been recd. Others laugh at the idea that the French fleet can even alarm the place or that the united efforts of French & Aman. Armys can endanger that garrison. Within this few days the ministry have hinted forth their alarms for the safety of Hallifax. On enquiry from a pretty good line, I find that on the 14th at night an Express arrivd from Sr. Jo: Yorke with a discovery of his "that Ternays fleet & an Army of Amns & french were actually meant against Hallifax before the close of the Season."

Mr R Temple has not yet finally succeeded as to getting a protection for the Cartel to depart for some port of Spain or France. The Vessel will be obligd to clear out for Oporto & so make her way to Bilboa at the risque of Mr Temple. All idea of Exchanging an equal number of Americans in confinement here for those who came on Parole in that Cartel is at an end; The application was scouted, & the Parole Prisoners were told to go back to N York & there give themselves up for an equal number of *Rebels* exchangable in that place only with British prisoners taken &

1. The ships of the line were the *Boyne,* 70, and *Preston,* 50: *London Courant, and Westminster Chronicle,* Sept. 16, 1780.

2. North needed to borrow only £12,000,000: *Annual Register . . .* for 1781, p. 183 of first pagination.

carryd into America. The Insolence of People in Office here, & their inattention to the solicitations of their own subjects in cases of this sort, seem to encrease with the impotence of Government. They seem determind never to do a good natured or a conciliatory act.

There have been two Tobo [Tobacco] Ships from Balte [Baltimore] to Holland lately brot. into the Thames. They saild as late as the 6 or 8th of Augt. from Hampton, as did one also from No Carolina, yet we have no accots or any kind of news by these Vessels—the papers & letters have been all seizd & sent to the Ministry. The men (wch will add 70 or 80 to our numbers in Forton) have been put on board men of war to be sent thither, & the accots from them being all in possession of the Torey merchts & owners of these privateers, none are comeatable.— They cannot however be bad for Ama. or they would be let out, & it does not indicate that Cornwallis has over run *all* No Carolina & Virga.

I expected to have given you further accots of Mr Goddard & the Bills, but have not been able to see him. He is not visible. I sent you the 5th a Copy of his letter to me,[3] acknowledging they were his acceptances (consequently he must pay the Bill) & am waiting your ansr. I think you better send the bill to me endorsd & I will contrive to get it paid, at least as much as you have advanced on it.

I am anxious to hear if the Bishops picture got safe as well as the one sent you from Amm by M De Neufville, lodgd there by M Champion of Bristol.[4] I would not have the Bishop lost in the carriage on any accot, as that worthy family is in the Country, there is no knowing from them.

I expect to write you in 8 or 10 days by a *frd* who came in the Cartel & who has letters for you. One of the Instruments of writing you gave Capt. C—rp———r[5] in Apr. or May last, has

3. Goddard's letter was dated Sept. 5; Digges forwarded it to BF on the 8th, above.

4. The portrait was Georgiana Shipley's of her father: Digges to BF, July 12, above. Neufville sent it from Amsterdam. The other picture probably was the porcelain representation of Washington mentioned in Digges's Aug. 18 letter, above, and acknowledged by BF on Oct. 9, below.

5. Capt. Benjamin Carpenter, to whom BF had issued a passport: XXXII, 22–3, 103n.

not been used & shall be sent back (at least a part of it) to you by the above conveyance. Mitchell I understand has got safe into Boston, *by the fortune of war a prize to the Dean.* He had a fine useful Vessel of 18 Guns & carryd near twenty Captives with him hence.[6] His business was well done. Tho I am at present in a calamitous situation in consequence of my name being on 2 bills of 500 £ ea, wch were paid him by the Admiralty (thro an under Clerk of theirs Mr J. Jackson)[7] for the Cartel vessel wch. was seizd from Him at Bristol. These bills were drawn by Mitchell on Jackson & accepd to be paid at *the Bank of Engd* the 29th Augt. When the day came they were noted for non payment & are yet unpaid but in a fair way to be recoverd.

I expect my Reverend & Good frd Mr W———[8] here every day, when we will settle your donation of 8 pr week to each prisoner most likely in a post or two, I shall draw for 30 or 35 £ the then advance— The Bill will be on Mr Grand for accot B F & I will give him a line of advice with it. You will please also to mention it to Him.

As there is no domestic occurrence but Wch my friends the Bearers are acquainted with, I beg leave to refer you to them and to assure you that I am with the highest esteem Dr Sir Yr obligd & Obt Sert   T. D

Please to forward the inclosd in safety to Mr Carmichael Mr. Petree has been some days in England & has lately returnd to Town as unsuccessful Candidate for Cricklade—a very extraordinary attempt![9] I do not know him personally so that we have not met tho He is frequently with two or three valuable acquaintances of mine.

Notation: Sept. 18. 1780.

6. Capt. Henry Mitchell was brought into Boston aboard the brigantine *Adventure* in July, 1780: XXXI, 365n. The *Deane* was a Connecticut privateer: Louis F. Middlebrook, *History of Maritime Connecticut during the American Revolution, 1775–1783* (2 vols., Salem, Mass., 1925), II, 66–7.

7. George Jackson.
8. Wren.
9. See Samuel Petrie's letter of Sept. 22, below.

From the Loge des Commandeurs du Temple

ALS: American Philosophical Society

A L'O∴[1] de Carcassonne d'un lieu éclairé,
ou regnent le silence, la paix et la charité.
Le 18e du 7e mois de l'an de la V. L∴[2] 5780
[September 18, 1780]

A La Gloire du Grand Architecte de l'univers
La Loge Réguliere de st Jean de Jerusalem
sous le titre distinctif des Commandeurs du Temple[3]

Au très digne très vertueux & très réspectable Frére
Docteur Franklin, Ministre plénipotentiaire
des Etats-Unis de L'Amérique auprés de sa Majesté
très chrétienne S∴ F∴ U∴[4]

T∴ C∴ F∴[5]

Nous n'avions pas douté un seul instant, de vous voir sensible au malheur de la famille que nous vous recommandions, son état était un titre infaillible auprés de vous; Mais nous n'osions nous flatter de vous voir porter votre attention, jusques à nous offrir de faire passer vous-même nos Lettres à M. Le chevalier de la Luzerne. Une grande ame ne sait pas faire le bien à demi; vous nous l'aves prouvé plus que jamais en nous fesant une offre dont nous n'userons pas parceque la famille Andrieu, avoit déja écrit à Monsieur L'Ambassadeur avant votre réponse.[6] Nous

---

1. A L'Orient.
2. De l'an de la Vraie Lumière.
3. The lodge was known by its *titre distinctif.* Among BF's papers at the APS are several printed letters from the Commandeurs du Temple to "la R∴ L∴ de Saint-Jean de Jérusalem, régulièrement constituée à L'O∴ de Paris sous le titre distinctif des Neuf Soeurs." For the Carcassonne lodge see Alain Le Bihan, *Loges et chapitres de la Grande Loge et du Grand Orient de France . . .* (Commission d'histoire économique et sociale de la Révolution française, *Mémoires et documents*, XX, Paris, 1967), 57–8.
4. Salut Force Union.
5. Très Cher Frère.
6. For Andrieu's undated letter see XXXI, 89. There we miscalculated the Masonic date of the present letter, which we refer to by the more general title, St. John of Jerusalem, a title they shared with the Neuf Soeurs.

ne laisserons pas perdre cépendant le fruit de votre bonté, & nous vous supplierons, de vouloir bien vous rappeller les promésses que vous nous avés faites d'écrire en Amérique. Vous mettrés le comble à vos bienfaits, si vous voulés vous interesser auprés de M. De la Luzerne. Reçeves en attendant pour tant de soins nos rémerciments. Les éloges les plus pompeux les suivraient, si votre modestie ne nous imposait le plus profond silence.

Vous adressant cette Planche,[7] nous croirions manquer à notre devoir, si nous ne vous faisions part de L'Evénément heureux, qui cause à tous nos fréres la plus sensible Joie.

Une nouvelle nomination d'officiers à mis à notre tête, L'illustre Prince Nicolas Alexis de Galitzin que nous avions le bonheur d'avoir pour affilié depuis quelques années.[8] Aprés avoir partagé notre sensibilité pour les Malheureux, vous partagerés nos transports pour ce choix glorieux. Nous L'avons annoncé de toute part, & nous joignons cy-inclus notre circulaire pour que par votre Canal, la loge, qui a la faveur d'admirer de prés vos vertus, Connaisse un évenement intéressant pour tout ce qui tient à l'art Royal.[9]

Notre bonheur sera parfait Si nous pouvons avoir le bonheur de vous voir affilié à notre temple, et figurer dignement à Côté des hommes illustres que nous Possedons déja.[1]

7. A Masonic term meaning any piece of writing sent by a lodge or brother: Daniel Ligou, ed., *Dictionnaire de la Franc-maçonnerie* (3d ed., Paris, 1991), p. 940.

8. The new officer, who was "Vénérable d'honneur," may have been Nicolas (b. 1751), son of Alexis Démétriewitch, but the Galitzins were a large princely family, many of whom were masons: *Dictionnaire de la noblesse*, VIII, 829–30; *tableau des officiers* for 1782, enclosed in a Sept. 4, 1782, letter from the Commandeurs du Temple to the Neuf Soeurs (APS). See also Tatiana Bakounine, *Le répertoire biographique des francs-maçons russes (XVIIIe et XIXe siècles)* (Brussels, 1940), pp. 179–81 under "Golicyn"; Le Bihan, *Francs-maçons parisiens*, under "Gallitzin."

9. A masonic term for masonry: Ligou, ed., *Dictionnaire*, p. 79.

1. In the eighteenth century an individual Mason could be affiliated with another lodge in the manner of an *associé libre* or *correspondant* of an academy: Ligou, *Dictionnaire*, p. 15.

Nous avons la faveur d'etre avec les sentimens de la plus tendre fraternité par les N∴ M∴ A∴ V∴ C∴[2]
T∴ C∴ F∴ Vos affectionnés & fideles freres
    ROQUES Vble en Exercice
    Par mandement de la R∴ L∴[3]
    des Commandeurs du Temple
    ASTOIN Sre.
    Timbré & Sçellé par nous Garde des Sçeaux,
    Timbres & Archives.
    MÊRIC DE RIEÛX[4]

From Jean de Neufville & fils

ALS: American Philosophical Society

Honourd Sir: AmtDm, the 18th. Sept 1780

May it please your Excellency, that on Covering the inclosed, recomanded to our Care, We crave reference to our last Respects of the 31th. of August and that we were as happy as to engage the Chevalier de Luxenbourg,[5] on his return to Paris to charge himself with the delivery of a box containing a very fine Portrait in Chinea of the Great Generall Washington which we were desired sometime ago to forward, butt for Which we have only waited for a good and Safe opportunity, and which our good friend Mr. Diggs in Londo. permitted us since to offer you in his name[6] we Shall be very glad and happy at any opportunity we might meet with to be of any Service to the American Cause, and in particular to your Excellency as having the honour to be with

2. Par les nombres mystérieux à vous connus.

3. La Respectable Loge.

4. Roques was a merchant, Astoin, *avocat en Parlement*, and Meric de Rieux, *prieur de Notre-Dame de Roumanou* and *avocat en Parlement: tableau des officiers* for 1782, cited above.

5. Anne-Paul-Emmanuel-Sigismond, chevalier de Montmorency-Luxembourg (1742–1790), who leased the frigate *South Carolina* to Alexander Gillon (for which see XXXI, 184n): *Dictionnaire de la noblesse*, XIV, 393–4; Lewis, *Walpole Correspondence*, XXXIX, 361n; D.E. Huger Smith, "The Luxembourg Claims," *S.C. Gen. and Hist. Mag.* X (1909), 92–115.

6. See Digges to BF, Aug. 18.

all respectfull Regard Honourd Sir Your Excellencys most devoted and most obed humb Servt. JOHN DE NEUFVILLE & SON

From John Bondfield

ALS: American Philosophical Society

Sr.   Bordx 19 Sepr 1780

I am honord with your favor 15th[7] I have given Notice to the Merchants equiping the Marquis de la Fayette that I have receivd your orders to ship 56 pieces Cannon I have laying in the arsenal belonging to Congress which at their first requission shall be shipt— I write you from my Bed where I have been confind upwards of a month by a violent fever so soon as I am able to attend to Buissness shall transmit you the general accounts of my disburstments on this Account— I have the honor to be with due respect Sr Your very hhb Servt   JOHN BONDFIELD

His Excellce. B. Franklin Esqr

Addressed: A son Excellence / Benj Franklin Esqr / Ministre Plenipotentiaire des Etats Unis / a / Paris

Notation: Bondfield John 19. Sept. 1780.

From Dumas

ALS: American Philosophical Society

Monsieur,   La Haie 19e. 7bre. 1780

Vous verrez par le feuillet ci-joint,[8] que nous ne nous lassons point de profiter de tout pour donner au public une idée des affaires en Amérique bien opposée à celle que l'ennemi avoit excitée depuis l'affaire de Charlestown. Aussi le Succès répond à notre attente; & les Anglomanes enragent. J'espere que le Vent, qui vient de se mettre à l'Ouest, amenera bientôt quelque navire

7. Published above under Sept. 11.
8. We suspect that Dumas enclosed a copy of an article datelined Leiden, Sept. 19, and appearing in the supplement to the *Gaz. de Leyde* of that date. It gave an extract of a July 13 letter from Newport describing the joy at the arrival of Ternay's fleet.

avec de bonnes nouvelles; & je me recommande d'avance pour les avoir d'abord. Rien de nouveau ici. Je suis avec un très-grand respect, Monsieur Votre très-humble & très obeissant serviteur

DUMAS

Passy à Son Exc. M. B. Franklin

Addressed: à Son Excellence / Monsieur B. Franklin / Mine. Plenipe. des Etats-Unis / &c. / Passy./.

Notation: Dumas la haie Sept 19. 80

To Vergennes

LS:[9] Archives du Ministère des affaires étrangères; AL (draft) and copy: Library of Congress

Sir,   Passy Septr. 20. 1780.

Since I have the honour of speaking to your Excellency on the Subject of a farther Loan of Money to the United States, our Banker M. Grand has given me a State of the Funds necessary to be provided, which I beg leave to lay before you.[1]

I have frequently written to Congress to draw no farther upon me, but to make me Remittances; for that the inevitable Expences of France in this War were immense, and that I could not presume to make repeated Applications for more Money with any Prospect of Success.[2] Your Excellency will see this acknowledg'd in their late Letters to me, of which I inclose

9. In WTF's hand.
1. The enclosed memorandum itemizes the 4,900,000 *l.t.* that would be needed through the end of 1781: 4,000,000 for loan office certificates, 144,000 to pay interest on loans and to reimburse Beaumarchais, 125,000 for funds drawn on BF by the congressional resolution of May 19, 125,000 for funds drawn on Jay by the same resolution, 24,000 (£1,000) for the bureau of foreign affairs (*i.e.*, for Searle; see Huntington to BF, July 12), 24,000 to pay bills drawn by Henry Laurens, 300,000 to cover JW's remaining expenses, and 158,000 to cover current and unforeseen expenses. The memorandum points out that the remaining funds from the French government for 1780 were already committed. Copies made by WTF and by L'Air de Lamotte are at the Library of Congress.
2. See XXX, 466, 473; XXXI, 420, 465; BF to Huntington, Aug. 10, above.

Copies;[3] and that they would have avoided drawing on me any more, if the present Conjuncture in which they were obliged to make vast Preparations to act effectually with your Troops, had not laid them under the absolute Necessity.[4]

The present State of their Currency rendring it insufficient for the maintaining of their Troops, they provide for a great Part of the Expence by furnishing Provisions in kind: but some more hard Money than came in by Taxes, was wanted, and could only be obtained by these fresh Drafts.

Their former unexpected Drafts, had already absorbed much of the Money put into my Hands, and I am now put into a Situation that distresses me exceedingly. I dread the Consequences of protesting their Bills. The Credit of Congress being thereby destroyed at home, the People will be unable to act or exert their Force. The Enemy will find them in a State similar to that of being bound hand & foot.

We have had Hopes of some Aid from Spain; but they are vanished.

The Expectation of a Loan in Holland has also failed.

I submit these important Circumstances to your Excellency's wise Consideration. The States will be well able in a few Years of Peace, to repay all that shall be advanc'd to them in this time of Difficulty: & they will repay it with Gratitude. The Good Work of establishing a free Government *for them,* and a free Commerce with them *for France,* is nearly compleated: It is pity it should now miscarry for want of 4, or 5 millions of Livres, to be furnished, not immediately, but in the Course of the ensuing Year.[5]

---

3. The enclosures were: (1) the first July 11 letter from the committee for foreign affairs, above; (2) the May 19 congressional resolution which it enclosed; (3) an extract from Huntington to BF, July 12, above, regarding James Searle's mission. Two copies in L'Air de Lamotte's hand are at the Library of Congress.

4. In his draft BF continued, and then deleted: "of asking such Assistance. They have [*interlined:* I understand] great Quantities of Tobacco as I am informed ready to ship to".

5. BF's pleading met with some success: on Oct. 5 the French paid the last quarterly installment of its existing 3,000,000 *l.t.* loan and on Nov. 27 they provided an additional 1,000,000 *l.t.*: XXXI, 267n; Morris, *Jay: Revolutionary,* p. 834. Vergennes also promised similar assistance for the coming year: Vergennes to BF, Nov. 26, 1780 (AAE).

With the greatest & most sincere Respect, I have the honour to be, Sir, Your Excellency's, most obedient, & most humble Ser.

B FRANKLIN

His Exy the Count De Vergennes.

Notation: 20 7bre

From Thomas Digges

ALS: Historical Society of Pennsylvania

Dr. Sir   London 20th. Sept. 1780

The Inclosd will inform you fully of some applications made Mr H for the release of some Prisoners now at St. Omers which seem to have passd your notice. They are American—Capturd & have lately petitiond the admiralty to procure their release. The Capt Scott mentiond also in the inclosd Letter, will I hope stand against Capt Manley; The Board of Sick & hurt have promisd his release & that an order shall be sent down for this Purpose to Plymo. in a day or two.⁶ A good word has been spoken for Capn C——m but he being a more recent offender, it was refusd; not however without some tokens of attention to the application.

The Board of Sick & Hurt seem wonderfully civil of late, (indeed they have always been attentive to our applications) and I am led to think therefrom, that they begin to see how likely it is that America will succeed & how better it is for them to temporise & be civil. A small vessel from No Carolina to France, wch. saild abot. the 6th of Augt., and two others from Baltimore to Holland, Tobo. [Tobacco] loaded, wch saild in a fleet of 30 from Hampton the 8th. Augt. have been taken by English Cruisers & brot in—⁷ The two latter into the Thames. All papers, Letters &ca &ca have been seizd & kept secret, and eight of the Crew

6. The enclosure is missing. Mr. H. is William Hodgson. For Scott see Hodgson's letter immediately below. His release had been considerably delayed: Elias and Finch, *Letters of Digges,* p. 279n.

7. According to the Sept. 20 issue of the *London Courant, and Westminster Chronicle* one of the prizes was a 14-gun brig captured by the *Surprize,* a Guernsey privateer. The Sept. 22 issue of the *Gaz. de Leyde* (sup.) reported captures from a convoy of a dozen ships bound for the Texel, which left Hampton, Va., in early August, quite possibly the same convoy.

of one of them put on board the Tender at the Tower for his Majestys Service. I do suppose that the accots by these vessels are such as our great folks do not like, or they would have been let out—nay I think these very accots have been the reason of so much civility in office. I told you in a late letter that the Cartel Brige [Brigantine] Temple had got permission *to return.*[8] On Mr H——s mentioning to day at the board of sick & hurt, that it would be impossible for this vessel to return *without Seamen,* Mr H was desird to get Mr Temple to petition for these 8 Seamen on board the Nightingale Tender at the Tower, to be releasd & sent to Bristol to navigate the Ship away. I shall draw up the Petition tomorrow & Mr T will give it into the Admiralty, where I have reason to think it will be granted. As these men are only pressd by the Gangs for this work, & have not yet been committd for Treason or Piracy, there can be no plea (as there was in the case of the Parole Prisoners by the Cartel) "that prisoners committed by a Magistrate for Treason &ca cannot be releasd but by certain forms &ca".

I am expecting dayly a line from you about Goddards Bill as well as an ansr. to Mr Bowmans supplication for a pass *for His necessary Baggage* in case the Ship He is going in to Charles Town may be taken by an Amn Privateer.

No authentic news yet from N York but much rumour is going about that the ministers have for some days had possession of bad accots from that quarter.

The General cry of all partys is that the Amn War is intollerable & so little to be born, that the new Parliament is speedily to go upon the business of accomodation if at the expence of the Declaration of Independence. I reely beleive the Cabinet have determind to abandon that war, & look to their affairs nearer home. A Privateer just arrivd from Lisbon says there was an Embargo laid there on all English Ships the morning that He slipt away.—[9] This has causd some little alarm in the City.

8. Above, Sept. 8.

9. This news was reported in the Sept. 21 issue of the *London Courant, and Westminster Chronicle.* The embargo seems to have been a response to the use of Portuguese sailors by British privateers and merchant ships frequenting the Tagus: *Gaz. de Leyde,* Oct. 3. Portugal had the right by the 1654 Treaty of Westminster to prohibit British warships from using the port of Lisbon in time of war.

The Portugue Envoy set out yesterday for Lisbon, but *apparently* only to bring to England a few months hence His Lady.[1] The one coming so immediately on the back of the other causes much conversation. The Lisbon Merchts tho apparently frightend say it is only some partial embargo to detect or take some State Prisoner or publick thief. A few days will shew the truth. I wrote you on the 18th. by two frds. going directly to P——s. This will be put into the Post office in Ostend or Holland most likely before the next foreign mail gets across the Channel.

I am with the highest respect Dr Sir Yr obligd & ob Ser

W. S. CHURCH

Addressed: Dr. Franklin / Passy

Endorsed: Sept. 20. 80.

Notation: Sept. 20. 80

From William Hodgson

ALS: American Philosophical Society

Dear sir London 20 Sepr. 1780

'Twas only a day or two ago, that your Letter of the 25th Ultimo was delivered me. I have since been with the Commissioners of Sick & Hurt, who admit to have recd the Men whom your Certificates specify— Your Accot Stands as under

America Dr. [Debtor] to Prisoners sent to Morlaix	119
Cr. [Creditor] by Prisoners and from L'Orient & Morlaix	67
due to England on Ballance	52

I hope you will be able to pay off this ballance that we may have a fresh exchange, it grieves me much to think how very long some of the poor fellows have been confined— There is a Capt Robert Scott, who was commander of a Privateer called the Golden Eagle taken the 2d. June last by the Genl. Pickering Privateer of Salem Capt Harrabin & carried into Bilbao.[2] Capt.

1. Luís Pinto de Sousa Coutinho, visconde de Balsamaõ (1735–1804) served as Portuguese minister to the British court from 1774 to 1789: Elias and Finch, *Letters of Digges,* p. 279n; *Repertorium der diplomatischen Vertreter,* III, 317.

2. See XXXII, 563–4. The American captain was Jonathan Haraden.

Harrabin suffered Capt Scott to return to England upon his parole engaging either to return or procure the release of an American prisoner here, the Commissioners assured me they were ready to acknowledge Capt Scott as a prisoner discharged & to be reckoned in Acc't as if he came in a Cartel you consenting thereto & agreeing that his Parole is thereby fulfilled to which, I presume, you can have no Objection, 'Tis strange to me that we have not heard of the Crew of this Privateer, they must be prisoners as well as their Captain, I submitt it to you whether it is not a matter worthy your enquiry what are become of them, as also of other English prisoners in Spain of whom you formerly made mention,[3] I think I see a mode of Settlement opening by this that will answer the purposes of Humanity to improve— It seems to me, that, the Board of Sick & Hurt, by this precedent, will, in future have no Objection to admitt Parole engagements from Prisoners who have been *carried in to Ports in Europe* as exchanges made within the meaning of the Cartel & that they will be allowed as such in the general Acco't— I am the more founded in this Idea because they[4] have given me a List of some other prisoners taken by American Cruisers & now confined at st Omers, who if you will cause to be discharged, they promise to allow in Acco't alltho they do not expect you shou'd be at the trouble of sending them to any particular Port, their bare discharge with leave to get home as they can being all they seemed to think necessary on your part, I hope therefore you will take the first Opportunity of making application in consequence, the names of the Prisoners as under
John Bell of the Hopewell
Henry Davis[5]
George Fisher
Philip Bailleau of the May Flower of Jersey
James Bailleau
Philip Bisson

3. XXXI, 398.
4. Here BF has interlined "The Commissioners." Brackets mark a long passage, including the list of names of prisoners, that runs from "have given ... " through "to the Board."
5. Sartine had inquired about Capt. Bell and Davis, his pilot: above, Aug. 5.

Philip Bertram
Josuaricole
Philip Bisson
George Laurens— I think it will be necessary to have a Certificate of the discharge of these Men to produce to the Board. Your reply will oblige yr most Obedt sert   WILLIAM HODGSON

P.S. Your Secy. writes my address Messrs. Gill, Hodgson & Co making my Xtian name a Surname, it misled mr Petrie, Guillme you Know being only Wm.

Addressed: Dr. Franklin / Passy

From George Logan

ALS: Richmond Academy of Medicine

Dear Sir   Philadelphia Sepr: 20th. 1780.

Your polite attention during my short stay at Paris,[6] demands my most grateful acknowledgment. It would have afforded me particular pleasure to have returned to Paris, before sailing for America; but the reduced state of my Finances in Europe, & the situation of my affairs in this State, demanded my immediate presence, & attention.

I wrote to you twice from London, giving you an account of the situation of Great Brittain &c&c—[7] With respect to Public Affairs on this Continent, they are in a much better situation than I had any idea of. The Farmers, & the Quakers in general make use of little but their own manufactures. You would be astonished, & highly pleased to observe the improvements which are daily making every where in this Infant Country— I wish I could say as much for our Public spirit, & unanimity. Many individuals are charged with betraying the Interests of their Country willing to sacrifice every thing to their own ambition & emolument. Others, influenced by the prejudices of education still retain a strong prejudice in favor of their ancient constitution. I am however happy in informing you that different parties appear to be better reconciled to each other than formerly, & there is a great prospect of our becoming a united and happy People.

6. During the winter of 1779–80: XXXI, 302n.
7. Only one letter from Logan to BF from London is extant: XXXII, 257–8.

I can give you no Public information but what you will receive from Gentlemen much more capable of the task. With respect to private affairs I may inform you, that I arrived here about two months since,[8] & expect [to] reside here for life wishing to follow your laudable example in being constantly employed to the good of mankind in general, & in a particular manner to the prosperity of this rising Country— I am at present librarian to the Loganian Library;[9] I wish you to write on this subject, when at leisure I wish to put it on the most resp[*torn:* ectable?] footing.

Dr: Bond Mr: Rhoads[1] & your Friends in this City are in general well—

I am with great respect your much obliged Friend

GEORGE LOGAN

Addressed: A son Excelle: / Dr: Benjn: Franklin / a Paris

Notation: George Logan, Sept. 20. 1780

From Dumas

ALS: American Philosophical Society

Monsieur,   La Haie 21e. 7br. 1780

Je soupçonne que ce que j'ai eu l'honneur de vous écrire dans une de mes dernieres touchant Mr. Searce,[2] a été cru par mon ami, & débité par des Américains, un peu trop légerement: car voici ce qu'il me marque dans une Lettre suivante.

"Nous avons ici Mr. Austin revenu de Paris: comme aussi Mr. Francis Denca,[3] & un grand nombre d'Américains.— J'ai fait mon possible pour savoir la mission de Mr. Searce; mais qu'elle soit pour ici, ou pour des affaires publiques, il en est moins question qu'au premier abord. Le temps nous l'éclaircira. Il se pour-

8. He apparently sailed from Liverpool in late May: XXXII, 437.

9. The Loganian Library was assembled by George Logan's grandfather James Logan (I, 191n). After his death it became a public trust and BF served as a trustee. The librarianship was to pass through the male heirs of Logan's eldest son, William, George's father. In 1792 the Library was annexed to the Library Company of Philadelphia: I, 191n; V, 423–6; IX, 36–7.

1. Thomas Bond and Samuel Rhoads.

2. On Sept. 17, above.

3. Dana arrived in Amsterdam on Sept. 16: *Adams Correspondence,* III, 417n. Austin lodged with him.

roit bien même qu'il n'eût que ses propres affaires, relatives à sa maison de Madere encore, qui le conduisissent en Hollande. Si j'en apprends quelque autre chose, je vous le marquerai." Je suis fort curieux de ce qui se passera en Irlande pendant que le Parlement y est prorogé jusqu'au 10 du prochain mois, sans avoir revoqué ses arrêtés du 21 Août contre les Résolutions des Corps volontaires.[4] J'espere qu'on y sera assez insensé pour faire valoir ces arrêtés, & poursuivre criminellement ces Corps volontaires: cela joint à l'association qui vient de s'y former *pour cesser toute importation de la Grande Bretagne,*—pour *demander au Roi la dissolution du présent Parlement,* & pour *ne pas s'abandonner les uns les autres au ressentiment du parti de la Cour,* pourra produire là des effets délicieux.[5]

Nous attendons ici le Roi de Suede Samedi ou Dimanche, qu'on m'a promis de me faire voir de près.

Le vent reste bon, pour nous apporter des nouvelles de l'Ouest. Dieu nous les donne bonnes & décisives Je suis avec tout mon respectueux attachement, Monsieur Votre très humble & très obéissant serviteur   DUMAS

Passy à S.E.M. B. Franklin

Addressed: à Son Excellence / Monsieur B. Franklin / Mine. Plénipe. des Etats-Unis / &c. / Passy./.

Notation: Dumas la haie Sept 21. 80

To John Bondfield

Copy: Library of Congress

Sir,   Passy, Sept. 22. 1780.

In mine of the 11th. Instant, I desired you to Ship any Cannon that might be in your hands, on board the marquis de la Fayette.

4. We describe the Aug. 21 resolutions in our annotation of Newenham to BF, Sept. 9. The Irish Parliament's adjournment was reported in the Sept. 19 issue (sup.) of the *Gaz. de Leyde.*

5. This new and short-lived nonimportation movement had been provoked by the Irish Parliament's accepting a new sugar tariff just before adjournment: Maurice A. O'Connell, *Irish Politics and Social Conflict in the Age of the American Revolution* (Philadelphia, 1965), pp. 247–8, 253–4.

I am since informed, that you have 28 Eighteen Pounders, & 28. Twenty four Pounders. As I owe to M. de Chaumont 28 Eighteen Pounders, to replace an equal Number of the same bore which with others, he advanced to me at l'Orient to ballast the Alliance,[6] this is to request that those 28. Eighteen Pounders in your Hands may be delivered for his account to Messrs. S. Jauge & Fils. The twenty four Punders, are to go in the Vessel, as per my last.

I have the Honour to be &c.

M. Bondfield

From John Jay

> Copies: Library of Congress, National Archives, Henry E. Huntington Library, Columbia University Library

Dear Sir,   St. Il de fonse 22 Sept 1780

I have lately written to you several Letters. Enclosed is a Copy of one to Count de Vergennes,[7] which Ct. de Montmorin, who also writes to him on the same Subject,[8] is so obliging as to send together with this, by a Courier to bayonne. The Papers you have heretofore recd. from me, with those now sent will enable you to understand it; and I am persuaded your Abilities and Enfluence will be exerted to promote the Success of the applica-

6. On March 21–24 the *Alliance* took aboard twenty-eight 18-pounders and twelve 9-pounders: John S. Barnes, ed., *The Logs of the Serapis-Alliance-Ariel under the Command of John Paul Jones 1779–1780* (New York, 1911), pp. 75–6.

7. With the present document at the Library of Congress is a copy of the enclosure, Jay's Sept. 22 letter to Vergennes: Wharton, *Diplomatic Correspondence*, IV, 63–6. This lengthy document describes Jay's financial difficulties (including $50,000 in as-yet-unaccepted bills of exchange) and his unsuccessful negotiations. Jay asks Vergennes "to enterpose the amity of France" to rescue American credit.

8. Vergennes replied to Montmorin that he doubted he could help Jay, as BF had asked for an extra 1,000,000 *l.t.* to meet congressional drafts through the end of the year; he would do the best he could. Jay sent a copy of Vergennes' response to President of Congress Huntington on Nov. 6: Morris, *Jay: Revolutionary*, p. 834.

tion contained in it. It appears to me absolutely necessary that the Bills drawn on me be saved at all events. If contrary to my Ideas of the Wisdom & affection of France, She should not lend us Money for the Purpose we must endeavour to borrow it of Individuals, tho' at a higher than usual Interest, nay on any Terms rather than not get it. Almost anything will be better than a protest, for exclusive of Disgrace, which is intolerable, the Consequences of it would cost Congress more than the Expence of saving their Credit, be it almost what it will.

With very sincere Regard & Esteem your most hble Servt.

(signed) JOHN JAY

His Excellency Dr. Franklin.

From Juvel Neveux & Cauchoit

ALS: American Philosophical Society

Monsieur   Rouen le 22 7bre. 1780

Il nous a Eté negocié ce jour un effet tiré de lorient le 6 Ct. [courant] par gourlade et moylens a deux usances ordre de Maurice Sur vous de troix cens livres,[9] nous vous Serons obligé de nous marquer Si vous avés quelqu'un a paris ou vous fassiés élection de domicile pour payer les traites qui Sont faittes Sur vous, la ditte traite est payable le 15 9bre. prochain, nous avons l'honneur de vous Etre avec Respect Monsieur Vos tres humbles et obts Srs. JUVEL NEVEUX & CAUCHOIT

mds [marchands] Rue grand pont

Addressed: A Monsieur / Monsieur franklin ministre / plenipotentiaire des Etats unis de / lamerique. a passy pres paris / a Passy

Notations: Juvel neveu & Cochoit Rouen 22. 7bre. 1780. / [*in William Temple Franklin's hand:*] Rep. 23

---

9. This sum in favor of M. Maurice appears on WTF's list of bills drawn on BF by Gourlade & Moylan (for which see our annotation of BF to Gourlade & Moylan, July 5).

From [Samuel Petrie][1]   AL: American Philosophical Society

Dear Sir   London. Sept. 22d. 1780.

Circumstances unforeseen will detain me here longer than I intended, when I left Paris. Venality & Corruption have not decreased in this Country, during my absence; & the Confusion of a General Election, has given full play to the depraved disposition of the People. Accidentally landing in England, on the very Day the Proclamation was publish'd, for the dissolution of the last Parliament,[2] I found it impossible to restrain myself, from joining in the activity which Surrounded me on every Side. I posted down to a Borough in the West, where I had a right to expect to be received, as I was received, with open Arms, amidst the general Acclamations of the People, above five Sixths of whom, immediately enlisted under my Standard. My Competitors were Eastern Nabobs,— the one possessing about a Million of Money,— the other, possibly not more than a tenth of that Sum, but who is going out, under the Auspices of Lord North, President of the Council to Madrass.[3] I was not intimidated with the potent Qualifications, of these Gentlemen, and certain Victory was on my Side, till the Evening preceding the Election. A corrupt Manoeuvre then turn'd the Scale, & a venal Majority the next Day, poll'd against me; but the virtuous Minority must ultimately carry the Election, unless the Majority of the Committee who will determine on the Merits, Shou'd prove as venal as the Majority that poll'd.[4] This unexpected Business, will keep

1. Identified by the handwriting.

2. The proclamation dissolving Parliament appeared in the newspapers, e.g., *The London Courant, and Westminster Chronicle*, on Sept. 2. After arriving in England Petrie made his way to Crickdale, Wilts., where with John Wilkes's support he had stood for Parliament in 1775. On Sept. 11, he polled only eleven votes: Namier and Brooke, *House of Commons*, I, 409; John Cannon, "Samuel Petrie and the Borough of Crickdale," *Wilts. Archaeol. and Natural History Mag.*, LVI (1955–56), 371–87.

3. His opponents were John MacPherson, a wealthy Indian administrator, and Paul Benfield, who had amassed a large fortune in India: Namier and Brooke, *House of Commons*, II, 81–2; III, 96–7.

4. Petrie challenged the results of the election by presenting a petition to the House of Commons and by commencing actions against Benfield and MacPherson for bribery: Cannon, "Petrie and the Borough of Crickdale," p. 376.

me here, longer than I proposed, but I Still hope to be able to Set out, long before the meeting of Parliament;[5] tho' its not impossible, but it may be necessary for me to be upon the Spot at that Time.

It was whisper'd me a Day or two ago, from an intelligent Quarter, that the Speech at the Opening of Parliament, will breathe the Spirit of Peace & Reconciliation. I Suspect much, if it Shou'd do So, that they will be found only in Words.

At present there is no public News here of any Kind. The Conversation in all Companies, is altogether confined to the different Elections. Royal Influence has driven Kepple from the Borough of Windsor, but there is no doubt of his Election for the County of Surry. Hartley has lost his Election for Hull, & I fancy will be out of Parliament. Burke is in the same Predicament for Bristol, but he will assuredly be brought in for some other Place, tho' he holds the Same Language in private, as he does in his public Address.[6]

I call'd on Woodmason,[7] who Says he waits to know the Quantity of Paper he is to send, & that he has wrote fully upon the Subject, but has hitherto received no Reply. Command me freely any where, & in any Thing, in which I can render the Smallest Service.

Remember me where you know I wish to be remember'd, & believe me always sincerely & faithfully Yrs.

Letters address'd for me, under Cover to James Chalmer Esqr., Leicester fields, London, will be deliver'd Safe.

Notation: B. Sept 22. 1780.

5. The opening day of the first session of the fifteenth Parliament was Oct. 31: Cobbett, *Parliamentary History,* XXI (1780–81), 768.

6. Adm. Augustus Keppel was defeated at New Windsor, Berks., but elected for the county of Surrey on Sept. 27. Hartley ran a poor third in the contest for Kingston-upon-Hull, losing to the long-time incumbent Robert Manners and the new young radical William Wilberforce (*DNB*). Edmund Burke, defeated at Bristol, was returned on Dec. 7 for Malton, Yorks., a borough that he previously had represented: Namier and Brooke, *House of Commons,* I, 210–11, 383–4, 434–5, 436; II, 145–53, 592–3; III, 7–11.

7. James Woodmason. See his letter of Sept. 12, above, and BF's reply of Sept. 26, below.

From John Thaxter, Jr.[8]

AL: American Philosophical Society

Friday Septr. 22d. 1780

Mr. Thaxter presents his respects to his Excellency Doctor Franklin, and will do himself the Honor of dining with his Excellency on Sunday next.[9]

Addressed: A Son Excellence / Monsieur Franklin, / Ministre Plenipotentiaire / des Etats Unis de l'Amérique, / en son hôtel. / à Passi

Notation: Thaxter Mr. Paris Sept. 22. 1780

To Juvel Neveux & Cauchoit

L (draft):[1] American Philosophical Society

Passy le 23 sept. 1780

M. Franklin a reçu la Lettre que Messrs. Juvel neveux et Cauchoit lui ont fait l'honneur de lui ecrire hier.

Toute Lettre de Change tirée sur M. Franklin, doit lui etre presentée pour l'Acceptation à son Domicile à Passy. Et toutes celles qui ont passé par cette formalité sont payées à leurs Echéances chez M. Grand, Banquier Rue Montmartre, vis à vis St Joseph—[2] à Paris.[3]

8. Thaxter, left behind when JA went to the Netherlands, described himself on Sept. 19 to his cousin Abigail Adams as "a miserable, solitary lonely Being": *Adams Correspondence,* III, 418. His isolation would soon end. On Sept. 23 JA, learning that he was authorized to remain in the Netherlands, summoned Thaxter, probably to help care for his sons John Quincy and Charles: *ibid,* III, 417n, 423–4.

9. Jeremiah Allen, who had traveled to France with the Adams party (XXX, 536n), also wrote BF on Sept. 22 that he would dine with him "on Sunday next." APS.

1. Drafted by WTF, with minor corrections written in red ink in another hand.

2. The cemetery which served the parish of Saint Eustache was called St. Joseph. It housed the sepulcher of Molière: Hillairet, *Rues de Paris,* II, 154.

3. Juvel neveux & Cauchoit wrote again on Sept. 27, enclosing their bill of exchange. WTF noted on that letter that the bill was returned, accepted. APS.

321

From J.F. Frin & Co.

LS: American Philosophical Society

Monsieur   Paris 23. 7bre. 1780

Nous avons l'honneur de vous remettre cijoint d'une part 34 effets du Congrès passès a notre ordre montant ensemble à Drs. [Dollars] 1578.

D'autre part 4 autres Semblables effets ensemble Drs. 1500 que nous vous prions d'accepter et de nous renvoyer ensuite. Nous prenons le parti de vous les remettre directement parceque nos amis d'hollande Mrs. D. Crommelin & Fs.[4] en nous les envoyant nous ont fait l'observation suivante que nous croyons devoir vous participer; la Voici:

"Nous avons à vous Faire observer à l'egard des deux Effets No. 228 pour 120 Dollars No. 641 pour autres 120 Dollars que notre ami nous marque qu'il avoit envoyé la troisieme de la pre. [première] & la premiere de la 2eme. endossées en blanc par un navire qui a eu le malheur d'etre pris et qu'il craint qu'on n'en fait un mauvais usage pour quoi il Sera à propos d'en prévenir M Le Docteur Franklin."

Nous avons l'honneur d'etre avec respect Monsieur Vos très humbles et obeissant Serviteurs   J. F. FRIN ET COMP.

M le Docteur Franklin à Passy.

Notations in different hands: j. f. Frin et Cie. Paris 23. 7bre. 1780. /23d / Ansd 10 Oct. 1780[5]

From John Paul Jones

ALS: American Philosophical Society; AL (draft): Library of Congress

Honored and dear Sir   Ariel, at Sea Septr. 23d. 1780

I duely received your Excellencies Letter, Orders, and Publick dispatches by Count De Vauban.[6] I received also the Letter

---

4. Daniel Crommelin & fils was the Amsterdam correspondent of J.F. Frin & Co.: XXXI, 269n.

5. The latter notation is in the hand of WTF. We have not located the answer of Oct. 10.

6. BF had been told Vauban would soon return to the *Ariel* and apparently used the opportunity to send dispatches: Jones to BF, Aug. 7.

you did me the honor to write me the 21st. Ult. containing a list of Men who had Served in the Privateer Madame &c.; Upon receipt of which, I immediately made a proper inquiry, and found that my Officer had really followed my Orders at St. Malo. He (Mr. Wheeler the Gunner)[7] took with him Letters from Gourlade and Moylan to the American Agent as well as from M. De La Grandville the King's Commissary at L'Orient to his relation the King's Commissary at St. Malo;[8] in Order to procure him the necessary facility in Enlisting and conducting to L'Orient some foreign Seamen who might be found at St. Malo free from Engagement.— These Men mentioned in the Within List[9] were found free from the Madame and actually on Board an Armed Vessel belonging to the King and destined for Brest. From that Situation they were given up to Mr. Wheeler *by the Kings Commissary* at St. Malo; and Mr. Wheeler brought no other Men from thence. I know not what became of the remainder of the list you sent me, as I never received any of them.—I should have given you an immediate Account of this; but the Captain and Owners of the privateer immediately after, sent two Gentlemen to me to examine the Crew— I went with them on Board and had them brought before them; they were at once undeceived with respect to the Number, but seemed to wish to take them back. I told them that though I had received the Men from legal Authority and with their own consent, yet I would give them Up on being reimbursed for what they had Coast the United States in Advance, Charges, and Victuals, which was but reasonable as the States had then received no benefit from their Service. They seemed to think my Offer frank and liberal, and went away so well Satisfied to all Appearance, that I conclude the

7. Wheeler had been sent to find thirty or forty American seamen: Jones to BF, July 12, above.

8. Frédéric-Joseph-Adrien Guillot (1736–1813) was *commissaire général* at St. Malo: Didier Neuville, ed., *Etat sommaire des Archives de la Marine antérieures à la Révolution* (Paris, 1898), pp. 142–3n.

9. Jones's list (Bradford, *Jones Papers*, reel 6, no. 1227, enclosure) gives the names of sixteen crewmen from St. Malo, four of whom had deserted. Among BF's papers at the University of Pa. Library are a Sept. 23 list signed by Jones of all the crewmen of the *Ariel*, an undated crew list including the prospective passengers for the ship and volunteers, and an undated list in French of the volunteers aboard.

foolish Claim of the Captain of the privateer and his Owners must have been given up. I have been Wind bound ever Since— and in the Road of Groix since the 4th.—[1] With respect to the Expence of the Ariel— It is certain that had circumstances been foreseen I should not have been for asking her from Government.— When I made the Application I had 400 Men in the Alliance Eating and Drinking at the publick expence. Besides the Ship being Copper Bottomed could have been prepared for Sea along Side of the Alliance in a Week, which would not have been the Case had I asked for a larger Ship.— Upon the whole I have Acted for the Best from the Beginning. I have done with Chaumont.— I had born his base conduct too long; but have now sent such proofs to Versailles as will I hope prevent his doing farther Publick Mischief.—[2] The Monies you entrusted to my distribution were applied agreeable to your Orders.— I shall be very happy if I am sometimes honored with a Letter from you. No Man loves, and esteems, and Venerates you with a more honest and grateful Heart than Honored and dear Sir Your Excellencies Most Obliged Most Obedient and most humble Servant

JNO P JONES

His Excellency Benjamin Franklin Esqr. &c. &c. &c.

Notation: Capt. Jones Sept. 23 1780

From Sartine

Copy: Library of Congress

Versailles le 23. Sept. 1780.

L'Intendant de la Marine à Brest,[3] Monsieur, m'a prévenu qu'il avoit fait avancer par le Trésorier de ce port à Mr. James Searle, Colonel au Service du Congrès arrivé depuis peu sur un Bâtiment Americain, une Somme de 2,400 *l.t.* dont cet Officier avoit besoin pour se rendre à Paris. Je vous serai tres obligé des soins

1. The *Ariel* was wind-bound in the roadstead for more than a month: Morison, *Jones,* p. 304.

2. He enclosed his "proofs" (now missing) in a Sept. 21 letter to Genet, the head of the bureau of interpreters for both the naval and foreign ministries: Bradford, *Jones Papers,* reel 6, no. 1216.

3. Arnauld de La Porte.

que vous voudrez bien vous donner pour que cette somme Soit remise à M. de Ste. James General de la Marine à Paris[4] qui est porteur de la Reconnoissance de M. Searle.

J'ai l'honneur d'etre avec une tres parfaite consideration, Monsieur, Votre tres humble et tres obeissant Serviteur.

(signé) DE SARTINE.

M Franklin

From George Scott

ALS: American Philosophical Society

Honourable Sir — Naples the 23d Sepr. 1780

I confirm the contents of my two letters which I had the pleasure to write you from hence on the 13th. & 17th. May last,[5] to which I hope you paid the necessary attention. By the last post I received a letter from our very worthy friend Dr. P—— who desires me, in case I shall return thro' Paris, to communicate to you certain events respecting his parting from Ld. Shelburne, & his present sittuation; but as I think of going home by Sea, I shall not have the pleasure to pay my personal respects to you, & therefore, I have resolved to send you an exact copy of his letter here enclosed.[6] I have engaged a passage in a Dutch Ship for Leghorn, & the Captain says he will sail tomorrow. I am with a lively esteem Honbl. Sir Your very Obedt Servt — GEO: SCOTT

I have been rather disappointed in not having the pleasure of a

---

4. In 1780 Claude Baudard de Saint James (1738–1787) was *trésorier général de la marine et des colonies*: J.F. Bosher, *French Finances 1770–1795: From Business to Bureaucracy* (Cambridge, Eng., 1970), pp. 185–6, 320; Henri Legohérel, *Les Trésoriers généraux de la marine (1517–1788)* (Paris, 1963), pp. 325, 331–3.

5. XXXII, 383–5, 384n. The present letter is the last extant one from Scott.

6. Scott apparently enclosed a copy of a letter from Joseph Priestley dated Sept. 1. Priestley reported that he had been ill of a bilious disorder for nearly six months and hence almost incapable of writing and that he was going to live in Birmingham on the £150 per annum allowed him by Lord Shelburne (XXXI, 456n). Some friends talked of supporting him so he could pursue his experiments; otherwise he planned to take in boarders. He asked Scott to convey his respects to BF and acquaint him with the change in his situation. APS.

few Lines from you to meet me here, however a line or two ad-dres[sed: *torn*] Crommelins in Amst[erdam: *torn*]

Addressed: The Honourable / Benjn. Franklin Esqr. / Passy

Notation: George Scott. Naples Sept 23. 1780

To Benjamin Franklin Bache

Copy: Mrs. Carl H. Ernlund (Cambridge, Massachusetts, 1958)

Passy, Sept. 25. 1780

I received a Letter the other day from my dear Boy, without Date.[7] It always gives me Pleasure to hear from you, to be in-form'd of your Welfare, and that you mind your Learning. It is now the Season for you to acquire that, at the Expence of your Friends, which may be of Use to you when they are dead and gone, and qualify you to fill some Station in Life, that will afford you a decent Subsistance. You see every where two Sorts of Peo-ple. One who are well dress'd, live comfortably in Good Houses, whose Conversation is sensible and instructive, and who are Re-spected for their Virtue. The other Sort are poor, and dirty, and ragged and ignorant, and vicious, & live in miserable Cabbins or Garrets, on Coarse Provisions, which they must work hard to obtain, or which if they are idle, they must go without or Starve. The first had a good Education given them by their Friends, and they took pains when at School to improve their Time and in-crease their Knowledge; The others either had no Friend to pay for their Schooling, and so never were taught; or else when they were at School, they Neglected their Studies, were idle, and wicked, and disobedient to their Masters, and would not be in-structed; and now they Suffer. Take care therefore, my dear Child, to make a good Use of every moment of the present Op-portunity that is afforded You; and bring away with you from Geneva such a Stock of Good Learning & Good Morals, as may recommend you to your Friends and Country when you return home, make glad the Hearts of your Father and Mother, and be

7. From BFB, *c.* Sept. 15, above.

326

a Credit to the Place where you receiv'd your Education, and to the Masters who have been so good as to take the pains of Instructing You.

Mr. Adams is gone to Holland, and has taken his Sons with him. Your friend Cochran is still at the Old Pension,[8] but I believe would be glad to be with you. I inclose a Letter from him to you.

I lately received a Letter from your Father which contains some of the latest News from Philadelphia, and inclos'd a Letter to you from your dear Mother, I send them both to you.[9] Write a Letter to each of them. I shall have an Opportunity in about three Weeks of sending Letters, and will take care to forward yours, if I have them in time.

Present my best Respects to Madame Cramer, & to M. Marignac, and to Mr Grands Sister, whose Name I do not at present recollect.[1] Let them know that I am very sensible of their Goodness to you, and that I hope to have an Opportunity of thanking them in person.

I am ever, my dear Child, Your affectionate Grandfather

B FRANKLIN

B F Bache

From Jean de Neufville & fils

ALS: American Philosophical Society

Honourd Sir.   Amsterdam the 25th. sept: 1780.

May it please your Excellency, That as some new draufts have apeared lately on Mr Laurence, we have continued to give our Acceptance to the Same as usuall; we specifie them in the List here inclosed; for which we begg for your Excellencys approbation; and to lett us know in time if there might become any alteration in her dispositions on the Subject.

8. BFB had attended the Pension Le Coeur in Passy with Charles Cochran and John Quincy Adams: XXV, 91–2, 646; XXVIII, 326n.

9. In his letter to RB and SB of Oct. 4, below, BF mentions having received several of theirs.

1. Agathe Silvestre Arthaud, sister of Mme Ferdinand Grand: XXX, 587n.

Further as the payments to be made are not of a Sufficient importance, we have thought not to divide them, butt to draw on Your Excellency the 1t. October at 3 Months what will be due in the Month of december And so Consecutively every month, in which we shall with pleasure Conform our selfs to what she may be pleased to prescribe, of all which we shall have the honour to give due notice, and as we have taken out our List we begg leave to observe that fr. what is due in in Xber [December] is f12366—to be drawn the ft. Octr.

in January 8800: . . .   the first 9ber
in February 11272 . .   the first Xber

In Case your Excellency might wish to know some more particulars, we will take care to provide for them.

We have received Remittes fr. Dollars 486 making £ 2430— from John Leverer passenger on a Vessell to our Consignment which we suppose to be lost, we wish'd now She was taken for the Souls on board, butt we have not heard anything about her; we have taken the Liberty to endorse them to our Banker with the endorsement under Guarantie; and we hope this may be sufficient for their paÿment. We languish very much here for Accounts from America and the Continent, we wish they may be favourable, as we may flatter ourselfs from every generall good Account we have from there. We have the honour to be with all devoted Regard and Esteem Honourd Sir Your Excellencys most obedient and most humble Servants

JOHN DE NEUFVILLE & SON

Notation in Franklin's hand:

```
    12366
     8800
    11272
florins 32438
```

To Sartine

Copy: Library of Congress

Sir,   Passy, Sept. 26. 1780.

As soon as I received the Letter your Excellency did me the honour of Writing to me relative to the Exchange of Capt. John

Bell & his Son, I wrote to the Owner of the Black Prince to know if they were not Hostages for the Ransom of their Vessel.[2] I have now received an Answer, that they are not Ransomers, but merely Prisoners, their Brigantine Hopewell having been taken by the Black Prince and afterwards retaken by the Enemy.[3] There is therefore no Objection to their being exchanged for Americans by the first Opportunity.— With great Respect I am, Sir, &c.

M. De Sartine

To [Vergennes][4]

Copy:[5] Archives du Ministère des affaires étrangères; copy: Library of Congress

à Passy ce 26 sept. 1780

N'ayant aucun moyen de Satisfaire aux payemens de Sommes aussi considerables & ne pouvant Supporter l'Idée de perdre le reste de Confiance que nous avons acquis en Europe par un retour à protest qui apprêteroit à rire aux Anglois à nos dépens en leur fournissant les moyens d'ajouter des realites aux fictions qu'ils ne cessent de répandre partout.

Le Poids de la Guerre ne permettant pas au Gouvernement de diviser ses Moyens pour la pousser avec vigueur je lui ai proposé un expédient qui peut nous Secourir Sans lui étre à charge c'est à dire que je M'engagerois envers lui que le Congrès fourniroit par lui même, ou par les Agents françois à ses Fraix les Vivres nécessaires aux Troupes de France en Amerique jusqu'à la Con-

2. Sartine to BF, Aug. 5, above; BF to Torris, Aug. 7, above.
3. Torris to BF, Aug. 11, above. On Sept. 20 William Hodgson had written BF, above, to ask their exchange, but we do not know if BF had received it yet.
4. The copy made by L'Air de Lamotte (Library of Congress) gives Vergennes as the recipient.
5. We presume this copy, in a hand we do not recognize, was made from the recipient's copy. Although it bears a "B Franklin" signature, it appears to be an imitation. We doubt that it is a translation of a now-missing English version, as L'Air de Lamotte's copy is also in French.

currence de nos besoins, Suivant l'Etat ci joint,[6] & pour le payement desquels il fournira ici les Sommes nécessaires aux Epoques fixées.

Tout ce que le Congrès fourniroit au dela Seroit remboursé ici & employé à lui faire passer les Articles d'Europe qui lui Seroit Nécessaires, on éviteroit par là tous les fraix, les inconvéniens, les longueurs, & les risques qui resultent nécessairement d'une aussi grande distance.   B FRANKLIN

Notation: 1780. Septembre 26

To James Woodmason   Copy: Library of Congress

Sir,   Passy, Sept. 26. 1780.

I have just received yours of the 12th. Instant. Inclosed I send you a Bill for twenty five Pounds Sterling, which will more than pay for the Machines, Cases, three Reams of the Paper & 1 Doz. of Inkpowder.[7] You will account to me for the overplus if any,

6. A copy in WTF's hand is at the AAE and one in L'Air de Lamotte's is at the Library of Congress. This financial statement differs considerably from the one BF enclosed with his letter to Vergennes of the 20th, above. WTF estimates that 5,176,000 *l.t.* will be needed by the end of 1781 and breaks the request into five periods of three months each: (1) for the remainder of the present year, 1,024,000 *l.t.* (500,000 for loan office certificates, 300,000 for purchases at Nantes, 200,000 to lease and arm the *Marquis de la Fayette*, 24,000 or £1,000 sterling for congressional requirements); (2) for the first three months of 1781, a million *l.t.* (800,000 for loan office certificates, 25,000 for congressional obligations, 24,000 for Laurens, 26,000 for current expenses); (3) 1,080,000 *l.t.* for April, May and June (800,000 for loan office certificates, 144,000 for Beaumarchais, 100,000 for cloth, 36,000 for current expenses); (4) 934,000 *l.t.* for July, August, and September (800,000 for loan office certificates, 100,000 for cloth, 34,000 for current expenses;) (5) 1,138,000 *l.t.* for October, November, and December (900,000 for loan office certificates, 200,000 for cloth, 38,000 for current expenses). L'Air de la Motte's calculations for the first quarter of 1781 differ (700,000 for loan office certificates, 250,000 for congressional expenses, *viz.*, $50,000 at 5:1); since these figures do add up to 1,000,000 *l.t.* we suspect it was WTF who copied them incorrectly.

7. BF wrote, on the address sheet of a letter from Dumas of Sept. 17, above, an accounting of how much the three machines and other supplies would cost. The total came to £23.8.0. Account VI (XXIII, 21) lists Grand's payment to Woodmason on Sept. 22 of 610 *l.t.*, 3 *s.*, 6 *d.*

after paying the Freight & Charges; for having no one in London to receive them. I must request you to take the Trouble of Shipping them in the Packet Boat that goes to Ostend, address'd to M. Francis Bowens Merchant, there. who will forward them to me. It was not my Intention to desire Credit. I approve much of the Resolution of Messrs. Bolton & Watt to give none: And I wish all the World would follow their Exemple, for I think Credit is upon the Whole, of more Mischief than Benefit to Mankind.— I am, Sir &c.

P.S. Please to send an Account which I may Show to the other Subscribers.

M. Woodmason.

From Joseph Caillot[8]

AL: American Philosophical Society

ce 26 7bre 80

Le Pere Caillot assure Monsieur franklin de Son Respect et de sa Reconnoissance; il ne peut pas Lui promettre D'aller le voir diner vendredy prochain a cause de versailles, Si caillot est libre il aura le plaisir de jouir du bon appeti de monsieur franklin. La petite Mere[9] et son Enfant lui disent mille choses; toutes deux se portent a merveille.

Addressed: A Monsieur / Monsieur franklin / Pere / A Passy

8. The actor (1733–1816), who at this time was BF's neighbor at Passy: XXVIII, 215n, 316. Retired from the Théâtre des Italiens in 1772, he continued to act and coach others in performances at court. In August he had helped the Queen and the comte d'Artois perform in several plays at the Petit Trianon: *DBF;* Maurice Tourneux, ed., *Correspondance littéraire, philosophique et critique par Grimm, Diderot, Raynal, Meister, etc.* (16 vols., Paris, 1877–82), XII, 427–8; Bachaumont, *Mémoires secrets,* XV, 303; François-Joseph Fétis, comp., *Biographie universelle des musiciens et bibliographie générale de la musique* (2nd ed., 8 vols., Paris, 1875–89).
9. The nickname given Blanchette, his wife (XXVIII, 215–16n).

From Thomas Digges

ALS: Historical Society of Pennsylvania

Dr. Sir   London 26. Sept 1780

My friend Mr Bromfield can best explain to You the business He is going upon as well as give you every accot. of the proceedings relative to the Brigantine Temple (the Cartel) in which He came from Boston. As I forwarded five Seamen from among our frds. to that vessel this day, I hope it will not be many days before She sails. There being nine Seamen, taken in a Ship of Ridleys bound from Baltime to Holland[1] now on board the Tender at the Tower for after commitment to Forton, I got Mr Temple to Petition the admiralty that these men be allowd to navigate the Cartel away; for every favour has been shewn towards the getting the vessel away but allowing Her American Seamen to navigate Her back. I am to have an ansr. tomorrow & from appearances hitherto I have reason to expect it will be granted, as there is not the old stale plea that americans Committed for Treason cannot be releasd from Prison without tryal or pardon.

I begin now to expect Mr Saml H——ys return hither. I should be glad to get by Him your passport for Mr Jno Bowmans baggage to Carolina, & to hear if the Picture sent by Miss Georgiana got safe, for she has once or twice applyd to me with anxiety about it.[2] Mr Bowens some time ago recd it & wrote me it should be soon forwarded by a safe conveyance. I should be also glad to hear of the safe arrival of that from Amsterdam left by Mr Champion.

I mentiond in my late letter to you,[3] an appearance here that the Cabinet had seemingly abandond the American war; for several days past the reports & conversations among a certain description of men seem to give weight to this opinion—most likely it is necessity & not the will that assents to the adoption of

1. Charles Henry Lincoln, comp., *Naval Records of the American Revolution 1775–1788* (Washington, D.C., 1906), pp. 315, 329, 339, 398, 402, 476, lists seven ships of which Matthew Ridley was owner or co-owner in 1779 or 1780.

2. Samuel Hartley and his wife, who had come to Paris in August, were still there in early October: Digges to BF, Aug. 18, and the Hartleys and Mr. Batley to BF, Oct. 4. For Georgiana Shipley's portrait see Digges's letters of July 12 and Sept. 18.

3. Of Sept. 20, above.

such a measure. The affairs at Home & in all the Dependencies of Britain were such a gloomy aspect as might frighten bolder men than those who compose the British Council.

Some flying reports from Portugal frighten them a little. A few days ago a privateer wch. had touchd at the Entrance of the Tagus brought accots to England that an Embargo had been laid on all English ships at Lisbon & the report of the day is, that a French fleet has enterd the Tagus to demand of Portugal an acquiescence to the neutral Confederacy or declare which side they will take in the war. The more thinking part of this metropolis say that England ought to trust as little as possible to the fidelity & firmness of a power situated as Portugal is, subject to the immedeate controul & even compulsion of arbitrary, powerful, & daring Enemys—most likely the accot may be premature, yet there may be some foundation for it from the Complexion of things between Spain & portugal.[4]

Every day produces some new instance of the wretched state both of the English army & navy in the Wt Indies. Rodnys fleet seem fixd to the harbours of St. Christophers *inactive* till the herricane months drive Him away or until some succour is sent from hence.[5] Eight ships of the Line are preparing with all Expedition to go thither. This fleet is orderd out in consequence of ministry having recd advice that a like number was dispatchd about five weeks ago from France to martinico.[6]

The Virginia frigate[7] is arrivd express from N York, but as the

4. Digges was right to be skeptical about the rumors. In 1777 Spain and Portugal had engaged in hostilities about the borders of their South American possessions but relations had improved and Portugal continued to play no direct role in the War for American Independence.

5. On Sept. 14 Rodney arrived at New York with a part of his fleet and claimed the right to exercise naval command there: N.A.M. Rodger, *The Insatiable Earl: a Life of John Montagu, Fourth Earl of Sandwich 1718–1792* (New York and London, 1994), pp. 284–7.

6. The government planned to send Rodney ten ships of the line from England and five from North America as replacements for the ships in the worst condition in his fleet; Rear Adm. Samuel Hood (*DNB*), commanding the contingent from England, did not sail until late November, however: Mackesy, *War for America*, pp. 375–7. Not only had the French not sent reinforcements for Martinique, but most of Guichen's fleet was en route to Cadiz, where it arrived on Oct. 22: Dull, *French Navy*, p. 189.

7. H.M.S. *Virginia*, formerly of the American Navy.

Bearer will not deliver this letter for many days to come & long after your getting more authentic accots of the news she brings, I need not mention particulars here—indeed we have nothing as yet but reports, & these are all spoken of as unfavorable to England. Every Countenance speak them *bad.*

I am with very great respect Your Ob Ser   T D

Notation: Sept. 26. 1780

From Dumas

             ALS: American Philosophical Society

Monsieur,   La Haie 26e. 7bre. 1780

Le Roi de Suede arrivera, dit-on, ce soir. Ce qui est sûr, c'est que *Notre Ami* arrivera, & que j'espere de le voir ce soir. Il ne pourra pas me dire grand'chose: car on continue de rester ici dans la plus profonde apathie. Rien n'étoit mieux calculé par les Anglomanes, que le voyage des Plenipes. à Pétersbourg. En attendant, le Lion Belgique dort à son aise.

La Gazette ci-jointe[8] vous fera voir que les amis de l'Amérique ne dorment pas, & qu'au moins ils font ce qu'ils peuvent, & pelotent, en attendant partie. Vous en direz autant du Mémoire, dont voici copie, que je remettrai demain aux Ministres de Suede & de Russie.[9] D'accord. Mais cela vaut mieux encore que rien du tout, en attendant que le vent vous amene quelque grande nouvelle, & que vous ayiez la bonté de me la faire parvenir d'abord, afin que je puisse l'apprendre le premier à ces Messieurs, au gd. Facteur au Gd. Pe. [Pensionnaire] & à notre Ami.

Il y a un Grand dans cette rep., que je vois quelquefois, qui

8. Dumas enclosed the first half of the Sept. 26 issue of the *Gaʒ. de Leyde*, presumably because it included a lengthy article carrying the dateline of Philadelphia, July 15, in praise of the American war effort.

9. The two-page memoir for the Russian and Swedish ministers gave a brief history of the English Navigation Acts and described the economy and exports of the U.S. The Russian minister was Prince Golitsyn, and the Swedish envoy was the newly arrived Baron Gustaf Johan von Ehrensvärd (1746–1783) for whom see the *Repertorium der diplomatischen Vertreter*, III, 412, and the *Svenska Män och Kvinnor: Biografisk Uppslagsbok* (8 vols., Stockholm, 1942–55), II, 332.

m'a dit en confidence, que dès que l'Amérique sera reconnue par cette rep., il briguera pour y être envoyé comme Ambr.

S'il se passe quelque chose d'intéressant à l'Assemblée d'Hollde., qui commencera demain, je ne manquerai pas de vous en rendre compte. Je suis toujours, Monsieur, avec le plus respectueux attachement Votre très-humble & très obeissant serviteur DUMAS

Passy à S.E. Mr. B. Franklin

Addressed: à Son Excellence / Monsieur B. Franklin / Mine. Plénipe. des Et. Un. / &c. / Passy./.

Notation: Dumas la haie Sept. 26. 80

From Jonathan Williams, Jr.

ALS: University of Pennsylvania Library; copy: Yale University Library

Dear & hond Sir   Nantes Sept. 26. 1780

I have received your kind Favour of the 18 Instant. You may depend that not a Moments Time shall be lost in sending all the Goods to L'orient; the Cloathing that I made up is already there & the Goods you took of M de Chaumont will be on the Road as soon as I can find Roulliers[1] sufficient which I hope will be in a few Days. The moment I hear of the Ships arrival at L'orient I shall set out to meet her there, and I will not ask ten Days to load her so that if there is no Delay elsewhere she will be quickly dispatched. I have written to Messrs De Segray & Co. at St Malo & have requested them to send off the Salt Petre with all possible Expedition, as it will be necessary to put it in the Bottom of the Ship for Ballast, it would not do to send it by Water, because of the uncertainty of its arriving in Time, even if there was no Risque in the Question. As I thought it necessary to put the Salt Petre in motion as soon as possible I have ventured to give absolute Directions to Mr De Segray & assured him that by the next Courier after you should receive this Letter he would receive from you a Confirmation of my Orders. Please therefore

1. Wagoners.

to write accordingly & tell him to send by Land to Gourlade & Moylan subject to my Disposal. I have also notified Mr Schweighauser to send all the Arms round, & as this is a heavy Article of inconsiderable value, & as the risque from this to L'Orient is not great, I have advised Mr Schweighauser to freight a Chassemarée & send them round by Water.

I have no power to dispose of Mr Hutchins' Charts, I sent them by his Order to Messrs Puech & Co *Rue Montorguil au coin de celle du bout du monde,* for Sale.[2] I told Mr Le Rouge, when I was last in Paris, to apply to these People & if they think proper they may employ him in the Sale, but I can give no Orders about the matter.

Mrs Williams and Chrystie[3] are both well & desire their affectionate Respects to you.

I am as ever Dear & hond Sir most affectionately & dutifully Yours   JONA WILLIAMS J

I inclose a Copy of the agreement with Mr de Chaumont about the Ship.[4] I wrote to Billy last Post about M Rasquins complaint which I hope is satisfactory to you.[5]

Notation: J Williams Sept 26. 1780

2. See jw's letter of Aug. 3.

3. Christine was Mariamne Williams' sister.

4. One of the three originals of this freight contract, dated Aug. 30, 1780, in French, and signed by both Chaumont and jw, is at the APS. In it, Chaumont agrees to charter the *Marquis de Lafayette,* formerly the *Breton,* to jw, acting on behalf of the Congress of the United States. The total amount, calculated at 200 *l.t.* per ton, would be set in advance, payable on bills charged to BF. The vessel would be ready to load in Bordeaux at the end of September or the beginning of October. It would then proceed to Lorient to take on the remainder of whatever cargo jw had prepared, and sail directly for America. Chaumont would bear the risks on the vessel, and jw the risks on the cargo.

5. WTF had forwarded Rasquin's letter to jw on Sept. 14, and jw answered on the 23rd: he returns the letter without any defense other than to enclose copies of six letters he had written, at various times, to Rasquin. "His protector Mr Mercier lost his cause with me, & I hope I never shall lose a cause with any Chicaneur." He apologizes for the trouble this is causing BF. Hist. Soc. of Pa. BF forwarded these letters to Vergennes in November, after Rasquin appealed directly to the government: BF to Vergennes, Nov. 24 (AAE). He had sent BF a second, angry letter on Oct. 30, this time threatening to sue jw (APS), which apparently BF ignored.

To Jonathan Williams, Jr.   Copy: Library of Congress

Dear Jonathan,   Passy, Sept. 27. 1780.

I have mislaid your Account of the Drafts you had made on M. De Chaumont, and want it much. Send me by the Return of the Post, either a Copy or an Abstract of it, expressing the Gross Sum & times of Payment. As soon as the Acct. is compleated I should be glad to have it.

I received yours of Augt. 26 & Sept. 14.— I approve of your Proposition about the Sailors, and will endeavour to do what you propose. I have spoken to the farmers Generals, and am promised a Passport in 2 or 3. Days for the Saltpetre, to transport it from St. Malo's to L'Orient, by Land or Sea.—[6] Mr. Ross has Shipt his Goods at l'Orient, at least 123 Bales.

Capt. Samson is returned to Nantes, Messrs. Adams, Dana, & Austin to whom he was recommended being all in Holland. He brought a little Box for me, to Nantes, but forgot it when he came up to Paris. Be so good as to take care of it, and send it to me when you have a convenient Opportunity.

His Portuguese Prize having nothing on Board that appears to be English Property, besides the Salt, must be after delivering up the Vessel & paying all Damages; an affair of no Profit. It will rather prove an Irish Prize in the sense of him who said he had *got a Loss.*

If Mr. Jay Accepts the Bills you mention; there is no doubt but, he will pay them. Love to your Family, and believe me ever. Your Affectionate Uncle.

M. Williams.

6. BF's contact in the *ferme* was Lavoisier; see BF to Lavoisier, Oct. 22. For Lavoisier's part in helping to get the saltpetre transported see Claude A. Lopez, "Saltpetre, Tin and Gunpowder: Addenda to the Correspondence of Lavoisier and Franklin," *Annals of Science*, XVI (1960), 83–94; Lopez, *Lafayette*, pp. 205–6.

From Thomas Collins[7]

ALS: American Philosophical Society

Sir　　　　　　　　　　　　Hotel De York 28 Septr 1780

I am fearfull, that my very honorable Friend, Sir Edward Newenham Inserted my Sons name, in place of mine, (thro' mistake,) therefore hope, you will be so kind as to forgive my acquainting you therewith; I have the honor of being with the greatest respect Sir Your most Obedient and most Humble servant[8]

THOMS COLLINS

Notation: Thom. Collin 28. 7bre. 1780

From Pierre Turini

ALS: American Philosophical Society

Monsieur　　　　　　　　　　Venise 28 Septbre 1780.

Il y a longtems Monsr. que la renommée la plus eclatante à fait retentir votre nom dans toutes les parties du Monde. L'Europe éntiere vous admire, et persone n'est plus vivement penetré, que moi de L'estime, et de la Veneration, qui vous sont dues à tant de titres. Vos Ouvrages, que j'ai devoré avec la plus grande avidité, et dont j'ai tiré les plus utiles instructions, m'ont fait comprendre l'immense etendue des vos rares connoissances, et des vos talens.

7. Newenham apparently had mistaken the first name; see his letter of introduction for John Collins, Sept. 9. See also BF to Sartine, Oct. 4, and Sartine to BF, Oct. 7.

8. Collins on Sept. 30 signed three documents pertaining to his proposed emigration from Ireland. One is an oath (in WTF's hand and signed by BF) that renounces allegiance to George III and promises to "support maintain & defend" the U.S. against him. The other two (in L'Air de Lamotte's hand with insertions by WTF and signed by both of them) are bonds in the amount of $2,000 for each of two ships, the brig *Lord Charlemont*, 100 tons, and the *Newenham*, 60 tons. A fourth document is a passport (undated, and in WTF's hand) for some natives of Ireland who have expressed a desire to settle in the U.S. They are traveling on the *Newenham*, bound from Dublin with a cargo of salt, silk, haberdashery, coarse linens, and woolens. A blank, not filled in, is provided for the names of the proposed settlers. A separate piece of paper, in WTF's hand, gives the weight, cargo, and number of travelers for each vessel (three on the *Newenham* and five on the *Lord Charlemont*). All of these documents are at the APS.

338

La Theorie de l'Electricité fixà d'abord, et fixerà toujours L'attention humaine. Une decouverte aussi interessante, reservèe à la Sublimité de votre Genie, devoit necessairement entrainer une diference sensible dans l'Explication des principaux Phenomenes de la nature, et des plusieurs de ses loix. En effet l'on explique à L'aide du feu electrique la plupart des Phenomenes Aeriens, et Terrestres, avec une facilitè, et une precision convainquante.

La salutaire Theorie des Conducteurs, fruit, tres important des vos applications, fait tous les jours des nouveaux progrès: l'unanime consentement des hommes prouve la verité du systeme, et sa pratique universellement adoptée montre combien on est generalement persuadé des avantages qui en resultent.

La methode, dont L'on s'est servi, jusqu'à present dans Chaque partie de la Terre, pour eriger des Conducteurs sur les Edifices est essentiellement la meme, et s'il-y-a quelque diference elle consiste dans quelques Scrupules, et attentions de plus ou de moins, qui dependent bien souvent de L'idée de ceux, qui sont chargès de leur erection: neammoins il faut avouer, que cette methode á des defauts essentiels, qui peuvent tot, ou tard causer des ruines irreparables: les Magazins à Poudre restent sourtout exposés aux insultes terribles de la Foudre, et il faut en redouter les funestes consequences.

Vous trouverez Mr. dans le petit ouvrage cÿ joint, que j'ai L'honneur de vous adresser[9] l'exposition des raisons, qui m'ont convaincú de L'insufisance des preservatifs generalement adoptés: j'espere avoir trouvé le Moÿen de mettre entierement à l'Abri de la Foudre ces Edifices, qui sont les plus importants, et d'avoir generalement adopté plus de sureté aux autres. Les progrés de l'esprit humain sont bien rarement rapides, au contraire il s'avance peu a peu, et par degrés, et ils sont fort rares des Ge-

9. Pietro Turini, *Considerazioni intorno all'elettricità delle nubi, ed al modo di applicare i conduttori alle fabbriche, e di preservare dal fulmine i depositi della polvere* . . . (Venice, 1780). The title translates as: *Considerations on the Electricity of Clouds and on the Manner of Applying Conductors on Buildings and Protecting Powder Magazines from Lightning.* Turini mentioned BF in his introduction as a "rare and sublime genius." We have no record of BF's reply, but the book itself is now at the Hist. Soc. of Pa. See Antonio Pace, *Benjamin Franklin and Italy* (Philadelphia, 1958), pp. 27, 39, 122–3, 417.

nies, qui vous ressemblent, et qui puissent etendre leur vues aussi loin qu'elles peuvent aller, et fixer les veritables principes d'une importante Theorie, telle que celle, Monsieur, dont vous etes l'Auteur. Je n'ai fait, qu'appliquer precisement les regles les plus connués à la pratique la plus exacte: Ce seroit une temerité que de pretendre beaucoup apres vos immortelles decouvertes. Da lunge il seguo, e sue Vestigia adoro.

Je m'empresse de soumettre cet essai à vos lumieres, et je sérai bien flatté s'il pouvoit meriter votre approbation. Il est en Italien: J'ai dú ecrire pour Ma Nation. L'importance de la matiere m'a enhardi à prendre la libertè de vous l'envoÿer tel, qu'il se trouve. J'aurai du moins la satisfaction d'avoir saisi cette occasion de vous exprimer les sentimens de l'admiration, et du respect, avec lequel j'ai l'honneur d'etre, Monsieur Votre tres humble, et tres obeissant serviteur

> Pierre Turini
> Lieutenant des Ingenieurs. au Caffè
> de Florian, a la Place S. Marc.

Addressed: A Monsieur / Monsieur Benjamin Franklin. / Ministre des treize etats unis d'Amerique; / de la Societé Roÿale de Paris. / A Paris.

Endorsed: Lieut Pierre Turini

From Jonathan Williams, Jr.

ALS: University of Pennsylvania Library

Dear & hond sir.   Nantes 28 Sept. 1780

The Bearer is Mr George Moore son of Mr Phillip Moore in Philadelphia,[1] He has been near two Years under my direction in this Place but is now written for by his Grandfather in the Isle of Man who wishes to see him; His Intention is therefore to pay his Duty to his aged parent & probably will return to America. I beg

1. Phillip Moore was a Philadelphia merchant who owned many ships during the course of the Revolution, and who had had business dealings with JW for years: *PMHB*, XIX (1895), 400; LV (1931), 226–7; Charles Henry Lincoln, comp., *Naval Records of the American Revolution 1775–1788* (Washington, D.C., 1906), *passim;* JW Letterbooks, Yale University Library.

leave to introduce him to your Notice & to request you will favour him with a Passport to England, & such advice as he may stand in need of.—[2] I have sent two Copies of my Accots by Mr Moore, as I have sent both those you certified to America & mean to send a third I request you will please to certify these two Copies, I have desired Mr Moore to assist Billy in the Examination of them which will save him some Trouble.[3] With the greatest Respect I am ever most dutifully & affectionately Yours

JONA WILLIAMS J

Addressed: His Excelly / Doctor Franklin

Notation: J Williams 28 Sept 1780

From John Adams

ALS: American Philosophical Society

Sir   Amsterdam September 29. 1780

Mr Samuel Andrews, formely of Boston lately of Demarara, is going to Paris upon Business, respecting a Vessell taken by the French and carried into Martinico.[4]

He will lay before you his Papers, and hopes for your Countenance, in the Prosecution of his Appeal, altho he claims as a Dutchman. I have the Honour to recommend him to your Excellencys Notice.

I have written to Mr Thaxter to ask the Favour of you to take into your Custody my Books and Trunks of Cloaths.— I dont know but I asked too much; perhaps you may not have Room,

2. We have not located the passport, but on Dec. 3 JW wrote to Phillip Moore that George had reportedly arrived in England. Yale University Library.

3. JW also wrote to WTF on Sept. 28, explaining that while WTF had had the accounts copied, he had forgotten to get them examined and approved by BF. He should have BF certify and sign both sets in as many places as the arbitrators had signed them, and append a general certificate at the end. APS. For these accounts see XXXII, 480n.

4. Andrews was the captain of the *Sally,* owned by the Boston merchant Ellis Gray, which had been condemned by a court in Martinique; although the ship and cargo were registered as Dutch its crew was English: *Adams Correspondence,* III, 420; *Adams Papers,* X, 186n.

without Inconvenience.— If so, Mr Thaxter, will locke all up in Trunks and get, some store for them.

My Affairs will oblige me to stay here, if Mr Laurens dont Arrive: and if he does, it will be proper for me to stay untill I can communicate all that I know to him, at least.—

I have heard often mention of a Letter from your Excellency to the Grand Pensionary of Holland, near a Year ago.[5] It is much esteemed here—but I cant get a sight of it.— I should be glad to support the sentiments in it, as far as I have learned them, but could do it to better Purpose if I Could obtain a Copy, which if there is no material objection to I request of your Excellency.

What this Republick will do in the Northern Confederation is a Question that divides all Parties.— Neither Stadhouderians nor Republicans. Neither Anglomanes nor Francomanes are agreed. Time will shew. I have the Honour to be, &c

JOHN ADAMS

His Excellency Mr Franklin

Endorsed: Answer'd Oct. 8.

Notation: J. Adams. Sept 29. 1780

From Thomas Digges

ALS: Historical Society of Pennsylvania

Dr. Sir [September 29, 1780][6]

You have intimated in a late letter to me, in answer to one wherein I attempted to describe the folly & infatuation of these people in their extraordinary exultations ever since the taking of Charles Town, "That the *second* 'hour of their Insolence' might be of as short duration as the *first*".[7] This has been strictly veryfyd, & the whole City is as much chap fallen & in the dumps as they were ever elated. The general cry for two days past is that "we are undone & ruind"—all is over—We always had hopes till now—our Army will be Burgoind &ca. &a. The affairs of

5. In his Oct. 8 reply, below, BF said he could not recollect such a letter.

6. It reports much of the same information as a Digges letter of that date to JA: *Adams Papers*, X, 186–8.

7. BF to Digges, July 30, above.

New York were in such a state as to induce Genl Clinton to send away a packet *out of time* on the 28th. of last month wch is not yet arrivd; and in a very few days after the Virginia Frigate with other alarming intelligences & of the discovery of the approach of Washingtons army towards New York.[8] She saild the 1st Int. and her arrival has thrown an unusual damp upon the Spirits of the Court, its creatures & their out runners & advocates. The heads of the news brought by this vessel, wch I have collected from the best quarter of information is,[9] That Monsr Terney arrivd at Rhode Island the 10th. & landed His Army the 12th. This arrival or landing was not known to Clinton for nine days after— Admiral Greaves arrivd at nearly the same period at N York & his Fleet was cruising between Rhode Island & N York when the Virginia Frigate Saild. As soon as Clinton heard of the arrival he determind on an Expedition to attack the French army at Rhode Island, & embarkd a large force on board Transports at N York. Adml Arbuthnot (who Commands) did not think the measure prudent, for reasons that there was not provision enough to victual the Transports, (there being scarcely sufficient for 2 months at short allowance and no supplys soon expected) and that by such an Embarkation the Garrison might be so weakend that Genl Washington might attack & take the City. This last reason only founded in speculation was soon realizd into fact; for after the Troops had been many days embarkd Genl Washington passd the No [North] River & approachd by regular march towards N York with 16,000 men. The British Troops were in consequence all disembarkd, and on hearing it, Genl. W——— halted and retreated a few miles back. Dalrymple (who brings the dispatches)[1] says that Washingtons Army is 20,000 Effective men, exclusive of French. The French Admiral had issued a

8. Washington had planned to attack New York if Clinton attacked Newport: Fitzpatrick, *Writings of Washington*, XIX, 318.

9. Most of the information below appeared in the Sept. 27 and 28 issues of the *London Courant, and Westminster Chronicle*. Clinton's failure to attack Newport is discussed in Willcox, *Portrait of a General*, pp. 326–40.

1. Clinton selected his quartermaster general, Brig. Gen. William Dalrymple, to carry his dispatches to Secretary of State Germain: William B. Willcox, ed., *The American Rebellion: Sir Henry Clinton's Narrative of His Campaigns, 1775–1782* ... (New Haven, 1954, reprinted Hamden, Conn., 1971), p. 205.

proclamation in the name of the Congress & King of France, assuring the People they should receive every support, & that the King his master had resolvd upon the Conquest of Canada & of ceeding that province to the United States, & that He was in dayly expectation of a considerable rienforcement. Before the Virga. Frigate Saild, Sir H Clinton had receivd advices of a late date from Lord Cornwallis, informing that his detachd partys had had several Skirmishes with Detatchments from Gates's army, & had been repulsd in all of them; That the People of Carolina who had taken up arms in the Royal Cause, had revolted & joind Genl Gates, to whom they had given up all their officers. In consequence of these disasters, Lord Cornwallis had determind to abandon all the interior Country of So Carolina & retire within the lines of Charles Town, in which place during Lord Cornwallis absence, there had been an insurrection of the People agt. the Soldiery, which had been quelld at the Expence of 4 or five hundd Amns. killd & wounded and near Eighty Soldiers.

A Sloop from the West Indies wch arrivd at N York the 30 Augt. brought an accot of Monsr. Guichens Fleet being seen on the 28th July steering for Jamaica & not far from it— His fleet consisted of 32 Sail of the line several frigates & lesser Ships making in the whole 76 Sail & having 16,000 Troops on board. There are an hundred other accots of lesser note, among them, that Monsieur Rochambeau had strongly entrenchd himself on Rhode Island, & that the June & July packets from England had been both taken by Amn. Privateers very near to Sandy hook.

The Quebec Spring fleet wch saild in June from Spithead were met on & near the banks of Newfoundland by some American Privateers which took twenty two out of the 30 Sail. The list of 20 of them is on Loyds book as arrivd in N England brought by a passenger who was allowd to come immediately frm. Boston to N York & so home in the Virginia. This is a greater blow *to Loyds* that the late capture of the West India Ships near £400,000 having been Insurd on them at Coffee House. I am told most of these Ships are worth from £30 to 35,000 & some of them above forty. O Rare Yankee! Well done Yankee!

A Report is very prevalent & much Credited that seven homeward bound East India men are also Capturd.

I am with very high Esteem Dr Sir Yr. obligd & obt Servt

W. S. C

I wrote you on tuesday last[2] by Mr B——f——d who will stop a day or two in Amsterdam. He can give you an accot of the Cartel to B——l [Bristol] &ca.

Addressed: A Monsieur / Monsieur B: F: / Passy

Notations: Sept 29 1780 / [*in William Temple Franklin's hand:*] Extrait d'une lettre de Londres a M. Franklin datté 29 Sep. 80.

From Dumas

ALS: American Philosophical Society

Monsieur   Lahaie 29. 7bre 1780

Le Roi de Suede arriva ici le 26 au soir & repart ce soir.[3] Il a soupé le 26 & le 27 chez Mr. l'Ambr. de France; & le 28 chez l'Ambr. d'Angle. qui s'est donné beaucoup de mouvement pour cela; & l'on a eu quelque peine a engager le Roi d'y aller. Comme le Spectacle est suspendu pendant ces 2 semaines, Mr. l'Ambr. de France a donné le 27 & le 28 ce Spectacle dans un hotel particulier où il a fait ériger un Théatre, & fait jouer les Comédiens, qui ont donné le premier jour *la Ve. de Malabar*,[4] & le jour suivant la *Fausse Agnès*.[5] Cette derniere Piece a beaucoup diverti le Roi, que j'ai vu à mon aise, & entendu rire fréquemment: car Mr. l'Ambr. a eu la bonté de me donner lui-même 6 billets, pour mon Epouse, ma Fille & moi.

Je verrai ce soir notre ami, quoique je sache d'avance qu'il ne s'y est rien passé d'intéressant.

Vous verrez sans doute avec plaisir les insertions dans la Gazette & supplément ci-joints de Leide.[6]

2. Sept. 26. Henry Bromfield, Jr., carried the letter, above.

3. King Gustavus III used a pseudonym, "the comte de Haga," during his unofficial visit: *Gaʒ. de Leyde*, issues of Sept. 29 and Oct. 3 (sup.).

4. Antoine-Marin Le Mierre, *La Veuve de Malabar . . .* (Paris, 1780, first performed 1770).

5. Philippe Néricault Destouches, *La Fausse Agnès . . .* (Paris, 1736).

6. Probably an article on the first page of the Sept. 29 issue of the *Gaʒ. de Leyde* entitled "Suite des Nouvelles de Philadelphie du 15. Juillet" and two letters from Boston in the supplement of the same issue.

Je suis avec un grand respect, Monsieur Votre très-humble & très-obéissant serviteur   DUMAS

Passy à Son Exc. M. B. Franklin

Addressed: à Son Excellence / Monsieur B. Franklin / Mine. Plenipe. des E. U. / &c. / Passy./.

Notation: Mr Dumas la haie Sept 29. 80

From Poliange

ALS: American Philosophical Society

Monsieur   Paris rue des Sts. peres no. 59 Le 29 7bre. 1780/.

Vous n'avez Sans doute pas reçu la lettre que j'eus Lhonneur de vous adresser le 18 aout dernier[7] dans laquelle je vous rapellais les promesses que vous eutes la bonté de me faire verballement au mois de juin a loccasion de mr. vigeral mon parent pris par les anglais le 5 mars 1778 sur un Corsaire americain, et duquel Sa famille desireroit avoir des nouvelles. La reputation que vous vous etes acquise, la place que vous occupez, tout me prouve que vous etes trop honnete pour differer plus longtems de minstruire du succes de vos recherches si Cette lettre vous parvient Comme je n'en doute pas. Dans le Cas ou elle resterait encore Sans réponce, je Concluerai que nos usages vous Sont inconnus, et que Ceux de votre nation sont tout à fait differens. Je Concluerai encore qu'on est bien malheureux dexposer Sa vie pour defendre la liberté d'autrui, si Ce Sacrifice doit etre paié par loubli Le plus affligeant pour une ame Sensible. Pardon Monsieur, Cest une femme qui parle et qui se Connait bien peu en matiere de guerre. Cest de plus une femme française, et mon Sexe dans ce païs Saccoutume tres difficilement a Ce qui peut blesser Son amour propre votre silence est dans Ce Cas par rapport a moy et jose esperer que Cette légere Considération jointe à tant dautres que je ne vous Suggere point, mais que vous ferez Sans doute, vous engagera enfin à m'honorer d'un mot

7. Above.

346

de reponse.[8] C'est dans Cet espoir que jai Lhonneur detre avec un profond respect Monsieur Votre tres humble et tres obeïssante servante

DE POLIANGE./.

Notation: De Poliange, Paris 29. 7bre. 1780.

From Thomas Ruston   ALS: American Philosophical Society

Sir   London Sept 29th 1780
   The most profound secrecy is studied with respect to the dispatches brought by General Dalrymple. He left N York about the begining of Sept. All those who have calld upon him have been refused admittance. The friends of Ministry acknowlege the news he brings is very bad. The scraps that are to be picked up are, that they were in the utmost consternation at new York, in consequence of de Ternays arrival at Rhode Island. Troops were embarked in order to attack him, but Arbuthnot and Sr Harry Clinton disagreed about the expediency of it, as Washington was in great force ready to attack N York.[9] in consequence of which they were disembarked. The loyalists are said to have laid down their arms. Lord Cornwallis is said to be Burgoyned in Carolina. Farther reinforcements were expected from France, in consequence of which the Americans were exerting themselves with the greatest spirit. The greatest part of the Quebec fleet which consisted of about 44 Sail have been taken and carried into new England. The Ministerialests here seem more

8. Mlle de Poliange wrote again on Oct. 16 to thank BF for his detailed answer (now missing). She notes that Vigeral has two sisters whose fortunes would be greatly affected if their brother were dead. She encloses two copies of the June memoir (mentioned in her Aug. 18 letter), adding to one of them her address and a personal plea to BF to order a search into the whereabouts of Vigeral. APS. It was apparently not until three years later that BF forwarded the memoir to Congress: BF to Charles Thomson, Sept. 13, 1783 (Library of Congress).

9. Vice Adm. Arbuthnot, the British naval commander, bore much of the responsibility for the failure of the British to attack Newport, but it was Clinton who feared for New York: Willcox, *Portrait of a General,* pp. 328–30.

heartily sick then ever they were upon any former occasion. Two opineons prevail here at present, the public one is that fifteen million will be wanted for the service of the next year. The more private one is that the K—g will open the Session of the new Parlt. with an inclination to accede to the Am———n Independence, which of them is the most likely to be true I shall not take upon me to determine.

I took the liberty of troubling you with a few thoughts the 9th instant on the subject of Am———n financ, if you think them worth your notice, or if you wish to have any farther communication on that Subject be so good as to direct to Dr Ruston at the Carolina Coffee house Birchin Lane *for the Author.* Pray what is the precise state of their debt. Who is at the head of their finance. I am Dr Sr with the most profound respect Yr obedt humble Servt   T. R.

Addressed: His Excellency / Doctr: Franklin / Paris

Notation: T R. London Sept. 29. 1780.

Receipt Written for Thomas-François Stanley[1]

DS: American Philosophical Society

Passy, Sept. 29. 1780

Receiv'd of Benjamin Franklin Eight Guineas in full for a Pendule which I left with him in London seven years since, when the above mentioned Sum was borrowed of him, and which he now agrees to give me for the said Pendule. Witness my hand—a prouvé Lescriture cy Desus   STANLEY

1. Written by BF for Stanley to sign; only the last phrase, in French, and the signature are in Stanley's hand. For this Parisian watch-maker whom BF had aided in 1773 see XX, 483n, 488.

From David Gregorie[2]

ALS: American Philosophical Society

Sir   Dunkerque 30th Septemb. 1780

I am desired to lay before your Excellency the Subjoined vouchers to Establish a proof of the atrocious abuse made by Capt Edward Macatter Commander of the black Princess Privateer, of the Power vested in him by the United States of America.

The paper N° 1 is a regular Protest taken by John McIsaac master of the Brig the John, at Dublin the 13 July last and by him & his Crew the next day affirmed upon Oath before the Lord Mayor of that City, Setting forth, That having been Captured by the abovenamed Privateer on the 8 July, one of the Officers compelled him by holding a Pistol to his breast to signe a Ransombill for £ 400 Sterling altho the Veshel burthen about 70 Tuns & her Cargo of Coals[3] were not in his own estimation worth above half that Sume—. I having with this proof in hand ineffectually offred Mr John Torris who is Capt Macatters Agent in this Town to pay half the Ransom by way of Composition, McIsaac the master of the Brigg found a necessity to Sell the Ship & Cargo by Publick Auction for behoof of the Captors that they might touch to the utmost extent of what the Subject might be worth.

The paper marked N° 2 leads a proof of this having been done in a regular manner & that both Ship & Cargo produced Net only about £193—Irish mony from which some expences on the Cargo are yet to be deducted, the Coals not being delivred when the Attestation was Sent away, but whatever may remain after all Charges are defrayed the Master offers to pay to the last Shilling, provided Capt Macatter or his Agent will accept of it as a full compensation for the Ransom, and further discharge all the expences of Duncan Flemings detention who was sent as hostage & furnish him besides a sume Sufficient to bear his charges home, Since no more mony can be drawn from the concerned, the Master himself and ev'n the owners of the Veshell being insolvent.

2. Gregorie (or Gregory) was a Dunkirk merchant specializing in the West Indies trade: *Almanach des marchands,* p. 193. The enclosures to his letter apparently were returned to him; see our annotation of BF's response, Oct. 9.
3. Being brought to Dublin from Campbeltown, Scotland: Clark, *Ben Franklin's Privateers,* p. 148.

After this plain State of the Case permit me to represent to your Excy. that any deed executed by a Man when under the fear of his Life becomes Nul & of no avail— McIsaac however has done ev'rything in his power towards fulfilling the engagement he contracted under these circumstances, and he now further has recourse to the Justice & humanity of your Excellency to Request he may be pleased to interpose his Authority that Duncan Fleming the hostage be released upon the terms before Specify'd and sent home to his own Country—.

I have the honor to be—Sir Your Excellency's most obedient and most faithfull Servant   DAVID GREGORIE—.
                                                                Merchant at Dunkirk

Benjamin Franklin Esqr Minister Plenipotentiary from the United / States of America at his Seat at Passy

Endorsed: Answer'd Oct. 9.

Notation: David Gregorie Dunkirk Sept 30. 1780

From Jonathan Williams, Jr.

ALS: University of Pennsylvania Library; copy: Yale University Library

Dear & hond Sir   Nantes Sept. 30. 1780.

I have received a Letter from Mr DeSegray at St Malo of which I send inclosed a Copy.[4] You will see by it the Difficulties that will attend the Transportation of the Saltpetre; That relative to Mr Schweighauser I have obviated by desiring him to write & relinquish his Pretentions, which he has promised in consequence of a Discharge from you which I have engaged he shall receive by return of Post; notwithstanding the Difficulties Mr DeSegray mentions the Salt Petre must come by Land to L'orient or we must renounce the Expectation of getting it out in the Breton, for it is almost certain Loss to send it by Sea, & it will not do to wait for it if the Winds should not be favourable for its

4. Missing.

coming round. The only Thing we can do will be to persuade the Farmers to dispence with the formalitys of leading the Bags & to grant a Permit to transport as if it belonged to the King, which would save, Time & Expence; but as I much Doubt the Success of the application & as I know you do not like to ask Favours of these People, I hardly think it worth the Pains; But if you could persuade Mr de Sartine to take the 100 Tons of Salt petre at St Malo & deliver the same Quantity from the Salt petre Works at L'orient, it would be an excellent arrangement, & I should think he would not refuse it, for as St Malo & L'orient are at nearly the same Distance from Brest, the Kings Salt Petre in either of this Ports is nearly the same thing as to convenience; If however this cannot be done immediately I think the best Way is to determine on having the Salt Petre transported to L'orient in spight of all Expence & Difficulty, and for this Purpose I request you to give immediate Orders as you may decide.

Capt Samson is returned without doing anything, & no Letters are yet come to hand from Holland about him so I do not know what he is to do: We sometimes laugh at the foolish & Extravagant Ideas of the French who go to america to make themselves, Generals or Senators & who expect to find Riches only for the Trouble of gathering them; but I think the laugh may be turned on our Borrowers of Money, for one would suppose they thought this Country paved with Gold & Silver and that they had only to send out a Ship to bring home a load of it.— The portuguese Capitaine who was taken by Capt Samson is trying to get him into a Law Suit but I believe I shall prevent it by having the matter refered to the Portuguese Ambassador & you, who are in my Opinion the only Persons who have a Right to interfere.

Mr Schweighauser is getting the Arms ready to send round to L'orient agreeable to my Desire.

I am ever with the greatest Respect Dear & hond Sir Yours dutifully & affectionately   JONA WILLIAMS J

Notation: J Williams Sept 30 1780

From George Woulfe

ALS: American Philosophical Society

sir.   saturday morn 30th. 7ber. [1780][5]

On my return home late yesterday Evening I found a letter from my Friend M. Petrie with the inclosed,[6] wch. he desires I Shou'd get carefully delivered into your or your Grandson's hands. I am sorry to have been detained so long yesterday where I dined, wch. prevented your receiving it yesterday Evening.

I am with the truest respect sir your most humble & most obedt. servant[7]   G: WOULFE

Notations in different hands: Ansd / G. Woulfe

To Jean de Neufville & fils

LS:[8] National Archives; copy: Library of Congress

Gentlemen,   Passy Oct. 1. 1780.

I have just received your respected Letter of the 25th. past, and take this first Opportunity of answering, that I approve of your making the Drafts upon me which you therein mention, and which I shall duly honour. But as Mr Lawrens, who was to sail three Days after Mr Searle,[9] may now be expected in Holland every Day, I could wish that you would not proceed in farther Acceptances before his Arrival, unless in case of absolute Necessity to prevent a Protest; as by the Resolve of Congress, which you acquainted me with in a former Letter it is probable that he brings Effects with him. Therefore in Case other Bills are offer'd to you, before his Arrival, I desire you would acquaint me with the Amount before you accept them, unless as above. When

5. The only year during BF's stay in France when Sept. 30 fell on a Saturday.

6. The letter was probably Petrie's of Sept. 22, above.

7. Woulfe wrote to BF twice more, on Oct. 14 in English and on the 18th in French; both times he forwarded newspapers from Petrie. APS.

8. In WTF's hand.

9. Searle sailed on July 14; see our annotation of Searle to BF, Sept. 11. The *Mercury,* carrying Henry Laurens, had sailed from Philadelphia on Aug. 13 and was captured on Sept. 3: Smith, *Letters,* XV, 533n; Digges to BF, Oct. 3, below.

that Gentleman arrives be pleased to present to him my Congratulations and Respects.

Your Guarrantee of the Bills you recd from John Leverer is sufficient in my Esteem, and they will be paid.

With great Regard, I have the honour to be, Gentlemen, Your most obedient & most humble Servant   B FRANKLIN

Mess. John De Neufville & Sons—

Addressed: A. Messieurs / Messrs. John De Neufville & Sons Negotiants / à Amsterdam

Notation: Oct 1780

To John Adams

LS:[1] Massachusetts Historical Society; AL (draft) and copy: Library of Congress[2]

Sir,   Passy Oct. 2. 1780.

By all our late Advices from America the Hopes you expressed that our Countrymen, instead of amusing themselves any longer with delusive Dreams of Peace, would bend the whole force of their Minds to find out their own Strength & Resources, and to depend upon themselves,[3] are actually accomplished. All the Accounts I have seen, agree, that the Spirit of our People was never higher than at present, nor their Exertions more vigorous.

Inclosed I send you Extracts of some Letters from two French Officers, a Colonel & Lieutenant Colonel in the Army of M. De Rochambeau,[4] which are the more pleasing, as they not only give a good Character of our Troops, but show the good Understanding that subsists between them and those of our Allys. I hope we shall soon hear of something decisive performed by their joint Operations, for your Observation is just that Specu-

1. In WTF's hand.
2. The draft and copy contain a postscript which is missing from the LS that JA received: "My compliments to Messrs Dana & Austin."
3. JA to BF, Aug. 17, above.
4. See our annotation of BF to Dumas, immediately below.

lations & Disputations do us little Service. Our Credit & Weight in Europe depend more on what we do than on what we say: And I have long been humiliated with the Idea of our running about from Court to Court begging for Money and Friendship, which are the more withheld the more eagerly they are sollicited, and would perhaps have been offer'd if they had not been asked. The supposed Necessity is our only Excuse. The Proverb says *God helps them that helps themselves,*[5] and the World too in this Sense is very Godly.

As the English Papers have pretended to Intelligence that our Troops disagree, perhaps it would not be amiss to get these Extracts inserted in the Amsterdam Gazette.

With great Respect I have the honour to be, Sir, Your Excellency's most obedt & most humble Servant   B Franklin

His Exy: John Adams Esqr.

To Dumas

ls:[6] American Philosophical Society; copy: Library of Congress; transcript: National Archives

Dear Sir   Pasy, Oct. 2. 1780

I received duly your several Letters of the 12th. 15th. 17th. 19th and 21st of September. I am much pleas'd with the Intelligence you send me, and with the Papers you have had printed.

Mr Searle is a military Officer in the Pensilvania Troops, and a Member of Congress. He has some Commission to execute for that Province, but none that I know of from Congress. He has an open Letter for you from Mr. Lovel,[7] which he has shewn me, It is full of Expressions of his Esteem; and I understand from Mr Searle, that you stand exceeding well with the Committee & with the Congress in general. I am sorry to see any Marks of Uneasiness & Apprehension in your Letters. Mr Chaumont tells me that you want some Assurance of being continued. The Congress it-

5. bf used the proverb in the guise of both "Poor Richard" and "Father Abraham": II, 140; VII, 341.

6. In wtf's hand.

7. Of July 10: Smith, *Letters,* xv, 421–2.

self is changeable at the Pleasure of their Electors, and none of
their Servants have, or can have any such Assurance. If therefore any thing better for you, & more substantial should offer,
no body can blame you for accepting it, however satisfied they
may be with your Services. But as to the Continuance of what
you now enjoy, or of something as valuable in the Service of the
Congress, I think you may make your self easy, for that your Appointment seems more likely to be increased than diminish'd,
tho' it does not belong to me to promise any thing.[8]

Mr. Laurens was to sail 3 Days after Mr Searle, who begins to
fear he must be lost, as it was a small Vessel he intended to embark in.— He was bound directly to Holland.

I enclose some Extracts of Letters from two French Officers
of Distinction in the Army of M. de Rochcambault, wich are
pleasing, as they mark the good Intelligence that subsists between the Troops, contrary to the Reports circulated by the English. They will do perhaps for your Leiden Gazette.[9]

With great Esteem & Affection I am ever Your faithful Friend
& Servt.   B FRANKLIN

Mr Dumas.

Notation: Passy 2e. Octobr. 1780 Mr. B. Franklin

To John Jay

LS:[1] Columbia University Library; copies (two): Library of Congress

Dear Sir,   Passy Oct. 2. 1780.
I received duly and in good Order the several Letters you
have written to me of Augt. 16. 19. Sept. 8. & 22.[2] The Papers

8. Congress, however, did nothing for Dumas: Schulte Nordholt, *Dutch Republic*, pp. 230–3.
9. Transcripts of the two unsigned letters are filed with the present letter at the National Archives. Dated July 29[–Aug. 3] and July 31[–Aug. 4], they are printed in the supplement to the Oct. 10 issue of the *Gaz. de Leyde*. They praise the Americans whom they met at Newport, particularly their enthusiasm and hospitality.
1. In WTF's hand. The last five words of the complimentary close are in BF's.
2. We have no record of the Aug. 19 letter; the others are above.

that accompanied them of your writing, gave me the Pleasure of seeing the Affairs of our Country in such good Hands, and the Prospect from your Youth of its having the Service of so able a Minister for a great Number of Years: But the little Success that has attended your late Applications for Money mortified me exceedingly; and the Storm of Bills which I found coming upon us both, has terrified and vexed me to such a Degree that I have been deprived of Sleep, and so much indisposed by continual Anxiety as to be render'd almost incapable of Writing.

At length I got over a Reluctance that was almost invincible, and made another Application to the Government here for more Money. I drew up and presented a State of Debts and newly expected Demands, and requested its Aid to extricate me. Judging from your Letters that you were not likely to obtain anything considerable from your Court, I put down in my Estimate the 25,000 Dollars drawn upon you with the same Sum drawn upon me, as what would probably come to me for Payment.[3] I have now the Pleasure to acquaint you that my Memorial was received in the kindest & most friendly Manner; and tho' the Court here is not without its Embarrasments, on Account of Money, I was told to make myself easy, for that I should be assisted with what was necessary. Mr Searle arriving about this Time, and assuring me there had been a plentiful Harvest, and great Crops of all Kinds; that the Congress had demanded of the several States, Contributions in Produce; which would be chearfully given; that they would therefore have Plenty of Provisions to dispose of; & I being much pleased with the generous Behavior just experienced, I presented another Paper, proposing in order to ease the Government here, which had been so willing to ease us, that the Congress might furnish their Army in America with Provisions in Part of Payment for the Sums lent us.[4] This Proposition I was told was well taken: But it being consider'd that the States having the Enemy in their Country and obliged to make great Expences for the present Campaign, the furnishing so much Provisions as the French Army would need might straiten & be inconvenient to the Congress; his Majesty did not at this time

3. BF had asked Vergennes for 125,000 *l.t.* ($25,000 in specie) on Sept. 20, above.

4. See BF to Vergennes, Sept. 26, above.

think it right to accept the Offer.— You will not wonder at my loving this good Prince: He will win the Hearts of all America.

If you are not so fortunate in Spain, continue however the even good Temper you have hitherto manifested. Spain owes us nothing, therefore whatever Friendship she shows us in lending Money or furnishing Cloathing, &ca. tho' not equal to our Wants and Wishes, is however *tant de gagné;* those who have begun to assist us are more likely to continue than to decline, and we are still so much oblig'd as their Aids amount to. But I hope and am confident that Court will be wiser than to take Advantage of our Distress and insist on our making Sacrifices by an Agreement, which the Circumstances of such Distress would hereafter weaken, and the very Proposition can only give Disgust at present. Poor as we are, yet as I know we shall be rich, I would rather agree with them to buy at a great Price the whole of their Right on the Missisipi than sell a Drop of its Waters.— A Neighbour might as well ask me to sell my Street Door.

I wish you could obtain an Account of what they have supplied us with already, in Money and Goods.

Mr. Grand informing me that one of the Bills drawn on you, having been sent from hence to Madrid, was come back unaccepted, I have directed him to pay it; and he has at my Request undertaken to write to the Marquis D'Yranda, to assist you with Money to answer such Bills as you are not otherwise enabled to pay, and to draw on him for the Amount, which Drafts I shall answer here, as far as twenty five thousand Dollars.— If you expect more acquaint me. But pray write to Congress as I do to forbear this Practice, which is so extreamly hazardous and may some time or other prove very mischevous to their Credit & Affairs. I have undertaken too for all the Bills drawn on Mr Lawrens that have yet appear'd. He was to have sailed 3 Days after Mr Searle, that is the 18th. of July. Mr Searle begins to be in pain for him, having no good Opinion of the little Vessel he was to embark in.

We have Letters from America to the 7th of August. The Spirit of our People was never higher. Vast Exertions making preparatory for some important Action. Great Harmony & Affection between the Troops of the two Nations. The New Money in good Credit &ca &ca.

I will write to you again shortly & to Mr Carmichael. I shall now be able to pay up your Salaries compleat for the Year. But as Demands unforeseen are continually coming upon me I still retain the Expectations you have given me of being reimbursed out of the first Remittances you receive.[5]

If you find any Inclination to hug me for the good News of this Letter, I constitute and appoint Mrs. Jay my Attorney to receive in my Behalf your Embraces.

With great and sincere Esteem, I have the honour to be, Dear Sir, Your most obedient and most humble Servant

B FRANKLIN

His Exy. John Jay Esqr.

Addressed: A son Excellence / Monsieur Jay, / Ministre Plenipotentiaire / des Etats Unis de l'Amerique / à Madrid.

Endorsed: Dr. Franklin 2 Octr 1780 ansd. 30 Inst. / Recd 12 Octr.

To Sartine
Copy: Library of Congress

Monseigneur,   Passy, le 2. Oct. 1780.

J'ai l'honneur de vous envoyer cy joint la traduction d'une lettre que je viens de recevoir du Capitaine Conklin qui se plaint beaucoup de la Detention de sa Cargaison par l'Amirauté des Sables d'Olones.[6] Votre Excellence a deja eu la bonté de me promettre la main levée de cette Cargaison,[7] mais restant toujours dans la même Situation, je prie V. E. de vouloir bien reiterer ses Ordres à cet effet.[8] Je suis avec Respect, Monseigneur Votre tres humble et tres obeissant Serv.

Monsieur De Sartine.

5. See Jay to BF, July 17, above.
6. Undoubtedly Conkling to BF, Sept. 14, above.
7. Presumably in his Aug. 19 letter to BF, above.
8. Sartine replied on Oct. 10. He has received BF's letter and the enclosed copy of Capt. Conkling's complaint that his cargo is being held. Sartine will forward it to "M. L'Amiral" (the duc de Penthièvre) and request him to rule on the cargo that is subject to spoilage. Library of Congress.

From Joseph Ceronio

ALS: American Philosophical Society

Sir   Genoa the 2d. 8ber 1780

Please to accept of my sincere acknowledgements for the trouble you have had some time ago of forwarding a Letter to my Son at St. Domingo,[9] which got safely to his hands, and upon the encouragement I have had from him, have sent my Second Son to Philadelphia under the Care of Mr. Morris;[1] I have two Left, which I intend likewise to dedicate to America, for I hope in time it will [be] the greatest Empire in the World; I shall take it as a particular favor, if you will be so kind to forward the inclosed, and if attended with any expence please to inform me of it, that I may reimburse you with many thanks besides for your kindness. Honour me with your Commands, and believe me with the greatest regard— Sir Your most Obedient & very humble Sert.   JOSEPH CERONIO

Addressed: A Monsieur / Mr: Le Docteur B. Franklin / Paris

From Harmon Courter

ALS: American Philosophical Society

Sir   L'Orient. Octr. 2. 1780

The dispatches you intrusted me with some time past, I had the pleasure of duly delivering to Congress—[2] altho your Joint letter with Messrs. Deane & Lee,[3] for which am much Oblidged, must say met with but a Cool reception, scarsely gave me money sufficient to bear my travelling expences from the place they set to a sea port after waiting three weeks for their answer, I consider the whole but a very insufficient compensation for my long Stay under my heavy expences at Paris.— but believe it would not have been the case had it not been for the influence the

9. Stephen Ceronio was at Cap Français serving as an agent for the Philadelphia firm of Willing and Morris and for Congress. His father had asked BF to forward letters to him: XXII, 633, 664–5; XXIV, 340–1; XXV, 42, 640–1.

1. This son was probably Ange Ceronio, who came to Philadelphia in 1780 under Robert Morris' sponsorship: *Morris Papers,* I, 170–2.

2. In May, 1778: XXV, 682–3; XXVI, 105–6, 400, 662.

3. The commissioners' recommendation of him: XXV, 682.

Messrs. Lee & their friends had in Congress which did not Intrust in my favour, but believe they prevented my having had the Command of the Alliance.—

I am now in L'Orient with the Ship Jay mounting Eighteen Nines burthen Abt. 400 Tuns Ninety men second Voyage,[4] am under some expectations of seling, which should not do if I had a full freight back to America, if in your way to give me Any should be much Oblidged,— if I should sell & in your Power to serve me any Other way the favour should be ever acknowledg'd by your most Obedt. & Hble. Sarvt.   HARMON COURTER

The Honourable Benjn. Franklin Passie

A few lines in answer should be much Oblidg'd for. Jes now A vessel Arived from Philadeliphia but Cold not Larn the Nuse

Addressed: The Honourable Benjn. Franklin. / Minister Plenipotentary at the Court of France; / at / Passie, / [*in another hand:*] pres Paris. / per post.

Notation: Harman Courter.— L'Orient Oct 2. 1780

From Jean de Neufville & fils

ALS: American Philosophical Society

Honourd Sir!   Amsterdam the 2d. October 1780.

My it please your Excellency, that on examination of those bills, which we shall have to pay in the Month of decemr: next, we found they were only amounting to Bk. Mey [Bank Money][5] *f.* 12316—instead of *f.* 12366—as we adviced wrong by our last

---

4. The first voyage was during or soon after August, 1779: Charles Henry Lincoln, comp., *Naval Records of the American Revolution 1775–1788* (Washington, D.C., 1906), p. 357. For his current voyage see Cuming's letter of Sept. 8.

5. The Bank of Amsterdam (*Wisselbank van Amsterdam*) listed its transactions in bank money, whereas businessmen listed theirs in current money, which was worth somewhat less: John J. McCusker, *Money and Exchange in Europe and America, 1600–1775: a Handbook* (Chapel Hill, 1978), pp. 43–4.

of the 25th. September and that we have now taken the liberty to draw in consequence on Your Excellency our three Bills for.

écus 2000 ⎫
    3000 ⎬ to our own order at three usance
   4295:5:8 ⎭

écus 9295:5.8 amounting at 53 grooten to the mentiond Summ of Bk. Mey *f.* 12316.[6] We beg leave to recomand them to your Excellency's protection and Acceptance. The Charges of brokerage and postage which naturaly attends them, will be found in future, desiring we might be able to show your Excellency at all opportunities our most devoted regard, we have the honour to be respectfully Honourd Sir Your Excellencys Most obedient and Most humble Servants   JOHN DE NEUFVILLE & SON

Endorsed: Answer'd Oct 5[7]

From John Paradise

ALS: American Philosophical Society

Dear Sir,   Hotel de Dannemarc Ruë Jacob 2 Octr. 1780.

Since I shall have the honour (and I shall ever esteem it a great one) of seeing you at Passy to-morrow morning,[8] I would not at this hour trouble you with a letter, if I were not extremely anxious to be honoured with your company at dinner, and consequently fearful lest you should be previously engaged on the day when I shall have the happiness of becoming a complete member of an American republick, a day, on which I shall through life reflect with pleasure, and which I therefore am desirous of

6. *I.e.,* 53 *grooten* per *écu.* At current exchange rates 9,295 *écus,* 5*s.,* 8*d.* was equivalent to 12,316 *f.* bank money; see our annotation of the firm's Nov. 2 letter. Our thanks to Professor John J. McCusker for his assistance on both letters.

7. We have no record of a response. It is unlikely that BF could have received this letter by Oct. 5.

8. Paradise and his friend William Jones had been in Paris during the spring of 1779 but they returned to England in June of that year. They came back to Paris in September, 1780: XXIX, 596–7; Digges to BF, Sept. 18, above; Archibald B. Shepperson, *John Paradise and Lucy Ludwell of London and Williamsburg* (Richmond, Va., 1942), p. 149.

celebrating with the sincerest joy.[9] What higher pleasure, indeed, can be felt by a man, who may without vanity profess himself a lover of liberty and virtue, than to be admitted as an affectionate and zealous citizen by one of those illustrious states, who by the noblest exertions of unexampled virtue, have established their liberty on the surest basis! Mr. Searle and such American gentlemen as I have the honour of knowing at Paris, will favour me with their company at half an hour after two o'Clock; and, if dining in town be not contrary to any rule that you may have made, I cannot express how much I shall think myself honoured and flattered if the excellent Ambassadour of those States and his amiable grandson will partake a republican dinner with, dear Sir, Your much obliged and ever grateful servant

JOHN PARADISE

Notation: John Paradise. 2. Oct. 1780.

From Thomas Digges   ALS: Historical Society of Pennsylvania

Dr. Sir   London Octo. 3. 1780

I am very sorry to inform you that Capt. Keppel of the vestal frigate arrivd here on Saty Eveng with an accot. of his having taken abot: 28 days ago on the Banks of New foundland a Packet calld the Congress bound from Philaa to Holland on board wch. was Mr Heny Laurens, His Secy, and another American genn

---

9. BF and WTF dined at the "Hotel de Dannemarc" on Oct. 3, as we know from bills submitted by their servants (for which see our annotation to the Editorial Note on Accounts). That must have been the day on which Paradise signed an oath of allegiance to the U.S. That oath is missing, but several years later BF provided a certified copy of it: Certificate regarding John Paradise, Aug. 3, 1789, Library of Congress. The precise nature of his citizenship, however, was unclear. According to Thomas Jefferson, Paradise was a foreigner under American law; even though in spirit he was "zealously a citizen" the law required that the oath be taken before a magistrate in the United States: *Jefferson Papers*, X, 199.

On Oct. 8, BF issued a printed passport for Paradise and Jones. Signed by BF with blanks filled in by WTF, it recognized the two men as "Citoyens des dits Etats" and was valid for one month: Yale University Library. (This was the second passport that BF had granted to the two men; see XXIX, 596–7.)

[gentleman].[1] It appears that the Man of Wars boat took up the mail before they boarded the prize, it being a pitchd leather bag & too boyannt for the weights fixd to it.[2] The friends to ministry give out that Mr Laurens's papers were also securd, but this I have no reason to beleive, and that they discover an intended Expedition agt. Hallifax wch was expected to arrive in that quarter between the 20th Sept & 1st Octor. also that a small fleet was going from France to Chesapeak bay.

Mr Laurens being much indisposd was put on shore at Dartmouth, where He yet is, but I learn He will soon be in London, probably put upon parole.[3] There is not the least appearance of exultation on accot of this capture, tho it appeard to Adml Edwards of such consequence as to induce Him to dispatch a frigate immediately from N foundland.[4] No particular news from that quarter, save that the number of Yankee privateers this summer out upon the banks & Coasts of that Island, as to have in a manner totally ruind the fishery for this Season. Another sloop of war arrivd Express from thence yesterday at Portsmouth, The news is not given to the publick, but must be of consequence from her being dispatchd so immediately upon the heels of the

1. On Sept. 3 the *Mercury* was captured by the 28-gun frigate H.M.S. *Vestal*, Capt. George Keppel: "A Narrative of the Capture of Henry Laurens, of his Confinement in the Tower of London &c. 1780, 1781, 1782," S.C. Hist. Soc. *Coll.* 1 (1857), 19–20; David D. Wallace, *The Life of Henry Laurens* . . . (New York, 1915), pp. 358. Laurens' secretary, Maj. Moses Young, was also captured; a prisoner at Newfoundland, Winslow Warren (son of James and Mercy Otis Warren), joined Laurens on his passage to England: Elias and Finch, *Letters of Digges*, pp. 291–3.

2. Among the captured papers was a copy of the American-Dutch commercial treaty drafted in 1778 by William Lee and Jean de Neufville: xxvii, 344n; Wallace, *Life of Henry Laurens*, pp. 358–61.

3. Laurens, considering himself treated as if he were on parole, refused an opportunity to escape while en route from Dartmouth to London: "Narrative of the Capture of Henry Laurens," p. 23. This is an excellent source, to which we refer the reader for details of Laurens' capture and imprisonment. Digges's prediction that Laurens would soon be given parole would prove incorrect.

4. Rear Adm. Richard Edwards (d. 1794) was governor of Newfoundland and commander of the naval station where Laurens was taken before being sent to England; Laurens praised his courtesy: John Charnock, *Biographia Navalis* . . . (6 vols., London, 1794–98), VI, 105–6; "Narrative of the Capture of Henry Laurens," pp. 21–2.

Vestal Frigate—report says this latter vessel was dispatchd with an accot of the discovery of a small french fleet in that quarter, supposd to have an intention to attack the Island.

The late news from N York & So Carolina, even garbled as it is [*in*] the last Gazettes is lookd upon as very bad & the cry still is "that we are all ruind in America." Yet there is an appearance of four Ships of the line intended to go soon to rienforce Adml Graves, and eight are talkd of for the Leeward Island Station.

I am respectfully Dr Sir Yr Obligd & Ob Ser   Wm. S. C.

Addressed: A Monsieur / Monsieur B. F / Passy

Endorsed: Oct. 3. 80

From Dumas

ALS: American Philosophical Society; AL (draft):[5] Algemeen Rijksarchief

Monsieur,   La haie 3e. Octobe. 1780.

J'eus Vendredi passé un Entretien avec *notre Ami*, qui sachant que je vois quelquefois 873. 64. 610. 783.[6] me pria de m'informer là, S'il étoit vrai (comme l'avoit dit à plusieurs grands personnages 873. 30.[7] sans date d'apres 958[8]) que le Danemarc fût convenu avec l'Angleterre de renoncer à la Neutralité armée.[9] Je

5. Dumas also sent an abstract of this letter as an enclosure to an Oct. 4 letter to President of Congress Huntington (both of which are at the National Archives). An English translation of that abstract is published in Wharton, *Diplomatic Correspondence*, IV, 76–7.
6. "The ambassador of Russia."
7. "The stadholder."
8. "Yorke."
9. On Oct. 3 Denmark presented the ratification of a July 4 agreement with Britain modifying their 1670 commercial treaty; in exchange for the freedom to carry provisions to the ports of the belligerents the Danes agreed not to attempt to carry naval stores. The Russians treated the Danish action as a betrayal of Denmark's accession to the League of Armed Neutrality: Madariaga, *Harris's Mission*, pp. 187–9, 233; Sir Francis Piggott and G.W.T. Omond, eds., *Documentary History of the Armed Neutralities 1780 and 1800* (London, 1919), pp. 222–3.

fis mes diligences en conséquence: & j'écrivis Dimanche la Lettre ci-jointe[1] à notre ami.

Rien de nouveau au reste, sinon qu'il est arrivé des Lettres de Petersbourg, portant que les plénipes. de la rep. ont commencé leurs conférences avec les Mines. [Ministres] russes.

Notre Ami croit que Mrs. d'hollde. resteront assemblés cette semaine & l'autre. Il me demande avec empressement des nouvelles d'Amérique. Puissiez-vous bientôt me mettre en état de lui en annoncer, à lui & d'autres, de victorieuses! Je suis, avec un grand respect, Monsieur Votre très-humble & très-obéissant serviteur   DUMAS

Je reviens de parler à notre Ami. Il est effectivement arrivé un Courier de Petersbourg, avec la convention dressée de la part de l'Impe. [Imperatrice] L. H. P. ne peuvent plus reculer de la signer. Voilà qui est bien expéditif, & montre que la Cour de Petersbourg ne lambine pas, & traite cette affaire avec le dernier serieux. J'ai des choses bien curieuses à vous marquer sur ce sujet par la Poste d'après demain.

P.S. Cette Lettre ecrite Dimanche devoit partir hier de Rotterdam. Toute réflexion faite, je l'ai retenue; & vous verrez ciderriere les particularités dont je parle.

Nos amis sont très-contents des Plenipes. de la Rep. & de leur Dépêche, portant 1°. Une Convention, dressée de la part de Sa Maj. Impe. qui a pour base celle faite avec les Cours du Nord;[2] & l'on y a ajouté deux articles, un 7e. & un 8e., dont le premier a pour objet la réclame & restitution des Vaisseaux saisis aux sujets de la rep.; le 8e. que si, en haine de cette convention & de ses suites, la Rep. se trouvoit attaquée, molestée, inquiétée, les autres feront cause commune pour cela avec elle, & la défendront.[3] A cela est joint un article séparé, portant que le but de la neutralité armée est aussi, dès qu'elle aura toute sa consistance,

1. We have located no copy of a letter from Dumas to van Berckel.
2. For the July 9 Russo-Danish convention, the Aug. 1 Russo-Swedish convention, and associated documents see Piggott and Omond, *Documentary History of the Armed Neutralities*, pp. 233–46.
3. In fact van Wassenaer Starrenburg and van Heeckeren tot Brantsenburg had already met a rebuff on their most important demand, that of a Russian guarantee of Dutch colonies: Madariaga, *Harris's Mission*, p. 231.

de procurer la paix entre les Puissances belligérantes.— (J'ai demandé Si je pourrois avoir une copie de cette convention: mais notre ami m'a dit, que les Plenipes. avoient exigé que leur dépêche ne fût communiquée à aucun Mine. étranger, par conséquent pas à Mr. Y.[4] Nous sommes persuadés pourtant que S. J. l'a déjà. Pour nous qui avons la conscience délicate, nous aimons mieux patienter, moi à demander, les autres à m'accorder la communication.)

2°. La Dépêche porte, que les Plenipes. tiennent du Mine. de Pe. [Prusse] que l'Envoyé d'Angle à Petersbourg a déclaré à S. M. Impe. que *Sa Cour respectera la neutralité armée des Puissces. du Nord*, POURVU QUE LA HOLLDE. EN SOIT EXCLUE.—[5] Voilà qui est impayable. Si l'on ne sent pas vivement ici cette *vraie hostilité* des prétendus bons voisins & amis de la rep., il faut qu'on soit bien incurablement ladre.

J'ai laissé notre Ami d'extraordinairement bonne humeur. Il m'assure qu'on ne pourra plus reculer; & que la Convention devra se signer, quelque que soit l'embarras des temporiseurs, qui n'ont plus de prétexte; qui puisse servir de *rémore* sans les rendre absolument odieux & responsables.

Le Gd. Fr. a aussi reçu des Dépêches de son Confrere à Petersbourg.

Nre. ami ne doute pas que le R— de Pe.[6] n'accede aussi à la Neutralité Armée. Il croit que l'Empr. en fera de même; puisque l'Impe. de Rie. [Russie] a été si contente de sa visite, qu'elle lui a

4. Sir Joseph Yorke.
5. Britain took a far different approach to counter the danger of the Dutch joining and thereby strengthening the League of Armed Neutrality. Ambassador Harris was told to warn the Russians that Britain was prepared to declare war on the Netherlands if they did so. When the Dutch persisted, the British opened hostilities, using the Neufville-Lee draft treaty as a pretext: Madariaga, *Harris's Mission*, pp. 234–8.
6. "Roi de Prusse." King Frederick II joined the League in May, 1781, Emperor Joseph II in October, 1781, and Queen Maria I of Portugal in July, 1782: Piggott and Omond, *Documentary History of the Armed Neutrality*, pp. 252–6, 270–4, 276–8. Joseph's visit to Russia in the summer of 1780 had gone well; he and Catherine took great care to impress each other and the first steps were taken toward an Austro-Russian alliance: Madariaga, *Harris's Mission*, pp. 216–17.

fait présent d'un Vaisseau de guerre.— Enfin, il y a beaucoup à parier que le Portugal y a accedé aussi.

Enfin je tiens de la meilleure part, que l'Impe. ne démordra pas de son Plan, aussi simple que noble, de procurer à toutes les nations maritimes de l'Europe un Code maritime, fondé sur le Droit naturel des gens, également respecté à l'avenir de toutes, & également utile & salutair[e à] toutes. Deux autres circonstances d'ailleurs me le pro[*torn:* uvent?] 1. le concert visible des Mines. du Nord, & de ceux de [*torn: word or words missing*] de Pe. [Prusse?], avec le Cabinet à Petersb— 2°. les ordres donnés en Russie & en Suede, tout récemment, d'équiper & mettre incessamment en mer de quoi doubler les Escadres Russe & Suedoise.

La populace & valetaille Anglomane ici, crient contre le sage & aimable Monarque qui a passé ici,[7] de ce qu'il ne leur a pas prodigué l'or à pleines mains; & ils l'appellent par dérision le *Roi de Cuivre:* d'autres d'un plus gros calibre enragent, aussi bas que la passion le leur permet, de ce que dans tout Son Voyage il a montré un éloignement marqué pour tout A———s [Anglais]. On a eu beaucoup de peine à le déterminer à accepter le souper chez S. J.

Addition au Mémoire pour les Minres. de Russie & de Suede, remis en 7bre. 1780[8]

Trois millions d'hommes, ayant derriere eux de vastes & fertiles contrées à défricher encore, ne s'appliqueront pas de longtemps aux Manufactures en grand. Il leur faudra celles de l'Europe pendant des siecles; & l'accroissement d'une telle consommation sera prodigieuse de génération en génération. Si l'Angleterre avoit su se conserver son empire sur eux, avec leur affection, elle devenoit réellement la reine du Commerce & des Mers du Globe entier; & par conséquent elle lui eût fait la Loi.

Passy à S. E. M. B. Franklin

Addressed: à Son Excellence / Monsieur B. Franklin / Min. Plénipe. des Etats-Unis / d'Amerique &c. / Passy./.

7. King Gustavus III of Sweden.
8. Of which Dumas had sent BF a copy on Sept. 26; see above.

To Sarah and Richard Bache

Reprinted from the Union Art Galleries Sales Catalogue (February 27, 1934), p. 28.[9]

Dear Son and Daughter,   [October 4, 1780]
I received yours of March 29 by the Nephew of Mr. Gerard; of April 29 by Mrs. Foulk and Fox; of May 2 & July 22.[1] I continue in health, notwithstanding the omission of my yearly Journies, which I have never been able to take since my being in France; being confined necessarily by the Business; but I have a large Garden to walk in, and I take some advantage from that.

I enclose Ben's last Letter to me, and a copy of mine to him, as you like to see our Correspondence.[2] I gave you in a former letter the Account of his gaining a Prize by having made the best Translation from Latin into French.[3] You will see in his Letter that he is— aiming at another.

I am glad to see the American Spirit rous'd again and I am much pleased with the Subscriptions of the Ladies and Merchants. They have confuted the assertion of the Scotch Writer, who says that Women have not the amor Patrie and that Merchants are attach'd to no Country.[4]

Send me your German as well as English News-Papers. I want

9. This possibly is an extract, as the sales catalogue refers to a lengthy letter of Oct. 4 that is given in part.

1. The March 29 letter (carried by Pierre Prothais Meyer) and the one of April 29 (carried by John Foulke and George Fox) were from RB; he and his wife both wrote on May 2: XXXII, 175–6, 325, 336–8. RB wrote on July 22, above.

2. BFB's letter, which we have dated c. Sept. 15, and his grandfather's reply of Sept. 25 are both above.

3. XXXII, 610–11.

4. RB had written about the Ladies Association on July 22, above. BF may be combining two Scottish writers into one. His old friend and correspondent Henry Home, Lord Kames (IX, 5n) wrote that as wives, children, and servants are connected with their country only through the master of the family, women "have less patriotism than men": *Sketches of the History of Man* (2nd ed., 4 vols., Edinburgh, 1778), II, 4–5. It was Adam Smith who said that "A merchant, it has been said very properly, is not necessarily the citizen of any particular country": *An Inquiry into the Nature and Causes of the Wealth of Nations* (2 vols., London, 1776), I, 509, (Book III, chapter 4).

also for a Friend a little piece on the Delaware Indian Language, printed by Mr. Miller for the Moravians.[5]

Temple is well and sends his Duty. He is my right hand. I am ever, with love to the Children Your affectionate Father

B. FRANKLIN

To Sartine

Copy: Library of Congress

Sir,   Passy, 4 Oct. 1780.

Your Excellency will perceive by the inclosed Passports the Grounds on which they were given.[6] The Person to whom they were granted is apprehensive that they will not be a Sufficient Protection against French armed Vessels, & desires to have like passes from your Excellency, which if there is no impropriety, I beg may be granted to him.

With great Respect, I have the Honour to be, Sir, Your Excellency's &c.

M. De Sartine.

From Mr. and Mrs. Samuel Hartley and John(?) Batley[7]

AL:[8] American Philosophical Society

Hotel de Louis seize Wednesday 4th Octr 1780

Mr & Mrs Hartley & Mr Batley present their respectfull compliments to Dr Franklin—they will do themselves the honour of accepting his kind invitation on Fryday next.

5. RB sent one German newspaper on Oct. 30, below. BF wanted John Henry Miller's *Essay of a Delaware-Indian and English Spelling-Book, for the Use of the Schools of the Christian Indians on Muskingum River* (XXXII, 609n) for Court de Gebelin, who on May 6, 1781, acknowledged receiving it (APS).

6. The passports were for Thomas Collins, who wrote BF on Sept. 28, above.

7. Possibly John Batley, like Hartley, a London merchant. A lacemaker, he is listed at 8 Bell-court, St. Martin's-le-grand, in *Kent's Directory* for 1779, p. 16.

8. In Samuel Hartley's hand.

Addressed: To / His Excellency / Dr Franklin / &c &c &c / Passy

Notation: Mr. & Mrs. Hartley. Paris 4 Oct. 1780

From ———— de Leempoel[9] AL: American Philosophical Society

Paris ce 4 8bre 1780.

Le Professeur de philosophie *de Leempoel* étant obligé de partir incessamment pour Louvain à cause de l'indisposition d'un de Ses confreres, il lui est impossible de venir en personne remercier Votre Excellence des bontes qu'elle a eû pour lui, Sur tout de l'admettre à Sa table dimanche dernier. Il en a le plus vif regret: il prie Votre Excellence, de vouloir disposer de lui, Si par hasard il pourroit lui être bon à quelque chose dans Son paÿs. Il finit par prier Votre Excellence d'être persuadée de Sa réconnoissance et de Son profond respect pour Elle.

Lotelle dartois Rue du [?]

Addressed: A Son Excellence / Le Docteur Franklin / Ambassadeur des Etats / Unis de l'Amérique / à / Passy

From John Jay   Copy: Library of Congress

Dear Sir,   Madrid 5. Oct. 1780.

Altho' you have not informed me that you had recd. my Letter from St. Ildefonso, yet I find it has not only come safe to your Hands, but that Mr. Grand (to whom I wrote a few Lines by last Post) is actually engaged in obtaining the Object of it. I thank you for this in both the Capacities of American & Friend. How far the Responsibility of the King of Spain may be a means of opening the Chests of your Money holders, I know not—but that nothing on my Part might be wanting, I applied lately to be

---

9. The writer is either Guillaume-Waléric de Leempoel (born *c.* 1750), professor of philosophy at the University of Louvain and later *recteur magnifique* of that university, or his brother Jean-Guillaume, professor of medicine, who also became *recteur magnifique.* Baron I. de Stein d'Altenstein, *Annuaire de la noblesse de Belgique* (Brussels, 1860), pp. 272–3.

furnished with some Evidence of it, and to be informed of the manner in which it should be given.— The Answer was that proper Instructions on this Head should be sent to the Spanish Ambassadors in France and Holland, and that they would on Application give this Responsibility in due Form to such Persons as might consent to lend Money on the Credit of it in those Countries and that the Ministry would do the Same there with respect to those in Spain.—[1] By this Opportunity I ought to add nothing further, than that I am, Dear Sir, Your affect: Friend &c.

(signed) JOHN JAY.

P.S. I have received Mr. Deane's two last Letters & written him two others.[2] If the Paper he sent by the Courier in August, be the Original, he has in my Opinion cut his Business short—for to this Day all my Inquiries about it have proved fruitless.[3]

His Exy. Doctor Franklin.

From Samuel Wharton   ALS: American Philosophical Society

Dear Sir   Off Groix October 5 1780

I have at last the Prospect of leaving this Country,[4] as Commodore Jones has every Thing on Board, and a favorable Wind is springing up. The Brigantine Duke of Leinster, Capt. Souder, & the Brigantine Luke, Capt. Clark for Philadelphia, and a french Lougre for Maryland sail under Convoy of the Ariel. If at any Time I can be any ways useful to you in america, I beg the Favor of you freely to command Me, as, I hope, I need not as-

---

1. James (Diego) de Gardoqui so informed Jay on behalf of Floridablanca: Morris, *Jay: Revolutionary*, pp. 717–18, 833.

2. *Deane Papers*, IV, 225–6, 227–31; Wharton, *Diplomatic Correspondence*, IV, 49–50. The last Jay letter (mentioned in *Deane Papers*, IV, 244) apparently is no longer extant.

3. Deane had sent by diplomatic courier a sealed letter from the late unofficial Spanish representative in Philadelphia, Juan de Miralles, whom Jay had much admired. For some reason Jay did not receive the letter: *ibid.*, IV, 244; Light Townsend Cummins, *Spanish Observers and the American Revolution, 1775–1783* (Baton Rouge and London, 1991), pp. 162–3.

4. Wharton had left Paris on March 17 to return to America: XXXII, 129–30.

sure you, I shall always be ambitious to prove the Sincerity of my Friendship and Attachment to you. We hear no News here, except Captain Landais is under an arrest by Order of Congress,[5] and a glorious Spirit is prevailing through the United States. My affectionate Regards to Billy, and in much haste, The Boat waiting, I beg leave to subscribe myself, with the greatest Respect, and sincerity, My dear Friend, Your's affectionately   S WHARTON

His Excellency Benjamin Franklin Esqr.

Notation: S. Wharton Oct 5. 1780

To Sartine   Copy: Library of Congress

Sir,   Passy, 6. Oct. 1780.

I have the honour of Sending your Excellency inclosed, an extract of a Letter I have lately recd. from London, desiring the release of certain Prisoners therein named, taken by American Privateers, & now confined at St. Omers.[6] Being desirous of repaying as soon as possible the Prisoners I owe, for those I recd. from England some time past,[7] & being promised that if these are set at liberty they will be carried to my Account. I request your Exy. would give immediate Orders for their Release.

With great Esteem & Respect, I am Sir, your Exy.

M. De Sartine.

---

5. Wharton had planned to sail with Jones on the *Alliance* and protested Landais' seizure of the ship: XXXII, 390, 525, 607–8. On Sept. 5 the American Board of Admiralty had suspended Landais from command of the *Alliance* and had ordered the Eastern Navy Board to hold an inquiry: Charles O. Paullin, ed., *Out-Letters of the Continental Marine Committee and Board of Admiralty August, 1776–September, 1780* (2 vols., New York, 1914), II, 260–1.

6. Undoubtedly Hodgson's Sept. 20 letter, above.

7. *I.e.,* those brought to Morlaix in March. The cartel had returned to England empty: XXXII, 167–8, 237–8, 305–6.

From Madame Brillon

AL: American Philosophical Society

Mon bon papa,   ce 6 au matin [October, 1780?]⁸

Mon premier soin avant de rentrer chés moi a été d'aller demander a Mr le curé⁹ si les porteurs de Mr Terrasson¹ étoient des doméstiques a lui et si cela le gésneroit [de] vous les préster, le curé m'a dit que les porteurs étoient deux ouvriérs du village qui appartenoient a tous ceux qui les payoient; j'en ai fait venir un qui vous reméttra cette léttre et prendra votre heure et vos ordres pour vous promener soit au jardin, soit au bois, soit chés vos amis, j'ai souffért souvent phisiquement et morallement ce qui est pir, la vuë et la jouissance de mes amis calmoit et adoucissoit mes meaux, l'air de ma térrasse est bon, et mon coeur est entier tout entier a vous: voyés mon ami si cétte nouvelle voiture vous fatiguera moins que le carrosse, éssayons d'éstre moins mal quand nous sommes mal pour tâcher d'attraper le bien, et si ce conseil ne vous paroist pas util n'en prisés que le motif et ne le suivés pas, songés que j'aime mon papa en fille bien tendre et que ma teste s'agitte pour le soulager en proportion de la chaleur de mon áme qui est pour lui au plus haut dégré.

Addressed: A Monsieur / Monsieur Benjamin / Franklin / a Passy

---

8. BF's attack of the gout seems to have begun around the middle of October and peaked in early November. The present letter may date from the earliest stage of the gout's onset when BF could still contemplate going out. It might also have been written in December when his health was improving.

9. Clément Noguères was the parish priest of Passy: XXX, 295.

1. Possibly Antoine Terrasson (1705–1782), a distinguished jurist. He was a professor at the Collège royal, a royal censor, and an *avocat du clergé.* He was also an amateur musician and played the hurdy-gurdy, the flute, and the musette, instruments made popular by the pastoral vogue in music: *Almanach royal* for 1780, pp. 67, 341, 464–5; *Biographie universelle;* François-Joseph Fétis, comp., *Biographie universelle des musiciens et bibliographie générale de la musique* (2nd ed., 8 vols., Paris, 1875–89).

From Thomas Digges

ALS: Historical Society of Pennsylvania

Dear Sir   London Octo 6. 1780 Fryday

Mr Laurens has been so ill as to retard his journy up to London very much. He arrivd in rather better health on Thursday night, & was this day examind at Lord G Germaines office & committed to the Tower—[2] The first night he was kept at the Messengers House in Scotland Yard, & taken from thence to Lord Go Gs office about noon. He was watchd & kept very close, so that no one of His frds. could even offer him any assistance. As those folks are ever in extreems, perhaps this regour will be soon removd, & Mr L allowd to speak to his friends. They boast much of discoverys made from His papers *all* as they say being taken; but I beleive my share of this. Not a word of any other news.

I am with great Esteem Sir Your obedt Ser   WM. C. C

One report is that He is not to be sent to the Tower till tomorrow but, I have good reason to think He went this afternoon.

To Desegray, Beaugeard fils & Cie.[3]

Copy: Library of Congress

Gentlemen,   Passy, Oct. 7. 1780.

We formerly requested you to hold the Salpetre in your Hands at the Disposition of M. Schweighauser, having given him Directions to Ship it to America. As he has not had an Opportunity of doing it conveniently, and we have a Ship that can

---

2. After spending the night at Scotland Yard, Laurens was interviewed on Friday, Oct. 6, by Secretaries of State George Germain, Hillsborough, and Stormont and by others. He was then committed to the Tower of London on "suspicion of high treason"; he later said that during his confinement the people there (exclusive of the governor of the Tower) were "respectful and kindly attentive": "A Narrative of the Capture of Henry Laurens, of his Confinement in the Tower of London, &c., 1780, 1781, 1782," S.C. Hist. Soc. *Coll.* 1 (1857), 23–5.

3. Written in response to JW's letter of Sept. 30 and its enclosure.

take it at l'Orient, I desire you would forward it thither by Land Cariage as soon as possible. In which you will much oblige.

Messrs. Desegray & Co.

To Sartine

Copy: Library of Congress

Sir, Passy, 7. Oct. 1780.

Your Excellency will perceive by the inclosed Extract of a Letter to me, from Messrs. Parsons Alston & Co. of Martinique, that certain Prisoners made by American Vessels, & carried in there were with others taken by French Vessels, sent to France via St. Domingo in order to be exchanged.[4]

If the sd. Prisoners are arrived, or when they do arrive, I desire your Excellency would cause those captured by the Americans (of which inclosed is a List)[5] to be deliver'd as such to the Capt. of the Cartel & a Rect. in Consequence taken for the same.

With great Respect & Esteem, I am Sir, Your Exy.

M. De Sartine.

4. William Bingham had chosen the firm of Parsons and Alston to represent American commercial interests in Martinique after his departure. It provided intelligence, but conducted little public business: Elizabeth M. Nuxoll, *Congress and the Munitions Merchants: the Secret Committee of Trade during the American Revolution, 1775–1777* (New York and London, 1985), p. 452; Smith, *Letters*, XVII, 175n. The firm did, however, write BF on Aug. 1 (APS). BF indicated on that letter that an extract should be made of its first two paragraphs. These, after announcing the firm's appointment, reported that Bingham had arranged that prisoners made by American ships and confined at Martinique should be exchanged by the French commandant, the marquis de Bouillé (XXIV, 60n); when Admiral Rodney refused to exchange prisoners with Bouillé, he sent them to France for exchange. In the remainder of the letter the firm gave naval intelligence and volunteered to send news in the future.

5. This Aug. 1 list sent by Parsons and Alston contains the names and nautical titles of 34 British subjects captured at sea by American armed vessels. APS.

To Schweighauser
Copy: Library of Congress

Sir,   Passy, Oct. 7. 1780.

This is to request you would write to Messrs. DeSegray & Company to forward the Saltpetre by land to L'Orient, where M. Williams will be ready to receive it & ship it with other Goods in his Hands for America. By doing this immediately you will much oblige me. With great Esteem I have the Honour to be,

M. Schweighauser.

To Jonathan Williams, Jr.
Copy: Library of Congress

Dear Jonathan,   Passy Oct 7. 1780.

Enclosed is the passport for the Saltpetre. I found no Difficulty is obtaining it from the Farmers General.[6] They would have made the Exchange if ours had been at Bordeaux or Marseilles; but at St. Maloes they have no Refinery.

I have received yours of the 26th. & 30th.

I enclose Letters also for M. Schweighauser & Messrs. Desegray & Co.

If it Should come too late for your Ship, you can Ship it in the Jay.[7]

I am, Your affectionate Uncle.

M. Williams.

From ——— Branco
ALS: American Philosophical Society

Monsieur   à Brou[8] ce 7 Octobre 1780

Je n'ai reçu que hier le Decret de la Reyne de Portugal: Je serai

---

6. That passport proved to be ineffective; see BF to Lavoisier, Oct. 22.

7. JW does not seem to have seriously considered using the *Jay*. In any case, the vessel, lying at Lorient, was lost on Oct. 10: from Harmon Courter, Oct. 30, below.

8. Near Chartres.

charmé qu'il vous plaise: J'y ajoutai une traduction litteraire, que faira bien comprendre l'esprit, malgré le defaut de phrase.[9]

J'aurai l'honneur de vous faire ma Cour lorsque je recevrai les pieces justificatives concernant la prise faite par le Corsaire de l'Amerique:[1] Le Capitaine du Brigantin améne à Bosthon vient d'arriver à Paris.

Je suis avec la plus parfaite et respectueuse consideration, Monsieur, Votre très humble et très obeissant Serviteur

BRANCO

Notation: Braner, a Bruce ce 7 October 1780

From Sartine

Copy: Library of Congress

Versailles le 7. 8bre. 1780.

J'ai reçu, Monsieur, avec la Lettre que vous m'avez fait l'honneur de m'écrire le 4. de ce mois les deux Passeports que vous avez jugé convenable d'accorder pour deux batimens anglois qui doivent transporter de Dublin dans l'un des ports des Etats unis et le Sr. Collins qui se propose de s'y établir avec sa Famille. J'ai rendu compte au Roi de la demande que vous m'avez faite de deux semblables passeports pour assurer plus particulierement la Navigation de ces Navires, et sa Majesté, pour entrer dans les vues qui vous ont determiné a Proteger, cet Irlandois devenu sujet des Etats unis ses Alliés, a bien voulu consentir à les accorder, J'ai l'honneur de vous les envoyer ci joints revetus de toutes les

9. The now-missing enclosure probably was a copy of Queen Maria's Aug. 30 decree forbidding privateers or prizes from any country to enter Portuguese ports: Wharton, *Diplomatic Correspondence*, IV, 83–4.

1. The ship undoubtedly was the *Nossa Senhora do Livramento e Senhor do Bomfim* (Joze da Fonseca Soarez de Figueiredo, captain), which had been captured on Aug. 31 by the *Mars* (Simeon Samson, captain) and sent to Boston: JW to BF, Sept. 14, above; Smith, *Letters*, XVII, 286n; John A. Mc-Manemin, *Captains of the State Navies during the Revolutionary War* (Ho-Ho-Kus, N.J., 1984), pp. 165–6. On Dec. 19, Branco forwarded the documents to BF; his covering letter is at the APS. By then BF had already discussed the case with the Portuguese ambassador: Wharton, *Diplomatic Correspondence*, IV, 180.

formalités necessaires.[2] Je vous prie de vouloir bien recommander à cet officier de remplir avec la plus grande exactitude les Conditions qu'ils renferment.

J'ai l'honneur d'être avec la Consideration la plus distinguée, Monsieur votre très humble et très obeissant Serviteur.

(signé) DE SARTINE.

M. Franklin

From Jonathan Williams, Jr.

ALS: University of Pennsylvania Library; copy: Yale University Library

Dear & hond Sir   Nantes Octor. 7. 1780

I received your Favour of the 27 Sept too late to answer it by the last Post. The Accot of Bills and the other Cloathing Accounts are making out as fast as possible, they are very long so I cannot send them by this Post but you shall have them in a Day or two.

I am glad to hear you are likely to get a Pasport for the Salt Petre—that article should be the first shipped but I am afraid it will not be in Time.

The Admiralty here have lately sent you some Papers relative to a retaken Spanish Snow by the Hercules Capt Carey[3] to my Address. I shall be obliged to you if you will return them as soon as you can as I want to finish the ships Business.

The Case you speak of Capt Samson tells me he sent by Mr Moore so I suppose you have before this received it.

I am with great Respect in which Mrs Williams Joins Your ever dutifull & affectionate kinsman   JONA WILLIAMS J

2. We have not found the enclosures. After a fruitless visit to Versailles Thomas Collins asked WTF on Oct. 11 to forward the passports (APS), but probably he did not leave for America immediately. In June, 1781, Sir Edward Newenham provided either Collins or his brother James with a letter of introduction to George Washington. James Collins reached Philadelphia by February, 1782, and the following month one of the brothers dined with Washington at the St. Patrick Society of Philadelphia: W.W. Abbot and Dorothy Twohig, eds., *The Papers of George Washington: Confederation Series* (6 vols., Charlottesville and London, 1992–97), I, 440n.

3. John Carey of Baltimore: Claghorn, *Naval Officers*, p. 49.

Please to tell Mr Deane that the post Departure does not permit me to write him but his Case of Papers is found & will go to him by the Messagerie, I will answer his Letter next Post.

Notation: J Williams Octo. 7 1780

To John Adams

ʟs:[4] Massachusetts Historical Society; copy: Library of Congress

Sir, Passy, Oct. 8. 1780

I received the letter you did me the Honour of writing to me by Mr. Andrews,[5] and shall render him every Service I can in his Application.

Your Books & Trunks have been lodged here by Mr. Thaxter, and will be taken care of. They are of no Inconvenience to me.

We begin to be in pain for Mr. Laurens who was to have sailed 3 Days after M. Searle. If that took place, he has been out 10. or 11. Weeks. I hope he did not sail so soon, otherwise it would be probable that he is either lost or taken.

I do not just now recollect my having written, as from myself, any Letter to the Grand Pensionary. I drew indeed the Letter that was sent by the Commissioners acquainting him with the Treaty of Commerce,[6] to which we had no Answer. But I will search, and If I can find such a one will send you a Copy, with a Copy of the other.

I shall be glad to hear if you are like to make any Progress in the Affair of a Loan, which I understand M. Laurens was charged with. I send you enclosed a Copy of a Vote of Congress, respecting your Salaries.[7] I hope you will be able to do without my Assistance. If not, I must furnish you. But I have been obliged to accept

4. In the hand of L'Air de Lamotte, as is the copy. The postscript, which is missing from the copy, is in ʙғ's hand.

5. ᴊᴀ to ʙғ, Sept. 29, above.

6. xxvi, 267–8.

7. Probably a resolution of May 31 ordering ʙғ to pay ᴊᴀ and Dana's drafts to the amount of their salaries: *JCC*, xvii, 476. There are copies among both ʙғ's papers and ᴊᴀ's (APS; Mass. Hist. Soc.).

Mr. Neufville's Bills on Acct. of his Acceptances of those drawn on Mr. Laurens, and I shall, with some Difficulty, be able to pay them; tho' these extra Demands often embarras me excedingly.

We hear that the Alliance is arriv'd at Boston.

I beg leave to recommend to your Civilities M. Searle a Member of Congress for Pensilvania, with whose conversation you will be pleased, as he can give you good Information of the State of our Affairs when he left America.

I ought to acquaint you, *a governo*,[8] as the Merchants Say; that M. Le Comte de V. having taken much amiss some Passages in your Letters to him, sent the whole Correspondence to me, requesting that I would transmit it to Congress. I was myself sorry to see those Passages. If they were the Effects merely of Inadvertance, and you do not on Reflection approve of them, perhaps you may think it proper to write something for effacing the Impressions made by them. I do not presume to advise you; but mention it only for your Consideration.

The Vessel is not yet gone, which carries the Papers.

With great Regard, I have the honour to be Sir, Your most obedient and most humble Servant. B FRANKLIN

[*in Franklin's hand:*] Perhaps the Letter you desire is one I wrote to M. Dumas, who might show it to the G. P.[9]

His Excy. John Adams Esqr.

Endorsed: His Excellency Dr. Franklin. 8. Oct. 1780 by Mr Searle.

To Sartine
Copy: Library of Congress[1]

Sir, Passy, 8— Oct. 1780.

Messrs. delap Merchant at Bordeaux desires your Excellency's Permission to expedite two american Vessels to the West

8. "For guidance" (in Italian).
9. Perhaps XXVII, 448.
1. BF's letterbook contains a brief, earlier version of this letter, dated Oct. 2 and marked "not sent." It simply asks that the Delaps' request be granted if consistent with the laws of commerce. Library of Congress.

indies without being obliged to pay the Duties. If this may be granted to them consistent with your established Laws of Commerce, I shall be much obliged to your Excellency to comply with their Request. They are satisfied to pay the Duties, if they do not return the necessary Acquits à Caution duly discharged in the time prescribed. The Vessels they wish the permission for are the *Polly* of Boston Capt. Eliphalet Ripley,[2] and the *Favorite of North Carolina.* Capt. Jeremiah Morgan.[3] With &c.

M. De Sartine.

To Georgiana Shipley
AL (draft): Library of Congress

Passy, Oct. 8. 1780

It is long, very long, my dear Friend, since I had the great Pleasure of hearing from you, and receiving any of your very pleasing Letters.[4] But it is my fault. I have long omitted my Part of the Correspondence. Those who love to receive Letters should write Letters. I wish I could safely promise an Amendment of that Fault. But besides the Indolence attending Age, and growing upon us with it, my Time is engross'd by too much Business, and I have too many Inducements to postpone doing, what I feel I ought to do for my own Sake, & what I can never resolve to omit entirely.

Your Translations from Horace, as far as I can judge of Poetry & Translations, are very good. That of the *Quò quò ruitis,* is so suitable to the Times, that the Conclusion (in your Version) seems to threaten like a Prophecy, and methinks there is at least some Appearance of Danger that it may be fulfilled.—[5] I am unhappily an Enemy, yet I think there has been enough of Blood spilt, and I wish what is left in the Veins of that once lov'd People, may be spared, by a Peace solid & everlasting.

2. The *Polly,* 8, had a crew of twenty men: Claghorn, *Naval Officers,* p. 259.

3. Morgan was soon captured: *ibid.,* p. 213.

4. Two letters from her in 1780 are extant: XXXI, 444–5; XXXII, 432–3.

5. "Quo quo scelesti ruitis": Horace, *Epodes,* VII, I. It can be translated as "Whither, whither are you rushing to ruin?"

It is a great while since I have heard any thing of the *good Bishop*. Strange that so simple a Character should sufficiently distinguish one of that sacred Body!— *Donnez moi de ses Nouvelles.*— I have been some time flatter'd with the Expectation of seeing the Countenance of that most honour'd & ever beloved Friend, delineated by your Pencil. The Portrait is said to have been long on the way, but is not yet arriv'd: Nor can I hear where it is.[6]

Indolent as I have confess'd myself to be, I could not, you see, miss this good & safe Opportunity of sending you a few Lines, with my best Wishes for your Happiness and that of the whole dear & amiable Family in whose sweet Society I have spent so many happy Hours. Mr Jones[7] tells me he shall have a Pleasure in being the Bearer of my Letter, of which I make no doubt; I learn from him, that to your Drawing, & Music, & Painting & Poetry, & Latin, you have added a Proficiency in Chess; so that you are, as the French say, *tout plein de Talens.*[8] May they & you fall to the Lot of One that shall duly value them, and love you as much as I do. Adieu.

Miss Georgiana Shipley

From Jean-Hyacinthe de Magellan

ALS: American Philosophical Society

Mon Cher Doctr. & très respectable ami   Ce 8 Octbre.[9] 80

Excusez ma liberté. Cet extrait bien plus ample, (mais necessaire pour le faire entendre en France) que Celui de notre ami Vaughan, est destiné pour paroitre dans le Journal de Rozier après etre lu a l'Academie.[1] Je l'envoye ouvert pour que Vous

6. For the drawing she had made of her father see Digges to BF, July 12 and Sept. 18.

7. William Jones.

8. BF had originally—and correctly—drafted the phrase in the feminine: "toute pleine de Talens".

9. Or possibly, "Decbre"; the handwriting is unclear.

1. This sentence holds an unsolved mystery. Vaughan's manuscript has disappeared and we have not been able to find any trace of it in BF's correspondence, the records of the Académie des sciences, or Rozier's *Journal de Physique*.

puissiez vous amusé à le lire dans quelques momens de loisir.
Corrigez, voyez, & faites y comm'il vous plaira. Vous en enten-
dez mieux que moi la matiere.

Soiez autant heureux dans tout ce qui vous regarde & le bien
public, que vous Le souhaite Votre du fond du coeur & ame pour
La vie   MAGELLAN

Notation: Magellan 8 Oct. 1780.

From Le Roy   AL: American Philosophical Society

Jeudy matin [after October 8, 1780][2]
On m'a dit Mon Illustre Docteur que vous aviez de la goutte hier.
J'espere qu'elle s'est contentée de vous tourmenter le Jour et
qu'elle vous a laissé tranquile la nuit. Vous avez au moins la re-
cette de M. Small.[3] Voici les livres que Je vous ai promis. Vous les
trouverez marqués à Larticle de LOrthographe. Les deux gram-
maires Sont précieuses et le traité du Mécanisme du langage un
Ouvrage de génie.[4] Si la goutte vous permet de vous en escrimer

2. Actually, between Oct. 8 and Oct. 20, when (judging by BF's letters to
JA of those dates) BF learned the news about Laurens. The two possible
Thursdays were Oct. 12 and 19.

3. See BF to Alexander Small, July 22.

4. Le Roy may only have been lending these works, but several French
grammar titles appear on the five-page list of books that BF apparently owned
in France ("List of Books," undated, APS, in the hands of WTF and Gurdon
S. Mumford). These are: "*Langue Françoise* par Mr de Wally," doubtless one
of the works by the distinguished linguist Noël-François de Wailly, and possibly his *Grammaire française* (Paris, 1754); "Boyer's *French Grammar,*" probably Abel Boyer, *The Compleat French Master for Ladies and Gentlemen . . .*
(London, 1694 and later), Part One of which was a grammar; *Dictionnaire
des proverbes françois*, which could have been one of two works published
anonymously under that title, one by Joseph Panckoucke (Paris, 1749 and
1758) and the other by Georges de Backer (Brussels, 1710); Pierre Restaut,
"*Grammaire Françoise,*" (either his *Abrégé des principes de la grammaire
françoise* or *Principes généraux et raisonnés de la grammaire françoise . . .*, both
of which went through many editions); Abbé Pierre-Joseph Thoulier d'Oli-
vet, *Remarques sur la langue françoise* (Paris, 1767 and later); and two other
titles: "*Dictionnaire des mots,*" and "*Homonymes de la langue Françoise.*"

The last work that Le Roy mentions is most likely Noël-Antoine Pluche,
La Mécanique des langues, et l'art de les enseigner (Paris, 1751).

aux Echecs dans la Soirée Vous Savez mon Illustre Docteur que Je suis votre homme. En lisant hier L'article de M. Laurens dans Le Courier de LEurope⁵ la joie que j'ai eue à votre arivée de ce que vous êties echappé à tant de dangers s'est renouvellée de la manière la plus vive.

Addressed: A Monsieur / Monsieur Franklin

Notation: Le Roy

To Thomas Digges

Copy: Library of Congress

Dear Sir, Passy, Oct. 9. 1780

I received the China portrait of Washington in good order, But no other you mention. Nor has the Picture of the good Bishop ever yet appeared, I begin to be in pain about it, having heard nothing of it from any Place on this Side of the Water, and I have more than one Reason for setting a high Value on it.

Your Favour of the 20th. & 29th. past came duly to hand, and are very pleasing. Inclos'd is my answer to a Letter from some Persons recommended by you.[6]

I have already written to you about Goddard's Bill,[7] and I sent you Jones's, which I hope you received.

I have been made happy by Visits from your two friends.[8] I send this by them, & hope they will have a prosperous Journey. They are worthy & amiable Men.

There is no News here at present but what comes in your news papers.

I am, with great Regard. Sir, Your most obedient humble Servant.

M. Digges.

---

5. Articles about Laurens being sent to the Tower appeared in the *Courier de l'Europe*, VIII (1780), 221–2, 230–1 (issues of Oct. 6 and 10).

6. To McCausland *et al.* of this date, below.

7. Above, Sept. 18.

8. William Jones and John Paradise: Digges to BF, Sept. 18, above.

To Dumas Copy: Library of Congress; transcript:[9] National Archives

Dear Sir,   Passy Oct. 9. 1780.

I received yours of 29th. Sept. & 3d. Oct. It is a very good Addition you made to your Memoire for the Ministers of Russia & Sweden. I am glad to find you are again on such good Terms with the Ambassador, as to be invited to his Comedy. I doubt not of your continuing to cultivate that good understanding. I like much your Insertions in the Gazettes. Such Things have good effect.

Your Informations relative to the Transactions at Petersbourg, & in Denmark are very interesting, & afford me a good deal of Satisfaction; particularly the former.

Mr. Searle will have the Pleasure of seeing you. I recommend him warmly to your Civilities. He is much your Friend, and will advise M. Laurens to make you his Secretary, which I hope you will accept. I have given it as my Opinion, that Mr. L. can no where find one better qualified, or more deserving. The Choice is left to that Minister, and he is impowered to give a salary of 500£ Sterling a year.[1] I am in pain on Account of his not being yet arrived; but hope you will see him soon. I request you would find means to introduce M. Searle to the Portuguese Ambassador.

Pray consider the enclos'd Papers, and after advising with Your friend, give me your Opinion as to the manner of the Application to the States general, whether I should make it, thro' their Ambassador, or directly with a Letter to the G. P. or in what other manner. You know we wrote to him formerly and receiv'd no answer.[2]

With great Esteem, I am, your faithful Friend.

M. Dumas.

9. The transcript contains a postscript (to which Dumas responded on Oct. 20, below): "You say nothing of Mr. adams. How do you stand with him? What is he doing?"

1. Laurens was authorized to employ "a proper secretary upon the most reasonable terms," but was not authorized to pay him more than £300 per year: *JCC*, xv, 1235.

2. American Commissioners to Grand Pensionary van Bleiswijk, April 10, 1778, xxvi, 267–8. The intended application to the States General must have been by Searle; see Dumas to BF, Oct. 20. The Portuguese minister at The Hague was Envoy Extraordinary Agosto Antonio de Souza Holstein (for whom see *Repertorium der diplomatischen Vertreter*, III, 318).

To David Gregorie

Copy: Library of Congress

Sir,   Passy, Oct. 9. 1780.

I received the Letter you did me the honour of writing to me the 30th. past. The king having by a late Ordinance directed the Council of Prizes to take Cognisance of Causes arising from the Conduct of Privateers fitted out in France by his Subjects, tho' under American Commissions, I apprehend that your proper Application for Redress will be to that Council. As you may in the Course of Such Application have occasion for the papers you enclos'd to me, I shall hold them ready to be deliver'd to any Person you may appoint to call for them.[3] I have the Honour to be, Sir,

M. David Gregorie, Mt. at Dunkirk.

To Gardoqui & fils

Copy: Library of Congress

Gentlemen,   Passy, Oct. 9. 1780.

I have long been made sensible by many Instances, of your Friendship for America, & of the kindness you have Shewn to many of my Countrymen;[4] I beg you to accept my thankful acknowledgements.

We have an Exchange of Prisoners here with England, which gives us Americans for all the English taken by American armed

---

3. On Oct. 21 Gregorie acknowledged BF's letter, reported he was awaiting orders on whether to apply to French courts for redress, and asked BF to send the papers relating to the case to Girardot, Haller & Co. for forwarding to him (APS). WTF made a notation on it that this was done. There are no further letters from Gregorie among BF's papers.

4. The firm had served for several years as an unofficial link between Spain and the United States: XXIII, 498–9. James (Diego) de Gardoqui (1735–1798), a son of Joseph Gardoqui, the founder of the company, was presently serving as Floridablanca's representative in discussions with John Jay. After the war he became Spain's first official diplomatic representative in the United States: W.W. Abbot and Dorothy Twohig, eds., *The Papers of George Washington: Confederation Series* (6 vols., Charlottesville and London, 1992–97), II, 362n; Light Townsend Cummins, *Spanish Observers and the American Revolution, 1775–1783* (Baton Rouge and London, 1991), p. 193.

Vessels. I have heard from time to time of English Prisoners carried unto the Ports of Spain by our Privateers, but I never knew or heard what became of Such Prisoners.[5]

If any now remain there I shall be glad of Information, what Number there may be, & whether they could not be sent to England on American Acct. to deliver so many Countrymen confined in Prisons there.[6] If it be not too troublesome for you to obtain and send me such information, it will very much oblige me.

I have the honour to be &c.

Messrs. Guardoqui & sons.

To William Hodgson

Copy: Library of Congress

Dear Sir,   Passy, Oct. 9. 1780.

I received your favour of the 20th. Past, containing the account of Prisonners as it stands between the Board & me. I do hereby agree that Capt. Scott of the Golden Eagle Privateer, taken by Capt. Harrabin of the General Pickering, and carried into Bilbao, and allowed to go to England on his Parole, be considered exchanged by one of the 119 Americans Landed at Morlaix; and that he be accordingly discharged from his Parole.— I have written to Bilbao to enquire about the Crew of that Privateer & other Prisoners in Spain.[7] As to the Others contain'd in the list you send me, who are confin'd in the Prison of St. Omers, I have apply'd for an Order to discharge them taking their acknowledgement of Such Discharge,[8] which I shall send you as soon as I receive it. And I wish to know whether if I discharge the Prisoners in the same manner that are in Spain, they will be

5. Generally, American-made prisoners in Spain had been released, but rumors persisted that some were still there: XXVII, 551, 575; XXVIII, 85–6; XXX, 380; Neeser, *Conyngham*, p. 138.

6. John Bondfield and David Hartley separately had suggested the idea in 1779 and since then BF had been pursuing in vain information on the subject: XXIX, 373, 733; XXX, 94, 140, 355; XXXI, 255, 398.

7. BF to Gardoqui & fils, immediately above.

8. BF to Sartine, Oct. 6, above.

allow'd in Account. I send you herewith a few American News-papers, and am, with the greatest Esteem, Dear Sir,

M. William Hodgson Mercht. London.

To Connolly McCausland *et al.*   Copy: Library of Congress

Gentlemen,   Passy, Oct. 9. 1780.

I received yours dated the 10th. past,[9] Tho' the Commission-ers of Sick and Hurt did not think fit to release any Actual Pris-oners in Exchange for you, perhaps they may be willing to re-ceive you in part Payment of a Debt I owe them of English in Exchange for Americans they have already delivered here.[1] In that Case, on your sending me their Receipit as for four Persons, I will send you such Certificates as may secure you from Blame, as well as from Danger in case of being again taken.[2] I am, Gen-tlemen, Your most obedt. h. Servant.

W. Connolly Mc. Causland, Wm. Stewart, James Campbell, Marms Mc.Causland.

9. Described in our annotation of Digges to BF, Sept. 8.

1. On Nov. 9 Connolly McCausland wrote BF that he and Robert Temple had applied to the Board of Sick and Hurt, but that they had refused the offer. McCausland asks whether the four prisoners can be exchanged in France "so as to Cancell our Parole." Until their case is settled they are determined to abide by their agreement. APS.

2. Before hearing again from them BF launched another plan for their as-sistance. On Oct. 18 he prepared a passport for Henry Bromfield, Jr., the two McCauslands, Stewart, and John Snelling (XXXII, 124n) to travel with Capt. John Fletcher; a rough draft is at the APS. On Oct. 23 Bromfield signed an oath of allegiance and a bond for £2000 (APS). On Feb. 5, 1781, however, Bromfield writes from Amsterdam that Fletcher has decided to cancel the voyage, fearing to go to London, and has destroyed the passport; he encloses an undated certificate from Fletcher stating he had done so. (Both of these documents are at the APS.) Bromfield asks WTF to cancel the bond. WTF responds on the 25th that he has to retain the bond "for the office," but reassures him that it would have applied only if the goods men-tioned in it had been deliberately carried into an enemy port (Library of Congress).

To Richard Price AL (draft) and two copies: Library of Congress

Dear Sir, Passy, Oct. 9. 1780

Besides the Pleasure of their Company, I had the great Satisfaction of hearing by your two valuable Friends, & learning from your Letter, that you enjoy a good State of Health.[3] May God continue it as well for the Good of Mankind as for your Comfort. I thank you much for the second Edition of your excellent Pamphlet.[4] I forwarded that you sent to Mr. Dana, he being in Holland.—[5] I wish also to see the Piece you have written as Mr Jones tells me, on Toleration.—[6] I do not expect that your new Parliament will be either wiser or honester than the last. All Projects to procure an Honest one, by Place Bills, &c appear to me vain and Impracticable. The true Cure I imagine is to be found only in rendring all Places unprofitable, and the King too poor to give Bribes & Pensions. Till this is done, which can only be by a Revolution, and I think you have not Virtue enough left to procure one, your Nation will always be plundered; & obliged to pay by Taxes the Plunderers for Plundering & Ruining. Liberty & Virtue therefore join in the Call, COME OUT OF HER, MY PEOPLE![7] I am fully of your Opinion respecting Religious Tests; but tho' the People of Massachusetts have not in their new Constitution kept quite clear of them; yet if we consider what that People were 100 Years ago, we must allow they have gone great Lengths in Liberality of Sentiment, on religious Subjects; and

---

3. The two friends were John Paradise and William Jones. Price's most recent extant letter, which BF had already answered, was sent the previous October: XXX, 532–3; XXXI, 452–3.

4. *An Essay on the Population of England, from the Revolution to the Present Time* (1st separate edition, London, 1780). Benjamin Vaughan had sent the pamphlet to BF in May: XXXII, 380.

5. Price became acquainted with Francis Dana when he was in London in 1775: D.O. Thomas and W. Bernard Peach, eds., *The Correspondence of Richard Price* (3 vols., Durham, N.C., and Cardiff, Wales, 1983–94), I, 200–1. BF also passed on a copy of the pamphlet to Turgot: *ibid.*, II, 68.

6. Price replied on Dec. 22, 1780, that although he had written a great deal on toleration he had not published on the subject: *Correspondence of Price*, II, 91.

7. "And I heard another voice from heaven, saying, Come out of her, my people, that ye be not partakers of her sins, and that ye receive not of her plagues." Revelation 18:4.

we may hope for greater Degrees of Perfection when their Constitution some years hence shall be revised.[8] If Christian Preachers had continued to teach as Christ & his Apostles did, without Salaries, and as the Quakers now do, I imagine Tests would never have existed: For I think they were invented not so much to secure Religion itself, as the Emoluments of it.— When a Religion is good, I conceive that it will support itself; and when it cannot support itself, and God does not take care to support, so that its Professors are oblig'd to call for the help of the Civil Power, 'tis a Sign, I apprehend, of its being a bad one. But I shall be out of my Depth if I wade any deeper in Theology, & I will not trouble you with Politicks, nor with News which are almost as uncertain: But conclude with a heartfelt Wish, to embrace you once more, & enjoy your sweet Society in Peace, among our honest, worthy, ingenious Friends at the London.

Adieu

Dr Price

To Thomas Ruston

ʟs:[9] Yale University Library; ᴀʟ (draft): Library of Congress

Sir,   Passy Oct. 9. 1780.

I received and read with Pleasure your Thoughts on American Finance, and your Scheme of a Bank. I communicated them to the Abbé Morellet, who is a good Judge of the Subject, and he has translated them into French.[1] He thinks them generally very just, and very clearly exprest. I shall forward them to a Friend in

8. The draft of the Massachusetts Constitution of 1780 stipulated that no person be eligible for election to the House of Representatives "unless he be of the christian religion." Although the provision was deleted, attempts were made in the convention to restore it and add "Protestant" to the requirement. The constitution did require the governor to be a Christian: *Adams Papers*, VIII, 248, 250, 267.

9. In ᴡᴛꜰ's hand. A fragment of the letter, comprising only the first two lines, appears at the bottom of a page in ʙꜰ's letterbook at the Library of Congress.

1. See our résumé of Ruston's Sept. 9 letter.

the Congress.[2] That Body is, as you well suppose not well skilled in Financing. But their Deficiency in Knowledge has been amply supply'd by Good Luck. They issued an immence Quantity of Paper Bills, to pay, clothe, arm & feed their Troops, & fit out Ships, and with this Paper, without Taxes for the first three Years, they fought & baffled one of the most powerful Nations of Europe. They hoped notwithstanding its Quantity to have kept up the Value of their Paper. In this they were mistaken. It depreciated gradually. But this Depreciation, tho' in some Circumstances inconvenient, has had the general good and great Effect, of operating as a Tax, and perhaps the most equal of all Taxes,[3] since it depreciated in the Hands of the Holders of the Money, and thereby taxed them in proportion to the Sums they hold and the Time they held it, which is generally in proportion to Mens Wealth. Thus after having done its Business the Paper is reduced to about a sixtieth Part of its original Value. Having issued 200 Millions of Dollars, the Congress stopt, and supplyed themselves by borrowing.[4] These Sums were borrowed at different Periods during the Progress of the Depreciation. Those who lent to the Publick, thereby fixed the Value of the Paper they lent, since it is to be repaid in silver according to its Value at the Time of the Loan. The rest went on Depreciating; and the Depreciation is at length only stopt by the vast nominal Sums called in easily by Taxes, and which will be by that means destroyed. Thus so much of the Publick Debt has been in this Manner insensibly paid that the Remainder, which you desire to know, does not exceed six Millions sterling. And now they are working with new Paper exprest to be equal in Value to silver, which they have made to bear Interest, and have provided such Funds to pay that Interest, that probably its original Value will be supported. In the

2. Ruston later surmised that the friend was Robert Morris (Ruston to BF, May 2, 1782), but we find no record of this in Morris' papers.

3. Immediately following this word BF interlined " a Tax set upon Money, a thing heretofore always found most difficult to tax," and then deleted it.

4. The ratio of currency to specie in July, 1780, was 62.5 to 1; by October it had reached to 77.5 to 1. On Sept. 3, 1779, Congress had set a limit of $200,000,000 in emissions, but in fact had issued $226,200,000 before the devaluation and new emission in March, 1780: Ferguson, *Power of the Purse*, pp. 30, 32, 46. For Congress' borrowing see pp. 35–42.

meantime the Vigour of their Military Operations is again re-
vived; and they are now as able, with respect to Money, to carry
on the War, as they were at the Beginning, and much more so
with regard to Troops Arms & Discipline. It is also an encreas-
ing Nation, Sixty thousand Children having been born annually
in the United States since the Beginning of the War;[5] while their
Enemies are said to be diminishing.

I am, Sir, Your most obedient and most humble Servant B F.

Mr. T. R.

Addressed: To / Dr Ruston / Exeter

Notations in different hands: B. Franklin. To Dr Ruston Octr 19th
1780 / with Mr Digges's Compliments

To ——— Viel[6]   Copy: Library of Congress

Monsieur,   Passy, 9 oct. 1780.

J'ai appris par une Lettre du ministre de la marine, que le
bateau sur lequel six americains se sont echappés d'angleterre il
y a quelque tems, avoit été vendu et que cette vente n'avoit produit que 34. Livres: que les frais relatifs à cette vente et autres depenses montoient à 139 livres que vous avez eu la bonté d'avancer.[7] Comme vous n'avez reçu que le produit du dit bateau, je
vous suis encore redevable de 105. et vous pouvez pour vous
rembourser de cette somme tirer une Lettre de change sur moi
et elle sera payée a vue,

J'ai l'honneur d'être, &c.

M. Viel, Grefier de l'amirauté de Coutances.

5. A very reasonable guess given what we now know of 18th-century de-
mography. The pre-war population of the colonies which became the United
States was about 2,200,000; an annual birth rate of about 27 per thousand
would produce 60,000 births per year. For pre-war population and birth rates
see Robert V. Wells, *The Population of the British Colonies in America before
1776: a Survey of Census Data* (Princeton, 1975), pp. 141, 260, 284.

6. Who had reported the sale of the boat discussed here: XXXI, 511–12n.

7. See Sartine's Feb. 21 letter to BF (XXXI, 511–12), which had enclosed a
memoir from Viel.

From Chaumont: Two Letters

(I) and (II) ALS: American Philosophical Society

I.

a Passi ce 9. 8bre. 1780

Je prie Monsieur franklin de me donner un mandat sur M. grand payable au quinze Novembre prochain Sur M. grand pour me Servir de valeur a mes acceptations des traittes de William pour Compte du Congrès.   LERAY DE CHAUMONT

Endorsed: Demand from M. de Chaumont of an Order on Mr Grand, for Money to pay his Acceptations of Mr Williams's Bills. Oct. 9. 1780

II.

a Passi ce 9. 8bre 1780

Je prie M. franklin de donner ordre a Bordeau qu'on Charge sur le Vau. qui S'appelloit Le Breton et actuellement le Marquis de la fayette, touttes Les Munitions quil peut y avoir pour Les etats unis de L'amerique.   LERAY DE CHAUMONT.

Addressed: a Monsieur / Monsieur le Docteur / franklin / à Passi

Notation: Le Ray de Chaumont Passy ce 9. 8bre. 1780.

From Joseph Conkling   ALS: American Philosophical Society

Sir   La float in Isle Deree[8] 9th. Octobr 1780
    The Gentelman that Waits on Your Excelency With this Letter is An Officer with me in the Brign. Whim the Season Being fair Relapts so that in A few weeks more shall Not be Able to Git my Cargo from La. France this fall thair fore have sent Mr. Pinkham[9] to wait on Your Excelency And pray Your Excelency

8. La Flotte is southeast of St. Martin-de-Ré.
    9. As Conkling and his ship were from Connecticut, this may well be Sylvanus Pinkham, who had served in 1776–77 as a Connecticut Navy midshipman aboard the *Oliver Cromwell:* Claghorn, *Naval Officers,* p. 243; Louis F. Middlebrook, *History of Maritime Connecticut during the American Revolution 1775–1783* (2 vols., Salem, Mass., 1925), I, 109.

to Asist him in Obtaining An Order as soon as posable for the Admeralty of Sab Daloon [Les Sables d'Olonne] to Deliver my Cargo Guns And Efects to me.

I have the honour to Be Sr. Your Excelencys most Obideant And Most Humble Servent   JOSEPH CONKLING

Doctr Franklin

Addressed: His Excelency Doctor Franklin / at / Perace / fvord pr Mr. Pinkham

Notation: Joseph Conkling. La Flott Oct 9 1780

From Francis Dana   ALS: American Philosophical Society

Sir   Antwerp Octr. 9th. 1780

The five enclosed bills were this day deliver'd me under cover— they are the property of Mr: Jona: L. Austin. I shall commit them to the care of Mr: Saml: Bradford[1] who goes on for Nantes (by the way of Paris) where he will meet with Mr. Austin. I have requested him to present the Bills for acceptance.

Mr Adams is at Amsterdam where I am about going tomorrow.— We have nothing new. Your letter to him has been received.[2] I am dear Sir with much respect and esteem your most obedient and most humble Servant   F M DANA

His Excellency Benjamin Franklin

Addressed: His Excellency / Benjamin Franklin / Passy.

Notations in different hands: Francis Dana. Antwerp Oct 9 1780 / Recd 14th Do. Presented 14 Oct. 1780.

---

1. Samuel Bradford (XXVIII, 278n) had made a brief trip to Europe at the beginning of 1779: XXIX, 358. By July 31, 1780, he was back in Europe, as on that date he wrote JW from Amsterdam and forwarded him letters from his friends: JW to Bradford, Aug. 29, 1780 (Yale University Library). He was in Passy on Nov. 6; BF gave him a passport to Nantes, good for one month (Dartmouth College Library).

2. Presumably BF to JA, Oct. 2, above.

From the Marquis de Lafayette

ALS: American Philosophical Society

light Camp Totawa Bridge Passaic River
Dear Sir   october the 9th 1780

I Wish it was in My power to Give you some *Grand* intelligence from this part of the world—But Considering the Naval Superiority which the Ennemy have hitherto kept on our Coasts, You will not wonder at our finding it Rather difficult to Cooperate against Maritime points, or such points as are at an immence distance from us.

The Arrival of the french Succour has however Been Attended With happy Circumstances—it has Serv'd as A check upon Sir harry clinton, and has forc'd him Both to leave off any offensive plan this way and to keep in Newyork Such troops as Should have Reinforc'd lord Cornwallis— From the Collection of the Ennemy's Men of War, our trade, and privateering have deriv'd Great Benefits— The Expectation of the Succour has also Wakened the States into spirited (tho Momentary,) Measures Which have Enabled our Army to Cut a figure this Campaign in the Neighborod of Newyork and to offer the Battle to the Ennemy upon Equal terms and Equal ground.

A Naval Superiority is to us of an immence importance—let us But Gain that point and we May be able to do Some thing— No intelligence about the Cloathing— We are Nack'd, Schokingly Nack'd, and worse off on that Respect than we have ever been— For God's Sake, my dear friend, let us have Any how fifteen or twenty thousand Compleat Suits (exclusive of what is expected) and let it be done in Such a way as will insure theyr timely departure from france— Cloathing for officers is Absolutely Necessary— No Cloth to be Got— No Monney to purchase— I hope the fifteen thousand stands of Arms will at lenght Arrive— We Shall also want a large Quantity of powder—how did it happen that Nothing is Yet Come to hand? Expectations were Rais'd—the disappointment is of Course attended with Bad Consequences— You have no idea of the shoking Situation the Army is in.

The Battle of Camden you will Certainly hear off— From General Gates's first Accounts we thought it was Much Worse, But was afterwards happy to find there had been a strange Mistake of the General— The Militia Ran Shamefully— The Continental troops Behav'd to A Charm.[3]

The french fleet and Army are at Rhode island. Rodney's fleet Consists of 19 of the line, and many fifties, frigats &c our Army is Encamp'd Near this place and here I am with the light Camp— The Conduct of the Ennemy is alwaïs the same, base, insolent, and cruel.

The Eastern States talk of adopting a plan which if Agreed to will insure our independency—[4] Newyork seems willing to fall in— Returning to Congress those powers which they Gave up, I don't know why— Raising An Army for war—subsiting that Army are the three heads of this truly patriotic project.

You will fully hear of Arnold's treachery—of Andre's execution—[5] What Miraculous escape we had—here are some papers which I have pick'd up for you— My Compliments wait on your Grand son, doctor Bancroft, monsieur de Chaumont, and My American Acquaintances on the other Side of the Great Water.

With the highest Regard and most sincere Attachment, My dear friend Yours   LAFAYETTE

General Washington Requests that his Compliments be presented to Your excellency.

his excellency Monsieur B. franklin [Esq]

Notation: La Fayette Octr 9. 1780

3. Gates's 3,000-man army was crushed at Camden, S.C., on Aug. 16: Ward, *War of the Revolution*, II, 722–30.

4. Lafayette was less cryptic in a September letter to the Prince de Poix, his wife's cousin: Idzerda, *Lafayette Papers*, III, 164–7. He is referring to an August meeting of Massachusetts, Connecticut, and New Hampshire delegates which urged various reforms and recommended adoption of the Articles of Confederation: Franklin B. Hough, ed., *Proceedings of a Convention of Delegates from Several of the New-England States, Held at Boston, August 3–9, 1780 . . .* (Albany, 1867), pp. 35–52.

5. The spy Maj. John André was captured on Sept. 23 with documents incriminating Gen. Benedict Arnold, who fled to the British two days later. André was executed on Oct. 2: Freeman, *Washington*, V, 196–222.

From Jean de Neufville & fils

ALS: American Philosophical Society

Honourd Sir!   Amsterdam the 9th. Oct 1780.

We begg leave to thank your Excellency for her most obliging favour of the 1st. instant, promising to honour our draufts in
the manner we have mention'd, and which we will Continue in
Consequence; when any other bills will appear, we propose to
follow exactly your Excellencys orders in mentioning the
summs, except when a protest should be enthreathend, in such a
case we won't hesitate to accept of such bills immediately; and
we are the more satisfied and pleased with this arrangement as
we learnd last saturday morning[6] by an express from Londo. the
misfortune of Mr Laurens being taken and carried in to Darthmouth, it was confirmd next day by the mail, and we doubt not
butt your Excellency must have gott already the same intelligence by the way of Ostende. This we look upon to be a greater
misfortune then the Tabacco which was send here on acct. of
Congress and was likewise taken, The publicq news says that the
papers of Mr Lawrence were thrown overboard butt seized Since
little damaged;[7] so they were afraid of it in London this to be
true. My Son,[8] who happens to be there will Certainly vizit this
worthy Gentleman, if there is any possibility, and as we are
favoured there with the acquaintance of many worthy frinds to
the American Cause we doubt not butt he will be the most fitt
to execute any Comissions thereto relating which I make bold to
mention as your Excellency will find him disposed to execute any
orders she might find proper to honour him with on the occasion, with any other commands she may think proper to favour
him with his adress is to Mr. Van Boiset, under a Cover a
Messieurs Jean Noël Famin & Co[9] Negts. a Londres. And your
Excellency will every way find us most Willing to serve her with
Zeal and integrity; by first maill I intend to write to Mr. Laurens,

6. Oct. 7.

7. Laurens' capture and arrival at Dartmouth were reported in the Oct. 10
issue of the *Gaz. de Leyde,* but the recovery of his papers was not reported
until the next issue, that of Oct. 13 (sup.).

8. Leendert de Neufville: XXIX, 566n.

9. For whom see XXVI, 389n.

and mentioning your Excellencys Civilities will be obeying her Comands as Circumstances will permitt, though it would Certainly have been the greatest satisfaction if we could have had the honour to congratulate in her name as well as in our own, on his Safe arrivell in Holland; This disappointment however, we hope, wont hurt the Cause, we expect to hear something more about it, and in which way we might be able to promote any good, our hearth and Soul will be in it.

We have again to thank your Excellency for paying the bills fr. Mr. John Leveret on our Guarantie and to assure her that with the highest Esteem & regard we wish for ever to be Honourd Sir Your Excellencys most devoted And most obedient humble servt.   JOHN DE NEUFVILLE & SON

From George Washington

ALS: New Jersey Historical Society; draft:[1] Library of Congress

Bergen County in the State of N: Jersey
Dear Sir,   Oct 9th. 1780.

I was very much obliged by the letter which you did me the honor to write me by our amiable young friend the Marquis De La Fayette,[2] whose exertions to serve this Country in his own are additional proofs of his zealous attachment to our cause, and has endeared him to us still more.

He came out flushed with expectations of a decisive campaign and fired with hopes of acquiring fresh laurels, but in both he has been disappointed; for we have been condemned to an inactivity as inconsistent with the situation of our affairs as with the ardor of his temper.

I am sensible of all I owe you My Dear Sir for your sentiments of me, and while I am happy in your esteem, I cannot but wish for occasions of giving you marks of mine.

The idea of making a tour together, which you suggest after the war, would be one of the strongest motives I could have to

1. Dated Oct. 11, and in the hand of Alexander Hamilton.
2. XXXII, 56–7.

postpone my plan of retirement and make a visit to Europe, if my domestic habits which seem to acquire strength from restraint did not tell me, I shall find it impossible to resist them longer than my duty to the public calls for the sacrafice of my inclinations.

I doubt not you are so fully informed by Congress of our political and military State that it would be superfluous to trouble you with any thing relating to either— If I were to speak on topics of the kind it would be to shew that our present situation makes one of two things essential to us—A Peace—or the most vigorous aid of our allies particularly in the article of money.— Of their disposition to serve us we cannot doubt; their generosity will do everything their means will permit.

With my best wishes for the preservation of your useful life and for every happiness that can attend you which a sincere attachment can dictate I am—My Dear Sir—Yr. Most Obedt. Hble. Servt   Go: Washington

His Excelly Doc B Franklin

To Gourlade & Moylan   Copy: Library of Congress

Gentlemen,   Passy Oct. 10. 1780.

The foregoing is Copy of a Letter[3] to which I have received no answer. In the mean time Sundry other Bills have been presented to me viz

For 672. 13s. in fav. of Parementier ⎫
For 5608. 2. fav. of Laurent Bené   ⎬ dated 7 Sept. 80.
For 300. fav. of Maurice   dated 6. Do.

all which I have accepted.[4] But am much dissatisfied with being so continually drawn upon without receiving any Advice or any Accounts, I have the Honour to be.

Messrs. Gourlade et Moylan.

3. An asterisk here in the text refers to a marginal note identifying the letter as BF's to Gourlade & Moylan of Sept. 7.

4. These were presented by Richard le jeune, Grand, and Juvel neveux & Cauchoit (see that firm's letter, of Sept. 22 above): WTF's list of bills drawn on BF by Gourlade & Moylan, APS.

From Thomas Digges

ALS: Historical Society of Pennsylvania

Dr. Sir   London Octor 10. 1780

Since I wrote you the 6th. Int. no alteration has taken place with regard to Mr Laurens confinement & treatment. No person whatever has been permitted to speak to Him, but it is said any person may who will apply for a Secy of States order to do so.— I hear of none of his friends who have made any attempts to do so; I suppose from thinking any stir made to see Him may be disadvantageous to Mr L———.

A torey Cozen or two, & his Correspondent in trade, Mr Manning,[5] have made unsuccessful attempts. It is thought this rigour will be relaxd in a few days, & most likely it will for these folks are ever acting in Extreems. Nothing can more strictly verify it than their behaviour at the present moment. Last week & indeed until last night the general cry was "we are undone—we can never do any thing in America—the War must be given up— our armys will be Burgoind—our fleets beaten" &ca &a &a. Yesterday an officer arrivd Express from Cornwallis with an accot of a victory over Gates's Army at Cambden in So Carolina,[6] and now they are all in the Skies again— The whole Southern America is theirs—Virginia will "come in" on a certainty—the Rebels will be beat every where—a few thousand more regulars sent over directly will insure the subjugation of America—let us persue the war vigorously &ca. &a— their folly is enough to make one sick.

For several days before this arrival, it was the general talk that the cabinet had absolutely determind on pushing the war in Ama with vigour & that 10 Ships of the line & as many thousand men were to immideately be sent. If there are as great fools within as there are out of the Cabinet, most likely this measure will be adopted. There are appearances of four Ships of the line & some troops being intended for No America but this may be a necessary measure even if it is determind to relinquish the american War.

---

5. Laurens' business agent William Manning (xxx, 503n), whose daughter married Laurens' son John.

6. An Aug. 21 letter from Cornwallis to Germain reporting the victory was published in the Oct. 10 issue of the *London Courant, and Westminster Chronicle.*

I inclose you the gazettes accot. of Engagement in So Carolina. A report is going about, that while Cornwallis was out, there was an insurrection in the Town which was quelld at the expence of near 400 lives of americans & about 80 British, but the report does not gain much credit.

I am with the highest Esteem Dr Sir Yr. obligd & ob Ser

W S. C

I expect the Revd Mr W [Wren] in Town soon to settle the amot. of your donation weekly to our Captive friends. I will draw a Bill on Monsr. Grand for its amount & give notice by the same post of the draft.

Addressed: A Monsieur / Monsieur B. F—— / Passy

Endorsed: Oct. 10. 80

From Dumas

ALS: American Philosophical Society; AL (draft): Algemeen Rijksarchief

Monsieur   La Haie 10e.[–12] Oct. 1780

Je commence cette Lettre aujourd'hui, mais vraisemblablement je ne l'enverrai qu'après demain dans l'espoir de pouvoir y ajouter quelque chose sur ce qu'on aura dit ou fait dans l'Assemblée d'Hollde. En attendant je vous dois prévenir d'une incorrection & d'une omission qu'il y a dans le compte que j'ai eu l'honneur de vous rendre de la Dépêche de Petersbourg.[7] 1°. Ce que j'ai dit, touchant la déclaration que l'Envoyé Britannique a faite, "que Sa Cour aura Soin que les navires de la *Neutralité armée*. Soient respectés, pourvu que cette rep. en soit exclue," les Plénipotentiaires l'ont avancé dans leur Dépêche, non comme ne le tenant que de l'Envoyé de Prusse,[8] mais *comme le tenant de Source*. 2°. Et quant à l'accession du R— de P—— à cette neutralité, ce n'est pas une simple conjecture de notre ami, c'est l'Envoyé de Pe. à Petersbourg, qui a dit aux Plénipes. que le R— son Mre. [Maitre] accedera à cette Neutralité armée.

7. Dumas to BF, Oct. 3, above.
8. The Prussian envoy was Count Johann Eustach von Goertz.

Je vous suis très-obligé, Monsieur, de ce que vous m'apprenez par la vôtre du 2e touchant Mr. Searle. Je languis de le voir, & de lui témoigner toute l'amitié & tout le respect, & rendre tous les services dont je suis capable. Mais où est-il présentement? Si j'ai bien compris notre Ami, qui m'en a parlé, il a été à Amsterdam auprès de Mr. Adams; notre Ami l'a vû, & m'en a parlé en termes remplis d'estime. J'en Suis d'autant plus mortifié de ne pas l'avoir vu encore: & je regrette aussi de n'avoir pas la Lettre de Mr. James Lovell dont il est porteur.

Je vous ai bien des Obligations, Monsieur, des Assurances que vous avez bien voulu & pu me donner. Il ne s'offre rien qui surpasse ni équivale ma situation actuelle, les ennemis de l'am—— ont mis ordre à cela depuis longtemps. Je n'en ai pas non plus cherché les occasions; & celles qu'on m'a présentées par le passé, étoient de nature à être rejetées avec le dernier mépris par un brave homme.— J'ajouterai seulement, que la rage de ces ennemis croît, à mesure qu'ils voient croître leurs propres embarras & que ne pouvant plus rien m'ôter, ils me persécutent sourdement jusque chez moi, en rendant malheureux ce qui m'est le plus cher.

Vous aurez déjà appris, Monsieur, le malheur arrivé à Mr. Laurens d'être pris avec son Secretaire, & conduit à Darthmouth en Angle. Je lui ai écrit, par une main sure, une Lettre pour lui offrir les services qu'il pourroit me croire capable de lui rendre.

Vous verrez, par l'Imprimé ci-joint, que j'ai été diligent à faire insérer ce que vous avez eu la bonté de me communiquer.[9]

L'Assemblée d'Hollde. n'a rien décidé encore sur les Dépêches de Petersbourg. On y lut hier une Dépêche du Gouvr. De Graaf de St. Eustache, laquelle confirme authentiquement tout ce qui a été publié dans les Gazettes touchant les hostilités exercées par les Angl. & NB. par ordre exprès de leur Cour, contre l'Isle holl. de St. Martin aux Indes occid.—[1] Il faut avouer que cette Rep. ici est bien malheureuse.— Mais on peut lui dire ce

9. Dumas must have sent a copy of the Oct. 10 issue of the *Gaz. de Leyde*, which printed the letters BF had forwarded to him on Oct. 2.

1. The same issue of the *Gaz. de Leyde* reported that Adm. Rodney had violated the neutrality of the Dutch Caribbean colony of St. Maarten to seize American ships.

que vous m'avez dit sur un autre sujet: *Tu l'as voulu Ge. [George] Dandin.*[2]

Je suis, Monsieur, avec le plus ferme & respectueux attachement, Votre très-humble, très-obéissant & fidele serviteur

DUMAS

12e. Octobe. 1780

Addressed: A Son Excellence / Monsieur B. Franklin, Esqr. / Min. Plenipe. des Et. Un. / &c. / Passy./.

From Fleury & Demadières ᴀʟs: American Philosophical Society

Monsieur   a orleans ce 10e 8bre 1780

Nous recevons dans le moment d'envoy de mr Jn Williams de nantes pour votre Compte 6 Caisses de madere, a leur arrivées nous les avons examinées, il sen est trouvé quelsqunes de Cassées & ce parcequ'elles etoient fort mal Embalées, & si il faut vous les expedier dans le tat ou elles sonts vous En aurez plus de la moitié de Cassées dicy Chez vous En Consequence, nous vous prions, nous marquer En reponse si vous voulez, que nous les faisions mettre En etat de vous parvenir sans risque, nous attendrons votre reponse auparavant de vous les expedier & avons l'honneur detre avec Le plus profond respect Monsieur Vos tres humbles & tres obeissants serviteurs

VE F. FLEURY & PRE. DEMADIÊRES

Notre addresse est a Ve fleury & Pre Demadieres negts a orleans si vous avez besoin de nos services En cette ville soit En draperies, Bas, & autres articles pour vos etats unis, nous sommes a Lieu de vous les procurer a bons Comptes, & de la meilleur qualité.

A son Excellence monsieur franklin ministre Plenipotentaire des Etas unis a paris

Addressed: A son Excellence / Monsieur franklin Ministre / Plenipotentaire des Etats Unis / A Paris

2. Dumas himself had earlier made reference to this title character of a Molière play about a jealous husband: xxx, 605.

Notations: J. f Fleury et Pre. Demandieres Orleans. 10. Oct. 1780. / [*in William Temple Franklin's hand:*] Ansd[3]

From Ezra Stiles

ALS: University of Pennsylvania Library; copy: Yale University Library

Dear Sir   Newport Rhode Isld October. 10. 1780.

Mechanical Inventions, and Improvements in every Branch of experimental Philosophy, are at all times so agreeable to you, that it must give you pleasure to be informed of a Grist-mill, newly invented by an American which will soon come into general use, not only in America but in Europe & thro' the World. There are but 4 or 5 already built. I give you the Description from my own autoptical examination.

It has but one Wheel and that horizontal, constructed like the frustrum of a Cone inverted.[4] Mr. Kelsy the inventor[5] made it, in his first mill, six feet high, three feet diameter at one End & eighteen Inches diameter at the other: but that which I saw was according to the Dimensions in the Margin. It is made like an inverted pyramidical Barrel secured with 2 or 3 Iron Hoops; and affixed to or connected with the perpendicular wooden Shaft of perhaps four Inches Diameter with two radial crosses near the top & bottom. On the Inside are affixed sixteen narrow pieces of board two or 3 Inches wide & half an Inch thick, each running down the Length of the Vessel. These make interior Buckets, the Section of which exhibits this appearance. The Column of Water carrying this Wheel is but *five Inches* broad and *three Inches*

3. The answer (missing) was dated Nov. 14, according to the firm's reply of Dec. 6 (APS).

4. Kelsy had constructed a tapered variation of the "tub wheel," a horizontal water wheel that was destined to be replaced by more efficient vertical ones. See Charles Howell, "Colonial Watermills in the Wooden Age," in Brooke Hindle, ed., *America's Wooden Age: Aspects of Its Early Technology* (Tarrytown, N.Y., 1975), pp. 125–7; Oliver Evans, *The Young Mill-Wright and Miller's Guide* (13th ed., Philadelphia, 1850; reprinted New York, 1972), pp. 167–72, plate IV.

5. The first several letters of this word and of "feet" are obscured by sealing wax. We have supplied them from the copy.

thick, and is introduced atop and operates on the inside by percussion on the Valves or vertical slips of board, performing its circumgyrations in lateral Spirals five Inches in diameter: so that in a Wheel 5 feet high the water performs 12 Revolutions before it passes out at bottom. And altho' I am apprehensive that there is dead water towards the bottom of so high a wheel, yet I doubt not the operative momentum of the water continues for 3 or four Revolutions at least. In a common Water Wheel this momentum is lost after its operation upon one quarter or at most one third of the wheel. There may be probably an Amendment of this horizontal wheel by a Diminution of its length to perhps about three feet.

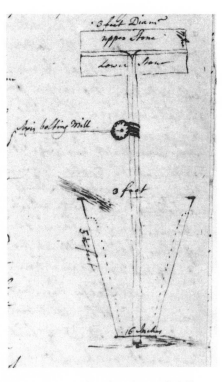

A usual height of Water is necessary or 4 feet head & 4 f. fall, altho' this which I saw went well with only six feet superincumbent water including the descent. However while a smaller Quantity of Water answers, it is necessary there should be as much greater a Descent as the altitude of the wheel, that the water which comes in atop may flow from the bottom & be carried off horizontally. The wheel is inclosed in a Cellar, so that being thereby preserved from freezing, it goes all winter. No larger stones than three feet Diameter & 7 or 8 Inches thick have been tried; tho' doubtless with a bigger Column of Water the largest may be carried. The Mill I saw would grind 40 Bushels or more per day without heating. It ground into excellent Flour a Bushel of Wheat in *twelve Minutes* by the Watch. A spiral on the upper end of the vertical Shaft turns a wheel affixed to the Axis of a bolting mill into which the meal passes as it comes from the Stones. In the same Mill House may be carried half a dozen of these *Kelsy Mills* at the same Time & with the same Quantity of Water as carries one common mill. Mr Kelsy the Inventor is of Middletown in Connecticutt where he built his first mill. He intended to have kept it's construction a secret. He offered to build for £20. Silver L.M. [lawful money] a piece, accounting he should make £10 profit. He made the Owner enter into Bond to keep the Wheel concealed in the Cellar. However the Depreciation of money has annihilated that security, besides one of the mills by Death or otherwise has shifted its possessor & has been seen by him who constructed from his Recollection that which I saw. The poor man is chagrined, & builds no more. The old millers are also against it. However it will soon get abroad, & will be found of great public Utility. I think the principle of an interior operation on the Wheel will apply to other Water Works, whereby they may be reduced to greater Simplicity and be carried with less Water than usuall. I think the Inventor merits such Gratuities from the public at large as would give him Independence.[6]

I am now on a Visit to Newport, where we have a fine French Army with a naval Force. The Chevalier de Chatelux, the second Major Generàl under M. de Rochambeau, is a Lover of Literature as well as of every Thing tending to the happiness of Society & the aggrandizement of Republics. He does me the honor of conveying this to your hands, by the Ship now bound from hence for France.[7] By this Ship you will receive an account of the Treason & Apostacy of one of our greatest Generals (who went over from us to the Enemy 25th of September last), and the

6. Stiles had seen one of Kelsy's mills on Sept. 18 and was struck by how little water was necessary to grind a reasonable amount of grain. He reported in his diary that there were only four of them in the world, all in Connecticut, with a fifth under contruction in Lenox, Mass. Stiles presented a description of the "new American Invention" to the chevalier de Chastellux (XXI, 505n; XXXII, 135n) on Oct. 18, but the following month he learned that a similar mill was in use in Carolina, and began to doubt whether Kelsy was truly the inventor. Franklin Bowditch Dexter, ed., *The Literary Diary of Ezra Stiles, D.D., LL. D.* (3 vols.; New York, 1901), II, 420–1, 470–1, 474, 481.

7. Stiles had been sumptuously entertained by Chastellux on Oct. 9, and had the highest regard for him: *Literary Diary of Ezra Stiles*, II, 473.

happy Detection of it before the Treason was carried into Execution. General Arnold has buried all his military Glory, and sends his Name down in History execrated with Contempt & Infamy. He will be despised not only by us in the United States, but by all the Nations of Europe & in all future Ages. There is reason to believe that he meditated with the reddition of Westpoint on 27th. Sept., the betraying at the same time of General Washington and the Minister of France into the hands of the Enemy. For his Excellency the Chevalier de la Luzerne told me that passing thro' Westpt in his Way hither on 24th or the day before the Detection, General Arnold importuned him even to Indecency to tarry & rest there 4 or 5 days. And Arnold also knew General Washington would meet there at the same time on his Return from an Interview with the French Officers at Hartford.[8] G. Arnold is a Loss! But America is so fertile in Patriots that we can afford to sell a capital Patriot or two every year without any essential Injury to the glorious Cause of *Liberty* & *Independence*. The greatest Injury he can do us will be in Information. However the present State of the American Army is now so good, as that the most thoro' knowledge of it will rather do us a benefit than an Injury. The seasonable Execution of Major Andre, (the Seducer,) Adjutant General of the British Army, on 2d Inst. will probably deter such Adventurers for the future.

Congress & the *Assemblies* thro' the States continue firm & unshaken; & they have a cordial Support in the Union of the main body of the People at large; notwithstanding the Efforts of Tories & governmental Connexions intermixt in all parts, whose sysiphean Labors only pull down ruin upon themselves. A greater Mortification one can scarcely wish them than with an ultimate Disappointment to be subject *to Congress* & to pay *Continental* Taxes. The Storm still blows heavy—but our Ship will ride it thro'. With joy we look forward & with undoubting Assurance anticipate the Sweets & the final Triumph of American

8. Washington met La Luzerne between West Point and Fishkill on Sept. 24 and arrived at West Point the following day. Arnold, learning of André's arrest, fled just before his arrival: Freeman, *Washington*, v, 196–201. The Hartford conference had been held between Sept. 20 and Sept. 22: Lee Kennett, *The French Forces in America, 1780–1783* (Westport, Conn., and London, 1977), pp. 59–61.

Liberty! Wishing you every Blessing, I am, Dear sir, Your most obliged most obedt & very humble Servant   EZRA STILES

Dr. Franklin

Addressed: His Excellency Benjamin Franklin Esq LL. D. / Minister Plenipotentiary from the Congress / of the United States / to the Court of / Paris

Notation: Stiles Octr. 10 1780

From Jonathan Williams, Jr.

ALS: American Philosophical Society; copy: Yale University Library

Dear & hond Sir   Nantes Octor 10. 1780.

The present serves only to hand you a small Dft which Messrs De Segray & Co sent me for a little Balance due to him on the Dolphin Capt Nicholson in Decr 1777, being for some Charges after the Accots were closed, As it is a trifle I paid it & have charged it to the public please therefore to return me the note with your Signature to serve as a Voucher to my accots.[9]

I send you also inclosed a Letter which I have lately received from Capt Manly in Mill Prison,[1] I wish it were possible to get all these poor Fellows exchanged before the Marquis de la Fayette sails as they might then go home in that Ship.

I am ever with the greatest Respect Dear & hond Sir Yours most dutifully & affectionately   JONA WILLIAMS J

Hon: Doctor Franklin

Notation: J Williams Octo. 10 80

---

9. BF did not; it is among his papers at the APS. The undated draft, signed by the firm, asks that BF pay to JW the sum of 29 *l.t.* 12 *s.* for expenses of the *Dolphin,* Capt. Samuel Nicholson, at St. Malo, Dec. 10, 1777 (for which see XXV, 160n, 194, 426–7). JW noted at the bottom: "Mr Williams / Pay the above & charge it to the Public of America Passy Octor   1780."

1. This one is missing, but JW had forwarded a previous letter on July 25.

From John Jebb[2]

Reprinted from William Temple Franklin, *The Private Correspondence of Benjamin Franklin, LL.D., F.R.S., &c...* (2nd ed., 2 vols., London, 1817), I, 456–61.

London, Oct. 11, 1780.

The consciousness of a sincere desire to promote the interests of human kind, as far as my confined abilities and humble station will permit, induce me to give you my sentiments upon a subject which, I have no doubt, is ever present to your thoughts. Excuse the presumption; the intention is honest; let this consideration compensate for the want of every other qualification. Independent in my principles and unconnected with party, I speak those sentiments, which circumstances appear to me to dictate, and I speak them without reserve.

A federal union between America and England, upon the broad basis of mutual convenience, appears to me a point of so much consequence, that I cannot conceive, in the present circumstances, how either country can fully enjoy the means of happiness, which indulgent Providence has poured forth on each with so much profusion, unless such union immediately take place.

I also am persuaded, that the present war, between this country and the House of Bourbon, is of so peculiar a kind, that no solid reason can be assigned for its continuance, a moment after America and England shall cordially agree upon a termination of their dispute.

It is obviously for the advantage of England, that America should employ her manufacturers, and that her fleets should have free access to the shores, from whence she derived those various sources of strength, which enabled her so long to reign the unrivalled mistress of the deep.

On the other hand, the rising States of America, wisely intent on such measures, as tend to increase their population, and per-

2. The English radical. Benjamin Vaughan had sent what we believe was one of Jebb's pamphlets to BF in May (XXXII, 380). In 1783 Jebb wrote that he had been in BF's company only twice (Jebb to BF, Aug. 15, 1783, APS), and no letters to him from BF are extant.

fect those forms of civil polity, which, at the same time that they promise internal security and happiness, will probably establish an asylum for the rest of mankind, must derive considerable advantage from the free importation of those articles, which, in their present circumstances, they cannot with convenience manufacture themselves.

And why should England envy to France and Spain, nay, to all the world, that portion of trade, whatever that be, which suits the circumstances of each power; and from which all deriving the sources of rational enjoyment would, perhaps, remain in the same ratio as at present, with respect to relative strength?

How strange therefore to persevere in an appeal to arms, when neutral interest, and the ties of blood; the sameness of religion, language, and laws, so loudly call for peace! We might reasonably have hoped, that in the course of eighteen centuries the gospel of peace might have suggested to us a more rational mode of terminating our contests.

As it never was the interest, so neither was it in fact the inclination of the English people, to break the bonds of union with their American brethren, until seduced thereto by the arts of designing men. Their motives I leave to themselves—they will be revealed in their day.

Had the English people been equally represented in an annual Parliament, that Parliament, acting in strict conformity with the interests of its constituents, would have seen that every consideration required, that the bond of union between the countries should be preserved inviolate.— It would have perceived, that those restrictions, which were the offspring of the occasion, or suggested by narrow systems of policy, ought to have been removed, the moment that they occasioned the first murmur of complaint.— But unhappily for England, the love of arbitrary sway so far operated upon those, who most are exposed to its temptations, as to engage them in the desperate measure of deluding one half of the empire, in order to subjugate the rest.

The period of this delusion, however, is now rapidly advancing to its termination.— Calamity has brought home the perception of the consequences, attendant upon national error, to every private breast.— It has taught us wisdom—and has begun to humanise our hearts.— The many are now ready to exclaim, in the expressive language of scripture, "We are verily guilty concerning our brother, in that we saw the anguish of his soul when he besought us, and we would not hear; *therefore is this evil come upon us.*"[3]

But although the people are disposed to accommodation, a mighty power continues to oppose itself to the general wish.

And were the aristocratic strength of our constitution to prevail in its conflict with that power, I am far from being satisfied, that a general and permanent pacification would be the result.

The restoration of the English constitution to its primeval purity, appears to be an essential preliminary to an honorable and lasting peace.

Peace and war are relations which the inhabitants of different countries stand in to each other. In this sense the people of America are not at war with the people of England. The latter having lost their power of self-government are merely the instruments of administration. *The present war is a war between the people of America and the administration of this country.* Were the inhabitants of this country restored to their elective rights, and other constitutional franchises, a state of peace would immediately ensue.

Upon this idea alone can America have a proper security for the due observance of that solemn compact, which I should rejoice to see established between my native country, and her free and independent states.

The supporters of the septennial bill, at the time that ruinous and unconstitutional measure took place,[4] strongly insisted upon the advantage that would ensue from that increased confidence, which foreign nations would thenceforth repose in us, on account of the consequent stability of our public counsels.

Experience has shown this measure to have been founded in policy the most unwise.

Reason surely dictates, that the confidence, which nations re-

---

3. " . . . therefore is this distress come upon us": Genesis 42: 21.

4. The Septennial Act, passed in 1716 in the aftermath of the Jacobite uprising of 1715, extended the legal life of the sitting and subsequent parliaments from three to seven years. Opposition politicians throughout the eighteenth century routinely called for its repeal.

pose in each other's public counsels, must be the greatest, when the agents speak the real sentiments of their constituent bodies.

It is also to be considered, that the changes of sentiment, in the constituent body of the nation, must unavoidably be gradual, as general interest, always slowly unveiling itself, shall direct. Whereas the agent, who has a permanent estate in his office, will vary his conduct in conformity to the quick revolutions of those numerous temptations, to which views of private interest, and prospects of power hourly expose him.

For England therefore to be free, and to regain the confidence of nations, her parliaments must be free and independent: and the same measure which gives independency to the English parliament, will, under God's providence, restore to us peace with America and with all the world.

I write not thus, induced thereto solely from an attachment to my native soil—the world is my country—and the region which is the seat of freedom has in my eyes charms more attractive than my native soil. I write not thus from an attachment to a favorite measure, but from a full conviction that such a preliminary as I have mentioned, being inserted in every proposition for peace on the part of America, would lay a lasting foundation for that peace—and would be a perpetual security that the independence, which America so justly claims, and in the establishment of which every nation under Heaven is interested, would never be brought into question to the end of time.

The sum and substance of what I urge is this—That as a more equal representation of the English people, in annual parliaments, is a point essential to the restoration of our freedom;[5] it is equally essential, as a foundation for a federal union with the American states.

After all—the changes in the affairs of men, whether they be revolutions in the fortunes of nations, or of individuals, are in the hands of Providence; and are directed by its resistless power to the general good. That good will finally prevail, whatever the

5. Annual parliaments were a fundamental tenet of the radical reform platform: H.T. Dickinson, *Liberty and Property: Political Ideology in Eighteenth-Century Britain* (London, 1977), pp. 219–20; Eugene C. Black, *The Association: British Extraparliamentary Political Organization, 1769–1793* (Cambridge, Mass., 1963), pp. 60–1.

hearts and heads of politicians may devise. The only differences will be, a difference in the time and manner in which the ends of providence are brought to pass; and a difference in the final fate of those who are employed as the means of their accomplishment.

The fell destroyers of their species shall see their measures, though planned with Machiavelian policy, and for a time successful, finally abortive—failing in the attainment of the evil wished for, and productive of the good they hate.

On the contrary, if virtue, honor, zeal for the interests of our country and of human kind form the outline of the character, the agent of heaven will be renowned in his day; and long futurity, through every successive age, shall impart increase of glory. The joys of self-complacency shall gild the evening of his days. They will also be the earnest of an happiness which will know no bounds.   JOHN JEBB.

From Jean de Neufville & fils

ALS: American Philosophical Society

Honourd Sir   Amsterdam the 12th. Oct: 1780.

Since our last respects to your Excellency,[6] we have only now to mention, that of the bills on Mr. Laurens we gott yesterday seven more to the Amount of Three thousand eight hundred and fifty Gilders, for which we have promisd an Answer by the return of the maill, and your Excellency will find us ready to Accept of them and any others, as we only wish now fr. her comands.

May we begg leave Honourd Sir by this opportunity to enquire about John Searle Esqr. Whome we heard to be in France and even by some report to have been in Amsterdam, we have some conections with his Mercantile House at Madeira, Which he probabely will not be Acquainted with though relating to American Correspondance,[7] so we wished (?) to pay our Respects to him or in person or by Letter, the more as a Gentleman of his Caracter we should be glad to be acquainted with him, and

6. Above, Oct. 9.

7. Searle had spent sixteen years in Madeira as a member of his brother's firm, John Searle & Co.: *DAB*.

your Excellency procuring us those means will encrease our obligations to her, [*word illegible*] as we have the honour to be with all respectfull Regard. Honourd Sir Your Excellencys most devoted and most obedient humble Servant,

JOHN DE NEUFVILLE AND SON

Notation: Ansd the 26th. Oct. 1780

From James Pemberton[8]

ALS: Frederic R. Kirkland (Philadelphia, 1955)

Esteemed friend   Philadelpa. Octr. 12th: 1780

Encouraged by thy kindness in forwarding to our mutual friend Dr: Fothergill in London the letter which I took the liberty to transmit to thy care about a year since, I make use of the same freedom to request again the like favour of sending the Inclosed to him by the first speedy & safe conveyance;—[9] I had made up & sealed it with an intention of conveying it via' Statia & Holland, not knowing of this oppo: or should not have sealed it, that thou might have been satisfied the Contents do not relate to any political matters injurious or justly exceptionable.

I heartily wish to see the[e] safely returned among thy Country-men, & friends here with the desireable Olive Branch, that thou might be enabled to cultivate peace & establish it on so firm a bottom, as that all parties may be reconciled and unite in securing to each other domestic harmony & Concord.

Considering the extremities of distress to which war necessarily subjects a people, we enjoy in this City more plenty and quietude than the gloomy prospect gave us reason to apprehend, our markets are well supplied with provisions, our last harvest has been favourable, many people are taught frugality by neces-

8. The Philadelphia Quaker merchant and politician. During the winter of 1777–78 he had been interned in Virginia along with several other Quakers who were thought to be dangerous to the American cause: XIII, 260n; Betsy C. Corner and Christopher C. Booth, eds., *Chain of Friendship: Selected Letters of Dr. John Fothergill of London, 1735–1780* (Cambridge, Mass., 1971), p. 482n.

9. Neither of the letters mentioned is extant. The two men were long-time friends and they had exchanged messages through BF in the past: XXI, 537–8.

sity, but many others are abandoned to extravagance and dissipation, at the public expence, imitating the vices & follies of G B to great excess, which produce animosities & party divisions to the manifest injury of the whole, and the ruin of individuals;— Thy Old Opposer our former C Justice is lately deceased,[1] having had the mortification to see his power and influence long before depart from him, many others of thy Acquaintance are also no more; So passeth away as a Shadow this world's Glory— I am Thy respectfull friend

JAMS. PEMBERTON

[B] Franklin Esqr

Addressed: To Dr: Benjamin Franklin / at Passey / near / Paris / per Cap: Bell

From John Paul Jones

ALS: University of Pennsylvania Library; AL (draft): National Archives

Honored & dear Sir   Ariel, L'Orient Octr. 13. 1780.

When I had the honor of writing to your Excellency the 23. Ult. I hoped about the end of this Month to have set foot on the Continent beyond the Atlantic. The prospect changed however, immediately after I had sent away my dispatches, and Prudence bid me again drop Anchor at Groix.— The within Declaration of my Officers will explain, in some degree, the difficulties I have since met with.[2] My Heart tells me I have done my Best, however

1. William Allen, a prominent Philadelphia citizen and public official who served as chief justice of the province from 1750 to 1774, died on Sept. 6. *DAB.* He appears frequently in our earlier volumes. At first Allen encouraged BF's career, recommending him for the office of Deputy Postmaster General in 1751. But he went on to oppose BF bitterly and, said Joseph Galloway, his malevolence would never end, "but with his Breath" (XIII, 295). For BF and Allen's relationship, see, in particular, III, 296–7n; IV, 134–5; VI, 409–10; VII, 363n; XI, 328, 407–12; XIII, 317, 320, 429, 499.

2. The enclosed certificate, signed by eight of the *Ariel*'s officers, described the terrible storm of Oct. 8–10 in which their ship was dismasted and almost driven onto the rocks: Bradford, *Jones Papers,* reel 6, no. 1231. See also reel 9, no. 1920, pp. 88–9 and John S. Barnes, ed., *The Logs of the Serapis-Alliance-Ariel . . .* (New York, 1911), pp. 135–6.

Unfortunate I have been. I can give you no Just Idea of the terrible Storm of the 8 & 9th.—part of it exceeded my Utmost conception of Tempest and of Ship Wreck; and I believe no Ship was ever before Saved from an equal Danger off the point of the Penmark Rocks.—[3] I owe the warmest thanks to the Spirited and Unremitting assistance of my Officers, who beheaved with a steady composed Courage that does them the highest Honor; and I have no fault to find with the conduct of any person under my Command: They all beheaved remarkably Well. The Gentlemen Passengers shewed a manly Spirit and true greatness of Mind, even when Death in all its pomp stared them in the Face, and I am sure not one among them ever expected to See a returning Sun.

I have been with my good friend the Commandant of the Marine, M. le Chr. de Thevenard; he has already given Orders to make a set of New Masts and Sails to replace those we have lost, and that work goes on with all possible dilligence.— We will loose no time in examining the situation of the public Stores and if any of them are damaged the necessary steps will be taken by Mr. Moylan and myself for their preservation.— The Lugger[4] is arrived here Dismasted, and the Brig Luke is in a small river in Quiberon Bay; having followed an English Twenty Gun Ship that had been given up by the Captain and Officers to the prisoners for the preservation of Lives.— The Duke of Linster is not yet heard of, and I have great fears for Mr. Ross.[5] I am, in all changes of good or bad Fortune, with an Affection and respect proceeding from the Heart Your Excellencies' most Obliged and most humble Servant   JNO P JONES

His Excellency B. Franklin Esquire American Minister at the Court of France &c &c.

Notation: J.P. Jones 13 Oct. 1780

3. The Pointe de Penmarch.
4. According to the officers' certificate cited above this was a French lugger which accompanied the *Ariel, Luke,* and *Duke of Leinster.*
5. The brigantine *Duke of Leinster* reached Philadelphia on Nov. 29 and soon thereafter Ross was in contact with the American Board of Admiralty: *Pennsylvania Packet, or the General Advertiser,* Dec. 2, 1780; Claghorn, *Naval Officers,* p. 291; Ross to Secretary of the Board of Admiralty John Brown, Dec. 13, 1780 (National Archives). The *Luke* sailed again, but was captured by the privateer *Tamer* and taken to Helford, Cornwall: *Courier de l'Europe,* VIII (1780), 304.

From Sartine: Two Letters[6]

(I) and (II) Copy: Library of Congress

I.

A Versailles le 13. 8bre. 1780.

Je m'empresse, Monsieur, ainsi que vous me le demandez par la Lettre que vous m'avez fait l'honneur de m'écrire le 6. de ce mois de donner ordre à l'Intendant de la Marine à Brest de faire expedier des Passeports pour les Prisonniers Anglois conduits en France par des Corsaires Americains et detenus à St. Omer, Je lui recommande d'exiger d'eux des Certificats qui constatent que la liberté ne leur a été accordée qu'a titre d'Echange.

J'ai l'honneur d'etre avec la Consideration la plus distinguée, Monsieur, Votre très humble et très obeissant Serviteur,

(signé) DE SARTINE.

M. Franklin.

II.

Paris le 13. 8bre. 1780.

Je n'ai point Connoissance, Monsieur, que les Prisonniers Anglois qui ont été conduits à la Martinique par des Bâtimens Americains et qui doivent repasser en France,[7] soient arrivés dans le Royaume, aussitot que je serai instruit de leur arrivée je m'empresserai de donner des ordres pour qu'ils soient renvoyés en Angleterre, et remis au Capitaine d'un Navire Parlementaire

---

6. Written on Sartine's final day as French naval minister, these letters are the last extant correspondence between BF and him. On that day he was handed a letter from the King relieving him of office. Although he was a political ally of Maurepas and Vergennes, they failed to save him. The Spanish court blamed him for the lack of a decisive naval victory. He, moreover, had challenged Necker's authority over French royal finances. For his six years of ministerial service he was rewarded with a large pension and by being named comte d'Alby: Dull, *French Navy*, pp. 194–202; Jacques Michel, *Du Paris de Louis XV à la marine de Louis XVI: L'œuvre de Monsieur de Sartine* (2 vols., Paris, 1983–4), II, 191–9; John Hardman, *French Politics, 1774–1789: From the Accession of Louis XVI to the Fall of the Bastille* (London and New York, 1995), pp. 55–6.

7. For which see BF to Sartine, Oct. 7.

Anglois qui en donnera une reconnoissance que j'aurai soin de vous adresser.

J'ai l'honneur d'etre avec la Consideration la plus distinguée, Monsieur, votre tres humble et tres obeissant serviteur,

(signé) DE SARTINE

From the Comtesse de La Rouërie[8]

AL: American Philosophical Society

[after October 13, 1780][9]

Une mere dont l'inquietude ne peut s'exprimer, suplie Monsieur franckin, de vouloir bien lui apprendre le sort du Colonel Armand, son fils, qui sert dans l'armée amériquaine et dont elle n'a eu aucune nouvelle depuis l'affaire de Camden, ou, elle à appris par les papiers publics qu'il étoit, sous les ordres du Général Gates.

Notation: La mere du Colonel Armand

From John Adams

LS:[1] American Philosophical Society

Sir,   Amsterdam October 14th. 1780.

The Extracts of Letters You was so good as to send me,[2] have been inserted in the Papers, and I should be obliged to You, for future Communications of the same kind.

Notwithstanding the flow of Spirits, and the vigorous Exertions of our Countrymen this Year, I am sorry to say I cannot see

8. Thérèse de La Belinaye, widow of Anne-Joseph-Jacques Tuffin, comte de La Rouërie (1725–1754) was the mother of Charles-Armand Tuffin, marquis de La Rouërie, known also as Col. Armand (xxv, 383n): Bodinier, *Dictionnaire;* Lasseray, *Les Français,* II, 454. The abbés Chalut and Arnoux had written on her behalf, we think in late 1777: xxv, 382–3.

9. The day on which the *Courier de l'Europe* (VIII [1780], 236) reported on the battle of Camden. Col. Armand's regiment appears on the list of Gen. Gates's forces.

1. In John Thaxter's hand.

2. With his letter of Oct. 2, above.

a prospect of any thing decisive this Campaign. The fatal defect in the plan of the Campaign in not sending a sufficient number of Ships with M. de Ternay, or soon after him, will render abortive all the great Exertions, and immense Expences of the Year.

And at the same time Cornwallis will spread too much devastation at the Southward, where the want of numbers of Whites, the great numbers of Blacks, and above all the want of Discipline and Experience, will make the People long unhappy and unfortunate.

The ill luck of Carolina pursues her Citizens even to Sea, and to Europe I think. Can nothing be done for the Relief of Mr. Laurens? Will You be so good as to apply to Court, and see if they will lend Us somebody of Mark to exchange for him? After exchanging so many military Men as prisoners of War, it is pitifully spightfull to use Mr. Laurens as they do: but they cannot conceal the Meanness of their Character.

I have felt the mortification of soliciting for Money as well as You: but it has been because the solicitations have not succeeded. I see no reason at all that We should be ashamed of asking to borrow Money after maintaining a War against Great Britain and her Allies for almost six years, without borrowing any thing abroad, when England has been all the time borrowing of all the Nations of Europe, even of Individuals among our Allies, it cannot be unnatural, surprising or culpable or dishonourable for Us to borrow Money.

When England borrows annually a Sum equal to all her Exports, We ought not to be laughed at for wishing to borrow a Sum annually equal to a twelfth part of our annual Exports.

We may, and We shall wade through, if We cannot obtain a Loan: but We could certainly go forward with more Ease, Convenience and Safety, by the help of one.

I think We have not meanly solicited for Friendship any where. But to send Ministers to every great Court in Europe, especially the Maritime Courts, to propose an acknowledgment of the Independence of America, and Treaties of Amity and of Commerce is no more than becomes Us, and in my Opinion is our Duty to do: it is perfectly consistent with the genuine System of American Policy, and a piece of Respect due from new

Nations to old ones. The United Provinces did the same thing, and were never censured for it, but in the End they succeeded. It is necessary for America to have Agents in different parts of Europe, to give some Information concerning our affairs, and to refute the abominable Lies that the hired Emissaries of Great Britain circulate in every Corner of Europe, by which they keep up their own Credit and ruin ours. I have been more convinced of this since my Peregrinations in this Country, than ever. The universal and profound Ignorance of America here, has astonished me. It will require Time, and a great deal of Prudence and Delicacy too to undecieve them. The method You have obligingly begun, of transmitting me Intelligence from America, will assist me in doing, or at least attempting something of this kind, and I therefore request the Continuance of it, and have the Honour to be, with respectful Compliments to Mr. Franklin and all Friends, Sir, your most obedient Servant   JOHN ADAMS

His Excellency Dr. Franklin.

Notation: J Adams Oct. 14. 1780

From Samuel Wharton   ALS: American Philosophical Society

My dear Sir   L'Orient 14 Ocr. 1780

Little did I expect to address you again from any part of this Kingdom, But you will hear from your other Correspondents, The Cause of Commodore Jones returning to L'orient. I will not attempt to describe the Horrors of the dreadful, or as the Seamen express it,— unequalled Tempest, We have been in, nor the miraculous Delivery from Death, We have had.— We were all summoned on Deck to meet our Fate, and had taken a solemn Farewell of each other;— But thro' the matchless Skill, and cool, and unshaken Intrepidity of our Captain—"Who truly rode in the Whirlwind, and directed the Storm"—[3] We were saved, When We momentarily expected to founder.— He with a fortu-

3. As Addison described Marlborough in *The Campaign* . . . , line 292: A. C. Guthkelch, ed., *The Miscellaneous Works of Joseph Addison* (2 vols., London, 1914), I, 165.

nate Celerity of Thought ordered the Anchor to be dropped, and not finding the Ship to rise in Consequence of it (which at that Time was fast filling with Water, overpowering the Pumps)— cried out, cut away the Foremast. Happily She began to rise, and in a few Minutes obeyed the Rudder, and became upright. Soon after The Storm increased with redoubled Fury, and the Main, and Mizen Masts were found to be shaken from their places, and no Safety remained for us, But in quickly cutting away the mainmast, which in going over the Side, carried the Mizen Mast with it. In Brief the Ship was left a hopeless Wreck, exposed to the Rage of a wild, bellowing Sea, and depending only on an Anchor, cast in unknown Ground with Breakers, and Rocks at a little Distance from Us, and our Men quite worn Out with the Severity of Duty, They had undergone. The next Day was employed in collecting Materials to erect Jury Masts, and the following Day in preparing and fixing Them, and the suceding Night at 11 oClock, We sailed, and made Groa in the Evening. I cannot too much praise the Skill, Fortitude, and Vigilance of the first Lieutent Mr. Deale (a Virginian) The second Lieutent Mr. Lunt, and the Master Mr. Stacy (both New England Men) and all the midshipmen.[4] The Sailors also deserve the highest Commendations. Captain Clarke, who saild with Us is got into the River Ven [Vilaine?], But We have no Intelligence of poor Mr Ross, on Board Captain Souder.[5] We suffer much on his account.

I must pray your Excuse for the Brevity of this Letter, as I am a good Deal hurried in getting Lodgings, and am scarcely recovered from the Fatigues of our Disaster. Will you be pleased to present my affectionate Respects to Monsr. de Chaumont, Mr. Dean, Dr. Bancroft (To Whom I will write soon) and Billy; And Permit Me to subscribe myself, with real Attachment, My dear Friend yours most affectionately   S. WHARTON

Notation: S Wharton. L'Orient Oct. 14. 1780—

4. Wharton is praising Lt. Richard Dale, Lt. Henry Lunt, and Master Samuel Stacey; the midshipmen aboard the *Ariel* were Thomas Potter, Beaumont Groube, Nathaniel Fanning, Joseph Hitchborn, and Arthur Robinson: John S. Barnes, ed., *The Logs of the Serapis-Alliance-Ariel under the Command of John Paul Jones 1779–1780* (New York, 1911), pp. 20, 135–6.

5. John Souder was captain of the *Duke of Leinster,* Joseph Clark of the *Luke:* Claghorn, *Naval Officers,* pp. 60, 291.

From Jonathan Williams, Jr.

ALS: University of Pennsylvania Library; copy: Yale University Library

Dear & honoured Sir   Nantes Octor 14. 1780.

I hear that my Friend & Correspondent Mr French of Bordeaux is now in Paris & intends to wait on you. I therefore beg leave to reccommend him to your Friendship & Civilities and I shall consider your Notice of him as an Obligation on me.[6]

I long to hear of the great Ships being at L'Orient as I am ready for her, & you may depend there will be no fault to find with my Dispatch.

I am as ever Yours most dutifully & affectionately

JONA WILLIAMS J

Notation: J Williams Octo. 14. 1780

From Vergennes   LS: American Philosophical Society

A Versailles le 15. 8bre 1780.

J'ai reçu, Monsieur, la lettre que vous m'avez fait l'honneur de m'écrire aujourd'hui.[7] Je joins ici celle que vous me demandez pour M. le Cte. de Montmorin, ainsi que le Passeport pour le Courier que vous expédiez à M. Jay.

J'ai l'honneur d'être très sincèrement, Monsieur, votre très humble et très obéissant Serviteur.   DE VERGENNES

M. Franklin

Notation: Count de Vergennes Oct. 15. 1780

From Isaac All   ALS: American Philosophical Society

Dear Sir   Port L'Orient 16th Octobr. 1780

Altho I flatter my self it will not be disagreable to you to hear of my safe arrival in this Country I did intend to defer doing my

6. JW wrote V. & P. French & nephew on the same date, discussing their proposed shipment of 100 cases of claret from Bordeaux to Lorient on the *Marquis de Lafayette*, and telling them he had written to BF. Yale University Library.

7. Missing.

self the honour of writing to you untill next Post and had your Letters sent to the office yesterday morning, but in the course of the day I was informed by Capn. Jones of this Conveyance. I therefore embrace the Opportunity to inform you that the Family were all well on the Eleventh of Sept. one or two days latter then their Letters,[8] as I was detained in Town longer then I expected— I will not pretend to enter into any information from the other side well knowing you have every Circumstance respecting the public affairs of our Country from abler hands. Therefore shall only say that Mrs. Beache was Just returned to Town from Mr. Duffelds where she had spent some time in the very warm weather and was busily employed in cutting out and making up shirts for the Soldiers of Gen. Washington's Army of the linning purchased with the money Collected by herself and a number of the Patriotic Ladies of Philadelphia—a business she entered into with all that spirit and zeal you know her to be possesed of. In short the Ladies concerned in this affair have gained immortal Honour, of which Mrs. B. might Claim a Capital Share.—

As I have been only two days at this place, I cannot say any thing about the time of my departure from hence, but hope it will not be more than three weeks, in which time I hope to have the pleasure of hearing from you and receiving any Commands you may please to Commit to my Care, pray make my best Compliments to Temple he will I hope pardon the familar manner of my expression— Accept Dear Sir My most Sincere Wishes for your long life and perfect health. And believe me to be with the Greatest Respect and Esteem Your Affectionate & Very Humble. Servt   ISAAC ALL

Addressed: His Excellency / Benjamin Franklin / Minister Plenipotentiary from the United / States / To the Court of France / a Passy pres Paris

Notations: Isaac Ally, l'orient 16. Oct. 1780. / Ansd

---

8. He carried SB's of Sept. 9 and RB's of Sept. 10, above.

From Jonathan Loring Austin

ALS: American Philosophical Society

Sir,   Nantes 17 October 1780

The Nature of my Errand to Europe I had the Honor to communicate to your Excellency soon after my Arrival,[9] the Difficulties which have occur'd to accomplish it if possible, have verified your Predictions. Altho' disappointed & often mortified in every Attempt I have made to execute this Commission entrusted to me by the State, my Anxiety was however greatly alleiviated on the Receipt of a Letter from the Committee of foreign Affairs, ordering me to freight their Goods, as the Ship they proposed sending out was detain'd for the protection of the Trade. Contrary to my Expectations the Ship Mars Capt Sampson has arrived here at a critical Season of the Year, not only to receive a Cargo of Cloathing, the State was too sanguine I had procured, but I am order'd to give her every necessary Supply, & to pay the Crew a proportion of their Wages. Situated as I am its impossible for me to answer their Expectations, & unless I can procure a Freight for her, she must return charged with a heavy Debt, & to detain her here any considerable time to accomplish this only point, would not perhaps be adequate to the Expence. Since my Arrival my Friend Mr Williams has informed me of a Quantity of Warlike Stores, laying here, belonging to the United States. I beg leave to refer your Excellency to a Letter he now writes you respecting them.[1] Should you consent to send them to America, I should be glad to take on Board the Ship Mars such a Quantity as could be conveniently ship'd, & at a Freight to be paid here, which shall be deemed equitable, this I imagine will be more satisfactory than to leave it for future decission— These Goods are of such a sort that Vessels in general would not incline to take them on Freight, & probably a better Opportunity to ship them will not soon offer. I therefore doubt not, as your Excellency can herein serve the State of Massachusetts Bay & the Continent in general, you will please to give the necessary Orders for shipping them—

9. He arrived in May (xxxii, 250–1n); this is the first extant letter from him since his arrival.

1. Of the same date, below.

I shall be carefull to enclose your Excellency by this or next Post a Draft on Paris for the Money you was pleased to lend me[2] & am with the greatest Respect Your Excellency's Most Obedient & very humble Servant   JONA. LORING AUSTIN

His Excellency Dr Franklin—

Notation: J. L. Austin. Nantes Oct 17. 80

From Benjamin Franklin Bache

ALS: American Philosophical Society

Mon Cher grand papa   Geneve 17 8tobre 1780
Je vous écris cette lettre pour m'informer de vôtre santé parcequ'il y a assès longtems que je ne vous ai pas ecris et ayant beaucoup de temps parceque nous sommes dans les congès des vandanges quoique j'aie des taches davant les congès l'on m'invite quelque fois avec le fils de Madame Cramer[3] alors je me rejouis parceque l'occasion ne se presente pas souvent. Je ne peux vous envoyer que 3 pièces de dessing parceque mon maitre a eu des affaires pendant quelque temps qui m'ont beaucoup retardées ne voulant pas differer plus longtemps pour ne pas laisser passer cette occasion ne pouvant en trouver que rarement.[4] Il me faudroit bien à genève quelques uns de mes amis comme Cockran. Je vous prie de me dire si les deux adams dont vous m'avès parlés viendront.[5] J'espére que je raprendrois facilement l'anglois ayant un maître.[6] Je commence à faire des progrès ou du moins Je fais mes efforts pour en faire.

2. 600 *l.t.*, which BF gave him on Oct. 12: Cash Book. See also Austin's letter of Oct. 19.
3. Gabriel Cramer: XXX, 248n; XXXI, 363.
4. He had first promised a drawing in his letter of May 30: XXXII, 444.
5. See BF's letter of Sept. 25, above. Charles and John Quincy did not go to Geneva. They were enrolled at the Latin School in Amsterdam from Aug. 30 until Nov. 10, 1780, after which they had a preceptor at home. John Quincy matriculated at the University of Leyden on Jan. 11, 1781: Butterfield, *John Adams Diary,* II, 448, 451–2; Taylor, *J. Q. Adams Diary,* I, 35n, 62–4, 75n.
6. Marignac's bills for BFB's schooling mention a *maître d'anglois* beginning with the statement for Oct. 5, 1779–Jan. 5, 1780: XXX, 481. See also his most recent bill, beginning Sept. 5, above.

J'ai l'honneur d'être mon cher bon papa Votre très humble et obeissant petit fils   B FRANKLIN B

Mon cher grand Papa Je vous envoye aussi mon prix parceque Je pense qu'il vous fera plaisir.

From Thomas Digges

ALS: Historical Society of Pennsylvania; copy: Public Record Office, London[7]

Dr. Sir   London 17. Octo 1780

It was not until the 14th. inst that *any person whatever* was permitted to see Mr Laurens in the Tower— *Then* after repeated applications for admission Mr. Manning and Mr L——ns's Son,[8] a Youth of 17 or 18 who has been some years at Warrington School,[9] got admission to Him. A permit was given them, signd by the Lds. Hillsborough, Stormont & Germain "for *half an hours* interview & that the permit did not extend to any future visit." They found Him very ill of a lax, much emaciated, not low spirited, & bitterly invective against the people here for his harsh treatment. He spoke handsomely of his treatment while on board ship, & of the Capn. (Keppel) & Lieut Norris who attended him to London, but from the period of his landing He was treated with a brutality wch. He did not expect even from Englishmen. His weakness from sickness & the agitation on seeing his Son took up the first *ten* of the 30 minutes allowd him to con-

---

7. Reproduced in Stevens, *Facsimiles*, X, no. 952. This is the first of three letters from Digges to BF intercepted by the British post office; the others are below, under Oct. 27 and 31. Apparently the British did not penetrate Digges's aliases, but on Nov. 20 his connections with the American painter John Trumbull caused him to be interrogated. He was saved from immediate arrest because he had not kept copies of any incriminating letters at his residence: William Bell Clark, "In Defense of Thomas Digges," *PMHB*, LXXVII (1953), 421–4.

8. Henry Laurens, Jr. (1763–1821) had been sent to England in 1771 for his education: *Laurens Papers*, IV, 153; VII, 480, and *passim*.

9. Warrington Academy, where Joseph Priestley had taught from 1761 to 1767: John T. Rutt, ed., *Life and Correspondence of Joseph Priestley, LL.D., F.R.S., &c.* (2 vols., London, 1831–2), I, 48; *DNB* under Priestley.

verse with His friends;—the rest was filld with invective against the authors of his harsh treatment. His outer room is but a mean one, not more than twelve feet square, a *dark* close bed room adjoining, both indifferently furnishd, & a few books on his table, no pen and Ink has been yet allowd him, but He has a pencil & memdm book in wch. He occasionally notes things. The Warden of the Tower & a Yeoman constantly at his elbow tho they make no attempts to stop his conversation. Mr Mannings being the first visit he has had, perhaps He said every thing He could about the severity of his treatment, in order that it might get out & contradict the general report of His being exceedingly well treated. He has hitherto declind any Phisical advice, or the visits of any of those Creatures about Him who may be set on to Pump. Mr Penn[1] is making application to see Him, & will likely get leave. It is doubtful if the Son will be able to get admission a second time. His treatment being *now* very generally known every person is crying out shame upon it & the authors thereof are very much abusd. It is a strange thing to go forth, but it is the general receivd opinion that the orders for such harsh treatment were in consequence of an intimation from the *first* man in this Country, now generally known by the appellation of *White Eyes.*[2]

Every appearance indicates that this Mr White Eyes is determind on prosecuting the Amn. War vigorously. New Regiments are raising—10 or 12,000 Men under orders to go & transports actually got & getting at unusual high prices. Nothing can exceed such folly but it actually appears the determind resolution of the Cabinet to risque every thing upon a last stake— The inactivity of the French in Ama. & the West Indies, seems to be the bait of inducement for these folks to go on. Abot a month ago, before the arrivals from N York & Carolina & Jamaica, there was every appearance of the cabinet having given up the Amn War.

I am without any of Your favrs. lately. I wish to know if You got the picture of the Bishop safe. What is further to be done

1. Richard Penn, Jr. (XII, 94n).

2. Possibly the King, whose worsening eyesight caused him to acquire a peering look: John Brooke, *King George III* (New York, St. Louis, San Francisco, 1972), p. 288.

about Jones's Bill on Goddard. What ansr. to the Letter sent by the parole Prisoners who came over in the Temple, Cartel to Bristol. & if Mr B—w—n [Bowman] may Expect a pass for his baggage.

I drew a Bill on Monsr. G——d the 16th. 10 days sight for 48 £ payle to the person You write to frequently about the Prisoners.[3]

I am wth Esteem &ca &ca— W S. C

Addressed: A Monsieur / Monsieur B. F— / Passy

Notation: Oct. 17. 1780.

From Jonathan Williams, Jr.[4]

LS: University of Pennsylvania Library; copy: Yale University Library

Dear & Hond. Sir Nantes 17 October 1780

I have already mentioned to you the Arrival of the Massachusetts State Ship Mars & I suppose both Mr Austin & Capt Samson have told you her Situation; I need not therefore make any further Introduction to this Letter, which I shall confine to that Subject.

It seems the State expected Mr Austin would have succeeded in obtaining a Loan, or at least in obtaining a Quantity of Goods on the States Credit, & so sure were they of his Success that they have not made the smallest Provision for his Failure. In consequence of this incautious Proceeding the Ship is here at a heavy daily Expence, considerable Sums to be paid to the Officers & Crew per Agreement, & in want of great Supplies of every kind, without any Means of answering these Demands; in this Situation the only Method that occurs to me is to get as much Freight, payable here, as will defray the Ships Expences, and send her

3. The bill on Grand was to be payable to Digges himself; see his letter of Oct. 10.

4. On the same day, JW wrote BF a brief general letter of introduction for Jean Conrad Zollickoffer (University of Pa. Library). Although Zollickoffer was already known to BF, their acquaintance had been some years prior to this: XXV, 61n; XXVIII, 66n; XXXII, 228–9.

back again as soon as possible. There will remain in the Arsenal after I have taken what I can put in the Marquis de la Fayettes Hold a Quantity perhaps about 20,000 old Gun Barrells with an equal Number of Bayonnetts & Locks, besides 30 Casks of Flints & the Anchors that were bought in the Time of Mr Deanes Administration for our 74 Gun Ships,[5] which may together make an Object of an hundred Tons. It will be a public Benefit to send all these Things to America, for every Gun Barrell will be in use as soon as it gets there, & while they remain here they are as useless as if they had never been bought, It will also be a Benefit to the State to have their Ship sent back again without incurring a Debt, & I think you will be willing to do a Service to the State when you serve the Public in general at the same Time. If therefore you will consent to give this Freight we may probably in addition find private Freight sufficient to pay her Charges. The Price per Ton I think should be more than what I pay the Marquis de la Fayette, because my Tonnage is reckoned by measuring the Ship, which makes it, I suppose, about a quarter dearer than measuring the Goods, and indeed 250 Livres per Ton is as cheap, if not cheaper, than any Ship would now take Freight at. If the Marquis de la Fayette should not be able to take all the Saltpetre & other Articles, I may perhaps be able to give the Mars something more, but I would not choose to promise more than what comes more from the Arsenal, till the great Ship is loaded. Another Circumstance which I think makes this Scheme eligible is the Expiration of the Lease of the Arsenal at Christmas next, when Mr Schweighauser will be obliged to put you to the Expence of another Store & considerable Porterage. If you do not choose to make any Conditions about the Freight it may be left to be settled between Congress & the Massachusetts State, you advancing, on Accot of the State, sufficient money to dispatch the Ship; by this Mode the State will still owe the Money to Congress even if the Ship is taken, by the other the Freight being due on the Ships sailing, it will be a certain Expence to Congress whether the Ship arrives or not.— These are considerations which may be worth while between two Merchants, but as Congress & the State are both

5. XXIV, 360, 370, 385.

public Bodies, who have the same Interests, they may not be necessary, & either one or the other may be adopted. I thought of this Plan as the only one which would at once Serve the Public & releive the State, some time ago, but I did not choose to propose it till I saw Mr Austin, & he now thinks as I do.

I shall be glad to have your immediate Answer to this Letter, & if you Approve of my Proposal please to return me an Order on Mr Schweighauser to hold all the Goods in the Arsenal at my Disposal, & I will sett the Business agoing with the utmost Expedition. You I trust will beleive I have no Motive in what I write but the general Good, I have no Wish to serve the State to the Prejudice of Congress, but I think it my Duty to point out a Way of serving both at the same time.—

When you Answer this Letter please at the same time to inform me what is determined on relative to the Portuguese Captain who was taken by Capt Samson. There is no Doubt but the Man has a Right to his Ship & Freight, & the State I dare say would make him ample Amends if he was in Boston, but they cannott pay a Sol here unless the Ship is seized & sold, which I trust Government will not permit; Whatever is done however had better be done soon, so as we may know what is to be depended on.—

You have no doubt heard of Jones's Disaster, there will be probably part of the Ariels Cargo to ship in another Vessell, so that I imagine we shall have enough for bothe the Marquis de la Fayette & Samson.

If you give the order to Mr Schweighauser about the Arsenal let it be to *ship* all he has belonging to the Public in such Vessell or Vessells as I point out, not to *deliver* to me, because I desire not to take from him any Commission which may arise in the Operation, for my Motives in this Business are not interested ones.—

I am ever with the highest Respect Your dutifull & affectionate Kinsman[6] JONA WILLIAMS J

My Hurry of Business obliged me to make use of a Copyist for this Letter, which I never choose to do when I write to you if I can help it.

6. From this paragraph onward, the letter is in jw's hand.

I am ready for the great Ship without a moments Warning & wish she was at L'Orient. JW

Endorsed: Jona Williams Oct. 17. 1780

Notations: Jona Williams 17 Octo. 1780 / [*in William Temple Franklin's hand:*] Ansd by W.T.F.[7]

To Pierre-Joseph Macquer[8]   LS: Bibliothèque Nationale

Monsieur   Passy. Oct. 18. 1780:
Celui qui vous remettra cette lettre est M. Foulke de qui j'ai eu l'honneur de vous parler l'autre jour chèz M. L'Avoisier,[9] c'est un jeune Americain très honête qui est venu à Paris avec le dessein de se perfectionner dans la connoissance théorique et pratique de la medecine et de la Chirurgie: permettez moi de le recommander à vos bons offices et Conseils, et je vous serai très obligé des bontés que vous voudrez bien avoir pour lui.

J'ai l'honneur d'être avec beaucoup d'estime et de consideration, Monsieur, Votre très humble et tres obeissant Serviteur

B FRANKLIN

M. Macquer

7. Because BF was stricken with gout. The letter is below, Oct. 25, written in the presence of BF and Chaumont.

8. Macquer (1718–1784), the author of several works on chemistry, was interested in the applications of chemistry to medicine. He was a *docteur-régent* of the Faculté de médecine and lectured in chemistry at the Jardin du Roi. As consultant to the government's Bureau de commerce, which controlled French trade and industry, he was involved in the investigation of problems concerning saltpetre and the dyeing and ceramic industries. He was a member of the Société royale de médecine, the Académie royale des sciences, and, among other foreign societies, the APS: *Dictionary of Scientific Biography;* Larousse; Quérard, *France littéraire; Almanach royal* for 1780, pp. 455, 481, 501. For Macquer's contributions to French industry see Roger Hahn, *The Anatomy of a Scientific Institution: the Paris Academy of Sciences, 1666–1803* (Berkeley, Los Angeles, London, 1971; paperback ed., 1986), pp. 68–71, 117–20.

9. A bill for the expenses of BF's servant Arbelot shows that BF dined "a larsenal ches madame lavoisier" on Oct. 15. See the annotation of our editorial headnote on accounts.

From Ezra Stiles

ALS: American Philosophical Society

Sir   Newport 18. Octr 1780

John Bunnel of New Haven in Connecticutt Son of Mr Israel Bunnel,[1] was taken by the British June 25 1777 on board a Merchant Brig from Charlestown So. Caro. bound to France, and put on board the Valiant Man O' War a 74 Gun Ship; from which, while lying at Portsmouth in Engld, he wrote a Letter to his Father dated Octr 28 1777. This is the last time his Parents have heard from their Son. His Parents request that Dr Franklin would give himself the Trouble of handing this to the Commissary [for?] exchanging Prisoners, if perhaps their Son might be found and exchanged. I am, Sir, Your humble Servant

EZRA STILES

Dr Franklin

Addressed: The Honorable / Benjamin Franklin Esq L L. D. / Minister Plenipotentiary of / the United States / At the Court of / Versailles

From Jonathan Loring Austin

ALS: American Philosophical Society

Sir.   Nantes 19th October 1780

I had the Honor of writing you by last Post[2] relative to a Quantity of warlike Stores I wished to take on Freight for America, & hope in due time to be favored with your Excellency's Answer.

I now enclose your Excellency a Draft on Monsieur Grand for 330 Livres in part of the 600 you was pleased to lend me, I did

1. Israel Bunnell (1715–1781), a graduate of the Yale College class of 1743, was a former schoolmaster in New Haven: Franklin B. Dexter, *Biographical Sketches of the Graduates of Yale College . . .* (6 vols., New York, 1885–1912), I, 728. See also Zara Jones Powers, ed., *New Haven Colony Historical Society: Ancient Town Records*, vol. III, *New Haven Town Records 1684–1789* (New Haven, 1962), pp. 675, 815.

2. On Oct. 17, above.

not perceive till this Morning a Mistake had been made in drawing the Bills which occasions my not drawing for the whole Sum; I will desire Mr Williams to pass to your Credit the remaining 270 Livres; provided it will be as agreeable to you as having an Order on some Person in Paris—with which you'l please to acquaint me—

I am with great Respect sir Your most Obedient & very humble Servant   JONA. LORING AUSTIN

Addressed: Son Excellence / Monsieur Dr Franklin / à Passy / pres Paris

Notation: J. L Austin Nantes 19 Oct 80

From Jonathan Williams, Jr.

ALS: University of Pennsylvania Library; copy: Yale University Library

Dear & hond Sir   Nantes Octor 19. 1780.

I have just received a Letter from Mr De Segray of which he tells me he has sent you a Copy.[3] You will see by it that it is not the *Regisseurs des Poudre* but les *Fermier Genereaux* that must give the permission desired. Please to obtain this & send it to Mr De Segray as soon as possible, in the mean time I have desird him to try to forward the Business by engaging to pay all Duties in failure of the Permission, & to send it on, cost what it will, for the Salt Petre may as well be at the Bottom of the Sea as at St Malo, so far as relates to the public of America.

Our old acquaintance Capt Isaac All is arrived at L'orient by him you have no doubt advice of the Check Genl Gates has received.—[4]

I am ever with the greatest Respect Yours most dutifully & affectionately   JONA WILLIAMS J

Notation: Jona Williams Oct. 19. 80

3. Missing.
4. At the Battle of Camden. All did not mention the battle in his letter of Oct. 16, above.

To John Adams

LS:[5] Massachusetts Historical Society; copy: Library of Congress

Sir   Passy 20 Oct. 1780.

Understanding that in Case of Mr. Laurens's Absence, you are charged with the Affair of procuring a Loan in Holland, I think it Right to acquaint you, that by a Letter from Mr Jay of the 12th Inst,[6] from Madrid, we are informed that the King of Spain has been so good as to offer his Guarrantee for the Payment of the Interest and Principal of a Loan of Money for the Use of the United States. Mr Grand thinks that no considerable Use can be made here of that Guarrantee, on Account of the considerable Loan Mr. Necker is about to make; but that possibly it may have weight in Holland.— Orders will be sent to the Spanish Ambassador here, by the next Post respecting this Matter.

I regret much the taking of Mr. Lawrens. His Son, I understand sailed a Fortnight after him, for France;[7] but he has not yet arrived.

The Ariel has been at Sea, but meeting with a terrible Storm which carried away all her Masts, has return'd into Port to refit.

I have the honour to be with great Respect, Sir, Your Excellency's most obedient & most humble Sert.   B Franklin

P.S. By a former Letter from Mr Jay I find the Sum to be one hundred & fifty thousand Dollars, for which the King of Spain would be answerable payable in the Space of 3 Years.[8]

His Exy. John Adams Esqr.

Notation: His Excellency Dr Franklin recd and ansd 24. octr. 1780 warranty of Spain for a Loan.

---

5. In WTF's hand.

6. The recipient's copy is not extant; the copy in BF's letterbook (printed above) is dated Oct. 5.

7. BF's intelligence was wrong. Col. John Laurens had been captured at Charleston, and was not exchanged until November, 1780: Fitzpatrick, *Writings of Washington*, XX, 315.

8. This information is correct; see Morris, *Jay: Revolutionary*, p. 718. The letter BF refers to is not extant.

From Dumas

ALS: American Philosophical Society; AL (draft): Algemeen Rijksarchief

Monsieur,   Lahaie 20e. Oct. 1780.

La vraie amitié qui caractérise si bien vos Lettres du 2 & du 9 Octob. me remplit de gratitude. Je vous promets bien saintement de la mériter jusqu'au dernier soupir, avec votre approbation qui m'est aussi précieuse que la vie. J'eus la satisfaction, avanthier d'avoir ici Mr. Searle, & de passer la nuit avec lui à Leide, d'où je suis revenu hier un peu tard. Ah! l'excellent homme! Quand je vois de tels Américains, les Epines qui m'ont piqué pour eux se chargent de Roses.

C'est à force de patience, mais sans lâcheté, que j'ai vaincu le ressentiment du Gd. Fr. [Grand Facteur] Il étoit juste: une seule chose qu'il exigeoit, & à quoi j'espere qu'il ne pensera plus, ne l'étoit pas.

Hier 8 jours l'Amirauté d'hollde. donna son Préavis sur l'accession de la rep. conformément aux desirs de l'Imperatrice & de la Ville d'Amst. Hier Cet avis fut converti en Résolution unanime de la Province.[9] J'espere que les Etats-généraux, à qui elle va être communiquée, selon leur coutume d'adopter les resolutions d'Hollde. adopteront aussi unanimement celleci. *But let us not be too sanguine in our hopes.*

J'accepterai certainement le Secretariat en question avec l'appointement de 500 £.St. qui y est attaché par le Congrès; & je suis sûr que celui qui remplira la place de Mr. L—— [Laurens] sera content de moi. Voici ce que j'écris ce soir là-dessus à Mr. Searle:

"I can't help to be still vexed with the misfortune that has happened to his Exc. L——. The new arrangement of Such a Secretaryship, as the honble. J. Lowell speaks of in his Letter,[1] & to which, by your & his good advice, as well as by that of his Exc. Dr. Franklin, he would have chosen me, with a salary of 500 £.st: per annum would have made me (& my little family) very happy with him, & will so, I hope, with whoever will be appointed to

---

9. Authorizing the Dutch representatives in St. Petersburg to accede to the Russian agreements with Sweden and Denmark: Fauchille, *Diplomatie française*, p. 537.

1. On July 10 James Lovell wrote Dumas via Searle promising to help him obtain the official post he had solicited: Smith, *Letters*, XV, 421–2.

succeed him. Permit me only to wish, it might be your amiable person. Whenever you write to America, be pleased Dear Sir, to testify my chearfull as well as gratefull acquiescence, & acceptation of the said arrangement, or an equipollent one; & that my only ambition has been, from the beginning, & will be throug the remainder of my life, to be continued & maintain'd in the service of a cause, to which the having been so very unexpectedly or rather providentially called, has filled my mind with thoughts, & my heart with feelings, more comfortable for me, than any other grandeurs whatever could do."

J'aurai soin, Monsieur, de consulter avec notre Ami, sur ce qu'il faudra faire relativement à l'affaire de Saba,[2] & de vous rendre compte en son temps de ce qu'il en pense.

L'Envoyé de Portugal n'est pas ici actuellement; il est à Londres; & l'on ne sait encore quand il sera de retour. Comme la dite Cour, leurs Ministres ici, avoient paru jusqu'ici si bons amis de l'Angle. que je n'ai point formé de liaisons avec eux. J'ai donc besoin d'être introduit moi-même chez Mr. De Souza, avant de pouvoir lui présenter Mr. Searle: & Mr. Searle m'a chargé de vous prier de me procurer de la part de l'Envoyé de Portugal en France[3] une Lettre introductoire, ou de recommandation. J'aurai le temps de la recevoir avant que Mr. De Souza arrive. Je connois bien Son Aumônier ici; & je ferai quelques démarches auprès de lui. Mais une Lettre de l'Envoyé de Portugal, accordé à votre demande, si je puis la présenter, vaudra mieux, & abrégera les choses au contentement de Mr. Searle. Elle me donnera d'ailleurs un pied là pour toujours.

2. In November, 1779, the packet *Eagle*, owned by James Searle & Co. and carrying provisions for the French fleet in the West Indies, was chased by British privateers into the harbor at Saba (a Dutch island near St. Eustatius). The British succeeded in carrying her off to Nevis and selling her in spite of the Dutch governor's promise of protection to her American captain. After reviewing the case Congress ordered BF to seek the help of the States General in obtaining redress: William Bell Clark, "The John Ashmead Story 1738–1818," *PMHB*, LXXXII (1958), 27–32; *JCC*, XVI, 279–80, 286–7; Smith, *Letters*, XIV, 66, 89–90, 264. Undoubtedly Searle acted as an intermediary.

3. The conde de Sousa de Coutinho, probably a relative of Souza Holstein. The former's name is sometimes spelled Souza: *Repertorium der diplomatischen Vertreter*, III, 317.

I Say nothing of Mr. *****,[4] nor of what he is doing because I cannot say anything of neither, since we parted at Leiden. I hope only I stand well with him, because I have done my best to merit it. I hope to see him at Amsterdam, when this Assembly will separate. There are (between us) some good people that find him too much reserved, & do not agree with some of his ideas, or perhaps with the manner of his delivering them. But perhaps those good men would be the first of not supporting me, if they were to be called to account for what they said confidentially to me respecting him. You Know Dear Sir, I have not long since, paid very dearly (nearly with my life, & I fear with that of my wife) for too much unreservedness in writing.[5] I am, honoured and dear Sir, very happy in your everlasting friendship, & in the sincerity of my heart with which I am for ever, your most obedient, most humble & faithfull servant   DUMAS

Paris à S. E. Mr. B. Franklin

Addressed: à Son Excellence / Monsieur B. Franklin / Esqr. Min. Plenipe. / des Et. Unis &c. / Passy ./.

From John Paul Jones

ALS: American Philosophical Society; AL (draft): National Archives

Sir,   L'Orient Octr. 20. 1780
It being represented to me by Saml. Wharton Esqr. & Captain Hall of Philadelphia,[6] Mr. Robt. Mease Merchant of Virginia and Mr. Mathew Mease Purser of the Ariel that Five persons lately arrived here directly from Maryland and Pensylvania were Under the following circumstances Vizt. Mr. Cheston from Maryland confesses he has never taken an Oath of fidelity to the

4. Adams. Immediately below his signature Dumas drafted and then deleted the following sentence: "Je n'ai pas eu le temps de garder copie de la derniere partie de cette Lettre, touchant Mr.*****."
5. A reference to Georges Grand and La Vauguyon's quarrel with Dumas.
6. Probably Capt. John Hall of the brigantine *Friendship,* 12: Claghorn, *Naval Officers,* p. 133.

United States, nor taken any Active part in the Revolution, but has rather been a favorer of British Measures, and came here bound for England, as he Says, to settle his Affairs there and with intention to return to America.[7] Captain Smith from Maryland Appears to be nearly in the same situation; he says his fortune is in the British Funds.—[8] Mr. West from Philadelphia, is a Quaker, son of a Carpinter, and having a considerable intrest there has refused the Oath or Affirmation and was bound for England.—[9] Doctor Brown late of the Army is set out three Days ago, as I understand, either directly for Paris, or which is more likely *for St. Malo*—meaning to go along Shore and to remain in England. Doctor Wilson of St. Kitts also from America and now here is bound for England.— I thought it my Duty in conformity to the Advice of Mr. Wharton &c. to apply to Comte De Maillé[1] to prevent the Embarkation of the Four Suspected Persons above Mentioned in a Dutch Ship bound for Os-

7. James Cheston wrote to BF from Lorient, also on Oct. 20: he was born in Maryland and had a wife and three children there, although he was educated mostly in England. Between 1769 and 1775 he was a partner in the Bristol merchant firm of Stevenson, Randolph, and Cheston, but resided in Maryland. In August, 1779, he sailed for France. He seeks a passport in order to settle affairs in England and to gather his effects before returning to America. APS. BF witnessed his oath of allegiance on Nov. 19 (APS). It is possible he was the Maryland lawyer James Cheston (b. 1747) for whom see W.W. Abbot *et al.*, eds., *The Papers of George Washington: Colonial Series* (10 vols., Charlottesville, 1983–95), VIII, 215n.

8. Thomas Smith accompanied Cheston to France on the brig *Nesbitt*. On Oct. 20, he prepared his own memorial (APS). Presently 58 years old, he was born in England and served in the Maryland-London trade for 39 years, rising to the rank of captain. He resided in Maryland from 1775 to 1779, where he still owns land and slaves; until recently he had a wife and family there. He came to Europe in order to withdraw his funds from England and then plans to return to Maryland. He asks a passport if BF approves. BF also witnessed his oath of allegiance on Nov. 19 (APS).

9. Based on the additional information on West given by Wharton the same day, below, our guess is that he is a descendant of Charles West, owner of the West shipyard on Vine Street, perhaps his son James or a grandson: Harold E. Gillingham "Some Colonial Ships Built in Philadelphia," *PMHB*, LVI (1932), 171.

1. Charles-René de Maillé de La Tour-Landry, comte (later duc) de Maillé (1732–1791) for whom see the *Dictionnaire de la Noblesse*, XII, 822–3, and Croÿ, *Journal*, IV, 322n. Maillé, a *maréchal de camp* in the army, became inspector of troops in Brittany on Aug. 1, 1779: Bodinier.

tend, Until they had Obtained Your Excellencies Permission.—
I hope You will approve this Step I have taken, as there are now
Seven American Vessels here Richly Laden besides the Ariel;
and Mr. Cheston and his three Companions being Under no Tie
on their Arrival in England, would naturally give information
not only of what they know here, but of what they have Seen in
America.— These Men Say they are now willing to take the
Oath of fidelity to the United States.— I have been Actuated in
the matter only by Publick motives.— I have the honor to be
with the greatest respect Sir Your Excellencies' Most Obedient
very humble Servant   JNO. P JONES

His Excellency B. Franklin &c. &c.

Notation: J. P. Jones L'Orient Octr 20.80

From the Abbé André Morellet

L:[2] American Philosophical Society

[October 20, 1780?][3]
L'abbé Morellet Supplie Monsieur franklin de lui faire dire S'il
Sait quelque chose d'un officier Suisse nommé Mr. Bedault[4] qui
a quitté il y a quelques années le Service de hongrie pour passer
à celui du Congrès, a été pris par les anglois, a trouvé le moyen
de Se Sauver, est revenu à Paris, à passé en Amérique avec Mr.
de la fayette et a été récemment promu au grade de Lieutenant
colonel. Le bruit de Sa mort S'est répandu, mais on n'en a que

2. In the hand of his secretary, Poullard.
3. The day on which Morellet wrote to Ostervald and Bosset de Luze, the
Neuchâtel publishers, apologizing for not having answered several of their
letters. The editors of the Morellet edition suppose that in one of these unanswered letters, no longer extant, Ostervald and de Luze had requested Morellet to look into rumors of Charles-Frédéric Bedaulx's death, and that on the
same day Morellet replied to them he wrote to BF about Bedaulx: Dorothy
Medlin, Jean-Claude David, and Paul LeClerc, eds., *Lettres d'André Morellet* (3 vols., Oxford, 1991–96), I, 436–7, 438n.
4. Who had died in Charleston during the winter of 1779–80: XXIII,
39–40.

des avis vagues et indirects. On voudroit Savoir ce qu'il est devenu.[5]

Notation: Morellet

From Jonathan Nesbitt
ALS: American Philosophical Society

Sir!   L'Orient October 20th: 1780

I have the honor to inclose you Copy of a Letter which I receiv'd by the Brigantine Nesbitt from Mr. Stephen Stewart of West River, in Maryland. This Gentleman you will see recommends Mr. James Cheston, who came passenger in said Brign: in the warmest manner to my attention & Civilitys.[6] On Mr. Chestons arrival here he communicated to me his intentions of going to England by the way of Paris & Ostend, but a few days before he intended to depart, he met with the Captain of a Flemish Vessell ready to Sail for Ostend, and as this would save both time & Expence, he took his passage on board.— On Wednesday last as Mr. Cheston had prepared every thing for his departure, he was surpriz'd to find an order to attend the Commandant, who inform'd him that information had been lodged against him as a suspicious person, & required that he should give his Parole, not to depart from this Town untill further orders;—this Mr: Cheston comply'd with, by which means he has lost the opportunity of Sailing for Ostend.— I have not taken the pains to enquire who the *persons* are who have given the above information, or on what grounds it is founded;—no doubt they are warm friends to

5. The young man's family also sought news of him through other channels. On Nov. 1, A.-A.-J. Feutry wrote to WTF on behalf of Bedaulx's parents. APS. On Dec. 5, Ostervald requested Morellet, presumably on behalf of the family, to ask BF for any information on Bedaulx's death. A copy of this letter is preserved at the Bibliothèque publique et universitaire of Neuchâtel and was kindly communicated to us by Dorothy Medlin. On April 28, 1781, his uncle, J.H. Bedaulx, Major-General in the Dutch Service, sought help from Dumas who forwarded a translation of the uncle's letter to Congress: Wharton, *Diplomatic Correspondence*, IV, 390–1.

6. This June 24 letter called Cheston "a Merchant & Gentleman of honor & Integrity." APS.

America, and deeply Interested in the Consequences of any information that Mr. Cheston might give on his arrival in England, if it was his intention to have given any information,—but of this I would beg leave to assure you Sir, that it was not necessary for them to take the measures they have done to prevent him.— Had they express'd their disapprobation of his going to England by Sea, either to himself, or to me, it would have answer'd the same purpose— Mr. Chestons behavior since he came to this Port fully answers the Character given him by Mr. Stewart.— It has been such as to gain him the Esteem of every person with whom he has had any acquaintance.— Perhaps you may be acquainted wth. the Character of the person who recommends him.— He has allways been warmly attach'd to the American Cause, & would be very far from recommending any person whom he thought capable of doing it any Injury.— Mr. Cheston informs me that it has been Insinuated that he left America in a Clandestine Manner, to confute wch: he incloses you a Certeficate signed by Captain Forbes of the Brigantine Nesbitt, who has been in the American service Since the begining of the War, and bears an extraordinary good Character;—[7] I am well convinced he is not Capable of setting his hand to a falsehood.

I hope Sir! you will excuse my troubling you with so long a Letter on this occasion, but I am the only person in this Country to whom Mr. Cheston has brought Letters of recommendation, and cannot help thinking that those who have inform'd against him, have done him an Injury from which no advantage either to themselves or the publick can be derived.— Common Politeness (knowing him to be recommended to me,) might have dictated to them to have acquainted me with their Intentions, before they apply'd to the Commandant, which if they had done would have prevented my troubling you at present.—

7. For the numerous commands held by James Forbes of Philadelphia see Claghorn, *Naval Officers*, p. 112. His Oct. 20 certificate states that many inhabitants of Baltimore and Annapolis knew in advance that Cheston was sailing on the *Nesbitt* and that he had spent the evening before his departure with Col. William Fitzhugh, a member of the Maryland House of Delegates, and Maryland Chief Judge Nicholas Thomas. APS.

I have the honor to be, with Sentiments of great Respect.—
Sir! Your most Obedient humble Servt: JONAT: NESBITT
His Excellency B: Franklin

Notation: Nesbit Jona. L'Orient Oct. 20. 1780.

From Samuel Wharton   ALS: American Philosophical Society

Sir   L'Orient 20th October 1780
    In some of the late Vessels, arrived from Maryland, and Penn-
sylvania came passengers the following Gentlemen.— Messrs.
Cheston, and Captain Smith of the former; and Mr.   West,
and Dr. Wilson of the latter State, and They were preparing to
go in a Dutch Vessel to Ostend, and from Thence to England,
But Commodore Jones, upon the Advice of several American
Citizens and myself, judged it necessary to apply to the Commanding Officer of this Province to Stop Them, Until your
Pleasure was known. Mr. Cheston says, He will this Day before your Excellency a State of his Conduct in Maryland, and the
Reasons for his going to England. He acknowledges to have
acted uniformly against the Principles of the Revolution,— not
to have taken the usual Oath to the State, and to have departed
from Maryland, without permission of the Government, But at
the Same Time, He alledges has left his Wife, and Debts, and
Possessions to a considerable Amount there, and produces a
News Paper, wherein is an Advertisement avowing his Design of
going to Europe, and requesting all persons indebted to Him to
pay their Several Debts to his Attorney.— Mr. Cheston, before
the Revolution, was a Merchant in New Town on the Eastern
Shore of Maryland, and a Justice of Peace, in Governor's Eden's
Administration,[8] and appears a Gentleman of good Address and
Understanding. Captain Smith, I understand has always been
unfriendly to the new Government, and says his Business is to
sell some Stock, He has in the British Funds. He has no permission to go to England. Mr. West is a Quaker, and Son to the late
Mr. West a Ship Carpinter in Vine Street, Philadelphia. He has

8. Robert Eden (XVI, 185n) was governor from 1769 to 1776: *DAB.*

not taken an Affirmation of Allegiance and Fidelity to the Government nor cannot produce any Evidence of Liberty being granted Him, To pass from France to England, But says He has an Estate in Philadelphia, worth six thousand pounds. Dr. Wilson was employed as a Surgeon in the fedral Army, and is In the Same Predicament. His Design is to stay in England, and not return to the United States. It might be of injurious Consequence, if these persons were permitted to land in the Enemies Country, particularly at this Time, When the Frigate Ariel, and Seven Sail of American Vessels are in Port, loading with very valuable Cargoes;— And, perhaps, during the War, It might be impolitic to suffer the Enemies of America to come to the ports of this Kingdom without permission, and from thence to pass to England, Where They would be closely interrogated, as well with Respect to the Situation of Affairs in the States, as of all Vessels, and Armaments, in the Harbours of our Ally. I recommended to Mr. Cheston and the other Gentlemen to proceed to Passy, and lay before your Excellency a Brief state of their Affairs, and the Object of their Errand to England, But they seem to prefer staying here, Until They know your Pleasure, and flatter Themselves, You will allow Them to Carry their first Intention into Execution.

I have acted in this affair, in giving my opinion as above stated to Commodore Jones, wholy upon publick Grounds.— I have not been moved to it by any illiberal Motive, as I had not the least personal Knowledge of Mr. Cheston and his Companions.— I have the Honor to be, with great Respect your Excellency's most Obedient and most humble Servant

SAML. WHARTON

Be pleased to read Dr. Wilson, formerly of St. Kitts, Where I have written on a Razure.[9]

His Excellency Benjamin Franklin Esqr.

Notation: S Wharton. L'Orient. 20 Oct 80

---

9. An obsolete word for "erasure"; in the body of the letter "Wilson" is first written over a name which is no longer readable and later written below a name which has been scratched out.

From [the Marquis de Castries][1]

Copy: Archives Nationales, Paris

A Versailles le 21. Octobre 1780.

J'ai vû, Monsieur, la lettre que vous avez écrite à M. de sartine, au sujet de deux Bâtiments Américains que les Srs. de Lap, Négts. à Bordeaux, se proposent d'expédier pour les Colonies françoises de l'Amérique.[2] M. Necker, à qui M. de sartine avoit écrit pour un Armément semblable, projetté par les Srs. Bondfield, flaipood, et Compagnie, et que vous lui avez recommandé au mois de juin dernier,[3] a répondû qu'il avoit ordonné au Directeur des fermes à Bordeaux,[4] d'accorder, sans dificulté, les expéditions nécéssaires, tant pour les Bâtimens dont il s'agissoit, que pour ceux qui auroient, à l'avenir, la même destination. Il a même annoncé, en dernier lieu, qu'il avoit donné des Ordres pour que le droit du fret ne fut pas éxigé. D'un autre côté, les Bâtimens Américains seront admis, avec leurs Carguaisons, dans nos isles[5] où ils pourront prendre en retour des chargemens de denrées coloniales. Les Srs. de Lap peuvent s'adresser aux Srs. Bondfield et flaipood qui les instruiront de la maniere dont le Directeur des fermes en aura usé à leur égard./.

J'ai l'honneur d'etre avec la plus parfaite consideration, M., votre très humble &ca.

A M. Franklin

---

1. Charles-Eugène-Gabriel de La Croix, marquis de Castries (1727–1801), a lieutenant general in the French army and a hero of the Seven Years' War, had been named naval minister a week earlier. He owed his appointment to Necker and to the Queen, who were political rivals of Vergennes and Maurepas: *DBF;* Baron Jehan de Witte, ed., *Journal de l'abbé de Véri* (2 vols., Paris, [1928–30]), II, 397; John Hardman, *French Politics 1774–1789: from the Accession of Louis XVI to the Fall of the Bastille* (London and New York, 1995), pp. 56–8.
2. BF to Sartine, Oct. 8, above.
3. See XXXII, 445–6, 605–6.
4. *I.e.,* the local representative of the farmers general, probably either M. Dublanc or M. Bachelier: *Almanach Royal* for 1780, pp. 549, 551.
5. In the Caribbean.

From Jonathan Williams, Jr.

ALS: American Philosophical Society; copy: E. Marie Lorimer (Philadelphia, 1957)

Dear & hond Sr   Nantes Octor 21. 1780.

Inclosed is a List of all the Bills I have drawn on M. de Chaumont for accot of the Cloathing from the first Bill to the present Day with the No date Term & every particular relating to each amounting to 741095 *l.t.* 18 *s.* 4 *d.*[6]

I intended to send this List at the same Time I sent the Accounts of this Operation, but what I have this day learnt from Paris determines me to send it off immediately; I am told that M. de Chaumont has been exceedingly pressed for money so much so as to be obliged to suspend his Payments for two Days, and it is only through the Aids of Government that he has been able to continue his Payments, whether this aid will be continued to him or not I am also told is a matter of uncertainty.[7] In consequence of this I think it is proper & necessary you should have a State of the Bills immediately. The Accounts of the whole of this Operation will follow as soon as possible & will no doubt much exceed the Sums I have drawn for, but in the present State of Matters I cant venture to draw on M. de C for what I shall want more, for I should not like to push his Credit in such Circumstances for his Sake as well as my own. You will observe that upwards of 200,000 Livres of the Bills in the State are not yet due & consequently are unpaid, should these come back on me I should have a hard Struggle to get through them. I therefore hope you will

---

6. Although the list is missing, the figure corresponds to that cited in various of Chaumont's accounts (Account XIX, xxviii, 3; Account XXVI, xxxii, 3) for bills jw drew on him from February through September, 1780. It is the sum of the first 372 bills drawn on Chaumont that jw itemized in Account XXIV (xxxi, 3).

7. Chaumont's difficulties were reported on Oct. 22: "M. Le Roy de Chaumont, le grand munitionnaire des Américains, l'hôte et l'ami de M. Franklin, a suspendu ses payements pendant vingt-quatre heures. Sa faillite étoit déclarée, si M. Necker ne lui avoit fait fournir des secours par le Roi." Mathurin-François-Adolphe de Lescure, ed., *Correspondance secrète inédite sur Louis XVI, Marie-Antoinette, la cour et la ville de 1777 à 1792* (2 vols, Paris 1866) I, 324–5.

see them taken up. Please to let me know in answer whether you have paid into Mr de Chaumonts hands money enough to answer these Dfts. If not it will be well to secure it in such a manner as to appropriate it only to the payment of them, & for this Purpose it would be well to lodge in the Caisse d'Escompte a List of such of the dfts as are yet unpaid (which I suppose will be all subsequent to the 12 June last,) & give Directions that in Case of Failure on the part of Mr de Chaumont you will pay the Bills. You will excuse these Apprehensions in me, but my Credit is a very delicate point for if these Bills were to come back on me at once (tho' I should lose nothing in the End) it would ruin my Credit. Mr de Chaumont is I am sure one of the best men in the World, and so far as relates to himself the utmost Dependance is to be placed upon him, but from what I hear I am afraid he has undertaken too much. I beg this Letter may be between ourselves, I write to you freely & without reserve nor can I ever write to you otherways on any subject. I beg to hear from you on this Subject in the mean time shall draw no more Bills on M. de Chaumont.

I am ever your dutifull & affectionate Kinsman

JONA WILLIAMS J

P.S. I have written to M. d'arlincourt fils.[8] F G. who directs the Bureau of the Farmers General *Rue de Richelieu pres la petite Porte du palais Royale* about the Salt Petre which I mentioned to you in my last. If you see this Gentleman or M. Paulze or M. Necker the matter may be easily settled. JW

Endorsed: Mr. Williams Oct. 21. 1780 Relating to the Acceptances His good Opinion of M. de Chaumont—

Notation: Jona Williams Oct 21 1780

To Lavoisier

Copy: Library of Congress

Monsieur, Pasy, le 22 Oct. 1780.

Je prends la liberté de vous envoyer cy joint diverses Piéces que je viens de recevoir de Messrs. de Segray & Co. par les

---

8. Louis-Adrien Prévost d'Arlincourt: XXIX, 88n.

quelles vous verrez que l'Ordre que vous avez bien voulu m'accorder pour le Transport des Salpêtres de St. Malo à l'Orient, ne suffit pas[9] et qu'on m'en demande un de Messrs. les Fermiers généraux des cinq grosses Fermes.— Oserois-je vous prier, Monsieur, d'avoir la bonté de jetter les yeux sur ces Pieces et de me donner votre Conseil sur le parti que je dois prendre, vous rendrez un nouveau et très grand Service à celui qui a l'honneur d'être avec un très sincere attachement, Monsr., V. tr. h: et t: o: S.

M. La Voisier.

From Dumas

ALS: American Philosophical Society; AL (draft): Algemeen Rijksarchief

Monsieur   Lahaie 23e. Octobe. 1780
    Ma Lettre ci-jointe du 20e.[1] n'a pu partir vendredi, parce qu'il étoit trop tard.
    J'ai vu *notre Ami*. Il croit que l'Ambassadr. de la rep. à Paris[2] fera difficulté de se charger de votre Réclamation,[3] du moins de la maniere qu'il le faudroit. La même difficulté auroit lieu avec le G. P—— d'Hollde. Nous en avons conclu, que le meilleur parti à prendre, c'est que vous écriviez directement *à Leurs Hautes Puissances les États-Généraux des Provinces-Unies des Pays-Bas*. On leur dit, en les apostrophant, *Hauts & puissants Seigneurs (High & mighty Lords)*. Si vous m'envoyez la Lettre cachetée de votre cachet (volant), j'y joindrai les papiers que vous m'avez envoyés, avec la résolution annexe du Congrès, en

9. Lavoisier had learned this himself, from a M. Lechault in St. Malo (probably a customs officer) writing on Oct. 17 in answer to Lavoisier's of Oct. 4. Lechault had presented Lavoisier's passport to his *directeur des fermes*, who replied that the saltpetre, held by the farmers under lock and key, was an "article . . . prohibé," and had to be shipped in bond under the auspices of the customs office. BF must have misunderstood what was required. APS; the letter is reprinted in Claude A. Lopez, "Saltpetre, Tin and Gunpowder: Addenda to the Correspondence of Lavoisier and Franklin," *Annals of Science*, XVI (1960), 90–1.
    1. Above.
    2. Mattheus Lestevenon van Berkenrode: XXVIII, 324n.
    3. On behalf of Searle; see BF to Dumas, Oct. 9.

un paquet à part; & je porterai le tout au Président de semaine de L. h. p. Ce sera à elles alors à voir quand & comment elles répondront à Votre Lettre: & vous, Monsieur, de votre côté, aurez rempli la commission du Congrès, completement quant à vous. Je suis avec un grand respect, Monsieur Votre très-humble & très-obéissant serviteur   DUMAS

On a trouvé dans la Vallise de Mr. L——ns le projet d'un Traité entre l'Am—— & cette rep., dressé par Mrs. Wm. Lee & De Neufville, avec toute la correspondance entre ces Messieurs sur ce sujet, parmi laquelle diverses Lettres de Mr. Stockton,[4] où certain grand personnage ici se plaint d'avoir été traité avec peu de respect. On n'a pas manqué d'envoyer tous ces papiers à S. J. Y., pour les remettre au grand personnage,[5] afin de l'aigrir contre les Amns. Cela est facheux, & fait un éclat facheux, pour Mr. De Neufv. Je n'ai point caché à notre Ami qu'une démarche aussi prématurée, que l'étoit alors celle-ci, de ces têtes un peu trop chaudes, devoit naturellement avoir quelque suite semblable.

Passy à S. E. M. B. Franklin

Addressed: à Son Excellence / Monsieur B. Franklin / Mine. Plenipe. des Etats-Unis / &c. / Passy

From John Adams: Two Letters

(I) ALS: American Philosophical Society; (II) ALS: Reprinted from Stan V. Henkels sales catalogue no. 1415 (May 22, 1928), p. 8.

I.

Sir   Amsterdam October 24. 1780
   I have this moment the Honour of your Letter of the twentyeth of this Month and it is, as cold Water to a thirsty Soul.
   I have been busily employed in making Enquiries, in forming Acquaintances and in taking Advice.— In hopes of Mr Lau-

4. Samuel Stockton (XXII, 198n) had been William Lee's secretary: XXVI, 582–3.
   5. Undoubtedly the stadholder, who enjoyed close ties with Ambassador Yorke.

rens's Arrival, and wishing him to judge for himself, I have not decided, upon some Questions that necessarily arise. I am not able to promise any Thing but I am led to hope, for Something. The Contents of Mr Jays Letter, will certainly be of great Weight and Use.— I am assured of the good Will of a Number of very worthy and considerable People and that they will endeavour to assist a Loan.

Let me intreat your Excellency, to communicate to me every Thing you may further Learn respecting the benevolent Intentions of the Court of Madrid, respecting this Matter.— I will do myself the Honour, to acquaint you with the Progress I make,.— I was before in hopes of assisting you Somewhat, and your Letter has raised those hopes a great deal, for the English Credit certainly Staggers here, a little.

The Treatment of Mr Laurens is truly affecting. It will make a deep and lasting Impression on the Minds of the Americans. But this will not be a present Relief to him. You are no doubt minutely informed, of his ill Usage.— Can any Thing be done in Europe for his Comfort or Relief?

I have the Honour to be, with respectfull Compliments to all Friends, sir, your most obedient humble servant   JOHN ADAMS

His Excellency Dr Franklin

Notation: J. Adams. Oct 24. 1780

II.

Sir   Amsterdam october 24. 1780

Separated from Master S.C. Johonnot[6] for a longer time than I expected, I am under apprehensions about him, and therefore must request your Excellencys Attention to him;

6. Samuel Cooper's grandson Samuel Cooper Johonnot had been a classmate of JA's sons in Passy: XXXI, 85n; XXXII, 117n. When JA went to the Netherlands BF took over JA's responsibility for the boy's care and paid for his schooling: BF to Cooper, Dec. 2, 1780 (Henry E. Huntington Library). On March 4, 1781 BF prepared a record of what he had spent (APS): he had paid the schoolmaster M. Péchigny 345 *l.t.* 10 *s.* on Nov. 6 for a quarter's schooling and on Feb. 9, 1781, 374 *l.t.* 7 *s.* for another quarter. Meanwhile on Dec. 30 he had received two bills of exchange worth 900 *l.t.* from JA to cover the expenses, leaving a favorable balance of 180 *l.t.* 3 *s.* BF labeled this document "Johonnot's Acct Settled."

I have no Money in my Hands, which belongs to his Father,[7] but am informed he has sent a Remittance for him, which I hope will soon arrive.— I must however, be responsible, for his Expenses, whether Remittances arrive or not as long as he Stays. I have the Honour to be, sir, your humb. sert[8] JOHN ADAMS

His Excellency Dr Franklin

From Thomas Digges

ALS: Historical Society of Pennsylvania

Dr. Sir   Stepney 24 Octor 1780

The letter of Sepr. 18 with an inclosd Bill reachd me but a very few days ago, & I immeadiately made the necessary enquirys about Mr Jones. This Genn. [Gentleman] is not in England but I hear He is coming this way, & is at present in Amsterdam, where (I suppose) he is playing similar tricks to those He has imposd upon You. The good old Doctor[9] of whom I made my enquirys after Jones, tells me that He drew upon him from Paris for Eight Guineas "to keep him out of a French Goal". This draft was follwd a post or two after by another for 20 £ "to enable him to get to America". Besides these Bills, he, by imposing himself on Dr. F as a Bror [Brother] to Dr. Jones of N York,[1] obtain several small sums of money, & the old Dr. knows nothing of him at present. I will be upon the watch for Him & therefore hold the Bill you inclosd me; but I think your best & only remedy is on Goddard, Who having Acknowlegd His acceptance of such a bill, is in consequence thereof liable to pay what has been advancd on it.

7. Gabriel Johonnot, a Boston merchant whose wife Judith died in 1773: XXI, 124n. The bills of exchange mentioned in the previous note were his; he sent them to JA in September and came to Europe himself in 1781: *Adams Papers*, X, 139, 305n.

8. On Nov. 6 WTF, writing for his grandfather, informs JA that BF had been unable to answer JA's several letters because he is "laid up with the Gout." He hopes within a few days to be sufficiently recovered to write. WTF sends his regards to Mr. Dana and Mr. Thaxter (Mass. Hist. Soc.).

9. Undoubtedly Dr. John Fothergill.

1. Most probably the celebrated surgeon Dr. John Jones (1729–1791): *DAB*.

My two friends are arrivd & I red [received] the newspaper by them.[2] I am uneasy about the picture; upwards of two I believe three mos ago Mr. F Bowens at Ostend acknowlegd the save receival of it, & said it should be forwarded properly.[3] I will write to Him abot it, & desire Him to address you on the Subject. Three of the four men whom you address a line to[4] are gone to Ireland; but not till after (by the advice of Mr H———n [Hodgson] & myself) making the proper application for the Receipt for four men from the Sick & hurt, to stand against as many confind americans. There are above an hundred people in their predicament in England, & most of them seemingly very easy under their situation; many have behavd well & done everything in their power.

The Person whom I have lately wrote to you about the Confinemt of, is in much better health, tho rigorously confind as usual. I have communicated with Him. This is mentiond for your Government in case you have a word to say to Him. I am With the highest respect Your Obedt Servant   Wm. S. Ross

No Western news but appearances speak that Some Ships & troops are soon going to the Wt Inds. & No Ama.

A Bill on Monr. G———d dated 16 Octor. for 48 £ for Accot of Your Charity at F———n [Forton]

Notation: Oct. 24. 1780.

From the Marquise(?) de Rochambeau[5]

AL: American Philosophical Society

au Palais Royal ce 24 Octobre [1780]

Made. De Rochambeau est pénétrée de Reconnoissance des Bontés de Monsieur frankln, Elle lui demande en grâce de les lui con-

2. William Jones and John Paradise, who brought BF's Oct. 9 letter to Digges.

3. See Digges to BF, Sept. 26.

4. Connolly and Marcus McCausland, William Stewart, and James Campbell.

5. Probably the marquise de Rochambeau and not the countess, who will write (in a different hand) on Aug. 8, [1781] (APS). Marie-Claire-Thérèse

tinuer, et Elle lui demande la Permission d'aller quelque fois passer quelques moments avec lui, Il Seroit bien Aimable quand il passe au Palais Royal S'il vouloit bien l'honorer d'une petite Visite Elle loge dans la grande Cour,[6] et il ni a pas une Marche pour entrer chez Elle. Elle Espere que cette Comodité et sa Reconnoissance lui procureronts quelquefois cette honneur.

Addressed: A Monsieur / Monsieur francklin Ministre / Plénipotentiaire de la République / des Etats-unies de L'Amerique / Septentrionale / A Passi.

Notation: Rochambeau 24. Oct. 1780.

From Jonathan Williams, Jr.

ALS: University of Pennsylvania Library; copy: E. Marie Lorimer (Philadelphia, Pennsylvania, 1957)

Dear & honoured Sir—   Nantes le 24 Octor 1780

I wrote you last Post[7] a particular Letter relative to Mr de Chaumonts affairs since which I find they are publicly known & the alarm is general. Every man who has taken my Bills on him in this Place have mentioned to me his stoppage of payment, but I am happy to find they have great Confidence in my Signature and do not discover any distrust; My answer has uniformly been that my Bills would always be paid at the Caisse d'Escompte whether Mr de Chaumont failed or not, & that if any in the mean

---

Begon, marquise de Rochambeau (d. 1782), was the mother of the comte de Rochambeau. She had been *gouvernante* of the duc d'Orléans' children and lived in a small apartment at the Palais-Royal. Her husband, Joseph-Charles de Vimeur, died in December, 1779. See Bodinier, *Dictionnaire*, p. 480; Jean-Baptiste-Donatien de Vimeur, Comte de Rochambeau, *Mémoires militaires, historiques et politiques* (2 vols., Paris, 1809), I, 33, 320–1; Jean-Edmond Weelen, *Rochambeau* (Paris, 1934), pp. 32–5, 110.

6. The *cour d'honneur,* the courtyard beyond the *cour d'entrée* which at this time, before the 1781 addition of the shops and galleries, opened onto the gardens: Hillairet, *Rues de Paris,* II, 217; Pierre d'Espezel, *Le Palais-Royal* (Paris, 1936) p. 121.

7. Oct. 21, above.

time should come back, Cash would be found in my Counting House to pay them.— I have accordingly been collecting all the Cash I could, & putting off payments for Goods for a few Days, so as to keep myself strong in Cash in Case of Emergency.— I beg however you will particularly attend to the payment of my Bills at the Caisse d'Escompte as they become due for that is the only way to save our Credit perfectly— If Mr de Chaumont continues to pay it is undoubtedly the safest & most honourable Method, but Funds should be provided in case of his Failure.— Mr de Chaumont I very much respect & would do all in my power to oblige, I have always done so, & lately have furnished him about 60,000 Livres, which I remitted to his Bankers on their Bills at a longer date, he has desired me to assist him farther & to draw on him for my Reimbursement, which indeed I intended to do, but I cannot now negociate a Livre on his Name & I would not choose to strain my own Credit.—

I beg you will favour me with your answer in a particular Letter on this Subject which I may show so as to assure the Persons who have taken my Bills that they will not be dishonoured.

I am ever with the greatest Respect Your dutifull & affectionate Kinsman   JONA WILLIAMS J

Endorsed: has assisted M. de Chaumont

Notation: Jona Williams 24 Oct 1780

To Schweighauser   Copies: Library of Congress, Yale University Library

Sir,   Passy 25. Oct. 1780.

This is to request you would Ship all the Stores you have in your Possession belonging to the Public of America, whether in the Arsenal or elsewhere, on board such Vessel or Vessels as shall be pointed out to you by Mr. Jonathan Williams.

I have the Honour to be Sir, Your most humble Servant. B.F.

M. J. D. Schweighauser

From Amezaga AL: American Philosophical Society

Ce 25. 8re 1780

Mr. D'amezaga est dépuis Six semaines à la Campagne. Il meurent d'envie de voir son cher Monsieur de Franklin. Il â trouvé à la Campagne un Noble Genois qui S'apelle Mr. de sélezia[8] qui a porter chés Monsieur de Franklin, un Paquet dont on L'avoit changé [chargé]. Il n'a point trouvé Monsieur de Franklin chés luy et à Laissés Son Paquet. Mr. de Sélezia qui connois L'attachement qu'a Mr. D'amezaga, Pour Monsieur de Franklin, voudrois aller dinner a Passy. Le Jour que désirera Le Cher amis que Jaime et que Jembrasse de toute mon ame, Mr. Damezaga et Mr Selezia yront ensemble reponce Sil vous Plait.

Notation: D'amzaga 25. 8bre. 1780.

From William Carmichael: Two Letters

(I) and (II) Copy: Library of Congress

I.

Dear Sir,   Madrid 25th. Oct. 1780.

The Duke De Crillon,[9] and who hath not heard of the Name of Crillon? does me the honour of accepting of an Introduction to you, which give me an Occasion of boasting of any influence with you to him, and to you of the honor he has done me by his Acquaintance & Friendship here. This Must be Clear to you when I mentione his name, tho' that to those who know him, is his least Recommendation.— Have however the same Indulgence for my failings that you have always had, & if not for my sake, for that of the Duke who is every Way worthy of your Esteem. Receive him in a Manner that will do Credit to my Introduction for when you know him, I am sure you will have been

8. Pietro Paolo Celesia. See Mazzei to BF, Aug. 19.
9. Louis de Berton, duc de Crillon (1718–1796), a hero of the War of the Austrian Succession and the Seven Years' War, who in 1762 had entered Spanish service: *DBF*. His greatest accomplishment, however, was the 1782 capture of Minorca, a project already under Spanish consideration: Montmorin to Vergennes, Oct. 30, 1780, (AAE).

pleased to have done it for his, I am Your Excellency's, most
obliged & m: h. S.   W. CARMICHAEL

His Exy. B. Franklin.

II.

Dear Sir,   Madrid 25. Oct. 1780.

I little thought when I mentioned to you the Pleasure I received from an introduction to the Family of the Prince de
Masseran, that I should have ever had an Occasion of giving you
an Opportunity of participating that Pleasure with me, But to
the misfortune of all their Friends & of none more than myself,
The Princes officers call him from this Country, and he does me
the honor of accepting this Introduction to you, the only return
in my power to make for all these Marks of his & the Princesses
obliging notice, which they have shown me a Stranger in this
Country.— You see me therefore in the Situation of an Insolent
Debtor, with all the Inclination of an honest one to pay his just
Debts, but without the ability, unless you will afford him the
Means— Like him I am obliged to apply to my friends, and I certainly offer a great Interest, when I give you an Opportunity of
profiting at Paris in the same Way that I have done at Madrid of
a Society that will give you a pleasure in the Possession equal to
my regret in being deprived of it. I intended for the Princess one
of these engravings, for which I wrote to my name sake[1] but as
I am sure She will have much more Pleasure in the original than
in a Copy, I must beg you to show it to her to advantage, which
I am sure you much always do, if placed in the same Light as
when seen by your Excellency's Most obliged & humble Sert.

                                        W. CARMICHAEL.

His Excelly. B. Franklin.

From Castries   Copy: Library of Congress

                              Marly le 25. 8bre. 1780.

J'ai l'honneur, Monsieur, de vous envoyer differentes Lettres que
le Capitaine du Parlementaire Anglois le Dowe arrivé a Cher-

1. WTF. See also Carmichael to BF, Aug. 12.

bourg a remis à Mr. Deshays Commissaire des classes. Comme ces Lettres [*in the margin:* 11. Lettres] sont de quelques Prisonniers Americains detenus en Angleterre, et qu'elles sont adressées à des Particuliers de la nouvelle Angleterre, J'ai cru devoir vous les faire passer.[2]

J'ai l'honneur d'être avec la Consideration la plus distinguée, Monsieur, Votre très humble et très obeissant Serviteur,

(signé) CASTRIES.

M. Franklin.

From Dumas

ALS: American Philosophical Society; AL (draft): Algemeen Rijksarchief

Monsieur,   La haie 25e. Octobe. 1780

J'ai eu l'honneur de vous rendre compte de ce qui est arrivé aux papiers trouvés dans la Vallise de Mr. Lns.[3] Le grd. Persge. [grand Personnage] les a remis aux Etats; & en a voulu faire un crime à notre ami: mais la gde. Ville a pris fait & cause pour notre ami, qui y est allé en poste, & revenu avec une Déclaration, de n'avoir rien fait que par ordre de sa régence.[4] La ville demande en même temps que les Etats d'Hollde. approuvent par une résolution ce qu'elle a fait, sinon, qu'elle fera imprimer & publier elle-même sa Déclaration. Il s'agit du projet d'un Traité de Commerce, à conclure entre les deux rep., *quand l'Angleterre auroit reconnu l'Indépendance Américaine*, & de la Déclaration y jointe de notre amy, donnée en ce temps à Mr. De Neufv., qui la remit à Mr. Wm. Lee, que celui-ci vous montra, dont vous ne futes pas content, & qui effectivement n'exprimoit que la bonne

---

2. Apparently BF kept his promise to forward them (in his Oct. 31 response, below), as we have no other record of them.

3. In the postscript to his letter of Oct. 23, above.

4. On Oct. 25 the burgomasters and town councillors of Amsterdam replied officially to the demands of the States of the Province of Holland for an explanation. They argued that the Neufville-Lee treaty was obsolete and without effect and discussed its genesis. Their report was forwarded to the States General: Schulte Nordholt, *Dutch Republic*, p. 150; Edler, *Dutch Republic*, pp. 154–5.

volonté, ou le bon appétit de la Ville, d'avoir part au Commerce d'Amérique, quand l'Angleterre aura *reconnu* &c. C'est la peur d'être exclus dans la future pacification, qui les avoit engagés à cette démarche: & je leur avois inspiré & augmenté cette peur. Mr. Wm. Lee qui savoit toutes mes opérations antérieures, parce qu'il avoit eu communication, par son frere,[5] de toute ma correspondance avec la Commission Plénipe. d'alors à Paris, en a agi peu honnêtement, en manigançant cela à mon insu avec Mr. De Neufv., qui dans ce temps n'étoit point lié avec moi, & qui me voyoit lié avec une autre maison sa rivale.—[6] Je saurai aujourd'hui, ou demain, ce que les Et. d'hollde. auront résolu là-dessus; & vous aurez la déclaration d'Amsterdam, dès qu'elle m'aura été communiquée.

Les Lettres de Mr. Stockton, qui ont tant offensé le gd. Personnage (&, il faut l'avouer, avec raison) sont écrites *à Mr. Whitestone,*[7] que je ne connois pas. Il y dit entre autres, que ce gd. personnage veut faire ici, comme le R— son Cousin en Angle, savoir se rendre le maître &c. Du reste ces Lettres, qui ont été remises aux Etats avec le Traité, ne peuvent avoir d'autres suites, que d'aigrir ce gd. Personnage contre les Amns. en général, ce qui ne laisse pas d'être facheux pour nos opérations ici, qui en seront plus traversées; & de lui faire regarder Mr. Stokton de mauvais oeil toute sa vie, comme un ennemi personnel; ce qui est facheux pour Mr. Stokton, qui ne pourroit pas paroître ici,[8] sans s'exposer à quelque affront parce que son nom est signé tout du long dans ces Lettres.

J'écris *raptim* mais avec tout le respect qu'à pour vous Monsieur, Votre très-humble & tres obéissant serviteur   D

Passy à Son Exc. M. B. Franklin

Addressed: à Son Excellence / Monsieur B. Franklin / Mine. Plenipe. des Et. unis, / &c. / Passy ./.

---

5. William Lee's brother Arthur was one of the three commissioners to the French court (with BF and JA) when the treaty was drafted in September, 1778.

6. Perhaps de la Lande and Fynje; see XXVIII, 426–7.

7. Probably Stockton's friend Dr. John Witherspoon: XXIX, 391.

8. Stockton returned to America in 1779 and did not go back to Europe: XXIX, 696n.

From John Fothergill
ALS: American Philosophical Society

London 25 X [October] 1780

When I received, My honoured Friends obliging letter by Dr. Waterhouse,[9] little did I exspect, it would not be in my power to return a more speedy Answer. But I will not take up any more of my time in making apologys, as I mean this to be a long letter but to proceed to the business—after entreating my Friend to allow me to forget that I am writing to a Minister to one of the first courts of Europe from a State the most promising of any that ever inherited any part of this Globe.

My disorder was not the Strangury, but the Gout,[1] it fell upon the neck of the Bladder swelled the passage, prevented entirely the discharge of any urine, which was drawn off twice a day for a fortnight—or I had perished. The Operation was exquisitely painfull—as passing the instrument thro very tender parts occupied by a gouty swelling.— At length it gently touched my ancle left the passage free, and so it has remaind ever since.—

The Strangury is a different disease—it is properly such a kind of heat as attends blisters—creating an ineffectual nisus to discharge more, with a sense of great heat.— A solution of G. [gum] Arabick in water, used freely that is, an ounc dissolvd in Quarter of a pint of water, and a Spoonfull or two of this solution Strained & taken in evry liquor that is used—or in a little milk and water, often alleviates this disorder and gives ease by blunting the Acrimony of Urine. Should a tendency to any difficulty of this kind recur(?) pray describe the Sensation & Symp-

---

9. The letter is BF's of June 19: XXXII, 555–6. Dr. Benjamin Waterhouse (1754–1846) was born in Newport, R.I. He went to Europe in 1775 to complete his medical training and studied at London and Edinburgh. In the fall of 1778, at the suggestion of Fothergill (his mother's first cousin), he enrolled at Leyden. There he became a close friend of JA, whose acquaintance, according to Waterhouse's later recollection, he had first made at BF's. After returning to the U.S. in 1782, Waterhouse had a varied and controversial career as a physician, professor at Harvard College, and promoter of vaccination against smallpox: *Adams Correspondence,* IV, 32–4n, and *passim; DAB.*

1. Fothergill apparently was mistaken in diagnosing his own disease as gout: Betsy C. Corner and Christopher C. Booth, eds., *Chain of Friendship: Selected Letters of Dr. John Fothergill of London, 1735–1780* (Cambridge, Mass., 1971), p. 500.

toms pretty fully and in return I will say all that occurs to me worth saying on the subject.— I rejoice thankfully that I am free from this complaint and yet able in some degree to discharge the dutyes of a laborous station.

Lady H.[2] is much obliged to my Friend for his kind intelligence and will act conformably.

Much horrible mischief would indeed have been prevented had our Superiors thought fit to pay any regard to our humble endeavours. But their ears were shut, their hearts hardend, Kings became delerious, and the poor Greeks sufferd for it.[3]

Still we are all hope, all serenity—nay triumphant—Determined to prosecute the same plan. Pride and vengeance are very fallible counsellors— I think I see all Europe slowly leaguing against us, and for two of the strongest reasons in the world— and which cannot but pursue, unless for their sins, they become besotted—To retrench our power, and to increase their own by an open commerce with America.

In the warmth of my affection for mankind, I could wish to see engrafted into this league, a resolution to preclude the necessity of general wars—the great object of universal civilization. The institution of a college of Justice—where the claims of Sovereigns Should be weighed—an award given—and war only made on him who refused submission.— No one man in the world has it so much in his power as my honourd Friend to infuse this thought into the breasts of Princes, or those who rule them and their affairs.

Let me touch on a lesser point, in which I also wish to engage a moment of my Friends attention. The most entensive capacity—the greatest human mind may possibly overlook some humble, yet proper objects such perhaps is that which I am going to mention. Establish thro' all the united states as speedily as possible one general standard of weights and measures, and let this standard be directed, if I may use the expression by squares— The weights which the Apothecarys use is first a grain—20 make a Scruple—3 scruples a dram. It is impossible

---

2. The Countess of Huntington: XXXII, 555n.
3. "Quidquid delirant reges, plectuntur Achiui." For whatever folly kings commit, it is the Greek people who suffer: Horace *Epistolae*, I, ii, 14.

to reduce any of these weights to an unite without a fraction—
No more can the foot or the yard nor measures of capacity—Let
the Scruple consist of 16 grains. 4 Scruples to make one dram—
8 drams the ounce. 16 the pound—and pounds to be reckoned
by decimals if thought more convenient. I rather describe these
circumstances to explain my measures than as the identical rules
that ought to take place. Why not institute an American Standard, and at this moment, when your trade is less than it ever will
be hereafter, while you exist? The diversity and confusion in this
Island, not to say in Europe is a sufficient proof of the need there
is of such a reformation—no time more proper for it than the
present—no one more more capable of forming the basis of
such a regulation than my Friend—and if proper, I know it will
be encouraged.

I sent a long paper on *oaths*, by a Gentleman of my acquaintance from Maryland— Pray keep this subject in sight.— The
Massachusets Goverment has adopted such a plan in part—they
have allowed those who conscientiously refuse an Oath, to qualify themselves for offices, by an affirmation—[4] this is liberal—
and the more to be regarded, as I dare say it Sprung from the
breasts of those who had the modification of this goverment
committed to them and not from any solicitation of ours, or others who had similar Scruples.

It is a singular event in the history of the human mind, that a
state heretofore considered as one of the most intolerant—
should have framed one of the most liberal plans of Government
ever framed in the world.

My worthy Frd. D. Barclay and myself, not being able to influence our superiors, have become superiors ourselves.— We
have engaged the society we belong to, to purchase Ackworth
schoolhouse in Yorkshire, built as an appendix to the foundling
hospital— It is converted into a school for a plain English education for the children of such amongst us who are not in affluent
circumstances. We have got together near 300 children boys and

4. The Massachusetts Constitution of 1780 referred in several places to
oaths or affirmations, and Quakers were specifically allowed to affirm rather
than swear; see *Adams Papers*, VIII, 233–4, 251, 267.

Girls in less than a year— We have got people to superintend it diligently— We were there together this autumn and had the satisfaction to see a numerous and orderly family—[5]

I dare not touch upon our situation—but it is tending to the point, Slowly yet certainly, which may probably may prove extremely advantageous to us—poverty and distress—seldom enemys to virtue. Whilst a single man or a single guinea can be raised—peace is hardly to be hoped for—and while comissarys and a tribe of devourers are employed, they will always find means to urge a mind not disposed to relent in your favour—to proceed with vehemence however ineffectual— I think your business is, to risque nothing— You lose in Action for the most part, the advantages you reap from patienc— The late affair in Carolina is a manifest proof of it—and I fear if you prompt your general to do more than he ought you may still be sufferers— But I am not a judge of these matters— Accept my very cordial thanks, for thy great kindness to Dr. Waterhouse—a little Friend and relation of mine, who I hope will do his country no discredit. After he has had a little experience in the practice of Physick I think, should the States of Massachusets ever establish a school of medicine—and such there should be, that if he lives and has his health, he would fill a chair in it very properly. At present he is too young—too inexperienced but he has collected good materials, tho' I am confident without any such intention—for such a purpose.—

With cordial regard—and undiminished esteem I am thy affectionate Frd   J FOTHERGILL

Notation: Fothergill 25 Xbre. 1780

5. In late 1777 Fothergill learned that a large building suitable for a school was for sale at Ackworth, Yorkshire. He, David Barclay, and some other well-to-do Quaker friends arranged to place an option on the property, and the following year their proposal was accepted by the London Quaker Yearly Meeting. The school opened on Oct. 18, 1779: Corner and Booth, eds., *Chain of Friendship*, pp. 31–2, 490–1, 494, 495; R. Hingston Fox, *Dr. John Fothergill and His Friends: Chapters in Eighteenth Century Life* (London, 1919), pp. 281–9.

From John Jay

Copy: Library of Congress

Dear Sir, Madrid 25. Oct. 1780.

Your very agreable and friendly Letters I have recd. and shall take an early Opportunity of answering fully.— I have no Reason as yet to think a Loan here will be practicable. Bills on me arrive daily. Be pleased to send me a Credit for Residue of our Salaries.— America rises in the general Estimation here.

Tell Mr. Deane I have recd. four of his Letters & written three to him. He may expect to hear from me again soon.[6]

Prince Massarano sets out for France early in the Morng. I had intended to devote this Afternoon & evening to writing by him but have been prevented by Company. It is now late at Night and can see little.— I am much indebted to the Politeness of this Nobleman, and except at his Table have eaten no Spanish Bread that I have not paid for since my arrival in this City.— This Circumstance will I flatter myself recommend him to your particular Attention, which I have Reason to think would be very acceptable, from the Respect & Esteem which he frequently expresses for you. The Duke of Crillon who accompanies the Prince has also been polite to us.—& I fancy they will both receive Pleasure from finding me sensible of their attentions. The Princess appears to me to have much merit— I regret her Absence, and the more so perhaps as it will not be supplied. She is a Lady of much observation & Discernment.— God bless you my Dear Sir, I am affectionately & Sincerely your Friend & Servant— (signed) JOHN JAY

His Excelly. Dr. Franklin,

From Robert Morris

ALS: American Philosophical Society

Dear Sir Philada. Octr. 25th. 1780

I take the liberty to introduce an Old acquaintance of mine to your Patronage & Protection whilst he may Stay in Paris which I apprehend will be but a Short time, it is Mr. Isaac Hazelhurst of

---

6. Jay wrote Deane the following day: *Deane Papers*, IV, 248–50.

this place who Visits Europe on Commercial Views and who I fancy will transact his business chiefly in France & Holland.[7] Your Countenance cannot fail to be usefull to a Stranger and I wou'd not ask it, but in favour of a deserving Man.

Your Enemies are busy here but I hope their operations will not be able to touch you, If I can help to bear the shield that protects Your honour & your reputation I shall deem it no small happiness for I am Dr Sir Your sincere admirer & Obedt hble servt   ROBT MORRIS

His Excy Doctr Benjn. Franklin Esqr Minister Plenipy Paris

Addressed: His Excelly / Doctr Benjn. Franklin Esqr. / Minister Plenipoy / Paris / by Mr. Isaac Hazelhurst

From Jean de Neufville & fils

ALS: American Philosophical Society

Honourd Sir!   Amsterdam 25 Oct: 1780.

With all reverence we take leave to lay again before Your Excellency; that we have not yett received the permission for the Acceptance of the last mention'd bills[8] on Mr Laurens of which the bearers apply'd again, butt were persuaded to wait untill next maill, Should we then not find our Selfs favour'd with directions from your Excellency, we shall be obliged to accept them; there hath been presented Six— New bills to the Amount of three thousand three hund Gild. [Guilders] which we offer to your Excellencys notice as the bearers consented to wait a fourthnight for our consent butt as they Suspect us Some of them to contrive

7. Isaac Hazelhurst, Sr. (1742–1834), a Philadelphia merchant who had emigrated to America from Manchester, England, and contracted with Morris to purchase goods in Europe. By the end of February, 1781, at the latest, he was in Paris. He apparently returned to America a little more than a year later. His only daughter, Mary Elizabeth, married Benjamin Henry Latrobe in 1800: *Morris Papers,* 1, 10, 12n; John C. Van Horne and Lee W. Formwalt, eds. *The Correspondence and Miscellaneous Papers of Benjamin Henry Latrobe* (3 vols., New Haven and London, 1984–88), 1, 177n; 186n; Hazelhurst to BF, March 24, 1782 (APS).

8. See the firm's Oct. 12 letter to BF.

this to gain by those means a fourtnights time, we have gallantly consented, that when Accepted, it should be from the date of their presentation.

With all Respectfull Regard we have the honour to be Honourd Sir. Your Excellencys most devoted And most Obedt. hum Servt.   JOHN DE NEUFVILLE & SON.

William Temple Franklin to Jonathan Williams, Jr.

Copy: Library of Congress

Dear Jonathan,   Pasy 25. Oct. 1780.

My Grandfather is laid up with the Gout & cannot write. He directs me to acknowledge the Receipt of your letter of the 17th. Inst.— He is entirely unacquainted what the Freight you propose is worth, but in order to assist the Ship Mars in returning to Boston, he is willing to advance twelve thousand Livres, provided she will take a hundred Tons of the Military Stores now in the arsenal at Nantes. If Mr. Austin thinks fit he may take more. The 12,000 livs. is intended to be on Acct. of said Freight, The remainder to be paid by Congress when they shall have settled with State of Massachusetts, what they are to pay pr. Ton.

This is all my Grandfather can do: & he desires me to add that he hopes you will not by any Fresh Propositions endeavour to get more Money from him.

We have not as yet an Ans. from the Farmers General relative to the Order desired of *them* for the transport of the Saltpetre.

Your communicating this Letter to M. Austin, will render my writing to him unnecessary. Please to make him my Complts.

Inclosed you have the order you desired for Mr. Schweighauser.[9]

I am ever, my dear Friend.   (signed) W.T FRANKLIN

---

9. Of this same date, above. jw forwarded it to Schweighauser on Oct. 28 with a letter of instructions. The *Mars* will take on stores up to 100 tons; she is now ready for loading. Schweighauser should have the heavy articles weighed, and the "light bulky ones" measured; the latter will be taken at 42 cubic feet per ton. Yale University Library.

P.S. M. Chaumont who is present desires me to make you his Complts.

M. Williams.

To Jean de Neufville & fils

Copy: Library of Congress

Gentlemen, Passy 26. Oct. 1780.

I received duly your Favour of the 12th. Inst. & should have answer'd it sooner had not a very severe Access of the Gout obliged me to keep my Bed, & rendered me incapable of doing any Business.

I consent to your accepting the seven Bills you mention drawn on M. Lawrens, amounting in all to three thousand eight hundred and fifty Guilders; and to enable you to pay them, you may draw on me for the Amount, making your Drafts payable about the time sd. Bills become due.

Having lately recd. Advice from America of fresh and unexpected Bills on me to a very considerable amount,[1] which I am ill provided to answer I cannot for the future pay any more of those drawn on M. Lawrens: & if any more of them should appear you will present them to Mr. Adams, who replaces Mr. Laurens, & who I make no doubt will contrive means to honour them if possible.

With great Regard I have the honour to be Gentlemen, &c. &c.

Mess. Jean de Neufville & Sons

From John Bradford

ALS: American Philosophical Society

Sir, Boston 27th. Octobr 1780

I Beg Leave to Approach your Excellency with every sentiment of Esteem and Respect, and to Acquaint You with a very

---

1. Probably Lovell's Aug. 15 letter, above, although BF did not respond to it until Dec. 2 (Wharton, *Diplomatic Correspondence*, IV, 178).

extraordinary event having taken place, vizt. the Mail from Philaa, due last evening, was Seized in the dead of night at Stratford, by the Enemy And was Carried over to Long Island, they obliged the post rider to Accompany them to their Boat, and then discharg'd him. I have good reason to believe the Bills mention'd in the inclos'd Resolve,[2] were in that mail, I think it fortunate that this early Conveyance offers to Advise Your Excellency of this Circumstance, lest the Bills might reach You in an undue manner, the Youth, my Son, who paid his duty to Your excellency the last Year,[3] is Again on his travels in Europe, if he shou'd visit Paris a renewal of the civilities he before recieved, will meet with the most grateful acknowledgement.

I am happy in Assuring Your Excellency, that the demand on my Son from France, for which a power was sent here to receive it, under Your attestation, Was honorably acquitted; before the power Appear'd here, the Bills were in Holland. Lodg'd with Messrs. Denevill & Compy.[4] I am so well convinced of my Son's inflexible integrity, that I become his Sponsor for Any engagements he may enter into.

I am Sorry to Acquaint You Sir, that we have this hour receiv'd certain intelligence, of Mr. Lawrence being a prisoner at Newfound Land, taken in the Mercury packet bound to Europe.

I have the honor to be with the greatest veneration and Attachment Your Excellencys Most Obedient and Most Obliged humble. servt. J: BRADFORD

His Excellency Benj. Franklin Esqr.

Notation: Bradford Boston 27. Oct. 1780.

2. Quite likely a congressional resolution of Sept. 22 directing the sale of £4,000 worth of bills of exchange drawn on BF: *JCC,* XVIII, 848–9.

3. For Samuel Bradford's trip to France see XXVIII, 278, 304, 338, 355; XXIX, 206, 354, 358.

4. Undoubtedly Neufville & fils.

From Thomas Digges

ALS: Historical Society of Pennsylvania; copy: Public Record Office, London[5]

Dr. Sir   [on or before October 27, 1780]

I wrote you lately[6] that Jones was not to be found here consequently the Bill irrecoverable from Him. He is at Am——m. playing his tricks so I understand. The person who accepted the Bill & acknowleges the acceptance, may be obligd by Law to pay what has been advancd on it.

I hear our sick frd is better— His disorder being contageous I am afraid to visit him— He is getting better & I hear from Him & he from me now & then. There are many people here hurt & as much astonishd as you can be at Mr. L——s treatment, which still continues rigorous to an extreem— This, with Lord Cornwallis's military Executions & cool butcheries of defenceless People in So Carolina, irrevocably seals the perpetual disunion between Gt. Britain & America. Tis however to be lamented that Peace is so far-distant as appearances indicate, and come when it will, we may safely pronounce it will be accompanyd with anguish and humiliation to the Savage heart, that seems insatiable of human gore. No news but what the papers will inform you. The annexd note will explain itself.[7] Mr. W. S. C can do the needfull.

I am with high respect Your Servant   WM. FITZPATRICK

"Tho not personally known I am well acquainted with Yr. (*Mr. W S. Cs*) Character & attatchments & with his connexions *yonder*, & had letters to Him from ——— and ———. I am happy to be informd the bills are taken up—there will no more appear—had reprobated the premature & dangerous step of draw-

---

5. Reproduced in Stevens, *Facsimiles*, X, no. 953. Notations indicate that it was intercepted on Oct. 27 and that it had been sent under cover to Ferdinand Grand. On that date Digges wrote a similar letter to JA: *Adams Papers*, X, 308–9.

6. Digges to BF, Oct. 24, above.

7. Digges told JA that he had "lately got the annexd note": *Adams Papers*, X, 308. It actually is a copy in Digges's hand of a communication from an unnamed correspondent, possibly Henry Laurens himself. "William Singleton Church" and "William Fitzpatrick" were aliases used by Digges.

ing—should be glad were it possible to see You & the person concernd in taking up the Bills (*L—— De N——le*)—[8] The present confinement is cruel, the mode & terms aggravate, but there is no abatement on this or any other consideration of Spirits— These are calm & composd—had these faild, the flesh under the late malady would have sunk totally— Continue to keep those friends F and A——[9] informd, & communicate intelligence from them as soon as possible— Should not friends interpose for obtaining some Enlargement on parole, by bail or Exchange?—have no hint to communicate at the moment except that those papers said to be taken, which were intended to be sunk, are of no importance— A million of thanks to W S.C— but a snatchd moment to write all this."

Addressed: Dr. Franklin

Notation: sup Oct. 31.

From Pothonnier & Cie.   ALS: American Philosophical Society

Monsieur   Paris Le 27e 8bre 1780

Nous avons receu hyer l'honneur de votre Lettre, qui nous laisse dans l'Incertitude Si les lettres de Change en acquit de Compte du Vau. [Vaisseau] Lariel Seront acceptés,[1] nous avons

8. Leendert de Neufville.
9. Franklin and Adams.
1. BF's letter is missing. By "accepting" their bills of exchange, BF would be promising to pay them when due; when actually paying the sums (through his banker), he would be "acquitting" them. This is the distinction that Pothonnier & Cie. will draw about their own remittances, later in the present letter.
   Pothonnier & Cie. had presented one bill of exchange on July 19, two on July 21, and one on Oct. 4: WTF's list of bills drawn on BF by Gourlade & Moylan (APS). The first three are listed as having been accepted on July 29, and the fourth was accepted on Oct. 10. According to a letter from Ferdinand Grand to BF (undated, but after Nov. 16), the first three fell due on Oct. 27, but as of the time of his writing, had not been submitted for payment. APS.
   An undated note from BF to WTF may date from this period, when BF was still indisposed: "The enclosed Bills are Booked and only wait your Signiture to be sent to the Owner. They are those that came last Evening from M.

eu celuy de vous prevenir que cet [c'est] notre Maison qui à acquittée toute la dépense de ce Vaisseau, par les Traites que Mrs. Gourlade et Moylan ont fournies Sur nous dont la majeure partie Sont acquittés, et le restant acceptées, nous esperons que vous aurés Egard, a la bonne Volonté que nous avons apportée à ce qui vous Seroit agreable.

Il est arrivée dernierement à Lorient, Quinze Voiture chargées de marchandises, pour votre Compte, Sans aucun avis, Les Voitures ont Coutés 2400 *l.t.* et les dittes Marchises. [Marchandises] ont été Enmagazinée pour attendre vos ordres.

Nous desirons, que votre Santé, Sera retablie, nous l'apprendrons avec un vray plaisir, Nous avons l'honneur detre avec un tres respectueux attachement, Monsieur Vos tres humbles et tres obeissants Serviteurs POTHONNIER ET COMP.

M. Benj. franklin a Passy

Notation: Pothonnier et Compe. Paris 27. 8bre. 1780.

From the Abbé Rochon   AL: American Philosophical Society

[after October 27, 1780][2]

Mr. L'Abbé Rochon est prié instament de demander à Mr. Franklin, si l'Eclipse du Soleil vue totale à Penobscot a été ob-

---

Pothonnier. I would come down but am not dressed sufficiently. Is there any one who waits for them?" WTF answered, "Nobody; but I promised to *send* them this morning, and as I am a going to send to Town would profit of the Occasion." Hist. Soc. of Pa.

2. On Oct. 9, the newly formed American Academy of Arts and Sciences, in conjunction with Harvard College, launched a scientific expedition to Penobscot Bay to view the total eclipse of the sun predicted for Oct. 27. Headed by mathematics professor Samuel Williams and sailing in a vessel provided by the Commonwealth of Massachusetts, the delegation set up an observation station on Long-Island in Penobscot Bay, working under the constraints imposed by the occupying British troops. The weather being fair on Oct. 27, Williams succeeded in gathering detailed data. His observations were eventually published in the *Memoirs of the American Academy of Arts and Sciences*, 1 (Boston, 1785), pp. 86–102; the Academy most likely sent a version of this paper to the Académie des sciences shortly after it was written. For Williams see *Sibley's Harvard Graduates*, xv, 134–46.

servée à New-York ou à New-Cambrige, dont nous ignorons icy les observations à la Reserve de celle de Penobscot qui seule â été envoyée à l'Academie. On a besoin de celles de New Cambrige ou de New-York.[3]

To Jonathan Williams, Jr.

AL (draft): American Philosophical Society; copy: Library of Congress

Dear Jonathan,   Passy Oct. 28: 1780

I last night received together yours of the 21st & 24th.—I had before recd yours of the 19th.

I am glad you have sent me so exact an Acct of the Bills you have drawn on M. de Chaumont, and that you have concluded to draw no more on him, but on me directly. I never understood the Reason of his Proposing that circuitous Operation, & therefore never approv'd of it. Be assured that I have regularly furnish'd him with Funds for the Payment, amounting in the whole to 750,000 *l.t.* The last 250,000 *l.t.* was given him about a Month ago.[4] It seems to me that instead of obtaining a Credit by this Measure, I have, in a great Degree paid Ready Money. I think him as you do a very honest and good Man, and tho' I hear some few Bills on him met with a little Demur, yet I understand they were afterwards paid, & that his Payments go on. I suppose the Government owes him Money, & thence the Propriety of its supporting him. I have no question that his Circumstances are good at Bottom, even that he is rich; but he entreprises too much. As long as his Payments continue regular, I think the Measure you propose to be taken at the Caisse d'Escompte is unnecessary, and may even be hurtful. Mr Grand is of the same Opinion. You know that for our parts we have Sufficient in our hands, to reimburse us if he should fail, the Clothing you bought of him being

---

3. The American Academy's first volume of *Memoirs* also contained several other reports of the eclipse. One was indeed from Cambridge, but the southern-most set of observations came from Providence. We have no evidence that BF ever received any of these while he was in France.

4. BF authorized Grand to give Chaumont 250,000 *l.t.* on March 19, July 27, and Sept. 20: Accounts XIX and XXVI (XXVIII, 3; XXXII, 3).

estimated at 400,000 *l.t.* and then there is the Freight of the Ms. de la Fayette: If she is ever in a Capacity to receive it. By your State of the Bills, there cannot be near that Sum yet unpaid. You may however be assured of my taking Care of your Credit. I continue laid up with the Gout; & have had no Answer from M. Lavoisier. I am, your affectionate Uncle.

P.S. You forgot to send me the Invoice of the Goods which you promised.

Notation by Franklin: BF to Mr Williams Oct. 28. 1780 Glad of the Acct of Bills drawn on M. de Chaumont and that he has re-solv'd to draw no more. Never understood nor approv'd of that circuitous Operation. Ready money, as previous Funds were furnish'd.

From James Lovell

ALS: American Philosophical Society; copies: American Philosophical Society, National Archives; transcript: National Archives

Honble. Sir   Octr. 28th. 1780

A Committee was appointed in Congress on the 6th. to draught a "Letter to our Ministers at the Courts of Versailles & Madrid to enforce the Instructions given by Congress to Mr. Jay by their Resolutions of the 4th. Instant and to explain the Reasons & principles on which the same are founded, that they may respectively be enabled to satisfy those Courts of the Justice and Equity of the Intentions of Congress."[5]

That Comtee. reported a Draught of a Letter to Mr Jay "and that a Copy of it be communicated to Doctor Franklin together with the Resolution directing the Draught."[6]

There is no member of the Comtee. of forgn. Affairs attend-

5. *JCC*, XVIII, 908. The Oct. 4 instructions to Jay (*ibid.*, pp. 900–2) directed him not to relinquish the rights of the United States to free navigation of the Mississippi.

6. *JCC*, XVIII, 935n. On Oct. 17 Congress accepted the draft of a letter to Jay explaining the instructions (*ibid.*, pp. 935–47). Copies of the Oct. 4 and 17 documents are with BF's papers at the APS.

ing Congress but myself,[7] nor have the Comtee. had a Secretary or Clerk since T Payne's Resignation.[8] I must entreat you therefore Sir to excuse the Œconomy of my Request that you would transmit to Mr. Jay all of the Papers which happen to reach you directed for him taking Copies of such as are left open for your Information. I persuade myself that you will readily communicate to Mr Adams what appears so much connected with his Commission, though it has not been specially ordered by the Report of the Comtee. upon the Draught.

I am Sir your most humble Servant   JAMES LOVELL

Honble Doctor Franklin

copy

Addressed: Honble. / Doctor Franklin / France

From Desegray, Beaugeard fils & Cie.

LS: American Philosophical Society

Monsieur   St. Malo ce 29. 8bre. 1780.

Etant privés de reponse a la lettre que nous avons eu l'honneur de vous ecrire le 14 de ce mois,[9] la presente est pour vous annoncer que Monsieur Williams nous ayant mandé de nouveau que l'Envoy des salpêtres en question etait trés instant pour profiter d'un Vaisseau qui est en charge a Lorient pour les États unis de l'Amerique, nous venons de nous determiner a envoyer ces salpêtres par terre sous acquit a caution avec des Plombs &ca. et nous avons commencé a en charger 263 sacs par 7 Rouliers a la'dresse de Mrs. Gourlade et Moylan a Lorient a 6 *l.t.* 10 *s.* du Cent. Nous allons continuer, Monsieur, a mesure qu'il se presentera d'autres Rouliers, a moins que vous ne puissiez nous faire passer incessamment un ordre de Messrs. les fermiers Generaux pour la libre exportation de ce qui pourra nous rester

7. Lovell's colleague William Churchill Houston had signed with him the committee's letters of July 11 printed above. Three weeks after the present letter was written Houston was in Philadelphia: Smith, *Letters*, XVI, 351.

8. In January, 1779: XXIX, 47.

9. The firm sent the same letter to JW; see JW to BF, Oct. 19.

des 1520 sacs de salpêtre ce qui Eviterait beaucoup de fraix et d'Embarras. Nous desirons beaucoup que notre Conduite merite votre approbation, et nous serons toujours flattés de pouvoir vous temoigner le parfait devouement et le respect infini avec lequel nous avons l'honneur d'être Monsieur Vos très humbles et très Obeissants Serviteurs DeSegray & Cie.

Le Passeport de Mrs. Les Regisseurs des Poudres et Salpetres ne nous sert absolument en rien.

Son Exc. Monsieur Franklin a Passy.

Addressed: A Son Excellence / Monsieur Franklin, / Ministre des Etats unis de / L'amerique, / à Passy, / Près Paris.

Notation: Desegray &c Sept. 29. 1780

To Castries
Copy: Library of Congress

Sir, Passy 30. Oct. 1780.
Tho' late, it is with great Pleasure that I congratulate your Excellency, on the high and most important Office in which the discerning Eye of your souveireign has lately thought fit to place you.[1]

A severe Access of the Gout which has kept me for a fortnight past in continual Pain & Fever, prevented my sooner waiting on you with my Respects. They are however not the less sincere, and I beg you will accept them with my Best Wishes for your Success, Honour & Happiness— I am Sir, Your Excellency's &c.

His Excellency the Marquis de Castres.

From Richard Bache
ALS: American Philosophical Society

Dear & Hond. Sir Philadelphia Octr. 30th. 1780.
I still remain without any Letters from you; Our Kinsman Mr. Williams wrote me some time ago, that your Letters were put on

---

1. Castries had been naval minister since Oct. 14.

board the Kensington Capt. Smith, who sailed with the Alliance, but having sprung her Masts, was obliged to put back— She is not yet arrived—[2] I have a few Lines from Temple dated in March, desiring me to send you some Nuts & Apples.[3] I could not procure them in time for this Vessel, shall have a fine opportunity in a Week or two by a new twenty Gun Ship, called the Shelela—[4] Inclosd you have 1st. Bills for the Amount of Interest of your Money in the Loan Office to the 10th Sepr. 1780. I have never heard yet whether the Bills, for the last years Interest, got safe to hand, but suppose they did, as some of the set went with Mr. Gerard—[5] Besides the other weekly papers, you will receive herewith, the Dutch papers printed by Styner & Cist, formerly Apprentices with Mr. Miller, the old Gentleman has not done any Business for some time past; I saw him the other day, when he desired to be remembered to you.—[6]

Mr. Lee is at last arrived here, he & his friend are endeavoring to kick up a dust; on Thursday last notice was given by a Member in Congress; (one Mr. Mathews of South Carolina) that he should [of] this day move for your recall;[7] what the event will be I know not, but it is generally conjectured out of doors, that it will be a vain attempt.—

I have no news that the papers don't furnish, the Family is

2. JW's letter to RB is missing, but on May 3 he wrote SB from Nantes that the *Kensington* (XXXI, 461n) was proceeding downriver that day. Yale University Library.

3. Not found.

4. The *Shelala* (or *Sellelagh* or *Shellelagh*) carried a crew of 120: Charles H. Lincoln, comp., *Naval Records of the American Revolution 1775–1788* (Washington, D.C., 1906), p. 458.

5. RB regularly forwarded bills of exchange for the interest accrued on BF's loan office certificates (including those sent with former French Minister Conrad-Alexandre Gérard): XXIII, 280–1n; XXVII, 601; XXIX, 273–4; XXXI, 19; XXXII, 175–6.

6. The paper was the *Philadelphisches Staatsregister* and Mr. Miller was John Henry Miller, one of BF's former apprentices: XXXII, 609n.

7. John Mathews (1744–1802) was a congressional delegate from South Carolina: *DAB*. Congress did not take up the question of the French mission during the period covered by this volume. Mathews, Lee, and Izard were leaders in a successful attempt to weaken BF's authority, which will be discussed in vol. 34.

well, and join me in love & Duty to yourself & Temple. I remain
Dr. Sir Your ever affectionate son   RICH. BACHE

We long to hear from Ben, give our love to him.

Dr. Franklin

Addressed: Dr. Franklin

From Harmon Courter   ALS: American Philosophical Society

Sir   L'Orient 30th October 1780
    I wrote you the 2d Inst. again troubled you with a few lines.
I acquaint you that I have been unfortunate enough to loose
my Ship in this Harbour, by receiving much damage in a Gale of
Wind On the 10th. Inst.[8] In consequence of which thought well
to Overhall her, and found her unfit for Sea: As you are at the
helm Of affairs, and I entertaining the highest Oppinion of your
friendshipe for me; from a former Circemstance, thout it did
Not suceed requests your Interest in point of procuring me
A Ship, The Tarepscord[9] is now in this Harbour; and I undre-
stand no one as yet appointed to her Command; I am here with
100 Officers and men reaedy to Step on board Of a Ship; If you
think well should be happy to except Of her, or any other Ship
of Ware, upon due encouragement I can raise any number of
men here, that may be Necessary to compleat a Crew.[1]
    My Command that you'l be pleas'd to appoint Me too, will be
manfully and faithfully discharged by Honoured Sir your most
Obdt Humble Sarvt   HARMON COURTER

    8. The same storm which struck the *Ariel, Duke of Leinster,* and *Luke.*
    9. The *Terpsichore:* XXXII, 581n.
    1. On Nov. 5 WTF responds on behalf of his grandfather, who was inca-
pacitated by gout: "he cannot possibly undertake to sollicit this Government
to give you the Command of the Terpsicore or any other Vessel whatever.—
He has already been brought into so many Difficulties by making such Requests, that he has resolved never more to have anything to do with such
Business: In which he is totally ignorant." He has, however, desired a friend
to write to Dunkerque to ask whether there is any *armateur* there who is in
need of officers and men to equip her. As soon as he receives an answer he
will inform Courter. Library of Congress.

475

P.S. Sir I request you answer by the returne of the Post

The Honble: Benj Franklin

Addressed: The Honble: Benj Franklin Esqr. / pasay / Parris / per Post

Notations in different hands:[2] Hamon Couter. L'Orient. 30 Oct 1780. / Ansd 5 Nov 80 by W.T.F.

From Marie-Elisabeth Fournier[3]

ALS: American Philosophical Society

Monsieur   de paris ce 30 8bre 1780

Connoissant votre bon Coeur toujours disposé à obligér et mon mari et moy nous trouvans forcés de Chercher à nous procurer quelque dedomagement des pertes que nous avons essuyes par des Banqueroute et en manquant douvrage de notre État pour La fonderie. Permetez moy de madressér à vous pour vous prier trés instenment Monsieur de vouloir bien nous procurer quelque personnes de votre Connessance qui desireroient se mettre en pensions dans un Cartier en bon aier et prés du Jardin du Roy et prés des boulevars nous sommes actuellement Loges rûe Copeau au Coin de La rûe neuve st. Etienne La porte Cocher en face du sabot d'or. Notre appartement et au premier il à même remise et écurie dans La maison nous pouvont prendre Jusqu'a trois ou quatre pensionaires. Je vous seray obligé de vouloir bien penser à nous. Vous étez aporté de nous rendre ce service important par La quantité d'ameriquains qui vienne demeuré a paris et qui on L'honneur de vous voir. Daignez ne pas nous La refuser cette grace de vos bontes. Mon mari à L'honneur de vous presen-

2. The second of these is in WTF's hand.

3. Wife of typefounder Jean-François Fournier, a cousin of the more successful Simon-Pierre Fournier le jeune. Mme Fournier had met BF in August, 1777: XXIV, 500–1. BF ordered a font of type from her husband (XXVII, 618), which seems to have been their only transaction. Marie-Elisabeth was the daughter of François Gando, another important Parisian typefounder: Marius Audin, *Les Livrets typographiques des fonderies françaises créées avant 1800* (Paris, 1933), pp. 85–6.

ter ses très humble respects et moy celuy de me dire tres parfait-
tement, Monsieur Votre très humble et très obeissante servante

GANDO FEMME FOURNIER

Addressed: A Monsieur / Monsieur Francquailee / dans La maison de Mr. Chommont / A passÿ

Notation: Fournier. Paris ce 30. 8bre. 1780.

From John Jay

ALS (draft): Columbia University Library; copy: Library of Congress

Dr Sir   madrid 30 Oct 1780

The Pleasure given me by your Letter of the 2d. Inst may
more Easily be conceived than expressed. I am greatly obliged
by your Attention to my Embarrassmts. In my last on that Subject which you recd.[4] was a Copy of my Letter to Count D Vergennes from which it appeared that the Sum I shd. have occasion
for wd. probably be considerable and far exceed 25,000 Dollars,
Bills to the amt of 100,000 Dollars have arrived. A Loan cannot
be effected here. What the Court will do is as yet uncertain &
may long continue so. I should have replied to your Letter before but as I daily expected to hear from Ct. D Vergennes I
waited with a view of mentioning the Import to you. The enclosed Copy of a Note I recd from Count Montmorin contains
all the advices I have on that Head.[5] My Situation continues unpleasant and tho my Endeavours are not wanting to better it, future Events are too uncertain to be relied upon. To be active prudent & patient is in my Power, but whether I shall reap as well as
sow & water God only knows.

I have often been told of the former Supplies and asked how
they were to be reimbursed. My answer has uniformly been that

4. Jay to BF, Sept. 22, above.
5. At the Library of Congress are copies of the enclosed extracts, which
are from an Oct. 12 Vergennes letter to Montmorin and an Oct. 16 Montmorin letter to Jay. Vergennes promised to do his best to obtain money for
Jay but he cited BF's request for 1,000,000 *l.t.* as the reason why he could not
be certain of success.

I knew neither their amount or Terms, & that I wished to be furnished with an acct of both, &c &c. As yet I have not been able to obtain it.

Some Mistake must have given occasion to any of the Bills drawn on me being returnd. without Acceptance. The Fact is that tho I often delayed (with the Consent of the Holders) yet I never refused to accept any of them.

I have written several Letters to Congress requesting them to forbear drawing further Bills till proper Funds should be established for their Payment.[6] Mere contingent assurances or flattering Inferences drawn from flattering Expressions ought never to be considered as a sufficient Foundation for such serious Measures.

Cornwallis it seems has cropt some of Gates's Laurels, and Mr Laurens is in the Tower. European Policians will I suppose, tho often deceived in the same Way again think America on her Knees in the Dust,— Had Ternay been supported the Campaign wd. have had a different Termination. Much money and Spirit has been wasted by this Disappointmt.— Of the Latter indeed we shall never be in Want, and I shd be happy if the like cd. be said of the former. The Conduct of France towards us has been friendly,[7] and tho I cannot forbear to think she has been too inattentive to this Object, my Gratitude towards her is not impaired by it. I regret it as misfortune not blame it as a designed Omission.

I wrote to you last week and now enclose a Duplicate of another Letter. You may rely on my reimbursing You the Advances on Acct of our Salaries out of the first Remittances I receive.

I have often congratulated my Country and myself on your being at present in France, I once expected to have seen you there and to have profited by the Lessons which Time & much Experience have taught you. Miracles have ceased and my Constitution does not promise Length of Days[8] or I shd. probably desire you when you ascend to drop me your Manttle. That you may long retain it is one of the Prayers of your Frd & Servt   J.J.

To Dr Franklin 30 Octr 1780

6. See Wharton, *Diplomatic Correspondence*, III, 707–34, 843–4.

7. Jay here wrote and deleted "& noble".

8. His pessimism was unjustified; although often in ill health Jay lived to the age of 83: *DAB*.

From Jean de Neufville & fils

ALS: American Philosophical Society

Honourd Sir.   Amsterdam the 30th Oct: 1780.

May we be excused to trouble Your Excellency again with An Account of Four bills Amounting to four thousand four hundred Gelders on Mr. Laurens since our last;⁹ we wish we may receive now by the first mails directions About those we acquainted your Excellency with Some time ago,¹ for Satisfaction to the enquiries of the bearers.

Our newspapers mention that the papers found with Mr. Laurens Should partly relate to the City of Amsterdam, and that they Shall be printed.

We have the honour to be with the most respectfull Regard. Honourd sir Your Excellencys most devoted and most Obedient Humble Servants.   JOHN DE NEUFVILLE & SON.

To Castries

Copy: Library of Congress

Sir,   Passy 31. Oct. 1780.

I received duly the Letter your Excellency did me the honour of writing to me on the 17th. Inst. inclosing a List of Prisoners made by American Vessels & delivered to the Capt. of the British Cartel Ship the James, on Acct. of the United States,² I am very sensible of your Excellency attention in forwarding me this list and beg you to accept my thankful acknowledgments.

I am honour'd likewise with your Excellency's favour of the 17th.³ inclosing Letters from Americans, prisoners in England to their friends in America which I shall forward by the first Opportunity.

I have likewise to acknowledge the Rect. of another Letter from your Excellency relative to Messrs. Delap's Request⁴ I

9. Of Oct. 25, above.
1. Presumably a reference to the firm's letter of Oct. 12, above; it had not yet received BF's reply of the 26th, above.
2. The letter and its enclosure are missing.
3. Probably Castries' letter of Oct. 25, above.
4. Castries to BF, Oct. 21, above.

should not have thus long delay'd acknowledging the Reception of these several Letters, had not my Illness prevented me for some time past attending to any business—

With great Respect, I have the honour to be Sir, &c.

M. Marquis de Castries.

From Thomas Digges

ALS:[5] Public Record Office; copy: Library of Congress

Dr. Sir   [October 31, 1780]

The rigorous Confinement of Mr L yet Continues. I did hope eer this there would have been some abatement in it. There is no telling upon what principle it is they confine Him a *close* Prisoner of State after so many precedents have been set. Sullivan, Sterling, Lee, Lovell,[6] & many others. But why should we expect these folks to act upon any *principle*. To treat a Citizen of a State thus compleatly in possession of Sovereignty de facto, is very extraordinary. They apparently mean to exasperate America & drive them to acts of retaliation. They seem to govern without any reason or principle, & to conduct their affairs without System, delivering themselves up intirely to the Government of their Passions & their Caprice. This treatment of Mr L, together with Lord Cornwallis's late Military Executions & cool butchery of defenceless People in So Carolina will irrevocably seal the perpetual disunion between G. Britain and America. Cornwallis's & Tarletons late Gasconade serves to diminish the esteem of mankind for the People of England, by giving fuel to their passions, & making them throw off the masque. I dont believe that His advantage is half so great or the Amerin. loss half so much as they represent. Time you know is the mother of Truth. Audi

5. Reproduced in Stevens, *Facsimiles*, x, no. 954. The date is supplied from the copy.

6. All of whom had been exchanged, the three generals after being captured in battle, Lovell after being arrested as a spy: Elias and Finch, *Letters of Digges*, pp. 315–16n.

alteram partem,[7] & wait the consequences. Fighting is the thing—fighting will do the business—defeats will pave the way to Victories. Patience! Patience! Il y en a beaucoup en Amerique. Tis however to be lamented that peace is so far distant—at least appearances speak it so— Come when it will, we may safely pronounce that it will be accompanyd with anguish & humiliation to the Savage Heart (of "White-Eyes") that seems insatiable of human gore.

I shall keep this open to give You the substance of the Speech now about dilevering in the Ho Lords. That Society of worthies will be added to by abot. a dozen new plumpers for Ministry. I dare say He will find His usual majority in the other stable,[8] for there is a motley & a curious set got into it this sessions. It is not much to us who is out;— The nation will go to the end of its tether as your *friend* Govr Bernard did,[9] let who will be in or out.— We know the worst of it—& are prepard, let it come. The weaker our Enemies before they make Peace the safer we shall be & the longer the Peace will last. As to Friendship of Great Britain towards America it is gone to all Eternity. She never can forgive us the injuries She has done us.

Not a word from the wt.ward but what you have read in the news. The *talk* now of *10,000* Men going to Ama. is reducd to *six*—most likely these are only meant for the Wt Indies with the 4. Sail of the line going soon under Adl. Hood. A Small N York fleet lately saild without any. Our Gd. fleet passd Plymo. on a Cruize this 27th. Inst. 26 Ships.[1]

This frd. whom I have lately wrote to you about,[2] *has his Com-*

---

7. "Hear the other side."

8. The impact of the recent elections to the House of Commons was as yet uncertain: Namier and Brooke, *House of Commons*, 1, 80–87. The "plumpers" swelling the government's majority in the House of Lords presumably included six new barons named on Sept. 29 and two Scots peers recently elected to serve in the Lords: *The Royal Kalendar . . . for 1781* (London, 1781), pp. 14–15.

9. Sir Francis Bernard (x, 353n) who in 1769 had been removed as governor of Massachusetts.

1. Adm. Darby's fleet cruised during October in spite of bad weather: W.M. James, *The British Navy in Adversity: a Study of the War of American Independence* (London, New York, Toronto, 1926), p. 246.

2. Undoubtedly Laurens.

munications, & very lately expressd an expectation of hearing from You.

I am with the highest respect Yrs.   WM FITZPATRICK

There was no speech today—it is not to be given till tomorrow— the jet of it is said to be for a continuance of the Amn. War—that the success of Lord Cornwallis justifys the continuance of the war provided it is carryd on with spirit—much praise is given to His Lordships gallantry & conduct—comps. & prayer as usual for more money—that it shall be prudently and faithfully applyd &ca. &ca &ca

Cornwall[3] was proposd as Speaker by Lord G. Germaine

he had votes 234

Sr. Fletcher Norton . . . . <u>203</u>

Cornwall carryd by a Majority 31

Addressed: Monsieur B.F

Addressed: A Monsieur / Monsieur Grand / Banquier / Paris

From [Jean-Baptiste?] Vandenyver[4]

AL: American Philosophical Society

Paris ce 31 Octobre 1780

Vandenyver a Lhonneur dassurer Monsieur franklin de Ses tres humbles Respects et de Linformer que ce Sont Mrs Hope & Comp damsterdam[5] qui ont envoÿés les Effets pour etre acceptés avec ordre de les Leur renvoÿer revetu de cette formalité ou

3. Charles Wolfran Cornwall (1735–1789) who was elected speaker of the House of Commons on Oct. 31, replacing Sir Fletcher Norton (XXXII, 252n): Cobbett, *Parliamentary History,* XXI, 793–807; Namier and Brooke, *House of Commons,* II, 255–6.

4. Or his younger brother Guillaume-François-Eugène, partners in the banking firm of Vandenyver frères & Cie: Lüthy, *Banque protestante,* II, 322. As the firm was representing the owners of the *Flora* (XXXII, 435n, 576), presumably the effects mentioned below pertain to her cargo.

5. The banking firm of Thomas and Adrien Hope, taken over in 1780 by their nephew Henry: IX, 367n.

a protest. Je serai tres reconnoissant a Monsieur franklin Sil veut avoir la bonté de me les faire parvenir pour que je puisse Satisfaire Mrs Hope par premier Courier.

Notation: Vandyniver 31. Octr. 1780.

From Jonathan Williams, Jr.

ALS: University of Pennsylvania Library; copy: Yale University Library

Dear & hond Sir.   Nantes Octor 31. 1780.

I have received your Favour from Billy of the 25 Inst. & am sorry to hear you are laid up with the Gout, but I hope it will not last you long. The French say the Gout is a Brevet de Santé but it is a Commission which costs dear & I think not worth purchasing.

I have communicated to Mr Austin your Letter & he thanks you for the offer of 12000 Livres, I have given Mr Schweighauser the Order about the Arsenal and the Mars will take in as fast as he will ship: I shall be obliged to furnish what else the Ship wants, on the Credit of the State.

I hope you are not offended with me for making the Proposition about the Freight of the Mars: I have no desire to draw Money from you by my Propositions, my motive in this was only the general good; if I have erred I am sorry, and will do so no more.—

I have to day received a polite Letter from M. d'arlincourt Fermier General to whom I had written about the Salt Petre & he assures me that every difficulty shall be removed; So I suppose you have easily obtained the Pasport necessary. I impatiently wait to hear of the arrival of the Marquis de la Fayette at L'Orient, I am all ready for her & have been so some time.

I am ever Yours most dutifully & Affectionately

JONA WILLIAMS J

P.S. The prodigious length of my Accots prevents my sending them this Post. I hope to have them finished in a Day or two.—

Doctor Franklin

Notation: Jona Williams Octr 31 80

To John Paul Jones Copy: Library of Congress

Dear Sir, Passy, Nov. 1. 1780.

I received duly yours of Oct. 13 & 20th. I am extreamly sorry for your Misfortune. The Storm was a terrible one, it was well you escaped with your Lives.

Since your Departure I have received the Acct. of Messrs. Gourlade & Moylan,[6] and I am astonished to find that I am charged with so heavy a Sum as near 100,000 Livres for the Expences of the Ariel. After having twice entreated you for god Sake to consider my Circumstances,[7] the Difficultyes I had to provide for so many Expences, and not take any thing but what was absolutely necessary, which you promised me fully you would attend to, I am surprised to find a charge of near 6000 Livres for Shot, which cannot be wanted in America, where they are made in Plenty; 5566. Livres 16. s for Drugs, an enormous Quantity, and more than 20000 Livres for Slops. &c. after all the officers and Sailors had had considerable Advances made them, without consulting me. Perhaps it will be said, that the Drugs and Slops may be wanted or useful in America. But you will easily conceive on Reflection that if every Person in office in a Ship of the States takes the Liberty of judging what is wanted in America, and in what Quantities, and to order those Quantities leaving me to pay for them, I may not only be involved in unexpected Debt and Demands as at Present, but very unnecessary and unproportioned Supplies may be sent over to the Damage of the Publick.— I find myself therefore under the Necessity of putting stop to this Proceeding: And I know no other way of doing it, than by absolutely refusing Payment of such Charges, made without my Orders or Consent first obtained. Some Medecins & some Slops may be necessary, but those Quantities appear to me enormous.

I send you herewith Copies of the Oath taken by the Subjects of the United States, with Passes for such of the Gentlemen ar-

6. The account is missing.

7. Most likely in his letters of Feb. 19 (XXXI, 498–9), and Aug. 21, above. See XXXI, 524, for Jones's reply to the first admonition. During his April 17–June 2 visit to Paris, too, BF probably discussed with him the American mission's financial constraints.

rived from Maryland as chuse voluntarily to take the oath before you. to whom I hereby give all the Power that in me lies of administring those Oaths in my Stead.[8] Those who do not chuse to take the oath, can have no Claim to Passport from me; they must be considered as British Subjects, and in the Disposition of the Government. The Passes you give may be so worded, as to prevent the Gentlemen preceeding sooner than you judge proper, if you have any Suspicion that dangerous Information may be obtained from them. I have had a most severe Attack of the Gout which Still harasses me, and I write in great Pain. I am, with much Esteem, dear Sir. &c. &c.

Comme. Jones.

[*In the margin:*] Sent a Duplicate of this Letter on the 18 Nov. 80 the Original having miscarried—

To Jonathan Nesbitt
Copy: Library of Congress

Sir,   Passy, Nov. 1. 1780.

I duly received the Letter you did me the honour of writing to me the 20th. past. But have been too ill to answer sooner. I am sorry that anything happened in the Disention of your Friend, that is disagreable to you or to him. I send down by this Post Directions to Commodore Jones to receive his Oath to the States & deliver him a Passport. But as there are other Persons in Company, & I find there are Apprehensions that Intelligence early given in England either thro' Inadvertence or otherwise, may be prejudicial to the Interests of Persons concerned in the Ships going to America, and to the Publick I have left a little in M. Jones's Discretion as to the time of the Passports, commencing, which I hope will not be very Inconvenient to M. Cheston. I wish to know, if he is any Relation of a M. Daniel Cheston whom I knew about 40. Years ago, & who then lived I think on Chester River.[9]

8. The two gentlemen from Maryland subsequently took oaths of allegiance before BF himself; see our annotation of Jones to BF, Oct. 20.

9. This merchant, shipowner, and sheriff had written to BF from Chester in 1747: III, 166–7.

Please to present my Compliments, & excuse my not writing to him, as I am in continual Pain. I have the Honour to be, Sir, &c.

M. Nesbit.

To Samuel Wharton Copy: Library of Congress

Dear Sir, Passy, Nov. 1. 1780.
I received your Favours of the 14th. & 20th. past, But have been so continually harass'd by the Gout, as to be unable to write or think. I congratulate you on your mirculous Escape. But am extreamly concerned at the various Accidents that have so long delay'd & prevented your happy Return to your family, Friends & Country.— I thank you for the Information relating to the Passengers arrived from Maryland. I have impower'd Comme. Jones to receive their oaths to the State, & then to give them Passports, under such Restrictions as to the time of their Departure as he may think the public Good Shall require. I write in much Pain, & can only add that I am, Dear Sir, Your m. o. & m. h. S.

Samuel Wharton Esqr.

To Jonathan Williams, Jr. Copy: Library of Congress

Dear Jonathan, Passy, Nov. 1. 80.
Enclosed is a Letter from M. Lavosier, one of the Fermers General, by which you will see that the necessary papers for the Saltpetre are dispatched.[1]

I want much the Invoice you promised me of the Cloths bought of M. De Chaumont, and to know precisely the Terms of that Purchase & the Amount.

M. Austin tells me he will leave some Money in your Hands

---

1. JW forwarded Lavoisier's now-missing letter to Desegray, Beaugeard fils & Cie. on Nov. 5, adding that he hoped nothing further would impede the transportation of the saltpetre. Yale University Library.

for me, in 270 Livres;[2] Please to receive them and give me Credit.— Excuse to him my not writing at present.

M. De Ch. goes on paying, and I fancy the Difficulty is over for the present. But it is well for you to be cautious: for some times People drag down with them their best Friends. And I cannot answer paying for you any Bills you may have aided him with, as they are not a Publick Concern. I hope however that this Caution is unnecessary.

M. Johnson wrote me that he had lodg'd with you scealed up some Papers I had put into his Hands.[3] You may open and read them; & send them to me when you have a good Opportunity, with your Sentiments. I have Such another Dispute about accounts with M. Moylan.[4] He charges me among other unnecessary Articles with money paid you for Shot. Explain this to me.

I am Still ill of the Gout, and write in much Pain, But I am ever &. Your affectionate uncle.

M. Williams.

From James Woodmason   ALS: American Philosophical Society

Sir   Novemr. 1 1780

Your esteem'd favour of the 26 Sept: came duly to hand covering a Bill for 25 £. conformable to your Order I shipped 3 Copying Machines with Paper & Ink Powder. I doubt not but you will find the Machines much approved off. The Patentees have found that their Ink Powder will not entirely dissolve the best way of making Ink from it is to mix the Powder with proper quantity of Water in an open Vessel & to let it stand for 48 hours, & then pour it off. I find that the Patentees have also improved their Paper, but I have none of it yet.

I have the pleasure to acquaint you that I have receivd an Order for the finest Royal for the Large 4to: Edit of Voltaire. & I understand that they have not finally determined on what Paper

2. See Austin's letter of Oct. 19.
3. We have not located Johnson's letter, but for the papers see BF to Johnson, Sept. 18.
4. See BF to Jones of this date, above.

to have for the other 4to: Edition. I must beg you to accept of my warmest thanks for your friendly recommendation.[5] I am Sir Your most Obedt. hble Servt   JAMES WOODMASON

P.S. Freight cou'd not be paid in London, the Captain not knowing the Exchange

Bot of James Watt & Co.

3 Patent Copying Machines	@£6/6s.	£18.18.	0
3 Sett of Case's for do	6s.	18	
3 Ream's Extra la thin			
Copying Post	18s.	2.14.	0
1 dozen Copyg Ink Powder		9.	0
Packing Case to Contain the whole		15.	0
Entry Shipping Expences &c		1. 0.	0
		£24.14.	0

Address'd to Mr. Francis Bowen Mercht Ostend

Benjn. Franklin Esqr.

Addressed: Dr: Franklin / a Passey near / Paris

Notations: Woodmason. Nov. 1. 1780. / Ansd May 81

5. Woodmason had traveled to Paris with samples of fine wove paper in June, 1779, hoping to secure an order from Beaumarchais for the playwright's projected publication in Kehl of Voltaire's writings: xxx, 609–10. Over the course of the project's troubled history, Beaumarchais' plans for editions of various dimensions and quality changed several times. The prospectus of January, 1781, advertised an octavo edition and two limited quarto editions, one of which would be a deluxe publication on royal stock (presumably this paper from Woodmason). Eventually, both quarto editions were abandoned; when volumes finally began to appear nearly four years after the prospectus, they were available in either octavo or duodecimo. A portion of Woodmason's paper may have gone into the select "English paper" edition of Beaumarchais' *Mariage de Figaro,* issued from the Kehl presses during this period: Giles Barber, "The Financial History of the Kehl Voltaire," in *The Age of Enlightenment: Studies presented to Theodore Besterman,* W. H. Barber, *et al.,* eds. (Edinburgh and London, 1967), pp. 155–60, 162; see also the references cited in xxx, 609n.

From Desegray, Beaugeard fils & Cie.

ALS: American Philosophical Society

Monsieur   St. Malo 2. 9bre. 1780.

Nous avons eu l'honneur de vous ecrire le 29. 8bre, et le 31 ditto on recut icy l'ordre de Mrs Les fermiers Generaux pour la libre Exportation de vos salpêtres,[6] mais en même tems nous avons recus des avis de Lorient qui nous en ont fait suspendre l'Expedition, comme il est plus au long detaillé dans notre lettre de ce jour a Monsieur Williams, dont nous avons l'honneur de vous remettre cy joint Copie;[7] et nous attendons maintenant des ordres ulterieurs a cet egard.

---

6. Presumably the orders that Lavoisier had told BF were on their way: BF to JW, Nov. 1.

7. The firm enclosed an extract of their letter to JW:

"Le 31. 8bre. nous avions expedié a Lorient 9 Voitures de Salpêtres, pezant ensemble 41000 *l.t.* a 6 *l.t.* 10*s.* du%. Nous allions continuer et nous avions même arreté quelques autres Rouliers lorsque nous avons recu [*une*] lettre de Mrs. Gourlade et Moylan de Lorient qui nous engagent à suspendre ces Envoys. Nous n'avons pas cru devoir aller outre Jusqu'a recevoir de nouveaux avis Soit de leur part ou de Monsieur Franklin, et nous apprendrons avec plaisir que vous approuviez notre Conduite en toutes choses. Ce nouveau Contretems est d'autant plus facheux que le même Jour 31. 8bre. est parvenu icy l'ordre de Mrs. Les fermiers Generaux pour la Libre Expedition des dits Salpêtres Sans Plombs et sans être obligé de les faire voiturer icy, ce qui evitera beaucoup de fraix et d'Embarras lorsqu'on Sera determiné a faire passer le restant a Lorient, et vous pouvez compter qu'aussitôt que nous aurons recu les ordres convenables nous y donnerons tous nos soins.

Il parait, Mr, que Mrs. Les fermiers Generaux Se sont plaints de ce que nous avons porté dans notre Cte. Estimatif la Nourriture et Gratification des Employés des fermes. Quoiqu'en disent ces Mrs., il est certain qu'il est d'usage de donner une gratification aux Employés Suivant L'Embarras plus ou moins grand qu'ils peuvent avoir, et non Seulement ils ne la refusent pas, mais ils n'oublient point de la demander et Ceux des Negts. qui pourraient la refuser (puisque effectivement ce n'est pas un droit) n'en Seraient pas mieux pour leurs Operations. Il y avait 4 Employés qui etaient dernierement Employés pour les dits Salpêtres dont deux étaient Envoyés d'icy a St. Servan, et nous avons payé les Diners a l'auberge de ces 2 ders. ainsy que pour un de nos Commis, vu qu'autrement les dits Employés eussent quitté L'ouvrage a 11 heures pour venir diner a St. Malo, et ne Seraient partis d'icy qu'a 2 heures pour reprendre la Besogne et ouvrir le magazin vers les 3 heures. Il faut ensuite le fermer a 4 heures ½ pour revenir en Ville, vous pouvez juger de la Si nous avons exageré le dit appercu de Compte."

Nous sommes avec un prof[ond respect,][8] Monsieur, V[os trés humbles et] très [obéissants serviteu]rs   [DESEGRAY ET] CIE

S. Exc. Monsieur Fra[nklin]

Addressed: A Son Excellence / Monsieur Franklin / Ministre des Etats unis de / L'Amerique, / à Passy. / près Paris.

From Dumas

ALS: American Philosophical Society; AL (draft): Algemeen Rijksarchief

Monsieur,   Lahaie 2e.[–3] Nov. 1780

Le 27 du passé notre Ami me remit une Copie authentique, de l'Imprimerie des Etats, de la Résolution prise par les Etats d'Hollde. le 25. Je me mis tout de suite à en faire la traduction que voici, vous priant de vouloir bien la joindre à la premiere Dépêche que vous enverrez en Amérique.[9] Voilà Mr. V. B. le 1er. Pense. d'Amstm. hautement justifié.[1] Ceux d'Amsterdam, voyant qu'on ne laissoit pas, par des Emissaires, de représenter la chose autrement dans le public (car les Résolution, quoiqu'imprimées, ne sont point publiques) viennent de faire imprimer leur Lettre aux Etats chez l'Imprimeur de leur ville, avec les Armes de la Ville à la tête, & le nom de l'Imprimeur au bout, avec injonction d'en répandre les Exemplaires par toute la Rep. La Gazette de Rotterdam l'a exhibée ce matin toute entiere, avec ce qui la précede. Cela a furieusement piqué un grand personnage, & causé beaucoup de rumeur ici. Je vous divertirois, si je pouvois vous raconter des particularités là-dessus qu'il n'est pas bon d'écrire.

8. The bracketed passages are conjectural readings; the MS is torn.

9. Dumas enclosed his eight-page French translation of: (1) extracts from the Oct. 20 deliberations of the States of the Province of Holland forwarding to the burgomasters and regents of Amsterdam copies of Laurens' papers relative to the Neufville-Lee treaty and asking their response; (2) the Amsterdam officials' response of Oct. 25 (for which see Dumas to BF of that date).

1. For Pensionary of Amsterdam Van Berckel's role in the Lee-Neufville treaty see XXVII, 344–6; *Adams Papers,* VII, 5–6n; Samuel Flagg Bemis, *The Diplomacy of the American Revolution* (Bloomington, Ind., 1957), pp. 157–8.

Excepté la Frise & l'Overyssel, il n'y a pas d'autre Province encore qui se soit déclarée pour l'accession à la Neutralité armée. Cependant il est arrivé de nouvelles Dépêches de Petersbourg, "pour presser l'accession de la Rep., si elle ne veut pas se voir exclue, à la grande Satisfaction des Anglois, qui remuent ciel & terre à Pétersbourg, pour la faire exclure; à quoi ils ne réussiront pas, Si la Rep. elle-même ne s'exclut pas, en n'acquiesçant pas aux termes proposés comme un *non plus ultra* par l'Impce. [Imperatrice]," & dont je vous ai déjà rendu compte.

Je garde cette Lettre jusqu'à demain, pour voir S'il y a quelque chose à ajouter.

3e. Nov.

Ce matin l'Assemblée d'Hollde. ayant délibéré sur la conduite d'Amstm. relativement aux Papiers en question, Dort, & Harlem, l'ont avouée & approuvée hautement: les autres Villes ont pris la chose *ad referendum*. Vraisemblablement on laissera tomber cette matiere; & il n'en sera plus question: car elle embarrasse beaucoup ceux qui l'ont mise avec tant d'empressement sur le tapis. L'Assemblée se séparera demain: & l'on ne se rassemblera que dans la quinzaine.

Je profiterai de cet Intervalle pour aller passer quelques jours à Amsterdam. Je suis avec mon attachement respectueux, pour toujours Monsieur Votre très-humble & très-obéissant serviteur
DUMAS

Passy à S. E. Mr. B. Franklin, Esqr.

Addressed: à Son Excellence / Monsieur B. Franklin, Esqr. / Min. Plenipe. des Etats unis / &c. / Passy./.

From Jean de Neufville & fils

ALS: American Philosophical Society

Honourd sir!   Amsterdam 2 Nov: 1780
May this find Your Excellency in a better state of health, then we observed by the reception of her last favour,[2] she had been

2. BF to Neufville & fils, Oct. 26, above.

in, this being our wish, and to obey always her most respected Commands, we have Accepted, to be comprehended with those of the Month of October the three thousand eigt hundred and Fifty Gilders on Mr. Laurens, and we have taken the liberty to draw on Your Excellency *f*. 8800: is écu 6680. 54—[3] at the Exchange of 52 ¹¹/₁₆ grooten at 3 Usance to our own order in Three bills Dividd.

$$\left\{ \begin{array}{l} \text{écu 2000.—.—} \\ \text{2200.—.—} \\ \text{2480.54.} \end{array} \right.$$

On the due honour of Which we doubt not in the least, nor on those which shall remain, untill we are intirely reinbursed.

We have gott the honour to wait on Mr. Adams, and obtained his leave to present to H. Excy. the remaining bills; about which he certainly will write to your Excellency; may we begg leave to assure her, as we did verbally to Mr. Adams, that with proper orders we should have been intirely disposed to Continue to protect the bills on Mr. Laurens, for which in particular we thank Your Excellency She hath enabled us untill now.

We have the honour to be with all Respectfull Regard. Honourd Sir Your Excellencys most devoted And most Obedient humble Servants. JOHN DE NEUFVILLE & SON.

To Lavoisier

Copy: Library of Congress

Monsieur, Passy, le 3. Nov. 1780.

Je suis très reconnoissant de la permission que vous vous étes donné la peine de me procurer de la ferme Generale et je vous prie de recevoir mes très sinceres remercimens.[4] Dans ma Lettre du 22 du mois passé, j'ai eû l'honneur de vous envoyer une Lettre accompagnée de divers papiers que j'avois reçu de M. de-Segray & Co. lesquels je vous prie de me renvoyer pour me mettre à même de repondre à ces Messieurs. Je suis toujours harassé de la goute, sans quoi je serois venu moi même vous remercier des Services que vous m'avez rendus.

3. The 8,800 *f*. for which the firm had drawn on BF was equivalent, at the current exchange rate, to 6,680 écus and 54*s*. or 20,042 *l.t.*, 14 *s*.

4. BF had not yet received the bad news contained in Desegray, Beaugeard fils & Cie.'s letter of the previous day.

J'ai l'honneur d'être avec la considération la plus distinguée, Monsieur, &c.

M. LaVoisier.

From the Board of Treasury

LS:[5] American Philosophical Society

Sir.   Treasury Office November 3d. 1780

The Board do themselves the honor to transmit enclosed sundry orders respecting bills of Exchange together with the resolutions authorising them to be drawn, that you may be enabled to discover counterfeits— You will please to observe, that the several extracts from the Minutes of this Office refer to other Extracts which it is presumed are in your possession.

No. 2. is an order executing the Resolve of Congress of the nineteenth of May last with a Copy of that resolution inclosed.—[6] No. 3 is an order executing the resolve of the 9th. of August last—No. 5 an order executing the resolve of the 23d. of August last No. 6. an order executing the resolve of the 30th. of August last, a copy of all which resolves is inclosed in their respective orders— No. 4 is an order executing the resolve of the 3d of August last respecting bills of Exchange on the Commissionrs at Paris a Copy of which is inclosed.[7] It is necessary here to take notice that the printers have made a mistake in the second third and fourth bills of each set of the last mentioned Exchange of the Denomination of sixty dollars—the words "*inteterest of Money* instead of the words *interest due on Money*."

I have the honor to be with the greatest respect your most obt humble servant   CHAR LEE Secy.

5. In the hand of the Board's secretary, Charles Lee (*JCC*, XVI, 325–6).

6. The committee for foreign affairs had sent BF a copy of the resolve on July 11, above.

7. James Lovell told BF on Aug. 15–22 about the latest resolves and sent him copies of them on Sept. 7; both covering letters are above. Note that it was the Board of Treasury that was entrusted with preparing the bills of exchange which Congress had resolved should be drawn on BF: *JCC*, XVII, 763, 794.

The Hon'ble Benjamin Franklin Esqr. Minister plenipotentiary of the United States at the Court of Versailles

From Thomas Digges   ALS: Historical Society of Pennsylvania

Dr. Sir   Nov 3 1780

I hope e'er this that the picture of your valuable friend, has reachd you. I have been very uneasy abot. it & wrote to Mr Bowens (who long ago acknowlegd the Rect of it in safety & that it shoud be forwarded) to clear up to you where the stoppage was occasiond. I am almost afraid to pay your valuable frd. a visit till I hear it is in safety for the young Lady has it much at heart.[8]

The frd. of whom I have lately wrote[9] continues in the same situation—much rigour shewn him—his frds. absolutely denyd any further admittance—yet communications are kept up.

You will have read the Speech & debates upon it in the He. [House] Lords—[1] War! War! was the theme.— I was an attentive observer & tho it was full of big words, it did not strike me, nor did the conclusion of that day, that the *American* War would be pushd with vigour. If *that* war *could* be carryd on rigorously, I have no doubt but it *would*. The means the means are wanting. I see no likelihood of Troops going to the Contint. tho some few may be intended for Chs. Town in the fleet now about to sail.[2] 10 or 12,000 are I believe going to the Wt Indies but at present no appearces of any marching to the Sea Coasts, and there are none of Portsmo save the Corps of Fullartons raggamuffins,[3] who are a disgrace to the name of Soldier.

8. The valuable friend was Bishop Jonathan Shipley and the young lady, his daughter Georgiana.

9. Henry Laurens.

1. For the King's Nov. 1 speeches to the Houses of Parliament opening the new Parliamentary session and the related debates see Cobbett, *Parliamentary History*, XXI, 808–44.

2. Three battalions sailed for Charleston in January, 1781: Mackesy, *War for America*, pp. 376–7.

3. William Fullarton (*DNB*) and a fellow Scotsman had raised two regiments, the 98th and 100th Foot, at their own expense; they were scheduled to leave in December for an attack on the Pacific islands of Celebes and Mindanao: Mackesy, *War for America*, pp. 373–5.

Several Ships of the line, have during the last 8 or 10 days slid away *seperately* from Portso, but whether they are intended, as is now reported, to form a part of a fleet going from the Channel Squadron to Gibraltar; or, as was before given out, to reenforce the fleet in the West Indies, is not easy to say. I rather think they are gone for the West Inds., to which quarter Sr. Sam. Hood is to follow with abot 5 Ships. Troops are going with Sir Saml but in what numbers cannot be told.[4] As the Carolina fleet is to sail at the same time it will be difficult to say what part of them is intended for Chs. Town but the numr. talkd of for that quarter is 2,500. It is generally believd that Rodney has gone with his fleet from the Wt Indies to N York—.

I am respectfully Yrs &c   W HAMILTON

Notation: Nov 3 1780

From Robert Willcocks *et al.*:[5] Certificate

ADS: American Philosophical Society

Done in Forton Prison, Novemr. 3th. 1780
We the Subscribers American Officers Now Laying in Forton Prison, do Certify that Mr. Joseph Lunier, Was taken A passanger on Board, of the Makeral prise to the Brigg Noterdame, Belonging and Bound to the State of South Carolina and that he has Been Confined upwards of three Years in this place.[6]   ROBERT WILLCOCKS
JOSIAH ARNOLD
ELIAS PORTER
SAMUEL HAYWARD

---

4. Hood brought eight ships of the line and three battalions of troops: Mackesy, *War for America*, pp. 376–7; W.M. James, *The British Navy in Adversity: a Study of the War for American Independence* (London, New York, and Toronto, 1926), p. 440.

5. The four signers appear in Kaminkow, *Mariners*, pp. 6, 87, 154, 207.

6. Lunier was plotting an escape when he asked these "four american officers my fellow sufferers" to write this certificate. He enclosed it in his letter to BF of Dec. 3, written from Le Havre: APS.

From John Adams　　　　　　ʟs:[7] American Philosophical Society

Sir,　　　　　　　　　　　Amsterdam Novr. 4th 1780.

Mr. De Neufville, this morning brought to me a number of Bills of Exchange, drawn upon Mr. Laurens, in the Month of July, amounting to seven or eight hundred Pounds sterling, and informed me that your Excellency had declined becoming responsible for them and referred him to me.[8]

I have enquired of Mr. Searle, who informs me there are about twenty thousand Pounds in such Bills now on their Way.

If there were only seven or eight hundred Pounds, I would accept them for the Honour of the United States, and run the Venture of being able to pay them by borrowing or some way or other: but twenty thousand Pounds is much beyond my private Credit.

I have been and am pursuing, all those Measures to which I am advised by Gentlemen, in whose Judgment I can justify placing Confidence, and am not without hopes of succeeding in some Measure: but I have not as yet been able to obtain any Money, nor any Certainty of obtaining any in future.

I write this, therefore to your Excellency, that if You could see your way clear to become responsible for these Bills for the present, I will engage to see them paid with the Money I may borrow here, if I borrow enough before the Term for their payment expires, or as much of them as I shall be able to borrow: but in this Case if I should not succeed in obtaining the Money, your Excellency will be answerable.

I should be sorry that the Credit of the United States should suffer any Stain, and would prevent it if I could: but at present it is not in my power.

The Successes of the English at the southward, added to the many Causes that obstructed our Credit in this Republick before, some of which it would not be prudent to explain, will render a Loan here difficult: but I still hope not quite impracticable.

I have the Honour to be with great Respect, Sir, your Excellency's most obedient & most humble Servant.　　　Jᴏʜɴ Aᴅᴀᴍs

His Excellency Dr. Franklin.

Notation: J. Adams. Novr. 4. 1780

7. In John Thaxter's hand.
8. See ʙꜰ's Oct. 26 letter to Neufville & fils.

From Fizeaux, Grand & Cie.

LS: American Philosophical Society

Monsieur   [after November 4, 1780?][9]

Nous avons été privés depuis longtems de motifs pour avoir l'honneur de vous écrire,[1] nous Saisissons avec empressement celui qui se présente pour nous rappeller à votre Souvenir, & vous reiterer Monsieur Les Assurances de notre parfait dévouement.

Nous vous informons avec Satisfaction que Mr. J. Adams à bien voulu nous charger des Payemens qu'il à à faire ici pour Le Compte des Etats Unis de L'amerique, comme il nous à dit que ce Seroit avec vous Monsieur que nous aurions à nous entendre de nos frais d'usage, nous prennons la liberté de vous demander s'il vous sera agréable que nous vous remettions de tems à autre, le Compte de nos opérations avec ce Ministre, nous recevrons toujours avec plaisir vos ordres & nous nous flattons que vous ne doutés pas de nôtre empressement á les éxécuter.

Nous vous renouvellons Monsieur les assurances de la Consideration très distinguée avec la qu'elle nous avons l'honneur d'être, Monsieur Vos trés Humbles & trés Obeissans Serviteurs

FIZEAUX GRAND COMP.

S. E. Monsieur B. Franklin à Passi.

From William Carmichael

Copy: Library of Congress

Dear Sir,   Escurial 5th. Novr. 1780.

A Courier which the Ambassador of France dispatches from hence gives me an Opportunity of expressing the pleasure I received from your last to Mr. Jay,[2] and at the same time of communicating the only interesting News from this Country, viz the departure of the Count D'estaing the 30th. ulto. with 38. sail of

9. The date of the first recorded transaction between the firm and JA: *Adams Papers*, x, 385n.

1. The last time the firm wrote, as far as we know, was April, 1780: XXXII, 297.

2. Above, Oct. 2.

the Line & 70 Merchant men from Cadiz.[3] The next day Mr. Cordova sailed with 26. Spanish Ship of the Line. From what I have heard you may probably see the Count at Paris in December and have an opportunity of cultivating the Disposition which he manifested here for our Interests— I cannot help observing to you, that from an anxious attention to all that had passed between this Court, & us, I see no prospect, in our present Situation, of considerable Succours here. I knew well their own Embarassments for Money, & think that a Part a least of the Ministry seems to wish to be regarded as mediators for a general peace.— They are flattered by England with this Idea while perhaps that Country really means either to detach them from the alliance with France, or to make the Rest of Europe believe they are on the point of doing it. I ought to apologize for making these Observations to you, who have had an Opportunity of seeing the different Papers that have passed between the Minister and Mr. Jay, but permit me to add that these many minute Circumstances of which only a person on the Spot can judge.— The Cloathing so long promised is still at Cadiz, & no Directions were given, until last Night for its delivery to Mr. Harrison our Agent *there*[4] if *then*. I say this because more than a month ago we had the same assurances that orders had been given to that Purpose— Mr. Galvez with 3500 Troops is gone against Pensacola.[5] The Ct. de F. Blanca told his first Commis this day in my Pres-

3. The convoy was comprised of ships from the West Indies. Bad weather forced d'Estaing back to Cadiz. On Nov. 7 he sailed again, accompanied temporarily by six Spanish ships of the line. His journey to Brest, expected to take two or three weeks, required almost two months: Baron Jehan de Witte, ed., *Journal de l'abbé de Véri* (2 vols., Paris, 1928–30), II, 406, 418; Jacques Michel, *La Vie aventureuse et mouvementée de Charles-Henri, comte d'Estaing* (n.p., 1976), pp. 259–60.

4. In September, Floridablanca had promised Jay clothing for ten regiments which had been taken from the captured Jamaica convoy; the merchant Richard Harrison had recently arrived in Cadiz: Morris, *Jay: Revolutionary*, pp. 796, 826.

5. Louisiana Governor Bernardo de Gálvez had succeeded in convincing Spanish officials in Havana to outfit a squadron and expeditionary force to attack Pensacola. Hit by a hurricane during mid-October, however, they had to return to Cuba: John Walton Caughey, *Bernardo de Gálvez in Louisiana 1776–1783* (Berkeley, 1934), pp. 192–3.

ence in Spanish, of which he thinks me Ignorant, that Rodney with 14 Sail of the line had sailed to North America. Our late Misfortune in Carolina hath had a bad effect here. Mr Cumberland is still at Madrid, waiting the return of the Abby Hussy who carried an answer to his last Propositions—[6] After his Departure the Minister assured Mr. Jay, that the king wou'd listen to none but those tending to a general Peace— I have received a Letter from America since the arrival of the Alliance, that Mr. Lee was opening his Batteries in form, having employed T. Paine & others as Pioners & Infants perdus—[7] I mention this to you in Confidence & also permit me to observe to you, that there have been Letters written to america that you have done all in your power to evade the Settlement of Mr. Deans accounts &c. I am well convinced of falsehood of the Insinuations contained in those Letters, but at the same time I should be wanting to the Friendship by which I have always thought myself honoured by you, if I did not give you this Notice— I took the Liberty of introducing the Prince & Princess Massaran to you[8] & hope you will excuse this Freedom when I assure you it was sollicited by them & that I had no other means of showing my sense of the Friendship which they have on every Occasion evinced to me here, I beg you to present the proper Compliments for me to my namesake and other acquaintances & to believe me always, Your obliged & humble Sert.   (signed) W. Carmichael.

His Exy Dr. Franklin.

6. On Oct. 19 the British government had decided to suspend the negotiations with Spain carried on by Richard Cumberland and Rev. Thomas Hussey. The priest did not report the news until December, however: Samuel Flagg Bemis, *The Hussey-Cumberland Mission and American Independence: an Essay in the Diplomacy of the American Revolution* (Princeton, 1931), p. 94.

7. After a month's stay in Boston, Arthur Lee proceeded to Philadelphia, arriving in mid-October. He attacked BF's supposed business dealings and accused him of neglecting public business: Louis W. Potts, *Arthur Lee, a Virtuous Revolutionary* (Baton Rouge and London, 1981), pp. 243–5. Paine, however, who had been engaged in a newspaper war with BF's friend Silas Deane, made no attacks on Deane between September, 1779, and March, 1782: Philip S. Foner, ed., *The Complete Writings of Thomas Paine* (2 vols., New York, 1945), II, 96–7, 181–6, 186–8.

8. Above, Oct. 25.

From Benjamin Gale[9]

ALS: American Philosophical Society

Honored and Dear Sr   Killingworth 5 Novr 1780

The Important Affairs In which You have been Engaged, Since Your Residence at the Court of France, I have Esteemed a Sufficient Bar to prevent my Writing You, on Matters which Relate to my Private Affairs, But must now beg Leave to Sollicit Your Assistance, on a Subject which may be an Advantage to me, and our Family, and perhaps Eventually to This Whole Continent.

I have ever been Zealous to promote our own Manufactures in Domestick Life, But Since Our Rupture with Great Brittain, I have been Convinced, we Could not Secure our Independance so Effectually, as by promoting our own Manufactures, Accordingly In Conjunction with Two of my Sons in Law, and Some Others, have Erected a Furnace in this State, for Casting Hollow Ware, and have Contracted to Supply the Continent with 60 Tons of Shot and Shells, and are now going on with our Second Blast Successfully, and This Summer have Erected a Potters Manufactory, which I purpose to Enlarge and Extend to All the Branches of it—, And am Now Aiming to Introduce The French Delph Ware, Commonly Imported to America, and For That End Want to Introduce a Manufacturer From France, who well Understands every Branch of That Bussiness,— The Ware I mean is Commonly of a Chocalat Coulour on The Outside, White within, and Painted with Blue; To Effect which, Under the Present Situation of National Affairs, without Your Kind Interposition and Aid, I Look upon Impossible; I may not Expect You will personally Act In This Affair— But I may not doubt But That Your Request, to Any American Gentleman, who may be on the Spot, will Engage him In That Matter— Dr Bancroft if he is With You, would do Thus much for his Old Preceptor—[1] But if that is not The Case, There is Now with Coll Elliot, a

9. BF's old friend, a physician in Killingworth, Conn., is identified in XI, 183n.

1. Bancroft evidently studied with Gale in Killingworth between 1760 and 1763, when, at the age of eighteen, he ran away to Barbados: Julian P. Boyd, "Silas Deane: Death by a Kindly Teacher of Treason?" *W&MQ*, 3rd ser., XVI (1959), 177.

French Gentleman who on his Passage from the Cape to France, was Last winter Wrecked on this Coast, Who says, he is a Son of Mr Robt(?) Fitz of Havre de Grace, a Captain in the Kings Guards, who he says has the Honour of Your Acquaintance, and owns such a Manufactory near Havre de Grace, if this Account is true, it may be Easy by him to procure a Manufacturer that may well Answer my Designs, if you should request That Favour for me.

I herewith Enclose some Proposals that I would make to any that would be proper to Engage in such an Undertaking, which if You will Condescent to Deliver to Dr Bancroft or any Other Person that You may Judge Proper, to Carry the Same Into Execution, and Give me the Necessary Information it will by me be Esteemed as a high Obligation.[2]

We have been This summer shockd by the Loss of Charlestown— More Recently by the Scandelous Desertion of Arnold, The Ravages of Brittish and Indian Savages in the North, and The Incursions of the Brittish in the Southern States, Although they have Just Receivd a Severe Check Lately, of which You will be Better Advised before this Reaches You— Many are disapointed by the Failure of the Arival of the Second Division of the French Fleet—for my own Part, I do not pretend to be Acquainted With the Secrets of The Cabinet, but have raised Expectations from The Quadruple Alliance of the North,[3] which I hope will at Least produce a Truce during the Course of this Winter— In the Multiplicity of Important Affairs which Lye Upon Your Mind, I may not Expect the Favour of a Line from Your own Hand, But I pray God Your Life may be protracted, Untill Peace is Restored to this Empire, of which You will Ever be Esteemed The Founder.— With The Greatest

2. Gale enclosed a two-page proposal on behalf of Benjamin Gale and Company, dated Nov. 6 and addressed to "Any Potter, well skilld in Every Branch of The Manufacture of French Delph Ware, who will Come to America, for the Purpose of Manufacturing the same." The firm pledged that, upon selection of a potter, they would immediately build any structures he specified and order equipment from France. Once in America he would receive food, lodging, wages as agreed upon, and a constant supply of clay and glaze. This proposal is among BF's papers at the APS, and Gale does not reappear in his correspondence.

3. Russia, Sweden, Denmark, and the Netherlands.

Respect and Esteem, I have The Honr to be Your Excellencys Most Obedt and Most Humle Servt BENJA GALE

To His Excellency Dr B Franklin Esqr

William Temple Franklin to John Paul Jones

ALS: National Archives; copy: Library of Congress

My dear Sir, Passy 5 Nov. 1780.

My Grandfather who is still obliged to keep his Bed and unable to write, directs me to send you the enclosed Extract of a Letter, he last Night recd from Dr Cooper of Boston.[4]

We desire much to know when you will be able to put again to Sea; That you may have a prosperous Voyage, is the sincere Wish of, Your very affectionate Friend W. T. FRANKLIN

Honble. Com: Jones. L'Orient[5]

Addressed: A Monsieur / Monsieur le Comme Jones /chez M. Gourlade / Negt. / à L'Orient

Notation: Pasy 5 Novemr. 1780. a B Franklin.

From Sir Edward Newenham

ALS: American Philosophical Society

Sir Dublin 6 Novr. 1780

I take the immediate opportunity of Mr: John Collin's return from Paris, to Express my sincere and most Gratefull thanks to you, for your repeated favors, which have left Impressions on my

4. WTF enclosed a copy of the third paragraph of Samuel Cooper's Sept. 8 letter, above. It was also copied into BF's letterbook along with the present letter.

5. Jones acknowledged the present letter and its enclosure on Nov. 11. He expressed concern about BF's health and complained that he had received neither passports for James Cheston and others nor powers to administer oaths of allegiance to them. He advised sending dispatches to him as soon as possible, and promised that when he returned to America he would "endeavour to prove the wondrous Wisdom of Doctor Lee": Bradford, *Jones Papers*, reel 6, no. 1264.

mind that no Time can Efface; Happy shall I Esteem myself in every opportunity of Shewing my respect to so Great & Eminently distinguished a Character; May The Almighty long bless the United States of North America, by preserving and prolonging your Life,

There is one return which is within my own power to make to your Excellency, that is, an Earnest and friendly attention to such Americans, as the Chance of War may occasion their being Prisoners within this Kingdom; I Entreat the favor of your Excellency, if any come within your Knowledge, who may want assistance in this Kingdom, that I may be honoured with the Knowledge thereof, and nothing shall be wanting to obtain their release or render their Captivity comfortable; I already got thirteen released since the first of last July; but I wish their agent was ordered to apply to me, whereby I would be enabled to make my actions correspond with my wishes.

The same sentiments of Brotherly Love and Esteem possess the hearts of my countrymen, in general, towards the Virtuous and Magnanimous United States, as in the beginning of the Contest, between Liberty and Haughty Brittain; I do not, among my most Numerous and Extensive acquaintance, find the smallest falling off; on the Contrary, I find their love Doubled; the whole force of our Corrupted Government has been exerted to obtain addresses inimical to virtue and contrary to the spirit of our once Glorious, but nearly annihilated Constitution, but the people have remained firm; our Parliament shewed some Spirit in the beginning of last session, but towards the End they became infamously Corrupted; they denied their own words; the Declaration of rights was treated with Contempt; The Freedom of Trade was reversed, & the oeconomy of Lord Buckingham was closed with the Grossest prodigality & Corruption, we are now to have red-heeled Carlisle & Commissioner Eden,[6] Men whose principles & Characters cannot agree with those who love

6. The earl of Buckinghamshire had come to Dublin as lord lieutenant of Ireland in January, 1777, and was recalled in the fall of 1780. He was replaced by the earl of Carlisle, who brought William Eden as his chief secretary: J.C. Beckett, *The Making of Modern Ireland, 1603–1923* (New York, 1966), pp. 209, 220–1. Both men had been members of the Carlisle Commission in 1778: XXVI, 108.

the Just rights of mankind; for my part, I am convinced I shall Ever oppose them, while I am in the Irish Parliament, being firmly persuaded that their Views cannot tend to the Good of this Kingdom;— There are five new peers to be Created, three reversions of Great Employments & Nine Considerable pensions to be distributed to Satisfy the Undbounded avarice of some parracidical Members of both houses of the Irish Parliament; these Measures will occasion Such an accumulation of New-Taxes, as must soon make the Landlord feel the oppression of Government in the tenderest point; their rents ill paid; their Tenants Emigrating to the Continent of America;— I am so convinced of the truth of these opinions, that I do not mean to place any of my Sons in the Army, Law or Mercantile Line in this Kingdom; Last month I brought from England three of my Sons, two of them I have put to a marine academy, the other I intend Shall Study Physic; My Eldest is Educating under a most respectable Gentleman in the Pais de Vaud,[7] the fifth is very young, & I have not yet fixed his Line of Life;— If I live, & America, which I ardently hope, rises in honor & Glory, I shall personaly accompany three of my Sons & fix them there; in the year 1777 I had Shipped my travelling things on Board the Isabella, Captain Thompson, & was on the point of Sailing for New-Yorke, but, to me, an unlucky accident happened the Ship, she was Stopped by an order from the Irish Revenue Commissioners—

I send this Letter under Cover to my Son at Lauzanne, as the only safe mode of convying; Happy will I Esteem myself to have the honor of a Line in return; for I own, that your health and happiness and the Prosperity of the United States, have my most sincere and Warm wishes—

I have the Honor to remain with Every Sentiment of respect Your Excellencys Most Obliged and Obt: Humble Servant

EDWD NEWENHAM

Addressed: To / His Excellency Dr: Benjamin Franklin / Minister Plenipotentiary / of the United States / Paris

Notation: Edwd. Newenham 6 Nov. 1780.

7. Edward Newenham, who wrote from there to BF on Jan. 8,1781 (APS).

From ———— Tardiveaux   ALS: American Philosophical Society

coüeron près nantes en Bretagne le 6 9bre 1780.
Monseigneur

Le choix merité que la Republique des provinces unies de l'Amerique Septentrionale a fait de Votre Excellence pour la Representer à la cour de france et les Savantes decouvertes sur la nature de l'Electricité, me font prendre la liberté de lui offrir un discours sur les sentimens que doit avoir et la conduite que tout sujet fidel et Religieux est obligé de tenir Specialement au tems de la guerre actuelle, mue entre la france et les isles Britanniques.[8]

Je desire ne mêtre point Ecarté des Regles de mon ministere et avoir justement employé les maximes de la Religion au Bien social: du moins mon intention a été de dire des choses permises et salutaires puisées dans les livres sacrés aux fins de fortifier mes paroissiens dans l'amour pour leur bon Roy, de les consoler au sein des peines que les hostilités leur font eprouver, de les engager a servir la patrie, selon la position où la providence les a placés et de leur enseigner les moyens propres a attirer les fa[veurs] du ciel sur le sort de nos armes.

Je supplie Votre Excellence d'excuser le defaut de style et le vice d'enchainement d'idées qui se trouvent dans cette production agreste; elle est l'effet de la naiveté et du zele d'un pauvre curé de campagne qui ignore les methodes litteraires et les formes academiques et qui ne scait parfaitement que l'assurer de son profond respect je suis Monseigneur De Votre Excellence le très humble et le très obeissant serviteur   TARDIVEAUX
                                                curé de coüeron

monseigneur francklin.

8. We have not found his enclosure but he apparently continued his involvement in public affairs. Among the holdings of the Bibliothèque Nationale is an eight-page publication in quarto, "Discours prononcé par M. Tardiveaux, recteur de Coüeron, lors du serment civique prêté du 14 juillet 1790 par les habitants de sa paroisse": *Catalogue général des livres imprimés de la Bibliothèque Nationale* (231 vols., Paris, 1897–1981), CLXXXII, 665.

William Temple Franklin to Dumas

Copies: National Archives, Library of Congress

Dear Sir   Passy 6 Nov. 1780.

My Grand father has been for a long time past laid up with the Gout, and is so still. He directs me to inform you, that he has recd. Several of your Letters, which he has not as yet been able to answer; he hopes however that in a few Days he shall be able to do it, as his Sufferings are much diminished.

You have heard I suppose of the arrival at Brest of M. De Guichen.[9]

I am as ever my dear sir, your Very affectionate humble Servant   W.T. FRANKLIN

M. Dumas.

To Grey Cooper[1]

Copy,[2] press copy, and transcript: National Archives; copy: Library of Congress

Sir,   Passy, Nov. 7. 1780.

I understand that Mr. Laurens an American Gentleman for whom I have a great Esteem, is a Prisoner in the Tower, and that his Health suffers by the Closeness and Rigour of his Confinement. As I do not think that your Affairs receive any Advantage from the Harshness of this Proceeding, I take the Freedom of requesting your kind Interposition, to obtain for him such a degree of Air & Liberty, on his Parole, or otherwise, as may be necessary for his Health and Comfort. The Fortune of War, which is daily changing, may possibly put it in my Power to do the Like good Office for some Friend of yours, which I shall perform with

9. Guichen had arrived not at Brest but at Cadiz, although the news would not reach Paris for almost another week: *Courier de l'Europe,* VIII (1780), 323, issue of Nov. 21 (item of Nov. 12). On Nov. 7 WTF wrote to tell Dumas that the news of Guichen's arrival at Brest was unfounded. National Archives.

1. As secretary to the Treasury Board, BF's former friend Cooper (x, 185n) was an obvious channel to First Lord of the Treasury North.

2. In the hand of L'Air de Lamotte.

Henry Laurens

much Pleasure, not only for the Sake of Humanity, but in Respect to the Ashes of our former Friendship.— With great Regard I have the Honour to be, Sir, &c. &c.

[*in Franklin's hand:*] Copy of a Letter from B Franklin to Sir Grey Cooper, Baronet, Secretary to the Treasury.

To Thomas Digges   Copy: Library of Congress

Dear Sir,   Nov. 7. 1780.

I have received several Letters from you lately which I have been unable to answer, a severe Fit of the Gout having confined me to my bed for these three Weeks past.

I inclose the Bill accepted by Mr. Goddard: But I do not clearly see how it is to be managed; for I gave a little Note to Jones acknowledging my having received such a Bill of Security for the Sum lent; and I think the Bill, being for a much larger Sum cannot safely be given up to the Endorser on the Payment of the Small Sum, perhaps it will be best to receive the whole, and put what does not belong to me into the Hands of Dr. Fothergil, as so much Security to him.— The Sharper is as you suppose playing the Same Tricks at Amsterdam,[3] having borrowed Money of M. de Neufville & others there.

I am glad to hear that the unfortunate Gentleman[4] is better, with regard to his Illness, and that his Sprits are good. I think he is in no Danger from his Enemies, tho' they are not deficient in Malice: I imagine the Principal Danger is of his Health from too close a Confinement. I shall try what care [can] be done by a Letter to an old Friend[5] towards procuring some Relaxation on Parole.

It may be some Satisfaction to him to know that a dirty Attempt to deprive him of some of his Property has not succeeded. A Number of Bills of Exchange, some for considerable Sums drawn upon me in his Favour, others purchas'd by him in America have been presented to me for Acceptance. Their not being

3. See Digges to BF, Oct. 24.
4. Laurens; see Digges to BF, on or before Oct. 27.
5. Grey Cooper; BF's letter to him is immediately above.

endors'd by him occasioned at first some Suspicion, & on Examination of the Bill Book, it was found that precisely the same Bills, endorsed by him to Veuve Babut & Co. at Nantes had already been accepted. On enquiry of the Dutch Banker here how he came by those Bills we learnt that they were sent to him by Mrs. Hopes of Amsterdam, who are intimate Friends, It is said of Sir Joseph York,[6] who probably had them from the Ministers, who found them among our Friends Papers— This may be but [*one*] among the many other Instances of British Meaness, that tend to make one regret the generous Civilities we have Shown to their People, by delivering up to Passengers & Captains taken Prisoners every Pennyworth of Property they could claim as belonging to them Personally. There is one Instance that Many Gentlemen & Ladies in England may remember, to wit the Treatment they received from Capt. Conyngham, when he took them in the Packet Boat between Holland & Hariwich.[7] By the Way what is become of that honest brave Fellow. Has M. Hartley done any thing for him?

I think the Protection desired for M. Bowman Baggage was sent.[8] As it seem to be lost, I enclose another.

Your Bill for 48 £ on Acct. of the Prisoners[9] will be duly honoured, when it appears.

I wish you would find some Opportunity of sending me the following Books, viz Croxall's Esop, Watts's Songs for Children, Watts's Logic, Lord Mahon's & M. Lyon's Treatises on Electriticity[1] and the Nautical Almanach for the Years 1778. 1779. 1780. & 1781. I am with great Esteem, Dear Sir, &c.

Mr. Digges.

6. Dumas had warned against Thomas and Adrien Hope: XXVII, 129–30.
7. Conyngham's prize was the packet *Prince of Orange:* XXIV, 48.
8. See Digges to BF, Aug. 25. We have not located the enclosure.
9. Mentioned in a postscript to Digges's Oct. 24 letter.
1. Samuel Croxall, ed., *Fables of Æsop and others . . .* (London, 1722, and numerous other editions); Isaac Watts, *Divine Songs attempted in easy language for the use of children* (London, 1715, and numerous other editions); Isaac Watts, *Logick: or the right use of reason in the enquiry after truth . . .* (London, 1725, and numerous other editions); Charles Stanhope [Viscount Mahon], *Principles of Electricity, concerning divers new theorems and experiments . . .* (London, 1779); Rev. John Lyon, *Experiments and Observations;*

From Jonathan Williams, Jr.

ALS: American Philosophical Society; copy: E. Marie Lorimer (Philadelphia, 1957)

Dear & hond Sir.   Nantes Nov. 7. 1780.

I have before me your two Favours of the 28 Ulto and 1st Instant.— I understand as little as you do the Reason of drawing on M. de Chaumont, but he ordered me to do so and you had previously put me under his Orders about the Cloathing;[2] the only Reason I ever heard was a supposed incompatibility between your public Character and an acceptor of Bills: For my own Part I should have been equaly satisfied to have drawn on you directly. As to the Motives of Mr de C in this Business I am ignorant of any other than what he professed, which were, to preserve a consistincy in your Character as a Minister, & to save you trouble. I think with you that no Step should be taken at the Caisse d'Escompte, while the Payments go on, but a good watch should be kept so as not to let our Credit suffer an hour: All the Bills I have drawn for the public will be found marked HS (habilement de Soldat) these are all in the List I sent to you and all I expect you to pay for me in the Case of failure on the part of M. de C. I have besides drawn on him ten Bills marked HO (habilement d'Officier) agreeable to the List inclosed amo [amounting] to 25551. [*l.t.*] 19 [*s.*]—[3] These Goods he Ordered on his own accot, & the Officers in America are to buy them of Mr Holker, If however Mr C should fail I shall be obliged to reimburse this money, but in that Case I shall retain the Goods if they are not gone; So that I should not lose much in the End, tho' it would be disagreeable to pay Cash, which I can't well spare, & take Goods which I do not want. All my other Bills for Mr de C *for aids* are

---

made with a view to point out the errors of the present received theory of Electricity . . . (London, 1780). BF had ordered several volumes of Watts's works in 1745: III, 50. The first two items on the present list may have been intended for BFB: XXX, 587; XXXI, 361. BF had recently borrowed Lord Mahon's book: XXXII, 405–6.

2. See XXXI, 284, 353, 435.

3. The enclosure, dated Nov. 7, is entitled "List of Bills drawn by Jona Williams on M. de Chaumont in Payment for Officers Cloathing." It shows bills no. 343 through 352, all drawn on Sept. 16 at 4 usances.

paid, except what I lately furnished him, & the amount of these are under the Acceptance of Messrs Cottin fils & Jauge his Bankers, so that I think I am on all sides perfectly safe.— I forwarded your Letter from M Lavoisier to Messrs De Segray & Co at St Malo, and the same day I received a Letter from them[4] informing me that all former Obstacles were removed, but they tell me of a new & unexpected one, which is Mr Moylans want of Cash to pay the Lettres de Voiture on their arrival & this Gentleman has for that Reason desired the Expedition to be stopped, I shall immediately direct the Business to go on again & if Messrs Gourlade & Moylan cannot or do not choose to find Cash I will find somebody that will, which I trust you will not disapprove.

Mr Johnson has given me the Papers & agreeable to your Desire[5] I broke the Seals and read them, I think their cannot remain Doubt as to the propriety of your Conduct relative to Mr. S,[6] and of the impropriety of his relative to you. I have Letters from Boston which inform me that Landais was turned out of his Command on the passage as being *insane:* It did not require much Penetration to find this out before he sailed.— I suspect Mr S intends to keep the public Goods in his Hands untill you pay his Bills, for, notwithstanding your Orders & Mr Austins constant application to him the loading is not begun, tho' the Mars has been waiting for nothing else this week past.

I wish it had been in my power to send you the Invoice of the Goods taken of Mr de C before this time, but it is an immense Work of about 100 pages in folio, full of additions & Calculations and all this to be copied before I can send it,[7] after which I

4. A copy of which was enclosed in theirs to BF of Nov. 2, above.

5. Expressed on Nov. 1, above.

6. Schweighauser.

7. JW did not send this invoice to Passy until Feb. 1, 1781, and it was addressed to Chaumont (JW to BF, Feb. 1, 1781, APS). A duplicate of the invoice that finally accompanied the goods is at the National Archives: 91 pages long, it is entitled "Invoice of 321 Bales of Cloaths Shipped by Order of the Honourable Doctor Franklin on board the Ship Marquis de la Fayette Captain De Galatheau, on account & risque of Congress & bound for Philadelphia by Jonathan Williams Junr of Nantes." JW dated it Aug. 30, 1780, and signed it. There are actually 369 bales whose contents are broken down by number of ells of fabric in each, for a total cost of 428,328 *l.t.*, 12 *s.*, 8 *d.* (This sum differs by a couple of *livres* from the figure JW reported to BF on Dec. 19, 1780: APS.)

shall have 4 more Copies to make. I hope to get through the two first this Week & as soon as I do you shall have it, in the mean time I send inclosed a note of the Terms as Mr de C wrote it himself:[8] The price I understood to be the Cost & Charges & thus I have calculated it.—

I send inclosed a model of a Bill of Exchange such as I suppose will answer your Purpose & Mr de Chaumonts equaly, I have not put the Names of the Persons you draw on because I do not know whether you will choose to draw on the Congress or the Committee. Mr de Chaumont in one of his Letters to me mentioned that the Bills should be paid in either *hard* money or other Bills on you, as the Option of this, lays with Congress I see no objection to drawing the Bills in that manner, but you may alter it or not as you please.—[9]

I am very impatient to hear if the Marquis de la Fayettes having quitted Bordeaux,[1] that Ship might have been now under Sail for America if she had arrivd at L'orient when I expected.—

I am ever with the greatest Respect Yours most dutifully & affectionately   JONA WILLIAMS J

The Goods you take of M. de C will exceed 400,000 so that if you give him Bills now, you may safely do it for that Sum & the Balance may be drawn for afterwards.

Mr Moylan has paid me for Shott I sent for the Alliance which was ordered by Capt Jones, I send you the Invoice of it inclosed,[2] with its voucher please to return me the latter.

Once fees were added for storage and porterage, and a 2½% commission was calculated, the total came to 439,546 *l.t.*, 17 *s.*, 5 *d.*

8. This is probably the undated note in JW's hand, also at the APS, that reads: "Extrait du marché fait par M. de Chaumont avec Mr Williams pour Compte de M. Franklin. `M. Franklin prendra mes marchandises contre des Traittes sur le Congrès a mon Ordre qui les remboursera par des Traittes sur M. Franklin ordre de Holker.'" BF endorsed this, "Marché fait par M. de Chaumont pour les Draps. No Date."

9. JW's draft, with emendations by BF, formed the basis for the bills of exchange BF sent to Samuel Huntington, dated Nov. 23 (APS). They will be discussed in vol. 34, under BF's receipt for Chaumont, Nov. 23.

1. She had not; the vessel did not arrive in Lorient until Feb. 9, 1781. Lopez, *Lafayette*, p. 216.

2. This and the enclosure mentioned in the following paragraph have not been found.

I also inclose you the Letter & Invo I have recd from Messrs French & Co of Bordeaux, relative to the choice Claret I promised to procure for you,— I hope the Quality will answer the Price,—there are under your mark 5 Cases for Doctor Bancroft which please to deliver him, the other 5 are for Mr Adams which please to keep for his Orders. I shall in the mean time only charge you with 500 for the 5 Cases you receive. JW

Endorsed: Letter from M. Williams Nov. 7. 1780. Answer to the Question, Why were your Bills drawn on M. de Chaumont? Schweighauser   Terms of Purchase of the Cloths from M. de Chaumont

Notation: Jona Williams

From Dumas

ALS: American Philosophical Society

Monsieur   Lahaie 9e. Nov. 1780.

Son Exce. M. l'Ambr. de fce. [France], qui étoit allé accompagner Made. la Duchesse Son Épouse retournant en fce., est revenu. Il doit être parti pour Amsterdam. Je le saurai demain, Avant Son voyage, je lui avois fait ouverture de l'affaire de *Saba*, & des papiers que vous m'avez envoyés à ce sujet. Il est disposé à interposer ses bons offices dans cette affaire.[3] Ainsi, dès que vous m'aurez envoyé la Lettre pour Leurs H. PP., ouverte à cachet volant, je la lui ferai voir, ainsi qu'à notre Ami; & je me conduirai en conséquence de leurs directions. Vous verrez, Monsieur, par la feuille ci-jointe, comment on en agit avec Mr. Lns. Je tiens ces Extraits de Mr. Adams, qui m'en garantit la véracité & l'exactitude.[4] Je ne puis encore me consoler de sa capture, tant pour les affaires en géneral, que pour lui & pour moi en particulier. L'arrangement du Sécrétariat en Ma faveur, m'auroit rendu heureux & tiré de toutes mes peines, qui Sont cruelles. Ce n'est point l'ambition, ni une avidité sordide qui les rend telles,

---

3. The affair of the *Eagle*, carried off from Saba.
4. These extracts were from Digges's letters to JA: *Adams Papers*, X, 256, 260–1, 276–7, 332–3; *Gaz. de Leyde*, Nov. 10, 1780; Wharton, *Diplomatic Correspondence*, IV, 84–5.

mais deux circonstances où je me trouve pour le Service Américain, & de l'une desquelles les 500 £. st. attachés au Sécrétariat
qui m'étoit destiné, m'auroit Sûrement tiré en 2 ans de temps ou
environ, par les Epargnes que j'aurois faites Sur cette somme, en
acquittant une Hypotheque de 300 £. St que j'ai dû mettre Sur
une petite terre destinée à servir de derniere ressource à ma
famille en cas de malheur: l'autre dépend plus de la grace de
Dieu, c'est la santé d'une personne qui m'est & doit m'être infiniment chere, & qui a excessivement souffert depuis quelque
temps;—[5] Mais rompons là-dessus. Je n'ai d'autre but, en vous
en parlant, que de me Soulager un instant, par la douceur qu'il y
a de verser ses peines dans un sein amical. Je vis à présent dans
l'espoir que Mr. Searle m'a donné, d'écrire en Amérique pour
qu'il soit pourvu à mon sort de quelque maniere équivalente, le
plutôt possible. Daignez, Monsieur, écrire de-même.

Je regarde l'affaire des *Papiers* de Mrs. Lee & Stockton,
comme finie ici, après la démarche vigoureuse de la Ville d'Amstm. Le gd. Fr. & notre Ami, disent à présent qu'il n'y a pas de
mal que cette affaire Soit arrivée. Cela est vrai, sans doute, dans
le sens qu'ils l'entendent: mais cela ne peut l'être quant aux in-
térêts politiques de l'Ame. ici; & l'éclat que cela a fait, rend ma
marche & ma contenance beaucoup plus délicate qu'elle ne l'é-
toit. La démarche de Mr. Lee, il y a 2 ans, étoit prématurée & im-
prudente. Si j'avois voulu me contenter de Si peu de chose, j'aurois pu l'obtenir longtemps avant lui. Faute de lumieres
suffisantes, il s'est fait une illusion, qu'il a fait valoir en Ame.
comme quelque chose de réel. Vous vous apperçutes fort bien,
Monsieur, dès-lors, de son illusion:[6] mais il n'a tenu compte de
votre sentiment, est allé son chemin dans ses Dépêches en Ame.,
& n'a fait que de la mauvaise besogne, en gâtant la mienne.

Je compte de partir Vendredi pour Amsterdam, où toutes
sortes de bonnes raisons m'appellent depuis longtemps; Je ne
puis plus différer d'y aller, & d'y passer quelques jours. J'y verrai Mrs. [*torn:* Searle?] & Adams.

5. Undoubtedly his wife, Maria Loder Dumas, who had been reduced to
despair by La Vauguyon's criticism of her husband: XXXII, 165, 226, 263.

6. In 1778 BF had refused a mission to the Netherlands because he was uncertain he would be welcome. At that time he told Dumas that America
should not actively court an alliance with the Dutch: XXVII, 448.

Je Suis pour toujours avec le plus respectueux attachement Monsieur, Votre très-humble, obéisst. & fidele serviteur ᴅᴜᴍᴀs

Je viens de voir Son E. Mr. l'Ambr. Il n'ira que la semaine prochaine à Amst. Ce que j'ai dit dans la Lettre, qu'il interposera ses bons offices dans l'affaire de Saba, doit s'entendre person-nellement, & non officiellement. En un mot, il me dirigera avec notre Ami; ce qui est à propos & nécessaire, après l'éclat Si re-cent qu'ont fait les papiers de Mrs Lee & Stocton, & la mauvaise humeur que les derniers s[ur]tout ont donnée à un gd. persge.[7]

Passy à Son Exce. Mr. B. Franklin

Addressed: à Son Excellence / Monsieur B. Franklin, Esqr. / Min. Plenipe. des E. U. / &c. / Passy./.

From Thomas Digges

ᴀʟ: Historical Society of Pennsylvania

Dr. Sir   London 10 Novmr 1780

I have seen Miss Georgiana & sympathisd with Her for the present appearance of the picture She sent you in June or July last being stopt somewhere between Ostend & Paris.

It was carryd safely by my frd. Mr. Champion of Bristol and lodgd with Mr F Bowens at Ostend for forwardance to You; that Gentn. was *then* in the habits of sending parcells of Pamphlets News papers &ca. &ca forward to Paris for J. A—— almost weekly from me,[8] & none of them having miscarryd I trusted the picture by a like conveyance would be safe also. He acknowlegd the safe Rect of it a very few days after Mr Champion left it in June or July, & has acknowlegd to me in two letters since, that He held it for a safer conveyance than the dilligence. I have also more than once wrote to Him to make You acquainted where it was, thinking You might point out a safe way of getting it, & from a long silence from both of you, I made sure it had got safe. Your letter of the 9th. Octor. cleard up to me You had not recd

7. "Grand personnage," *viz.*, the stadholder.
8. More than fifty letters from Digges to ᴊᴀ are published in Elias and Finch, *Letters of Digges.*

it. I cannot accot for the delay, & have lately wrote repeatedly to Mr Bowens to give You a line about it. When it gets to hand I beg to be informd of it, that I may satisfy Miss Georgianas uneasiness's therefor.

I hear now & then from the frd. I have lately mentiond in Letters to you, & he express's wishes to hear from others & to know what can be done in His case. His son[9] is now with me.

Mr. L.s confinement has been rigorous as usual till the 8th. inst. His son & Mr Manning were on that day allowd another half hours visit wch was extended to one hour, & the same day He got an order to be permitted to walk round the Tower whenever he chose to apply to the Dep Govr. for leave to do so.[1] His health & spirits are good. During His illness he was honourd with a visit from Lord Hillsborough & Stormont, a jesuitical visit no doubt, & with a visible meaning to pump or get at some thing. This, without any *particulars,* has got out from his late Visitors, only by the Prisoners expressing the extreem complaisance of his two ministerial visitors, particularly in the point of the cringing complementary offers of services from Lord H—— and I dare say the Scotsman was not behind hand.[2] I cannot accot for this lenity towards the Prisoner in no Other way (for they very lately peremptorily & rudely refusd the Son a second Visit) but from a whisper going about that a motion was to be made in Parlit. for a relaxation in the Severity of treatmt to Mr L, & that He should be put upon Parole or baild— This *was* in agitation, & the now granting Mr L a walk out will be brought an argument that He is not a *close* prisoner or ill treated. As appearances speak our *wise* rulers are not well pleasd with the treatment they have shewn Mr L, I doubt not but they will soon allow Him further favours & most likely give him parole.

9. Henry Laurens, Jr.
1. The terms were in fact much more restrictive. Laurens, believing Col. Gore, the residing governor, hypocritical, "treated his kindness with contempt, and refused to walk": "A Narrative of the Capture of Henry Laurens, of his Confinement in the Tower of London, &c., 1780, 1781, 1782," S.C. Hist. Soc. *Coll.* 1 (1857), 29.
2. A meeting with Hillsborough and Stormont occurred before Laurens was sent to the Tower: *ibid,* pp. 24–5. There is no record in Laurens' account of his captivity of a subsequent meeting.

We have no news yet from Ama. or any other but what you read in the publick prints.

I am with very great respect Yrs &ca

Addressed: A Monsieur Monsr. B.F / Passy

Notation: Novr. 10. 1780.

From Lavoisier

ALS: American Philosophical Society

Monsieur   10. 9bre. 1780./.

Je vous prie de m'excuser, si je n'ai pas eu l'honneur de vous renvoyer plustost Les lettres et autres pieces relatives à votre expedition de salpetre de st. malo à Lorient. Ayant été obligé de les communiquer, et de les joindre au mémoire dont Le rapport a été fait à la compagnie, elles étoient restées dans les bureaux de l'hotel des fermes, et on ne me les a fait repasser qu'aujourdhuy.

Je suis avec un proffond respect Monsieur Votre tres humble Et très obeissant serviteur   LAVOISIER

Notation: Lavoisier Novr 9. 1780

From Jonathan Nesbitt

ALS: American Philosophical Society

Sir   L'Orient Novr: 10th: 1780

I had the honor in due time to receive your Excellencys Letter of the 1st. Inst: & have to return you my most sincere acknowledgments for the attention that you have been pleas'd to pay to my Letter of the 20th: Octor: & to the Memorial of my worthy friend Mr: James Cheston.

I am exceedingly sorry for your Indisposition, & most sincerely hope that Mr: Cheston (who will have the honor to deliver you this Letter) will find you perfectly recover'd.— No doubt it was a continuation of your illness that prevented your giving orders to Commodore Jones to receive Mr: Chestons oath to the States and deliver him a Pasport.—for which reason, and being determind to go to England by the way of Ostend, he has taken the Resolution of waiting on your Excellency.—[3] He is Son to your old acquaintance Mr: Danl. Cheston who lived on Chester River.

I cannot too often repeat my wishes that this may find your Excellency perfectly recoverd from your Indisposition, & have the honor to be, with Sentiments of the most perfect Respect.— Sir Your most Obedient humble Servant JONATN: NESBITT

His Excellency B: Franklin

Addressed: His Excellency / Benjn: Franklin Esqr: / Passy

Notation: Jona. Nesbitt L'Orient Nov 10. 1780—

From Vergennes

L (draft):[4] Archives du Ministère des affaires étrangères

A Versailles le 12 9bre. 1780.

Je viens d'être informé, M, que le Sr. Dohrmans, négt. à lisbonne, chargé de pourvoir aux besoins des prisonniers américains qui peuvent Se trouver en Portugal, néglige depuis quelque tems entiérement ce Service; le Consul du Roi à Lisbonne à écrit en conséquence à ce négociant la lettre dont je joins ici la copie;[5] mais celuy cy a jugé à propos de la laisser Sans réponse, en sorte que les matelots américains Se trouveroient depourvûs de tout secours Si un nommé Baptiste, agent du Consulat de france, ne les assistoit pas. J'ay crû devoir, M. vous transmettre ces détails, afin que vous puissiez prendre les mesures quil vous paroitroit exiger de votre part.

M. franklin

3. He was in Passy on Nov. 19 to take the oath of allegiance; see our annotation of Jones to BF, Oct. 20. Jones wrote WTF on Nov. 11 wondering why authorization had not been sent him to administer the oath. APS.

4. In the hand of Gérard de Rayneval.

5. He enclosed an Oct. 7 letter from Consul General Brochier (*Almanach Royal* for 1780, p. 251) to Dohrman, which noted that American prisoners were in need and asked his intentions, so that Vergennes and BF could be informed (AAE). In June, 1780, Congress had appointed Dohrman American agent in Portugal, partly in recognition for his services to American prisoners stranded there: XXVI, 211n. See also Digges to BF, Aug. 18.

To John Adams

LS:[6] Massachusetts Historical Society; copy: Library of Congress

Sir   Passy Nov. 13. 1780.

I am honour'd by your Excellency's Letter of the 4th Instant, relating to the Bills drawn on Mr Lawrens. I recommended their being presented to you, as I understood you supply'd his Place during his Absence, and I thought it more reputable to our Affairs, that they should be accepted by you for him, than that their Credit should depend on the Good-Will of a Dutch Merchant, who, except a few of the first, does not accept them but as I guarrantee their Payment, and will perhaps besides making a great Merit of it, charge 5 per Cent Commission for his Service. I therefore still wish you would accept them, and if you should not before they become due be enabled otherwise to pay them, you can draw on me so as to be furnished in time with the Money. I have other Letters from your Excellency to answer, which I must at present postpone, as I continue ill with the Gout, and write this in my Bed with Difficulty.

With great Respect, I have the honour to be Sir, Your Excellency's most obedt & most humble Servant   B Franklin

His Exy J. Adams Esqr

Endorsed: His Ex. Dr Franklin 13 Nov. [*in John Thaxter's hand:* 1780] desiring me to accept the Bills

To Edward Nairne

Two LS:[7] Library of Congress, Yale University Library; AL (draft) and press copy: Library of Congress

Sir,   Passy, near Paris Nov. 13. 1780.[–October 18, 1783][8]

The Qualities hitherto sought in a Hygrometer, or Instrument to discover the Degrees of Moisture & Dryness in the Air,

6. In WTF's hand.

7. Both of these are in the hand of L'Air de Lamotte. The press copy was made from the LS at the Library of Congress.

8. BF did not send this letter until Oct. 18, 1783, when he enclosed it with another letter to Nairne of that date. As he explained there, after writing

seem to have been, an Aptitude to receive Humidity readily from a moist Air, and to part with it as readily to a dry Air. Different Substances have been found to possess more or less of this Quality; but when we shall have found the Substance that has it in the greatest Perfection, there will still remain some Uncertainty in the Conclusions to be drawn from the Degree shown by the Instrument, arising from the actual State of the Instrument itself as to Heat & Cold. Thus if two Bottles or vessels of Glass or Metal being filled, the one with cold & the other with hot-Water, are brought into a Room; the Moisture of the Air in the Room will attach itself in Quantities to the Surface of the cold Vessel, while if you actually wet the surface of the hot Vessel, the Moisture will immediately quit it, and be absorbed by the same Air. And thus in a sudden Change of the Air from cold to warm, the Instrument remaining longer Cold may condense & absorb more Moisture, and mark the Air as having become more humid than it is in Reality; and the contrary in a Change from warm to cold.

But if such a suddenly changing Instrument could be freed from these Imperfections, yet when the Design is to discover the different Degrees of Humidity in the Air of different Countries; I apprehend the quick Sensibility of the Instrument to be rather a Disadvantage; since to draw the desired Conclusions from it, a constant & frequent Observation Day & Night in each Country will be necessary for a Year or Years, and the mean of each different Set of Observations is to be found & determined. After all which some Uncertainty will remain respecting the different Degrees of Exactitude with which different Persons may have made and taken Notes of their Observations.

For these Reasons I apprehend that a Substance which tho' capable of being distended by Moisture & contracted by Dryness, is so slow in receiving and parting with its Humidity that the frequent Changes in the Atmosphere have not time to affect it sensi-

---

three pages he was "interrupted by some business; and before I had time to finish it I had mislaid it." When he found it, three years later, he continued with "what I suppose I had intended to add" (Smyth, *Writings*, IX, 108–9). BF submitted the paper to the APS in 1786, and it was published in the *Transactions*, II (1786), 51–6.

bly, and which therefore should gradually take nearly the Medium of all those Changes & preserve it constantly, would be the most proper Substance of which to make Such an Hygrometer.

Such an Instrument, you, my dear Sir, tho' without intending it, have made for me; and I without desiring or expecting it have received from you. It is therefore with Propriety that I address to you the following Account of it, and the more as you have both a Head to contrive and a hand to execute the Means of perfecting it. And I do this with greater Pleasure as it affords me the Opportunity of renewing that antient Correspondence & Acquaintance with you, which to me was always so pleasing & so instructive.

You may possibly remember that in or about the Year 1758, you made for me a Set of artificial Magnets, Six in Number, each 5 ½ Inches Long, ½ an Inch broad, & ⅙ of an Inch thick.[9] These with two Pieces of Soft Iron which together equalled one of the Magnets were inclos'd in a little Box of Mahogony Wood, the Grain of which ran with, & not across, the Length of the Box; and the Box was clos'd by a Little Shutter of the same Wood, the Grain of which ran across the Box; and the Ends of this shutting Piece were bevel'd so as to fit & slide in a kind of Dovetail Groove when the Box was to be shut or open'd.

I had been of Opinion that good Mahogony Wood was not affected by Moisture so as to change its Dimensions, & that it was always to be found as the Tools of the Workman left it. Indeed the Difference at different Times in the same Country is so small as to be scarcely in a common Way observable. Hence the Box which was made so as to allow sufficient Room for the Magnets to Slide out and in freely, and when in, afforded them so much Play that by shaking the Box one could make them strike the opposite Sides alternately, continued in the same State all the Time I remain'd in England, which was four Years, without any apparent Alteration. I left England in August 1762 and arriv'd at Philadelphia in October the same Year. In a few Weeks after my Arrival, being desirous of showing your Magnets to a Philosophical Friend, I found them so tight in the Box, that it was with Difficulty I got them out; and constantly during the two Years I

---

9. For the purchase of these magnets and the achromatic pocket telescope mentioned later in this letter see X, 171; XII, 259.

remain'd there, Viz till November 1764, this Difficulty of getting them out and in continued. The little Shutter too, as Wood does not shrink lengthways of the Grain, was found too long to enter its Grooves, & not being us'd was mislaid and Lost, and I afterwards had another made that fitted.

In December 1764 I returned to England and after some time I observed that my Box was become full big enough for my Magnets, and too wide for my new Shutter; which was so much too Short for its Grooves, that it was apt to fall out; and to make it keep in, I lengthen'd it by adding to each End a little Coat of Sealing Wax.

I continued in England more than 10 Years, and During all that time after the first Change, I perceived no Alteration. The Magnets had the same Freedom in their Box, and the little Shutter continued with the added Sealing Wax to fit its Grooves, till some Weeks after my second Return to America.

As I could not imagine any other Cause for this Change of Dimensions in the Box, when in the different Countries, I concluded first generally that the Air of England was moister than that of America. And this I supposed an Effect of its being an Island, where every Wind that blew must necessarily pass over some Sea before it arrived, and of Course lick up some Vapour. I afterwards indeed doubted whether I had not been too general in my Conclusion; and whether it might not be just only so far as related to the City of London, where I resided; because there are many Causes of Moisture in the City Air, which do not exist to the same Degree in the Country; such as the Brewers' & Dyers' boiling Cauldrons, and the great Number of Pots and Teakettles continually on the Fire, sending forth abundance of Vapour; and also the Number of Animals who by their Breath constantly increase it, to which may be added that even the vast Quantity of Sea Coals burnt there, in kindling discharge a great deal of Moisture.

When I was in England the last time, you also made for me a little Achromatic Pocket Telescope. The Body was Brass, and it had a round Case (I think of thin Wood) covered with Shagrin. All the while I remained in England, tho' possibly there might be some small Changes in the Dimensions of this Case, I neither perceived nor suspected any. There was always comfortable Room for the Telescope to slip in and out. But soon after I arrived in America, which was in May 1775, the Case became too small for the Instrument, it was with much Difficulty & various Contrivances that I got it out, and I could never after get it in again; during my Stay there, which was 18 Months. I brought it with me to Europe, but left the Case as useless, imagining that I should find the continental Air of France as dry as that of Pensilvania where my Magnet Box had also returned a second time to its Narrowness, & pinched the Pieces as heretofore, obliging me, too, to scrape the Sealing Wax off the Ends of the Shutter.[1]

I had not been long in France, before I was surprized to find, that my Box was become as large as it had always been in England, the Magnets enter'd and came out with the same Freedom, and when in, I could rattle them against its Sides; this has continued to be the Case without sensible Variation. My Habitation is out of Paris, distant almost a league, so that the moist Air of the City cannot be supposed to have much Effect upon the Box: & I am on a high dry Hill in a free Air, as likely to be dry as any Air in France. Whence it seems probable, that the Air of England in general may, as well as that of London, be moister than the Air of America, since that of France is so, and in a Part so distant from the Sea.

The greater Dryness of the Air in America appears from some other observations. The Cabinet Work formerly sent us from London, which consisted in thin Plates of fine Wood glu'd upon Fir, never would stand with us, the Vaneering, as those Plates are call'd, would get loose & come off; both Woods shrinking, and their Grains often crossing, they were forever cracking and flying. And in my Electrical Experiments there, it was remarkable, that a Mahogony Table on which my Jars stood under the Prime Conductor to be charged, would often be so dry particularly when the Wind had been some time at N. W. which with us is a very drying Wind, as to isolate the Jars, and prevent their being charged till I had formed a Communication between their Coatings and the Earth. I had a like Table in London which I us'd for the same Purpose all the time I resided there; but it was never so dry as to refuse conducting the Electricity.

1. This marks the end of folio sheet three of the draft, where BF left off the writing of this letter.

Now what I would beg leave to recommend to you, is, that you would recollect if you can, the Species of Mahogony of which you made my Box, for you know there is a good deal of Difference in Woods that go under that Name; or if that cannot be, that you would take a Number of Pieces of the closest and finest grain'd Mahogony that you can meet with, plane them to the thinness of about a Line, and the Width of about two Inches across the Grain; and fix each of the Pieces in some Instrument that you can contrive, which will permit them to contract & dilate, and will show in sensible Degrees, by a moveable Hand upon a marked Scale, the otherwise less sensible Quantities of such Contraction and Dilatation. If these Instruments are all kept in the same Place while making, and are graduated together while subject to the same Degrees of Moisture or Dryness, I apprehend you will have so many comparable Hygrometors which being sent into different Countries, and continued there for some time will find and show there the Mean of the different Dryness & Moisture of the Air of those Countries; and that with much less Trouble than by any other Hygrometer hitherto in use. With great Esteem I am, dear Sir, Your most obedient & most humble Servant B FRANKLIN

Mr. Nairne.

1780

To Jean de Neufville & fils

Copy: Library of Congress

Gentlemen, Passy, Nov. 13. 1780.

I received your Favour of the 2d. Instant, and shall duly honour your Bills therein mentioned. I have this Day written to Mr. Adams, on the Subject of the Bills on Mr. Laurens which you have not accepted, & such as may arrive hereafter, and believe he will accept them. I thank you much for the Services you have done, and your kind offer of continuing them, & have the honour to be, Gentlemen, Y. m. o. &. m. h. S.

Mrs. John Neufville & fils.

From Thomas Digges: Two Letters

(I) and (II) ALS: Historical Society of Pennsylvania

I.

Dr Sir Novr. 13. 1780

The Bearer of this, Capn. Benjamin Joy, waits upon Your Excellency on a matter of Business which will be explaind by Himself to You. He is so well recommended and His attatchment & active services for the cause of His Country are so well known to me, that I cannot but back His solicitation to Your Excellency with my strongest wishes that You gratify Him.[2]

His Business is on a similar nature with that I wishd Your Excellency to grant a Friend I recommended in a letter the 26th Septr; and I am the more anxious for its completion, because the adventure is meant for the State of Virginia now very much in want of Blue & Coulord army Cloths, Blanketts, Coarse Woolens, Tent Linin, Sail-Duck &ca. &ca, which Captain Joy has been recommended to carry out at every risque by some of the distinguishd leaders of the People in that Quarter; particulary James Barron Esqr of the Board of War, Duncan Rose Esqr of the board of Trade and General Weeden.[3]

For the accomplishment of His purpose, Captain Joy means to vest His property & effects in Europe in such articles as are specifyd above and to Conduct them to Virginia, on board His vessell the Brigantine Swallow of about 150 Tons Burthen, mannd with fourteen or fifteen Seamen & carrying Six Carrigge Guns four pounders—a Copper sheathd vessel of the Bermudean mould having a square tuck &ca.

2. On Dec. 4, BF prepared a passport for Joy (the draft of which is at the APS): XXXII, 103n. Also on that date Joy signed a bond attested by BF for £2000 that he would land his goods in an unoccupied American port (APS). Benjamin Joy (1757–1829) was the son of John Joy (1727–1804), a Loyalist who had emigrated from Boston. After the war Benjamin was involved in the East India trade and became the first American consul general in Calcutta: James Richard Joy, comp., *Thomas Joy and His Descendants* (New York, 1900), pp. 75-85; *Jefferson Papers*, IX, 238; XVI, 284–5n.

3. James Barron was a member of the Virginia Board of War, Duncan Rose of the Virginia Board of Trade; Gen. George Weedon was presently at Richmond arranging for that city's defense: *Jefferson Papers*, III, 17n, 58n; IV, 78.

If such vessel and Her intended Contents can be protected by Your Passport from any stoppage by the Cruisers of America or Her Allies, I am very sure the scheme will turn out of great publick benefit to my Country.

I am very Respectfully Dr Sir Yr Obligd & Obt Servt.

T. DIGGES

His Excelly B. Franklin Esqr

Addressed: His Excellency / Benjn. Franklin Esqr / Passy

Notation: Novr. 13. 1780.

II.

Dr Sir   London 13 Nov 1780

Since I wrote You last, on the 10 Int, I have had another letter from Mr F Bowens at ostend relative to the picture, for the safe delivery of which I am so anxious as to be frequently troublesome to You. Mr. Bowens by letter the 4th Int. informs me He has wrote to the necessary stages abot it, particularly to his frd at Lisle (to wch place it got in safety) and He thinks it has been detaind at and may be found *at the Bureau des Delegences de Flandres a Paris.* If it has not got to hand, be pleasd to order your Servant to enquire at that Bureau for it; for it would give me, as well as the Young Lady who sent it, the greatest satisfaction to hear *by the Bearer* it had reachd you in safety.

Your two packages by Mr Jones[4] went thro my hands in safety to Mr Hodgson— He will write You in case there is any new move relative to the Prisoners. At present all is at a stand with the board here, for want of hearing from You with the specification of numbers on hand in France, & which I fear very much you will not have in Yr. power to give while the american Cruizers continue the abominable & impolitic practice of not holding their Prisoners, but suffering them to go at large whenever they have opportunity. Numbers have reducd lately at Forton, owing to the exemplary exertions of a very worthy little agent; numbers having found their way over to a certain *House* in Amsterm. At Plymo. there are 135 the 2d Int. & their numbers woud have been greater had 15 or 16 remaind, who in a fit of dispair of get-

---

4. William Jones; see BF to Digges, Oct. 9.

ting Exchang'd, lately enterd into the British service. I cannot here omit the extraordinary Conduct of one lately (of the name of Laurance, rather above the common level, a Yankee, well read & informd) who glancing over a Chapter of the bible that expressd "Eunucks had a better chance for the Kingdom of Heaven than men in perfect verility"[5] immediately with a sharp knife committed the operation on Himself, and is now perfectly recoverd. Man——y [Manley] & Co——g—m [Conyngham] are still in their old quarters & have been very roughly treated & punishd for two attempts to elope. Your former charity of 25£ to M——y, has been servicable to them both, and the 6 d pr week to each man is a good help.

Every day here produces some new proofs of the inattention in the Captains of American Cruizers towards holding their Prisoners for Exchange. The Pilgrim Cap Robinson[6] of Salem, 18. 6 prs. & 150 Men, landed about a month ago six or seven Captns & 53 Seamen near to Cape Clear in Ireland. Capt. Ferguson (one of the Captns.) who relates this says that during the 15 days he was on board, The Pilgrim took 7 homewd bound Wt Inda Men (four of them from monserrat out of the 5, the only ships wch came from thence this year, & sent them all for boston) and that His ship was the 79th. prize the Pilgrim had taken— The Pilgrim has only been 20 months off the Stocks.

Your letter in ansr. to that wrote by the Parole Prisoners which came by Capt Fletcher from Boston, has been recd; and they made the requisite application at the board of Sick & hurt *to be exchangd by rect. & stand in accot. with you,* as you recommended; This has been refusd them as unprecedented, & Capt. McCausland wrote you last post about it; praying to know if it was necessary for Him to go to Paris & surrender themselves to You.[7] If you can favour them with an ansr. by *the Bearer* it will be a great obligation on some good men who seemingly wish to do every thing in their power to comply with their parole agreement.

No new movement with respect to Mr L——ns since my late

5. "There be eunuchs, which have made themselves eunuchs for the kingdom of heaven's sake": Matthew 19:12.

6. Capt. Joseph Robinson: Claghorn, *Naval Officers,* p. 261; Allen, *Mass. Privateers,* p. 237.

7. See our annotation of BF to Digges, Oct. 9.

letters. It is the opinion of some, that there will be soon a further relaxation of sevirty towards him, & that there will be a probability of his getting out soon on Parole. The Papers wch our ministry took from Him & sent over to the States General, made their appearance in the English news today, & causes much exultation, such as by the message of the Statholder &ca &ca it is *apparant* Holland will stick to the Interest of England &ca. &ca. They boast the same way too of affairs in Portugal. Spain too is *certainly* (say they) listening to overtures lately sent over by the Priest Hussy; & the cry of many is, that our ministry will do well to detach Spain from the American Interest at the expence of submitting to let Gibraltar be taken, to give the Dons East & Wt Florida the whole of the Campechy Lod [Log] Wood trade &ca &ca. Time, the mother of Truth, will discover what all this will come to; at present the fashion is to beleive that our wise ministers will certainly seperate Spain from the Bourbon Compact ha! ha! ha!

I inclose You a Certificate which you formerly granted to Carpenter. As I found the partys concernd in it, were not expressly going according to the tenor of that pass, (not that I mean they intended to go to an Enemys port) I refusd to give it to the partys, & they proceeded out in a Strong armd vessel & have got to B——n [Boston]; where every thing went well.

You recollect, Mitchells Cartel was after much trouble paid for by bills of 500 each on Jackson at the Admeralty who accepted them *payable at the Bank*.[8] When the bills became due they were refused payment & are still unpaid, & unfortunately for me (who had no other motive or benefits in them but to get them discounted) my name stands upon two, wch has much distressd me.

Your last to me is of the 9th. Octor. & I expected to hear further from You about your bill from Jones on Goddard— If I can be any ways servicable you may freely command me— I have informd You how the same Jones took in Dr. Fothergill.

My late Dates have been the 3d Octor giving an Accot of H L——ns capture. also the 6th, 10th, 17th, 24th, 31st; and the 3d & 10th Int. I am rather curious to know whether *one* of these got safe—it contain an extract from a captive & is dated I think the

8. For Henry Mitchell, the lawsuit involving the cartel ship *Polly*, and the lawyer John Jackson see XXXI, 365n, 366n.

31st Octor—⁹ The getting this information, as well as to have *a name* to direct to instead of the B. F a Passy wch. I always cover to Grand will be servicable & safer to me.

The bearer will give you the current news of the day & carry a few news Papers. He is a young man who has renderd services to the Cause particularly in the quarter of virga. & on whom I have very good reasons for placing strict confidence & good opinion.

I am with the highest Esteem Yr most Obedt Servt W: S: C

Monday night¹

P.S. Since writing the foregoing, I find there is a Capt St George² arrivd at the Secys office with Dispatches from N York of a late date— The Town is in a hub-bub to get at their *real* contents— accots are so incoherent that it is impossible for me (before I am obligd to seal & deliver this to the Bearer) to obtain any thing like the true accot; but this will be remedyd to you by the Bearer fulfilling his promise to carry the tomorrow mornings papers & add them to the few of today that I send you. It appears that Rodney wth 11 Ships saild from the Wt Indies the 24 Augt. & got to Rd Island the 20th Sept. lookd into that port, did nothing, touchd at N York, and returnd to His Wt Inda Station Pts on the *26th*. One accot (tho not a beleivd one) says his fleet remain at N York when this last packet saild.³ It is with concern I inform you that arnold has turnd Traitor to His Country & got into N York— It appears by the todays yet incorrect accot He had obtaind some secondary Command under Washington near N York, they say some Posts or Fort. He had prior to that made *his bargain* with an Emissary of Genl Clintons to betray the Amn

9. We have dated it as "on or before Oct. 27"; it and the other Digges letters are above.

1. Nov. 13, 1780, was a Monday, so this was written in the evening of the same day.

2. A captain in the 44th Foot who became an aide to Clinton: Worthington C. Ford, comp., *British Officers Serving in the American Revolution, 1774–1783* (Brooklyn, 1897), p. 156. His arrival was noted in the Nov. 14 issue of the *London Courant, and Westminster Chronicle*.

3. Rodney's squadron did not sail from New York until Nov. 16: William B. Willcox, ed., *The American Rebellion: Sir Henry Clinton's Narrative of His Campaigns, 1775–1782* . . . (New Haven, 1954, reprinted Hamden, Conn., 1971), p. 234n.

Army & direct the British where to Surprize it. On the day fixd for this acheivement, Clinton sent out a major St André to inform Arnold of His movement— He went in the Character of a deserter valet de Chambre, was known on his landing, apprehended, detected & immediately hangd— Drafts of the Amn. Army plan of its lines, & the plan fixd between arnold & Clinton was found upon Him. Arnold immediately fled & got by water into N York. The accots further say that Gen Washn improvd this settled plan to his own advantage & strengthend a Post wch. Arnold had declard would be but feintly defended, & by that means routed the British army who went to possess it & had advancd too far before they heard of Major St. Andre's fate.

Altho these accots have been bandied about ever since ten o Clk. this morning, there is no exact recital given from the quarter of authority—there they are rather mute, do not exult in the least, & by every appearance the accounts are in the lump highly dissatisfactory.

Notations in different hands: Nov 13. 1780 / Nov. 13. 1780.

[From Madame Brillon]: Le Sage et La Goutte[4]

Printed by Benjamin Franklin, Passy [1784]: Yale University Library

[before November 14, 1780]

LE SAGE ET LA GOUTTE.

Un fléau des[5] plus redoutable,
La Goutte, ce mal incurable,

4. This is the first of several literary pieces exchanged between BF and Mme Brillon during the period when she was in bed with depression and he was confined with gout. The MS versions of this little fable, in the style of La Fontaine, have disappeared. When BF received the original he evidently kept it and returned a copy made by WTF; in her letter of [Nov. 14], below, she asks for it back and sends him an improved version. BF printed the fable on his Passy press in 1784, and included it among the several printed bagatelles he sent her on April 8, 1784 (APS). See Lopez, *Mon Cher Papa*, pp. 77–8, where the fable is discussed and the opening verses are translated. For a complete verse translation see *The Bagatelles from Passy* (New York, 1967), pp. 32–3.

5. "De" is what was printed; the "s" was added by hand, in pen.

Chez un Sage alla se loger,
Et pensa le désespérer:
Il se plaignit. La sagesse a beau faire,
Alors qu'on souffre, on ne l'entend plus guère:
A la fin cependant, la raison l'emporta.
Contra le mal mon Sage disputa:
Chacun employa l'éloquence
Pour se prouver qu'il avoit tort.
La Goutte disoit; la prudence,
Mon cher Docteur, n'est pas ton fort;
Tu manges trop, tu convoites les femmes,
Tu ne promenes plus, & tu passes ton temps
Aux échecs, & par fois aux dames;⁶
Tu bois un peu. Dans ces doux passe-temps
L'humeur s'amasse, & c'est un grand service
De venir t'en débarrasser.
Tu devrois m'en remercier;
Mais depuis un long tems je connois l'injustice.
Le Sage reprit à son tour
Et dit: Je l'avouerai, les attraits de l'amour
De l'austere raison tolerant la rudesse
Semblent prolonger la jeunesse.
J'aime, j'aimai & j'aimerai toujours;
On m'aime aussi. Dois-je passer mes jours
A me priver? Non, non, la vraie sagesse
Est de jouir des biens que le ciel nous donna;
Un peu de punch;—une jolie Maîtresse;
Deux quelquefois,—trois,—quatre, & cetera:
De toutes celles à qui je pourrai plaire
Aucunes ne m'échappera:
Ma femme me le pardonna;
Et tu voudrois ici trancher de la sévere.
Pour les échecs, si j'y suis le plus fort,
Je m'y complais;⁷ mais lorsque par caprice
Fortune fuit, ils m'ennuyent à la mort,
Et j'en ferois alors le sacrifice—.
Par le secours de la Philosophie,

6. "Jeu de dames" is the French name for checkers.
7. As above, the final "s" was a later insertion, in pen.

Tout Sage ainsi sçait borner ses desirs,
Se consoler des peines de la vie.
Dupes & sots renoncent aux plaisirs.

From Madame Brillon
AL: American Philosophical Society

ce mardi de mon lit [November 14, 1780?][8]
Je vous renvoye mon chér papa une copie bien propre d'un brouillon que je vous redemande;[9] je ne vous aurois pas cru capable de manquer a votre parolle, vous aviés promis a Brillon de lui rendre la folie qu'un moment de liberté de teste, m'a inspirée pour mon amusement et pour votre distraction; vous deviés vous contentér de la relire; primo, vous en avés tiré copie; secundo, malgré l'air de famille, j'ai reconnu l'écriture de mr votre fils; il l'a donc vuë! Il l'a donc luë! Je vous pardonne mon ami ce petit écart, lorsqu'une fautte est faitte il faut peu grondér, mais avértir qu'on s'en est apérçu pour empêcher les rechuttes: au surplus mon bon papa je suis enchanté que la petite fable vous ait fait rire, si quelques nuits il me passe encore quelques rêveries par la cérvelle, je vous l'envoyerai et je consens que mr votre fils la métte au nét; mais de grace ne les montrés à personne; je ne veux pas qu'on dise de moi, ce que le Misantrope disoit a mr Oronte—j'en pourrois par malheur faire d'aussi méchants—mais je me garderois de les montrér aux gents—[1] Je suis fémme, mon lot et mon gout sont la modéstie; j'ai la teste vive, rien ne me déffend de l'occupér; mais pour moi, et pour mes amis les plus intimes—Adieu mon bon papa donnés moi des nouvélles de la goutte du sage, je souhaitte qu'elle aille mieux que les nérfs de votre fille:

J'ai corrigé quelques fauttes a la fable, il y auroit encore beaucoup a faire mais j'aurois peur de réssemblér a certain statuaire qui trouvant le nei d'une teste de fantaisie un peu trop gros, le diminua tant qu'il n'en résta plus:/:

Mr votre fils m'avoit dit que vous m'écririés; une coréspondance avéc vous seroit surement une grande distraction a mes meaux: *faittes le donc, et je répondra:/:*

8. The Tuesday before Nov. 17, when BF responded to this request and returned her rough draft.
9. "Le Sage et La Goutte," the preceding document.
1. Molière, *Le Misanthrope*, Act I, Scene 2.

From Chalut and Arnoux

AL:[2] American Philosophical Society

paris mardi 14 9bre 1780

Les abbés de chalut et arnoux se rejouissent du meilleur état de la santé de leur respectable ami, ils l'assurent de leur estime et de leur amitié.

Voici un projet de lettre pour M. et Mde poivre.[3] Monsieur franklin y ajoutera ou y retranchera tout ce qu'il jugera à propos.[4] Ce qu'il y a de vrai c'est qu'on ne sçauroit dire trop de bien de Monsieur et de Madame poivre.

Nos amitiés s'il vous plait à Monsieur votre petit fils.

L'adresse de la lettre doit étre à Monsieur et à Madame poivre à lyon.

Addressed: A Monsieur / Monsieur franklin / Ministre plenipotentiaire / des etats unis d'Amerique / à Passy.

To Vergennes

LS:[5] Archives du Ministère des affaires étrangères; copy: Library of Congress

Sir,   Passy, Nov. 15. 1780

I thank your Excellency for the Information contain'd in the Letter you did me honour of writing to me the 12th. Instant, re-

2. In the hand of Arnoux.

3. Pierre Poivre (1719–1786), botanist, traveler, and colonial administrator, spent his early years in India and China. From 1766 to 1773, he served as *intendant* of Ile de France and Ile de Bourbon, now Mauritius and La Réunion. He was a member of the Académie de Lyon and from 1754, a correspondent of the Académie royale des sciences. His widow, Françoise Robin de Livet (1748–1841), married Dupont de Nemours and traveled to America: Larousse; Institut de France, *Index biographique des membres et correspondants de l'Académie des sciences de 1666 à 1939* (Paris, 1939), p. 370; Anne Blanchard, *Dictionnaire des ingénieurs militaires . . .* (Montpellier, France: 1981), p. 116. For a contemporary appreciation of Poivre and his wife see Anacharsis Brissot de Warville, ed., *Mémoires de Brissot . . .* (4 vols., Paris, 1830–32), II, 94–104. This edition includes an extract of a biographical note by Dupont de Nemours.

4. Neither the abbés' draft of the letter to the Poivres nor an amended version by BF has been found.

5. In WTF's hand.

lating to the American Prisoners at Lisbon. Mr. Dohrman was, I think, appointed by the Congress to take care of them. I do not know the Reason of his Discontinuing that Care. But if he has not resumed it, or does not chuse to do it, I will thankfully repay any Expence the Consul of France may judge proper to order for the relief of those unfortunate People, as well as what has already been incurr'd; and shall write accordingly to Lisbon.

With the greatest Respect I am, Sir, Your Excellency's most obedient and most humble Sert.   B FRANKLIN

His Exy the Count De Vergennes

Notation: envoyé la lettre à M Brochier

To ——— Brochier   Copy: Library of Congress

Sir,   Passy, Nov. 15. 1780.
I am much obliged by the Care you have so kindly taken of the poor American Prisoners that has been brought into Lisbon.[6] I beg you to accept my Thankfull acknowledgements and that you will be assured, that what you have already disbursed, or may hereafter think proper to disburse for their Relief in furnishing them with Necessaries, Mr. dohrman continuing to neglect them, Shall be repaid with Thanks, on Sight of the Account. I have the Honour to be, with much Respect, Sir &c.

Mr. Brochier, Consul de France à Lisbonne.

6. About which Vergennes had informed him on Nov. 12, above.

Index

Cadwalader, Dr. Thomas, 69
Caillot, Blanchette (Joseph's wife), 331
Caillot, Joseph (actor): identified, 331n; invited to dinner, 331; letter from, 331
Cains, Robert: signs promissory note, 33n
Caisse d'escompte, 446, 452–3, 470, 509
Calder, Hannah Ogden, 120
Calder, Rev. James (Hannah's husband), 120n
Calonne, Charles-Alexandre de (intendant of Flanders), 139–40
Calonne (French privateer), 26n
Calypso (literary figure), 85
Cambridge, Mass.: solar eclipse viewed from, 470n
Camden, Battle of (S.C.), lv–lvi, 10n, 194n, 280–1, 396, 400, 418, 478
Campaign . . ., The (Addison), 420
Campbell, Capt. Duncan, 33n
Campbell, James (paroled prisoner): wishes exchange, 267n, 388, 451, 526; letter to, *inter alia*, 388
Campbell, Maj. Gen. John, 12
Canada: Louis XVI resolved to conquer, says Ternay, 344
Canals: used to transport masts, 283
Cannon: Bondfield's, to be shipped aboard *Marquis de Lafayette*, liv, 281, 292, 307, 316–17; Delmot offers to supply, 107; Chaumont's, used to ballast *Alliance*, 156, 317; Jauge & fils requests, 292, 317
Cape Clear, Ireland, 526
Cape Spartel, Morocco: Franco-Spanish fleet reported off, 11
Cape Ste. Marie (Cabo de Santa Maria), Portugal: Franco-Spanish fleet reported off, 11
Cape St. Vincent's, Portugal, 237
Capricieuse (French frigate), 11
Carcassonne: masonic lodge at, 304–6
Carey, Capt. John, 378
Carleton, Sir Guy, 33
Carlisle, Frederick Howard, Earl of, 503
Carmichael, William (Jay's secretary of legation, xxii, 487n): and Hopkinson, 54; Jay, 83, 86, 188; Md. bank stock, 176; Montmorin, 187–8, 497; wtf, 188, 455; voyage of, to Spain, 54n; finances of, 83n, 138, 187n, 188, 358, 462; reports

court news, 86–7, 186–9, 498–9; hopes for information about America from Deane, 187; criticizes A. Lee, 188; wishes print for Princess Masserano, 188; sends greetings to Ramel, 189; military intelligence, 497–9; Digges sends letter to be forwarded to, 303; introduces Crillon, 454–5; Masserano, 455, 499; asks bf's intervention with Vergennes, 498; letters from, 86–7, 186–9, 454–5, 497–9
Carolina Coffeehouse, 278, 348
Carpenter, Capt. Benjamin, 302–3, 527
Cartel ships: Hodgson hopes may sail again, 61; return empty to Britain, 61n; sent to France, 108–9, 142–3, 144, 152, 155, 158–9, 198–9, 229, 234, 372n, 387, 455–6, 479; captain of, sends receipt for prisoners to bf, 229; from Boston, R. Temple accompanies, 236, 247, 266, 301–2, 332, 428; not to be allowed to carry back American prisoners, 247–8; Mitchell's, seized at Bristol, 247, 267, 303, 527; to Bristol, Bromfield reports on, 345; bf asks Sartine to deliver prisoners from Martinique to, 375, 417–18. See also *Bob*; *Polly*; Prisoners, American; Prisoners, British
Castration, 526
Castries, Charles-Eugène-Gabriel de La Croix, marquis de (French naval minister): identified, 444n; bf gives map of Gulf Stream to, xxix; congratulates on appointment as naval minister, 473; becomes naval minister, 36; and Douillemond's commission seeker, 49; approves American trade with French West Indies, 444, 479–80; sends letters from prisoners for forwarding, 455–6, 479; list of American-made prisoners delivered to *Jane*, 479; letters from, 444, 455–6; letters to, 473, 479–80
Castries, Gabrielle-Isabeau-Thérèse de Rosset de Fleury, marquise de: asks news of son, 36
Cathelin, Louis-Jacques, xxvii
Catherine II, Empress of Russia: engraving of West family dedicated to, xxviii; and League of Armed Neutrality, 11n,

Continental Congress (*continued*)
change, 126; Fouquet wishes reimbursement from, 129; signs contract with Francy, 136n; considers Fouquet memorial, 144n; will not approve of JA's indiscretions, claims BF, 145; decides to exchange only army officers, 150n; protects holders of loan office certificates, 153; BF asks to appoint consuls, send no more warships to his care, 161, 167: for copies of complaints against him, 168; Ross ships goods to, 161, 296, 297; should write Danish court, recommends BF, 161; sends instructions on fisheries, 163; expresses gratitude to Louis XVI, 163n; Jones to deliver military supplies to, 183; defrays De Boy's expenses, 186; fails to vote secretary for BF, 193n; Schweighauser claims to have authorization of, for disbursements, 225; loan attempts are on behalf of, 241n; Vergennes wishes to negotiate consular convention with, 251, 256; draws on states for funding, 260; BF shows Vergennes resolutions of, 260n; Ruston's suggestions to, on strengthening of public credit, 275–8; Bondfield assembles supplies for, 281, 307; authorizes JA to procure loan, 287n: to remain in Netherlands, 321n; calls for payments in kind to support troops, 309, 356; will be able to repay debts after a few years of peace, predicts BF, 309; will provision Rochambeau's army, proposes BF, 330, 356–7; BF estimates his financial obligations toward, 330n; Ternay issues proclamation in name of, 343–4; Searle has no mission on behalf of, 354; serves at pleasure of electors, 354–5; does not adequately compensate him, complains Courter, 359–60; Miralles serves as Spanish contact with, 371n; borrows money from public, 391; continues firm and unshaken, says Stiles, 407; can settle with Mass. costs of sending goods on *Mars*, 429–30, 464; rumored move in, to recall BF, 474; mentioned, 56, 65, 90n, 128, 293, 347n, 399, 435. *See also* Loans, American

Convoys: British, from Baltic carrying naval stores, expected arrival of, 10–11: to West Indies, captured by Córdoba, 11n, 187n, 230, 240, 258–9, 300–1, 344, 498n: to, from N.Y., 62–3, 210–11, 481: to, from West Indies, 63, 526: from Quebec, captured off Newfoundland, 259, 301, 344; French, from Toulon, arrive at Cadiz, 11: from St. Domingue, reach Cadiz, 187; American, from Chesapeake Bay, escorted by *Fier Roderigue*, 11–12, 161, 168, 210; Dutch, warships outfitted to protect, 23: intercepted by British, 23n; Spanish, to Havana, 258n

Conway, Thomas, 197

Conway, Col. Thomas, 48, 197

Conyngham, Gustavus (privateer captain, XXIII, 585n): Digges helps, 60, 79–80, 137–8, 207–8, 310, 508; possible exchange of, 60, 79, 208; arrives at Mill Prison, 125n; treatment of, 134n, 209, 526; Coffyn asks help for, 134–5; Nesbitt asks help for, 135n; treated British prisoners well, says BF, 508

Cook, Capt. James, 61

Cooper, Sir Grey: asked to help H. Laurens, liv, 506–7; letter to, 506–7

Cooper, Richard Wibird (Samuel's nephew), 120–1

Cooper, Samuel (clergyman, IV, 69–70n): writes via Austin, *Rambler*, *Pallas*, 77–8, 121; introduces Bromfield, 78: R. Cooper, 120–1: Appleton, 142n; reports political news, 119–20, 262–4; on importance of naval superiority, 120, 264; and grandson S. Johonnot, 121, 264, 449n; supports French alliance, 264; extract from letter of, sent to Jones, 502; letters from, 77–8, 119–21, 262–4

Cooper, William (Samuel's brother), 121

Copley, John Singleton, xxix

Copying machine: invented by Watt, 115–18, 286, 487–8

Córdoba y Córdoba, Adm. Luis de: commands fleet, captures British convoy, 11, 165, 187, 230, 240, 246–7, 258–9, 498

Cornu. *See* Corun

Cornwall, Charles Wolfran, 482

Cornwallis, Gen. Charles, 258, 302, 344, 347, 395, 400–1, 467, 478, 480–1